Also by Justin Spring

Fairfield Porter: A Life in Art
Paul Cadmus: The Male Nude

SECRET HISTORIAN

SECRET HISTORIAN

The Life and Times of

SAMUEL STEWARD,

Professor, Tattoo Artist, and Sexual Renegade

JUSTIN SPRING

Farrar, Straus and Giroux

New York

Farrar, Straus and Giroux
18 West 18th Street, New York 10011

Library of Congress Cataloging-in-Publication Data
Spring, Justin, 1962–
    Secret historian : the life and times of Samuel Steward, professor, tattoo artist,
and sexual renegade / Justin Spring — 1st ed.
        p.   cm.
    Includes bibliographical references.
    ISBN: 978-0-374-28134-2
    1. Steward, Samuel M.   2. Authors, American—20th century—Biography.
3. Poets, American—20th century—Biography.   4. Novelists, American—
20th century—Biography.   5. Gay authors—United States—Biography.
6. College teachers—Illinois—Chicago—Biography.   7. Tattoo artists—
New York (State)—New York—Biography.   8. Sexology—Research—
United States—History—20th century.   9. Pornography—United States—
History—20th century.   I. Title.

CT275.S6966S676 2010
810.9'005—dc22
[B]
                                                                2009043086

Designed by Jonathan D. Lippincott

www.fsgbooks.com

1   3   5   7   9   10   8   6   4   2

. . . the question of being important inside in one . . .

—Gertrude Stein to Samuel Steward,
letter of January 12, 1938

CONTENTS

PREFACE

Samuel M. Steward—a poet, novelist, and university professor who left the world of higher education to become a sex researcher, skid-row tattoo artist, and pornographer—may seem at first an odd candidate for a biography, for he is practically unknown and nearly all his writing is out of print.

I first ran across Steward's name in the gay pulp fiction archive and database at the John Hay Special Collections Library at Brown University, where I had gone to research the social and literary challenges that a particular group of artists and writers had faced during the still largely undocumented years before gay liberation. As a biographer and art historian, I knew only a little about pulp fiction before visiting Brown, and was unaware of how many of these cheap paperbacks of the 1950s and '60s had described the "secret" world of American homosexuals. But pulp fiction writers had been among the first to chronicle the homosexual subculture for the popular reading public, skirting the stringent antiobscenity laws of the time by describing the homosexual "illness" in ways that were melodramatic and grotesque. While I was at first titillated by the lurid cover illustrations and outrageous titles I found in the archive—*Flight into Sodomy*, *Kept Boy*, and *Naked to the Night* all looked like great fun—the books themselves quickly proved just the opposite: they were, for the most part, badly written tales of loneliness, alcohol, and psychic defeat, often concluding in suicide or murder (or both).

While browsing through these depressing paperbacks, I recalled a very different series of novels and stories I had come across a decade

earlier at A Different Light bookstore. Erotic comedies, they had chronicled the adventures of a hustler named Phil Andros, an improbably literate Ohio State University graduate turned leather-jacketed hustler. Phil
lived a happy-go-lucky life, for his general interest in human nature made
each of his paid sexual encounters a sort of learning experience. The tone
of the Phil Andros books had been resolutely sex-affirmative, despite the
dark, antihomosexual atmosphere of the times they had described; Phil
liked sex—and was good at it—and had apparently become a hustler to
have as much of it as possible.

The Phil Andros books I had purchased (seven titles all told) had
been reissued versions of previously published books. They were published in the early 1980s by a house called Perineum Press, and their
cover illustrations featured drawings—presumably of Phil Andros—by
Touko Laaksonen/Tom of Finland, an erotic illustrator who had begun his
career in the mid-1950s but achieved his greatest popularity nearly twenty
years later. The Perineum edition, despite its 1980s publication, held no
detailed information about the original printings of the books, nor did it
explain what connection Phil Andros had (if any) with Tom of Finland;
nor did it give the real name of the author—only the pseudonym Phil
Andros. I remained puzzled about these literate, well-written social comedies featuring detailed descriptions of men having sex with men for the
better part of a decade; as a result, the novels lingered on my bookshelf,
and occasionally I shared them with fellow writers who took an interest
in such things. When a Pulitzer Prize–winning playwright returned one
to me, she observed that it was the happiest, most well-adjusted pornography she had ever read.

Though most of the Phil Andros novels and stories were set in the late
1950s and early '60s, I soon learned from Brown's pulp fiction database that
they had originally been published as paperbacks starting in 1970. (Only the
story collection $TUD had been published in hardcover, by a house called
Guild Press in 1966.) As for the pseudonymous Phil Andros: he had published under many other names as well—Donald Bishop, Thomas Cave,
John McAndrews, Phil Sparrow, Philip Sparrow, Ward Stames, D.O.C., Ted
Kramer, and Biff Thomas, among others—but his real name was Samuel M.
Steward. I subsequently discovered that Steward had begun his career as a
poet, literary novelist, and short story writer. He published three significant
nonfiction books in his later years, however: *Bad Boys and Tough Tattoos*, a

social history of American tattooing; *Dear Sammy: Letters from Gertrude Stein and Alice B. Toklas*, a memoir of his friendship with the two great literary women; and finally *Chapters from an Autobiography*, a modest memoir of his own life and times.

•

Several months later, while writing a book on the artist Paul Cadmus, I found a group of letters from Steward in the Beinecke Rare Book and Manuscripts Library at Yale. The letters amazed and delighted me, for they were highly risqué and often very funny. Through them I discovered that Steward had traveled frequently to Paris, that he had worked with Alfred Kinsey's Institute for Sex Research, that he had kept a tattoo parlor on Chicago's South State Street, and that he had been the single most important American contributor to the vanguard European homophile publication *Der Kreis*.

My curiosity aroused, I subsequently read several biographies of Kinsey, from which I learned that Kinsey had been fascinated by Steward's lifelong project of documenting his sex life in every particular. Upon being interviewed by Kinsey in late 1949, Steward had agreed to share this secret documentation. His later contributions to the Kinsey archive included drawings, photographs, sexual paraphernalia, homemade erotic decorative objects, and—most important—a vast compilation of numerical data and written material, including correspondence, fiction, personal narratives, diaries, and journals.

In his extraordinary openness about his sexuality, Steward was quite the opposite of nearly all the homosexual artists and writers I had been researching. Even Paul Cadmus, who had launched his career through scandalous depictions of homosexuality in his paintings, had been enormously careful about sharing the details of his personal life, and had left behind few written records of it for posterity. Likewise, most of the artists and writers of Steward's generation had either concealed any references to their homosexuality in their private writings and correspondence, or else rigorously edited it out in the years that followed. As a result, firsthand accounts of homosexual lives during the middle years of the twentieth century have remained underchronicled. As I considered this gap in available information, Steward's papers began to seem increasingly rare, valuable, and interesting to me.

But what had become of them? Though Steward had died in 1993, few of his papers had entered public collections. Despite his close association with Kinsey, the library at the Kinsey Institute listed only a few books by Steward in its online database, which made no mention whatsoever of his papers, artworks, or data. Yale had a few of his letters, and so, too, did Berkeley, thanks mostly to Steward's friendships with Gertrude Stein and Alice Toklas. There were also two boxes of his papers at Boston University's special collections library. But on the basis of what I subsequently found there—most of it dating from the 1980s—I sensed there once had been more. The question, now, was whether it still existed.

After tracking down a manuscripts dealer in Berkeley who owned some artwork by Steward, I came up with two possible addresses for his executor, but no phone number, and was also told he might have either died or moved away. I wrote to him at the addresses I had been given, but received nothing back. Several months later, though, my phone rang in New York. It was the executor; he was in town on a brief visit, was I possibly free to meet in the next hour or so? I was; he came by. After a long and friendly conversation, he invited me to come visit him in San Francisco—for, as he then revealed, he had been keeping Steward's papers in his attic for nearly a decade.

Only when I turned up on his doorstep a month or so later, however, did the executor let me know the extent of his holdings. Steward's effects filled nearly the whole of his attic. I spent the days that followed unpacking and photographing this enormous trove of objects, papers, drawings, photographs, manuscripts, home furnishings, and sexual paraphernalia—sensing, as I did so, that among this vast and bewildering collection I had found one of the more sensational secret lives of the twentieth century.

In the years that followed, I have come to know my subject as a complicated man of many identities. Among them are Samuel M. Steward, the mild-mannered poet, literary novelist, and professor of English literature at a Catholic university in Chicago; "Sammy" Steward, adoring young friend and fan of Gertrude Stein, Alice B. Toklas, and Thornton Wilder; Thomas Cave, spiritual seeker; Sam Steward, unofficial sex researcher for Alfred Kinsey's Institute for Sex Research; Phil Sparrow, streetwise Chicago tattoo artist; "Phil" and "Philip von Chicago," homoerotic illustrator; Ward Stames, homophile journalist; "Doc" Sparrow, official tattoo artist of the Oakland Hells Angels motorcycle gang; and, finally, Phil Andros, the homophile pulp pornographer who described the sexual underground of the American 1950s with passion, good humor, and charm. Steward's journals, letters, memoirs, diaries, and archive of published materials brought all these various identities together into one man.

While Steward's various writings were introspective, he was far from solipsistic. In fact, quite the opposite: his writings evoked the world in which he moved more vividly than any anthropologist or social historian I had ever read. Steward was indeed a born observer, and as a result, he described the world around him with extraordinary clarity and empathy. Like most diarists and record keepers, however, his first concern was with himself and his inner life.

Starting with the the vast amount of primary source material I discovered in that San Francisco attic, and then continuing my research at a number of archival collections around the United States, I have worked for nearly a decade to combine Steward's various unpublished memoirs, fiction, journalism, letters, journals, diaries, artwork, photography, and sexual records into one single, detailed story of a man who literally spent his entire life pondering the nature of his sexual identity even as he devoted the better part of it to sexual activity. My touchstone, throughout, has been his "Stud File," a whimsically annotated and cross-referenced 746-card card catalog in which Steward documented his sex life in its entirety from the years 1924 through 1974. I have also drawn extensively upon his neatly typed, thousand-page, single-spaced confessional journal, a document that he created at Alfred Kinsey's specific request. This journal is not only vastly entertaining, but also rich in specific descriptions of people, places, and activities that have otherwise gone largely undocumented in our culture. Perhaps in years to come it will find publication in its own right, for it is both an extraordinary social document and an oddly entertaining intimate personal record.

That Steward could have had the many sexual experiences he described so thoroughly in his Phil Andros fiction, his homophile reportage, his journals, his artwork, and his Stud File seemed to me at the outset of my research hardly possible. But because he kept such complete (and in many instances DNA-verifiable) records of his myriad sexual contacts, my connection of events in his private life to events in his writing is the opposite of speculative. As a result, I consider this biography in many ways a completion of his own life's work: that is, a full and thoughtful account of one man's highly sexual life, as carefully documented as possible, from birth to death.

Steward's many forms of self-documentation now seem to me, in retrospect, a single, lifelong body of work through which he hoped to demystify homosexuality for generations to come. As a young man Steward had hoped to establish himself as a popular novelist, but by his early forties he realized he would not be able to do so without censoring, condemning, and pathologizing his own homosexuality to suit the expectations of his publishers. And so instead, he decided to write a secret history—one that was playfully cross-referenced, illustrated, and footnoted—telling the absolute truth about his sex life in every particular and detail. Doing so would, he hoped, further the cause of Kinsey's sex research. But the project was primarily undertaken for himself; it was, in fact, his great consolation in a life that was otherwise characterized by constant disappointment, discouragement, isolation, and rejection. Following Steward's whimsical-serious example, I have attempted to write a biography that is similarly playful in its cross-references, illustrations, and footnotes, and at the same time similarly responsible in its commitment to sexual and emotional truth. Though the story is not without darkness—for it is, in many ways, a story of obsession, isolation, and failure—I have nonetheless attempted to tell it just as Steward might have: with a minumum of moralizing, and the lightest possible touch.

Author's Note

Steward was careful throughout his life to respect the sexual privacy of others. In writing his biography I have attempted to be similarly respectful by creating pseudonyms for nearly all those living individuals included in the biography whom Steward discussed intimately in his diaries, journals, correspondence, and Stud File. In instances where Steward created his own pseudonyms for real-life intimate acquaintances in order to include them in nonfiction works that he published during his lifetime, I have used Steward's pseudonyms rather than creating new ones. A small number of Steward's surviving intimate friends have welcomed my inclusion of their names in this book, and in these instances I have used their real names in preference to pseudonyms. For the most part, however, readers of this biography should assume that all the names given for Steward's sexual contacts are not the individuals' real names, but rather pseudonyms, and also that all those acquaintances of Steward's whose personal lives he discussed in an intimate manner have also been given pseudonyms.

SECRET HISTORIAN

1

"Wild—Hog Wild"

Samuel Morris Steward was born July 23, 1909, in Woodsfield, the seat of Monroe County in southeastern Ohio, a county bordering on Appalachia, and in many ways just as impoverished as that region. His modest, small-town beginnings are important to an understanding of the man he later became, for his plainspoken humor and openness to all things sexual are surely related to his country roots. At the same time, his lifelong preoccupation with the nature of his homosexuality can be seen as a direct response to the "stern and austere Puritanism of my Methodist maiden aunts."

Outside accounts of Steward's early life are basically nonexistent, and he himself wrote of it only in passing; those few sentimental memories he retained of his childhood—whether shared in letters to his sister, or else recounted in his journals or unpublished memoirs—seem to have made him too sad to dwell on it for long. And indeed he had a painful early life. His academically brilliant mother had died of an intestinal obstruction when he was only six, and his father, who had both drug and alcohol addictions, was essentially unable to care for either Steward or his baby sister. As a result, Steward grew up in a boardinghouse run by his mother's sister and two stepsisters. These three older spinsters—Elizabeth Rose and Minnie Rose, and their half sister Amy Morris—spent most of their day "cooking and serving, making beds and washing, and hoeing in the garden behind the house when there was time for it."

The Morris, Rose, and Steward families had resided in the Woodsfield area for generations, and were well established in the professional class; even Steward's father, despite his drinking and drug problems, had served for a time as Monroe County's deputy auditor, and despite his multiple addictions taught a weekly Methodist Bible class for more than twenty years. Steward's paternal grandfather, meanwhile, was a respected country doctor. All of Steward's family on his deceased mother's side were teetotalers as well as devout Methodists, and the church literally loomed large in their lives, for the town's imposing redbrick church stood just across the street from the boardinghouse. The town had no Catholics, and the one black who had attempted to settle there had been run out of town on a rail. As a result, Steward grew up seeing the world as basically divided between those who devoted their lives to Protestant churchgoing and Christian good works (such as his aunts and maternal grandparents), and those who had, for whatever reason, fallen away.

Faced both with the death of his mother and the improvidential absence of his father, the six-year-old Steward might well have withdrawn into grief or shocked stupor. But with the resilience of a child, he did just the opposite, dedicating himself energetically to becoming a highly sympathetic companion to the work-worn aunts who had taken him in. By stepping away from his own feelings and concerning himself primarily with the management and care of others, he was insuring he would not once again be discarded, and in so doing he was also setting the pattern for his later life. But as a result he also grew up feeling very much an outsider, and relatively at a distance from his own feelings and impulses, for he naturally had a great deal of grief and sadness about his own life situation. His aunts seemed not to notice, however, for they had any number of problems and concerns of their own, and moreover they themselves were not very happy people. Worn down by endless amounts of domestic work and by constant money worries, they seem to have lavished most of the joy and attention they had on Steward's very beautiful baby sister. Steward was after all a boy, and seemed relatively capable of taking care of himself. None of the three aunts had much understanding of males: after all, none of them had married or had children or even had brothers. As adult women living in a home owned by aged parents, their own lives were, in a very real sense, a surrender to womanly duty: their personal frustrations and domestic claustrophobia were something they accepted as their lot. These were the three adults who populated Steward's childhood—stern, comfortless, deeply religious women who could not quite understand him or his ways, and yet whom he felt an urgent, almost desperate need to comfort, accommodate, and appease.

Out of the double loss of his mother and father—one loss permanent and abrupt, the other ongoing and perpetually inconclusive—Steward seems to have accepted from a very early moment that his life's essential condition would be one of loneliness and exclusion. Deprived of parental love and recognition, he would grow up expecting very little love from others. Likewise, having experienced very little touching, warmth, or affection as a child, he would eventually find that prolonged physical intimacy made him extremely uncomfortable, and that those who expected the same from him were destined for disappointment. He would grow up to be a very sociable man, highly skilled at managing and seducing others, but unable to cope with everyday closeness. As a boy, he did his best to fit in, but at the same time he spent a good deal of time by himself. His preference for solitude eventually led this gifted young boy to develop a rich private fantasy life, one in which he thought of himself as someone special, separate, and apart.

Steward was very intelligent, like his mother, and he worked very hard in school. His aunts had high expectations for him, for although they were stuck in the boardinghouse, they wanted something better for him, and also for his sister. They saw to it that he earned top grades, kept fastidiously clean, had perfect manners, and in general did everything right. Wanting so much to please and amuse his aunts, Steward not only worked hard at his studies but also quickly mastered the piano, and soon specialized in "showy little pieces" that he picked out specifically to delight them. They, in turn, made a great fuss about his looks, which were delicate and refined. In an early set of photographs, he is beautifully turned out in a Little Lord Fauntleroy suit featuring velvet breeches, a matching jacket, and a delicate round white collar. In many ways, he seemed like a perfect little doll.

Whatever ambivalence Steward may have felt about his childhood in later life, he never denied the goodness of his aunts, or their love of him, or the many great sacrifices they made on his behalf. And, in fact, he would portray them quite tenderly in his first literary novel. But he was also exhausted by them—for the perfect, doll-like, self-contained little man they so much wanted him to be was very far from the complicated, fallible, and emotionally deprived young boy that he was, or the troubled teen he eventually became.

Because of his extraordinary academic achievements, Steward seems to have felt from a very early moment that the great awareness of "difference" he had from the people around him was primarily due to his intelligence. And indeed he was very intelligent: brilliant not only at all his school subjects, but also at music, amateur dramatics, and drawing. Among these many activities, though, he found his greatest pleasure in reading and writing, for through them he began to imagine himself in the outside world. From his earliest days Steward read everything he could lay his hands on: popular fiction, poetry, and the great classics of Western literature. He borrowed vast numbers of books from the local library, and also purchased books and magazines by mail. Because silent films were shown weekly in town, Steward became a great fan of film and stage celebrities—men and women whose lives and careers seemed so real to him in the pages of *Photoplay* that he began to write them letters. Much to his amazement, several wrote back. In this way, reading and writing served from earliest childhood to create for Steward an intimate conduit to the world of his dreams and fantasies—a world full of glamorous and fascinating people so very different from the simple folk of Woodsfield. Before long Steward was writing to nearly every celebrity he could think of—authors, musicians, and film stars—and assiduously collecting and cataloging their autographs and letters. He cherished their responses to him as proof positive of his own specialness. Through his collection of celebrity letters and autographs, he had created a world in which he stood at the absolute center.

In his unpublished memoirs, Steward makes clear that while he spent many of his leisure hours reading and writing and chasing down autographs, he also spent a good deal of time playing with other boys and girls. He may have been thought of by his contemporaries as "different" because of his bookishness, but he was always treated with respect. The facility with which he handled nearly everyone around him—from his aunts to his teachers to his fellow high school students—suggests that Steward had a talent for communication. He was by no means a leader, but by the time he reached high school (and the emotional and physical changes that come with the onset of puberty), he was well known for playing any number of sly pranks and practical jokes. Duplicity was something in which, for whatever reason, he took an enormous and childlike delight: being bad, misbehaving, and "crossing the line" between acceptable and unacceptable behavior were in many ways central to his character from boyhood onward. This love of duplicity became even stronger when Steward discovered sex.

Growing up under the watchful eyes of spinsters, Steward had known that sex was "wrong" long before he knew what it was. He later remembered, only half jokingly, that "in my sheltered little-boy Methodist way, the talk [of sex] caused me much agony. The slightest brushing of my hand against my penis was not only a religious sin, but would lead to blindness and pimples, kidney disease, bed-wetting, stooped shoulders, insomnia, weight loss, fatigue, stomach trouble, impotence, genital cancer, and ulcers." In fact, he so deeply internalized his aunts' great fear of sexual "filth" that the unintentional discovery that his foreskin could retract (and the sudden sight of his filth-encrusted glans) shocked him so deeply that he passed out cold.

Not surprisingly, then, Steward experienced a series of significant physical and emotional upsets as his body entered puberty. Sexual thoughts and desires began to surface within him despite his best efforts to exclude them from consciousness. It was at roughly this time that he began to engage in various forms of aggression and bad behavior, including pranks and practical jokes. As a result, he wrote, "The meek mild little mama's boy, the potential sissy, may have remained that on the outside, but inside there was a curious change to a twelve-year-old devil."

He began to do a lot of spying and eavesdropping. Steward's growing curiosity about other people's private lives and personal habits presumably led him first to peep through the many keyholes available to him in his aunts' boardinghouse. There he could watch and listen to whatever the various male lodgers might be getting up to in their rooms. He also began to spy on various other people throughout Woodsfield, including a girl who lived next door. In one of his earliest surviving short stories, written while still a preadolescent, Steward describes spying on a teenage boy and girl who have gone skinny-dipping together; while he senses something momentous is about to happen between them, he does not yet know what it is.

Steward's first introduction to sexual self-pleasure came about through instruction by another boy in the practice of masturbation. He achieved orgasm some time later, in private. Some time after this first orgasm, Steward began to realize that he was sexually excited by other boys. While he found the realization troubling, he also seems to have realized in short order that he could do nothing about it—just as, indeed, he could do nothing to control his interest in sex. As he later observed, "'Choice' had no part in [my sexual identity.] When I discovered what I wanted [sexually], every corpuscle, every instinct I had, drove me unerringly in that direction."

Steward later wrote that he could recall no real concern among the adult population of Woodsfield about the sex games he and the other boys in town sometimes played, at least insofar as these games might potentially cause them to develop into homosexuals. He credited this lack of concern to a simple, widespread disinclination to discuss sexuality in general, and on top of that, an almost complete, culture-wide ignorance about the existence of homosexuality:

> Midwest American views on homosexuality in the 1920s were very quaint, and were based on the assumption that all people raised in civilized Christian countries knew better than to fall in love with, or bed, persons of the same sex. Knowing better, then, the Fundamentalist mind made two breathtaking leaps of illogic: people did not do such things, and therefore such things must be nonexistent. This kind of thinking protected us all during the 1920s and 30s. Though one might be teased for being a sissy, no one could believe that any person actually engaged in the "abominable sin." We lived under the shadow and cover of such naiveté.

Thus while Steward recalled many injunctions against "sin" in his religious upbringing—both in church and at home—he recalled no specific early injunctions against homosexuality. Through his own investigations, however, Steward soon ascertained that sexual acts between men were not only strictly illegal in Ohio, but also punishable by incarceration. In his unpublished memoirs, he concludes the story of his first nonmasturbatory sexual experience with another boy—"a big guy" football player who had convinced him to engage in an act of oral sex that was "over in less than two minutes"—by going on to note that the punishment for such activities in Ohio at that moment so far exceeded the "crime" as to make the whole situation absurd: "So began my criminal life, then punishable by the laws of the state of Ohio—at that time—by about twenty years of imprisonment, I guess. Each time. Total incarceration in Ohio: between five and six thousand years."

Steward had enjoyed the encounter with the football player, and as a result, he subsequently provoked similar encounters with other (usually older, better developed) boys in locations all over Woodsfield: in the town graveyard, in a neighbor's attic, in the courthouse bell tower, and even in the same room at the Methodist church where his father taught his Sunday Bible class. Since Steward usually proposed and intiated these activities, he felt no sense of coercion by the older boys. Rather, he considered himself unique:

> I figgered I was put in that town just to bring pleasure to the guys I admired . . . In that small (about 350 students) high school, the word got around quickly enough, and (I think) they all came to look on me as . . . a dandy substitute for their girls . . . I felt different from those boys—superior in a way, because I could give them something they wanted (and needed?) . . . I thought I was the only one, and grew somewhat proud that I could satisfy these boys, most of whom I looked up to and admired because they were my adolescent "heroes." [And] they [in turn] treated me with a funny kind of respect, as if they knew that if they made me mad, they wouldn't get any more . . . I was not patronized or made fun of. In those far-gone days, everything seemed "natural."

Even so, these new activities made Steward ever more clearly an outsider. To his teachers and his aunts he may well have seemed a handsome young man of great academic promise, but to himself—and among the boys with whom he was active—he was not only a rebel (a boy who stole from the cash register in his uncle's store, got drunk on stolen wine, and once even threw a pumpkin through the window of the high school principal's house), but also an oddity (because he was a boy who enjoyed pleasuring other boys sexually, and seemed to have no shame about doing so). To Steward, who had basically already accepted that he would never quite "fit in," his sexual activities were just another aspect of his teenage rebellion. With puberty, he later observed, "the birth of desire had taken place in me, and the patterns that I needed to survive were firmly imprinted by the time I left the town [of Woodsfield]: concealment and pretense, duplicity, a guise of wide-eyed innocence—and a kind of 'passive aggression' [unusual] in such a shy-seeming young man."

Of course, Steward was hardly alone in adopting such a strategy; most homosexual young men of his generation found themselves facing a similar crisis of disconnection from the society around them as they became sexually active. Just as the orphaned and rejected Jean Genet (Steward's exact contemporary) would note that through homosexuality, violent crime, and thievery he had "resolutely rejected a world which had rejected me," Steward took a similar view of his departure from the upstanding life into which he had been born, and toward which his aunts had so earnestly propelled him:

> The personality which has been kept repressed, as mine had been by the strict Methodist upbringing my aunts had given me, and kept within the strictest lines and boundaries, really goes wild—hog wild—when it finally breaks away. And although I was still living within the family walls, the rebellious spirit was growing daily stronger . . . I *had* to be free.

Steward's ability to think clearly and without too much anxiety or self-blame about his sexual activities (or at least to view them with a certain degree of humorous detachment, and to recognize them not as aberrant behaviors, but rather as aspects of an essential self that absolutely *had* to find expression) is something he later credited to an extraordinary boyhood find: a copy of Havelock Ellis's *Studies in the Psychology of Sex, Volume II: Sexual Inversion*. Steward had serendipitously discovered the book under a bed in the boardinghouse, where a traveling salesman, after stealing it from the "restricted" section of an Ohio library, had subsequently left it behind.

A voracious reader even in his early teens, Steward had already special-ordered Freud's *Beyond the Pleasure Principle* and *The Interpretation of Dreams* through the Woodsfield confectioner by the time he found the Ellis volume. But the latter book was a unique godsend, for this landmark of early-twentieth-century sex research was particularly sympathetic toward "sexual inverts" and "sexual inversion"—that is, to homosexuals and to homosexuality. The book immediately set Steward's mind at ease about just who and what he was, and proved a welcome alternative to the vague but terrifying sermons he had heard all through childhood about "sexual sin." Thanks to Ellis, "not only did I discover that I was not insane or alone in a world of heteros—but I [also] learned many new things to do. I made a secret hiding place for the book under the attic stairs, and read and read and read. Thus I became an expert in the field of [sex] theory (by the time I finished the book I probably knew more about sex than anyone else in the county) and then began to make practical applications of this vast storehouse of material."

Steward affects nonchalance about his sexual identity in his memoirs, and doubtless he was nonchalant about it for much of the time. But he also faced a very difficult moment of self-recognition in mid-adolescence, as he realized that what he was getting up to with other boys was simply not acceptable. The realization became manifest in an incident involving, of all people, his father.

Steward's father had been largely absent throughout his childhood; during that time, Samuel Vernon Steward's brief, rare visits to the board-inghouse were almost always painful ones, for his inability (or unwilling-ness) to provide for his children had complicated the lives of Steward's aunts considerably, and they resented him. They also resented his in-volvement with other women, since they felt he ought to have remained faithful to the memory of their sister. His ongoing dependence on drugs and alcohol, meanwhile, had led him to ignore both the emotional and the financial needs of his children.

The son of a country doctor, he had dabbled with drugs since boy-hood. He had obtained virtually unlimited access to drugs as a young adult by securing a pharmacist's license through the study of pharmacy in college. His subsequent experiments had led him to become a frequently relapsing opium addict* who also "dabbled largely in [other] drugs, espe-cially laudanum and morphine." Though in many ways a weak man, he was capable of unexpected violence; one of Steward's few early childhood memories was of watching his father hit his mother hard across the face, merely for having dropped and broken his bottle of ketchup.

In later life, Steward kept no photographs of his father, only a couple of inconsequential letters and a small book of occasional speeches. The contents of these documents suggest he was a man inclined to sancti-mony. The fact that he went on to spend twenty years teaching a Sunday

---

*Steward's father took the Keeley cure for opium several times, a quack cure invented by Dr. Leslie Keeley in 1879 that relied on the injection of "bichloride of gold" to remedy alcohol and narcotic addiction.

Bible class at the church across the street from the boardinghouse where his children were growing up without his financial support suggests that there was much about him that Steward might justifiably have disliked.

According to Steward, his relationship with his father worsened after the two were tested for their IQ:

> The propagandizing of my aunts against whomever [my father] looked upon as a possible new bride had affected me; they some-how felt that he should remain true all his life to the memory of my mother [and so did I]. An additional strain was that I had earned my own way during the high school years, since with his meager salary he could not support either myself or my sister. And finally, the superintendent of schools had given both my fa-ther and myself the same IQ test—which had just then been in-vented. When the weighting of the scores was adjusted for our ages, it was discovered that my result topped his. I do not believe he ever forgave me, and was jealous of that small detail the rest of his life; he often referred to it, but never in my hearing.

The final break between father and son came after. Steward wrote a sexually suggestive note to a handsome young traveling salesman at the boardinghouse, and the salesman, outraged, subsequently gave the note to the proprietor of the town's only restaurant, thereby making the prop-osition—and the proof of it—town-wide public knowledge. Publicly shamed by his son, Samuel Vernon Steward drove the boy out to the countryside to discuss the matter in the privacy of his car. There, as Stew-ard later recalled, his father had bawled him out:

> "I want to know what the hell a son of mine is doing writing love letters to another man."
>
> "I think," I said, drawing on my new vocabulary from Have-lock Ellis, "that I am homosexual."
>
> ". . . Don't give me any of your smartaleck high school rheto-ric!" He bellowed . . . [And] that was the way the conversation went on for about a half hour. When I saw that he *wanted* to believe that I had not actually sinned, the game became fairly easy . . . I pretended to be chastened, to be horror-struck at the

enormity of [what I had proposed to the salesman] . . . I worked
it to the hilt, falling in easily with his suggestion that perhaps I
should go to see a professional whore—that such an experience
might start me on a heterosexual (he said "normal") path.

And Steward did go to the professional whore, too—using his own five
dollars, since his father declined to pay for it. He described the encounter
with the girl in the neighboring town as "a sad little experience . . . [which]
took me a long time—and finally the girl herself had an orgasm. My own
was brought about by thinking of [my friend] Carl."

The matter might have ended there, but Steward sneaked a look at
his father's diary a couple of weeks later. There, to his enormous shame,
he read his father's account of the situation, one which noted that the
experience had, in his father's words, "cut my heart out." Much as Steward would have liked to discount both his father and his opinions, he
could not deny his father's great sorrow, shame, and embarrassment at
the public revelation of his son's homosexuality, for the facts were all too
plain upon the page.

In a letter Steward wrote to Alfred Kinsey shortly after their first
meeting in 1950—a year and a half after his father's death by an overdose
of amphetamines mixed with alcohol, and more than twenty-five years
after being confronted by his father with the note to the traveling salesman—Steward wrote Kinsey, "I guess the psychic trauma of my father's
rejection of me went much deeper than I realized."

He then added,

It was not until [a day after you took my sexual history] that [I]
realize[d] what a deep and profound psychological need it [had]
answered . . . Two or three times during [our] interview I found
myself thinking: "If only my father had been like this man!" and
instead of his profane Pilate's gesture* regarding me, [he] had
given me the sympathy and comprehension that you extended . . .
[As a result of my meeting with you,] the great dry wasteland of
my psyche, the bitterness, the unwanted feeling—all have [now]

---

*With "Pilate's gesture," Steward is suggesting that his father had, like Pontius Pilate, "publicly
washed his hands" of any responsibility for his son (Matthew 27:24).

begun to change; I am conscious of great alterations somewhere within.

The note is telling, for it suggests that with the public revelation of his homosexuality, Steward felt that he had been cast off not only by his father, but also from his father's religion—and with it, all that had up to that point made him secure in the world. But apart from Steward's disconnection from both his father and his religion, there was a loss of something even more important: a loss of connection to truthfulness. Steward was, despite his playful love of duplicity, a person for whom truth was of primary importance. Even if he had felt no shame about his homosexuality, Steward must at least have been shamed by his own dishonesty. And of course, Steward had no one to blame for this dishonesty but himself. He lived in a world where the truth about his sexuality was simply not acceptable, and so, when pressed, he had done the only thing he could do: he lied.

•

Two of Steward's aunts moved to Columbus in 1926, selling their share of the Woodsfield boardinghouse in order to buy and run a boardinghouse that was just a short walk from the Ohio State University campus. They did so for the express purpose of seeing Steward and his little sister, Virginia, through their college years at OSU, for they had resolved to provide their children with the best possible university education despite their extremely limited income. Taking his last year at a public high school in Columbus rather than in Woodsfield, Steward helped out at the new boardinghouse in whatever way he could; he also continued to write poetry and fiction, play jazz piano, and collect celebrity autographs and letters. Since many entertainers passed through Columbus on whistle-stop tours, he was now able to pursue them in person, simply by waiting outside their theater or else in the lobby of the town's best hotel.

Steward was by now also having a good deal of casual sex, mostly with the undergraduate males with whom he shared his home. "My aunts' house on Seventeenth Avenue had about eleven rooms," Steward later recalled. "Six of the bedrooms were rented to two boys each, making a full house of a dozen young men. Over the years I managed to have about half the population of the place—some reluctant, some returning again and again." Steward's most remarkable sexual experience, however, happened as a result of his autograph-collecting* adventures, and took place in downtown Columbus.

Although Steward never mentioned the encounter in his published memoirs, he detailed its specifics in an interview he granted to a friend just four years before his death:

> I had a friend at the best hotel in Columbus, the Deschler-Wallich . . . He called up one night and said, "Somebody has registered here. I don't know whether you'd be interested or not. His name is Rudolph Guglielmo" [sic]. That was [Rudolph] Valentino's real name, of course. And I said, "Oh, my God, I'll be down in a minute." That was July 24, 1926.

The great silent-film actor Rudolph Valentino was always assumed to be forcefully heterosexual, even while under attack by the popular press as a promoter of male effeminacy. Steward had long been in awe of him, for throughout the 1920s Valentino had been a top Hollywood star worshipped as a paragon of virility. Just six days before coming to Columbus, however, Valentino had been lambasted for his mannerisms in the *Chicago Tribune*, in what later became known as the "Pink Powder Puffs" incident. Steward later described it in his account of their meeting:

> [Valentino] was returning from Chicago, where he had gone a second time to challenge the writer of that editorial that called him a "powder puff," who never showed up [for the duel to which Valentino had challenged him]. He was coming back on the train,

*The autograph book in which Steward collected celebrity signatures during the period 1926 to 1929 remained with him throughout his life. Distributed among the signatures of his fifty high school classmates are autographs by the stage actor Otis Skinner; the bestselling author Will Durant; the silent film star Rudolph Valentino; the pianist and composer Percy Grainger; the *prima donna assoluta* Mary Garden; the silent film comedian Roscoe "Fatty" Arbuckle; the Viennese architect and designer Josef Hoffmann; the violin virtuoso Fritz Kreisler; the bestselling author-adventurer Richard Halliburton; the coloratura soprano Amelita Galli-Curci; the silent film actress Pauline Lord; Ziegfeld's "Girl with the Bee-Stung Lips," Mae Murray; the Pulitzer Prize–winning playwright Zona Gale; the author and poet Hamlin Garland; the Russian composer Sergei Rachmaninoff; the biographer Emil Ludwig; the jazz orchestra leader Paul Whiteman; the psychologist Alfred Adler; and the playwright and novelist Thornton Wilder, whom he would meet again in 1937.

and I don't know why he stopped in Columbus, but there he was, absolutely incognito, because he would have been mobbed otherwise. So I went down to the hotel, my autograph book in hand, and knocked on the door, and he signed it . . . [He had been showering and wore only a towel but] he took the book and sat down and signed it. For a long time [after], there was the imprint of his damp palm on the page [of the autograph book]. He stood up . . . and I was about to leave, and he said, "Is there anything else you want? I'm very tired."

I said, "Yes, I'd like to have *you*." And then he really did smile . . . He reached over and pushed the door shut. I had it half open, my hand on the knob—I was about to exit—and he pushed the door shut with that hand, and with the other hand he undid his towel. And then he sat down on the edge of the bed.

Though pressed by his interviewer, Steward declined to give any further details of the sexual encounter.* But young Steward emerged from the hotel room not only with the autograph, but also with a swatch of Valentino's pubic hair,† which he subsequently kept in a monstrance at his bedside until the end of his life.‡ The experience was all the more trenchant for Steward because within a month Valentino suddenly ruptured his appendix and died, aged thirty-one.

Though unable to discuss his encounter with high school friends, Steward memorialized this and other sexual experiences by keeping records and collecting memorabilia. Steward's first sexual experience had taken place only two years before, but he already had a secret list of all his encounters that he had transcribed in coded notations, occasionally supplementing these notes with physical souvenirs that carried their own erotic charge. Through these collections of facts, figures, and objects, Steward was able to put the experiences into order, to consider their relative importance (or unimportance), and, essentially, to daydream about his own risk-

---

*The Stud File notes (in code) that Steward performed oral sex on Valentino. He filed the card under the name "Guglielmi" rather than "Valentino," and his one comment about the encounter (apart from a coded note on Valentino's penile dimensions) is "Nuf sed."
†Steward's interviewer never asked how he had attained this prize. In a later, unpublished interview with Jack Fritscher, however, Steward mentioned using a blunt-tipped manicure scissors.
‡The monstrance is now in a private collection in Rome.

taking sexual activities with a sense of both detachment and control. Through them he would enter a state of erotic reverie—one in which he saw himself not only as safe, secure, and very much at the center of his sexuality, but also as a daredevil, a risk taker, and a sexual hero—a young man both larger than life and impervious to its cruelties.

•

By the time he finished high school in 1927, Steward was eager to begin a new phase of exploring his sexuality, this time through writing:

> For my entrance essay [for Ohio State University] I chose Walt Whitman as a topic, and let fly with all the accumulated but un-digested wisdom—and none of the caution—of an eighteen-year-old who had read Havelock Ellis, and also through him investigated John Addington Symonds and found out about Horace Traubel[*] and Peter Doyle.[†] Moreover, instead of writing on *Leaves of Grass* in general, I chose the homosexual "Calamus" section in particular. I [even] quoted *The Invert*[‡] (by "Anomaly") on why inverts made such good nurses . . .
>
> This amazing little essay I later learned landed in 1927 in the midst of a staidly closeted English department with the disruptive force of several pounds of TNT . . .

Paying his way through school as a part-time librarian, Steward took a BA with honors in 1931. As an undergraduate he helped organize student protests against the racial segregation of the fraternity system (despite having grown up in a segregated town, Steward maintained friendships with blacks throughout his life) and also against the presence of the ROTC on campus. He also participated in amateur theatricals, wrote poetry and prose for the school literary magazine and newspaper, and played in a jazz combo at school dances and mixers.

---

[*]Traubel (1858–1919), the self-described "spirit child" of Whitman, published a nine-volume biography of the poet and was an active executor of his estate. He was fifteen when the two first met.
[†]Doyle (1843–1907) was the confederate army veteran and bus conductor whom Whitman met shortly after the end of the Civil War in Washington, D.C. The two were (in Doyle's words) "the biggest sort of friends" until Whitman's death in 1892.
[‡]London, 1927.

Steward found significant inspiration at OSU in a sympathetic mentor—a professor upon whom he would later model himself as both a teacher and a literary dandy. Clarence "Clare" Andrews, an elegant man of letters, had published several books, including the novel *The Innocents of Paris* (1928), which had been turned into a 1929 film starring Maurice Chevalier. He regularly summered in Europe and was a friend of Gertrude Stein and Alice Toklas; on one occasion he had even helped eject Hemingway (who was drunk) from their home. "Always elegantly groomed, tie carefully knotted . . . [he was] the very model of a professor," Steward later wrote. "I *inhaled* him, I worshipped his intellect and understanding, and I patterned my teaching career around him."

While Andrews was homosexual, he was discreet about it, and partnered, and he wisely kept Steward at a careful arm's length. "[When] I wrote a short novel (imitative of *Death in Venice*, I fear) . . . Andrews read it, and scolded me for my preoccupation with sex." Nonetheless Steward met a number of established literary figures through him, including William Butler Yeats.

Even while an undergraduate, Steward dabbled in various forms of literary bohemianism, for he had read all about bohemian life in Ben Hecht's *Count Bruga*,* and he had joined a group of young people crafting similarly "artistic" lives for themselves in a tenement building at 31 East Long Street in downtown Columbus. Though far from Greenwich Village, these young artists and writers listened to *Le Sacre du Printemps* on the Victrola at their cocktail parties, and read all the latest art and literary magazines. The group included Steward's best friend and classmate Marie Anderson, a stylish lesbian who ultimately left Columbus to become a Communist, and Bobbie Creighton, a worldly young prostitute with a substantial collection of literary erotica and pornography. According to Steward, Creighton gladly lent him copies of "early poetry by Pound, the work of Joyce and Stein and e.e. cummings, the suppressed drawings of Felicien Robs,† [and] the work of J. K. Huysmans." Creighton's collection

---

*Best remembered today as a screenwriter, Hecht (1894–1964) began his professional career as a hard-boiled Chicago newspaperman, and his lifelong love of Chicago found its way into his many story collections and novels, which also included *1001 Afternoons in Chicago* (1922), *Fantazius Mallare* (1922), *Gargoyles* (1922), *The Florentine Dagger* (1923), *Tales of Chicago Streets* (1924), *Broken Necks* (1924), *Humpty Dumpty* (1924), and *The Kingdom of Evil* (1924). Steward loved and collected Hecht's books throughout his life.

†Felicien Robs (more commonly, Rops), Belgian symbolist artist and engraver (1833–1898), whose work was often erotic.

of erotic books, poems, and pictures was profoundly important to Steward, for it described many varieties of sexual awareness—including homosexual ones—at a time when, according to the novelist Carl van Vechten, there was not "a single English or American novel of the first rank that deal[t] with [homosexuality] save in a perfunctory or passing way." (In fact, her pornography collection fascinated him to the point of complete distraction, in a way he would later describe in his first novel, *Angels on the Bough*.) But by far the most important works that he found in her collection were the "decadent" early novels of Huysmans, for they were works upon which Steward would fashion his life.

As a slight but handsome young man now sporting a mildly outrageous pompadour and a racy pencil mustache, Steward had an easy enough time convincing young male undergraduates to have sex with him. He noted in his memoirs, "I went to Columbus with the major purpose of bringing pleasure to others, mainly straight young men." He also observed that "none of us was coy in those days . . . We all liked to experiment [and] we found the direct approach daring." In one instance, while fooling around in a frat house with an old friend from Woodsfield,[*] the two were discovered by another frat member. In order to help his friend save face, Steward then pleasured a number of other frat members—for among these young men, only those who performed oral sex were considered homosexual.[†]

Steward had been exploring his sexual attraction to boys in his own writings beginning at age fourteen,[‡] and he continued to address the topic of homosexuality in his academic writings throughout his college and graduate school career. The question of how to discuss homosexuality would, in fact, be the central question of his writing life; not only would it preoccupy Steward during his early literary and academic career, but it would also be central to his later work as a diarist, sex researcher, and erotic author.

---

[*]Steward notes in the Stud File that he first had reciprocal oral sex with Junior Stewart sometime in 1924, and that they continued to have reciprocal oral sex ten more times. The interruption at the OSU frat house, while not specifically mentioned in the Stud File, is recollected in the SMS *Straight to Hell* interview and also is mentioned in the Phil Andros novel *Shuttlecock* (p. 102).

[†]Definitions of homosexuality vary from culture to culture and period to period. For an intriguing account of the varying ways in which sexual acts have defined sexual identity in the United States in the first half of the twentieth century, see George Chauncey, *Gay New York: Gender, Urban Culture, and the Making of the Gay Male World (1890–1940)* (New York: Basic Books, 1993).

[‡]These stories by Steward, written in his early teens, are in the collection of the Kinsey Institute for Sex Research.

None of Steward's academic writings on homosexuality ever achieved mainstream publication,* but his poems and short stories from the same period have survived, and in both the stories and the poems, sexuality is often the subject. He began publishing his romantic verses in the *Columbus Dispatch* starting at age eighteen, and by March 1930, his junior year, he had published a poem in the magazine *Contemporary Verse*. Benjamin Musser, the editor of that magazine, took a special interest in Steward, and eventually obtained a small yearly college stipend for him from the philanthropist Cora Smith Gould.

Musser (1889–1951) was a very minor poet, and he would eventually leave literary publishing for a religious vocation,† but at the time Steward met him in 1928, he was best known as the publisher of two small magazines, *Contemporary Verse* and *JAPM: The Poetry Weekly*.‡ Though closeted, Musser had written and privately published the anonymous homoerotic novel *The Strange Confession of Monsieur Montcairn*. Through marriage, meanwhile, he had become wealthy enough to set himself up as a publisher of new and emerging (young male) poets.

Steward met Musser at a poetry reading at Columbus's Chittenden Hotel and later noted, "From that chance meeting (as Huysmans wrote in *A Rebours*§) sprang a mistrustful friendship that endured for several years." Musser, then in his forties, promptly became infatuated with Steward, and forthwith introduced him to a wider circle of poets and literary figures, including Harold Vinal, secretary of the Poetry Society of America.

Steward was himself an able poet. His Italian sonnet "Virginia to Harlotta," written at age nineteen, presciently describes a consciousness divided between virtuous chastity and thankless promiscuity:

> *This is yours: to lie beside him all the night*
> *And feel the steady heat come out from him;*

*Steward's PhD dissertation explored, tangentially, the probable homosexuality of Cardinal Newman.

†Musser converted to Catholicism, became a tertiary of the order of St. Francis, and devoted the remainder of his life to religious work as a lay monk.

‡"JAPM" is an acronym for "Just Another Poetry Magazine." In 1930, the two magazines were merged into his *Bozart: The Bi-Monthly Poetry Review*.

§Steward is citing a key moment in Huysmans's *Against the Grain*, in which Des Esseintes is accosted by a boy prostitute and so begins his first homosexual affair: "From this chance encounter there had sprung a mistrustful friendship that somehow lasted several months . . . never had [Des Esseintes] run such risks, yet never had he known such satisfaction mingled with distress . . . the recollection of this mutual attachment dominated all the rest."

The coolness of his hands, each slender limb
Made restless by the absence of the light . . .
To know the graceless touch, the never-quite-
Sufficient kiss of lip on lip, or breast,
And when the day comes, grey unwanted guest
To see love's death, each in each other's sight.

And this is mine: a solitary bed,
And I so still . . . unwarmed, untouched, unkissed,
With moonlight fingering flowers on my spread,
And moaning trees and crying winds and mist . . .
Weave me a spell, O bow-boy, so that he
Embracing her sends his caress to me!

In a sense, the poem serves as an emblem of Steward's sexuality during his early years in academe, as he pined for fine young men who would never love him, while at the same time he had any number of vigorous, semianonymous encounters with others about whom he had few illusions, and who in return had few illusions about him. The form of the poem, meanwhile, shows Steward's interest in the sonnets of Petrarch, on whom he would later publish an essay in the *Sewanee Review*.

Musser invited Steward to visit him in New York, and subsequently to a number of romantic getaways at his beach house in Margate, near Atlantic City. In his *Bozart* gossip column of March 1930, Musser gleefully noted, "Sam Steward made his very first visit to New York [this past month] and the greater thrill was mine in showing him around . . . we made New Year whoopee at Parker Tyler's* apartment; Idella Purnell lunched with us one day and Harold Vinal the next."

Apart from meeting these two poet-publishers† (the latter best remembered in E. E. Cummings's verse indictment of bad poetry, "poem, or beauty hurts mr. vinal"), Steward had a number of other New York ad-

---

*Parker Tyler (1904–1974), novelist, poet, and film critic who edited the surrealist magazine *View*. Steward, who had been told by Musser of Musser's sexual involvement with Tyler and Ford, met both of these raucously effeminate young men but never developed a friendship with either, and later wrote disparagingly (but only in passing) of their collaborative novel *The Young and Evil*.

†The poet Idella Purnell Stone (1901–?) published the verse magazine *Palms* from 1923 to May 1930; the poet Harold Vinal (1891–1965) was involved in many publishing ventures. Steward maintained a friendship with Vinal for over a decade; Vinal's self-published *Nor Youth, Nor Age: Poems 1924–25* was jointly dedicated to Sam Steward and Cora Smith Gould.

ventures, only one of which has survived in print: he traveled up to Harlem with an unnamed lesbian friend to visit the postal clerk Alexander Gumby in his large studio apartment on Fifth Avenue between 131st and 132nd streets. Gumby's gay literary salon drew many of Harlem's theatrical and artistic luminaries; Steward, who enjoyed the sexual company of black men throughout his life, later recalled it as an evening of "reefer, bathtub gin, a game of truth, and assorted homosexual carryings-on." But he was otherwise nonplussed by New York. "NYC is fun," he observed to a friend at the end of his life, "but it drains you quickly (or it always did me) and the entanglements and cross-purposes and switchings and turn-arounds make it seem like an emotional railroad yard, with everything working well but not much actually getting done."

•

Through Musser's financial assistance, Steward published his first book with the vanity press Henry Harrison in 1930, a short-story collection entitled *Pan and the fire-bird*. These early stories featured a sexually allusive prose style strongly influenced by James Branch Cabell, whose 1920 novel *Jurgen* (a fantasy tale about a medieval pawnbroker, rife with naughty double entendres and barely concealed allusions to phalluses and sexual activity) had first been suppressed on charges of lascivious obscenity, then subsequently published to scandal-driven success. The collection included, most notably, Steward's tribute to Valentino, a poem entitled "Libation to a Dead God."

"With an interweaving of classicism and modernism, a soupcon of delicate decadence and sophisticated naievety [*sic*], the young Ohio poet and word-artist in this first book has linked the later Hellenic spirit with today's art in storytelling," Benjamin Musser noted of the book. "In these tales and poem-sketches, Mr. Steward strikes an exquisite note." But Steward's collection received few favorable reviews. One noted their frequent use of phallic imagery (the "fire-bird" of the title was in fact a phallus; the bird's name, "cirpk," was a none-too-subtle anagram). "That much is subtly suggestive, with an apparent flavor of homosexuality, will make [these stories] popular in certain circles," the *Dallas News* reported, nonetheless genially adding that "Mr. Steward is worth watching." A columnist in *The Brooklyn Citizen*, however, took violent exception to the book's homosexual innuendo: "*Pan and the fire-bird* caught my eye as it lay supinely in our literary editor's waste basket. I picked it up, read into its mystic and ineffably beautiful (to the initiate) tales of sex life among the Greeks, and tossed it forthwith into my own."

While Steward might have moved to New York after graduation, he felt no need to "escape" to Greenwich Village. He was managing very well to have all the sex he wanted in Columbus, and moreover he was intent upon an academic career. The "screaming" effeminacy of Greenwich Village homosexuals like Parker Tyler and Charles Henri Ford was simply not for him; since he preferred encounters with masculine men, and since he was himself masculine in affect, the Village had little allure.

In mid-1930, while traveling out to the Jersey shore to see Musser, Steward had a spontaneous sexual encounter with a Pullman porter that resulted in a lesion upon his glans which his doctor shortly thereafter diagnosed as syphilis, then still a life-threatening disease.* "Given my loathing of uncleanliness and my early conditioning," Steward later recalled, "the shock [of it] nearly unravelled me." The best treatment then available was "a three year ordeal—[including] weekly shots of Neosalvarsan from a doctor . . . who had been a classmate of my father's. And my father had [needed] to know too . . ." Steward's father's only comment on learning of his son's condition was to repeat what his own father, a country doctor, used to say: "It's like backing into a buzz saw, ain't it? You can't tell which tooth bit you."

The painful weekly shots gave Steward both purpura and a skin ulcer. After the course of neosalvarsan came a mercury ointment that he had to rub into his armpits and groin, and then a course of saturated solution of potassium iodide "which caused the skin to erupt all over [my] back in what looked like Job's boils." The illness made Steward feel polluted, and the trauma brought on by the disease seriously curtailed his sexual activities for the next thirty-six months.

Having been inducted into Phi Beta Kappa in his junior year, Steward received a BA with Honors in 1931 and was awarded the title of University Scholar in 1932–33 and University Fellow in English from 1933 to 1934. During this time he worked on a novel (provisionally entitled "Eros in Intaglio"), short stories, and plays. By August 1932 the Columbus *Sunday Star* would note, "The most sought after man on the Ohio State Cam-

*Sulfa drugs would come into general use only a decade later, approximately in 1939.

pus is not a football player, but he's more elusive than Garbo and has a
more successful mustache than Menjou. Listen, gals, he's Sam Steward,
author of *Pan and the fire-bird* [and his] telephone number [is] WA1592."
The Ohio Stater of April 1933 likewise nominated Steward for the Ohio
State Hall of Fame. During this time, he wrote his master's thesis, "Mutability in Spenser," and his dissertation, "Provocatives of the Oxford
Movement and Its Nexus with English Literary Romanticism."

Steward's intense focus on his studies during the early thirties may
have been based primarily on his love of literature; but it was also driven
by his fear of both unemployment and poverty, for these were the darkest
days of the Great Depression, and neither Steward nor his aunts had
any money. During the summer of 1933, he taught creative writing without pay at a provisional summer school for the unemployed. As soon as
he was granted his PhD in 1934, he seized the first teaching post he
could find, a summer appointment at Davis and Elkins College in Elkins,
West Virginia.

•

Steward began a period of spiritual questioning as a graduate student that
resulted in his conversion to Catholicism. His journey to faith was not
one he ever cared to chronicle in depth, though he did describe a similar
journey for a character very much like himself in his 1936 novel *Angels on
the Bough*. He did, however, note in his unpublished memoirs that his
attraction to Roman Catholicism had been largely sensual, and that he
had come to that sensual response primarily through reading the novels
of Huysmans:

> I went into the church by the back door, as a kind of spiritual ex-
> periment . . . learn[ing] from Wilde's *The Picture of Dorian Gray*
> about a book, in which "in exquisite raiment, and to the delicate
> sound of flutes, the sins of the world were passing in dumb show
> before him,"* a book filled with "metaphors as monstrous as or-
> chids," a "poisonous" book about strange purple sins.

---

*Steward is quoting from the passage in *The Picture of Dorian Gray* in which Gray experiences a
sexual awakening as a result of reading *Against the Grain* (as indeed Wilde himself had). The passage
concludes, "Things that [Dorian] had dimly dreamed of were suddenly made real to him. Things of
which he had never dreamed were gradually revealed."

This book was *Against the Grain* [*A Rebours*] by [Joris-Karl] Huysmans. Its sensuality and erudition fascinated me, enchanted me, for it described the life of the senses in terms of mystical philosophy; and the exploits of its hero, Des Esseintes, seemed to range from the ecstasies of a Medieval saint to the confessions of a modern sinner.

Against the Grain was (and remains) the standard defining example of French decadent fiction, the story of a man who withdraws from society to live in elegant depravity; but it was also the story of homosexual awakening that had inspired Oscar Wilde in both thought and deed. Huysmans's subsequent work, *Down There* (*Là-Bas*), had combined fiction and autobiography in its study of the black mass and Satanism. "Having developed a passionate admiration for Huysmans," Steward noted, "I went with him on his climb back from atheism to the Church in *En Route*, *The Cathedral*, and finally *The Oblate*."*

While Steward credited Huysmans with his conversion to sensual Catholicism, he was surely also rebelling against his own very chilly Methodist upbringing. The anti-Catholic teachings of an Ohio State history professor had also roused his curiosity: he later wrote that this professor's "innuendoes and crafty indictments of the Catholic Church [in his course on the Protestant Reformation] made me stubbornly determined to find out more about Catholicism."

But there was another aspect of Catholicism that appealed most strongly to Steward: namely, the concept that through confession one could seek (and obtain) absolution. For Steward, who felt so strongly rejected, condemned, and shamed by his own church, the idea of sexual absolution through confession was entirely appealing. Steward's PhD dissertation on the Oxford Movement reflected his new embrace of Catholicism, for in it he discussed a movement that had sought (specifically through the work of John Henry Newman) to bring the Church of England back to its Catholic roots—but had ultimately resulted in a number of its participants, including Newman (whom Steward sensed was homosexual), instead converting to Catholicism.

---

*In his enthusiasm for Huysmans, Steward wrote a study of his influence upon the Paris-based Irish writer, poet, and art critic George Moore, publishing it in *The Romantic Review* in 1934.

Steward would not, however, remain a Catholic long, for in confessing the sin of his homosexual activities, he found that he was routinely asked by his confessor to promise he would cease to engage in them. Though Steward did so, as time passed he realized he could not make such promises in good faith, and his own rigorous truthfulness suddenly came into complete conflict with what he was doing:

> My allegiance to Catholicism lasted a year and a half, and then the boyhood indoctrination against the Whore of Babylon* won out. I had been attracted to the Catholic liturgy, and by Huysmans . . . I thought I had found a creed elastic enough to allow for my pagan love of life—but the basic honesty infused into me by my early training [as a Methodist] made me realize that I could never again make a perfect act of contrition . . . And celibacy was not for me . . . [My ultimate feeling was that] no one with honesty can be both a Catholic and a homosexual.

Steward's explorations of both Catholicism and homosexuality found their way into his dissertation. By detailing the probable homosexuality of the Oxford Movement's leader, the philosopher, writer, and (later) Catholic convert John Henry (later, Cardinal) Newman, Steward noted that he had created "almost as much of a bombshell [in the English Department] as [had] my early essay on Whitman." Nonetheless, the dissertation passed. He had earned his PhD.

Steward completed the dissertation at twenty-four, ten years after his first sexual experience, and just before beginning his first lonely winter of teaching English at a small Catholic college in Helena, Montana. He seems to have written an essay around this time, never published, in which he described the challenge of adjusting to his sexual nature. He signed it using an alias, and altered enough of the specifics of his own life story in it that he could not be concretely identified as its author. Entitled "The Homosexual's Adjustment," it features none of the humorous detachment of Steward's later writing; in fact, it is deadly earnest, and so remarkable

---

*By "Whore of Babylon," Steward means the Catholic church as it has been referred to by various fundamentalist denominations. The expression comes from a vision offered in the book of Revelation (17:18).

a document of his state of mind during these early years that it merits reproduction in its entirety:*

I am twenty-two years old. I was graduated from college last June and am at present an instructor in English at a western college. I have reason to believe that with hard work on my part, I shall be able to go a little further in my profession than does the average instructor. But for the past three years I have known that I am a homosexual [and] it is something that I must take into account in any plans I make for the future. I will not say that it is the fact of first importance in my life . . . But it is a fact that I can certainly not ignore—or only at a price that I should not care to pay. The acceptance of the fact does not come at such a cheap price either.

This knowledge of my homosexuality did not, of course, come as a sudden burst of intelligence. If at the age of sixteen I had known that there was such a thing as homosexuality, I might have understood myself better. As it was, I was finding sexual expression with boys of my own age who were perfectly normal boys [who] chose [me as] the next best means of expression. As I grew older and my friends' sexual interests became entirely taken up by the opposite sex, I began to wonder at the tardiness with which, in my case, these feelings put in their appearance. I did not at the time doubt that they would develop; I was concerned chiefly at the unconscionably long time it was taking them to do so.

In college they had not yet appeared, and in comparing my sexual reactions to those of my acquaintances, I began to worry about myself . . . I set about reading such books on psychiatry and psychopathology as I could get my hands on in an effort to

---

*The essay is signed "Michael Walters," an alias Steward never used again. It appears to have been composed in 1934, the year in which he took his teaching position at Carroll College. Since so much of this biography depends on Steward's credibility in his own writing, and since so much of what he did would seem almost beyond believing had not Steward himself been so good at documenting and recording his activities, it is worth noting that while Steward was utterly truthful always in his private records of his sexual activities (at first because he kept these records only for himself, and later because he kept them for Kinsey), he was, like all writers, capable of significant omissions or minor alterations of fact in writings about himself that he intended for anonymous or semi-anonymous publication.

understand myself better; then suddenly I felt that I had found out much more than I cared about knowing . . .

I was nineteen years old, a junior in college, when I made this discovery about myself . . . [But] if the price of . . . "belonging" was that I deceive myself and stifle some of my feelings, I was willing to pay the price . . . When I graduated three of my college friends—my roommate, another friend, and one of my professors—knew that I was a homosexual. To these three I had volunteered the information; I feel sure that neither of the three had previously suspected any such thing.

I do not know just when it was that I began to question the wisdom of my adjustment, to suspect, indeed, that it was no adjustment at all but merely a silly and futile effort to deceive myself into thinking that there was nothing the matter with me . . . But . . . I was not fooling myself. In the first place . . . I was also in less guarded moments building romantic notions about a future love affair of my own with another person like myself. Every new and attractive boy I met appeared as the possible fulfillment of this dream. In the second place, there was the conviction that my friendship with these normal boys was pretty one-sided. I understood them, even their love affairs, but they did not even begin to understand me. In the third place, I came to realize that I was living in a perpetual state of tension; at any moment something might snap and I would give myself away. Psychologists can perhaps explain the feeling of actual physical tension that seemed to accompany this mental state. I felt constantly on guard, and it seemed that I held my body rigid, so that I could not even relax in sleep.

Since my graduation last June, I have been trying to make a more mature adjustment to my condition. I realize that different inverts have made different adjustments and that there are perhaps as many types among homosexuals as there are among normal men . . .

The adjustment of one invert, whose book I have read, has largely been determined by his conversion to the Roman Catholic Church. Religion, especially the Catholic religion, expects a definite adjustment from its sexually abnormal believers . . . There is much to be said for such an attitude. In the first place, it is definite. It does not ignore homosexuality nor make light of it; it accepts its existence and has a definite program for dealing with it. To those inverts who do believe or can honestly come to a belief in revealed religion, it offers a program of action. But to suggest that one accept the Catholic religion, or any other religion in order that he may gain thereby a program for dealing with his homosexuality, is, it seems to me, to suggest a perversion of religion. For those inverts who cannot accept the tenets of revealed religion even though through such an acceptance might come a solution of their problems, there must be some other form of adjustment.

In my own case . . . I have taken what I think are two definite steps toward a more mature adjustment to my nature. In the first place, I have stopped pretending that I am normal. I do not say that I have cut out normal activities or cut myself off from normal people . . . But I know that the enjoyment I get from such activities is not the enjoyment that my heterosexual friends get. I know this and sometimes it makes me afraid. I am afraid that sometime a girl is going to take me too seriously, that some girl may even begin to fall in love with me. I shall hate to fail her then. For I know that whatever latent capacity for love I may have, it will never be awakened by a woman.

Secondly, I have learned not to look upon every good looking boy I meet as a possible lover. I pride myself that my attitude is realistic . . . This new attitude has saved me from a lot of futile day-dreaming; unfortunately it has not rendered me impervious to the attraction.

At the present time, that is about as far as my adjustment has got. When I think of the future I find that there are some other things that I must take into account.

I have said that I do not consider my homosexuality the most important fact in my life. I am an invert but I am also ambitious. Normal men have other interests than sex; so does the invert. But normal men do not often have to choose between love and a career . . . But the homosexual, it seems to me, often finds himself in a place where the choice between a career and love seems inevitable.

I want to teach. For the next four or five years I shall be so busy getting degrees that, even were I normal, I should probably not give marriage much consideration. But with a doctorate and an instructorship in some college, I would, were I normal, probably fall in love and marry. No one would bat an eyelash. But suppose that within the next four or five years, with my doctorate and an instructorship, I should fall in love with another instructor like myself or with one of my students. There would at first be gossip. It would develop into opinion. Whether I were teaching at a small denominational college or at a state university it would probably mean my dismissal. One might of course escape detection by being furtive and secretive. Undoubtedly there are many men, married and single, on the faculties of denominational colleges and of large universities who carry on clandestine love affairs and get away with them. I might put my love on such a compromise basis and be fairly happy. But people would wonder why I did not marry, why I did not fall in love with "some nice girl." It would be hard to escape detection . . . Of course, there is something to be said for announcing to the world what one is, for sending out wedding announcements as it were. And it is romantic and defiant. It is one way of solving the original difficulty—by creating thirty subsequent ones. And it would be one way of ensuring your dismissal from the faculty.

If one does not want to suppress his nature and yet is afraid of expressing it, what is he to do? I do not know. Not now. The homosexual, probably more than the normal man, learns the futility of mapping out a path for his emotions. I do not know what I shall be feeling or believing five years from now. I do not even want to know.

But this I do know. My friends are going to fall in love. They are going to get married. Try as we may, we shall never be able to regain the old intimacy of college days. My brothers and sisters will marry and raise families. My parents will not always be here. If I discover that I cannot have both love and a career and choose in favor of the career, I shall have the satisfaction of knowing that according to the standards of my age I have chosen the path of virtue and righteousness [and] perhaps in time I shall become a Grand Old Man.

That is one picture I see when I try to look into my own future. [But] there is [also] a blacker picture which I sometimes force myself to consider. That is the picture of arrest and imprisonment; in this country as in most of the countries of Europe, homosexual love is a crime, punished by fines and imprisonment.

There is, of course, a somewhat brighter picture. I may find a satisfying companion; I may fall in love, and because of love give up my career and find another career with which love would not be so likely to interfere. Up to the present time, although I have had infatuations for normal men, I have never been in love with another invert. Obviously I cannot predict what I might do should I fall in love. For love, my normal friends tell me, makes one do strange things.

In considering his future as dispassionately as possible, Steward admitted (as he would rarely do again) the many sorrows of his very solitary existence. What is most chilling about the essay, however (apart from its extraordinary focus and clarity), is its prescience. The bleak vision he offers of his future as a homosexual educator was entirely accurate, and does a good deal to explain his descent into alcoholism shortly after he wrote it. It also suggests that his conclusive departure from the world of academe (albeit nearly twenty years later) would be no mere accident of circumstance.

2

Teres Atque Rotundus

While Steward's job as an English instructor at Carroll College, a small Catholic institution in Helena, Montana, paid a much-needed hundred dollars a month with room and board, he soon realized that teaching in the wild west would hardly be the romantic idyll he had envisioned from his Columbus bedroom. "Trying to teach cowboys and the sons of cowboys about semicolons is not a rewarding pastime," he wrote years later, "[and] there was nothing to do in Helena . . . Almost every evening I would be tanked on sherry, for my life as an alcoholic was by now well under way." One night after too many whiskey sours with Monsignor Emmet Riley, president of the college, the two ended up in bed together and, in Steward's words, "enough happened to weaken my faith considerably . . . [for apparently] a cardinal sin in Ohio was [but] a peccadillo in Montana." In the course of the fall term, two other priests attempted to bed Steward, and a third "pop[ped] out of the confessional to see who had confessed such lurid sins." These and other acts of clerical hypocrisy quickly convinced Steward that Carroll was not for him, and also helped hasten his abandonment of Catholicism.

Apart from a clandestine sexual arrangement with a redheaded cowboy named Doug McCann, Steward found few diversions during the winter months. "We had a two-week period of minus 35 degree weather, warming up in the afternoons to minus thirty. Sometimes we amused ourselves by opening a third floor window and spitting out; the spittle would freeze . . . and a glass of water, if poured slowly in a thin stream, hit the earth with a tinkle of broken icicles." To combat boredom, Steward held an oratory contest, drove 115 miles to Missoula to speak on "Trends in Modern Literature," and took a bus full of students 250 miles to Billings to see a performance by the Ballets Russes. But for the most part he spent his evenings alone, working on the novel he had begun in Columbus, or else writing letters to anyone who interested him. The most successful of these correspondences was with Gertrude Stein.

Steward had first written to Stein from Columbus in 1932 to inform her of the death of Clare Andrews. By way of introduction, he had noted in a Stein-like pastiche that "one day in class he read your *As a Wife Has a Cow a Love Story* and he read it so well we were all thenceforth readers of Gertrude Stein." Stein's immediate openness to Steward and his ideas seems to have encouraged him to abandon his initial disingenuousness toward her, or rather to engage in it more playfully in the knowledge that she readily saw through it. In any event, he genuinely liked her writing and she genuinely liked his praise of it, and on that basis they began an increasingly intimate epistolary friendship. Though his own prose style had gone in other directions since *Pan and the fire-bird*, Steward genuinely loved Stein's continuing exploration of the abstract potential of language. He also loved her daring experiments with same-sex eroticism in works like "As a Wife Has a Cow" and "Lifting Belly." And yet while Steward's initial excitement about Stein had been a poet's excitement about innovative use of language, he found that Stein began almost immediately to reach out to him personally: to nurture him, encourage him, and share her life with him in a way he had never dreamt possible with anyone— much less a literary celebrity.

•

Steward's first letter to Stein from Helena noted his sadness at missing her when she visited Ohio State University on her speaking tour of the United States, for *The Autobiography of Alice B. Toklas* had just then established her as a national sensation. He quickly set up a speaking engagement for her in Helena, tempting her there with promised visits to a ghost town, a gold mine, and a hangman's tree—but in the end the trip fell through. "When the [cancellation] telegram came from Alice [Toklas] . . . I broke down and wept," he later wrote. "My regret and unhappiness were only slightly tempered by receiving one day a very large matted portrait of Gertrude [by] Carl Van Vechten" bearing an autographed personal inscription from her. Still, she was no pushover: In September 1935, Stein responded to his gift of *Pan and the fire-bird* by telling him that while "there are spots in it that I like very much . . . it is a mess."

By then Steward had left Carroll College; after writing a bitter account of his (nonsexual) experiences there as a much-exploited lay faculty member (and subsequently publishing it in the Catholic magazine *The Commonweal**), he had accepted a yearlong posting at the State College of Washington at Pullman, near the Idaho border. After spending the summer working as an information clerk in Glacier Park, he arrived in Pullman in late summer. "The whole scene around Pullman especially from my study window has the air of one of Grant Wood's Iowa interiors," he wrote Stein, "and with a little snow the other morning it was so clear and calm I felt a Wordsworthian tear very near." But he soon discovered that Pullman, too, was far from ideal, for it was an extremely conservative school with a faculty that was "dull, inbred, and disastrously gossipy." As a result Steward again found himself socially isolated, and again spending his free time mooning over the "fine upstanding young [male] heterosexual students, the western ideal that I had seen suggestions of in Montana . . . in the Housman manner I [then] wrote scores of melancholy poems about handsome young men I couldn't have."

A typical poem from this Housman-inspired series, dated November 16, 1936, reads:

> *I could not stand your presence here*
> *More than the sun's at noon,*
> *And yet I hope, but know you won't*
> *Come back so very soon.*
>
> *Two nights we've lain together there,*
> *And never dared a touch,*
> *For I would choke & you would curse*
> *If either tried as much.*

---

*The article (describing the routine exploitation of lay faculty by clergymen at the college) was published as "The Lay Faculty," *The Commonweal* 21:24 (April 12, 1935): 667–68. See also Jeremiah K. Durick, "The Lay Faculty: A Reply," *The Commonweal* 21:25 (April 19, 1935): 699–701.

Lad, lonely shall we go our ways,
No matter whom we choose,
You with the maid your eye lights on,
And I to tend my bruise.

Steward had few illusions about these verses, later noting they consisted of not much more than "a simple dingdong rhythm containing the
record of a 'pain.'" The only subtle note in the poem is in its final word,
"bruise"—for Steward was now beginning to acknowledge not only emotional bruises, but also physical ones, as the young men he attempted to
seduce sometimes responded to his overtures with a fist.

Housman's erotic longings for idealized young men at least held out
the possibility of creative sublimation for Steward as he struggled with his
own intense loneliness as an unattached and closeted academic.* As for
the poems' overtly homoerotic content, Steward felt simply, "If a don of
Cambridge could get away with it, so could I."

The suite of Housman-inspired poems also demonstrates a significant change in Steward's writing style. While *Pan and the fire-bird* had
abounded in florid word experiments, such things had now all but disappeared from Steward's writing, replaced instead by plainspoken expressions of grim and awkward truths. Steward never wrote directly about the
influence of Housman on his writing, but on his first trip to Europe a year
later, he would make a special journey to Cambridge specifically to pay
homage to the recently deceased scholar-poet.

By the time Steward received Stein's letter about *Pan and the fire-bird*
being "a mess," he readily agreed with her:

> When I wrote [*Pan and the fire-bird*] I had nothing to say, I was
> just writing. I had discovered that words were lovely and fascinat-
> ing and I was like a child with new toys. And I put words together
> without reason, attempting only rime . . . I cannot read a single
> page of [it] without hollowness settling wildly over me. But next

---

*Despite these longings for young men he could not have, Steward managed nonetheless "a consid-
erable number of sexual releases [while at Pullman] with handsome young animals who were not
gods but men." "I was drunk each time," he later noted, ". . . [and] somehow I didn't care for my
reputation, having usually managed . . . to get them to jack me off—which compromised them as
much as myself, so they wouldn't talk." (Steward, unpublished memoir.)

time when *Angels on the Bough* is published I hope you will let
me send you a copy of it to make some effort (which may fail!) to
redeem myself from the adolescence into which I must have
fallen in your regard. In this one which is a modern novel I do
have something to say I hope.

Stein's friendliness toward him was such that in his next letter he
ventured, "I have thought that in the summer of 1937 it would be nice to
come to Europe, [and] surely get to meet you at last." He then described
for her his growing popularity in Pullman as an English instructor: "I had
two hundred students for my first semester here and next year . . . I will
have a special course in creative writing all my own." He accepted a verbal
offer of reappointment to Pullman in April 1936.

A month later, in May, *Angels on the Bough* was published to uni-
formly positive reviews. Rather than submitting the novel to the top literary publishing houses in New York, Steward had simply placed the
manuscript with Caxton Publishers, a small commercial printer just three
hundred miles south of Pullman, in Caldwell, Idaho, which was developing a book-publishing venture as a sideline. Nonetheless, the novel received national attention, for it was a very fine first effort.

A collection of deftly juxtaposed character sketches of Columbus
bohemians, *Angels on the Bough* is a beautifully crafted narrative exploring
their intersecting lives during the toughest days of the Great Depression.
In its look at love, faith, and the erotic drives of young men and women
in a small Midwestern city, it is a comedy unique in its sexual candor. The
novel received a long, praise-filled review by Stanley Young in *The New
York Times* that noted that the novel's six characters were "illumined by a
very distinct gift above the usual. The inner motives of personality are so
skillfully turned outward that we see straight through to the[ir] heart[s]
and head[s]." Young went on to praise the novel's

direct, dramatic subjectivism that goes back to Henry James. Mr.
Steward has no thesis to impose upon us, nor any ulterior aesthetic intention. His object is to create character in much the
manner suggested by Woolf in her critical essay "Mr. Bennett and
Mrs. Brown"—that is, to picture people as distinct entities
[whose] lives are inseparably woven together. This author, in his

first novel, has carried out his purpose with architectural perfection. In so doing he rises considerably above the garden variety of first novelists.

Each of the characters in *Angels on the Bough* represents some aspect of Steward's own personality: Richard Dominay, a young man crushed by the endless duties and obligations of academe; Tom Cave, a spiritual seeker drawn toward Catholicism by Huysmans (and simultaneously drawn away from it by pornography); Jan Halladay, an artist incapacitated by his mother's suicide; Mary Nowell, a good-natured floozy; and Dora Milton, a young woman who feels immense relief in finally running away from the man who loves her, despite her own great love and need for him. Marie Anderson appears as Jean Anders, who marries a Communist and sets sail for the Soviet Union; Steward's aunts appear as the endlessly bickering Purfle sisters, who run a boardinghouse.

While deeply felt, the novel is also quite funny, particularly in its characterization of Mary Nowell, the homely young secretary whose private life revolves around the pickups she makes on the street. Steward delights in her rationalizations about her wanton ways, and his oddly empathetic portrayal of her makes the novel's denouement—when she discovers she has been infected with deadly syphilis by a young man she had hoped would marry her—all the more shocking. While favorable reviews of the book appeared nationwide in more than twenty newspapers, the critical success of the novel gave Steward only trouble—for as a result of his extremely sympathetic portrayal of that girl of easy virtue, the morally righteous president of the university fired him on the spot.

Steward was dumbfounded. As he told the *Columbus Dispatch* a month later, "Four hours after the president delivered his commencement address extolling the virtues of liberty and a free people, [E. O. Holland, the university president] summarily dismissed me for exercising a little academic freedom and told me my going was but the forerunner of six or eight more to go." When challenged, Holland stated that Steward had not only published an obscene novel, but also encouraged his students to engage in a strike against the administration. But an official investigation into the incident by the American Association of University Professors later found nothing to substantiate the latter charge and censured the university president.

At the moment of his dismissal, however, Steward had no legal recourse. He was without a job, and contesting his dismissal through the university system would have taken months. With little in savings, he could only pack his bags and leave town to find work elsewhere. But before returning to Columbus, he wrote Gertrude Stein:

> Tomorrow I am posting to you at Bilignin a copy of my novel and I hope I do indeed hope sincerely that you may like some of it. There was an awful squabble here, the people turned provincial on me, I was like to lose my position. But now all seems quiet although I am still wondering who won and how far a college teacher is limited in his extramural utterances and if I am to go through the creative life I may have thinking of every sentence phrase and word with it pass favorably under the eyes of my superiors. I feel this would be a very bad thing do not you.

Stein wrote back:

> My Dear Sam,
>   The book came and I have just finished it and I like it I like it a lot, you have really created a piece of something, by the way how old are you, I have just finished it and I am not sure that I am not going to read it again. It quite definitely did something to me . . . something came into xistence [sic] and remained there, I have to read it again to know more just what . . . I will read the book again and write again and I can tell you that I like it and that it did something to me.*

By the end of the summer Steward had found a job at Loyola University, a Jesuit school on Chicago's North Side. "I hardly wanted to go back into religious teaching," Steward later recalled (for he had long since abandoned Catholicism), "but I sent a copy of my novel to the dean there, explaining all. He found it innocuous, and I was hired to teach . . . under the direction of Morton Dauwen Zabel, one of the most feared and re-

---

*Stein later wrote in *Everybody's Autobiography* that "*Angels on the Bough* . . . is a very interesting book. It has something in it that makes it literature. I do not know quite what but there it is."

spected scholars in the field." Two months after arriving in Chicago, Steward wrote Stein describing his new situation:

> How I got here I am not sure, but they took a chance on me and I am in a very stronghold of Jesuitry, a blackbird warren, a place of four-square education. For there is a Wall around education here and beyond it in his thoughts, his reading, no good papist must go. For a time methought the Parcae* had something dire against me, to weave my poor strands into this desperate pattern but one discovers that if a thing is said in a skillful way, all things may be said . . .
>
> Strange that one can actually be lonely in a great city . . . I have a small little apartment and it is really rather nice . . . the lake is only a hundred yards away but I cannot see it unless I walk down the street. The other night at midnight I did walk down there, it was blowing and wild . . . You stand on an embankment overlooking darkness and see no line between sky and water but only a sullen void with whiteness fretting and circling at your feet, in a thin crisping edge of foam, and the winds are wild and roar in your ears, and at such moments you believe that you can do anything at all in the world.

Steward's first year at Loyola was exhausting, for Zabel, a brilliant Henry James scholar, leaned on him heavily from the start. A confirmed bachelor who lived with his mother, Zabel had little tolerance for fellow academics who could not keep up with his own exceptionally high level of productivity. "Zabel worked us unmercifully," Steward later noted. "His razor mind under his youthfully bald pate made him the archetypal egghead, with a soft voice that could cut like a blade of Toledo steel if necessary."

Though Steward was now regularly drinking alone at night to blackout state, he nonetheless came into his own as a scholar at Loyola, for in Zabel he had finally met a boss he genuinely respected and wanted to please. In his first year Steward would teach "Contemporary English and American Literature," "Pope and His Contemporaries," and "Middle English Poetry and Prose" to undergraduates, and "Modern Drama," "The

---

Parcae is the Latin word for the Fates of Roman mythology, the three goddesses of destiny.

Seventeenth Century," "The Modern Novel," and "Shakespeare Studies" to graduates. Over the coming years he would teach an extraordinary variety of other courses,* including undergraduate French. "If I accomplished nothing else [during my time at Loyola]," he later wrote, "it was to become *teres atque rotundus*—complete and well-rounded—in the field of English literature and its allied topics."

Despite the academic freedom granted by Zabel to his department, Steward remained closeted at Loyola, for the academic climate of the mid-1930s was, if not openly hostile to homosexuality, at least incapable of sympathy for it. Newton Arvin, a leading (and deeply closeted) critic of the time, wrote apologetically on Whitman in 1938 that "Whitman was no mere invert, no mere 'case': he remained to the end, in almost every real and visible sense, a sweet and sane human being." Participating in such maddening hypocrisy galled Steward, who after all had begun his academic career with a forthright reading of Whitman's "Calamus" poems by way of Havelock Ellis.

Even so, he profited from Zabel's example as a scholar, and for a while he was happy with his career:

> Zabel turned me into a better scholar than I had ever been as a PhD candidate. A perfectionist himself, he expected it in others—and although I never reached his degree of acumen or profundity, I did learn much from him and come to respect him as a talented and meticulous savant with an encyclopedic mind, a giant of learning. And I came also to sympathize with him and the tumult that his [closeted] sexual nature must have caused him.

Then again, Steward could hardly have objected to Zabel's closeted ways, for as he saw it, "If you were hypocrite enough to accept a job in a religious institution after having lost your religion—why should you expect perfection in anyone else? I tucked the whole problem away, drank a few more martinis, and did not bring it up again."

---

*Steward's courses (apart from introductory English courses and introductory French language courses) included: The American Novel; Dryden and Restoration Verse; English Literature from 450 to 1660; Contemporary British Literature; English Romanticism; Early Victorian Literature; Composition and Rhetoric; Literary Criticism; Tennyson and Browning; Elizabethan Drama; Contemporary French Literature; Shakespeare; The Age of Johnson; The English Renaissance; Wordsworth and Coleridge; *Beowulf*; and English Poetry and Prose of the Sixteenth and Seventeenth Centuries.

And drink Steward did. "By the time I reached Chicago," Steward later wrote, "I was fairly established as a secret drunk. Things grew steadily worse for the next ten years [until] I was consuming—at home in my apartment— a quart a day, to which must be added the shots I had *en route* to and from class. It was a period filled with dreadful scenes, the gradual loss of friend after friend, the deterioration of my health and sleep patterns, the inexorably growing loss of memory, and the slow ruin of my potency and my body." In another instance he observed,

> These were the vacant years, the empty years, when the blackouts steadily increased—until sometimes I had to take to marking the calendar with crosses, the way a convict might in prison, so that I could remember what day it was—and whether I had to teach . . . but I never landed in jail for drunkenness, nor did I miss classes, nor did I lose my position as a professor.

Steward had always been popular with his students, and at Loyola he became wildly so. "My classes are always full," he wrote Gertrude Stein, "but maybe that means I [just] put a lot of sex in my lectures. [Still] I try to liberate the students, or increase their backgrounds, or train them to teach themselves. They say I have a sharp tongue and am a disciplinarian. Once I overheard one say, when he got back a paper with a low mark, 'Oh, that Doctor Steward—I never know whether to kiss him or kill him.'"

Steward also quickly developed a number of friends away from Loyola, most of them living near the University of Chicago in Hyde Park. They included the surrealist painter Gertrude Abercrombie, a young black painter named Charles Sebree, and the pioneering black dancer-choreographer Katherine Dunham and her husband, the stage designer John Pratt. Thornton Wilder, who then held a part-time teaching position at the University of Chicago, would eventually become another acquaintance; so, too, would a struggling young novelist and short-story writer named Wendell Wilcox, who like Steward was being mentored by Stein. Last to join this loose-knit group in 1938 would be the young avant-garde writer James Purdy, with whom Steward had a brief fling, even though Purdy was still in his late teens.

Steward also befriended Emmy Curtis, a French teacher at Theodore Roosevelt High School in Albany Park, who was eighteen years his senior.

"When I first knew her, [she] looked like the stereotype of the old-maid schoolteacher," Steward noted, "greying brown hair parted in the middle . . . into a small bun low on the neck; thin-lipped, and seeming to be easily shocked. [But with]in a few years [of knowing me], both her appearance and attitudes were greatly changed." A war widow, Curtis lived with "her very German mother, Augusta 'Mutter' Dax," who disapproved of Steward entirely. Nonetheless "[Emmy] fell in love with me," Steward later wrote, "and in my peculiar way, I loved her. About 1943 we began to go to bed together, and continued this for about six years (211 times) until Kinsey said after our interview, 'why don't you stop?' And I, of course, was not heterosexual. I bought her a wedding ring as a common-law wife, both of [us] having fulfilled the legal aspects by announcing it to three people. We did not want to get married; it was as much her reluctance as mine, for she would have lost her husband's pension as a war-widow." Though it ceased to be sexual, their remarkably warm friendship would last until Curtis's death twenty years later, and during that time she would see Steward through many a crisis.

•

Having decided to visit Stein in Europe, Steward made no secret of his summer travel plans; the Loyola University newspaper noted that his ambitious program would include study at the British Museum in London, a tour of the Paris Exposition, and a journey to Bilignin in southern France to stay at Gertrude Stein's summer home. If the newspaper article was to be believed, Steward then planned to "sojourn the latter part of his six weeks abroad as the guest of Thomas Mann, famed German writer in exile."

As an ambitious young literary man patterning himself on his mentor Clare Andrews, Steward had long wanted to travel to Europe to immerse himself in the avant-garde milieu so amiably described by Andrews's friend Gertrude Stein in The Autobiography of Alice B. Toklas (1933). Moreover, by the mid-1930s a number of significant studies of contemporary literature, most notably Malcolm Cowley's Exile's Return: A Literary Odyssey of the 1920s (1934), had pinpointed Paris as a crucible for innovative American writing of the Jazz Age. So Steward's decision to travel to Paris seemed, on the face of it, entirely in keeping with his academic vocation. The large number of tête-à-têtes he had arranged with leading European literary figures impressed Morton Zaubel, who of course knew nothing of the won't-take-no-for-an-answer fan-mail letters Steward had been so assiduously writing these various literary figures for nearly a year on Loyola University stationery.

But Steward had more in mind than simply visiting these great writers as a scholar and student of literature. Since adolescence he had modeled himself on suave Continental sophisticates such as Adolphe Menjou. Now, having read all about French sexual sophistication, he hoped to establish himself in Paris as a writer and intellectual. Far from Woodsfield and its stodgy Methodists, Steward knew that in Europe (and particularly in Paris) he would finally fit in.

•

Steward memorialized his first trip to Europe in two diaries. The first was a simple travel diary noting random encounters with other tourists; the second was a secret diary describing his various literary and sexual adventures.* In advance of the trip he had arranged by letter to meet not only with Thomas Mann, but also with Lord Alfred Douglas, André Gide, and Romain Rolland. Of all the literary figures he had written, only James Joyce had declined a meeting with him outright.

After arriving in London, Steward traveled up to Trinity College, Cambridge, where, as he later wrote in his memoirs, he walked "to Whewell's Court and Great Court B2 where A.E. Housman had lived for twenty-five years," there "to stand silently weeping" in tribute to the poet and scholar. Upon his return to London, he telephoned the aged Lord Alfred Douglas. Steward had been corresponding with Douglas regularly since 1934, for Douglas had been hoping Steward might help him find a good American publisher for his *True History of Shakespeare's Sonnets*. While making his various plans for Europe, Steward had come up with the idea that through physical contact with Douglas he might establish physical contact, by extension, with his great literary hero Oscar Wilde.

Douglas's voice was "high-pitched and tinny over the phone," Steward later recalled, but "he seemed cordial enough, and invited me down to tea on an afternoon two days hence." Steward accordingly took the train to Brighton, "which was next door to Hove where he lived, connected in those days (and perhaps still) by a kind of boardwalk along the seafront . . .

---

*This second "secret" diary was unfortunately lost in a fire in 1970 (see pages 356–57).

[Douglas's home, St. Annes Court, Nizells Avenue] was a fifteen minute walk from Brighton past flimsy pavilions dingy from the sea air."* The place in which Lord Alfred Douglas lived, as Steward later wrote, was "hardly . . . Wordsworth's 'pastoral farms green to the very door,'† but it was pleasant and British and the sort of dwelling I was used to seeing in British movies."

As Steward later confessed:

> I must honestly admit that I had no interest whatsoever in Lord Alfred Douglas as a person or as a writer, but only in the fact that he and Oscar Wilde had been lovers,‡ and back in those shrouded days the name of Wilde had a magic all its own for those of us who had to live without the benefits of liberation or exposure of our wicked lives. Besides, I was in my twenties and Lord Alfred was by then sixty-seven, and in anyone's book that's *old*. To go to bed with him was hardly the most attractive prospect in the world—it was terrifying, even repulsive. But if I wanted to link myself to Oscar Wilde more directly than I was linked [by touch] to Whitman [through the novelist and poet Hamlin Garland, who

---

*The 1937 travel (as opposed to "secret") diary has no description of Steward's visit to Douglas in Hove, and while Douglas does appear in the Stud File, the date of the encounter is erroneously placed as "July 1937," which was impossible since Steward arrived in England only on August 10 and departed on August 19. Steward's Stud File notations for encounters previous to 1947 are often hazy, however, since through the late 1940s he kept the Stud File only for his own amusement (it became much more specific in its dates after Kinsey asked him to consider donating it to the Kinsey Archive in approximately 1950). Although Steward's "secret" diary was lost in a 1970 fire, Steward's various other written, published accounts of the visit to Douglas (which he published starting in the mid-1960s) are entirely consistent with the facts (only published much later) of Douglas's life in Hove. In 1937, Douglas did indeed have a flat at St. Annes Court, Hove, which had been rented for him by his nephew, the Marquess of Queensberry. Douglas was able to entertain Steward with assured privacy since he lived alone—for his wife, Olive, had by then abandoned him though she continued to live nearby (Douglas Murray, *Bosie: A Biography of Lord Alfred Douglas* [New York: Hyperion, 2000]). In autumn 2009, the copy of Douglas's *True History of Shakespeare's Sonnets* inscribed to Steward by Douglas surfaced at public auction; it is currently in the collection of the author.

†Steward is quoting from Wordsworth's "Lines Composed a Few Miles above Tintern Abbey" (1798).

‡At the time Steward visited him, Steward was unaware of Lord Alfred's character, for indeed very few people knew the truly awful behavior Douglas had shown toward Wilde before, during, and after Wilde's imprisonment—by 1937, Wilde's *De Profundis* had been published only in Robbie Ross's highly expurgated 1905 version, a version that had left out all of the many damning statements about Douglas by Wilde that might have been considered actionable. (The full text of Wilde's indictment of Douglas would be published in its entirety only in 1949, more than a decade after Steward's visit to Hove.)

had touched me on the head at an OSU literary reception], there was no other way.

Even so, the possibility seemed remote . . . He had married in 1902 and become a Roman Catholic in 1911, and thus put behind him all such childish things as fellatio, mutual masturbation, sodomy, and so on.

Steward then recalled the particulars of the visit:

[Lord Alfred Douglas] opened the door himself—a man of medium height with hairline receding on the right side where it was parted, and the somewhat lackluster straight mousy hair falling down towards his left eyebrow. His nose was very large and bulbous. The red rose-leaf lips* beloved by Wilde had long since vanished; the mouth was compressed and thin, pursed somewhat, and the corners turned slightly downwards. I looked in vain for a hint, even the barest suggestion, of the fair and dreamy youth of the early photographs with Wilde. None was visible.

He never stopped talking—a long monologue in which "As a poet I" and "As an artist I" recurred again and again and again. He seemed not even to realize the extent to which he revealed his violent prejudices and hates, nor the immaturity of his view of himself. It became obvious before very long that he had never really grown up. He remained psychologically (and in his own eyes perhaps physically) still the radiant and brilliant adolescent beloved by the gods. He was a man of vast essential egotism . . . As for homosexual leanings and entanglements—that had all been given up when he became a Catholic—oh yes. He still got hundreds of letters from curiosity seekers and homosexuals and he could have had his pick of any of them (my ears and armpits flamed), but that was all finished. Sins of the flesh were obnoxious and uninteresting.

---

*Steward's borrowed phrase about the "red rose-leaf lips" comes from the "madness of kisses" letter from Wilde to Douglas, a letter that was stolen from Douglas by a blackmailer and subsequently used against Wilde in court as damning evidence of his "sodomitical nature."

The conversation took a turn for the better, however, when Steward suggested they adjourn to a pub for a drink, and Douglas responded by opening a bottle of gin:

> Within an hour and a half we were in bed, the Church renounced, conscience vanquished, inhibitions overcome, revulsion conquered, pledges and vows and British laws all forgotten. Head down, my lips where Oscar's had been, I knew that I had won.
>
> After I finished my ministrations and settled back, his hand stole down to clamp itself around me. It began to move gently. Still moving it up and down, shafering me, he spoke: "You really needn't have gone to all that trouble, since this is almost all Oscar and I ever did with each other . . . We used to get boys for each other . . . We kissed a lot, but not much more."

"I got to Brighton for the ten o'clock train that night," Steward concluded. "Lord Alfred never wrote to me again, nor I to him. He died in 1945."

•

On August 19, Steward left London, taking the boat train to Paris. His visit took place during the Exposition Internationale des Arts et Techniques dans la Vie Moderne 1937, where, in the shadow of the Eiffel Tower, Boris Iofan's Soviet Pavilion confronted Albert Speer's German Pavilion, and Picasso's *Guernica* hung in protest against the atrocities of the Spanish Civil War.

Along with trips to the Exposition and to Paris's various monuments and museums, Steward met up daily with some fellow homosexuals he had met on his crossing on the *Aquitania*. One night he stayed out until 2 a.m. at a seedy dive on Rue de Lappe, where, as he noted in his diary, "*les hommes dansent ensembles*." He picked up several Frenchmen and sneaked each of them up to his hotel room, only to be horrified by their low standard of hygiene. Of one he noted, "Desire to give the whole French nation a collective bath." Of another, "The French get dirtier and dirtier, and I more odor conscious."

On August 23, he made his way to André Gide's apartment on Rue Vaneau, where a handsome eighteen-year-old Arab in a burnoose led him in to meet "a tall, slightly stooped man in his late sixties, wearing a shabby old unbuttoned brown cardigan that sagged from somewhat narrow shoulders. The face was sensitive and thin-lipped, and he was nearly bald . . . his cheekbones were high and hollowed underneath." Steward later felt that "Gide's troublesome puritan-Protestantism" was reflected in these gaunt features; roughly the same age as Lord Alfred Douglas, he seemed equally unappetizing to Steward as a potential sex partner.

While Steward had always found Gide's writing rather dry, he nonetheless thought Gide a heroic figure whose "brave and brilliant stand for homosexuality was like a lighthouse in those dark and stormy days of the 1930s . . . To me in my twenties, he was one of the first knights of Camelot." After all, Gide's *Si le grain ne meurt* had been the first book in which a respected public intellectual had openly described his homosexual history.* Steward admired both that book and *Corydon*, Gide's dialogue on homosexuality; but he loved *The Immoralist* best, thinking it the greatest novel of homosexual experience yet written. At the same time, he found Gide's metaphysical dualism—which distinguished sharply between body and spirit, and confined homosexuality to a purely physical realm from which all emotion (most notably love) was forever banished—much too rigid and confining for his own tastes. As a result, he respected Gide's work, but felt no immediate connection to it or to him. Gide himself seemed only an ancient, dried-up intellectual—one whose puritan upbringing had clearly left him unable to reconcile "base" homosexual desire with the realm of higher emotion. Steward (who at that moment in his life wanted strongly to reconcile emotion with desire) later observed in an interview, "[While] I think that *The Immoralist* [is a perfect homosexual novel], Gide has failed and fallen because of that thin-lipped fingernail-biting puritan Protestantism of his, which goes all through everything he has written; it doesn't essentially damage his creative work, but you always sense it behind his writing, so that he seems to be a *closed* spirit rather than a flowering one."

Steward was nonetheless delighted to be in the presence of a writer who had successfully presented his own homosexuality to the public without shame, fear, or embarrassment—and had moreover done so first, and to acclaim. Steward had come to France in search of the legendary

---

*It had appeared in a limited edition in 1920–21 (and was later published commercially in 1926).

Gallic sophistication about all things sexual, and in Gide he found it personified. The experience of meeting him was all the more fascinating since their interview took place in Gide's own bedroom, which to Steward's amazement "had a huge circular bed draped with a pink satin coverlet, and a frilly canopy at one end." After discussing the Paris Exposition with Gide, and then moving on to discuss various authors, Steward revealed he had just visited Lord Alfred Douglas in Hove. Gide was appalled, for he had met Douglas in Oscar Wilde's company many years earlier in Algeria, and he still considered him "a dreadful man . . . a shocking man." Their interview concluded, Gide invited Steward to return in ten days' time for a signed copy of *Les Caves du Vatican*.

When Steward did so, he was led once again to the room with the circular bed—but not to visit with Gide. The handsome Arab houseboy had mentioned to Gide that he had taken a fancy to Steward during his first visit; as a result, and with Gide's blessing, the two were given the use of Gide's bedroom for the afternoon.

In the days that followed, Steward visited Sylvia Beach's bookshop on Rue de l'Odeon, toured Notre Dame de Paris, and took a day trip to Versailles. Finally, after visiting the grave of Oscar Wilde at Père Lachaise, he boarded the train for the small town of Culoz in the Rhône-Alpes, not far from where Gertrude Stein and Alice Toklas had the annual rental of an eighteenth-century château. There he was finally to meet the world-famous author who had taken such an active interest in his writing.

•

Stein, aged sixty-six, was just then settling back into life in France after the tour of the United States that had followed the great popular success of *The Autobiography of Alice B. Toklas* (1933). During the course of the tour she had been not only widely recognized as a central figure of the Paris-based Modernist avant-garde, but also embraced as a lovable female American genius-eccentric. She had lived in Paris since 1902, supported by a trust fund, and with her brother, Leo, she had collected works by Matisse, Derain, Gris, Braque, and Picasso. Starting in 1909, Alice Toklas, a fellow Californian expatriate, had lived and worked with her as her secretary and business manager. During that time their salon at 27 Rue de Fleurus had become a gathering place for many of the most brilliant creative minds of the 1920s, including Sherwood Anderson, Ernest Hemingway, Thornton Wilder, Ezra Pound, and Guillaume Apollinaire.

By 1937, however, Stein's life was relatively quiet. While she still entertained a steady stream of guests at Rue de Fleurus and at Bilignin, she devoted most of her days to her writing and correspondence. Steward later wrote of his first visit, "I was not old enough then—nor indeed was anyone wise enough at that time—to evaluate accurately her place in literature, and certainly it was hard to be conscious of it while one was near her . . . [for she was] a great and very human woman, an intricate yet simple and earthy personality, tremendously alive."

With his slight frame, delicate constitution, and multiple food allergies (which included wheat flour), Steward immediately appealed to Stein and Toklas as an adorably childlike young man over whom they might fuss as much as they liked. They called him "Sammy" from their very first meeting, and would alternately pamper, scold, and praise him for years to come.* The small, robust, and motherly Stein took an immediate liking to him, and he in turn found himself surprisingly at ease with her, for she bore an uncanny resemblance to his favorite stepaunt, Elizabeth Rose.

From his very first day, Steward kept painstakingly detailed records of his visits to Bilignin, writing up a full account of the day's activities and conversations with Stein each evening after they had retired. He also photographed the ladies and their home with his little Argus camera, and took Stein's palmprint with a special kit designed for palmists.

Steward was delighted with the grand seventeenth-century château and its formal garden, which overlooked a small valley planted with corn, beyond which rose the wooded hills of Ain. He quickly adapted himself to a daily routine of dog walks, outings to local restaurants, and expeditions by car to view nearby alpine scenery. During the visit, Steward found himself welcomed as a fellow writer, and discussed with Stein the difficulty of writing good fiction while teaching, for he had an enormous workload at Loyola and little time in which to do anything truly creative.

---

*Steward was hardly alone in receiving such treatment; Thornton Wilder would later refer to "all of [Stein's] children," a group of friends including the so-called Kiddies (William G. Rogers and his wife, Mildred Weston Rogers); Robert Haas; and even Wilder himself. This game of parent-child make-believe had many permutations, however; with Carl van Vechten, Stein was the baby—"Baby Woojums"—with Toklas and Van Vechten taking the role of the parents.

Hoping to help him, Stein introduced him to a cadaverous-looking neighbor, Henri Daniel-Rops, who would eventually make a small fortune writing popular books on Catholic subjects, and become known as "the Dr. Goebbels of the Christian World by his jealous atheist enemies because of his strong resemblance to that german minister."* (The name Daniel-Rops was, in fact, a pseudonym; born Henri Petiot, the author had taken the name in admiration of the artist Felicien Rops.) For the next two years, Stein and Daniel-Rops would try repeatedly to secure Steward a teaching position in France.

At the end of a week, Stein wrote a note to Thornton Wilder, who was just then hidden away in Zurich, working on a play: "We have been having a young fellow here Sam Steward, he is the one who wrote *Angels on the Bough* and is a college professor we like him and he goes to Zurich [soon] . . . he will not interrupt your solitude much because he has to be in Cherbourg on the 15th."

Because Wilder had left a vest with Stein, Stein entrusted it to Steward, and thereby guaranteed the two would meet. Accordingly, on Thursday the ninth, Wilder wrote to Steward, who had just arrived in Zurich after a very warm good-bye from Stein and Toklas. "I am at the Carleton-Elite hotel," the note said, "and [I] would be delighted to see you at any time. I scarcely know anyone in town and will be free anytime so do not hesitate to call."

Wilder had not yet achieved acclaim as a playwright, but his novel *The Bridge of San Luis Rey* was a worldwide bestseller. The financial success of this novel had enabled him to live and work abroad, where his life was largely solitary. While as a younger man he had taught high school at Lawrenceville—and so he shared Steward's experience as an educator—it was really their shared love of Gertrude Stein and her work that first drew Wilder and Steward together.

Wilder never chose to acknowledge his homosexuality publicly, and was careful during his lifetime to suppress any information about it; perhaps as a result he destroyed his letters from Steward even as he praised them to Gertrude Stein. In this sense Wilder was not much different from many other celebrated men of his generation for whom such discre-

*So observed by Sir Francis Rose (*Saying Life*, p. 396), who met Daniel-Rops in 1939 and subsequently designed a book jacket for him.

tion was a necessity; but to Steward, Wilder's deeply closeted ways later seemed to indicate a "basic dishonesty [that he] lived with all his life." Remembering their first meeting in Zurich in 1937, Steward wrote in his memoirs,

> My feelings about [Wilder] in 1937 were different from those of the first time we had met [in 1929 in Columbus when he auto- graphed my copy of *The Angel That Troubled the Waters*]. I was eight years older and considered myself much more knowledge- able—[but] another thing marking a shift in my opinions about Thornton was Michael Gold's attack on him in *The New Republic* in 1930 . . . Gold had called Wilder a prophet of the genteel Christ, the Emily Post of culture, procurer of a chambermaid literature peopled with daydreams of homosexual figures in grace- ful gowns. Gold was simply following the Communist party line of attack, but I was not astute enough at the time to recog- nize it.

Much to his own surprise, Steward soon found himself entirely cap- tivated by Wilder—who, having spent a great deal of time alone to work on the play that would eventually become *Our Town*, was just then eager for literate and well-informed company. Though Steward initially thought Wilder rather schoolmarmish (fully twelve years older, Wilder had the affect of a much older man, and was visibly wide in the hips), he also quickly realized that Wilder was one of the most civilized and conversa- tionally brilliant men he had ever met:

> Our week began with a whirlwind of talk—eager, lively, and fas- cinating to me. The richness of his mind reminded me of that of Oscar Wilde . . . He had scores of little set speeches, and these issued forth automatically when properly triggered . . . During those days in Zurich we saw each other every afternoon and eve- ning . . . Of the six or seven afternoons and evenings in Zurich, there was one extraordinary night when it started to rain while we were walking around the town—not hard, but mostly a drizzle . . . [After staying up all night] he went to his hotel and that morning wrote the whole of the last act of *Our Town*. It was not until I saw

the play that I connected the umbrellas at the opening of that act
with my yelling for one that wet night in Zurich. He had, as Gertrude told me later, "struck a match on me."

As for myself, at the moment I was vaguely remembering a
short story I had read about an old man who had to have youth
around him to feed on. Thornton was only twelve years older than
myself, but it seemed more like thirty; he was a little too sweet
and old-maidish for my contemporary "slickness."

Wilder was pleased to mentor Steward during this brief overseas
meeting—particularly about ways in which he might best reconcile himself to his homosexuality. Yet even as he did so, Steward later recalled,
Wilder was maneuvering him into bed:

During those several days he lectured me about my homosexuality—which he had got me to confess early on—telling me how to
handle it in a kind of four-way treatment (which was, perhaps,
Thornton's own advice to himself): Think how to run your classes
most easily without draining yourself; write some essays (why, in
heaven's name?); consider your childhood and youth thoroughly,
seeking out and examining all the disgusting things regarding sex
until they are no longer repulsive; and study the lives and careers
of the great homosexuals from the beginning down to the present
day—Leonardo and Michelangelo to Whitman and beyond . . .

After this worldly intellectual preparation, sort of like tenderiz-
ing a tough cube steak, we climbed into bed together, myself half-
drunk as I had to be in those days to have an encounter.

Thornton went about sex almost as if he were looking the
other way, doing something else, and nothing happened that
could be prosecuted anywhere, unless frottage can be called a
crime. There was never even any kissing. On top of me, and after
ninety seconds and a dozen strokes against my belly he ejaculated.
At this he sprang from our bed of roses and exclaimed in his rapid
way: "Didntyoucome? Didntyoucome?"

No, I didn't.

Thus began the casual acquaintance with Thornton Wilder
that lasted through the war years and beyond, ending sometime in

1948.* I became his Chicago piece, possibly his only physical contact in the city. If there were others, I knew nothing of them, for there was a double lock on the door of the closet in which he lived . . . [Besides] he could never forthrightly discuss anything sexual; for him the act itself was quite literally unspeakable. His Puritan reluctance was inhibiting to me as well . . .

Steward next traveled to the suburb of Kuesnacht, where Thomas Mann was then residing, having fled Munich and the Nazis. Steward had lunch with Mann and his family, then spent the afternoon in private conversation with him, mostly discussing *The Magic Mountain.* "With what nervous heart and dryness of mouth I followed him upstairs to his study, to spend the hours alone in talking!" Steward later wrote. "Had I but known for sure that my instincts about [his sexuality] were true, who can say that I might not have laid a hand on his knee, or put my arm around his waist?" Mann's feeling for Steward remained warm enough that, on passing through Chicago two years later, he met Steward again, this time presenting him with a personally inscribed photograph of himself.†

•

Steward subsequently traveled to Montreux for a rendezvous with the French author and mystic Romain Rolland—but here, for the first time, he struck out. At Rolland's door he was abruptly informed by Rolland's sister that no matter what he may have told Steward by letter, the writer was currently incapable of receiving guests. And so, with nothing better to do, Steward visited the nearby castle of Chillon (which he knew through Byron's poem‡) and, suitably moved by this connection to literary history, made off with the key to the castle's men's room. "Montreux was frightfully dull," he wrote Stein, ". . . Lac Léman had colors not of this earth, and my soul reveled in them and in the Alps, on which fresh cold snow had fallen the day before I arrived. But the 'season' was over, and no

---

*Steward's entry for Wilder in the Stud File notes that he and Wilder engaged in frottage a total of twenty-six times during the course of their friendship starting in 1937, and that these meetings took place in Zurich, Paris, and Chicago.

†The inscribed, dated photograph (noting in German that they had met previously) remains in Steward's papers.

‡"The Prisoner of Chillon," a key work of English Romanticism, was a poem Steward taught regularly at Loyola.

one was there save old men with pipes, and tuberculosis babies. And I looked at the snow and the lake and the swans and decided not to stay too long."

Wilder and Stein meanwhile discussed Steward by mail. "Steward [is] a fine fella and it was a pleasure," he wrote her. "And one of the finest things about it was to learn that at your house he had written down twenty-five closely-written pages of Gertrude's talk." Stein responded, "I'm glad you liked Sam Steward . . . he is drowned at Loyola but perhaps Rops will get him a job in a lycée here and then he will have time to write. I think he will do something really good sometime." Wilder agreed with this opinion, praising Steward's abilities as a letter writer to Stein and calling him "the last of the elegants."

Wilder was just then in the midst of preparing three plays simultaneously—a translation of Ibsen's *A Doll's House*, *Our Town*, and *The Merchant of Yonkers* (which, though initially a failure, would eventually become *The Matchmaker*, and later *Hello, Dolly!*). Nonetheless he found time to send Steward a bon voyage telegram on the *Queen Mary*, and two weeks later a substantial note of farewell:

Dear Samuel,

Lord's sakes: you arrived in Zurich three weeks ago tonight. You arrived in my solitude and we had some very happy times and you left me to my solitude and I've missed you. The next week I went up among the peaks (it's now settled; there *are* mountains in Switzerland) to Nietzsche's beloved Sils Maria.* It's rained a lot, but it was fine just the same and the great ghost walked for me, and the play benefitted from it. Then I came back and moved out to a hotel about five miles from the city and worked some more, and walked some more (with a great black dog named Morro, half saint bernard).

I'm kinda pining for home . . . [After my travels to Paris and London I'll] go home. And then some time in the new year I'll come to the Hotel Stevens and sleep in Room 1000 for a while.†

---

*The little village in the Upper Engadine where Nietzsche had lived and worked.
†The hotel room Wilder considered his Chicago home, and in which he would repeatedly host Steward in years to come.

I think of you often and wonder how it's all going. I lectured you so much over here that I'm not going to put a single didactic word in this letter, but you know that's between the lines . . .

Give your boss* my regards.

I can see your letters have elegance—in that wonderful Roman sense. You can't help it, so this won't make you self-conscious. I look for more. And thanks a thousand times for your dropping-from-heaven, unexpected and felicitous.

Yr friend

Thornton

A month later, excited by the reception his agent had given *Our Town*, Wilder changed his plans; he would not immediately come to Chicago, so no meeting between him and Steward would be possible. But he had read *Angels on the Bough*, and in the brisk tone of a man who has much to do, he wrote Steward,

In the *Angels on the Bough* all I liked was the [spinster aunts]. Them I liked tremendously. We'll talk about it when I get to Chi[cago].

It's fine to have got it out of your system. Now the decks are clear. Everything's all ready—you have style, and observation, and everything. One can begin.

Wilder was right; *Angels on the Bough* was good, but it was only a first effort, and with that novel behind him, Steward needed to move on to bigger and better things. The talented young professor from Chicago had made a very good start; now it was time for him to write something truly exceptional.

---

*Morton Zabel.

3

The Chicago Novel

But as he settled back into his teaching routine at Loyola in the fall of 1937, Steward neglected his writing, and instead began to volunteer as a stage extra at the Civic Opera House,* appearing primarily in ballets. He had been fascinated by ballet as an art form since seeing the Ballets Russes perform in Washington, D.C., in 1935. After that, he wrote,

> I read books on the ballet—histories of its past, intimate memoirs of its internal life, snooty discussions of its aims, and naughty anecdotes about its personnel. I learned all the technical terms from *entrechat* to *glissade*. I worshipped Nijinsky and flung the names of Diaghilev and Fokine into all my talk . . . I thought and dreamed about the Ballets Russes . . .
>
> [Three years later in Chicago I began appearing as a supernumerary for the Ballets Russes, in their production of *Scheherazade*.] The "supering" went on for many years, until I had become a well-known regular, with several small roles distinctly my own when the Ballet Theater, the New York Ballet, or the American Ballet Theater came to Chicago.† I was the gondolier who poled the little princess across the stage in the last act of *The Nut-*

---

*Today known as the Lyric Opera House.
†Steward's mention of "Ballet Theater" and "the American Ballet Theater" is slightly confusing since they are one and the same. "American" was added by Sol Hurok when the company made its first foreign tour. The "New York Ballet," meanwhile, is the New York City Ballet. Steward cites Ballet Theater under both its names since he supered for both.

cracker, a eunuch in *Scheherazade*, a fiddler in the phony on-stage orchestra in *Gaieté Parisienne*; and [I had] a half dozen other roles [too] . . .

Like many of his generation, Steward found in the ballet not only an admirable art form in itself, but also an opportunity to admire male physical beauty in a public setting, and at the same time to mix with others who shared his taste for art, music, theater, and dance. To some extent, though, his enthusiasm was directly based on the sexual opportunities afforded by the performance: at a time when the public gathering of homosexuals in bars and nightclubs was essentially forbidden by law, the lobby of the Civic Opera House was one of the better places in Chicago to meet a friend or find a date. By working backstage, Steward was also able to befriend (and eventually bed) a number of dancers, whose names he later entered in the Stud File.

While the ballet was a leading form of artistic innovation during the first half of the twentieth century, it was also a highly physical art form that frequently asserted the validity (and delight) of sexual transgression and sexual release in a variety of ways, including through plotting, scoring, and choreography. Diaghilev's Ballets Russes had attracted both popular and critical attention under the direction of a publicly homosexual impresario with his known bisexual lover, Nijinsky, as its greatest star—so its vision was arguably an assertion of homosexual identity as well as of a modernist aesthetic. The two were in fact inseparable, for the modernist rebellion of this ballet troupe was based, in large part, upon various portrayals of romantic and sexual transgression. The overt sexuality articulated by the Ballets Russes accounts, in large part, for its sensational popularity in Paris (and, later, around the world). Erotically conceived ballets such as *L'Après-Midi d'un Faune* consciously fueled that popularity through the controversy they generated, thereby attracting scandal-driven public attention. In the coming decades, Steward's involvement with the ballet was such that he would befriend three significant homosexual men whose work and lives were intimately connected with the ballet: Paul Cadmus, Glenway Wescott, and George Platt Lynes. Compared to the ballet, Steward's own chosen art forms—poetry and fiction—were all just words on a page; but ballet was a living art in which bodies interacted directly with bodies, and where creative homosexuals existed not just in the pages of a book, but radiantly at the center of live performance, often working in celebrated collaboration. No wonder, then, that Steward yearned to be a part of it.

Apart from the Lyric Opera, Steward spent a lot of his early years in Chicago drinking and making pickups, and in that way life in the big city distracted him even more from the hard work of being a novelist. He had understood Chicago to be a place of both danger and sexual opportunity since first reading Ben Hecht's raffish Jazz Age story collection *1001 Afternoons in Chicago* in high school; since then, the city had become even more infamous for violent crime. All through the 1930s it was a rough, lawless city, and moreover one that became increasingly difficult for homosexuals to live in—particularly since, with the repeal of Prohibition, crooked police were once again able to monitor activities taking place in saloons, and thereby to shake down homosexuals by using threats of arrest and public exposure.

Despite the abundance of sexual opportunity, Steward nonetheless found city life an isolating existence. As he later told a sex researcher, "The only communal feeling that ever arose [among Chicago homosexuals in the 1930s] was at the Halloween drag balls . . . that was the only time of year that everyone came out. The rest of the time it was still an individual matter. We all went our separate, very lonesome, very lonely ways to our neighborhood bars, seeing whom we could make."

•

Steward's Stud File records a number of pickups in Chicago during the late 1930s that took place in bars or on the street—at least one of which, described simply as "Clark Street Roll," resulted in his being beaten and robbed (the card notes, "lost $$, shirt, etc."). Not all violent encounters were attacks, however; he also records a 1937 whipping administered by a man named John Thayer that he enjoyed well enough to repeat nine years later.

He also had sex at Chicago's Turkish baths. During the period 1936 through 1947, Steward had sex at "the tubs" on a total of fifty separate occasions, or roughly five times a year.* Chicago also gave him his first op-

---

*He would have additional encounters at the baths from 1947 through 1952, but bathhouses became far less appealing to him after he achieved lasting sobriety in 1947.

portunity to have sex with black men on a regular basis, for while he had known several in Columbus, he had not met any in Helena or Pullman. As he later told an interviewer, "There were two or three [clandestine gay bars] in Chicago—one [of them was] on the South Side, a black-and-tan joint—where blacks and whites mixed . . . That was unusual in the 20's 30s and 40s because racism was terrific." Although he had grown up in a small town that was totally segregated,* Steward had loved having sex with black men since his Columbus years,† and his first black male sexual contacts in Chicago began with the painter, musician, and writer Charles Sebree in 1938.‡ Most of his pickups, both black and white, were from working-class backgrounds; some were clearly thugs.

Asked about the danger of approaching and propositioning such men on the street, Steward later noted,

> I was not really "afraid." Liquor in those days had a lot to do with [that lack of fear, for at that point I needed to be drunk to attempt a pickup] . . . Once I got steel-knuckled in a Chicago alley and was in hospital for a few days; I had a good cover story for the dean who came to see me about getting mugged . . . I had several narrow escapes; once, being tied foursquare to the bed and whipped by a black, I lay there several hours unable to work loose because he had passed out [from drink]. Other times were equally dangerous. Next day I'd shake off my hangover and not be visibly deterred from trying the whole thing again in a few days.

Steward's fascination with rough trade was in fact part of a well-established tendency among middle- and upper-class homosexuals for taking their sexual adventures with men of working or criminal class, whose masculinity may have seemed greater due to their more violent, less predictable natures. Their potential criminality added to the excitement of the pursuit; to Steward, accosting rough trade seemed a fascinating high-stakes adventure, and moreover one that incidentally linked him

---

*Even as late as the 2000 U.S. census, Woodsfield, Ohio, has remained 99 percent white.

†Steward's Stud File uses the code letter "n" to denote each negro contact, "j" each Jewish one.

‡Steward remained friendly with Sebree for many years, buying ten of his paintings in total, and in 1954 attending a musical Sebree had written (entitled *Mrs. Osborne*, and starring Eartha Kitt). (Steward, *Journal*, Oct. 30, 1954.)

again to his great hero Oscar Wilde—who despite his idealized love for Lord Alfred Douglas had preferred erotic encounters with rough street boys, hustlers, and blackmailers. Wilde had in fact likened such activity to "feasting with panthers," later explaining "the danger was half the excitement."

Even if Steward hadn't been openly propositioning men in the street, his late-night drunken wanderings would still have left him vulnerable to robbery and murder. But, in the way of a drunk, he took such things in stride: "From an alley on La Salle Street," Steward wrote of his first holdup, "a guy emerged with a gun. He took my watch and told me not to move . . . After that I considered myself a True Native Chicagoan."

In fact, Steward was quickly coming to love Sandburg's "Stormy, husky, brawling / City" despite all its filth, poverty, corruption, and crime, and he took a certain pride in being a resident. He noted in the late 1940s that "there is a quality to the City of the Big Shoulders that grows on a person, like the taste of a martini, like learning to like pineapple and cottage cheese." It was, to his mind, "a man-city, healthy, sweaty and sensual. It is Gargantua with his head in Evanston, his feet in Gary, and he lies relaxed and smoldering along the lake front . . . the whole anatomy of the city his outstretched body."

Even as he became habituated to anonymous encounters and street pickups, Steward was seeing three sex partners regularly that he also considered good friends: a doctor named Jacob Cohen, a worker named Jimmy Taylor,* and a serviceman named Bill Collins.† Collins was not just a bedmate but a lover and intellectual equal whom Steward would eventually introduce to many of his literary friends, including Gertrude Stein.

Upon his return to the United States in the fall of 1937, Steward bought about twenty kitchen gadgets and sent them off to Stein and Toklas by way of a thank-you. Stein wrote back,

Alice is delighted with the gadgets she keeps them on a shelf on the best Italian furniture in the atelier with the best treasures, and she shows them with so much pride, they are so useful and

---

*Identified as "Jimmy Taylick" in Steward's memoirs, he was as close a friend as Steward ever had. The two men had sex regularly for eight years, through 1946.

†Collins was sexually active with Steward from 1938 until 1945, but because he spent much of that time away from Chicago (in the army), the two had sex only twenty-three times.

so beautiful and so pale blue and we are so pleased with our Sammy and [have] so much to tell you . . . we saw the Rops and we talked endlessly about you and I am writing a life in French of Picasso.

Like many of the literary and artistic men who flocked to Stein in her later life, Steward both admired her genius and craved her motherly warmth and support. Deeply alcoholic and massively overworked, he seemed to many on the verge of a breakdown. In a letter to her of late fall 1937 he wrote:

> To tell the truth, I am in a horrible state—one, I suppose, that has been growing for a long time. Something brought it to a climax and I can think of no other thing than that biography of Hart Crane which I have just finished. How horrible, how terrifying [his death was]—and particularly because I [sense] I am unconsciously following many of the same patterns he followed.* I think my personality has split—that sounds funny, but it has . . . In desperation I sat down last night and read some Whitman and for a little while forced myself into thinking he was right, and then I read one—oh, a very little one—in which he admitted he was wrong. It was "O Me! O Life!" . . . Do you remember it? "What good amidst these people, these faithless, these mean objects?" he asks. And his only answer: "that you are here—that life exists and identity, That the powerful play goes on, and you may contribute a verse." But *may* I? Have I anything to begin with?
> . . . Alas, I'm not drunk—I've found I can control that. And I feel I owe you an apology. I've just read this over, and I am strongly impelled to tear it up. But after an argument—no.

Stein responded calmly from her new home on Rue Christine, "We were all at dinner at the Rops and . . . they said if you were sad all you needed was Paris . . . I have meditated a lot about your letter perhaps it is

---

*The poet Hart Crane had killed himself in 1932 by jumping off the S.S. *Orizaba* into the Gulf of Mexico. He had reportedly done so after being publicly beaten by a sailor toward whom he had made drunken sexual advances.

better but you see the trouble it certainly was with Hart Crane, the question of being important inside in one . . ."

Steward would treasure this phrase ("the question of being important inside in one") for years to come, for the question—that is, the question of self-esteem—was, he felt, the key to his alcoholism, and also to his inability to develop as a novelist and writer. He responded: "You are right, the question of being important inside oneself can either cause or cure a lot of trouble . . . when I find the solution I think . . . I will be whole again and can write and do the things I want."

Steward was continuing his sexual acquaintance with Thornton Wilder during this time, but theirs was hardly a romance; although Wilder wrote to Steward with some regularity, he kept the contents of his letters breezily informal, and constantly misspelled Steward's name as "Stewart," as if to suggest the two men were barely acquainted. Even so, Steward noted in his memoirs,

> Every time Thornton came to Chicago I would receive in advance a phone call or one of his chatty postcards, containing about two hundred words in his minuscule handwriting; and I would go down to the Stevens Hotel (now the Conrad Hilton) to spend the appointed night in Room 1000. On such nights he might show me his elaborately annotated copy of *Finnegans Wake*, the margins so black with his innumerable notes that there was hardly any white to be seen; or he would draw a score of Palestrina out of his suitcase and tell me how he spent hours alone in his hotel room "reading" the music to himself, and enjoying it as much as he was hearing it . . . Occasionally he would come out to my northside apartment. Once he left his wristwatch on the night table beside the bed, and sent me a telegram the next day asking me to forward the watch to him in Arizona or else bring it to the hotel. The telegram was possibly one of the few bits of evidence he might have left that would have exposed his dread secret.

Wilder sent a follow-up note from Tucson after that March 1938 visit, thanking Steward for returning the watch but alluding to nothing more. In another letter, after briefly apologizing for two months of silence, he simply gave Steward more (unsolicited) writing advice: "Now do compose yourself to some critical articles 1/2 of them for the learned journals, and 1/2 of them for the better magazines. There lies (1) advancement (2) employment of your gifts. Then return to the novel." Steward was, however, far from heartbroken, having by now had enough experience, both sexual and romantic, to recognize Wilder's emotional limitations. With that recognition came a certain disillusionment, for this author who had written so brilliantly of love in *The Bridge of San Luis Rey* was apparently not capable of articulating such emotions in real life—or at least would not be doing so with Steward.

During early 1938, Steward applied to the International Institute of Education for an overseas scholarship, but nothing came of it. Loyola pressured him to teach over the 1938 summer vacation, and he needed the money, so he did. He also told Stein his latest scheme for financing a trip back to France: a Guggenheim Fellowship. He then asked her for a recommendation. "I am yours to command now and always," Stein responded, "but if you can get somebody with a pull do do so, because I do think that's the way it is done."* Steward responded that he was sure Stein would be the right person, then added some disturbing news:

> I got whapped by an automobile while I was crossing the street in Chicago, and [have a] sub-conjunctival haemorrhage in my eyeball [and] stitches in my lip . . . aside from all those varied lacerations and contusions on my face and knee etc there were no bones broken . . . but I am glad you two cannot see me . . . I will soon be well and hope you are too.

He gave the same (nonspecific) story about his injuries to Thornton Wilder, just then in Hollywood, when asking Wilder, too, for a Guggenheim recommendation. Wilder assented, concluding: "All my sympathy on your motor accident . . . try and write anyway. The WILL, the will is all we have. Don't postpone."

During this period, Steward struggled again with the question of faith. After an agonized reconsideration of Catholicism, however, he rejected it

---

*Stein wrote Steward a simple Guggenheim recommendation, saying that he was a scholar of distinction with an unusual gift for narrative writing, and commenting favorably on *Angels on the Bough*. She thought that his achievements would eventually be a credit to the Guggenheim Foundation. (Ulla Dydo to author, 2005.)

once and for all. Instead, "I think I am coming more and more to exist in
what Keats called a negative capability," he wrote Stein, "that is, no irri-
table reaching out after fact or reason, and a refusal to accept a universe
reducible to simple rules and terms." This willingness to abide by his own
constant uncertainty and spiritual discomfort would characterize not only
Steward's spiritual state from now on, but also his writing. In the years to
come he would return to Keats over and over again, finding consolation in
the example of Keats's own tortured, rejection-filled life and his ultimate
transcendence of that misery through creative brilliance.

By fall Thornton Wilder, Henri Daniel-Rops, André Maurois, and
Paul Morand had all agreed to recommend Steward for a Guggenheim,
and Steward began to think he had a chance of winning it. He wrote to
Stein that he was developing a new novel, one based on the myth of Hero
and Leander.

•

In his 1938 Christmas letter, Steward gave Stein some surprising news: "I
have finished a novel about Chicago but I do not know whether it is good,
it will need a lot of revision." He also noted, "I have completely stopped
drinking for awhile . . . I will need all my wits about me for [teaching]
Beowulf and anyway I want to start doing some more writing right away."
In February, when Steward learned that his application for the Guggenheim had survived a first round of cuts, Wilder congratulated him on
getting that far, then asked to know more about Steward's new "hard-
boiled" novel: "What do you mean—hardboiled novel? Did you write a
novel or did you pu[bli]sh a novel?"

The "hardboiled" novel was not the respectable Hero and Leander
project Steward had proposed in his Guggenheim application, but rather
a violent sexual tale set in the Chicago underworld, using "all the dirty
words there were and then some." He intended to offer this dark, homoerotic novel of murder and sexual dismemberment to Jack Kahane, publisher of Obelisk Press in Paris, before traveling on to Stein at Bilignin.

He wrote to Stein,

> The novel . . . is all about Chicago and it is very hard and not
> tender at all and I can't tell whether it is good or bad . . . But
> something else has happened to me and it is a very worthwhile

thing. Before, I was always trying not to be lonely and to be happy and all of a sudden it came to me that I should not struggle against feeling lonely . . . so I have just opened my arms to it and embraced it and become resigned to that particular thing and what is the result. I am feeling much better and feeling urges within myself and that is a wonderful good sign . . . the novel is imperfect but I will fix that.

But as winter turned to spring, he wrote her again with bad news: "The Ides of March in sooth was a blighted day . . . For we did not get the Goog,* no, neither Wendell nor myself . . . It was funny, I sat and looked at the letter for ten minutes, and then everything was over. But to thee much gratitude for helping."

Though disappointed, Steward continued to revise his Chicago novel and to make plans for his trip to France, booking passage on the *Normandie* even while writing Stein, "I have a strange feeling . . . there may be a war before [I arrive]." Wilder meanwhile responded to Steward's Guggenheim news (again misspelling his name "Stewart") with "Forgive a hasty [post]card . . . All 3 of my protégés lost out in the Guggenheim this year. Hmm, that's what I get for having a play *fail* on Broadway. Last year 2 of my protégés won."

•

"I met [William] Saroyan on the way over," Steward wrote to Stein in Bilignin immediately upon his arrival in Paris that June. "He was all you said of him, he was very annoying but it makes an amusing story." Steward had loved his passage over on the ultra-French *Normandie*, for its appointments had seemed lavish to him, even from his berth in third class. After settling in at the Hotel de Nice on Rue des Beaux Arts, he rented a typewriter "to do two or three solid weeks of writing," he wrote Stein, "because Paris brings it out in me." In fact, encouraged by the success of his 1937 visit, Steward had returned to Paris with the idea of establishing himself there as a writer—even as questions of income, academic career, and, above all, the looming world war seemed destined to thwart his plans. He had high hopes that Obelisk Press would welcome his shocking

*The Guggenheim Fellowship.

new manuscript; after all, Parker Tyler and Charles Henri Ford had published *The Young and Evil* with Kahane, even though it had been appallingly bad. Steward had met both young men through Benjamin Musser, hated their work, and felt sure his novel would do better, if only Jack Kahane would give him his chance. In the meanwhile, Steward continued forging various contacts in France—mostly through Stein and her French friends—that would help him, he hoped, either to emigrate to France to work there as a teacher, or else simply to spend extended periods of time in France, writing.

After a visit from Wilder a week later, Steward wrote to Stein again: "Dearest ones—well, Thornton came and it was huge fun for two or three days, but he read pages one and forty of the Chicago novel I am re-writing and while he didn't hit the ceiling he was so disturbed that I think I will take it over and throw it in the Seine."

Despite Wilder's dislike of Steward's novel (Wilder wrote to Stein, "Yes, you know me, I thought that Sammy Stewart's [*sic*] novel was a big mistake"), his visit to Steward was not without tenderness. Steward had been attacked in his hotel room earlier that week by a thug he had picked up on Rue de Lappe; after sex, the man had robbed him and "slugged [him] on the chin," causing Steward to bite his own tongue, which had then bled profusely. Wilder had comforted him about the injury while the two stood on a bridge looking down into the waters of the Seine. The two of course had sex; they also spent an afternoon at Shakespeare and Company, the famous bookshop Sylvia Beach had opened with the assistance of her lover, Adrienne Monnier. At Steward's suggestion, they had gone on to visit the room at the Hotel d'Alsace where Oscar Wilde had died (after legendarily observing, "My wallpaper and I are fighting a duel to the death. One or other of us has got to go"); there, in the melancholy half-light, Steward snapped a photo of Wilder sitting on the sill of the half-opened window. Wilder, however, apparently declined to snap one of him.

Knowing that Stein and Toklas would be receiving a number of guests over the summer, Steward visited them briefly at Bilignin, at the château they had rented each summer since 1929. His plan was to continue on from there to Algeria while they entertained others, and then return to them later in the summer for another, longer visit. On Steward's thirtieth birthday, Stein greeted him at breakfast with a kiss and a poem written in his honor.* More important to him, however, was her continuing belief in his talent, for she had begun encouraging him to undertake a comic novel based on the idea of the eleven women desperately seeking his hand in marriage. "You're a motherable person," Steward later recalled Stein as having said. "I think you really ought to do a book about the Eleven. You can begin it in [Algeria] . . . I do think you ought to be a writer Sammy, honest to God I do."

During the first part of the visit, they made assorted outings by car took daily dog walks in the countryside, and enjoyed good meals painstakingly prepared by the reclusive, chain-smoking Toklas. The three drove to Geneva to see "Les Chefs d'Oeuvre du Musée du Prado" at the Musées d'Art et d'Histoire; on Steward's last day, he took photographs when André Breton came over from Chamonix for a party, bringing with him an entourage of other artists including Yves Tanguy and Roberto Matta Echaurren.

Although he was intent upon being a "good Sammy" during his visit to Stein and Toklas, Steward drank heavily in his room at Bilignin after Stein and Toklas had retired for the evening. He also managed, against all odds, to have sex there—with Stein's Vietnamese houseboy, Chen:

> I suppose I might as well say that once upon a midnight dreary I ascended to the servants quarters at Bilignin, and came to know Chen better than I was supposed to know him . . . He was a nice kid, and I was grateful to him, for that was the only sex I had [in Bilignin] . . . Chen was terrified that I would tell Gertrude or Alice, but . . . I was just as terrified they might find out, so all ended happily.

Before leaving Paris, Steward had asked Jack Kahane to forward his "Chicago" manuscript to Stein, and Stein promised to read it while Steward was in Algeria. She also provided him with a letter of introduction to Picasso and quickly introduced him at the train station to her newly arriving houseguests, the painter Sir Francis Rose and the photographer Cecil Beaton.

Upon his arrival at the seaport Steward took an immediate liking to Marseilles, for its streets were full of sailors and thugs—just the type of men he found most attractive. Through an introduction from Stein, he

*Entitled "To Sammy on His Birthday."

also met J. Lambreghts Coulbaut, the Belgian consul-general in the city, a man of advanced years with whom he nonetheless enjoyed a brief sexual interlude. As he wrote to Stein and Toklas on July 25,

> Yesterday the "old part" of Marseilles took me driving with some friends down to the Cote d'Azur, to Cassis and Bandol . . . he is nice and likes me . . . this morning I walked all thru the vieux port and wouldn't dare it after night . . . In this French Chicago I am not at ease particularly because I am used to gangsters not being so *chic* and here they are but I guess looking like *un Anglais* helps protect me because everyone knows *les Anglais* have no money. The Old Part and his "jeune" ami have given me lots of warnings which I have heeded. But it is a fascinating and exciting town and even though it is very dirty I like it a lot.

•

Steward's decision to visit Algeria had been inspired by his reading of Gide's *The Immoralist*, which had described it as a place of romance, intrigue, and young men eager for sex for pay; and also by his knowledge that Oscar Wilde and Lord Alfred Douglas had engaged in a number of sexual adventures there. Steward's travel to the casbah was, in that sense, like travel to Marseilles: an opportunity to mix in the same rough, sexually available masculine company he most preferred, and at the same time to immerse himself in various literary associations and an utterly foreign culture. He quickly picked up a handsome young Arab named Mohammed Zenouhin to be his guide and escort.

A week into his visit, Steward wrote to Stein:

> Four things have kept me from working: Henri [Daniel-Rops's] friends, the awful humidity, the fascination of the life here, and my small Arab friend. At the moment I'm unhappy because I cut off my moustache; Mohammed [Zenouhin] didn't like it. I am taken for young without it, too young.
>
> You were right about the spoken word and it is a wonder you even could read a third of [my novel].* Kahane said

---

*This note seems to suggest that Stein had written Steward a note about the Chicago novel, but no note has survived.

no, that it went beyond publishing even in France, that the subject had been overdone lately even if not in such remarkably outspoken manner, which was his polite way of saying no.* But the MS will be nice to keep as a souvenir of my final immersion in sex.†

In later life, Steward recalled more specifically what Stein had told him about the novel:

In 1937–38 I wrote a novel about homosexuals in Chicago, a fearsome thing ending with a murder by some "dirt" and the subsequent actual emasculation of the protagonist; I did this in two versions—one with dirty language, and one using euphemisms. Gertrude read the first version in 1939 and said of it that the dirty book began very well, the church scene was very good, and then it went on and I varied the dirt a great deal and that was not easy.

While disappointed with the rejection, Steward nonetheless found Algeria to be "a thoroughly hedonistic and leisurely vacation." During his three weeks there, he had sex not only with his guide, but also with two Algerian soldiers. He later described these experiences in an erotic correspondence:

[One of the Arab soldiers was] very fancy, with a long red sash around his waist and a red fez. We went to a cheap hotel and he [had] me SEVEN times. The Arabs just love to [fuck]—and they know all the tricks. Two days after the soldier had so well-fucked me, I gave in to Mohammed. I couldn't get him past the doorman of my hotel, so we went back to the one where I'd taken the soldier . . . The goddamned clerk spoke in Arabic to Mohammed and told him I'd been there with [the soldier], and Mohammed was hurt and angry . . .

*No letter from Kahane survives.
†The manuscript, too, has been lost; though Steward donated a copy to the Kinsey Archive, the Archive cannot locate it.

After taking leave of Mohammed (giving him a generous gift of money and his Chicago address*), Steward hastened back to France—for a note had just arrived from Stein telling him to make haste, for "we are all afraid of war."[†]

Arriving back at Bilignin, he found his former room now occupied by Sir Francis Rose and Cecil Beaton. The very stylish Beaton took absolutely no interest in Steward, but Rose, who at five years younger than Beaton was exactly Steward's age, got on very well with him indeed—so well, in fact, that the two immediately began a friendship that would last for twenty-five years. Steward seems to have found in Rose a sort of doppelgänger, for despite their vastly different backgrounds and circumstances, Rose, too, had struggled throughout his life to reconcile an artistic vocation with a wildly adventurous (and self-destructive) sex life. Over the next thirty years, Steward would not only write several drafts of a novel based on Rose, but also save his correspondence, and even document various events in his life quite thoroughly in his memoir of Toklas and Stein.

Rose, unlike Steward, felt that the working-class men he preferred were fundamentally different from him. His memoirs note, "I was [always] fascinated by what were termed 'the lower orders' by my mother, and less generously 'the great unwashed' by Granny." He nonetheless enjoyed having sex with "the great unwashed" from early adolescence onward; the danger, transgression, and perceived self-degradation of these escapades contributed significantly to their erotic appeal.

Like Steward, Rose was bookish as well as artistic, and he had a playful, imaginative nature. His Scottish father, Sir Cyril Stanley Rose, had died when he was five, leaving him a small fortune and a baronetcy; his eccentric (and independently wealthy) Franco-Spanish mother, Laetitia Rouy, had subsequently preferred to live abroad. As a result, Rose had been involved since early adolescence with the French avant-garde—particularly with Jean Cocteau and his circle, whom he had come to know at the Welcome Hotel at Villefranche-sur-Mer. There he had befriended Isadora Duncan, Mary Butts, Glenway Wescott, Natalie Barney, Radclyffe Hall,

---

*Mohammed Zenouhin never made it to Chicago; he died young, poisoned by his father for refusing to marry. (Extensive details on Zenouhin's gruesome death, sent to him by Witold Pick, can be found in Steward, "Early Chapters" [unpublished], p. 224.)

†This note, like the one about Steward's novel, has not survived; Steward re-created it from memory in his Stein-Toklas memoir (p. 75).

Monroe Wheeler, Christian ("Bébé") Bérard, Max Jacob, and even the young George Platt Lynes—just then a recent Yale dropout.

By his early twenties (if his memoirs are to be believed) this wealthy, well-connected, opium-addicted young man had become closely associated with Captain Ernst Röhm, the first leader of the Nazi SA, to whom he had been introduced in Berlin in 1930 by his godfather, Franz von Papen.* Rose subsequently began a close, loving (but—he insisted—nonsexual†) four-year relationship with Röhm, who was twenty-three years his senior, in 1930. At the same time, he had his first major painting exhibition in Paris, sharing space with a kindred spirit, Salvador Dalí, at the gallery of Marie Cuttoli.‡ His introduction to Gertrude Stein took place shortly afterward, in 1931, when she bought one of his paintings. He would continue to exhibit and sell his paintings in London, Chicago, New York, and Paris throughout the 1930s.

When Ernst Röhm was assassinated on Hitler's "Night of the Long Knives,"§ Rose had been away from the house they shared in Bavaria, re-cuperating from hepatitis at his villa on the Riviera. The news of the murder devastated him; he subsequently left Europe to travel extensively in Asia, and finally to set up residence in Peking. He remained there, becoming friendly with the similarly half-English, Catholic, and homo-sexual aesthete Harold Acton (then also living in self-imposed exile) until both were driven out by the Japanese invasion of 1937. In 1938, Rose lost the better part of his fortune when Richard Whitney, the chairman of the New York Stock Exchange (to whom he had given power of attorney), was convicted of engaging in a massive embezzlement scheme and simultane-ously declared bankrupt. To make matters worse, Rose had picked up a handsome young American criminal on his travels back to Europe who subsequently defrauded him of his one significant remaining asset, his villa in the hills above Cannes. Thus at the time of his first meeting with Steward, Rose was in complete financial ruin.

---

*Von Papen (1879–1969) had briefly served as chancellor of Germany in 1932.
†Though Röhm had been named as a homosexual by the German press as early as 1925, Rose staunchly denies the fact in his memoirs (which are rife with contradiction, most particularly where homosexuality is concerned). "Ernst was not the debauched degenerate that the pitiful Hitler tried to make him out to be . . . Rohm loved men and youths with a Platonic ideal—it was a kind of Nietz-schean cult, although Ernst disliked Nietzsche and the philosophy of the superman. He was not a homosexual . . . [but] I loved Ernst Röhm and he loved me." (Rose, *Saying Life*, pp. 195, 234–35.)
‡Marie (Madame Paul) Cuttoli (1873–1973), artist and art dealer.
§June 29–30, 1934.

Steward found that Rose had artistic tastes and interests remarkably similar to his own. Rose had been inspired early on by Beardsley, Wilde, and Huysmans, for his Catholic paternal grandmother had introduced him to the work of all three. Moreover, like Steward, Rose had been electrified by the Ballets Russes. He was also particularly devoted to (and inspired by) Cocteau, who seemed to him to embody the contemporary French ideal of dandyism, aestheticism, and intellectual achievement. Rose later noted in his memoir that "like Icarus plunging into the sea, so was I plunged into that renaissance which is personified by that brilliant human firework, Jean Cocteau."

Though Toklas thought him a particularly difficult houseguest, Rose had been a frequent visitor to the Stein-Toklas homes in Paris and Bilignin for nearly eight years by the time Steward met him; he would also eventually illustrate two books by Stein and *The Alice B. Toklas Cook Book*. Stein had collected Rose's paintings steadily since 1933, and would ultimately own nearly a hundred of them. Cecil Beaton perhaps described him best, as "an Englishman . . . who looks like Toulouse-Lautrec and in graces is of the Horace Walpole period and in manner like an intelligent spinster. He is in character and tastes very much like Miss Stein and Miss Toklas."*

Rose had warm (if hazy) recollections of meeting Steward during the 1939 visit with Stein and Toklas in his memoirs, noting, "Sam Steward, a friend of Gertrude and Alice, was there too, and I enjoyed his company. He was a young professor of history [*sic*] from Chicago who had a great love for France but the wit of a cultured American. With him one always had great fun." Steward in turn would write of Rose, "I liked Francis. I did not find him 'wicked and evil' (to use another of Gertrude's phrases about him); I think that she was afraid he would 'corrupt' me." The fact that Stein feared for Steward's innocence is, if nothing else, an indication of just how little she knew of his private life, and how much (by comparison) she knew of Rose's—for his sexual indiscretions were legion.

During the visit to Bilignin, Steward had an extraordinarily intimate discussion with Stein, one that she apparently initiated in response to his

---

*Beaton also believed (incorrectly) that Stein's motto "Rose is a Rose is a Rose" had somehow been based upon Francis Rose, a misattribution that later featured prominently in Rose's various obituaries. ("A rose is a rose is a rose is a rose" is a line from a short piece called "Sacred Emily," which Stein had written twenty years before her first meeting with Francis Rose.)

"Chicago" novel. Steward later reconstructed the conversation from the extensive daily notes he had taken in shorthand while visiting:

"Did [Thornton] tell you [Alice and I were lesbian]?"

"Only when I asked him a direct question, and then he didn't want to answer, he didn't want to at all. He said yes he supposed in the beginning but that it was all over now."

Gertrude laughed. "How could he know. He doesn't know what love is. And that's just like Thornie. We are surrounded by homosexuals, they do all the good things in the arts, and when I ran down the male ones to Hemingway it was because I thought he was a secret one.* If Shakespeare had had a psychiatrist then we would never have had the plays or sonnets. I like all people who produce and Alice does too and what they do in bed is their own business, and what we do is not theirs. We saw a part of all this in you but there was a dark corner and we were puzzled and now we have the right answer, haven't we."

"Yes, you do," I said, "and I'll never say a word—"

"Pshaw," she interrupted. "Most of our really good friends don't care and they don't know all about everything. But perhaps considering Saint Paul it would be better not to talk about it, say for twenty years after I die, unless it's found out sooner or times change. But if you are alive and writing then you can go ahead and tell it, I would rather it came from a friend than an enemy or a stranger."

"Well, I can keep my mouth shut," I said.

"But your pen sometimes runs away with you," she said. "Now you take that novel you let me read, that one about the homosexual scene in Chicago, well, you used all the dirty words there were and then some, some I'd never even heard and I've heard a lot, but it didn't work, it was too sad, and then the ending was horrible, everything cut off that poor fellow. You tried to do Henry Miller but without the gusto."

My ears burned. Gertrude plowed on.

---

*Hemingway described Stein's comments to him about male homosexuals in *A Moveable Feast* (1964), in a chapter that also features an unsavory portrayal of Stein's relationship with Toklas.

"Now, that one I did, the one I mentioned to you the other day, the Q.E.D.* one, I wrote that about, oh, thirty-five years ago, it was about the same matters but it was all done with restraint, restraint of course was part of the times then. But naturally I was ashamed of it—"

"Why?" I interjected.

"Well for one thing it was too early to write about such things in our civilization, it was early in the century and everything was puritanical and so it was too soon . . . and of course it was a kind of therapy for me just like writing yours was for you, you had to get it off your chest. But once it was written I was ashamed, it was not done the way it should have been done, it was too outspoken for the times even though it was restrained."

"And are you going to let it be published?"

She shook her head. "No," she said, "maybe later, maybe after I'm dead and gone. Anyway, I took it and changed it around and made a man out of one of the women and it became *Melanctha*. But it would not have been a graceful thing to publish it then."

Steward had brought his graphically sexual novel to Paris in order to submit it to the one commercial publisher who had succeeded up to that moment in putting literary homosexual novels into print, and he was now having a significant discussion with a major literary figure about the ways in which homosexual acts could be brought into the cultural dialogue. But that novel would never be published, and Stein would never record the particulars of her conversation with Steward. Steward himself would allow more than thirty-five years to pass before publishing his own ac-count of this conversation with Stein, out of respect for her and Toklas's privacy. Toward the end of his life, Steward recalled (again, only in his unpublished autobiography) that Stein had not been at all averse to the violent sexual content of his "Chicago" novel (including violent castra-tion, a theme used two decades later by Tennessee Williams in *Sweet Bird of Youth*), but rather only to its obsession with street language and slang. "Gertrude . . . said . . . the thing that was wrong with Wendell [Wilcox]'s and Saroyan's and my novel-writing was that we were all haunted by the

*Stein's novel Q.E.D. (1903), published in 1950 as *Things as They Are*, is the story of a lesbian love triangle.

spoken word." The memory of her openness to his experimentation with sexual themes would sustain him in the years to come, even though she had told him quite bluntly that the "Chicago" novel was a failure.

•

By August 28 a declaration of war seemed so imminent that Stein advised Steward to leave as quickly as possible for Le Havre before the ports were closed. The *Normandie* had been scheduled to depart on September 6; unaware that it had never left New York, Steward boarded a train for Le Havre via Paris and so began a long and extremely difficult trip home.

In a note to Stein and Toklas written en route from Rouen, he described Paris as "ghastly" but went on to note that he had met up with Francis Rose at the "Cafe de Flore. [Where Francis] was tremendously upset—not over war, but leaving Cecil [Beaton]." After visiting Rose's lavish apartment on the Ile St. Louis, Steward and Rose "ate together, then had a tour of the bad places. There were some adventures . . . If *Normandie* doesn't sail, [I] will enlist. Could do something perhaps."

Though he arrived in Le Havre to discover the *Normandie* missing, Steward managed to obtain a last-minute berth on the S.S. *Harding* even as six thousand other panicked American passengers were redirected to Bordeaux. From his improvised bunk in a cargo hatch of the desperately overcrowded ship, Steward wrote Stein and Toklas:

[I have] been on this damned tub for a whole week today—it is bulging at the sides with people of all kinds, and rocking & pitching in a dreadful storm at the moment. But I am glad to be getting back . . . It was uneasy the first few nights because everyone was remembering the *Athenia*[*] and thinking of mines and torpedos they've seen in movies. Now it is better.

A whole oceanful of love to you and a hope we can see each other next year when all is calm again.

Xxxx

Sam

---

[*] The S.S. *Athenia*, a passenger ship carrying 1,103 civilians (including 300 Americans) bound from Liverpool to Montreal, had been torpedoed and sunk by a German U-boat on September 3, 1939, just twelve days before Steward wrote his letter.

4

"The navy has always had an attraction for me"

After Steward got back to Chicago, he offered to help Stein arrange a second lecture tour in the United States, for he worried about her safety in Europe. But upon finding he could do little for her, he came up instead with a project for her amusement. "Six weeks ago I started to work on this Mixmaster which I am going to send you," he wrote. Of this strange undertaking he later recalled,

> I remembered the village fair [we had attended together] at Virieu-le-Grand,* and how Gertrude had said she liked things that went around—gramophone records, whirling grouse, egg-beaters and the world. [So] the Mixmaster seemed like the perfect gift, and useful to Alice as well . . . [Though Stein wrote me not to send it] I thought of all the trouble [I had already taken]—the special wiring, the wire-strapped shipping box—and sent it anyway, by parcel post [in late November 1939].

Since Europe was now engulfed in a world war, Steward doubted the Mixmaster would ever arrive. In late spring 1940, however, he had a note:

My Dearest Sammy,
    The Mix master came Easter Sunday, and we have not had time to more than read the literature put it together and gloat, oh

---

*A small town near Bilignin. While at the fair, Steward took photos of Stein, Toklas, and Daniel-Rops trying their luck at a shooting gallery.

so beautiful is the Mix master, so beautiful . . . we are very happy to have it here, bless you Sammy, Madame Roux said oui il est si gentil, *et en effet* he is dear little Sammy, Easter morning, what a spring, lovely as I have never seen anything lovely . . . Alice all smiles and murmurs in her dreams, Mix master

Gertrude

Steward continued to entertain Stein during the bleak months that followed by filling her in on his various projects:

I'm writing . . . but the Eleven isn't ripe yet, I guess. Beginning in that vein, however, and using the details of a little story Sir Francis Rose told me (and changing the details to a situation I knew about myself) I am writing a novel in the light tone and being veddy veddy gay about it all, and have 120 pages done . . . If you come I hope you'll like it. (And everyone hopes you will come, and wonders when it would be.)

. . . This one is going to leave Loyola, next September at the latest . . . For 3 reasons: one, an e$pecially obviou$ and nece$$ary con$ideration; two, security of tenure; three, a pension for the twilight years . . . I am so tired of Catholics. For a long while I hated the idea of losing the "prestige" of teaching in a university; but . . . you can't put prestige in the bank. All the machinery for making a change is in motion now.

Steward contacted the film director William Dieterle with the idea of doing a movie about Stein's life, and in a subsequent note to Stein about it, he described his progress on his novel—"There is a lot of *Tristam Shandy* in it, and Ronald Firbank and Norman Douglas, and Richard Hughes' understatement, but more in it of Gertrude Stein and her influence than anything else." He then confessed obliquely that he had been beaten by a street pickup:

I have been in the hospital for five days, there are three stories to it all, the official, the semi-official, and the true . . . the official is that I was in an auto accident and had some stitches in my chin, and a subcorneal hemorrhage, and a cracked rib, etc. But I am definitely on the mend now and it was not bad so you mustn't worry, and the

Wilcoxes say it is all right because my ethereal beauty is not changed, except I look very distinguished with the goatee the stitches forced me to grow for a little while.

The "true story," as Steward later wrote in his unpublished memoir, was that "when prowling the dark alleys of the Chicago Loop, I was set upon by someone who disapproved of my tastes and inclinations, hit on the chin with a brass-knuckled fist (ten stitches) and laid to rest in a hospital for several days. My cover story that I had been mugged was accepted easily enough, Chicago's reputation being what it was." In fact, Steward's craving for rough and dangerous encounters had intensified in the past few months and would continue to do so during the war years; one such encounter, a bar pickup on the South Side of Chicago, resulted in a seven-hour ordeal as a sexual captive.*

On May 21, Steward (who had remained at Loyola despite his earlier plan to leave) wrote Stein that with Europe now impossible to reach, he hoped to summer among French-speaking people in Quebec, and added, "I have finished my little book at last—or think I have—it's only about 45,000 words long, but that's as long as any of Thornton's."

By midsummer, though, he wrote her that his plans had changed once again:

I'm leaving tomorrow to spend August on an island off the coast of Maine—Cora Gould that old lady with eight millions wrote and said, would you like to spend it here at my expense, and so naturally I said yes . . . the address will be The Moors, Vinalhaven, Maine . . . I guess I will not be drafted since my 31st birthday was the 23rd, I thought of Basket II's birthday[†] on July 22d, and of how last year I was with you . . . I was real unhappy thinking of all that . . .

I may see Thornton sometime in August or September, I suppose you know he is at Bass Rocks Theater in Gloucester playing

*Information about this encounter is listed in the Stud File under the subject heading "South Side," with the additional information "Chicago 1942 100 Seven hours!" "100" being Steward's code word for "jackpot," or "sex in all forms."
†When Stein's poodle, Basket, had died, she bought another, giving the new poodle puppy the same name.

in his play* just at the moment. He seems to be just about the same. I am going to write the 11 or make a good beginning while I am at Maine; I re-read it the other day and decided what was there was really good and I'm going on with it. I finished the other little thing, Houghton-Mifflin had been pestering me despite the fact I kept saying, no, how could anyone who published Keats and Hawthorne, how could they publish such a frivolous Firbankian thing, but they insisted on seeing it and of course didn't want it, so I am taking it to Bennett Cerf when I go to New York and then to Simon and Schuster after that if he doesn't want it.[†]

Steward's visit to Maine was not particularly exciting; he recalled it many years later as "Vinalhaven, that island off Rockland [where I had] more shore dinners than you c[oul]d count . . . And not much sex. The 'host' (whom one paid) was the ole broken-down 2-rate poet Harold Vinal; the island named for his ancestors, I guess." Even in that remote place, however, he managed to scare up some fun: one Dr. Ralph Bowen performed oral sex on him five times. Of it Steward later noted, "Mouth of emptiness, excellent."

Steward had hoped to see Wilder while vacationing in New England, but a brisk postcard from Wilder put an end to that plan: "Forgive the hurried card: working like a n[ig]g[e]r: acting, directing, & writing. I wish I could see Maine this summer and have some good long talks with you but when these present distractions are over I must nail myself down to my desk . . . Have a good rest, and once rested put pen to paper again. All my best as ever, Thornton."

By the end of summer 1940, Steward could barely reach Stein by mail; as a result "letters [from Stein and Toklas became] sporadic. Sometimes my letters stayed in occupied Paris a year before reaching them, and theirs to me were similarly delayed." Nonetheless, in October, he wrote Stein,

Well, Thornton was here and . . . he is the same old Thornton only he is talking a little more than usual about getting old and I think he is, I think maybe he needs a psychiatrist to work on him a little.

---

*Wilder had taken the role of the Narrator in his play *Our Town*.
†This never-published untitled manuscript has been lost.

He is more nervous and fussy and fidgety than he ever was before and he works very hard going places real fast and being athletic, I think to convince himself he is still young . . .

Everyone is becoming awfully patriotic . . . and quite naturally some of us even though we are patriotic are inclined *a vomir** at all the fuss . . . You can't walk a block without seeing someone in uniform . . .

[The military] would probably use me in the intelligence service whatever that may be . . . it is all very exciting, and with things outside you that exciting it matters less about your own importance to yourself inside yourself, or maybe not, maybe it is just that the excitement gets inside you as well and you temporarily are dulled and so don't notice the lack . . .

Wilder, in passing through Chicago, enjoyed a night with Steward at the Stevens Hotel, and wrote him a long letter afterward from Albany, New York, which concluded:

> . . . So many things come back to me that we didn't have time to talk about.
>
> But it was very fine seeing you and thanks . . .
>
> Do sit down some rainy afternoon and write me—anything, moods, anything.
>
> Ever y'r' old
Thornton

Although Steward kept no journals during the 1940s, letters from Wendell Wilcox to Stein indicate that Steward was significantly depressed in the fall of 1940: "Sam . . . is very unhappy and we are trying to soothe him. He is having a very trying time and Esther† thinks it is partly not wanting to be in a church any more." He also added that "Thornton's *Our Town* was in town . . . Sam saw it and cried."

In spring of 1941, Steward wrote Wilder in anticipation of Wilder's return to Chicago to teach the summer session at the University of

---

*"To vomit."
†Esther Wilcox, Wendell's wife.

Chicago. Though Wilder discarded the letter, Steward saved Wilder's response, written from Medellín, Colombia, which suggested a lover's quarrel: "So you do write letters after all! So you aren't mad at me! My God—after all that silence I thought you'd decided to efface me, so that I shrugged my shoulders with assured pique and said: all right, so I'll efface Sam."

•

Steward spent more time with Wilder that summer, but then traveled alone to Quebec for his August vacation, there writing Stein,

> It is Quebec now, out of my love for France, and I have a room with a little balcony looking out over an infinite expanse of the St. Lawrence and next door the *très elegant* Chateau Frontenac, and just a little below me the board-walk where all Quebec in the evenings parades endlessly, looking pathetically for sex and sin or excitement or something. The people are very strange . . . The first person [I have spoken to in five days] is a real French sailor, of a *sous-marin* crew that had been at Dakar, and it was strange and thrilling to hear good French again . . . Mostly I just sit on the promenade of afternoons and read a mystery, I read one a day now and the passion has more than got me . . .
>
> I think Thornton is a little sillier than he ever was [and] more hysterical than ever . . .
>
> It has been a sort of easy year for me, I am teaching entirely downtown now, and that is better, the people are much more mature. I suppose I shall stay on though I have been trying to get in the Naval Intelligence Service doing something, I would much rather be using my brains than my body when war comes, and of course it will in September sometime. I got deferred in the draft because of my aunts "partial dependence" but in case of actualities I'd be right in the middle of the senseless thing. And the navy has always had an attraction for me.

Steward's interest in joining the navy was based in no small part on his long-standing fascination with sailors—and indeed, Chicago was just then awash with them, for hordes of men in training for the United States Navy were doing so just forty miles north of Chicago. Of the four million

American men who saw active duty in the U.S. Navy during World War II, one million would be trained at Great Lakes Training Station, the nation's largest naval training facility. By September 1942, well over one hundred thousand sailors were enlisted there, and all of them were taking their liberty breaks in downtown Chicago.

Young, vital, socially unencumbered, and forced into celibacy during long months at sea, the sailor on shore leave has long been considered an archetype of sexual availability, and Steward, like many homosexuals of his generation, had an abiding interest in picking them up, for they were well known as easy "trade."* By World War II, the openness of sailors to any sort of sexual experience largely went without saying, and cultural references to it abounded—from the sly song lyrics of Cole Porter ("what's Central Park / without a sailor?"), to the scandalous homoerotic paintings of Paul Cadmus, to the intimate homoerotic watercolors of Charles Demuth. Plays, musicals, and ballets based on World War II experience would continue to establish the sailor as a figure of romantic and sexual longing in years to come, as evidenced by the tight-pantsed sailor in Tennessee Williams's drama *The Rose Tattoo*, as well as similarly attired young sailors in Jerome Robbins's ballet *Fancy Free*, and Comden and Green's musical *On the Town*.†

Of the sailor's uniform, Steward later wrote,

> Most uniforms make the bodies beneath them more exciting—some in greater degree than others. For me, and perhaps for a majority of others like me, the sailor's uniform top[s] the list.
> . . . The sailor's uniform, I decided . . . represents a way of life that most of us can never know . . . He fights for us who are left at home in the dull round of living . . . beneath the rough wool there beats a heart more brave and gallant than any we have ever known . . . The uniform surrounds him with the shimmering glitter of an illusion, and we are frozen into our positions of adoration and desire. The uniform is the psychic link—the gazing-glass through which we look into another world.

*"Trade" describes a man who, though self-identifying as heterosexual, will allow another man to perform nonreciprocal oral sex on him.
†For more on the phenomenon of homosexual desire and American sailor imagery, see the exhibition catalog "The Sailor: 1930–1945," from an exhibition by the same name curated by Tom Sokolowski at the Chrysler Museum in Norfolk, Virginia, in 1983.

Although at thirty-one Steward was too old to be drafted (the average American sailor in 1945 was approximately twenty-five, and only one in two had completed high school), he had a good ability with languages and had studied codebreaking through an army-sponsored course. As a result he began teaching cryptography at Loyola in anticipation of entering army intelligence. But when school let out in June of 1943, he impetuously enlisted instead as a seaman:

> Everything was beginning to point towards an army commission and a career for me in Intelligence. But . . . I loathed the color of khaki! . . . [So] I enlisted in the navy, was sworn in, and sent to the Great Lakes Naval Training Center a few miles north of Chicago [for training as a sailor]. No one [there] seemed to be interested in the fact that I had a considerable background in cryptography, and the Ph.D. stood for nothing.

If enlistment as a seaman did nothing else for Steward, it gave him an inside view of life at the enormous naval training station. But not for long: after initially passing the physical exam (during which he purposefully neglected to mention that he suffered from multiple food allergies), he was given his beloved uniform. Within minutes of eating his first meal of navy "chow," however, he experienced an allergic reaction so sudden and so violent that he was completely incapacitated. Sneezing, coughing, gasping for breath, covered in hives, his eyes swollen shut, he was sent to an infirmary where naval doctors interrogated him, determined him unfit for service, and immediately placed him in a holding tank to await discharge.

"I think I have about the shortest navy career of anybody," he wrote Stein and Toklas. "Just a graceful little pirouette with a coupla entrechats—and it was all over." His detention at the naval training station lasted several weeks, however, during which (according to his Stud File) he had sex with seven fellow detainees. At the end of that time, he was given a set of makeshift civilian clothes and sent back to Chicago as a reject. Only then did he learn that because of his medical discharge he was no longer eligible for work in any other branch of the armed services.

Though he made light of the rejection, Steward was devastated; with exclusion from the ranks of the navy, his desire to possess this uniformed masculine ideal—the sailor—grew ever stronger. And indeed, in the coming decade his sexual preoccupation with sailors would border on obsession.

•

Luckily for Steward, he did not need to be a sailor in order to have sex with one. In truth, by living alone in Chicago, he was in a much better position to have sex with sailors than he ever would have been while enlisted. At the time of his dismissal from the navy, an average of fifty thousand soldiers and sailors were pouring into the Loop each weekend in search of an inexpensive night out on the town, and with it some form of sexual relief. Steward was clean, handsome, and physically fit; he knew the Bluejacket manual cover to cover, and he now had firsthand knowledge of the Great Lakes Training Station, too. After years of picking up men in bars and on the street, he was no longer the least bit shy; and since most of the boot sailors were only slightly older than his students at Loyola, he knew how to approach them, and did so with confidence and ease.

The early years of the war were a time of erotic opportunity and discovery for many men and women in the armed services, most of whom were away from their families for the first time. The crowds of soldiers and sailors swarming through the Loop created what one veteran later described as a "gay ambiance" in which many of these young GIs felt entirely comfortable. Since the government's need for manpower was immediate, military authorities did little to crack down on possible homosexual activities among servicemen on liberty passes during the early stages of the war (only later, when men were no longer needed, would the large number of career-destroying expulsions begin). When local police and military police combined forces to control or shut down gatherings at which homosexual activities might be initiated, they unwittingly created "alternating periods of crackdown and openness [which] put urban gay life [in Chicago, San Francisco, and elsewhere] through major cycles of disruption and reorganization" that were not without their own illicit thrills. As a result, until the end of World War II, there was a new openness and activity among homosexuals who had been brought together by the American war machine—men and women who were, in the words of one historian, "not proclaiming or parading their homosexuality in public but [also] not willing to live lonely, isolated lives."

While Steward was far from unique in having sex with enlisted men, his documentation of these encounters was extraordinary, for it consisted not only of his Stud File records, but also of short stories based on real-life events. He also wrote a short novella entitled *Bell-Bottom Trousers* that was designed specifically for use with his military pickups; in order to create it, he commandeered a Loyola hectograph machine and used it as his printer. The story chronicled the sexual exploits of a virile sailor, and was meant to arouse servicemen visiting his home. After sex, Steward would give the serviceman a copy of the work (along with his name and address).* He later described the project to a sex researcher:

> [These] typewritten stories [were] the only pornography that we had . . . Everybody who could get his hands on them [would circulate them]. Some people tried their hands at writing these stories, and some of them were really good. It was all male oriented and homosexual . . . I wrote one during World War II, called "Bell Bottom Trousers," [making] copies of it on an old hectograph . . . The hectograph was jelly, and you wrote on paper with a special purple pen, or with purple ribbon in your typewriter, then put that face down and took copies off the jelly. It would last for only 25 copies, and that's the reason my first pornography was limited to an edition of 25. I sent those to all my friends in the services in various parts of the world, together with a note that said they had permission to reproduce it if they wanted to. It was about 5,000 words long. I still have a copy of it somewhere. It's got a heterosexual core to it, because a lot of my acquaintances were not gay; they had been trade, of course. There were homosexual incidents in it too . . .

In his later years, Steward would roughly estimate that of the 807 people he had had sex with up to that day of his life, servicemen comprised a significant number: "sailors—a coupla hundred; sergeants—about 30; marines—2 dozen." He would also tell an interviewer that his

---

*Steward later donated a copy of *Bell-Bottom Trousers* to the Institute for Sex Research, which for years listed its author as "Guy de Mereille." But this is clearly a pseudonym chosen by Steward (Guy de Mereille was the name of a 1937 Paris pickup about whom Steward had observed in his diary, "Desire to give the whole French nation a collective bath. Personally filthy"). The cover of the work, which features an illustration by Steward, also features a note reading, "Of this story twenty-five copies have been hectographed, five of which have been reserved for the author. It is particularly intended for the enjoyment of members of the armed services, and permission to reprint it is freely given." (KISR Library.)

most personally significant experience of sadomasochistic sex had been with an (unnamed) sailor he had met in Chicago during the war.

During the second and third years of the war, Steward could not travel on his summer vacation; wartime hardships and the limitations of his own meager salary (much of which he was spending in bars and on whiskey) kept him home in Chicago. As he wrote Stein and Toklas, "I have been doing a lot of lecturing around and about . . . but it's been mostly for love or peanuts . . . Mostly I've talked on literature or semantics or cryptography." He was forced to move twice, finally ending up in a one-bedroom apartment at 5441 North Kenmore Avenue, in a drab, crime-ridden neighborhood at the north end of Lincoln Park.

During the last three years of the war, which were also the worst years of his alcoholism, Steward did no writing apart from collecting and transcribing dirty limericks and sexual graffiti (which he termed "latriniana") from various public toilets around Chicago.* His abandonment of his literary vocation was due, in part, to an overwhelming sense of futility and exclusion, for as he later noted when interviewed for a study of the homosexual novel in America, "At the time it was more rewarding to play games with rough trade in a city park than with editors and publishers in the world of American letters, and to a considerable extent it is for this reason that we have so few gay novels to tell us what it was like to be in the 'shadow world' of the 1930s [and early 1940s]."

Following the suggestion of Thornton Wilder, however, Steward did try his hand at essays and reviews, which he began publishing monthly in a most unlikely venue. As he later explained,

> My dentist in Chicago . . . Willam P. Schoen, Jr. . . . was also the editor of the *Illinois Dental Journal*, and while I was at his mercy in the chair one day in 1943 he talked me into starting a series of articles for his *Journal*, giving me free rein to write on any topic I chose. So I began, using the name I was later to use as a tattoo artist, Philip Sparrow—using "Philip" instead of "Phil," since it was more dignified.
>
> For six years and over sixty articles I enjoyed [writing them] . . . Alice Toklas saw most of them and flattered me by liking them,

---

*Steward's notebook of neatly transcribed erotic limericks remains within his papers; other "latriniana" was donated to the Institute for Sex Research.

saying that they were filled with "Sammish impishness" and my "best whimsy and pretty lightness."

Steward's column appeared in the *Illinois Dental Journal* every month, with rare exceptions, from January 1944 through October 1949. Its name, "The Victim's Viewpoint," ostensibly referred to the dental patient; but it was also a private gesture of self-identification, for Steward was by now entirely aware of his masochistic preferences, particularly where handsome, authoritative men like his dentist* were concerned. (His first essay for the *Dental Journal* was in fact entitled "The Sublimated Sadist: The Dentist as Iago.") His subsequent writings for the *Dental Journal* wandered from food allergies to psychiatry, A. E. Housman to Gertrude Stein, schoolteaching to bodybuilding, and served as a lifeline to his nearly abandoned ambition of becoming a full-time writer.

In November 1944, Steward developed a sudden, massive inflammation in one of his testicles. Doctors were unable to determine the cause of the problem but Steward's pain was so acute that they immediately performed an orchiectomy, with surprising results. As Steward wrote Stein and Toklas several months later,

> It seems that all these years without knowing it I had been carrying a twin around with me, and all of a sudden it flourished, and had to come out. This set me awhirl with speculation about the old medieval theory that one soul is divided between two when twins are born, and such like, and I began to experience some of the surprise that Jove must have felt when Minerva jumped out of his brow full-grown.

Steward later described the traumatic amputation of his testicle—and the horror of the biopsy that followed—in greater detail:

> It was certainly cancer . . . [and] afterwards [the biopsy revealed a malignant teratoma† containing] hair follicles, sweat and sebaceous glands, nerve and teeth elements . . . And then I began to

---

*Steward privately referred to Dr. Schoen as "Dr. Pretty" (*Schöne* being German for "pretty"). Elsewhere he described Schoen as looking like the film star Gregory Peck.
†Malignant teratoma: a type of cancer that involves cysts that contain one or more of the three main types of cells found in a developing fetus (embryo).

remember other small details about myself . . . I had four fewer
teeth than usual [and a] tiny, rudimentary nipple two inches below my right one . . .

There was no getting around it! I had been meant to be a
twin, and it had not worked out right . . . Since I was an autosite*
for a twin, there were other metaphysical questions that began to
arise—the old wives' tale saying that if you were a twin, you
shared one soul with another—so quite possibly I had no more
than half a soul.

Steward was devastated by the operation, not least because of the
centrality of his genitalia to his everyday life. (But, as he soon discovered,
he functioned perfectly well with his one remaining testicle, and very few
of his partners seemed to notice or care about the missing one.) Still, the
surgery left him with a new awareness of his own mortality, and with it, a
growing desire to get sober.

Steward's life during 1945 is best chronicled in his correspondence
with Sergeant Bill Collins, the sex-and-drinking partner he had known
since 1938. The two wrote each other regularly while Collins was posted
in Europe.[†] With careful wording, Steward was able, despite wartime
censors, to describe his growing "latriniana" collection, and to tell salty
stories about various homosexual acquaintances, including a well-known
neighborhood hustler. Steward also regaled Collins with tales of his more
outrageous sexual escapades, for theirs was not a possessive relationship.
Yet despite the ribaldry, there are moments of genuine intimacy in the correspondence, during which a love relationship seems to exist between
them. During the summer of 1945, as he attempted to quit drinking,
Steward wrote Collins of a visit home:

Getting readjusted to my family has been a rather strange thing for
me. It's the first time they've seen me sober for the past fifteen years,
and I don't think they know me. It is even more strange for me—I
look at them, and suddenly see them for the first time: a somewhat

*Autosite: The usually larger component of abnormal, unequally conjoined twins that is able to live
independently and nourish the other parasitic component.
†Steward would later donate that correspondence to the Kinsey Institute, apparently to demonstrate
the nature of loving, erotic friendships between men.

valiant group of old people with a great many more interesting characteristics than I ever had attributed to them . . . It's too late, I guess, to do anything about it; they knew me as [the drunk] I used to be, and I doubt if they can change their opinion of what a general heel I am—and of course I cannot make them see or understand how they are to me at present. I can't get through to them. I can't say something like, "Look, I'm a new person and I find I really do like you somewhat, and do you like me?" That just wouldn't work; they'd think I was crazy. So I don't suppose anything will ever come of it, and I won't remember the moment's mood after two days go by.

Since Steward and Collins were at that point separated by an ocean and a war, the relationship never had a chance to deepen. Perhaps as a result, Collins was not the only enlisted man for whom Steward would have strong feelings during this time. He had recently been particularly moved by a sexual encounter with one Lieutenant Art Craine. In the months that followed that 1943 encounter, he sent Craine a series of highly erotic letters (which Craine, to Steward's chagrin, insisted that Steward sign as a woman). Three years after the war ended, Steward and Craine would meet again in Pittsburgh, and though that subsequent encounter did not amount to much, Craine would remain an erotic ideal to Steward for years afterward: his name would appear repeatedly not only in Steward's journal recollections, but also in his Phil Andros fiction.*

Though still a binge drinker, Steward was now working steadily toward sobriety, and with it a return to serious writing. In an April 1945 letter, he wrote Stein and Toklas:

No, believe me, I am through with drinking; and it makes me think of all the time I wasted doing it. I stopped October 1st and it is now six months without a drappie.† Already I am recovering and feeling ambition inside me (it is not too late I hope) and . . . turning to writing again after all these years of lapsing . . . I am coming to the conclusion that if I write to please myself there will be enough

---

*Art Craine appears as himself in Greek Ways; the novel ends at his home in a small town just outside Pittsburgh.

†Scottish dialect for "a drop," as in "A Wee Drappie Mair," an old Scottish drinking song.

other people who will be pleased, after all . . . I read very little now-adays except detective stories, dozens and dozens of those.

Steward's fascination with hard-boiled detective fiction and the American vernacular would ultimately contribute to the wisecracking tone of his erotic narratives, and it would also permeate his correspondence, his journals, and his Stud File.

Wilcox, meanwhile, gave Stein and Toklas a glimpse of Steward in relapse:

I talked to Sam today and his week end seemed to have started already.* I could get nothing very straight but it looks as if he had resigned completely from Loyola and it also looks as if he were considering rebecoming a Catholic. At least there is going to be Communion and a confession for the past ten years. The conversation however was pretty confusing.

In this particular instance, Steward's emotional crisis may have been triggered by a war fatality. His sister had married Lieutenant Arthur Ury in 1935, and Steward, who liked Ury very much, had recently sent him to Stein and Toklas bearing a gift for them and a letter of introduction. In April 1945, however, Steward wrote to them,

there will be no more deliveries from that direction; my sister got one of those wires from the War Department—he was killed March 4th during the first drive across the Rhine . . . The worst thing was that on Easter there came from him, thru a prearrangement, a corsage for my sister . . . it is just one of those things about which one can do nothing, nothing at all.

In any event, by the end of the 1945 spring semester, Steward had reached an emotional crisis greater than anything he had experienced previously. Despite now teaching exclusively at the graduate center on Franklin Street in downtown Chicago ("to effect my escape from the nauseating adolescent brats on [the main] campus"), he was nonetheless hav-

---

*To "start the weekend early" is a euphemism for getting drunk.

ing a job-related breakdown. After a weekend at the home of the sculptor John Rood in Athens, Ohio, Wilcox wrote Stein and Toklas,

> Sam has been and gone. The first night he was walking about the house all night long after people were in bed and I could hear him say *merde* and [he was] casting eerie glances this way and that, but he remembered nothing though he ran a great deal of water and splashed a lot all night. He must have been off on a life of his own we none of us saw. I had never believed very strongly in his sudden alarms, bursts of hopes, fears, etc. But when I heard him fussing in the hallway and talking to himself I did seem to get it that it was all going on.

Steward's crisis worsened that summer, when a psychologically unstable older woman in one of his classes became psychotically obsessed with him. She was, as he later wrote, "mad, utterly mad. Every day [I would arrive in class to find] one full square of blackboard filled with her [obscene] writing—most of it rambling and incoherent." When Steward demanded immediate action from the administration, however, the dean made no move to expel her from the class. Steward, enraged and powerless, did the only thing he could: he took an immediate leave of absence.* As he wrote Stein and Toklas:

> I suppose technically you would say that it was a case of menopausal paranoia, complicated with a sex obsession and a religious neurosis, with myself the focal center of everything. So that made my life very exciting . . .
> I have taken on another job, and I like it. It's nothing but hackwriting in a way, but for the first time I'm making money, and I *love* that! It all began when one of my former students who works for the World Book Encyclopedia said to me how would you like to do some articles in a clear and simple style? . . . So I sat and wrote them this summer . . . They scrambled all over themselves trying to pick me up for work, because with my simple child's mind I wrote

---

*Steward's account is supported by a letter from Loyola (now in the Steward papers) documenting his leave of absence, and also by a sympathetic letter on the situation from Morton Zabel (now in the Zabel papers at the Newberry Library, Chicago).

things the way a child could understand them. They loved me . . .
[At first] I had some trouble adjusting to the office mentality and
the business world . . . [But] it has made me feel that I can do something more than just teach school.

As he began his new job of rewriting *The World Book Encyclopedia*,
Steward suggested to his sister, who was still grieving for her husband,
that she join the project. Virginia Ury eventually did so, working with a
staff of fellow scholars in what became an increasingly frantic two-year
full-time endeavor. The challenge of rewriting the encyclopedia brought
about a noteworthy change in Steward's spirits. As he wrote to Collins,

You've no idea what new confidence this second job has instilled
in me. For 10 long years I've been at the mercy of the Jesuits . . .
Now when their pettinesses reveal themselves again, I shall be
able simply to tell them to open an umbrella up their ass, and
betake myself to green woods and pastures new. It may be, I
hope, the beginning of my long hard climb out of the r(o)ut(ine)
I landed in, back in 1936. Be happy for me, lad; 'tis a little enough
thing, I know, but infinitely pleasing.

Unfortunately, the encyclopedia job remained on-and-off freelance
work for the first year. Steward filled the empty hours at the opera house;
Wilcox noted to Toklas, "Sam's been very busy being a super in the ballets
and operas. It has got to almost a profession by now."*
Feeling the need to reconnect with Stein at the end of the war, Steward decided to splurge on a fantastically expensive overseas telephone call
to her home on Rue Christine. Scheduling it took from October 1945 to
January 13, 1946, but finally, on January 20, the call went through, and,
as he later wrote, "I heard her wonderful voice, straight from Olympus,
neo-Valkyrean, thrilling and delightful. Space and time were no more . . .
For three full minutes we shouted at each other, neither of us knowing
what the other said. But it was joyous."
Steward's telephone call was prescient, for six months later, during
the course of an exploratory operation for cancer, Stein died. Steward was

---

*Steward's Stud File, meanwhile, notes a number of sexual encounters backstage, including one with
a man named Charles Silver "in the opera donjon" in 1947.

devastated. Unemployed, low on funds, and deeply depressed, he could not bring himself to write Toklas anything more than a telegraph of condolence. But she nonetheless wrote back, "Your wire did me good because at once there came back to me the really good time you had given Gertrude—so many times . . . Gertrude was the happiest person that ever was but you found a way to give her a new pleasure—and so I will always love you. Basket and I stay on here alone—so if you come over we'll try to welcome you prettily in Gertrude's home." Several months later, she sent Steward one of Stein's silk scarves as a remembrance, and in response to his note of thanks, she wrote: "Are you being a good boy. Or are you like Basket—perfect with an occasional lapse. Have you seen Thornton. He wrote me that he expected to see you—he thinks you should teach—he's a firm believer in teaching. He is of course the best example of the benefits it is possible to achieve from learning and teaching."

Deeply disillusioned with teaching and strongly aware that he was very far from "perfect with an occasional lapse," Steward again could not bring himself to respond. For a long time he sent no more letters to Toklas.

•

The encyclopedia job soon proved more difficult than expected. The editorial team struggled mightily to keep to its deadlines, and Steward, finding the pace exhausting, began to long for "those dear departed halcyon academic days when I never had to get up before noon, and when the week's work consisted simply of lecturing with a certain ironic and aloof dignity for only sixteen hours a week." He later thought it "incredible that I voluntarily committed myself to [that] madhouse for two full years."

He nonetheless performed well as department editor for *The World Book*, a job that consisted not only of revising and updating seven million words of text, but also of simplifying that text to meet various levels of reading difficulty. His clarity and precision as a prose stylist were indeed extraordinary; so much so that the managing editor for the project noted at its conclusion, "Dr. Steward [was] one of our ablest and most brilliant editorial workers . . . [in] charge of some of the 'touchiest' and most difficult fields of knowledge within the province of a general encyclopedia." The articles on religion had particularly challenged Steward, for each of his efforts had needed to pass muster with a Protestant, a Catholic, and a Jewish theologian before being sent to press. In promotional photographs of the editorial team taken during 1946–1947, he is nattily dressed, with carefully pomaded hair and a pencil-thin mustache, but he is also pallid and bleary-eyed. On one recent drunken night out in search of sex he had witnessed a murder; as Wilcox wrote wonderingly to Toklas, "It seems as if all the murders and sex crimes take place in his block . . . There was actually [one] in his building."

Money, too, remained a problem—so much so that, during the last months of 1946, Steward took a job as holiday help at the bookstore in Marshall Field's department store. Steward had naively thought that his lifelong love of books would make working in a bookshop at Christmastime enjoyable. It was not. In a *Dental Journal* essay about the horrors of holiday employment at Marshall Field's, he observed, "It was a howling madhouse, a lunatic Sabbath, a frenzied nightmare of females and squalling brats." The retail environment was nonetheless not without diversions, for Field's had long been well-known in Chicago as a homosexual cruising ground, and many of its employees (including Steward's boss) were homosexual. One afternoon Steward's sexual interest was piqued by an extraordinarily handsome young man working in the gift-wrap department: tall and dark-haired, he had trained at Great Lakes, taken a first posting at the Naval Air Training Station in Glenview, and then done a brief tour of duty in the Philippines. Once again a civilian, Roy Fitzgerald was now spending the holidays wrapping presents. Steward learned that he was a "club-member" from his boss; after a brief conversation, Steward and Fitzgerald boarded a freight elevator and stopped it between floors for oral sex. The incident was a onetime thing; Fitzgerald would take a job after the holidays as a postman in Winnetka, and by September he would have moved to Los Angeles, there to begin a highly successful film career as Rock Hudson.*

•

In early 1947, at the end of the holidays, Steward fell into an incapacitating depression. Physically worn-out from years of heavy drinking, on leave from a teaching job that had exhausted him, unable to progress with his literary writing, emotionally disconnected from everyone he knew, Stew-

---

*The card in the Stud File notes: "Tall ex-sailor. Ami de John Scheele [manager of the bookstore at Field's]. Worked in gift wrap dept. Black curly hair. V gd-lking." The encounter took place in December 1946; Steward later shared other particulars of the encounter (namely the use of the elevator) with his friend and former pupil Douglas Martin. Hudson's work in the gift-wrap department is briefly mentioned in Hudson's memoirs. (Rock Hudson and Sara Davidson, *Rock Hudson: His Story* [New York: William Morrow, 1986], p. 156.)

ard was also feeling less desirable than ever before on account of his advancing age, amputated testicle, and debilitating alcoholism. In despair, he decided on suicide.

Though loath ever to discuss it, Steward had repeatedly contemplated suicide since adolescence; while still a young man he had stolen twenty-four quarter-grain tablets of morphine from his grandfather's medicine chest, expecting he might one day use them to end his life. More recently he had acquired a hypodermic syringe in order to inject massive doses of vitamin B_{12} into his arm, "so that my ragged nerves could face each new day's old pain." He decided to crush the twenty-four morphine pills, dissolve them in water, and inject the lethal solution into a vein.

In a sense, Steward had been primed for suicide by culture-wide perceptions of the homosexual as an individual intent upon self-destruction. In the words of Edward Sagarin/Donald Webster Cory, a pioneering homophile writer of the period, American society saw "the homosexual as a depressed, dejected person, frequently on the brink of suicide, or actually ending his hopeless life after many years of despondent struggle . . . [The] wide acceptance [of this myth] may be attributed to the novelists who have ended so many books on [the] subject [of homosexuality] in a mood of despair, violence, and even suicide. [Nearly all contemporary novels on homosexuality of the 1930s and '40s] end with hopelessness for the invert. Several of these books bring the invert to self-destruction; the others leave him no other path to follow."

And yet as he prepared to inject the morphine, Steward hesitated. Through sheer force of habit he had found himself sterilizing the hypodermic needle, and when he realized what he was doing—sterilizing a needle in order to kill himself—he had a revelation: "From my deep despair I leaped suddenly to a peak of laughter . . . Well, not quite, and not immediately, but within a week I had gone to my first Alcoholics Anonymous meeting, and though it took me some time before I stopped 'slipping,' I had my last drink in 1947." The fact that the twenty-five-year-old morphine tablets were most probably inert added further merriment to Steward's after-the-fact recollection of his suicide attempt, which he later published as a short, life-affirming confessional article entitled "Death Averted."

Though it began in 1935, the Alcoholics Anonymous organization was then relatively new to the Chicago area. Steward had never been a "joiner" and hated the idea of swapping misery stories with a group of fellow drinkers, but he also now knew he needed help by whatever means he could find. As he began attending meetings, he found he had a very particular problem: Alcoholics Anonymous insisted upon his appealing to "God" as part of his recovery process :

> I had . . . difficulty with the God business [in AA] . . . but [then] I found a group in Chicago, the old Water Tower group, made up of hard bitten radio announcers, commercial artists, and such like. This group all had trouble with admitting God into their lives. As a result, we decided that the "greater power" simply meant the stuff in the bottle was stronger than we were, and that was acceptable to all of us. The moving spirits of the Group were [recovering alcoholics] Dorothy "Dode" Brando and her husband [Marlon, Sr.].*

Steward relapsed throughout his first years in the program. Eventually, however, he noticed a pattern to his relapses:

> After about four years of meetings . . . I found that the only times I now thought of drinking or alcohol were after the AA meetings! . . . I spoke to several experienced AA members about my problem; they all told me that if I stopped going to meetings the chances were almost dead against me—I would "slip" back into the old ways. But it worked—for me. Gradually the thought of alcohol receded until it was no longer there. This took about a year.

"Only three of my 'old' [drinking] friends survived into my new period," he later wrote, "the others disappeared." But far from feeling any nostalgia for his life as a drunk, Steward sensed he had barely escaped self-destruction: a good friend with whom he attended Alcoholics Anonymous meetings, George Barker, was not so lucky. "Barker put his head in an oven in Belleville, Texas," Steward later noted. "He had become convinced that he could handle alcohol and started drinking again."

Friends soon noticed a difference in Steward. "Physically he does improve, he really does," Wilcox wrote Toklas about his dry-out. "It takes a long time I guess once you get really pickled in that stuff. He gradually

---

*Steward later noted in his memoirs that "though [I] assiduously courted Dode in the hope that [I] might be introduced to her handsome son, she was evidently wise to the world's ways . . . [I] never did meet Marlon."

comes back into focus however. For a long time he was distracted looking and tired as if it took every bit of his strength just realizing his own
presence, now there's enough left over for the outside world." Recovery
brought with it an almost overwhelming sense of sadness and loss, though,
for Steward knew he had wasted precious time and opportunity as a writer
with his drinking, and now he had to face starting over—doing what, he
did not yet know.

In a letter from the period urging him to come back and visit her in
Paris, Toklas wrote Steward of a similar instance of "reformation":

Oh, Sammy, aren't you good at all any more. I'll begin to worry
terribly about you if you're just adrift . . . Be careful, very careful . . . Do you remember Francis Rose? He remembers you and
sends you his greetings. He has completely reformed—strange to
say it is quite becoming though he has lost his looks—married a
quite poisonous Frederica who has done him a world of good and
[he] paints beautifully—surer and firmer than when you knew
his pictures in '39 . . . Frederica writes [books]. It is all so different than it was. Francis has kept his sweetness and his pretty
ways, but has lost the eccentricity and exotic color of his youth.

Steward answered:

[I haven't written you because] I was going through an extremely
difficult period . . . You said to me in that wondrous letter that I
should not become a "drifter"—and although I am not by nature
a person to whom that would appeal, I was in danger then, grave
danger. The whole business grows out of my firm resolve NOT to
go back to school teaching . . .

Spiritually I have been reasonably happy, although not quite
the same since July of 1946* . . . The drinking is now under control, but the money is gone until I make some more, and then I
AM coming [to Paris] . . .

---

*The month of Stein's death.

5

Sobriety and After

Upon quitting alcohol, Steward found himself much more interested in sex, and much more conscious of his sexual interests as well, for sobriety brought with it a greater day-to-day self-awareness. With the great increase in physical vitality that came with giving up drinking (not to mention the great increase in his free time), Steward began engaging in various forms of creative sex play on a regular basis, including a form that involved writing erotic fiction.

The activity developed out of a chance discovery. During his last months at *The World Book Encyclopedia*, Steward came across an anonymous note that had been left in a hidden nook in his office building's hall toilet. Interested, he answered it with a note of his own—so beginning a secret, anonymous sexual correspondence with a man who worked in the same building. Leaving a note every day at the "back of [the] top of [the] toilet bowl, in [a] hole where [the] mortar had fallen out," Steward wrote explicitly and enthusiastically about his various sexual adventures involving both men and women, and his reward for doing so was a note returned later the same day detailing similar adventures. Steward based his stories on anything that interested him—and they were, in a sense, the beginning of his life as a pornographer. The collected correspondence (his own, combined with that of his correspondent) would also serve as a calling card for the next great mentor to enter Steward's life, the sex researcher Alfred C. Kinsey.*

---

*Steward gave the entire correspondence to Kinsey in 1950 and a year later at Kinsey's specific request wrote explanatory notes on the correspondence.

Steward's "toilet correspondence" took place from March through June of 1947, and ultimately consisted of 126 pages of single-spaced, typed transcriptions of letters written by Steward to a man named "Bob," along with Bob's handwritten responses. The two never saw each other picking up notes, but they did meet briefly to take a look at each other during the first week of the correspondence, and later met once for oral sex. Steward's letters to "Bob" describing heterosexual sex were, by his own reckoning, 80 percent fictional, with the remaining 20 percent based on his own experiences. His descriptions of homosexual sex, meanwhile, were 30 percent fictional, with the remaining 70 percent based on actual experiences that he had "dressed up" to make better reading. Steward conjectured that "Bob's" letters, by comparison, were based mostly on fantasies, since many of the things he described were (as he later noted to Kinsey) "quite impossible . . . [He is] not married, lives with mother, advertises his interest in females but [this] may be only voyeurism or day dreams without experience . . . [He] spends much time at noon hour in Marshall Fields [sic] in [the] toilets."

The toilet correspondence offers a funhouse glimpse of Steward's otherwise underdescribed sexual experiences of the 1930s and '40s, for they feature a number of highly plausible scenarios that are corroborated by Steward's Stud File entries. They include an account of his experiences with the two soldiers in Morocco in 1939; another of an orgy of thirty-five men in the navy barracks at Great Lakes Naval Training Station (of whom Steward "had" seven*); and of a sailor and paratrooper duo whom Steward had hosted in his home for a threesome. They also describe Steward's frequent three-day-long sex-and-drinking benders with Bill Collins. The correspondence also provides "Bob" with the current reckonings of Steward's Stud File, which in spring of 1947 consisted of "902 parties† with 287 different people." "I hope you don't mind being 288," Steward writes in one note. "Soon as I hit 1000 I'll consider myself a whore." In another note Steward recalls being pimped out to six different men in a Columbus hotel room by his black friend Leo, who then concluded the experience by being the seventh man to "take" him—an experience that, according to the Stud File, had taken place in 1942, not in Columbus but on the South Side of Chicago.

---

*The number seven corresponds exactly to the number of men Steward records in his Stud File as having had encounters with at the Great Lakes Training Station.
†"Party" is period slang for "sexual encounter."

In his growing boredom and irritation with "Bob" (who prudishly insisted throughout the correspondence on his preference for sex with women), Steward undertook to educate him on the nature of sex between men, in one instance recommending that Bob read Havelock Ellis. In another Steward mentions his sex story *Bell-Bottom Trousers*, "about a sailor on a weekend liberty being entertained by a bunch of North Shore gals, along with some other young men." He also revisited his pickup of a street tough on Rue de Lappe, making no mention of the robbery and assault that had followed it in real life.

Like Scheherazade, Steward had to imagine more outrageous things with each new story to keep "Bob" entertained. As the correspondence neared its conclusion, he began to describe rough sex:

> Sure, once in a while the "rough trade" (that means sailors, truck drivers, taxi drivers, and others who won't do anything with you, who are tough, and whom you take an awful chance with) get rough but I love it . . . I love to be whipped, too, and there was one guy last summer who left such scars on me I couldn't go swimming for two weeks. As I say, the old usual ordinary fucking and sucking holds little pleasure for me any more—I've had too damned much of it and like the unusual things.

Steward's final fantasy for Bob was an elaborate one. In it, he announced that he had gone into business with a cabdriver who was now acting as his pimp, delivering clients to his apartment and taking 40 percent of his earnings. In describing this scenario, Steward mentioned a mural he had painted in his apartment, in order to arouse visiting clients: "a 'tantalizer' about 6' x 4' of a sailor fucking a whore."* After growing tired of Bob's repeated dismissals of homosexual sex, as well as bored with Bob's own barely literate tales, Steward decided to bring the correspondence to a conclusion. He did so by describing how Jimmy, the cabbie and pimp, being "more than wise to all the ways of the world," had been outraged to learn about Bob. "With typical Italian jealousy and quick reactions, he insisted I put myself *completely* in his hands and not have anything to do with anybody while he was

---

*A photograph taken by Bill Dellenback of Kinsey's Institute for Sex Research in approximately 1950 clearly shows this mural over Steward's Murphy bed.

'managing' me," Steward wrote Bob. "So this is the last from me, as I sort of like being bossed and having the private whore feeling."

Bob's response was conclusive: "Good whoring to you and please forget me entirely. Hope that you *destroyed* all these as I have being [*sic*] too *dangerous*. The pimp need not worry as I go for the babes and [am] not much on fruits. So long!"

Steward, however, would have the last word. As he later explained to Kinsey, "I left no more under the name of 'Phil' but discovered that B[ob had] started to leave preliminary notes all over again. I thereupon adopted a different personality ('Art,' 19, normal) and after a few illiterate exchanges, I ended it with a blast."

Steward's last note to Bob came from his new nineteen-year-old persona, "Art," who wrote, "I was disgusted with what you wrote . . . and have decided you're no good for me . . . So I am going to put my sign back here and hope for someone that seems to be less mixed up than you are and just wants a good old fashioned suck. You sound even queerer than I am. What do you do, jack off when you read shithouse messages?"

•

The toilet correspondence was but one of several new diversions Steward engaged in as he created a new life away from alcohol. Since he had always loved to draw, he signed up for classes at the Art Institute of Chicago with Salcia Bahnc, an accomplished Polish-born printmaker and illustrator, and there discovered he had a natural flair for line illustration. He simultaneously took up painting, clay modeling, and various other media, in each case working almost exclusively with the male nude as his subject. Over the next five years he would create murals, oil paintings, watercolors, scratchboard illustrations, wire sculptures, photography, incised metalwork, glass etchings, small clay sculptures, painted screens, and painted lampshades, all of them featuring homoerotic themes, and he would install all these various works of erotic art in his apartment. He also experimented with "small tempera portrait drawings with semen as a binder instead of egg white, the fluid being furnished by the subject of the drawing," thereby creating macabre souvenirs of specific dalliances with men he found particularly attractive.*

---

*Several of these small paintings survive in private collections, featuring the nature of the medium and the name of the portrayed individual inscribed on the verso.

In his free time he collected homoerotic fetish objects, objets d'art, curios, books, photographs, and prints. The collective result was an apartment *Gesamtkunstwerk* that made so bold an assertion of the homoerotic self that Alfred Kinsey, who first met Steward in late 1948 or early 1949, had the place photodocumented in its entirety for the Institute for Sex Research.

As Steward became ever more creative in his sobriety, he also became ever more diligent in his research into the nature of his sexual desires. Over the coming decade he would read extensively and in depth on the topic of human sexuality. Moved and inspired by the landmark statistical studies published by Kinsey in 1948, he also became ever more detailed in his own statistics keeping, journal writing, letter writing, and fiction writing about his sexual experiences. In alcohol Steward had sought only oblivion; but now, in sex, he was mindfully pursuing an activity that gave a new focus, meaning, and center to his life. Sexual activity, however much it might have limited or complicated his existence, was also becoming his vocation. Not content with being merely a sex enthusiast, he now sought to become a sex expert.

One of Steward's greatest interests during this period was exploring the nexus between sexual pleasure and physical pain through spanking, paddling, caning, whipping, and various other forms of physical punishment. Steward had enjoyed such activities since the mid-1930s, but only when he could find someone to engage in them with him, which was rare. While no networks then existed for people with such interests to meet one another, he responded to a carefully worded classified ad in *The Saturday Review of Literature* of August 1947 requesting correspondence from men interested in whips. In doing so, he met an educated man from New York who worked in magazine publishing whose name was Hal Baron.

While Baron wrote that he had read all about the desire to be beaten in studies of abnormal psychology, he quickly confessed to Steward that he was "much more interested in the experience than in sublimating my desires into reading." Starting in 1935, at age twenty-one, he had shipped around the world as an ordinary seaman, and during the war he had received a commission as a junior grade lieutenant. "Flogging was not something I ever ran into either in the Navy or the merchant marine," he wrote Steward; "however I now have a strong suspicion that was because it was not something I looked for." When Steward mentioned that he, too, was a writer, Baron responded,

While I regard my writing as a craft, not an art, still there are certainly artistic elements in my craft . . . [I feel that the] same elements of suspense, rhythm, crescendo, climax and satisfying conclusion . . . apply [both to writing and] to whipping. Never hit in the same place twice, for example, just [as you] don't repeat the same phrase constantly in a story—unless you're striving for a certain effect or working in some special way with words as [Gertrude] Stein did. (. . . I have great respect for that gal.) And there should be an alternation of cruelty and tenderness, the sting of the whip and affection. Or don't you agree?

Baron then introduced Steward to a professor from Ann Arbor named Hal Stevens, and according to the Stud File, Steward subsequently met and "beat the hell out of him." Stevens liked his beating enough to return to Chicago later in 1948 and 1949 for more of the same, and more than a decade later he arranged for Steward and two other men to abduct him, beat him, whip him, and "rape"* him.

After Steward's successful meeting with Stevens, Baron put him in touch with several other Midwesterners who had responded to his *Saturday Review* ad in search of a good erotic whipping. The fact that both Steward and Baron were willing to take the dominant as well as submissive roles in such activity (combined with their shared literary interests) resulted in a growing epistolary friendship. But when they met several months later, they felt no sexual attraction whatsoever, and no further relationship (apart from a cordial friendship) would ever develop between them.

•

In early 1948, Steward came to the end of his work on the encyclopedia. Though given a warm letter of recommendation, he had no luck finding another editorial position in Chicago, and his misery at the prospect of returning to teaching triggered a major alcoholic relapse. As he wrote Hal Baron in April:

I'm in a comparatively lucid interval at present because I haven't had a drink in four weeks; it probably won't last much longer. But

---

*Like Steward, Stevens was engaging in pleasurable, consensual sex play in which he had willingly arranged to take the role of "victim." Though Steward may have used the word in his Stud File entry, Stevens was not "raped."

when I wakened one Sunday afternoon and found a small quarter-sized anchor tattooed on my left shoulder, and heard later in the day I'd broken a woman's finger the night before,* I decided that maybe it was time to ease off a little. I don't recommend sobriety, however, to anyone; and as soon as a little more passing time erases the shame I feel . . . I'll probably be right back at the bottle.

He later articulated the circumstances surrounding the acquisition of this first tattoo somewhat differently:

Perhaps the first tangible sign of my "anti-intellectual" revolt was that I got a small tattoo very high on my left deltoid. This was an odd experience for me. I had been "supering" with all kinds of companies that came to Chicago . . . In the Ballets Russes version of the *Nutcracker* I was always the gondolier who in the last scene rowed the little girl heroine [back from] the land of make believe. For this the Ballets Russes furnished me with a gondolier's costume, a part of which was a knit sleeveless dark-green nylon shirt.

It occurred to me that a gondolier might very well have a small anchor on his shoulder . . . The idea of getting the anchor tattooed on me was both fascinating and terrifying. Accordingly, one rainy night before that year's arrival of the Ballets Russes, I fortified myself with a couple of drinks and went down to South State Street in Chicago to get one.

I got it, all right—from "Tatts" Thomas, a skinny, baldheaded man with a mustache, the ends of which were waxed to long fine points.

Steward was again binge-drinking heavily; while doing so in June, he met a blue-collar former marine who subsequently became a long-term sex partner. Steward's first account of him went to Baron:

I got to talking with a kind of long-nosed Pollack, an ex-marine who was very *sympathisant*—and he was going to get married—is

---

*During a blackout drunk he had unwittingly broken Emmy Curtis's finger.

going to—come this next weekend. Finally a lot of plain talk got him to say yes, he'd come home with me, "but," said he, "I'm broke and can't pay you anything for it." Lord God, I wanted to laugh but couldn't very well.

He later gave a more detailed account of the man, whose name was Bob Berbich, in his memoirs:

In all those [sixteen] years [of our acquaintance] Bob really answered several of my needs; he was [employed] successively [as] a sailor, a motorcycle delivery boy, a taxi-driver, a night steel worker, a truck driver and a uniformed guard. In my growing preference for the blue collar instead of the white, these occupations of his were just what I needed for my fantasex.

Over the summer, Steward traveled to New York. He wrote Thornton Wilder to say he was planning a visit to New Haven while on the East Coast, to arrange the donation of Stein's letters to the Yale library* (for he hoped to visit Wilder, who lived close by); but Wilder seems to have carefully set aside the letter until after Steward had come and gone, later writing him:

Oh, oh. I humbly beg your pardon . . . Tomorrow [my sister and I] sail for 6 months abroad . . . so please forgive my silence. I hope you did come to New Haven and consign your G.S. letters here . . . I shall be seeing Alice before long and we shall talk of you. As a sign of your forgiveness do write me a letter of what you finally settle down to do. And surely, Sam, you are also doing some writing.

The final break with Wilder took place later that fall. During the early 1940s, Steward's friend Wendell Wilcox (whose fiction was by then being published in *The New Yorker*) developed an idea for a novel based on a story from Catullus. In Steward's recollection, "Wendell made the mistake of detailing his carefully researched plot to Thornton, and some time later [in 1948] Thornton's [novel] *The Ides of March* appeared. Therein,

---

*Steward visited New Haven that summer, but his actual donation of the Stein letters to Yale did not take place until spring of 1958. (Steward to Toklas [April 19, 1958].)

alas! Wendell found his plot. After that Thornton found that many of his friends in Chicago disappeared or grew cool."

·

Steward's September was difficult in other ways as well. As he later wrote, "In autumn of 1948 my father died, sitting at a stool, from taking amphetamines too soon after a [drinking] binge . . . I did not go back for his funeral, money was low." Unemployed but unwilling to return to Loyola, he instead found himself wandering "casually and a bit uncertainly into the Dean's office at DePaul University, [where I] told him of my background and asked if there were any openings."

DePaul University was much less distinguished than Loyola: its students came largely from blue-collar backgrounds, and most had received only basic secondary educations. The school had only a small liberal arts faculty, and an even smaller English department. Worse yet, Steward soon made an appalling discovery about the pay scale: "Laymen at this college were salaried not so much on their educational accomplishments and qualifications as on their marital status and the number of children produced for Mother Church—a highly immoral view, it seemed to me, but nonetheless rigidly followed."

Steward was equally dismayed by his students: "Many entering freshmen could barely read . . . [And as a recovering alcoholic] I no longer had [my] boozy tolerance [of stupidity] . . . instead, I found myself more and more being forced to take a half-tablet of some amphetamine to be able to face the classes that I came more and more to dislike."

Since he had no potential for material advancement at DePaul (and no possibility of tenure), and since so much of what went on within the school simply disgusted him, Steward could hardly take his new job seriously. Instead, he later wrote, he chose to

> let the fog rise about myself . . . purposively. I had now been away from alcohol for over a year and was much more in control of myself than I had been formerly. Here and there I dropped a word—yes, I had known Gertrude Stein and Alice B. Toklas; yes I had written a novel . . . yes, I had known Thomas Mann, Thornton Wilder, André Gide and others . . .
>
> The technique worked wonderfully well; by the time I had

taught there a couple of years I was classed as a character, a personality—the campus paper interviewed me . . . the "literary" journal also carried a profile. By student request, I formed the arts club . . . and my classes grew more and more popular, until usually each term they had to be closed at eighty to a hundred persons, despite the fact that I worked them hard.

•

In July 1949, Steward turned forty. With no great interest in his work at DePaul, he instead spent more and more time in his apartment—reading, writing, drawing, or else simply puttering among his various erotic materials. In his correspondence with Hal Baron he noted that he was now searching as far as New York for particular rare erotic titles;* but he was also collecting contemporary literary fiction relating to or describing various forms of homosexual experience. Photographs of the apartment at the Kinsey Institute show bookcases full of hardcover first editions of contemporary novels such as James Barr's *Quatrefoil*, Charles Jackson's *The Fall of Valor*, and other literary novels and short-story collections that were addressing the topic of homosexuality much more capably than anything that had appeared from American publishers in the previous decade.

The increasingly dire social circumstances homosexuals faced in 1950 were best described at the time by *The Homosexual in America*, written by the sociologist Edward Sagarin and published under his pseudonym Donald Webster Cory.† Steward owned a first edition of the book, which described the legal, social, and economic discrimination then being routinely leveled against American homosexuals, and at the same time described something much more insidious. As Sagarin noted:

> As a minority . . . homosexuals are . . . caught in a particularly vicious circle. On the one hand, the shame of belonging and the social punishment of acknowledgment are so great that pretense is almost universal; on the other hand, only a leadership that would acknowledge [its own homosexuality] would be able to

---

*Steward particularly asked Baron to keep an eye out for Apollinaire's 1909 *L'Oeuvre du Marquis de Sade*, with its "wonderful" analysis of *Les 120 Journées de Sodome*.
†New York: Greenberg, 1951.

break down the barriers of shame and a resultant discrimination . . . Until we are willing to speak out openly and frankly in
defense of our activities, and to identify ourselves with the millions pursuing these activities, we are unlikely to find the attitudes of the world undergoing any significant change.

The homosexual of his generation, he went on to note, "is not quite
sure that it is wrong to practice discrimination against him . . . the worst
effect of discrimination has been to make the homosexuals doubt themselves and share in the general contempt for sexual inverts." Moreover,
Sagarin noted, the situation would not get better any time soon, due to the
growing public condemnation of homosexuality: "The homosexual's chief
concern is neither with civil rights nor with legal rights, important as these
are. His is the problem of condemnation, which involves the necessity for
concealment, imposes a burden of self-doubt and self-guilt, and creates a
condition which inhibits the struggle for amelioration."

•

Along with Sagarin's book, Steward had been especially impressed by
James Barr's literary novel *Quatrefoil*, which had described the new set of
circumstances faced by two post–World War II homosexual men as they
struggled to remain invisible to outsiders and yet true to their sexual and
emotional orientation. Steward had a particular liking for the book because it described a passion between two navy men; but he also thought
it beautifully articulate in its vision of two "sane and well-balanced" lovers
who, in his words, "with subterfuge and skill waged an eternal battle to
remain closeted . . . successfully conceal[ing] their love for each other,
living by a deceit which was forced upon them, dangerously skirting discovery and escaping it only by clever fabrications and skillfully invented
fictions, compelled to stand guard over every gesture." In later life Steward observed, "In some ways *Quatrefoil* was a wonderful treatise on how
to live happily in the closet in 1950 . . . [For here was] a graphic and accurate picture of the secrecy and concealment that was necessary in those
days . . . [including a] firm determination—common to so many homosexuals in the past—to be an individual, standing alone, finding all answers within [one]self, and never identifying with any group." Steward
had long since defined himself as just this sort of loner—a man who

found scant consolation among other homosexuals, and who maintained not just one, but a number of secret and highly compartmentalized identities. The isolation mandated by such circumstances was profound; but there was no option—and Steward, who had lived in this isolated way from earliest childhood, therefore saw in the novel a powerful evocation of the way in which he himself actually lived.

•

Disliking his new job, Steward continued to daydream about moving to France, and also made plans to take a summer vacation in Paris as soon as he could possibly afford one. He knew that once he was there, Alice B. Toklas would happily introduce him into a number of important intellectual and artistic circles, including that of Jean Cocteau. In a recent letter she had pressed him once again to visit her, then added,

> I've kept off the subject of your teaching again—fearful that you had once more thrown it over. I do hope not. You always made one feel that you were exceptionally good at it—making things come alive to the dullest of impossible boys . . . Don't you find subjects galore amongst their strange relationships—you ought to be able to do a smashing novel about them and no one has in the U.S. They do it all the time still in England—so try it.

Toklas was now working on a book project of her own, for in her bereavement she had decided to realize a long-held ambition of writing a cookbook. Writing, she found, had a tonic and stabilizing effect; she therefore encouraged Steward to do likewise, even as she encouraged him to persist in his sobriety, noting, "Gertrude always said that liquor only improved the *deséquilibres* and my dear we hope you are not that . . . I'm all for [Alcoholics Anonymous] since it has done so handsomely for you. The program is sensible and generous and for God's sake take it as yours and *doucement allez doucement* as they used to say in Bilignin."

She also expressed real enthusiasm for his newfound passion for painting and drawing, which he had described to her in an earlier letter—for through Stein and her paintings collection, Toklas had established a long and loving relationship with the world of visual art. In one instance she even wrote him that "painting as a diversion for you is perfect—the trouble with Picasso was that he allowed himself to be flattered into believing that he was a poet too . . . It will be the deepest satisfaction to me if you pull off something of your real quality—you know Gertrude expected it of you."

Steward quickly made plans for a trip overseas. Now forty and decidedly unaccomplished, he was eager to reacquaint himself with this peculiar, famous old lady who could so easily mention his efforts at painting in the same sentence that mentioned Picasso. He needed her. She in turn wanted to help him, and so kept his "reform" strongly in mind:

> It's all one to me how you achieve your salvation as long as you do—whatever makes you happy—the Church or Alcoholics Anonymous or anything else. I'm a good Jesuit—any means that suits you—why even what Francis Rose chose—a strong wife . . . So if a good looking female a very few years older than you are says she wants to marry you and you think she really is in love with you—why just let her have her way. Francis is really happy and it's [his wife] who has induced this . . . Is there anything like her in the offing for you. For you and Francis are not so awfully unlike.

But there would be no wife for Steward. The "salvation" that would knock on his door in late 1949 would instead be his new mentor, Alfred C. Kinsey.

6

Kinsey and Company

By the time Alfred Kinsey first visited Steward's apartment, his *Sexual Response in the Human Male* had been causing a sensation across the United States for more than a year. Based on data that had taken over a decade to amass, the first volume of the Kinsey studies (along with its companion volume, *Sexual Response in the Human Female*, published five years later, in 1953) was a landmark statistical study of American sexual behavior. Kinsey's study of human sexual response was in fact related, in its approach, to his previous great project as a zoologist, a twenty-year taxonomic study of gall wasps. Since publishing the *Male* volume, Kinsey had undertaken a yearlong speaking tour to raise public awareness about the usefulness of statistical studies in understanding human sexual activity.

Steward's meeting with Kinsey took place at the suggestion of a fellow DePaul professor named Theodore Kundrat. In his memoirs, Steward recalled, "The interview would last an hour, Theodore said, although sometimes they ran longer if the interviewee had a lot to say."

I opened the door to a solidly built man in his fifties wearing a rumpled grey suit. He had a friendly face. His greying buff-colored hair stood in a short unruly pompadour; his eyes were sometimes blue and sometimes hazel. He had a rather sensitive but tense wide mouth above a somewhat bulldog or prognathous jaw, which in turn jutted out above his ever-present bow tie.

Indeed, Theodore had been a bit misinformed. The interview [about my sex life] lasted five hours, and it seemed to me that I

answered thousands of questions—although there were in reality
only a few hundred.

Sexual Response in the Human Male had been a work of the utmost
importance to Steward, for its 804 pages of tables, charts, and statistics
based on interviews with 5,940 men about their sexual histories and activities had documented the widespread occurrence of sex between men
across the American population. According to the data, 37 percent of the
total male population of the United States had had at least some overt
homosexual experience to the point of orgasm between adolescence and
old age; 50 percent of the males who remained single until age thirty-five
had had overt homosexual experience to the point of orgasm since the
onset of adolescence; 13 percent of males (approximately) had reacted
erotically to other males without having had overt homosexual contacts
after the onset of adolescence; 18 percent of males had had at least as
much of the homosexual as the heterosexual in their histories for at least
three years between the ages of sixteen and fifty-five; 8 percent of males
were exclusively homosexual for at least three years between the ages of
sixteen and fifty-five; and, finally, 4 percent of white males were exclusively homosexual throughout their lives after the onset of adolescence.

Since the Kinsey data on homosexuality was by far the most sensational revelation made in *Sexual Response in the Human Male*, cultural
and media attention became fixed on male homosexuality in the years
immediately following its publication—often to the detriment of the
many closeted and semicloseted homosexuals who had, up until that moment, gone largely unnoticed in American society. Kinsey's associate
C. A. Tripp later noted that while homosexuality "was only one of the six
basic forms of sex considered [in the study] . . . nothing so disturbed the
critics nor brought them to such a fever pitch of hate as did the homosexual
findings. Preachers, pundits and prudes found much to lament, and a variety of ways to do the lamenting: some questioned the scientific accuracy of
the work—'homosexuality just can't be that prevalent.' Others feared the
sociological effects of even discussing such matters—'by talking about it
you encourage it.' But the most virulent resentments arose from the fact
that sex, particularly homosexual sex, was dealt with [in the Kinsey study]
without a word of moralizing. Emotional reactions to the homosexual
findings dominated every level of criticism, though they were frequently
disguised as purely technical concerns."

•

In the weeks and months following their first meeting, Kinsey and Steward developed a substantial friendship.* Kinsey's fascination with Steward was based, at least at first, on Steward's lifelong habit of sexual record keeping and his vast collection of sexual paraphernalia and memorabilia— for Kinsey, too, was a passionate collector and record keeper. As a zoology professor, Kinsey had collected gall wasps by the thousand; now, as a sex researcher, he was actively collecting not only thousands of sexual histories, but also what would eventually become the world's largest collection of sex-related materials.†

Kinsey was impressed by Steward's intellectual commitment to establishing the legitimacy of homosexual experience, which at that time was not only rare among academics or public intellectuals, but also quite dangerous for anyone pursuing a university career. Kinsey was himself well outside the mainstream of academia in this regard; in fact, *Sexual Response in the Human Male* was widely read at the time of its publication as an indictment of American society, specifically its obsession with controlling and restricting sexual freedom. Moreover, since his statistical studies demonstrated that Americans were engaging in a wide variety of sexual activities (of which only a few were then lawful), academic conservatives had quickly accused Kinsey of using his research to promote both indiscriminate and deviant sexual activity.

Kinsey soon discovered that he and Steward had very similar backgrounds and early life experiences. Both had grown up in strict Methodist households with fathers involved in the church. Both had been raised without sexual instruction in an atmosphere of deep sexual inhibition. Both had had rejecting fathers, and both had fought, despite a lack of parental encouragement, to achieve academic prominence. Both had eventually developed into strong-willed and charismatic educators. Both had strong sex drives and both were sexually conflicted, and both had chosen to devote their lives (in very different ways) to reconciling these strong sex drives with the sexually intolerant belief systems and institutions into which they had been born. Both were also extremely enterprising men

---

*It was in no way sexual, however: "There was never any physical contact between us except a handshake." (Steward, "Early Chapters," p. 266.) There is no "Kinsey" card in the Stud File.
†The Kinsey erotica collection in Bloomington is now easily the largest conglomeration of erotica in the world, worth an estimated $20 to $40 million. (Jones, *Kinsey*, p. 519.)

who coped with their considerable psychic anguish over their sexuality by immersing themselves in work that sought to address sex via the intellect.

Kinsey tended to perceive those who had rejected or discarded injunctions against sex at an early age as impressively self-possessed, and so he seems to have had a special admiration for Steward. The fact that Steward had been repeatedly rejected as a writer, had succumbed to alcoholism, and had reached a point of utter frustration as both a scholar and a teacher may have seemed tragically wasteful to Kinsey; but it probably also made Steward seem oddly heroic to him as well—for Steward was, if nothing else, a man who had dared to live his beliefs.

Kinsey, of course, had made very different choices in his life. At the time of his first meeting with Steward, he was a happily married family man, a highly admired professor, and a justly acclaimed researcher who had spent his entire professional life successfully engaged in statistical scientific studies. He was also just then at the height of his critical and popular success. Perhaps the greatest difference between Kinsey and Steward, though, was one of faith. Where Steward had resolved the early dilemma of paternal and religious rejection by in turn rejecting both his father and his father's religion, Kinsey had simply distanced himself from both, and at the same time embraced Darwinian evolutionary theory. Kinsey's core faith was in science, and he found it entirely sustaining: his belief in it gave his life purpose, direction, and hope.

Kinsey's belief in the naturalness of variations in human sexual behavior flowed directly from Darwin's theory of natural selection, which was based not only on the variation of species, but also on variations (sexual and otherwise) within species. By creating a broad-based statistical analysis of human sexual response, he had been able to demonstrate the existence of widespread variations throughout the American population at all levels of society. His findings suggested that variations in sexual behavior were not based on acts of will and individual choice, as religious teachings had always insisted. Rather they were based on widespread biological variations existing within the human population: in other words, on genetic variation. The discovery of widespread sexual deviation and the revelation of the full extent of this deviation would at first shock America, but, ultimately, help to shift American perceptions of sexuality quite substantially. In so doing, Kinsey's research would help make the case for increased sexual tolerance—a tolerance that today is taken so much for granted in some quarters that the great storm of controversy created by the Kinsey findings in the early 1950s is very nearly forgotten.

From the moment they were published, Kinsey's statistical discoveries had an immediately beneficial effect upon the many individuals suffering undue guilt and anxiety about their sexual desires, habits, and practices. Through statistics, Kinsey had presented these individuals with a whole new way of understanding the sexual self. Among those with a homosexual orientation, feelings of guilt, shame, anxiety, and depression could be particularly intense, and so Kinsey's findings were profoundly enlightening—and, by extension, healing—to these people. Certainly they were enormously healing for Steward.

In compiling his statistics on sexual activity, Kinsey had conducted thousands of anonymous interviews about sexuality with the help of three charismatic associates, all of whom Steward would come to know well in the coming decade: Wardell Pomeroy, Paul Gebhard, and Clyde Martin. Starting in 1938 (and continuing until 1956), Kinsey, Pomeroy, Gebhard, and Martin had crisscrossed America by car, interviewing people from all social levels and ethnic backgrounds in cities, towns, and villages across the country. The confidential interview they conducted had been carefully devised to obtain a complete sexual history from each participant within two hours; the results of the interviews were then recorded in code and kept entirely private. The team obtained eighteen thousand such interviews, after which Kinsey subjected the results to a complete statistical analysis. Despite being subjected to heavy scrutiny and revision, the findings remain fundamentally unchallenged and unaltered to this day.*

Kinsey's findings about homosexual activity suggested that the word *homosexual* ought not be used as a noun, but only as an adjective, for clearly many men who self-identified as heterosexual engaged in homo-

---

*Various conservative groups opposed to studies in human sexuality have repeatedly attempted to vilify Kinsey and discredit his findings, but their arguments and ad hominem attacks on Kinsey have done nothing to discredit the data, which have been tested and reviewed repeatedly (*The Modernization of Sex*, pp. 43–44). Subsequent analyses have revealed that the data, while enduringly solid, are only "incomplete in scope and method," since "the findings were limited to white, better educated, less religious, and largely youthful women and men from the northeastern United States who volunteered to be interviewed about their sexual lives . . . the effect of volunteer respondents was to inflate the reported levels of some aspects of sexual behavior. The interview schedule and the interviewing were of high quality, but they could not correct for [these] biases in sampling." (John Gagnon, Ph.D., reviewing the reprinted and updated Kinsey volumes in *The New England Journal of Medicine*, February 18, 1999.)

sexual activity. The idea that the population was not divided up between homosexuals and heterosexuals was not new to twentieth-century thought—Havelock Ellis had already hypothesized a sexual continuum (ranging from entirely heterosexual in activity to entirely homosexual in activity); so, too, had Freud. But Kinsey's data supported the hypothesis by offering statistical proof.

·

Steward later noted of his first meeting with Kinsey:

> The thing that amazed him most of all [about me] was that I was a "record keeper"—"something all too rare," he said. But I had an accurate count on the number of persons I had been to bed with, the total number of times of "releases" (as he termed them) with other persons, number of repeats, and all the usual statistical information, taken from the "Stud File" that I had kept on three-by-five cards from my very first contact many years before in Ohio. My information like Kinsey's was coded, but not so unbreakably or exhaustively. I showed him the file; he was fascinated.
>
> . . . I [soon] became one of the "unofficial collaborators" for the Institute for Sex Research [for at that time] no one could officially work for the Institute who was not of the "majority sexual orientation"; all his associates had to be married, preferably with children, or else be absolutely asexual . . . Unofficially, then, I steered people to him or him to people, [and] gave him samples of my literary [and artistic] production.
>
> . . . Kinsey favored me in return with the most flattering kind of attention—never coming to Chicago without writing to me in advance to arrange a meeting. In the eight years of our friendship I logged (as a record keeper again) about seven hundred hours of his pleasant company, the most fascinating in the world because all his shoptalk was of sex—and what is more interesting than that?
>
> In those early years he had one of the warmest personalities I had ever met—a cordial gregarious man as approachable as an old park bench, and just as much of an accomplished con-artist as I was later to become in my tattoo career. The "con" approach was deliberately cultivated by him, so that he could win the trust

of the person being interviewed; in like manner, he took up smoking and drinking (very, very gingerly) to put his interviewees at ease. His warmth and approachability were further improved by his talent for talking to the most uneducated hustlers and prostitutes and pimps in their own language, no matter how coarse. It gained trust for him among the suspicious ones, and word of his honesty and secrecy opened doors for him that would have remained closed forever to a more academic attitude.

I learned many things from him, and in a sense some degree of "transference" took place in me. Though there was a difference of only about fifteen years in our ages, after the initial interview he became for me a sort of father-figure as he did for so many . . . In him I saw the ideal father—who was never shocked, who never criticized, who always approved, who listened and sympathized. I suppose that to a degree I fell in love with him.

In Steward's first letter to Kinsey, written in February of 1950, just a short time after their first meeting, he wrote,

What I really wanted to say, I suppose, was something about meeting you and what it meant to me . . . I am conscious of great alterations somewhere within—where they will lead, if to anything at all, I don't know. I still can't think clearly about it, and if this seems fuzzy and complex, don't mind it at all. I'll let you know about it after I stop whirling.

In early March, Steward wrote to Kinsey again, this time about a new undertaking: "I've arranged a small *spintriae* of six for tomorrow evening; those things need a kind of Emily Post to be run successfully. I think that perhaps just for the hell of it I'll write one up for you, and tell you what has been my experience in arranging and conducting them."

The word *spintriae* was both concealing and revealing, for it was Steward's code word for the all-male group sex parties he had been hosting regularly in his home starting in September 1949.* He would con-

---

*Steward described these get-togethers in his journals and records alternately as "daisy chains," "*spintriae*," and "partouzies." The latter was Steward's whimsical adaptation of the French *partouze*, a sexual free-for-all.

tinue to host these gatherings for the next eight years, eventually hosting twenty-nine in all.

Steward's use of *spintriae* located him as a man with both a classical education and a sense of humor, for it is based on the first declension masculine noun *sp(h)intria*, the nominative plural of which is *spintriae*, or, literally translated, "sphincters." Tacitus had been the first to note the Latin word, which had been borrowed from the Greek under the reign of Emperor Tiberius, who had enjoyed having sex with young men.* The word *spintria* had thus entered Latin usage as a word describing a particular kind of male who had sex with other males; Steward's *spintriae*, by extension, meant a group of men who had sex with other men.†

Steward's collecting and sharing of erotic materials and information on his sexual activities was very dangerous. Yet his compulsive risk-taking seems to have thrilled him precisely because of the high stakes: namely, professional self-destruction. In 1950, the mere possession of obscene works was a crime punishable by imprisonment in most states, even if the possessor had no intention of selling or exhibiting the objects (only in 1960, with the Supreme Court review of *Mapp v. Ohio*, would these laws begin to be revised). Yet Steward now presided over a wildly obscene apartment in which nothing at all was hidden, and where large numbers of anonymous men were gathering regularly for sex parties. Any one of them might easily have betrayed him to the police.

In late May of 1950, Kinsey's photographer Bill Dellenback photographed Steward's apartment, then remained to take photos of Steward and other men having sex there while masked.‡ Kinsey and Pomeroy also

---

*Tacitus (*Annals* 6.1): "He [Tiberius] often landed at points in the neighborhood, visited the gardens by the Tiber, but went back again to the cliffs and to the solitude of the sea shores, in shame at the sexual vices into which he had plunged so unrestrainedly that in the fashion of a despot he debauched the children of free-born citizens. It was not merely beauty and a handsome person which fired his lust, but boyish modesty in some, and noble ancestry in others. Hitherto unknown terms such as 'sellarius' [literally, he who practiced lewdness upon a sofa] and 'spintria' were then for the first time invented, suggested by the vileness of the place and the countless variations upon the act of sodomy that were invented." (Professor Stephen Colvin of University College, London, to author, 2005.)

†Steward used other Latin words in his Stud File. Of a trick named Jim Rogers, in November 1950, he wrote "*podex lambere*. Yum, yum." (*Podex* is Latin for "anus"; *lambo*, "to lap or to lick.") Another common notation in the Stud File, *lues* (Latin for "plague"), was Steward's code word for syphilis.

‡For reasons of confidentiality, the sex photographs of Steward by Dellenback are not identified by the Kinsey library as being of Steward. The photographs record a group-sex gathering in which Steward (naked but nonetheless identifiable by his tattoos) wears a mask (identified in his journals as a "French gangster mask").

seem to have been present; the team returned to Bloomington with Steward's Stud File* and some of Steward's own erotic photographs, both of which they kept until the fall.†

•

Despite his excitement about working with Kinsey, Steward had been making plans for over a year to return to Paris in the summer of 1950, and as a result, just six days after Kinsey and his team came to the apartment to photograph one of his *spintriae*, he took the New York Central's *Pacemaker* from Chicago to New York, where he registered at the Pickwick Arms Hotel for a few days of sexual indulgence. He then embarked once again, this time for Paris. After his several very wild nights in Manhattan, he found the crossing a sexual anticlimax, for 1950 was a holy year, and the dingy, single-class S.S. *Washington* was crammed with fourteen hundred Catholic pilgrims headed for Paris, including enough Catholic sisters "to make a floating convent." Apart from a brief restroom encounter with a Puerto Rican father of four, Steward had no sex at all while at sea, feeling oppressed at every turn by the horde of watchful nuns.

Toklas had reserved a room for Steward in Paris at the Hotel Récamier, just beside the monumental église Saint-Sulpice. Upon arrival he went immediately to Toklas's apartment on Rue Christine for a reunion. It proved unexpectedly moving. "The number and length of [Toklas's] letters, the outpouring, seemed almost to result from the desolation that she felt because of Gertrude's absence," Steward later noted. "[It was] as if by maintaining a contact with those [like me] who had known them both she was drawing life from the past to help her continue in the present."

Steward recorded his 1950 trip to Paris in a diary that gave detailed

*Out of consideration for the privacy of the donors, the Kinsey Institute does not share individual sexual histories with researchers. Thus while researching Steward at the library of the Kinsey Institute, I was not allowed to read Steward's sex history interview, nor was I offered the institute's copy of Steward's Stud File, nor was I told whether it had a copy of the Stud File in its possession. There is no mention of the Kinsey copy of the Stud File in its Steward finding aid, though Steward's own correspondence does indicate that a copy of it was made by Kinsey for the institute's archive. Thus, only because I had access to Steward's papers outside of the Kinsey library was I able to research his sex life and document it.

†Steward notes to Kinsey in a letter of November 7, 1950, that he is very eager to see "the pictures [Dellenback] took in Chicago," and eager to have back his Stud File and his own erotic photo collection.

descriptions of the many sexual activities he engaged in throughout the course of his stay. In it, Steward writes with almost manic good humor about his daily adventures with a seemingly inexhaustible supply of sex-obsessed men—Americans, Frenchmen, Britons, and assorted Europeans. But there is a quiet pathos to his adventures, and to the diary as a whole, when considered in the context of Steward's original intentions for his long-awaited 1950 trip. He had, after all, been thinking quite seriously about emigrating to France since his first visit there in 1937, when Paris seemed to welcome him with open arms as an aspiring novelist, scholar, and man of letters. During World War II his passion for France and the French way of life had remained so strong that he had even written a letter (sealed, stamped, and sent to his own home address) in which he renounced his American citizenship in favor of fighting for and with the French. Throughout the postwar 1940s, Paris had continued to beckon him, promising him a return to the avant-garde literary life he had once so easily assumed he would eventually lead. The bohemian literary and artistic existence he had been dreaming about since his boyhood in Woodsfield would be his, he had then thought, if only he could find his way to Paris. There he would escape the dreary world of teaching, and instead live among artists and novelists, poets and aesthetes. In the city of Huysmans and Verlaine, of Cocteau and Diaghilev and Gide, of Gertrude Stein and Djuna Barnes, he had been sure he would find a place for himself. Alice B. Toklas was waiting there for him, ready to offer him entrée to the brillant world of Parisian arts and letters.

That, at least, had been the dream. The reality would be, in its way, literary; within forty-eight hours of his arrival, Steward noted in his diary that "after much deliberation, [I] bought *Querelle de Brest*, with the Cocteau illustrations—12,000 [francs]. Contracted for English *Our Lady of the Flowers* & Sade's *120 Journées de Sodome*. Must buy them before realization of the value of the franc descends on me." The book purchase was, in a sense, the emblem of his summer—a summer devoted only casually to literary pursuits, and primarily to sex.

Steward's purchase of the pornographic limited edition *Querelle de Brest* was a considerable expenditure: the same money would have paid Steward's bill in the Hotel Récamier for more than three weeks. Then again it was an exceptionally rare and daring edition, for Genet's landmark novel of brutal sexual passion between men had been published underground by Cocteau's secretary Paul Morihien, who had put out the novel in two editions, one of them featuring a shockingly graphic series of homoerotic line illustrations by Cocteau.* It was this rare, deluxe illustrated edition of 1948, with its close-up imagery of hairy anal sphincters and rigid phalluses, of sailors fucking sailors in cheap hotel rooms, that Steward had sought out and purchased.

When not reading Genet's novel and marveling at the power of Cocteau's seemingly casual erotic line illustrations, Steward soon established a daily routine in Paris of sunbathing every afternoon on the *quais* of the Ile de la Cité "among the beauties with bikinis," and then, later in the afternoon and evening, scoring pickups at La Reine Blanche, the wildly popular homosexual bar in St. Germain. There, too, he met up with Daniel Decure, a young French associate of *Der Kreis*, the Swiss homophile magazine that Kinsey had recently recommended to him. After having Decure back to the hotel for sex, Steward noted that he was "rather undistinguished, [a] talky but sensual (and nice) 25 yr old Frenchman . . . we had a mediocre 69." Before they parted, Steward showed Decure some of his own drawings, and promised to contribute some erotic illustrations to the magazine.

After a day of buying more books, including "a small dirty Apollinaire & *Pompes Funebres* & . . . *11,000 Vierges*"† (as well as purchasing another series of illustrations to *Querelle* by Leonor Fini), Steward had dinner at the Wagenende, a seedy St. Germain brasserie, with a street pickup, a young French lawyer named Jacques Delaunay. They concluded the meal with "a lovely two hours in bed," with Steward noting afterward that "he's had 61 lovers in 4 years—not bad. I just love to rim him—he's so clean & cute. Then I made a sketch, and after, he whipped me a little . . . Such mad love. He thinks I'm 35, was not disillusioned by me."

A week later Steward was reunited with his old friend Sir Francis Rose at a lunch at Alice Toklas's home on Rue Christine. The two agreed at the end of a very enjoyable afternoon to meet up again several days later, this time at Rose's apartment on Ile St. Louis. When they did, Steward arrived

---

*The obscenity of the illustrations made it impossible for Cocteau to acknowledge them with his signature at the time of the book's publication, but he was nonetheless widely known to have drawn them.

†Genet's *Pompes Funebres* (1949); Apollinaire's erotic novel *Les Onze Milles Vierges* (Paris, 1907).

to find Rose's place in a state of total uproar. His diary noted, "George Melrish* [sp?] was there & wild disorder in the apartment, wrecked by 2 Americans. Francis & I then went to see his landlord, then wandered in Montmartre, lunched at Wepler's† & went to his gallery, Renou."

As it happened, Rose frequented a bar in Montmartre often patronized by Genet, whom Steward now wanted very much to meet. Since Rose sometimes paid Genet's companion, a young hustler named André, for sex, Rose offered to introduce Steward to him. Accordingly, on July 22, Steward and Jacques Delaunay went with Rose to "the small bar on rue Lepic [in Montmartre], where Francis took up with a young convict" who was in fact Genet's hustler friend André.‡ Half French, half Russian, and powerfully built, André (or Java, or Dédé, for he went by all three names) was just then making the most of his money as a jackroller operating in and around a public toilet in the gardens at the bottom of the Champs-Elysées.

A couple of days later, Steward noted in his journal, "Mad, fascinating day. To Francis, & found him in bed with [André] the young murderer of Genet's *Notre Dame*, the 'Dédé aux beaux yeux' of Saturday night.§ Made a date with Dédé for Friday night & conceived the wild project of taking him to the country for 3–4 days. This is danger."

But Steward's adventures, dangerous and otherwise, were fast being compromised by an unremitting case of diarrhea. The following day he noted, "Alice, in lieu of taking me to see [the artist] Marie Laurencin (who is ill) took me to a frightfully expensive restaurant for bouillabaisse, which so overwhelmed me with three kinds of fish, lobster & garlic that I

---

*The Welsh painter George Melhuish (1916–1985), who was platonically infatuated with Rose for many years.

†A historic brasserie on Place de Clichy famous for its long association with painters and writers including Picasso, Apollinaire, and Henry Miller.

‡Genet lived with André (or André B., as he is also known) from 1947 to 1954 in a hotel room in Montmartre. See White, *Genet*, p. 310. A fictionalized version of Steward's and Rose's experiences of André can be found in Steward's *Parisian Lives*, in which André appears as André Vignot. (Steward also mentions a "story about André in Brittany from my novel" in a journal entry of September 22, 1959.) André B. also appears in the Genet film *Un Chant d'Amour* billed as Java. (White, *Genet*, p. 310.)

§Although everyone else called him "Dédé," Genet apparently called [André B.] "Java" because the hustler had been working aboard a boat named *Le Java* when the two first met (White, *Genet*, p. 310). (The nickname was not so unusual; "Le Java" was a highly popular dance of the Bal-Musette of the 1920s and '30s.)

had to go without dinner and subsist mainly on alkaseltzer . . . I . . . have had to take paregoric to offset the Perrier shits." He nonetheless managed to rally, picking up a twenty-year-old Scotsman that evening and sneaking him upstairs to the hotel room for sex.

On July 28, Toklas departed on a restorative trip to the country, suggesting to Steward he visit her there for a little rest and relaxation a week or so later. He had already set his sights on a weekend with Genet's murderous hustler, however, so he told her no. But by the next night, he had had a change of heart, for after a night out with André, Steward thought the fellow more boring than terrifying: "[He] drank beer all evening [and ignored me to speak with his friends] . . . I don't particularly want [to go to] bed with him . . . I went home—not feeling jilted but free."

Steward's stomach condition meanwhile grew so bad that on August 1 he wrote,

> If my diarrhea doesn't improve I'll have to go to the American hospital . . . Jacques [Delaunay] came for dinner, and then we went to bed. He wanted to *baiser** me as usual but I said no, & he replied, "*Mais ça arrive souvent qu'on se salisse.*"† Much joking about closed on *Mardi*s, closed for repairs, for *aggrandizement*, etc. Too bad, but he really doesn't excite me much any more, or maybe it's just my *maladie*. Or maybe I really am about to give up sex. Might be a Catholic for a while to appreciate the return to it more.

Two days later, he noted that "in addition to the [meddlesome] concierge, I have my shits and my inability to *bander*‡—I guess this burned out husk of an old Don Juan had better quit—or wasn't I always this way?"

Finally, Steward had no choice but to take a "long weary trek" out to the American Hospital in Neuilly for a sulfaquandine prescription. That same evening he had another date with the young Frenchman from *Der Kreis*, one that resulted in "a gathering of 9 French *pédés* at Daniel De-

---

*To fuck.
†"But it often happens that one soils oneself."
‡To get an erection. (But Steward's "inability" was simply due to sexual exhaustion.)

cure's, in a depressing stuffy little apartment . . . a smelly pile of perspir-
ing bodies on a scratchy sofa—all in all a most depressing partouzie. Still
we can put it down as an experience in Paris." The Stud File described it
even more vividly as "8 Frenchmen in a small hot room, messy and smelly,
with Camembert crotches."

By now Steward was in a state of perpetual nausea, so he decided to
give up sex for a while by joining Toklas at her rest home in Bourges. At
the back of his mind, he knew that it was time for him to focus on his
writing, and to explore with Toklas the possibility of somehow establishing himself for good in Paris. Before he left for Bourges, however, he met
up with Witold Pick, the cultured, Paris-based Pole who had written to
him a decade earlier to inform him of Mohammed Zenouhin's death.
"Long aperitifs hour with the mysterious 'Pick' from Alger," Steward noted
in his diary, also noting the presence of a young man whom Pick archly
called his "'cousin,' a handsome blond Nordic boy . . . Pick's queer as
pink ink." The evening ended with an invitation to dinner at Pick's home
the following evening. Steward went, and "as the evening grew later, Pick
pressed me to stay all night, baiting the invitation with John, the beautiful Polish 'cousin.' So I did, and [John and I] made mad love most of
the night. Whether from drink, or my unattractiveness or age, or general
hetero-disinclination, he never did come . . . It was like bedding a bas-
relief from the Parthenon."

The next day, however, brought with it a nasty surprise: "Jacques
[Delaunay told me] he had a discharge from his cock . . . Turns out my
pretty clean-cut French lover had gonorrhea last April . . . caught from a
Spanish lover. Certainly this news unanchors me somewhat, and is dis-
tressful."

The horror of venereal disease hit Steward hard, for it brought back
the trauma of his 1934 infection with syphilis. He canceled his plans to
visit Versailles the next day and instead kept to his room, where, feeling
very fragile, he "spent the afternoon finishing [tracing] the Cocteau drawings [from *Querelle*], and reading in *Querelle*, which is a very good book
indeed and about the only one I ever wanted to translate . . . [It is] a
remarkable satisfying book . . . Now even if the *douane** takes it [away

---

*Steward is referring to U.S. customs, which would surely have confiscated the book if it had been
found in his luggage.

from me], I [will still] have the memory in my head." That evening, having calmed himself somewhat, Steward had an awkward dinner at the Wagenende with Delaunay: "It could have—has—happened to any or all of us," Steward wrote upon his return. "The love is replaced by a kind of universal pity, of which we are all in need—(No tears, now)."

Despite his fear of possible infection, Steward was unable to keep himself from a rendezvous at his hotel that night with Pick's "cousin" Johnny. In keeping the date, Steward seems to have rationalized that the only activity they would engage in (nonreciprocal oral sex) would pose no danger to the boy—even if Steward did have an infection, which was still not even established, for he was so far free of any symptoms. Still, after Johnny left, Steward had a restless night. He spent the next day halfheartedly researching Fulbright topics at the Bibliothèque National, and returned to the hotel to find "a disturbing *pneu* from Jacques saying he really did have [gonorrhea]."

By Sunday, Steward had worked himself into such a state of anxiety about the possible infection that he had to hit a friend up for an amphetamine simply to get through the day. "I keep thinking of [a] friend who turned out to be a carrier and never could [have sex] again," he wrote in his diary. "But at the same time I've been threatening for months to give up *la vie sexuelle*—and maybe this is the time to do it."

He saw Delaunay's doctor the following morning, who calmly reassured him that he probably was not infected, but nonetheless offered him a course of penicillin just to be on the safe side. Steward would not be able to begin the injections until the following Friday, however, since he had already booked his visit to Toklas at Bourges that week, and the injections needed to be administered in a daily sequence. "It probably means no more fucking, ever," Steward noted grimly, for he was now convinced that he was infected, and was feeling very cast down. "Met Jacques, who was very *gentil* about it all . . . Good Lord, how I'd rather not go to the country, but begin the course [of drugs] immediately."

Instead, as promised, Steward took the train to Bourges, where Toklas had installed herself at a very simple rest home, La Régie. He spent the next few days chatting with her and trying (unsuccessfully) to make his way through Ivy Compton-Burnett's *More Women Than Men*. But neither Toklas nor the novel proved at all diverting. "I simply count the minutes until I can get on the train back to Paris," he wrote in his journal the first

night. "God, how awful it would be to spend a length of time here . . . I'd
be mad in a week."

The day he got back to Paris he saw the doctor for his first penicillin
injection. He then had yet another glum dinner with Jacques Delaunay at
the Wagenende, followed by a drink at a café with Pick. Steward had now
became obsessed with the idea that he had infected Johnny—an obsession that rapidly escalated as Pick repeated over and over that Steward
"looked sick."

With the summer winding down, Steward arranged a farewell dinner
with Delaunay, then made some last-minute purchases, which included a
copy of *Fanny Hill* to read on the ship home. On his last night he took
Delaunay's doctor to dinner at Le Cochon de Lait, as a gesture of thanks
for his discreet handling of Steward's possible infection. "He came up to
my room [afterward], and we talked for a long time," Steward wrote in his
diary. "He assur[ed] me my decision to give up sex was sulfa-induced and
I'd be rarin' by the time I hit N.Y."

·

Despite its wild vacillations, Steward's Paris diary of 1950 marked yet
another new direction in his writing—for rather than engaging in mere
pornographic fantasy (as in his toilet correspondence), he had chosen to
spend his summer sifting through, savoring, and preserving a series of
sexual experiences that were entirely private, intimate, and real. He had
also chosen not to compartmentalize these experiences, but to link them
to the larger picture of his life. In doing so he was gaining a much clearer
understanding of his newly sober sexual self. The more melancholy moments of the summer diary bear a striking similarity to the musings of
Genet's Lieutenant Seblon, the introverted naval officer who is incapacitated by his desire for Querelle, and who turns instead to the expression
of that desire in writing in order to ease his mind. The diaristic jottings of
the lieutenant—anxious and full of longing, but also themselves a form of
private erotic satisfaction—are described by Genet in the novel with
something close to ridicule, for Seblon takes great and foolish chances
by expressing his desires so openly on paper. Yet Genet, Steward, and
Seblon were all united in this perilous activity of self-discovery through
confessional writing. The way in which language described and defined
not only a sexual experience, but also the inner life and motivations of the

person engaging in it—and, in doing so, the opposing sexual mores of the society in which that person lived—would become ever more central to Steward's own artistic project in the coming decade, even as his dream of establishing himself as a Paris-based literary novelist became increasingly remote.

7

Living in Dreams

Steward's travel diary came to an end with his vacation, and for a year he wrote nothing more in the way of a journal. He recorded all the details of his increasingly active sex life in his Stud File, but his correspondence with Alice Toklas from the period was apparently lost, and hers to him consists, during fall 1950 through spring 1951, of just a handful of letters. She did not press him to visit in the coming summer of 1951, for she knew that his money situation was not good.

During that fall, Steward developed a powerful infatuation with a tall, brown-haired student named George Reginato.* Steward became so infatuated with Reginato that he created a captioned erotic watercolor for Kinsey portraying himself whiling away the hours between the young man's beautiful thighs. Reginato, who was then in danger of flunking out of DePaul, began visiting Steward's apartment that semester, for he had arranged to barter oral sex for homework help and doctored grades. Steward's note about him in the Stud File is *"figure d'ange, âme de cochon.*† Gangster. This is it . . ."* Whether "it" referred to the great passion of Steward's life or to the sexual adventure that undoubtedly would end in his murder is unclear. In any event, Steward would later consider his infatuation with Reginato as the most powerful he had ever known.

---

*Reginato is a pseudonym. The young man's real name appears in the Stud File, in the book of drawings at the Kinsey Institute, and throughout Steward's journals. Characters based upon him appear several instances in Steward's erotic fiction, most notably as the young gangster Luigi di Lupo in "I (Cupid) and the Gangster." Since Reginato is still living, however, I have withheld any more specific details about him from this biography.
†"Face of an angel, soul of a pig."

In March 1951 Steward purchased a Polaroid Land camera and began using it to document his sex life (with Reginato and many others[*]) more thoroughly than ever before. Along with these instant photographs, he kept charts of his daily sexual activities, noting (in code) which kinds of activities he had engaged in and when. The tally sheet for 1951 specifically noted the introduction of the Polaroid:

> Remarks: periodicity reduced from usual 48 hr to 40+ hrs (?) Great leap after March partly due to purchase of Polaroid camera . . . (9 more releases than 1950, 82 more contacts.) Word to the lonely: Buy a Polaroid.
> AETATIS XLII[†]

The 1951 tally sheet also noted a grand total of 197 releases[‡] in 1951, and a grand total of 184 contacts for that year: an orgasm every forty hours, in other words, and sex with a new man every other day.

•

Prior to the invention of the Polaroid Land camera, those without access to a photographic darkroom were unable to create photographs of their sexual activities, for the printing and distribution of sexually themed materials were both prohibited by law. Now, thanks to Polaroid's instant-development technology, anyone with a Polaroid could use photography spontaneously in sex play.[§] Steward wrote Kinsey in early March that "the camera works wonderfully well, and as time goes by and the subjects multiply, there will possibly be some interesting developments."

Steward's collection of more than three hundred early black-and-white Polaroid photographs of men engaging in individual and group sex activities in his apartment is the most extensive and disturbing imagery in his archive, for the flashbulb-lit scenes are not only remarkably detailed, but also quite harsh and graphic. Still, to Steward and his sex partners,

---

[*]Reginato appears repeatedly in erotic Polaroids taken by Steward in his apartment starting in early 1951, copies of which remain both in the Steward Papers and in the archives of the Institute for Sex Research.
[†]Aetatis XLII: Steward's note (in Latin) that he is "Age 42."
[‡]Orgasms.
[§]The first commercially released Polaroid camera, the Model 95, had become available only in November 1948; in that sense, Steward was on the cutting edge of the technology.

they were thrilling, transgressive, and hugely stimulating. As Steward wrote Kinsey,

> so far I have nearly a hundred snaps in the album (where you saw about eight, I believe) and have had fifteen or sixteen very cooperative models. It takes a bit of conning, sometimes; but I remember what you said about exhibitionism and the male, and have found it all too true. You'll be interested in the pictures, maybe; but again—maybe not. I find it difficult to consider them objectively, of course, but they're not actually different from the thousands in your files. The camera does, however, afford me a definite release.
>
> . . . you promised me a photograph of yourself, and this is to remind you please not to forget it completely. One should have a picture of one's guide, mentor, instructor, savior, and friend around, shouldn't one?

A short time later Steward snapped a Polaroid of Kinsey visiting his apartment; the location is immediately recognizable because of the antimacassar on the armchair upon which Kinsey sits, clothed, in a bow tie, taking notes (other photos show half-dressed young men sitting in the same chair). Kinsey had recently given Steward a signed eight-by-ten glossy portrait photo of himself, but Steward clearly cherished the Kinsey snapshot as documentary evidence of Kinsey's (admittedly passive) participation in the sex Polaroid project.

By June 1951, Steward began another project at Kinsey's request: duplicating his own private collection of sex-related disciplinary devices. This new, second set was destined for the archives of the Institute for Sex Research. He wrote Kinsey,

> Today the remainder of the collection goes off to you . . . In the package is . . . a cut-off strop, a many thonged martinet of the "crusher" type, and a plain unvarnished paddle.* I would say that now you have an implement for any mood, and one that would offer sufficient variety to satisfy most general tastes. Getting these little trinkets together for you has been a fascinating project . . .

---

*Steward's "spanking" paddle bore three Greek initials, in emulation of a fraternity-initiation paddle; but its Greek initials are ΦBK (phi beta kappa)—a private joke, for Steward was a member of the Phi Beta Kappa national honor society.

If there is any other way in which I can possibly be of service, please let me know. I love "helping" in any way I can.

The Land Polaroid camera was, I am almost convinced, invented especially for me; what ever I did without it during the long empty years I'm sure I'll never know. I have just closed Volume I, with about 150 pictures in it.

Steward mounted most of the Polaroids in albums. In some photos he is performing oral sex, and in some he is being anally penetrated; in others, men are either having sex with partners or else having sex as a group. Young men are also pictured lounging around the apartment in various stages of undress and arousal. Some wear leather jackets and motorcycle caps—props apparently provided by Steward—but others, being boot sailors, are wearing their (real) sailor uniforms. There are also several sequences of staged Polaroids, including one entitled "Surrender of Armed Forces" in which Steward and his friend Robert Dahm (dressed as a sailor) reenact the friendly seduction of a sailor by a civilian.

Steward seems to be playing with various fantasy identities throughout the Polaroids, sometimes appearing in a striped French *chemise de matelot* he had bought the previous summer in Paris. Elsewhere, in a series of staged and dramatically lit photographs, he wears a set of American sailor's dress blues. In others, he appears as a street tough in undershirt, dungarees, and motorcycle boots, sometimes administering discipline to another man with a paddle, belt, or tawse. In yet others he wears an outrageous French leopard-print bikini or else is simply naked, instantly recognizable by his bikini tan line.

The Polaroids chronicle not only sex acts, but also sex fantasies. Just as Genet had imagined an array of male sexual icons and postures within *Querelle*—the construction worker, the sailor, the police chief, and the pimp—so Steward, too, was now creating a fantasy world of masculine erotic archetypes engaging in various forms of domination and display. The young men Steward photographed in his apartment are fit and good-looking, but the expressions of many are disturbing, for they vary from amused to bored to self-conscious to contemptuous. None seems overly caught up in Steward's fantasies despite the wide variety of costumes and props available. None seems especially affectionate toward Steward, either—perhaps because, though still youthful in appearance, he was already past forty, and therefore much older (by far) than anyone else in the room. Ultimately, the most moving of all the images is a series of admirably composed chiaroscuro self-portraits, in which Steward wears the dress blues of a sailor in the U.S. Navy. In these pensive images, sporting jaunty white sailor cap and navy blue wool jumper, he is entirely alone.

•

Steward could not have picked a worse time to immerse himself in such dangerously indiscreet sexual adventures, for even as Kinsey was establishing the widespread incidence of homosexual activity within the American population, other forces within American society were marshaling to vilify it, further criminalize it, and, essentially, to stamp it out. The year 1950 may have been the one in which the Mattachine Society, the first American homophile organization, was founded in Los Angeles; but it was also the year in which a congressional report recommended that "perverts" (that is, homosexuals) be classified as unsuitable for employment in the federal government, with one congressional subcommittee going so far as to state, "There is no place in the United States Government for persons who violate the laws or accepted standards of morality . . . those who engage in acts of homosexuality and other perverted sex activities are unsuitable for employment in the Federal Government."

The issue of homosexuals in government came to widespread public attention in February 1950, when Senator Joseph McCarthy of Wisconsin made headlines with his claim that 205 Communists were working for the State Department, and a few days later, the undersecretary of state security announced in his response to McCarthy that 91 homosexuals in government had been identified and fired. By the summer, congressional leaders were railing about Communists and sexual deviates infiltrating the government in a way that suggested the two were one and the same. Many homosexually active men chose to quit their government posts rather than face the possible public disgrace of dismissal. Similar resignations (many forced) would continue within the federal government throughout the 1950s. The FBI, meanwhile, began a broad surveillance program of suspected homosexuals; working with the assistance of local police departments, the bureau compiled lists of allegedly homosexual bars and other meeting places, and developed extensive files of news clippings on homosexuals and homosexual life across the United States.

The newly founded *Mattachine Review* quietly chronicled the scape-goating of homosexuals throughout society during this time, noting that "among homosexuals, learning that someone of the group has lost a job is commonplace. Many can list acquaintances who have gone long periods without steady, gainful employment." To make matters worse, politicians avid in their denunciation of homosexuality interpreted resignations within the government as proof positive of homosexual "guilt": the Republican senator Kenneth Wherry of Nebraska, for example, noted to a reporter that "they resign voluntarily, don't they? That's an admission of their guilt. That's all I need." The action against homosexuals gained further credibility when, on April 23, 1953, President Eisenhower officially prohibited the employment of homosexuals in any branch of the civil service.

Steward's outrageously daring activities as a resolutely self-documenting homosexual therefore must be understood in the context of 1951, when American homosexuals were being persecuted not only in the military and in the government, but also throughout civilian life as well, where they had few if any protections under civil law. Given these circumstances, Steward was not simply playing at outré sex games; rather, he was taking a potentially disastrous stand on behalf of his own right to sexual freedom within the privacy of his home. Forced resignation and its social stigma had ruined many men far more discreet than Steward, yet he persisted in his activities despite his very public career as an educator. What many of his friends considered at the time to be a wildly self-destructive game of Russian roulette was, in Steward's own words, his stubborn insistence on his right "to be free."

Even as he compiled his Polaroid collection, Steward was well aware that in creating so much documentary evidence of his sexual activities he was essentially courting prison time. As if to demonstrate that awareness, he kept a newspaper clipping neatly folded at the back of his Stud File, one describing the recent arrest of a heterosexual woman in San Antonio, Texas, who was discovered to have kept extensive records of her sex life. The article is superficially amusing, and surely appealed to Steward's own dark sense of humor; but the consequences the woman had faced (a lunacy trial, forced commitment to a mental institution, and widespread public disgrace) were minor in comparison to the consequences that he himself would have encountered had his files and photographs been seized.

Steward's risk-taking became even more pronounced that following spring in his dealings with George Reginato. Because Reginato was now routinely swapping sex for better grades, Steward drafted up two copies of a "contract" that both he and Reginato then signed. Steward gave Reginato a copy of the countersigned document, and placed his own executed copy in the Stud File. It read:

CONTRACT June, 1951
Between George Reginato [party of the first part] and Sam Steward [party of the second part].
    Whereas, in consideration for certain favors bestowed upon the party of the first part by the party of the second part, (4 marks of A in 4 courses at De Paul University, and one more to follow . . .), as well as other favors such as the preparation of papers and examinations, party of first part agrees to let party of second part go down on him one time during each of the months of June thru December . . . with one extra time during each of the months of June and July . . .

                                        Signed George Reginato
                                        Signed Sam Steward

On the reverse of Steward's copy (which was filed on an index card behind Reginato's "regular" Stud File card), he taped a swatch of Reginato's pubic hair, and made notations of the dates on which he and Reginato had met for sex as agreed. In later journal entries, Steward acknowledged that Reginato got his promised A grades in exchange for the arrangement.*

None of Steward's journals, letters, or statistical compilations of his sexual activities hints even remotely at his great success as a teacher. And yet during the fall of 1951, Steward found himself so wildly popular with the DePaul student body that he was extensively interviewed and photographed for the school newspaper. When he sent Toklas a copy of the glowing profile—one in which Steward's erudition and dry sense of humor are

---

*Steward's short story "I (Cupid) and the Gangster" includes a character named Luigi diLupo, based upon Reginato. Another short story featuring a character named Reginato, "The Bargain Hunters" (*Der Kreis*, vol. 28, p. 29 [August 1960]), describes a lasting erotic bond between a professor and his student.

both very much in evidence—she wrote back, "It was a pleasure to have a glimpse of you in your professional role and a delightful surprise to find you more yourself than ever . . . Are you getting some of that into your writing— you should. Impish is altogether too easy for you—your writing should be quite new and fresh as you are."

Steward had in fact returned to writing, but had done so this time as a translator, for since purchasing Morihien's deluxe edition of *Querelle de Brest*, he had remained enthralled by both the novel and its illustrations. As a way of somehow inserting himself into Genet's fantasy world, he had decided to translate the novel into English, intending to present it to both Genet and Morihien in Paris the following summer. Since the book could not have been distributed in the United States or the United Kingdom, Steward seems to have hoped that Morihien might publish and sell the English translation in Paris.

Querelle de Brest surely appealed to Steward for its sexual glorification of the sailor, as well as its descriptions of rough, often violent sex between working-class heterosexually identifying men. But the novel also spoke to Steward's own troubled perception of his sexual nature, for Genet equates homosexual acts with criminal acts throughout the novel, and Genet's perception of homosexual identity (whether in describing the desires of Querelle, Lieutenant Seblon, or the other sexually "passive" characters) is always of something monstrous and criminal. And indeed the pleasure Steward took in his own sexual adventures seems to have been darkened and intensified, throughout his life, by a similar psychic conflict. His response to the tortured sexual fantasies of *Querelle* was therefore a response of immediate psychological recognition: Genet's dreamlike, erotic tale of crime and punishment among sailors and thugs in Brittany was no mere fantasy to him, but rather a vivid evocation of the secret, tortured, highly sexual world in which Steward had lived for the better part of his life.

•

After an introductory visit to the Institute for Sex Research in Bloomington, Steward contacted Kinsey over the summer of 1951 to arrange a number of book and magazine donations. Knowing of Kinsey's pleasure in nudity and near nudity (Kinsey's Bloomington neighbors were often scandalized by his outrageously skimpy clothing as he puttered among the irises in his backyard), Steward included a special present in the package, "a pair of Bikinis [from France] which I think will fit you . . . this very fancy pair has a *coquille* inside to hold your *couilles*, prov[id]ed *que vous n'avez pas plus que deux*."*

In November, Steward shipped Kinsey yet more documentation of his sexual activities and interests, and also included a copy of his Ph.D. dissertation, specifically pointing out the chapter that had described the probable homosexuality of Cardinal Newman. Kinsey wrote back, "I am very much impressed with your [dissertation's] chapter on Cardinal Neuman [*sic*] and Froude. It is very important material . . . You have a great mind . . . I wish there were more of these things that we could look forward to." In the months that followed, Kinsey in turn provided Steward introductions to the artist Paul Cadmus, the novelist Glenway Wescott, and the former book publisher Monroe Wheeler, noting that the last two "had a great deal to do with setting him [Morihien] up in business . . . and both of them are long-time friends of Genet . . . They could get Genet's interest and approval of a translation if it is worthwhile."

·

In his next letter to Kinsey, Steward suggested that if Kinsey and Dellenback cared to photograph him engaging in sadomasochistic activities, they might consider visiting him in Chicago while the ballet dancer Fernand Nault was in town, for Steward and Nault had already engaged in highly satisfying S/M play on a number of occasions, and he sensed they would probably be doing so again. He also noted, "My contacts still keep apace with my periodicity,† and I'll be sending you the 1951 statistics very soon."

When Glenway Wescott wrote back to Steward from New York that he would be pleased to read some of the *Querelle* translation, Steward responded:

> Querelle seems one of the most fascinating character creations in print [and] has come to be a kind of *Dopplegänger* for me . . . I began the translation out of a kind of fascinated love . . . Translating it was, then, a kind of philanthropic work (in the extreme

---

*"This very fancy pair has a shell inside to hold your testicles, prov[id]ed you have no more than two."
†"contacts . . . apace with periodicity": Steward's humorous way of saying, in technical jargon, that he continues to have sex with a new person each time he has sex.

semantic sense* of the term). So whatever trickiness may tran-
spire [with Morihien and Genet] is of not much concern to me. I
had originally planned merely to put the finished thing in a snap-
binder and merely let my friends read it . . . the idea of possible
publication was a very late development.

Upon hearing that Steward was hoping for Wescott's assistance, Alice
Toklas cautioned Steward that Wescott was well known in the literary
world as a malicious and self-serving gossip, noting specifically, "If Glenway Wescott could have been useful *bien* but as a judge of literature—
hell. He writes pretentious unreal stilted letters to any and every body.
I've seen a couple and it's my idea that he hopes that they are being kept
and published—in his lifetime. He has by untiring effort over some thirty
years become what he believes to be an ultimate man of the world."

This sharp warning from Toklas (which she sent on January 30, 1952)
may explain the uncharacteristically formal tone of Steward's subsequent
letters to Wescott. And indeed he was someone of whom to be wary, for
although Wescott's 1927 novel *The Grandmothers* had achieved critical
success, and although he had moved easily among Cocteau's circle while
a handsome adolescent living abroad, he had suffered increasingly from
writer's block as he aged. With that writer's block had come a tendency
to meddle in and gossip about the private lives of others. In 1940 he had
published an impressive novella, *The Pilgrim Hawk*, in *Harper's Magazine*,
and subsequently republished it in an elegant small hardcover edition.†
Since its appearance, however, he had published only one more short
novel (*Apartment in Athens*, 1945), which was a commercial failure;
moreover, during the period that followed, 1946 to 1949, he had abandoned five different starts at novels. During the same period he had kept
detailed diaries of his sex life, for, like Steward, he frequently initiated
group sexual activities with younger men, despite the great and inhibiting
shame that he felt at having but a single testicle and, in his own words, a
"horrid little penis."

Wescott's ambivalence to Steward's *Querelle* project may have been

*From the Greek *phil* (to love) and *anthropos* (human being).
†*The Pilgrim Hawk* can be read as a portrait of the tortured love triangle then existing between
Wescott, his longtime partner Monroe Wheeler, and the younger, handsome, and prodigiously tal-
ented photographer George Platt Lynes.

based in part on jealousy (sexual, literary, or otherwise); but it was also based upon a class distinction—for though he came from a modest Wisconsin background, Wescott had achieved financial independence by introducing his brother, Lloyd Wescott, to the heiress Barbara Harrison; after the two were married in 1937, Harrison had then settled an income on her new brother-in-law and given him the tenancy of a small house on her New Jersey estate. As a result, Wescott now considered himself a gentleman as well as a man of letters, and made a point of dressing in fine clothes and affecting an English accent. Steward, who had no such pretensions, would ultimately seem to Wescott very common and "Irish-looking."

Wescott's ambivalence to Steward may also have had something to do with the *Querelle* project, for Wescott both disliked Genet and envied his success, describing him to a friend as "that horrid author" and further noting that "my [own] preference in erotica is lower-class, simpler." Certainly Wescott was jealous of Steward's close, easy friendship with Kinsey, for during the years 1949 through 1951 Wescott had assisted Kinsey with various projects in Bloomington, and in July 1951 he had initiated a brief sexual affair with the professor—much to the alarm of Kinsey's associates, who sensed Wescott's gossiping ways might permanently damage the reputations of both Kinsey and the institute.

On April 5, Steward wrote Kinsey his latest news:

> [I] sent [the manuscript] off to Morihien by air-express . . . and it should be in Paris by now . . . Even if [Morihien] turns it down, I [might try] the Obelisk Press, though it would be a little strong for them, I reckon. Whatever happens, there will eventually be a copy of the typescript for your collection . . .
>
> when I get to France, where do you think I'm going first? To Brest of course, looking for the bar-brothel with the iron spikes on the door, haunting the streets and looking for Querelle, and sleeping down there on the slope of [La] Recouvrance amidst the piles of *merde* and snoring sailors just for the hell of it. I may never get to Paris at all . . .

He concluded by noting, "Present contacts continue to surpass periodicity,* an unusually satisfying occurrence."

---

*"contacts continue to surpass periodicity": Steward's (humorous) way of saying that he has had more sexual opportunity available to him than he was able to handle.

Before Steward left for Paris, however, he took a trip to Bloomington to assist in the documentation of a sexual encounter. He did so by "starring" in a Kinsey sex-research film of sadomasochistic sex between men. Kinsey—who was intent on documenting all aspects of human sexual response, and knew that Steward had now been enjoying rough sex for years—had accordingly arranged to film him in an encounter with Mike Miksche, a former air force officer originally from Texas whom Kinsey had first met through Wescott.

Miksche came from a Czech background and stood six foot three. Wescott later described him as "a giant Paul Bunyan type, very strong, with a magnificent physique [and a] tyrannous, psychological sadism . . . He wanted to dominate everybody . . . [He] was [also] a terrific performer [and] . . . a showoff." Since leaving the air force Miksche had gone into fashion illustration in New York and simultaneously established himself as the erotic artist Steve (or Scott*) Masters, whose pseudonymous initials ("SM") were a coded indication of his sexual interests.

Kinsey had sensed upon meeting Miksche that he might be dangerous or unbalanced. Wescott had gloatingly agreed with him, noting that "a good many of the young masochists express fear of him. They fancy he will murder someone someday." Miksche had, in fact, recently broken a lover's ribs. As a result, there was apprehension all around when Steward and Miksche first met in Kinsey's Bloomington backyard.

Only in 1972, in a biography by Wardell Pomeroy, would anyone from the Institute for Sex Research publicly acknowledge that Kinsey had created film studies of human sexual activity.† Funding for the film purchases had come out of monies earmarked for "mammalian studies." The Kinsey team shot the films in Kinsey's own home on First Street in Bloomington, in a gabled bedroom featuring only a single small window, a plain board floor, and a mattress.

The film of Miksche dominating Steward was the first homosexual film the team had ever shot. In the three years that followed, Kinsey would film eighteen more homosexual encounters, matching participants that had been suggested by Wescott with partners taken either from a pool of willing Kinsey interviewees or else from the institute's staff. Stew-

---

*In Wescott's recollection, Scott Masters; in the Kinsey collection, and in Steward's recollection, Steve Masters.

†". . . and Pomeroy only revealed the tip of the iceberg." (Gathorne-Hardy, *Kinsey*, p. 333.)

ard himself described the experience many years later in an article for *The Advocate*:

> Kinsey and I had known each other about a year when he proposed an "arrangement" to me. He was extremely scrupulous about the confidentiality of his "subjects" and never set up assignations of any kind—but his interest in sadomasochism had reached a point of intolerable tension. He knew that I had experimented in that arena and he wanted to find out more.
>
> He therefore asked me to fly down from Chicago, and from New York he invited a tall mean-looking sadist, Mike Miksche, with a crewcut and a great personality . . . We were to be filmed in an encounter.
>
> It was quite an experience. For two afternoons at Bloomington the camera whirred away. Kinsey prepared Mike by getting him half-drunk on gin—an advantage for him but a disadvantage for me, since I had stopped drinking and could no longer join him in his happy euphoria. Sitting under an apple tree in Kinsey's garden before the festivities began, the Imp of the Perverse made me look down at Miksche's stylish brown English riding-boots (black had not yet become the leather-boys standard color) that had a bit of lacing at the instep. I plucked at one end of the lace and untied it, saying, "Humph—you don't look so tough to me."
>
> That was a deliberate challenge, of course, for which I paid dearly again and again during the next two afternoons. Mike was quite a ham actor; every time he heard Bill Dellenback's camera start to turn, he renewed his vigor . . . at the end of the second afternoon I was exhausted, marked and marred, all muscles weakened. During the sessions I was vaguely conscious of people dropping in now and then to observe, while Mrs. Kinsey—a true scientist to the end—sat by, and once in a while calmly changed the sheets upon the workbench.
>
> At the end of the last session, when my jaws were so tired and unhinged I could scarcely close my mouth, let alone hold a cigarette between my lips, Mike got really angry and slapped me hard on each cheek, saying that I was the lousiest cocksucker he

had ever seen.* I could have killed him at that moment. I sprang from the bed and ran to the shower; he followed me, but I was still seething. Later that evening Kinsey left Mike and me in separate parts of the library to do some reading; and suddenly Mike appeared, wild-fire-eyed and excited—having stimulated himself with some typewritten s/m stories—and had his way with me on the cold cement floor of the library stacks.

When Kinsey heard of the encounter, he laughed and said, "I hope the blinds were closed."

Mike Miksche later bore out the theorizing of Theodore Reik, Wilhelm Stekel, and Kinsey himself that sadists were perhaps not as well balanced as masochists, for Mike—after attempting and failing to turn his directions to heterosexuality by getting married—jumped into the Hudson River one day and committed suicide.†

Steward recorded the experience on his index card for Miksche in the Stud File, observing that he had his first encounter with Miksche the day before filming began, on May 30, 1952. Notes at the bottom of the card read: "1 x 2 hrs px ACK; 5-31, 6-1," meaning that the two-hour filming session involving Alfred C. Kinsey had taken place over May 31 and June 1. The note goes on to add, "Tall handsome sadist. Two pms‡ of movies. Whoo!"§

•

Nine days later (but still aching and sore from Miksche's brutalization), Steward wrote Kinsey a brief note from the Hotel Taft in New York: "It

*Steward later described these words to an interviewer as "the supreme insult" one could offer a homosexual. ("Jack Fritscher Interview with Sam Steward," copyright Jack Fritscher 1974, 2004. Used by permission of the author.)

†Accounts differ about Miksche's suicide. Wescott (who probably stayed in closer contact with Miksche since he was based in the New York area) told his biographer, Jerry Roscoe, that after being pulled from the Hudson River and hospitalized in Bellevue, Miksche had ultimately ended his life with an overdose of pills on a Manhattan rooftop. (Roscoe, *Glenway Wescott Personally*, pp. 198–99.)

‡Afternoons.

§The Kinsey Institute keeps the only copy of the filmed encounter between Steward and Miksche in its archive, but its sex film collection is closed to all researchers, and cannot be viewed by anyone at all.

was an extremely enjoyable week-end, and I was especially glad to be able to spend some time in the library. We hope that our part in the experiences may have contributed somewhat, but we are still a bit dubious."

Steward, who was only in town for three nights, spent two of them with Witold Pick's Polish "cousin," Johnny, the young man whom Steward had bedded in Paris the summer before, and then worried he had infected with gonorrhea. Johnny (who had not been infected and was not Pick's cousin) had recently moved to New York. "He is really very sweet," Steward wrote, "and even better looking than in Paris. He's 28 now, lithe, blonde, *bien bâti*."*

Tuesday the tenth, Steward went to Monroe Wheeler and Glenway Wescott's apartment at 410 Park Avenue—for Wescott, though away, had provided Steward with an introduction to George Platt Lynes, the well-known dance and fashion photographer who had an ongoing intimate relationship with Wescott's longtime partner and lover Monroe Wheeler. Lynes had arranged a small dinner party that night which included the playwright William Inge as well as a dazzlingly handsome young man named Ralph Pomeroy, who frequently modeled for both Lynes and Paul Cadmus.

Steward and Lynes hit it off immediately, in part because of their shared friendship with Gertrude Stein and Alice B. Toklas (for the two ladies had mentored Lynes when he was an aspiring young writer in Paris), but also in part because both men were highly sexual, with many shared sexual contacts in the world of ballet. Steward later wrote of spending the hours after dinner "looking at Lynes incomparable nudes." By the end of this long and pleasurable evening, the two men were fast friends; Lynes cordially offered to give Steward any number of his nude figure studies if only Steward would visit again when passing through New York at summer's end. Steward thought the evening a very promising start to what he hoped would be his best Paris summer ever.

•

After a quick ocean crossing filled with a number of pleasant sexual interludes (one in particular, with a professor who had once dated Steward's sister, seems to have bordered on romance), Steward arrived in Paris

*Well built.

rested and refreshed, and spent his first day in St. Germain with Esther Wilcox and James Purdy at a fashionable café. He spent the next afternoon in bed with Jacques Delaunay. "We had a bit of *enculage** and he has turned a little sadist," Steward noted with satisfaction. Once again Steward had almost immediately found himself at cross-purposes in Paris, hoping at once to live the literary life of a novelist abroad, and at the same time to immerse himself in nonstop sex. At tea with Alice Toklas that afternoon he met up once again with Sir Francis Rose, who had of course been living a similar double life for many years, and the two once again hit it off enormously. The next night they had a tête-à-tête dinner together, predictably filled with sex talk and laughter. At the end of the evening, and at Steward's urging, Rose "picked up a little snappy-eyed black-haired [teenager] named Luis," Steward recorded that night in his diary. "Half-afraid, [Rose] wanted me to go home with him and the boy, but I said no, and off they went."

Saturday brought another sexual adventure with an American artist acquaintance: Steward "was *sadique* with R. McCarthy . . . beat him, whipped him, twisted his nipples, put wrench on head of cock, pissed in his mouth . . . Took a shower, and left my watch there." When the watch was subsequently turned in to the police for an advertised award, Steward paid far more than it was worth to get it back, for it had been a gift from George Reginato, his Chicago paramour, and so it had special significance to him.

The following Monday, Steward met up with Jacques Delaunay again, "but somehow all the old fire was lacking, as well it might be after what we went through two years ago." After sex, however, Delaunay was kind enough to help Steward draft an elegantly phrased letter to the publisher Paul Morihien about the new translation of *Querelle* that Steward had shipped to Morihien several weeks earlier via air express. The next day, after sunbathing among the muscle boys of the Quai de Grenelle, Steward returned "to find a letter from Glenway [Wescott] arranging all sorts of things with Fr[ancois] Reichenbach (who called yesterday inviting me to see the Genet film), J[acques] Guerin, [Jean] Cocteau, *et al.* [But] Morihien probably won't [attend]."

Reichenbach, a charming and amiable homosexual documentary filmmaker, had invited Steward to his apartment to view *Un Chant*

*Anal sex.

d'Amour, the twenty-six-minute silent film that Jean Genet had recently made starring André (the hustler Steward had met in 1950 through Francis Rose) and another of his companions, Lucien Senemaud. Using shots of faces, armpits, and semierect penises, Genet had evoked a dreamlike series of erotic activities in a prison. Steward went to the screening, and there met Cocteau (who had been involved in the filming) and also Jacques Guerin, the wealthy businessman and arts patron who had financed the film. Steward briefly discussed his translation of *Querelle* with Guerin, who advised him to approach Genet about it directly. Steward seems not to have managed a word with Cocteau, however; he apparently became tongue-tied in the volatile artist's presence, and was barely able to stammer out a few admiring remarks.

Sunday the twenty-ninth brought on a heat wave, so Steward stayed in his room writing post cards and only ventured out again the next day for sex with an artist, Jean Tsamis, followed by a cocktail party at the home of Francis Rose. He ended the night with more cruising. The following day he saw Max Ophuls's new film of Schnitzler's *La Ronde*, which impressed him deeply, and then had dinner with Pick. Later, over drinks at a café, "Francis, drunk and in *maillot barré*, joined us *au* Royal, a perfect ass and bore for two hours of talk of Luis." Steward had propositioned Luis the previous afternoon and been turned down cold, so he had little patience for Rose's increasingly obsessive talk of the young man, who was clearly moving in on Rose as a patron and sugar daddy. Steward concluded his journal that evening by noting yet another new prospect, a "crew-cut French boy."

The boy, a nineteen-year-old named Jean Magriz, proved the next day to be "charming, *gentil, mâle* . . . [in bed] he reciprocated *un peu*—not enough to be displeasing . . . This makes up for a lot . . . he is the most lovely *beau gar** that I've *ever* met in 4 trips to La Belle France!" But when Steward met him for dinner the day after their encounter, "something happened . . . [Jean suddenly] grew very sad—and almost wept. Back at the Reine [Blanche], he excused himself and went away, leaving me sitting there a bit dazed and not quite sure what happened."

Sunday was a disappointment, for Steward was still disturbed by Magriz's sudden disappearance the night before, and the Quai de Grenelle

*Handsome fellow.

turned out to be far too crowded and hot for sunbathing. That evening, Magriz didn't show up at the Reine Blanche, leaving Steward to wait out the evening by himself. Alone in a café later that night, Steward returned once again to his literary projects, writing notes to the filmmaker Kenneth Anger and the novelist Julien Green, two of the many artists and writers he still wanted to meet while in Paris. By the afternoon, however, his sadness over the loss of Magriz had deepened: "Maybe it's time *now* to give up sex," he wrote in his diary, "rather than wait two more years til I'm 45."

On the eighth, Steward met with Morihien's secretary, Mme. Baudoin, who informed him that "Morihien will not at this time take *Querelle*," as he recorded afterward in his diary with some disappointment. Still, "she said [the novelist] Julien Green thought it superb, read every word of it," and she suggested that, based on Green's response, Morihien might eventually reconsider taking it on. That evening Steward had a date with Bob Martinson, the professor who had once dated Steward's sister, and whom Steward had had a brief fling with during the Atlantic crossing. But Martinson "showed up with some little nance of a french teacher . . . from University of Pitt[sburgh], leaving me again dazed and hurt. Saw them later; we walked for a while and then I had Bob (the 2nd time that day for him, I fancy) but found I didn't want him at all. There's a limit."

Several days after, Steward had word from Jacques Guerin, Genet's patron, saying, "I must go to see Genet alone, and [he] sent me his address." Steward seems, however, to have hesitated—afraid not of Genet, but rather of his cadre of thugs, about whom Steward had now heard a great deal from Francis Rose,* for Genet was apparently angry Steward had undertaken an unauthorized translation of his novel. Steward later described the situation to an interviewer:

> I took my translation of *Querelle* to France in the middle 50s and let Julien Green read it. He liked it—and said that it was a very American translation, largely because I'd tried to render the French argot into American slang, although some of the argot really had no exact equivalent. And then I gave it to Paul Morihien, who was Genet's publisher for some things. Well—that cre-

---

*For more on Genet's hustlers, see White, *Genet*, pp. 84–111, 310–13; and *passim*.

ated a turbulence, because Genet thought that I was trying to pirate it for he had already suffered one pirating, when *Notre Dame des Fleurs* appeared as *Gutter in the Sky*. I had translated the book as a labor of love . . . but evidently Genet didn't interpret it that way.

•

The professional rejection by Morihien, the sexual rejection by Magriz, and now the irrationally angry response from Genet all led Steward to ask himself in his diary, "Why go to Paris when you're so successful in Chicago?"

On July 15 Steward's mood lifted when he discovered that George Platt Lynes's artist friend Paul Cadmus,* who was just then on his way to Brittany from Rome, had by chance registered that morning at the Recamier. Steward left a note at the front desk asking him to lunch. Emmy Curtis had just arrived from Chicago, so Steward spent the morning looking after her, but he was free to meet with Cadmus at noon, and in the end the two had a long and pleasant meal. "We talked of many things— *argot*, Italy, painting. He says I will like Italy; it's so 'unbuttoned.'"

The next day Steward visited the novelist Julien Green. Like many Americans, Steward knew little about Green's writing, for though born an American, Green had grown up in France and wrote in French. Along with Gide and Genet, he is today recognized as one of the three great figures of modern French literature to have given a substantial account of his homosexual life in his writing, even though he was strongly ambivalent about his homosexuality.

Throughout his life, Green struggled to reconcile his sexuality with his Catholic faith. In his earlier years, he had vacillated between recognizing the validity of his homosexual desires (at the urging of Gide) and, alternately, seeing homosexuality as sinful and wrong (at the urging of the dashing Catholic theologian Jacques Maritain, who had also "converted"†

---

*The painter and printmaker Paul Cadmus (1904–1999) had scandalized the nation with his satirical erotic paintings of sailors on shore leave during the mid-1930s. He was just then living in Europe with his lover of more than a decade, the artist Jared French, and French's wife, Margaret Hoening French.

†Cocteau's conversion to Catholicism was brief, and motivated in large part (according to his biographer Francis Steegmuller) by his attraction to Maritain.

Cocteau). Green had ultimately decided in favor of Catholicism, and in 1949 returned to the church. Nonetheless his interest in homoerotic imagery stayed with him; so, too, did his interest in anonymous sexual encounters. Like Gide, Green distinguished between those homosexual attachments that had an emotional foundation (which were acceptable) and those that were purely physical (and which were thus the work of the devil). As a result, he considered himself as existing within a fallen state, for quite apart from failing to answer a higher religious calling, he had failed even to put the indulgence of his sexual desires behind him with his return to Catholicism. Upon their first meeting, Green presented Steward with a first edition of *L'Autre Sommeil* (1930), his semiautobiographical novel of homosexual awakening.

At first the two men talked primarily about publishing. Like Steward, Green was acutely aware of the need to engage in a certain amount of sexual hypocrisy in his writing in order to be published; unlike Steward, however, he had long since reconciled himself to practicing that hypocrisy. "In hesitating to talk about the hero's love for a young man, I falsify truth and seemingly conform to accepted morality," he once noted in a journal entry; "it is behaving thus that one finally becomes a man of letters."

All the same, Steward was delighted with Green, noting in his diary, "Green . . . is charming, quiet—*en est*,* and said wonderful things about my translation . . . Much euphoria over this, and wrote at once to K[insey]."

His letter to Kinsey concerned a specific new project:

As you undoubtedly know, there are two great diaries in France . . . Undoubtedly the first is that of André Gide, large portions of which have already been published . . . The second is that of Julien Green, and five expurgated volumes of that have already appeared [in French]. He is now 51, and has been keeping it very seriously since he was 27. At my suggestion, he wants to give it to you.

To my mind, this is one of the really great windfalls for your collection. It is *absolutely truthful* and must probably be guarded secret *in perpetuo* . . . I need not tell you why I know the diary's subject matter will interest you, since you know me.

---

*A polite way of noting that a person is homosexual.

•

Over the next few days, when not shepherding Emmy Curtis on sightseeing expeditions around Paris, Steward was setting up and keeping various sexual rendezvous and at the same time congratulating himself on having acquired the Julien Green diary for Kinsey.

July 23, his forty-third birthday, brought Steward the usual depression about advancing age and lack of accomplishment, but this year his various projects (and ongoing sexual success) kept him from feeling it too deeply. His old friend Emmy Curtis helped, too. "Emmy took me to Maxim's—plusher than plush—and then on the Bateau-Mouche, which lasted a bit longer than necessary . . . In the evening [we went] to see Alice—with much trepidation on my part—but she seemed to like Emmy, and talked endlessly until 12:30." Two days later, Steward had another meeting with Julien Green. "[I] gave him some of my dirty pictures," Steward noted, "at which he seemed overwhelmed. Then we went to lunch and talked endlessly until 4:00 o'clock, about art, literature and mainly sex. He said he would introduce me to the charming young Polish boy I saw at his house." The novelist telephoned the next day, and invited Steward to come around again for a visit. Steward then finished out the week with three more sexual encounters, one of them with Jacques Delaunay.

On Sunday, he took Emmy to see Tamara Toumanova dance *Giselle*. Steward was in fact devoted to this sweet old schoolteacher friend eighteen years his senior, for she had become very dear to him over the years. She had recently become a little more vague and confused than usual, and also begun to show symptoms of polycythemia, the serious bone marrow disorder that would ultimately result in her death. Wanting to make the Paris visit as special for her as possible, he arranged that they spend Monday together, too: "We climbed up to Sacre-Coeur, and amongst other things located Genet's little house [in Montmartre], which we photographed. [I] bought a small pissoir as a souvenir . . . and then stopped at Gallimard on the way home to pick up *Le Langage Populaire*."*

On the twenty-ninth he wrote up yet another adventure, of having a series of portraits of himself taken while posed as rough trade: "Midsum-

---

*Charles Nisard's *Etude sur le Langage Populaire, ou Patois de Paris et de sa Bainlieu* (1872), a study of Parisian slang and street language.

mer madness in Paris! Your old mother went . . . to the photographer Rudolph (de Rohan, 5 rue Medicis) to have her picture taken as rough trade—in jeans, etc. R[udolph] a fantastic Yugoslave auntie, white skin and red wig." From there, he continued on to Julien Green's, where the two men passed the time "looking at [Green's] photos—hundreds of erotic ones, not many sexual. He gave me about 20 very nice ones which may give me difficulty with the *douane* . . . Later I conceived the idea of copying some pen and ink sketches, and must ask him if he will lend them for a little while."

Two days later, Steward saw the proofs of the photos taken by Rudolph de Rohan, noting that they had "turned out to be very good—a couple—but scarcely ones for the yearbook at DePaul." He spent the later part of the week copying some of the drawings in Green's collection, and at their next meeting Green even offered to take Steward "to the male brothel, Saids—[which he said would cost me] 3000 francs." Steward, however, declined, for he had limited funds, and moreover was experiencing a good deal of sexual success without paying for it. Over breakfast several mornings later, he noticed a handsome young black man who turned out to be a Chicago-based dancer for Steward's friend Katherine Dunham. "Thus before noon [of August 7]," Steward wrote that night in his diary, "I had his lovely body in my arms and his big black cock in my mouth."

The brutal fantasies of *Querelle* were by now so firmly established in Steward's mind that when he "saw a blindingly beautiful Querelle type," after attending a church service at the Église Saint Germain, he decided that he absolutely "had to have it at all costs." He subsequently invited the eighteen-year-old ruffian out for a beer and stayed on the town with him until two in the morning—at which point Pick stole the stud out from under him via a quickly concluded financial discussion. When the thug reappeared the next day, Steward had him up to his hotel room for sex, but afterward noted, "*Rien.* Pick had got all the gravy."

A subsequent bar pickup turned nasty, with the fellow revealing himself to be "a [complete] sadist—ropes, scissors, belt." The encounter was the most authentically violent and dangerous Steward had ever known; he later noted in his Stud File, "[I] tho[ugh]t my last hour had come." It ended in a substantial beating as well as in stab wounds from the scissors. The following day, Steward remained in great pain, and also "found great difficulty in eating . . . because of my ruptured throat." He concluded by noting, "This was a shocking experience . . . I was psychically unprepared."

While Steward was not yet weary of Paris, he was physically injured and sexually exhausted, and he knew from his past experiences that with the Feast of the Assumption in mid-August, most of Paris would shut down for vacation, and the streets become empty and dull. He therefore strategically bought himself a train ticket for Brest, made a few last-minute purchases, and ended the afternoon by taking Emmy to the Musée Grévin.* There, almost in spite of himself, he picked up an American air force corporal in uniform and bought him dinner. After sex that evening, the corporal begged Steward for seven thousand francs so he could fly back to England and not lose his stripes for overstaying his liberty. "Like a fool, I fell for it," he wrote afterward, "—and that's the last I ever expect to see of [the money] . . . Anyway, I had him, but $20 is too much for your old mother to pay for second rate goods."

•

Leaving Emmy behind to fend for himself, Steward boarded the train the next morning for the long, slow ride to Brest. Though it was a journey of 375 miles, he was determined to pay homage to the city he had come to know so well through Genet's novel, and about which he had now fanta-sized continually for more than two years.

Genet had lived in Brest briefly before World War II, and had based much of *Querelle* on his experience of this maritime city at the farthest reaches of the rugged Breton coast. An orphan born the same year as Steward, he had moved from orphanage to reform school to prison as a young man, and had been stationed in Brest in 1938 while enlisted in the Second Regiment of the Colonial Infantry under false pretenses (for, as a former convict, he was officially prohibited from joining the military). Brest had long been one of the great military and penal centers of France, with prison labor used in the construction of naval ships; by all accounts, it was a rough, oppressive military-dominated garrison city. After stealing four bottles of an aperitif from a bar, Genet had spent a week hiding out from the police in the backstreets before being betrayed by an accom-plice and imprisoned. These autobiographical details and the foggy, phan-tasmagorical city in which they had been set were the raw materials from which Genet had crafted his violent, dreamlike, and highly sexual novel.

*A wax museum, similar to Madame Tussaud's in London.

Steward had fantasized endlessly about Brest while translating *Querelle*, but the most picturesque parts of the old city were just then in complete ruin. The Allied bombardment of the port during World War II had destroyed most of the dismal landmarks Genet had described, and now only their place-names remained. "The rue de Siam, and rue Telegraphe . . . The town is all rebuilt and the old Brest all gone. And none of the new [buildings are] finished," Steward wrote of it. "Dark and sinister and quiet at night."

Staying at a cheap new hotel built on the site of Genet's old Hotel de Siam, Steward tried mightily to commune with the spirit of the novel by prowling the dark streets, and in fact on his first night he found that "an old sailor-boxer took me by the hand in [La] Recouvrance."* But of course the real Brest could never live up to Genet's tortured erotic evocation of it, or to Steward's equally tortured fantasies of *Querelle*. As he wrote Kinsey: "What a poor dead mysterious town it is—all new buildings not quite finished—dark wide silent streets at night—certainly worse events than those G[enet] wrote about could happen now. La Feria, the tavern, is gone in a bomb, I fear. The hotel I live in is brand new. Still, in its way it is an even more wonderful setting for a 1952 *Querelle*."

He also added, somewhat impatiently, "Did you ever get the letter I wrote about Julien Green's diary, or didn't you want it, for [Green] has as yet heard nothing [from you] on the subject."

On his last day in the city, Steward photographed the door to a place that might have been La Feria, the bar in *Querelle*.† He also narrowly escaped being jackrolled. In a last-ditch attempt to score with a French sailor, and thinking as well of Genet's Lieutenant Seblon, Steward left a note in the local pissoir. But when at long last a naval officer showed up looking for sex, he was too old and too ugly; Steward didn't want him and sent him away.

•

Once back in Paris, Steward assisted Emmy with her packing, her banking, and her luggage before taking her out for a final "farewell" dinner at the Wagenende. With her departure, he felt himself falling into a depres-

---

*The very old district on the right bank of the river Penfeld, opposite Brest proper.
†In *Querelle*, Genet describes the bar and brothel known as La Feria as having a spiked door; Steward found one.

sion, but then at the Café Flore he met an acquaintance who "talked so long and well of sex in Italy that he convinced me I should go to Rome for a week." By the next day Steward had noted in his diary, "The die is cast."* After one last escapade—an all-night six-way *partouze* featuring four young French workmen and a fellow American tourist—Steward packed his bags and caught his flight to Italy.

"Rome!" Steward wrote two days later. "Even the air smells thick and rich—of melons, hay, fountains, lights, people . . . [It's] lovely to look at . . . [I] walked until late, taking in everything . . . It's fantastic—colored ochre and red . . . And the grandeur of its dimensions!" Quite apart from loving the look and smell of the city, Steward was particularly excited by the good looks and candid stares of Roman men, who seemed to him far more lively, direct, and sexually engaged than their more formal and reserved Parisian equivalents—and indeed, many of them were just then actively caught up in trading sex for money, for postwar conditions had left many Italians desperate for currency, and the streets were now crowded with well-heeled, sex-hungry tourists.

His first stop, however, was the house just off the Spanish Steps where Keats had died, for Steward admired Keats above all other poets. "Visited its little museum, wept," he noted in his diary. He then described the heavy cruising scene in the nearby park of the Villa Borghese: "A boxer came and sat down beside me. Very sexy, about 35 . . . 'Tony' or some such. We ate . . . an expensive dinner [and] after sex in the hotel, he took me for 4000 lira."

Sex between men in Italy, Steward soon learned, nearly always involved some form of payment.† Steward had few qualms about paying in general, and in Rome none at all—for the Roman men were handsome, the act of payment carried its own powerful erotic charge, and the cost, given the exchange rate, was almost fantastically low.

Jacta alea est, or "the die is cast," was Caesar's famous utterance upon the crossing of the Rubicon, the first step in his conquest of Rome and his overthrow of the Roman Republic. Steward's fanciful notion that he, too, would conquer Rome (sexually) is reflected in his later Phil Andros novel *When in Rome, Do . . .* , which he subsequently republished as *Roman Conquests.*

†"Kinsey speculated [about the exchange of money in Italy for sex between men that] it was not poverty [that motivated them], but that they would lower their station if they offered themselves without asking for payment. [Kinsey] thought it was probably an historical carry-over from Greek and Phoenician backgrounds." (Gathorne-Hardy, *Kinsey,* p. 427.)

Steward was not alone in coming to Rome for an erotic getaway; since the end of World War II, large numbers of American tourists had flocked there, with American writers and artists in the vanguard. Tennessee Williams had been visiting regularly since 1948; Samuel Barber, Gore Vidal, Frederick Prokosch, Paul Cadmus, Jared French, James Merrill, Bernard Perlin, and many others were resident or semiresident in Rome at this time, creating a substantial artistic community of young, dynamic English-speaking homosexually active expatriates. The world of Roman men-for-hire in which they moved was probably most vividly evoked by Tennessee Williams's 1950 novel *The Roman Spring of Mrs. Stone*, the story of a faded American actress who seeks oblivion in her many anonymous sexual encounters with young Roman hustlers—just as, during that time, Williams had done.

After a busy second day of sightseeing, Steward met up with Glenway Wescott's lover, Monroe Wheeler, and learned from Wheeler that a number of their Paris acquaintances had recently arrived in Rome, too, including Francois Reichenbach and James Purdy. While Steward and Wheeler had their dinner, Steward caught sight of "Tony," the hustler who had stolen his four thousand lire; but he was sanguine about the robbery, later noting only, "I see now he's one of the best professionals in Rome."

Two days later Steward met up with James Purdy for breakfast, then took a taxi alone to the English Cemetery, where he plucked some "shrubbery and clover from Keats and Shelley's tombs" and meditated in silence by Keats's grave. Then, after a quiet lunch, he cruised the Baths of Caracalla and the Terme di Roma, finding the latter "Fantastic. Full of tired American queens. Francois Reichenbach . . . took an American boy from me. And [I met] Tennessee Williams! [But] where were the vaunted pretties?"

Steward was delighted to encounter Williams, and particularly under such louche circumstances, for he was a great admirer of Williams's work—particularly the short stories, in which Williams had daringly presented various dark, often masochistic homosexual dramas without hiding behind the tiresome change-of-sex strategy he so often resorted to in his plays. "[The] stories of *One Arm* have haunted me for years—the title one, and 'Death and the Black Masseur,'" Steward later wrote Williams, "[and] I shall dream and think of the description of the motorcyclist in 'Two on a Party' . . . for years to come." In the same letter, Steward recalled to Williams their brief, amusing conversation while chatting in the Roman cruising spot:

> I had gone in the late afternoon to the Terme di Roma near the Trevi fountain . . . The word had reached us in Chicago that it was *the* place: all you had to do was go there and be seen and lo! Within a few minutes a handsome young Roman would throw his arms around your neck and swear to be yours forever. Well, I went, and found no one there but some tired American queens who'd heard the same story. But suddenly . . . word flashed like an electric current through the place: "Tennessee is here!" So I went and looked and there you were, sitting in a peacock rattan chair, legs crossed and swinging your foot at the world. I said that the only reason I'd come to Rome was to find the gamin on the Spanish Steps that you'd written about in *The Roman Spring.* "And did you find him?" you asked. No, I said, but I did find a young Roman gladiator in the Borghese gardens.

Several days later, Steward met and bedded an extraordinarily handsome young hustler named Carlo Monti. On the thirtieth of August he noted, "Carlo came [again] at noon . . . This time he took me for 5000 with some cock and bull story about a suit in hock. However . . . [that evening when we went out] Carlo looked wonderful in his 'new' grey flannel—arrogant, proud, with a wonderful carriage—*un vero Romano di Roma!*"

An evening later, Steward cruised the ruined Colosseum, for though regularly patrolled by police, it was then still open to the public, and well known for anonymous sex.* Steward's elation at his sexual success there did not last long, however, for the next day Monti "discolored my whole stay [in Rome] by stealing my wristwatch [after sex]—very cleverly, too." Crushed at the loss of this cherished keepsake from George Reginato, Steward could only observe, "I'm thankful this didn't happen on my first night here, or it would all have been very unpleasant. Still, it is only a minor emotional shock which will be cured by a little time passing." He consoled himself, as usual, by meditating on the experience in his diary.

---

*The Stud File notes: "3–viii–52 'Pasquale,'" but the lack of a money symbol suggests that on that evening in the Colosseum Steward gave the 2,000 lire as a tip rather than by prearranged agreement.

Steward spent his final days in Europe back in rainy Paris. On the fourth of September, he took leave of Alice Toklas, then picked up the *Querelle* manuscript at Morihien's office and gave it to an expatriate friend who had promised to return it to Julien Green. Witold Pick and Georges Raveau, a waiter Steward had been seeing regularly for sex that summer, came down to the hotel to see him off. "I shed some tears going down the Blvd Raspail," Steward noted, but "was done by the time we got to Place de la Concorde."

By the end of the travel diary, Steward seems to have realized that his dream of living and writing in France was still very far from becoming a reality, and that moreover it probably never would. He had, after all, arrived in Paris that summer still thinking of himself as a promising young writer who would be welcome in any number of literary salons, and he had been particularly confident that his new translation of *Querelle* would open many doors. In short order, however, he had experienced the complete opposite. He was now at an impasse with both Paul Morihien and Jean Genet. Jean Cocteau, meanwhile, had thought very little of him at all, and despite Steward's great admiration for the artist and poet, no friendship had resulted from their meeting. Most of the educated Parisian men Steward had met and attempted to bed had seemed, in retrospect, rather stuffy and dull to him: unduly complicated, formal, and sexually reserved. True, he had had some sexual success with Parisian tradesmen and waiters; but none had made too deep an impression. Rome and its men, by comparison, had been a revelation.

The problem, of course, was not with Paris, but rather with Steward himself, for during the 1952 visit he had finally started to realize that being an American tourist in Paris—however well one might speak French—was not quite the same as being a participant in French social mores and French literary culture. While Steward was by now basically fluent in the language, he was hardly capable of conversing with much subtlety or grace among the Parisian literati. And really, what was the point of doing so? Despite his decade-long study of the language, most of his friends that summer (apart from Jacques Delaunay) had been Americans or other visiting foreigners. Among the French writers he had encountered, only one— Julien Green, himself American-born—had authentically befriended him, and even then the two had conversed entirely in English. While Steward was doubtless capable of improving his French, he now wondered how long it would take—and with whom he would converse—and to what end he might want to do so. Apart from Genet, there was no one then writing in French he much cared to translate. Moreover, he had no intention of writing anything in French himself. For years, Steward had imagined himself as a Continental sophisticate, a Parisian flaneur with the tailored clothes and pencil mustache of a latter-day Adolphe Menjou. By the end of the summer, however, Steward was basically done with Paris; if anything, he much preferred Rome.

Steward's 1952 diary chronicles, amid its many sexual adventures, a quiet change of heart. With that change of heart came a new energy and resolve. Though he was returning to the United States discouraged by his reception among the Paris literati, he was nonetheless doing so with a formidable set of new sexual statistics. Moreover, as he sailed back to the States, he felt ever more sure of himself and his projects. The encounters he had been pursuing so actively over the past few years now seemed to him no longer a distraction from his literary endeavors, but increasingly his central life focus—and perhaps, at some point, a topic on which he would write with real authority. Having sex, not writing, was now the thing he most wanted to do—and there were plenty of men waiting for him back in Chicago.

·

On the passage back to New York, Steward met and had a number of discussions about Catholicism with the French theologian Jacques Maritain, a friend to both Julien Green and Jean Cocteau. Steward had previously met Maritain through the translator and literary critic Charles du Bos, a French Catholic convert whom Steward had come to know better in Chicago, during the war, after du Bos had taken a position at Notre Dame University in South Bend. Though Steward had long since left the church, he still remained interested in the question of faith—and also in Maritain, who was handsome, brilliant, and utterly charismatic. Unfortunately, Steward did not relate the content of these conversations in his diaries, which were intended in large part for Kinsey.

New York, when Steward arrived, was the same wonderful adventure as ever. He noted briefly in his diary of September 11 that "John Leapheart—charming negro—came [to my hotel and] I did him. Then we had dinner, and he came back to the hotel, and [he] did me." There were two other liaisons, but the highlight of the stopoff was the return visit to

George Platt Lynes, toward whom Steward had already begun to feel a unique and extraordinary connection. In a fictional evocation of Lynes and his New York milieu, Steward would later describe attending a sex party with Lynes at about this time, but in fact their one evening together was spent mostly looking at Lynes's art collection and photographs before going out to a bar. As Steward later noted,

> George [Lynes] and I went to [the Stage Bar,] a hustler's bar on 42nd street near Times Square, and sat in a dim booth to meet Bill Inge, the enormously popular playwright of *Picnic* and *Come Back, Little Sheba*. [We spent most of the evening] listening to his agonizing over whether to order another drink (his problem with alcohol was reflected in almost everything he wrote), and then—having succumbed—whether George and I thought the particular hustler he was eyeing, in a kind of bastard Western outfit, would be "safe" to take home.
>
> "Do you think he'd murder me?" Bill Inge kept asking.
>
> "That's a hazard of our profession," George said. "Nothing ventured, y'know."
>
> Bill staggered out of the booth and approached the young man. They talked for a moment, then started to leave. Bill came to the booth for his raincoat, for it was drizzling outside. "He only wants ten," he said in a whiskey whisper.
>
> "Good luck," I said, and George made a circle with his thumb and forefinger.

The next day, after another rendezvous with Leapheart, Steward "saw Geo[rge] Lynes and met [one of his models, a weightlifter] from Boston." He also noted he had "conned George [Lynes] out of about 35 pictures." But in fact Lynes had offered Steward as many photographs as he cared to take away with him, and Steward, knowing of Lynes's significant financial difficulties,* would gladly have paid for them if only Lynes had allowed. Lynes would not; in taking money for nude male imagery, Lynes

---

*Though a proper biography of Lynes has not yet been written, Lynes's financial difficulties are detailed in William R. Thompson, "Sex, Lies and Photographs: Letters from George Platt Lynes" (master's thesis, Rice University, 1997). The bankruptcy is also mentioned in Woody, *George Platt Lynes* (p. 11), and in the Glenway Wescott journals.

would have exposed himself to criminal prosecution, and despite his pending bankruptcy he was unwilling to take that sort of risk, even with Steward.

Before boarding the *Pacemaker* back to Chicago, Steward drafted a hasty note:

Dear George,

You'd like this wonderful gentle good-looking (superb body!) negro named John Leapheart . . . He knows I'm giving you the number, so do call him if the mood is on you some dark evening—he'll delight you.

Thanks for everything.

Sam

8

Writing Lynes

That fall Steward devoted himself more than usual to erotic letter writing with several acquaintances.* He later noted that his new friendship with Lynes, which had intensified via such correspondence, was just then particularly important to him as he began another bleak year at DePaul, particularly since Lynes was such a fan of Steward's erotic writing:

> [Lynes] discovered that I liked to memorialize various [sexual] experiences of mine in a sort of narrative form, and so I began to send him single-spaced one-page accounts of those brief encounters. "More, more," he kept asking—and in return for these he would give me small segments of photographs . . .
>
> On one occasion I pimped for him,† sending him a particularly handsome young black whom I had met; [Lynes then] photographed Johnny L[eapheart] over and over, and sent me one of the best, with Johnny lying enfolded against a white boy's body, Johnny's face slumbrous and composed . . . [a photograph that Lynes] entitled "Man in his Element."

*Through an introduction made by Kinsey, Steward conducted an elaborate erotic correspondence with a man named Jorge da Silva, who was similarly inclined to record keeping about his sexual experiences, and similarly obsessed with "collecting" and "having" men in military uniform. Only da Silva's side of the correspondence (sent from Rio de Janeiro) remains in the Kinsey Library, however—donated by Steward.
†"On one occasion" is not strictly true; there were several others apart from Leapheart.

It was through these letters that Steward seems, finally, to have come into his own as a writer comfortable not only with the description of his sexual activities and interests, but also with himself as a person. When Lynes cautiously inquired if Leapheart might be a hustler, Steward wrote back,

> Worry no more . . . The stuff is free, and quite elegant too . . . perhaps his background is not very large, but that's a little winter project for you; you can spread it out and deepen it.
>
> The pretty, pretty pictures! I wanted to look at them a dozen times on the train, but didn't, and since I've been back I've really done little else . . . The trip home was almost uneventful—except that near Toledo at 4:00 AM a returning soldier in mufti (tall he was, and so broad-shouldered!) asked me to open his liquor bottle for him, and I did since he was so drunk, and then I opened something else for him too—and left him a little weak but happy. Just how he could manage to face his wife and two children twenty minutes after was not my problem, of course.

During the fall Steward also concluded his negotiations with Paul Morihien, writing him a long letter in French suggesting the *Querelle* manuscript would remain available to him in Paris should he ever care to reconsider it.*

Steward heard no more from Morihien, but Lynes contacted him again in mid-October to thank him for the introduction to Leapheart, whom he described as "heaven," and to introduce him in turn to Scott Douglas, a dancer with the Ballet Theater who in Lynes's words had recently been "a three day wonder in my life." (Douglas was just then on tour in Chicago.) At roughly the same time, Lynes mentioned in a letter to his friend the artist Bernard Perlin that Steward had just sent him a letter "typewritten over what appears to be a 'dirty drawing'—somebody appears to be going down on what appears to be a sailor." And, indeed,

---

Querelle de Brest would not be published in the United States until 1973. The first English translation, undertaken by Genet's friend and agent Bernard Frechtman, was rejected by Genet (who also broke with him; Frechtman subsequently hanged himself). The novel was published in English in the UK only in 1966, with a translation by Gregory Streatham; Frechtman's translation and another by Anselm Hollo were published subsequently.

Steward had recently created several kinds of erotic stationery featuring Cocteau-inspired line drawings of two men having sex.

To Lynes, Steward's total lack of discretion in sending such things through the mail was deeply alarming, for American anxieties about domestic communism and the postwar rise in sexual openness had merged during the early 1950s to create a violently antisexual (and particularly anti-homosexual) culture. Most homosexuals now lived lives of great secrecy, discretion, and fear as politicians such as Senator Joseph McCarthy and political appointees like Postmaster General Arthur Summerfield made names for themselves by prosecuting anyone who dared to express publicly any interest whatsoever in sex. Summerfield had in fact recently launched a national crusade against what he termed "pornographic filth in the family mailbox" by persuading Congress to grant the post office sweeping powers to inspect and seize all mail that he and his censors considered obscene. Homosexuality was particularly targeted and vilified. The seizure of mail featuring perceived homoerotic content in many instances led to FBI surveillance of the recipients, harassment by federal, state, and local authorities, and public exposure of both sender and recipient for "sexual deviance." Kinsey, Steward, and Lynes* were all sharply aware of these dangers—and of the three, only Steward dared to flout the law.

When not drawing or writing about sex, Steward continued to pursue any man he found desirable. In 1951 a brilliant coming-of-age novel about a love affair between a teenager and a young man, *Finistère*, had been published in New York. Its author was Arthur Anderson Peters, publishing under the name of Fritz Peters. Steward had loved the novel; he also knew that Peters was the adopted nephew of Margaret Anderson, former editor of *The Little Review*,† and that Peters had lived briefly with Gertrude Stein and Alice Toklas before being taken in and raised by the Greek Armenian mystic Georges Ivanovitch Gurdjieff. Steward therefore decided to track Peters down and bed him. As he described his actions to a poet friend in later life,

---

*Lynes never signed his name (instead merely writing "Thine") in any of his letters to Steward. He did so as a way of protecting himself from potential prosecution for sending (arguably) erotic material through the mail.

†*The Little Review*, founded in Chicago and published from 1914 to 1929, featured modernist writing (most notably sections from James Joyce's *Ulysses*) as well as Dadaist poetry and art. Its editors, Margaret Anderson and Jane Heap, were lovers.

Right after *Finistère* was published I was at the height of my "passive aggressive" stage, so what I wanted was to give Fritz Peters a
blowjob, and I sought him out in Chicago since he was living in
Rogers Park (as I remember) only a few blocks north of me, and
[I] succeeded . . . even though he was terribly evasive at first—
and reluctant when I finally did get him in bed because his under-
wear wasn't the cleanest—but I managed to have my way with
him—and that was the end of that . . . He was so difficult to know,
so withdrawn and afraid (¿was it?) of being near or around someone gay or being thought gay himself that I just couldn't spend
the time with him that I should have—Chicago just then being
remarkably filled with other dingdongs demanding my attention.

At age thirty-eight, Peters had just emerged from a nervous breakdown
and was still quite fragile—in part because he was deeply alcoholic, and in
part because his psychoanalyst had ordered him to abandon his homosexuality and live as a heterosexual. Moreover, Gurdjieff (who was essentially
Peters's adoptive father) despised male homosexuality, and his profound
disapproval of Peters's sexual orientation caused Peters lifelong unhappiness. As Steward later recalled, Peters "burst into tears about five minutes
after he shot his wad, and began to drink even more [and to] rant about how
he really wasn't gay, and I became more and more impatient and he finally
left, still teary, and me—I was also shaken and irritated . . ."

Shortly thereafter, Alice Toklas sent Steward some news about Francis Rose, who was having an equally difficult time: "[Francis] is in Portugal now . . . but before leaving he was in a good deal of trouble with Luis
his *valet de chambre* boyfriend who he now says is his illegitimate son.
Francis is saying that he is going to recognize [Luis] so that he will inherit
the title!"*

Steward was immediately fascinated by the perversity of the discovery (particularly since he had been present when Rose first met Luis). He
later gave an interviewer his own recollection of the Francis Rose–Luis
Rose story:

---

*While Luis could never inherit Rose's English title of baronet, Rose did hold several Spanish titles,
which can descend through female lines when there are no male heirs and which may also be left at
will to anyone—including an illegitimate child.

Francis had been screwing [Luis] for about four months, until there was an episode over a stolen bicycle, and for the first time Francis looked at Luis's papers, down at the police station, and discovered that he was the son of this Spanish girl, Pilar some-body, on whom Francis had fathered an illegitimate child some nineteen years before . . . [I don't think the boy suspected or knew] until it was finally brought into the open . . . But . . . the episode titillated international circles for quite a while.

Apparently Rose now hoped to recognize Luis as his son even while keeping him as a lover, an arrangement by which Luis would eventually gain Rose's Spanish titles, and Rose, for his part, would keep the desirable young man tied to him permanently. But opinions were divided from the first about Rose's "discovery" that Luis was his son, for it seemed an awfully convenient discovery. The painter George Melhuish, a longtime friend of Rose's, later noted that Rose "had apparently convinced himself that his fantasy was fact, even though most of his friends, [myself] included, had serious doubts."

Steward subsequently received a two-page letter from Rose in which Rose gave all the details of the discovery, explaining to him the circumstances of Luis's birth and upbringing, expressing concern over his lack of discipline, but at the same time proudly noting how similar Luis was to him in so many ways. Rose's story was this: He had quietly married into a noble Spanish family just before the Civil War, but his wife had died shortly after giving birth, and all the rest of her family (excepting his child) had then been murdered by "red Trotskyists."* (Frederica, Lady Rose, would later deny the veracity of Rose's claim to have fathered Luis, as indeed would nearly everyone who knew him.)

Steward gleefully passed along to Lynes the jaw-dropping news about Rose having unwittingly bedded his son. Lynes immediately dismissed it as nonsense: "The tale of Francis Rose is too pipe-dream for me. Incest taboo, indeed! . . . Did you see Jimmy Hicks (Scott Douglas,† I mean)? He wrote the other day that he had heard from you, that he meant to call."

---

*Rose also noted in his memoir that he had fathered an illegitimate girl when he was fifteen, and an illegitimate boy with another woman sometime after that.
†Scott Douglas, born Jimmy Hicks (1928–1996), joined the Ballet Theater in 1950 and became a principal dancer in the American Ballet Theater in 1953.

Lynes had enclosed a copy of his *Ballet Yearbook* with the note. In sending Lynes his grateful thanks for it, Steward replied, "No, alas, J[immy] H[icks] Scott Douglas never did call up, and I rather wish he had." He then went on to add,

> I'm delighted you like J. Leapheart . . . [and] I'm glad you say you're a voyeur because now I feel more at home since I'm one, too. I'm throwing a d[aisy]-chain this Friday night with eight coming, three of them as lovely as anything you'll find in Ch[ica]go—and when it gets well under way I'll do what I always do—memorialize the event with my Polaroid camera (I've now got a second album almost filled, though not with all d[aisy] c[hains]'s however). My voyeurism ought to be sated for a coupla weeks after Friday. The thought of Buddy and Johnny being in a thing together was quite exciting to me. Hope they didn't disappoint you . . .
>
> Thy old blackhearted Evil
Sambo

Lynes then sent Steward the nude study of Leapheart embracing the weightlifter from Boston as a thank-you for the introduction to Leapheart—who had turned out to be not just a good model, but also a kind and gentle young man who was also a skilled lover. Steward in turn thanked Lynes for the photograph in the way he knew Lynes would like best: by sending along some stories of his most recent sexual exploits. In the letter enclosing them, he wrote,

> I wish I could've been behind the screen and peeping out when John [Leapheart] & [the weightlifter] were playing . . . As I told you, I planned a *spintriae* for that weekend, and it worked out wonderfully well . . . Eight altogether, six of them as lovely as anything the Midwest puts out, including one blonde and stalwart twenty-year-old with a perfect navy face and body to whom all of us were drawn quite as naturally as flowers face the sun . . . and at one moment, there were six of us working on him. Poor boy! When he got to his feet finally, shaking his head and staggering a little, all he could say was, "My God! And to think I'd ever

wanted to be the center of attention!" He was one of three red-blooded butch boys here who are working out a novel arrangement: two of them had been living together for quite a while, when the blond came along—and instead of his breaking up the duo, they simply opened their arms and took him between their sheets with them—a perfect *ménage a trois*. They go everywhere together. On the surface it seems quite perfect, but old eagle-eye senses certain tensions here and there that may break it up sooner or later.* Too bad . . .

Lynes, after receiving several of Steward's typed "stories" along with the letter, responded, "I wish I could write pornography as well (half as well) as you; it makes good reading. What do I do to encourage you? Is asking enough?"

Steward was hugely gratified by Lynes's praise and encouragement. Coming from an established artist with his own broad range of erotic experience, Lynes's suggestion that Steward was exceptionally good at erotic writing seems to have brought Steward to the realization that, whatever his previous failures as a literary novelist and man of letters, he might yet establish himself as a brilliant writer of homosexual smut. He wrote back,

> You flatter me by telling me how well I write pornography. I like to write it, but sometimes I'm not conscious that I am. And you ask for a photograph of the Navy-type boy of the last *partouse*. I can't give it to you yet, because that night with the Polaroid I took only group pictures with faces more or less hidden, and I haven't seen the boy since. There were so many unfamiliar faces present that night that I couldn't get up the nerve to ask for permission to take "recognizeable" pictures, and I would probably have been denied if I had. There will come a day, however, and you can be sure I'll send one to you.
>
> You may be interested in a little vignette that took place in a Turkish bath last Saturday† . . .

---

*Steward would later fantasize about a similar living arrangement among "three red-blooded butch boys" in his Phil Andros novel of police life, *The Boys in Blue*.
†A long pornographic account follows.

This afternoon to see the Franklin-Slavenska-Danilova remnant of the old Ballet Russe, a doin' "[A] Streetcar [Named Desire]"—will it be horrid? *J'en ai peur.* Thanks again for the pitchures, lovelish, tumefacient . . .

Two weeks later, after receiving more nude photos from Lynes, Steward sent back a narrative calculated to arouse and give pleasure to his friend, and yet at the same time to reveal something quite personal about himself:

Something lovely happened last night. I know a guy from Chicago's west side who's a young executive downtown, and like me, he leads an extraordinary double or triple life—he's one of the "wild ones," about 34, and he likes me . . . he lives in Logan Square . . . [a] real tough neighborhood . . . He called me up last night to say he'd met [someone], and did I mind if he brought him over? Of course not, I said, except I've just painted my sailor-screwing-woman mural off the wall behind my bed and the place is a mess. Small matter, he said, and after a little while they came. The kid was eighteen, and cute as hell . . . He had slick black hair and was very polite and yet damned near took my hand off with his grip . . . He was very naïve still about the H life, Wally having introduced him to it not very long before. Well, it wasn't many minutes until we were all undressing—I was sitting on the edge of the bed naked, and Wally crossed-legged in the middle, and the kid was wrestling himself out of his jeans and jockstrap, and then he suddenly paused and looked over at us and said in a little boy voice: "Cheez! I feel just like da T'anksgivin' turkey!" It damned near broke up the whole party . . . but didn't . . . When he came, he said a little after: "Youse guys sure treat a fella okay. I hope I kin come back." And after the two of them left I sat there a little cold for a moment, thinking about two old queens using a kid that way—but if it's evil, I'm glad, and I'm for more of it . . . So do tell me if you mind if I go back into the past a little further, for I love to write about these little excitements, and if you can stand them, that's a wonderful incentive to me, because—

strange as it seems—I'm actually a very shy and timid lil sensitive
plant . . .*

88,†

Sam

But after a Christmas card from Lynes (of a photographed wall of
erotic graffiti, such as one might encounter in a public toilet, which Lynes
and his friends had actually created as a backdrop for Lynes's nude male
photography), Steward had to admit to some new difficulties, for in wanting to write well for Lynes, and at the same time wanting to write something "dirty," he found himself at cross-purposes:

> You've set up the d[a]m[n]d[e]st psychic block in me . . . I keep
> thinking that you, with your experience, would certainly not be
> interested in reading little commonplace eroticisms which I
> dredge up outa my past. And when I start to write one, I keep
> saying to myself "Will he be disgusted with this? Will he think
> this is silly?" and so on, until it [has] almost grown impossible for
> me to put a line down. That "lavatory correspondence" with a
> complete stranger, on the other hand, was different; I didn't care
> what he thought about me, and so it just poured out.

He then went on to describe his most recent attempt at a novel, one
in which he once again hoped to challenge the boundaries of what could
and could not be written for a literary readership about the male homosexual experience:

> The combined efforts of yourself and Glenway and Dr K[insey]
> have finally started me to writing again—I've been spending hours
> on that, and trying to work too—and I've got about sixty thousand
> words done on what is one of the queerest novels ever written, I'm
> sure—sex is woven all around and through it, every page, every line.
> I have a distinct feeling it's not for publication here, although I have
> kept the downright ~~erotic~~ (pornographic) out of it. Yet it still is ex-

---

*The episode is noted, as described, in the Stud File; the boy's name was Jimmy Hannigan.
†"88," in the sex code Steward had developed for his Stud File, meant "hugs and kisses."

tremely sexual, in the insidious and thinly disguised way I have learned to lecture to teen-agers sexually . . . one of the reasons why they flock to my classes. I can't talk about the novel until it's finished, but then I'll Tell All . . .

Steward heard again from Toklas just before the New Year, who wrote him with the sad news that Basket had finally died in November. Despite her grief, she was glad to hear that Steward was hard at work on yet another novel, and observed: "What a beautiful way to have recommenced—with a gushing flood."

She also shared her most recent news of Francis Rose:

About Francis—the story has become involved as only his can. Frederica has been dragged into it for material and practical reasons—not at all certain that Francis is the father [of Luis]. With her permission Francis has recognized him—giving him French nationality for the moment—but when the boy becomes of age [Francis] wishes him to take Spanish nationality so that he may have the Spanish titles . . . May one ask a leading question—the only one that interests me—When in the course of the story did Francis hear that the boy was his son—from the beginning—soon after—or just when.

The same question fascinated Steward, to the point that in his free time he began a novel about Francis Rose, with a plot featuring the question of Luis's paternity as its central aspect.

Steward continued meanwhile to work with Kinsey. In submitting his 1952 sexual data in January 1953, he included a note about the new wall mural he had put behind his bed, for he had replaced the rough mural of the sailor and his floozy with an elegant new one of two lounging, classically proportioned male nudes in a moment of post-coital relaxation. He suggested to Kinsey that it might be worthy of inclusion in Kinsey's already quite extensive photographic documentation of Steward's apartment. He then added a brief observation about his pornography writing for Lynes: "I've developed quite a correspondence with GPLynes, and we have a little barter arrangement [swapping photos for stories] . . . [But] somehow I don't seem to be able to write to him with the same freedom I wrote to 'B'* down in the old Pure Oil Building." He did not, however, mention that he was just then struggling to finish a first draft of a new novel based on the misadventures of Francis Rose. By coincidence, even as he wrote it, he received a semiliterate letter from Rose himself, one offering Steward all of his private papers, diaries, and "details and drawings," in the event that Steward ever cared to write his biography.[†]

As he struggled with the new novel, Steward continued sending long pornographic accounts of his sexual experiences to Lynes, including an account of a recent *spintriae* Polaroid party that Johnny Leapheart had taken part in while visiting Chicago. Lynes responded enthusiastically:

> I wish I had been there for your latest picture-taking session. Johnny [Leapheart tells me he] had a ball. He gurgled and geysered about it—like one of the famous familiar far-western marvels—but wasn't exactly explicit. I didn't make out just what you photographed, except that you got into the pictures yourself; of course I can imagine a lot. But when (when?) do I get to see this fabulous collection of yours? Its fame spreads. Isn't it (is it?) possible to make duplicates of Polaroid prints? Can't I, as well as our friend in Bloomington, have a set? Only business could take me to Chicago, and these days I have none in that direction. Too expensive just for a jaunt. Too bad.
>
> . . . I see Johnny [Leapheart] now and then, preferably with his friend Bill—what wonderful names they have!—as a combination they're fantastic, irresistible.
>
> . . . Did I (didn't I?) thank you for your lst contribution to the general gayerty of nations, as KAP[‡] calls it . . . It's a good one and rather frightening. My favorite so far is the piece about Wally Kargol. How well I'm getting to know these characters! Keep them coming when their composition doesn't impede and interfere. The rate at which your novel progresses, according to your

---

*"Bob" Churchill, with whom Steward had conducted his "toilet correspondence."
†Though Steward eventually sold all his other letters from Rose, he specifically saved this letter because in it Rose had expressed the wish that Steward write his life story.
‡Katherine Anne Porter, short story writer and novelist, a good friend to Lynes.

report, indicates you're the demon sort of writer. Wish some of my other friends could "turn it out."* God bless . . .

Steward was glad that Lynes had been aroused by the episode featuring Wally Kargol, a former marine he had picked up one summer afternoon in the Indiana sand dunes bordering on Lake Michigan, and whom he had been continuing to see for years. Brutal, muscular, and strongly dominant, Kargol was just the sort of hypermasculine blue-collar worker Steward found most appealing as a sex partner—particularly since Kargol took great pleasure in slapping Steward around, giving him orders, and humiliating him as part of their sex play. In sharing the story of his exploits with Kargol with Lynes, Steward was not only savoring his memory of the experience, but also establishing a commonality of this extreme form of sexual activity with Lynes, one that served to draw the two men closer. Such intimacy was precious to Steward, for he had no friend like Lynes in Chicago, and few people with whom he could ever discuss such things, save Kinsey and his associates. Another note to Lynes suggests in an aside just how lonely (despite his ongoing sexual success) Steward's single life in Chicago actually was:

> The holidays were just other days for me. New Year's Eve found me without plans, and sitting home alone doing a sketch. Just when I was beginning to feel a little sorry for myself and swear at A[lcoholics] A[nonymous] for its proscriptions (but not really . . .), the phone rang—and a charming young man, similarly lonesome on such a night, came over to call. So I cocked a snoot at the old year, and bent to taste firmer delights just as the hour was stroking . . . How pleasant to look down the long vista of 1953 through a fine young pair of extraordinarily hairy legs!

Steward included a new erotic episode in the same envelope, along with a closing observation, half apologetic, that "they come out very quickly and are somewhat repetitious as most pornography should be for its best effect." But since erotic excitement was itself so evanescent, Steward protested that he could not dwell too long on the composition of the pieces. Rather, he told Lynes, "I have to catch them as they come."

---

*The reference is to Lynes's housemate, Glenway Wescott, who had chronic writer's block.

•

Because Lynes was experiencing severe personal and professional difficulties, his correspondence with Steward subsequently became more sporadic; he wrote his next note to Steward on Saint Patrick's Day 1953,
mostly just to say he had found a new apartment and was having a group
of handsome young men around for a party.

Steward, preoccupied with his new novel, responded a month later:

> Now it's your turn to get an apology . . . You can imagine what has
> been [going on] with me—guiding Sir Arthur Lyly* through the
> tortured and ludicrous web that he spun out of himself . . . [The
> novel] is all done right now, finished a few weeks back; and I loathe
> it, it is all I can do to look at it . . . but maybe a cut or two above
> most of the Greenberg† crap . . . thank god it's come to an end. I
> hate writing; it stops almost everything else . . .
>
> . . . except, of course, a modicum of sex . . . that has been
> taking a good deal of time, too: a few *spintriae* with some new
> people, some of them quite nice . . .
>
> There is no news . . . Spring is beginning to come to Ch[ica]
> go, and I'm not sure I'll be able to hold out until term's end; for
> every day, more strong and lovely forearms appear, and the tan be-
> gins to deepen, and baskets bulge beneath the straining paper-thin
> pale-blue denim . . . and with my x-ray eyes I can see the level of
> the compelling white sap churning breast-high in their translucent
> young bodies—ah me, so much denied to one in my position.

Steward also mentioned his novel to Kinsey: "[It's] not a very good
novel, I'm afraid, but at any rate it's a novel, which is quite an accomplishment for me, after a silence that I thought was going to last for the rest of
my unnatural life. [It's so obscene that] I'm gonna have to submit it under
a double pen-name."

By mid-May, Lynes had established himself at his new apartment,
and he wrote Steward,

---

*Lyly was the Francis Rose–like character in *A-Hunting We Will Go!*, a manuscript that, after many
years of heavy revision, would ultimately be published as *Parisian Lives*.
†Greenberg publishers, one of very few houses that dared to publish homosexually themed fiction
and nonfiction during the 1940s and '50s.

I'm glad you came out of the shadows. Stay out a while. It's nice out. I know. I was in them too . . . But all is relatively sunshiny now. The flat is settled enough . . . the end is in sight. Most important, I'm pleased with it . . .

Let me see that novel—how about it—even if you go on taking the dim view . . . Do you go to Yurp this year? If so, surely you'll be coming this way soon.

But Steward responded in mid-June that, due to time and money constraints, he would be traveling west that summer, not east:

That damned novel has taken ALL my fuckin time for months, and yesterday when I finally typed the last word and fell over the machine in exhaustion, I was gladder than I've been in a long time. So today the thing went off into the wild blue and I'd be just as happy if I never heard of it again . . .

And tomorrow morning I'm wild-blueing too, but in the opposite direction—San Francisco, where I'll be until about the first of August. And guess where I'm staying: the Embarcadero YMCA, the "armed services branch"! [It's a] Christian bordello . . . If you happen to know any excitingly evil ones in SF you might send me a name; my address is 166 Embarcadero, SF 5.

The winter partouzie season is closed for me—somehow they never seem to be successful in hot weather. But the last was a howling success of ten, among who were 1) a weightlifter, 22, who looked like a living bas-relief from the Parthenon, 2) a young soldier, paratrooper, with lustrous boots and smoky eyes, 3) a sailor who must have looked like Querelle de Brest, cruel mouth and tangled yellow hair, and 4) a *jeune dur** from the West side, complete with motorcycle boots and leather jacket. My god, is *tout le monde en est*† nowadays?

Come my return, I'll begin sending you little pornograffies again . . . Meanwhile, have a luscious summer and lots of playboys, light and dark and gentle and rough, and send me a note to the western world if the spirit moveth.

---

dur: French slang for "tough guy."
†"Is everybody homosexual?"

Steward had decided to go to San Francisco instead of Paris because of time limitations: he had only a month of vacation, and a transatlantic crossing (with transfers through New York) would have taken him nearly a week. Moreover, he was curious about the Embarcadero YMCA, which was said to be inhabited primarily by men freshly returned from the armed forces and merchant marine, and desperate for sexual release. Nonetheless he regretted that he would not get to see Alice Toklas, who wrote in late June to explain that her silence had been due to a long bout of hepatitis "and to the equally bothersome writing (?) of a 75,000 word cook book—the latter to earn the pennies to pay for the former."* After thanking him for a recent gift, she added, "In return for all your news there is little to offer. Francis has changed his mind about making his son a Spanish duke—Luis is to learn English and go into the British army—first having taken British nationality. They spent the spring in Minarco (the winter on the coast near Toulon) and are now in Madrid. A visit from Luis is announced for early next month. All through this turmoil and restless moving about Francis has done a great deal of work . . . Is he not incredible."

•

After arriving at the Embarcadero YMCA, Steward began a journal using code numbers to describe his sexual activities, and describing those activities circumspectly (and largely in French) just in case the document should be seized by the police. In its opening pages he described his initial disappointment with the Y, for his room was merely "a front cubicle on the 4th floor, very noisy." The elevated Embarcadero Freeway ran right past his only window.

After a few days Steward began to note the many sexual goings-on. "A *choice* motorcyclist in [room] 633," he noted in his diary. "Sailors everywhere! All branches [of the service]!" But with so many other older men camped out in various rooms, the competition for young sailors was keen. Experiencing only a minimum of sexual success, Steward began instead to explore the nearby nightlife: "356 Taylor, [a] club [full] of queens . . . then to Keeno's, a fantastic queer joint, and after [that I] walk[ed] the

*Despite her hepatitis, Toklas had written a superbly entertaining cookbook-memoir, *The Alice B. Toklas Cook Book*, which featured contributions from various friends, including Francis Rose, who was also the book's illustrator. The most notorious of the recipes came from the artist Brion Gysin, whose Haschich Fudge—a concoction of dried fruit and nuts based on an old Moroccan recipe—had called for a liberal dose of *Cannabis sativa*, or marijuana.

long way home down Market, to see the doorways filled with young toughs, available for $$, dangerous—very like Rome . . . very exciting."

In an effort to secure the favors of younger men, he helped several with small loans and in one case paid a week's rent for one named Jeff Brash. Brash then promised to join him that evening at "Chilli's, [a] queer low level joint on Embarcadero." But Brash never showed, "and in the agony ridden hour from 12 to 1, a Gesthsemane like some of Paris," Steward wrote, "my adoration changed from love to hate in one of those dreadful incomplete catharses that only belles can have." His night ended, however, with a pleasant surprise: at 3 a.m., he looked out his window and saw a nude man in a window across the courtyard. Steward made a sign, and the man came down to Steward's room in a towel to have sex.

"A week here," Steward reflected several days later in the hours following a sexual three-way, "seems like a month . . . At [our sunbath] this PM Jeff [Brash] showed [up] with a cute little ventriloquist . . . I took him back to my room (not too willingly) for a tongue bath." That evening, however, Steward's mood darkened after "a *pédé* was arrested this afternoon at the Y—I'm sure it was the one in room 733, a real auntie."

As the days passed Steward learned that another Y resident who had been arrested "got 3–5 years [in prison] for sodomy, poor guy." He then added, "This place is like a disease . . . The same old round of the chase, the orgasm, the farewell. I found nothing tonight, being always so slow and timid in my cruising . . . It's unthinkable that I may be here until Aug 1st and never get one sailor."

Despite the cold and damp of the San Francisco summer, he slowly settled into a routine of napping, sunbathing, and sketching between assignations. The twenty-ninth was particularly successful; he scored with an air force sergeant in the afternoon, then in the evening had sex with Johnny Clark, a handsome young man in room 730, and after that had sex again with a new arrival, Edgar Patterson. Since Clark and Patterson liked each other, the three subsequently met up for a night in the bars; the following day they hiked to an area under the Golden Gate Bridge, "a secluded wind-broken sandy stretch, [where] in a Whitman idyll [we all had sex together.]" Steward would later use the memory of this afternoon of sex *en plein air* in his first Phil Andros novel, *My Brother, the Hustler.*

Steward now began to notice the finer points of etiquette between the Y's resident homosexuals. "In the hierarchy of *pédés* here," he wrote

on July 2, "the mark of friendship is 'Do you go to dinner with him?'—
Whereas the blow job means *rien* . . . and comes first."

Just as in Paris, no sooner had Steward established intimacy with a
man than he began to find the fellow tiresome. Patterson was the first to
be crossed off his list. But when handsome Johnny Clark slipped out of
Steward's grasp, the loss caused him real anguish: "Of course, no one
here can hold anyone," he confided in his journal, "but this is awful."
Moreover, because the Y was full of uniformed sailors, Steward found
himself in a state of permanent sexual arousal, and as the weeks
passed, the condition left him exhausted. "Saw a fantastic thing down
by the piers," he noted one afternoon, "—two sailors standing watch for
passersby while a third went down on a fourth. Wanted to bust in, but
[was] afraid." Needing to give expression to his state of sexual overstimu-
lation, he went back to his room and painted a detailed watercolor of the
scene.

Seeking new thrills, he convinced a friend named Fritz Christenson
to pimp for him, for the idea of being a whore in the service of another
man was a fantasy that had captivated him for years. On the Fourth of
July, Christenson delighted Steward by sending up "a sailor, a little pudgy
one . . . But at any rate, a sailor. [I had him] twice." After another unsuc-
cessful night out cruising the Paper Doll, the 356, Keeno's, the Black Cat,
and Chilli's, Steward had Christenson pimp for him again, and was "wakened ungodly early to go to Fritz' room to do a bald mechanic." That evening, over dinner with Edgar Patterson, Steward found himself growing
weary and disgusted with himself, and noted that he "grew teary over the
prospect of our life . . . [It may have been] very adolescent, but I'm happy
I can still feel about something."

Cruising, Steward found, made him increasingly anxious and lonely,
for there was very little tenderness in the encounters and absolutely no
continuity. He was therefore delighted two nights later to note in his diary
that "at 12:30 Tommy Tomlin (real name: Emmet) called, to stay all
night . . . It was a very Whitman thing, 'his arm around me—that night I
was happy.'"* Tomlin proved a charming dinner companion as well as bed-

---

*". . . the one I love most lay sleeping by me under the same cover in / the cool night, / In the stillness
in the autumn moonbeams his face was inclined toward me, / And his arm lay lightly around my
breast—and that night I was happy." (Walt Whitman, *Leaves of Grass*, Book V, Calamus, "When I
Heard at the Close of the Day.")

mate, and in the days that followed, Steward took a great liking to him. Apart from having sex with him and dinner with him, Steward sketched him repeatedly, and described him in his diary as a "charming elfboy."

Even as yet another man was arrested at the YMCA for homosexual activity, Steward could not help writing in his diary about the elation he felt in being there. "SF induces a lyric mood in me," he wrote, "a feeling of high destinies working out. My perceptions, reactions increased. Sense of wonder and freedom." That feeling of exhilaration reached a high point on the fourteenth, which he described as "one of the really perfect days of my life . . . Johnny Clark took me in his car to Twin Peaks, Sea Cliff, Cliff House, Gold[en] Gate Park, [the] de Young Museum, Sausalito, Stinson Beach (for a wonderful hour in the sun)—radio music, the mountains, vistas, the sea, Coit Tower—everything. I had a feeling of climax, riding along nearly naked in the car with him. Superb."

One trick now followed another, and in the journal Steward did little to distinguish among them. There were, however, some emotional ups and downs: on the eighteenth, he watched two young air force recruits horse around affectionately, and was moved almost to tears; on the nineteenth, he took a day trip to Lake Temescal with two buddies and gave way to melancholy; on the twentieth, it was "dinner alone (Trocadero [restaurant]) . . . In the evening, befuddled by poor lighting, went to [room] 643 to bring succor to some poor old ex-seaman, and I *do* mean *old*." July 21 brought "good mail from Kinsey . . . asking about [my] Emb[arcadero] record . . . and one from Julien Green, [and] also [one from] Jorge da Silva with porny excerpts from his journal." The letters cheered him up—even though Kinsey had taken Steward to task for his lax record-keeping at the YMCA, writing,

> Why on earth haven't you kept a day-by-day record for us which would be something permanent instead of mere memory which persons connected with the research may have, but which cannot be utilized in a specific record until we get it down in black and white. If you do not have the record, I should like to get some hours of your time to get the specific data when you get home.

Steward wrote back that he would be pleased and flattered to make such a contribution to the Institute for Sex Research, and added by way of explanation that "this time—largely because I really had the intention of gathering material for another novel, a kind of h[omosexual] 'Grand Hotel,'* I've been typing up voluminous notes on the various *modi operandi* and the personalities here. I have about ten pages already typed, and some five or six thousand words . . . I've also done about twelve or thirteen sketches, all 'inspired' by Embarcadero events, and some accomplished with the assistance of willing posers (or *poseurs?*) that you may be interested in seeing." He went on to note that, out of frustration with Morihien,

> I started a rumor with Julien Green and another friend in Paris, to the effect that someone in New York had done a translation which was going to be published and bootlegged in this country (of *Querelle de Brest*, of course) and that I didn't want M. Morihien to think it was mine. It may be a way of goosing Morihien along—again it may not. All's fair, etc, and those French are so furtive anyway. Besides, it just *might* be that Ben Abramson† *would* pirate it here and publish it in this country; I must introduce myself to him when I get back.

Steward had no intention of actually publishing a bootleg *Querelle*, but Kinsey, deeply alarmed by the idea, responded, "May I save you the prospect of considerable difficulty by advising you not to have business dealings with Ben Abrahamsen [*sic*]. We can talk that over when I come to Chicago."

On the twenty-second, Steward put on his leather jacket and went out for another night of cruising at the Paper Doll and the Black Cat, but no one was interested in him, and he came home alone. The twenty-third was his forty-fourth birthday, and he sank into his usual birthday depression. On the twenty-fourth, he tricked with a straight-looking railroad worker who turned out to have a male lover; on the twenty-fifth he participated in two three-ways. On the twenty-seventh, just a few days before the end of his vacation, he got up "bright and early, finding my way to

---

Grand Hotel: a well-known Hollywood film of 1932, which had described various melodramas taking place within a luxury hotel in Berlin.
†Ben Abramson (1898–1955), proprietor of the Argus Bookshop in Chicago and a well-known dealer in rare and used books.

SF State College (both branches) and arrang[ing] an interview [there] tomorrow. A brand new campus—new, modern, colorful buildings— sunlight—my God, that's where I should be teaching!"

Upon his return to the YMCA he wrote: "I find my mood changing . . . For a while I thought it would be amusing to have two [men] a day in July . . . [But] that no longer seems important . . . [I have undergone] a psychic shift [away from sex]."

On his last day in San Francisco, Steward received a note from his former army lover, Bill Collins, inviting him down to La Jolla—but it was too late: the man who had once meant so much to him was simply too far away to visit. Similarly, he had never gotten around to seriously interviewing in the Bay Area for a teaching job. Steward's sex vacation was over, and he was heading back to Chicago with very little to show for it apart from a diary full of sex records and the outline for a sex novel based on all he had seen and heard and done.

The San Francisco journal ends abruptly. In his later tally for Kinsey, Steward noted that in his forty-two days there, he had had sex sixty-three times with thirty-eight new people. In the months that followed, he would attempt to draft up the many small dramas and cruising rituals he had witnessed at the Embarcadero YMCA into a novel, but it never got further than an outline—one he later donated to the Institute for Sex Research. Such a novel would of course have been unpublishable, and Steward knew it, so he abandoned it.

Even so, the story of his summer was not over, for Steward received two substantial letters that autumn. He sent them on to Kinsey in late November of 1953, and Kinsey, after reading them, placed them into Steward's Embarcadero journal as an addendum. The first of the letters had been dictated by Emmet "Tommy" Tomlin, the "charming elfboy" in whose arms Steward had passed the night in a Whitmanesque idyll, to his friend Bob Newton. The second came from Newton himself. Newton's letter explained that shortly after Steward's departure, Tomlin had been arrested and charged with section 288-a of the California penal code— Newton's discreet way of noting that Tomlin had been arrested for having sex with a minor. It went on to explain that when Tomlin had been unable to raise the five hundred dollars bail money, he had been thrown in jail. He then spent seven weeks waiting for his case to come up. The trial was to take place sixty days later and last three weeks; as a result, Tomlin would have spent four months in jail even before the case against him was decided.

The letter from Tomlin pleaded with Steward to help in any way he could, for Tomlin had neither money nor legal contacts. Since Tomlin himself was not much older than a minor, he was presumably being threatened with rape and brutalization by his fellow inmates on a day-to-day basis. Unable to send a letter directly to Steward from prison, he had dictated it instead to Newton, who had sent it from outside.

"Charming elfboy," Steward had noted of Tomlin in the Stud File. "Big head, perfect small body. Affectionate, sucked nipples, liked me. Made a sketch of him, want to go on knowing him." But from his apartment in Chicago, Steward could do nothing more on Tomlin's behalf than to share the story of his misfortune with Kinsey, and to write the young man a note of consolation.

9

"A kind of obscene diary, actually"

Steward had to start teaching a five-week summer course as soon as he returned to Chicago, and in the effort to do so he paid little attention to what at first seemed merely a summer cold or flu. By the third week of school, however, he was running a fever, was unable to keep down food, and his skin began to itch. He was deeply tanned from sunbathing in San Francisco, but when the whites of his eyes turned bright yellow, his doctor immediately diagnosed his illness as "jaundice." Steward had, in fact, contracted hepatitis, and though he was able to avoid hospitalization by living for a month on nothing more than a sugar-water solution made out of Karo syrup, the condition left him entirely exhausted.

When a gossipy letter from Lynes arrived that September, Steward took a month before responding, explaining about his jaundice,

> I resisted the hospital and went on working; it was quite a drag, and I'm glad it's all over now. But San Francisco, my lad, was a marvel . . . Sex in Chicago's a tired old thing with little excitement of the chase—but there's a kind of frenzied wonderful excitement surrounding it out there . . . I stayed at the "most notorious Y in the States" (says Kinsey) a kind of Christian bordello, and I am full of tales about it . . . All in all, I don't know when I've had a more sucksexful summer.

He went on to give Lynes the latest news about his fiction writing, which unfortunately was not good, for his novel had been rejected by

Greenberg Publishers. Greenberg was at that moment the only house in the United States specifically interested in publishing homosexually themed fiction:

My novel is [now] in the hands of an agent, Greenberg being afraid to publish it although thinking it publishable. I take it they were afeard because of the three lawsuits in which they are involved in southern states over the publication of *The Divided Path*** and *Quatrefoil*.† I am not sanguine about anyone's taking it, however, this side of the Atlantic. For the next winter I'd like to do a kind of "Grand Hotel" about the Embarcadero Y, but am not sure the subject could ever be cleared up enough to be written in a saleable non-porno book.

Steward had taken a jocular and dismissive tone about his hepatitis, but the illness was serious enough that it permanently affected his sexual desires and practices. He later noted to a friend that "an old-fashioned doctor got me through it [on Karo syrup] . . . Needless to say, I never rimmed anyone after that." Although Steward had been preoccupied with sexual hygiene since his early bout with syphilis, he was of course unable to eliminate the risk of various forms of sexually transmitted infection, and the severity of this particular illness had been a sobering reminder of the many grave physical risks he was now taking almost daily in his endless pursuit of sex.

Lynes, meanwhile, had been struggling for some time with a much graver illness, for he had cancer. In late November he responded sympathetically to his "dear old poor old Sam" that "there's scarcely an ache or pain I haven't had . . . in the lesser not-lethal categories. I have 20-odd kinds of pills which I take or don't take, on discretion. Maybe . . . I'll start feeling well again. Maybe I've already started . . . But what of your book? What about it? And what about your unacademic life? I've been expecting, though surely am undeserving of, new chapters

---

*The Divided Path, by Nial Kent (pseudonym of William LeRoy Thomas), tells the story of a young man growing up in a small town and discovering his homosexuality through his feelings for his heterosexual best friend. The book was published (by Greenberg) in 1949.

†*Quatrefoil* (1950), by James Barr (a pseudonym for James Barr Fugate). For more on this novel, see pages 108–109.

of the San Francisco saga . . . Be big about these things. Live big and tell all."

Steward was troubled by Lynes's illness and disappointed by the rejection of his novel by Greenberg, but otherwise had a relatively quiet fall. During that time, however, he came across a local newspaper article describing how a Chicago judge, John T. Dempsey, had been seized and roughed up by two policemen while walking his dog in Humboldt Park on Chicago's northwest side. The policemen afterward claimed Dempsey had seemed to them to be molesting park visitors, but Steward, recognizing it as part of a well-known shakedown racket, immediately wrote Dempsey otherwise, hoping that in his position as judge Dempsey might be able to do something about a situation that had by now become all too common among Steward's friends. As he wrote Dempsey,

> A man walking alone is considered fair game for the police, who either singly or in pairs—or working in collaboration with a district police branch—accuse him of homosexuality. The man is taken to the station, not booked, but terrified psychologically: his identity is learned, and then the sergeant suggests that he "talk things over with the arresting officer" who may or may not be in plainclothes. The arresting officer then suggests that for the payment of some money—from fifty to $750—depending on his estimate of how much the man has—all charges will be dropped. Usually the frightened victim will pay to avoid scandal, even if he be completely innocent . . . Unwittingly you have thus had opened before you a situation under which we have all suffered for a long time. Is it too much to hope that out of your brush against it will come some eventual good?

Steward had himself recently attempted to do something about the racket when a fellow professor of English literature and journalism at DePaul had been shaken down in just such a manner. Professor Art Lennon was a charming, charismatic, closeted professional colleague who had attended at least one of the sex parties at Steward's apartment.* Steward later gave the details of Lennon's ordeal in an oral history of Chicago:

---

*Lennon appears, masked, in Steward's Polaroid sex albums; Steward pasted Lennon's yearbook photo in the album beside the sex Polaroids in which he appears.

[Art] had cruised a plain clothes cop in the Chicago Public Library, and had been taken over to the station in Grant Park, and scared to death, and shaken down for three or five hundred dollars . . . [So I] call[ed] [George Reginato] . . . And [he] said . . . I'll ask my old man [to help.] So . . . [he came back to me and] said well, I know this captain in Summerdale station and he owes my father a favor, so I'll go talk to him and spread a few bucks around. And he did. The captain went down to the Summerdale Police Station and just raised hell. He said you have put your finger on the wrong guy this time, and if you ever do it again to any of my friends, I'm going to come down here and there'll be badges flying all over the place. So [Lennon] got [off] scot-free, except [that Lennon then] with typical bitch perversity went out the following Saturday and got stinking drunk in the same gay bars on Clark Street that he had been to [before], and of course the cops were laying for him. And they picked him up, took him out, and beat the hell out of him, you know, put him in the hospital. Ah, he couldn't do anything about that because he'd been warned . . . to stay out of sight for the next month.*

Steward's concern was not just on Lennon's behalf; after all, he himself was now enormously vulnerable to blackmail, for if police were to enter his home, his entire professional life would come to an end, and he would probably face prison time, too. Among the hundreds of sex photographs in his apartment—all of which were technically illegal to possess—many featured young men who might well have been below the age of consent. Steward had in fact been steadily involved with a sexually experienced sixteen-year-old named Bobby Krauss since March of 1953. In his zeal for record-keeping, Steward had kept Krauss's name, age, and other detailed statistics and particulars of their many encounters on a card in the Stud File, and also written his name on the back of several of the Polaroids featuring him. Thus, even as Steward disparaged Lennon's "bitch perversity," he recognized a similar streak of perversity within himself: a desire—conscious or not—to self-destruct.

January brought a letter from Alice Toklas commiserating with Steward about his hepatitis, since she, too, had just recovered from it. She also

---

*Steward later fictionalized Lennon's ordeal in his short story "Pig in a Poke."

sent more news of Francis Rose: "Francis has done some really beautiful line drawings for [my cookbook] and a dust cover [too] . . . He and Frederica are reconciled. She has bought the small top story of an old house in Ajaccio overlooking the bay and is building a small studio on the roof for Francis who in return seems to have offered the sacrifice (?) of renouncing his son Luis."

She went on to observe, "Without any unfaithfulness to [your sister] or to legendary Emmy [Curtis] isn't it time you found an Egeria*—what Thornton might call a serpent of the Wabash."

Steward was moving further and further from any possibility of marriage, however. Having entirely ceased sexual relations with Emmy Curtis in 1950, he had gone on to develop a network of male sexual partners, pickups, and prospects far more extensive than any he had maintained as a younger man. One of the most regular contacts was the former serviceman Bob Berbich, a married man about whom Steward recorded, quite typically,

> [Berbich] stopped in briefly around 9 to "invite" me over [to the Sun Times building]. We drove [to] the lower level to the parking lot south of the Trib[une Building], and there in a whirl of snow and reflected whiteness, I had him again. [He] made two large splotches on my black overcoat; I noticed them after I got on the El at the Mart—and wore my badge home proudly, reminding myself of an entry or two in Seblon's diary in *Querelle de Brest*.

Immersing himself in a world of increasingly masochistic fantasy sex, feeling far closer to the dream world of *Querelle* than to the everyday world of academe, Steward was now seriously ignoring his work at DePaul and entering yet another period of extremely erratic behavior. In mid-February, after another visit by Johnny Leapheart, he wrote Lynes, "You will say I've been working, and I wish you were right—but I suddenly reached one of those complete and terrifying dead-ends with my writing . . . my invention has failed me completely . . . [and] it's stopped everything else in me—except, of course, me 'love life' . . ."

---

*In Roman mythology, Egeria was the Roman who inspired and led Numa Pompilius, the king who succeeded Romulus; she existed both as his goddess and as his wife.

Leaving aside all questions of his career and his fiction-writing, Steward went on to describe his sex-party photography, for Lynes had been fascinated by Johnny Leapheart's description of the Polaroid collection:

> It was a lot of fun with Johnny, and we did take several px to add to the collection, which grows apace. It's really a kind of obscene diary, actually; there's no art connected with my picture taking—and I rarely use anything but flashbulbs (so they're all pretty flat) but Dr. K has thought them interesting and copied one entire volume, and will get the other one (he says he wants it) when it's full. I see no reason at all why you shouldn't copy some of them if you would want them, but my face appears freely in almost all (well, a great many) so you would please have to be discreet. They stimulate some people, but wouldn't you—and I must confess—they leave me fairly cold.

A month later, he wrote Lynes again with more news of his erotic, artistic, and pornographic activities:

> Ask me what I have been doing. Lotsa, lotsa . . . "Thor" (a corporation of three persons selling those sex drawings under this silly name) has taken four of my drawings of motorcyclists and will shortly splash them across the country, advertising in various [publications] like *Tomorrow's Man*, etc. I've re-drawn the "Motorcycle Pickup" series of 12 obscenities (you know it, certainly—the motorcyclist and the farm boy in the barn?) to suit my own tastes, and then was struck with the happy thought of writing a story to go with the 12 pictures—and I am sending you a copy [of the story] herewith, hoping your hard heart will melt. Then, an addition: I decided to make another *Reigen*,* a *Ronde* with it—long-term project, 8 episodes, 8 times 12 illustrations. I've been

---

Der Reigen, by Arthur Schnitzler, also known as *La Ronde* or *Hands Around*, was a privately printed novel of 1903, and later (more famously) a play first produced in 1920. The play features ten dialogues (by five men and five women) about the interlinked sexual activities of each of the characters. Steward had seen Max Ophuls's film version (in French, starring Anton Walbrook and Simone Signoret) in the summer of 1952.

also adding dozens of Polaroid pictures to my collection, am well into volume III at the moment. And I have shelved my novel about Sir Rose, at least temporarily—everyone said it was indecent and libelous. I guess I'm just ahead of my time. Morihien writes thru an intermediary that he will willingly transfer the rights to *Querelle* to any American publisher who wants 'em.*
But try to find, to find.

The day after writing this letter, Steward began to consider another tattoo, this time an extremely large one, describing his rationale for doing so in a journal he had begun keeping at Kinsey's suggestion:

I simply must have a rose in the center of my chest, whether or not I have finished my sixth hundredth contact—this being an early self-prohibition† to help me resist too many tattoos, for the lust is in me now . . . Why not be honest and admit that I'm narcissistic, even with this old body, and this combines with my exhibitionism, plus a hope that it will make me sexually attractive, or tougher than I am.

Even as Steward was becoming increasingly interested in tattoos and tattooing, Lynes wrote him in early April to urge him on in his erotic writing: "The [motorcyclist] story you sent—oh, it has had a success! . . . More, much more, please. Make it soon. G[lenway] W[escott] was appreciative too; he went so far as to borrow and to copy it. Ditto Neel Bate, who, as you probably know, was responsible for that series in the first place."‡ Lynes then went on to give Steward news of his own, for as his illness had progressed, he had been forced to think of a future home for his photographic studies of the male nude: "I am, it appears, giving all my negs of nudes into the custody of the good doctor [Kinsey], giving him

---

*This letter is missing from Steward's papers.
†Steward had decided, after his first few tattoos, to allow himself one new tattoo for each hundredth sexual contact.
‡Neel Bate, also known as "Blade," was a former merchant seaman turned erotic illustrator living in New York. His series of illustrations of a farmboy and a motorcyclist having sex in a barn during a rainstorm had been widely circulated for several years by the time Steward created his own illustrated version of the story. Bate and Lynes were friends.

(them) permanent possession eventually* . . . I've been lazy or uninspired in the picture making dept [recently]; not for lack of subjects, either."

Despite Lynes's enthusiasm for Steward's sex Polaroid and erotic fiction projects, Steward found himself suddenly overwhelmed by an interest in tattooing, and in his distraction he began networking throughout Chicago to find out more about it. Through a local character named Tattooed Larry, he gained an insider's view of tattooing and the tattooing community. During one such conversation with Larry, Steward seized upon an erotic image that would change his life forever. As he wrote in the journal he was keeping for Kinsey,

> [Tattooed] Larry . . . said [we should go] up to Milwaukee on a Sunday that was between paydays at Great Lakes—for if it were right after payday, Dietzel's shop was full of "sailors waiting in line" for a tattoo. He said it twice—and then it hit me. That idea of sailors waiting in line has been the longest-enduring, most-potently-effective fantasy of my whole life . . . I have always been powerfully stimulated by the idea of a line of naked young men, preferably sailors, waiting in line for me to go down on them. Pictures of young men in line have always excited me. I have several . . . And in the small book of [fantasies I drew for Kinsey] I [made] a similar sketch in inks.
>
> Sailors in line, waiting! How odd that this should be my strongest fantasy. I am reminded of Julien Green's reaction to the painting "The Bearers of Evil Tidings"† . . . I long for the day when—in my own tattoo shop in San Francisco on a Sunday morning, I can peek between the curtains, and find my own waiting room filled with nonchalant tanned young men, smoking, chatting—laughing . . . and waiting for me to leave my mark upon them.

*The question then of what to do with Lynes's negatives and prints of male nudes was a troubling one, since the works were considered obscene—and so illegal to sell or possess. More than 1,700 negatives of male nudes (and nearly 600 original prints) were eventually donated to the Institute for Sex Research.

†As a young man, Green had seen Lecomte de Nuoy's painting *The Bearers of Evil Tidings* in the Musée de Luxembourg. He felt a lasting erotic response to the work, in which several barely clothed black slaves have just been put to death by a muscular and fiercely handsome Pharaoh (see illustration 315b of Rappoport's *History of Egypt*, available on the Web at www.gutenberg.org/files/17330/17330-h/v10c.htm).

Steward now began to investigate tattooing more closely, enrolling in a correspondence course and researching possible injunctions by the church against tattooing. On April 24 he wrote, "I went to the library [at DePaul] . . . not a word in the *Catholic Encyclopedia*, and not a word in the index to St. Thomas. It looks as if I were disgustingly safe on that score." A week later, he added,

> Without too much alarm, and yet with a kind of hypnotized immobility, I watch the progress of the tattoo complex in me. I find that I think about it much of the time during the day, and that I dream of it almost every night. A recurring theme in these almost-nightmares is that I have great huge ones on my body, and experience a kind of wild regret, a feeling of being lost, at having them there without any possibility of removal. The urge to put another on my self, and yet another, comes on me like the urge to go out and cruise . . . so strong you feel almost choked beneath it . . .

Just as he had thrown himself into sex after quitting drinking, now Steward had begun focusing upon a new compulsion: tattooing. Both tattooing and being tattooed seemed to Steward highly erotic. The horror of being indelibly marked upon the flesh—or, better yet, of administering that mark upon a pure and innocent other—had utterly seized his imagination. In a letter written at the end of May, Steward wrote Lynes:

> [I have been suffering from] a vast ennui, a dreadful *Weltschmerz*— well, not so much Schmerz as just plain *Trägheit**—and so many other things to do—sixteenyearolds, sailors, truckdrivers, big ones all—and a coupla little ones. [Most particularly there was] a tattooed boy, a sailor—ears pierced for rings—his small hard body lay on the bed in the dusky near-dark, the dragon curling upon his belly, the mermaid long on his thigh, the eagle wings touching the collar bone on each side, the nippled eyes staring unwinking through the gloom. In a kind of ecstasy of disbelief at what I saw,

---

*Trägheit is German for "inertia"; *schmertz* for "sorrow"; and *Weltschmerz* (world sorrow) describes a state of general sorrow or pessimism over the condition of the world.

almost afraid to touch these designs, I at last ran my tongue along the length of the great dragon, beginning low at his tail almost within the bramble patch of pubic hair, and running in bending up-curves towards his right nipple. I sucked the unwinking eyes drawn upon the nipples, and licked the two sharks above his armpits, and then I pointed the arrowhead (on the head of his cock) straight down my throat until he came . . . and then relaxed, but pleasantly co-operative, he lay on his side and took hold of my cock and gently masturbated me, while my fascinated fingers, hypnotized, fled back and forth over the eagle's wings, the dragon's head on his chest and belly. Here, at long last, was the essence of the Sailor, his motions sure and deft. Here was the hand that had knotted the rope and spliced it, the Sailor who knew the far suns and seas, the bamboo huts of savages and the stone lacework of Indian castles, crystal pools and sand of Persia, white columns against dark blue Greek skies, the golden suns and fountains of red-walled Rome. Here was the distillate of the Sailor— dark, romantic, strange, bizarre and sexual under his tattoos, his muscles working to bring me pleasure, his body close curving . . . The old professor exploded in a lyric burst of semen, star-sprinkled . . .

And now how did I ever get into *that*? Enclosed please find a business card,* the which I trust you will hand to a sailor in Times Square, headed west. Some fun with all this tattoo business— real sexual. Sad-mashy.† Hooboy!

Lynes wrote back at the end of June, using a printed photographic negative of a male nude as his typing paper, and working the image into the text of the letter: "Do you do the tattooing, anything anywhere? For example just here?‡ And—you do neglect me—where is the typescript of

*Steward had printed up business cards advertising his services as a tattoo artist and providing his home phone number.

†"Sad-mashy," like "sadie-maisie," is a slang way of referring to "sadomasochism." (Steward had long known and used both expressions.)

‡The original letter is printed on a negative print of a young man, naked except for socks, viewed from the back as he lies on his stomach with legs curled up behind him, ankles crossed. The words "just here" are centered on the buttocks. Steward later described it to Lynes as "quite the loveliest letter I ever received." (Steward to Lynes, August [?] 1954.)

the sequel to the motorcycle story you promised? What other goodies? Alibis enough. Now I want action."

Glenway Wescott (who to this point had never actually met Steward) came to Chicago shortly thereafter,* and later described the meeting with Steward to his biographer in a way that makes clear not only Wescott's gossipy habits of exaggeration, but also (and more important) just how shocking Steward's lifestyle then seemed, even to a man of considerable sexual experience. As Wescott told his biographer,

> Sam Steward . . . was a smallish, lean, wiry, Irish-looking man . . . I would have liked a tattoo from him but I didn't trust him, he was such a sadomasochistic character. He [lived in] a small ground-floor apartment, with one small room and one immensely large room, and a tiny kitchen and bathroom. The walls above the bookshelves and the ceiling were covered with scenes of intercourse. There were penises this big and people that big fornicating all over the walls, painted by bad amateur artists of his acquaintance.† Hair-raising from the point of view of a cop coming in, you know, who would then want to know what all these boxes and file cabinets were. And scrapbooks. All over the walls were pornographic photographs. And furthermore he had a photographic journal of his sex life, which he showed me. It was the most astonishing thing I'd ever known anybody to have. He had a camera . . . and he had pictures of himself making love to every type of person you can imagine, and especially young boys. He had their names and their addresses and he told me who they

*Wescott has in fact conflated his three separate meetings with Steward in Chicago in this interview, for he visited again in July 1956 and in April (or May) of 1958. During the July 1956 visit he might have visited the tattoo cage at the Sportland Arcade, but only during the 1958 visit would he have been able to visit the tattoo parlor he describes in the interview (Steward opened it in November 1956). However, only on this first visit (and not the second or third) did he see the interior of Steward's (old) apartment, which was highly decorated with erotic drawings and murals. By the time of the second visit (during which Steward purposefully avoided inviting Wescott to his home), he had already moved uptown to a new second-floor apartment.

†Unlike the elegant mural of two men over the Murphy bed (which had been created by Steward himself, and which remained on the wall for as long as Steward kept the apartment), these wall drawings had apparently been scrawled crudely in advance of a sex party (Steward to Lynes, December 19, 1953). Steward had done something similar in the late 1940s, judging from descriptions of a similar mural in the toilet correspondence. Steward kept a Polaroid of the later "rough" mural.

were . . . I said, "I can't remember such a courageous man as you. It doesn't shock me a bit, and it gives me great pleasure to look at it all. But it alarms me. Aren't you running a frightful risk?" He answered, "Of course, I wouldn't dare do it, except that my dream all my life has been to be in prison, and to be fucked morning, noon and night by everyone, and beaten." I said, "If I hadn't seen this I wouldn't believe it, because what you say is so extreme, and you're so rational and intelligent and gentle and cultivated, and not the least bit cruel yourself, I should think. You wouldn't want to hurt anybody, and you're so vigorous, I can't imagine you letting someone hurt you." I felt really frightened. And all through dinner he had been talking Jean Genet talk, about how thrilling it would be to be in prison . . . He was the most extreme masochist that Kinsey ever found.

While Steward was by no means "the most extreme masochist that Kinsey ever found," Wescott was nonetheless correct in his observation that Steward had set himself on an extremely self-destructive course. Indeed, during that very spring of 1954, Steward began to tattoo by appointment out of the very same highly pornographic apartment—hoping as much to seduce the men who came to him as to build himself a small business. He began actively visiting the Great Lakes base a short while later in his search for business, writing Kinsey in late May, "I go out to Great Lakes every Friday night under the auspices of the Red Cross, in one of their buses, to play chess with the poor sick sailor lads in the hospital—and of course I leave a paper trail of [my business] cards everywhere . . . If this keeps up long enough, I'm bound to get a call sooner or later." In his free time, he continued to create more homoerotic visual material with which to decorate his home, adding in his note to Kinsey, "[I] have lotsa new photographs to show you, and Thor has bought eight pictures of mine to sell—they are just now being advertised."

Steward sent one of his new tattooing business cards to Alice Toklas with the suggestion she show it to Francis Rose, for Rose had long been passionate about sailors. She declined to do so, however, explaining that "*entre nous* I have engaged to keep him fairly respectable—he has cost his wife too much—probably in [both] tears and dinero."

Shortly thereafter Steward wrote Lynes to apologize for not having sent any more stories, and he explained that his new tattooing business was partly to blame:

> Yes, I know—I have been delinquent in typing off that second episode to follow the motorcycle story I sent you, but there's been so many things . . . Maybe in California there'll be time. I know that last year, despite all the s-x-l encounters there (hush, hush!) I got sixteen watercolors done—who can say what I'll accomplish in the six weeks I'll be [at the Embarcadero YMCA] this summer? . . . It'll be nice to see young Mr. Leapheart there [too] . . .
>
> There ain't no news, really. The summer has been sexually fruitful, and still I'm not sure it was fruit-filled as jam-filled.* Such lovely trade—ah *le bon dieu* is good! Such youth, such truck drivers! Part of it arises from the tattooing business, and much of it comes from my following the old "link" method of meeting new ones. That's why, once a year, I like to flex my cruising muscles in a place like the Embarcadero Y, where the competition is keen and cut-throat and high, and he who hesitates gets nothing but dregs.

•

As in 1953, Steward kept a detailed journal of his 1954 San Francisco summer vacation, but this time he did so with Kinsey strongly in mind as his ideal reader, making detailed notations about each and every sexual encounter. Even so, all did not go immediately as planned. Shortly after arriving on August 5, he noted:

> From the very first moment of setting foot in the [YMCA] this summer, [I] could tell that something had changed. There was a kind of furtiveness everywhere: people were quiet, there was no loud talk of any kind, and everyone walked with eyes almost painfully (and certainly maidenly) downcast. Perhaps there was an explanation for the surface dullness in the set of "House Rules" that old Pruneface handed me—saying in effect that since they wanted to establish a "Christian atmosphere" here in this Y, that absolutely

---

*Jam: a pun on the homosexual slang term "jam," describing a heterosexually identified man who will sometimes have sex with other men.

no one would ever be allowed up on the residence floors . . . and that even among residents there would be no visiting after 11:30, and that if anyone were caught loitering in the halls or toilets he would be asked to give up his residence . . . I don't see why they didn't simply say "we're trying to get rid of the homos here," and let it go at that. And they certainly seem to have succeeded.

Three days later he noted, "The place is like a tomb . . . I might as well face it: I 'operate' better at home in Chicago, with my clientele, than I do anywhere else in the world. I think about sending a note to Tommy Tomlin [who is now out of prison] but do nothing about it." He did, however, begin contacting other friends from the year before, including an acquaintance named Audrien Bingleman, who soon became a close and trusted confidant.

Through Bingleman, Steward learned that "the reason for the quiet at the Y . . . [is that] a sailor committed suicide there, and that called the military police in, who questioned everyone on the sailor's floor. The old-time residents said that there was a lot of h[omosexual]-goings-on . . . and the MP's went to the management and said looky here . . . clean it up. It's a logical story . . . B[ingleman] told me to move to the Golden Gate Y— and Monday night when I see Johnny Leapheart, I'll ask [Johnny] what he thinks about it."

Leapheart was in fact already staying at the Golden Gate YMCA. The next night Steward called for him there, and found that, unlike at the Embarcadero, at the Golden Gate "one simply went up in the elevator without difficulty. [Johnny] was bronze and naked under the silk lounging robe, smooth as satin and twice as animated. We had a lovely session of dalliance and innocent evil . . . After that we dressed and had a lovely large meal . . . and . . . he walked me clear home to the gate of the Reformed church of the Puritan Brotherhood. I couldn't ask him up—and was tired anyway."

Steward then attempted to move into the Golden Gate YMCA, but when the desk clerk discovered he was attempting to move in from the Embarcadero YMCA, he was denied a room. Steward then realized that he had been recognized and identified as a homosexual. "Baffled, bewildered, and feeling somewhat as if I had leprosy, I went out into the street . . . This kind of thing carries a shock with it," Steward wrote in his journal. "I felt (with the usual h-guilt complex) that something had been found out about me . . . I went around the corner to the YMCA hotel for men and women on Turk Street, only to discover I had been blacklisted at that place [too] . . . I began to toy with the idea of returning at once to Chicago."

It took Steward "24 hours to get over the shock of the Y episode." As he tried to decide what to do next, he registered at a small, noisy family hotel called the Roosevelt, where he then spent a "dull week of suspended animation" having no sex at all. Finally, and after much searching, he found a place that would accommodate his sexual needs: "the 'bargain basement' of the Stanford Court Apartments (Hotel) at 901 California Avenue, corner of Powell, right on the top of Nob Hill, next to the Fairmont and the Mark Hopkins." There, according to Steward, "for $50 a month, you live in a plush little room with wall-to-wall carpeting, quiet corridors, community showers—and absolutely no surveillance of any kind! *Vraiment*, they expect you to be queer—no kidding, and said to one complainer [about all the sexual activity] (he was a desk clerk at the St. Francis) that they really didn't very much care at all what went on in the showers." The ejection from the YMCA had, however, left Steward deeply shaken. Describing it in his journal as a "minor Gethsemane," he went on to note that Bingleman had been a huge reassurance to him during that difficult time. "Almost every afternoon I went over and lay on his roof in the sun, and [there, with him] my spirit began to heal . . . My shell is paperthin."

Steward was much happier in his new place of residence. He later described the Stanford Court Apartments in his Phil Andros fiction as being "for men only—rooms with community showers and toilets . . . a great place for the gay ones to stay when they came to town. The freedom was so nice and the management so liberal that a lot of people paid for the whole month willingly [even if only staying a week]." There Steward finally began to enjoy himself in San Francisco, noting in his journal of Sunday, August 23,

Went down an spoke to "Pop" Eddy* in his spotless tattoo joint. I introduced myself . . . and . . . he opened up and talked at length about business (not good) [and] other tattooers . . . He rather

---

*Clement John "Pop" Eddy (?–1957), a celebrated San Francisco tattooist who also sold tattooing supplies and machines.

wistfully wished (though not saying it outright) for another war, to make things a bit better . . . When the moment seemed psychologically right, I showed him the rose [I had tattooed] on my ankle, whereupon he congratulated me warmly, and said my work was more professional than that of many so-styling themselves.

Steward was energized by the meeting, for he was beginning to think he might really make a career for himself as a tattooist. But his mood darkened again two days later when he received a haircut so bad that it affected his ability to find sex partners—for, as he wrote in his journal, "I look like one of those creatures from the *Oz* books, exactly." Moreover, the weather had turned cold and overcast, putting an end to his daily sunbathing routine and sending him back once again to his dark room in the basement of the Stanford Court. There, with little else to do during the early part of the day, he read the local newspapers and brooded in his journal. On August 27, he noted with mixed feelings reading about a landmark ruling that had just been made involving the question of homosexuality:

Two things happened today that bear noting. One: an announcement in the papers of the reversal of the guilty-of-treason verdict of Sergeant Provoo of Berkeley. Reason: the prosecution had introduced "irrelevant testimony" regarding defendant's homosexuality.* Did I feel the world shift just a little under my feet at that moment? My first interpretation was to read it as a kind of victory for enlarging mores, a feeling that such a thing didn't matter, but a further amplification and quotation in the *Examiner* pointed out that the court had said: *"obviously [the] charge [of homosexuality] was utterly irrelevant to the issue of whether he had committed treason while a prisoner of war. The sole purpose and effect . . . was to humiliate and degrade the defendant, and increase the probability that he would be convicted, not for the crime charged, but for his generally unsavory character. We can conceive of no accusation which*

---

*Sergeant John David Provoo had been captured by the Japanese during World War II and his alleged collaboration had caused the death of another American POW. The U.S. government spent six years and over a million dollars prosecuting him, only to have the conviction overturned by the U.S. Court of Appeals on the grounds that the prosecution had unnecessarily introduced evidence of his homosexuality into the proceedings in an attempt to prejudice the jury against him.

could have been more degrading in the eyes of the jury or more irrele-vant to the issue of treason."

The last [sentence], of course, dashes all idealistic hopes groundward. Still, there may be some small profit: it may be an object lesson to the army (and others) that they ought to tread lightly on such matters.

The second, and far more interesting matter, concerned two clippings Emmy sent. The story told of the holding of thirty young Chanute Field* airmen for being members of Pachuco† gangs—violence and sadism. They were all tattooed with the mark of Pachuco—the cross with "merit badges" for outstanding acts of violence.

•

Without the YMCA as a center for sexual opportunity, Steward had to spend his nights out, cruising the bars. As an older man, and moreover as a recovering alcoholic, he did not find the scene an easy one. While many of his sexual fantasies involved tough guys in uniform—like the airmen who were also pachuco gang members in the article sent to him by Emmy—he nonetheless found the San Francisco bar scene much too violent and unpredictable:

the club-cruising here seems utterly unsatisfactory and frantic to me; I actually much prefer the *modus operandi* I have worked out at home. True, the excitement of the chase is lacking in my method—but so are the hazards of black eyes, rolling, beating, and (to a large extent) blackmail. Here, *tout n'est que désordre, tourbillon, mélée.*‡

. . . I never did find Larry [Ferguson] (we were to go drinking) but I walked miles—to the Sundown, Black Cat, Gordon's, Paper

---

*An air force base in Rantoul, Illinois, approximately one hundred miles south of Chicago.
†Pachucos (or Pachukes) were Mexican American youth gangs who developed a dandyish subculture in the 1930s and '40s that gradually merged into the greater American street gang subculture of the 1950s and '60s.
‡"All is disorder, whirlwind, free-for-all." Steward is riffing on Baudelaire's "L'Invitation au voyage," the last lines of which are: *"Là, tout n'est qu'ordre et beauté, / Luxe, calme, et volupté."* ("There, all is order and beauty, / Luxury, calm, and pleasure.")

Doll (it was so packed they were drinking outside on the steps—is this a purge town?) and finally Dolan's. All of a sudden I felt as empty as Mrs. Viveash in *Antic Hay*—when she and Gumbril, lost and alone in London, were taxi-riding to find someone they knew. No one at home, or all busy—or about to commit suicide. "Let us go back by way of Piccadilly," Mrs. V. kept saying; "the lights at least give the impression of being cheerful."

The loneliness and sense of exclusion from which he was suffering moderated, however, after a friendly encounter with an older naval officer:

at the Stanford [Apartments I met] a sailor with a hairdo . . . He is a great tall kind of bleached out thing, not too swish but a little . . . This evening he was in uniform and despite the "old salt" weatherbeaten quality of him and the bleaching and toupee (all curls in front like one of Louisa Alcott's Little Women), he looked authentically Navy in his uniform. I introduced myself—and to an airman named George, too, who was tying his tie; they'd just finished something—and learned he was on an admiral's staff (the admiral's a gay one, too) and had been in the Navy 10 years—achieving by his position a kind of maritime diplomatic immunity. He and the flyboy went out to dinner, and then he came back alone—read the motorcyclist's story, got hot, and when I asked him if he wanted a blow job, he lay back on the bed without undressing, his hands behind his head, and let me go at it—very wise as to what I wanted* . . . Then he looked at more pictures, posed for a sketch,—and later went and knocked up Ken McGrath (the Amer[ican] airlines boy . . .) and the two of them posed for a loose quick sketch, and then we had a three-way do, with myself going down on Ken, and Ken taking Mike the sailor, and then Mike going down on Ken (after I let go, Ken having come). This is the kind of wonderful goings-on to which I am accustomed, and I am certainly glad that some of it happened this summer! The Ancient Mariner's name is Michael Duke, and he seems to be independently wealthy . . .

*That is, to have sex with a navy officer in uniform.

The next day, after "breakfast with the Ancient Mariner" up at Gene's Coffee Shop, Steward's mood had lightened, and he went down to "Pop" Eddy's to have a tattoo put on. "We had a long talk, very pleasant; more and more I come to admire the relaxed easy philosophy of the tattooers," Steward recorded afterward. "He's had 44 years of experience, is one of the few old masters left—Dietzel and Tatts Thomas being others. The vacation has taken, on the whole, a decided turn for the better, and I find myself a little reluctant to leave on [September] the 9th."

•

The following day Steward got a number of supplies from "Pop" Eddy, as well as some technical tips on tattooing. He then met up with his sister at her elegant suite of rooms at the St. Francis Hotel, for she was just then visiting San Francisco with her new fiancé, Joe Harper, a highly placed hotel executive who always traveled in great style. By the end of the week, however, Steward had had quite enough of them, for seeing his sister so happily in love seems to have triggered in him an acute awareness of his own perpetual isolation. In a desire to escape these feelings, he once more went out cruising:

> Broke away from Jinny and Joe after dinner at Tommy's, and Bing and I went cruising in Sausalito . . . we came shortly back to SF, entering once more on the horrible empty Mrs. Viveash rounds . . . In the [Black] Cat I fell to talking with a wonderful little butch motorcyclist, complete with fancy leather jacket and untidy crewcut and pug nose—a solid little *dur*, very fascinating . . . We knew many of the same s-m crew in New York, though he made it quite clear he didn't "go in for that" in the least, whereupon I poohpoohed it myself. But I had a lovely fantasy of his tight little hard body sitting on my face—and his leather jacket still on.
> . . . [Later] I was turned down for the second time in one evening. This caused me to put my head against the doorjamb for a moment after he had gone, and wonder if perhaps the moment had not come when I should give it ALL up entirely . . . Then the pang passed, and I went to what I thought was the room of that little dish-faced blackhaired boy . . . who (being small) had a cock that actually did hang halfway down to his knee. Unfortunately, the

only open door was to the bed of someone else—and I was startled
at the stranger's face, and left hurriedly.

Though feeling his age and isolation more deeply than ever before,
Steward wrote his final journal entry the next day, September 8:

I made at least one good and permanent friend this summer, and
that's Bing[leman] . . . [Today] he said, in his quiet way, "You'll
never be lonesome, not with the richness of your mind," and a
little later, "it will seem like the end of summer, when you go."
These two small things I'll certainly treasure, for they mean a lot
coming from him. And then, so as to be able to put him in the
studfile, and really because I was dreadfully fond of him, I went
down on him a little—not much—standing there in the kitchen,
naked from our sunbaths, and kind of smelly—and he so exhausted and bitten and bloody from Jimmy of the night before
that he could barely raise a hardon. It was a kind of tribute, and
we both knew it—unimportant to be carried further.

[Afterward], I went back to the Stanford Court and packed—
and then towards midnight saw the ugly-faced little blackhaired
boy with the malocclusion. I asked him if he would like a blow
job. "If you're good," he said rather slowly. I grinned and said I
was reasonably proficient. So we went to his room, and he threw
the blind up so that there was light from Powell Street . . .
He was most appreciative, and grew quite hot, and pushed with
his hands on my head, and then called me up to kiss him somewhat. And when—panting, excited, his legs threshing—he grew
ready to come, he grabbed it and squeezed it with both hands on
it . . . I asked him why, and he said the orgasm was so violent with
him that often he went unconscious, and stayed out for half
an hour.

It was a nice ending to a stay in California.

The next morning I got up and took the morning plane home.
There were no more adventures worth recording—a Filipino U of
Michigan medical student sitting beside me, a mild flirt with a
redcap at the airport. Emmy was there; it was grey and raining—
and the key was melancholy, the drama ended, the "fun" over.

10

"Mr. Chips of the Tattoo World"

Several months after his lengthy conversations with "Pop" Eddy in San Francisco, Steward decided in early November of 1954 to try his hand at tattooing out of an amusement arcade in downtown Chicago. The decision was not one he made lightly; if his activities were to be discovered, he knew he would face immediate dismissal from DePaul. Even so, he seems to have felt that by doing something as dangerous and seemingly irrational as moonlighting as a tattoo artist he was somehow starting a new life. After all, he had been fantasizing about quitting academia to become a tattoo artist for nearly a year; as early as December of 1953, he had written Lynes that his great dream was to "hie me to a seaport town, rent a shack and hang out a shingle, and spend my golden twilight years putting lovely designs on strong young brown arms and shoulders—and thighs and buttocks and phalli, if the request arises. All my life has suddenly fallen into place with this resolve—and why should I else have been drawing for these years, and why do I like sailors? This is my *ultimathule*,* my dream of nirvana. I shall be called 'Professor Sparrow' and be the Mr. Chips of the tattoo world. *Ave atque vale*, for I am about to leave the world we know! (Blow jobs furnished free.)"

Although he had begun his study of tattooing via a correspondence course† a year earlier, Steward had soon realized that "learning to tattoo

---

Ultima thule (Latin): an expression probably best translated as "something we strive for but never quite reach."
†The course was offered by the tattooist Milton Zeis; Steward later contributed material to Zeis for inclusion in it. (Steward, *Bad Boys*; Don Ed Hardy to author.)

from a book [was] just about as successfully accomplished as learning to swim from a book in your living room." He later acknowledged, "It was not until I began to go to [Amund] Dietzel, the old master in Milwaukee, that I really learned how to tattoo." And indeed, while Steward knew enough about color and line from his art studies to draw illustrations on skin, tattooing required something much more technical: the precise insertion of ink below the skin using a rapidly vibrating mechanized needle. Mechanized tattooing needles were at that time almost impossible to obtain, so while searching for one, Steward purchased an electric engraving tool. He experimented with it on metal and glass, and used it to create a number of striking home furnishings: engraved aluminum tumblers and plates, engraved glassware, and an engraved brass cigarette box, all of them featuring images of nude males.

Steward soon realized why no practicing tattoo artist would willingly help him find tattooing equipment: with each new machine came a new source of business competition. Nevertheless, through Tattooed Larry, Steward finally learned of some available machinery. It was just then in the hands of a local wino (and sometime tattoo artist) named Mickey Kellet. Steward bought the entire outfit from Kellet—design sheets, machines, and stencils—for thirty-five dollars. "There were eight machines in various states of disrepair, a transformer and a rheostat, and hundreds of ancient stencils, all coated with greasy smearings of Vaseline and black powder," Steward later recalled. "There was [also] a two-foot high stack of hundreds of [tattoo] sketches." His first challenge lay in cleaning all these filthy things to make them fit for service. "It took [me] a week . . . [and even after] I scrubbed every stencil with detergent, they still stank."

Steward's decision to set up as a tattoo artist had been based, in large part, on his ignorance of the dangers of the tattooing life. "Could I have seen all the eighteen years ahead suddenly unrolled in their complexity," he wrote after his career had finally ended, "I might never have plunged into the tattoo world. It would have frightened the hell out of me." Indeed, apart from a highly unpredictable, often criminal clientele, Steward would also have to deal with a motley assortment of double-crossing fellow tattoo artists. "There is little that can compare with the cutthroat tactics, the trickery and chicanery of the tattoo world," he later wrote. "And why should it not be so? A good forty percent of its practitioners in those days was composed of ex-cons or con-men, drunks, wife-beaters, military deserters, [drug] pushers, [and] murderers . . . This was the world I had joined."

In an effort to keep his tattooing life separate from his life as a university professor, Steward decided to open his business using the pseudonym of Phil Sparrow. He later explained the name to friends by saying that a tattoo artist, like a sparrow, must peck (with his needle) to make his way in life; but Steward had in fact used a similar pseudonym (Philip Sparrow) while writing his columns for the *Illinois Dental Journal*. Given his wiry frame and small size, Steward was well suited to the name Sparrow. But it also had a literary precedent: John Skelton's Catullus-inspired poem "The Boke of Phyllyp Sparrowe," the mock lament of a young lady for her pet sparrow—a little bird that had, in happier moments,

> . . . *many tymes and ofte,*
> *Betwene my brestes softe*
> *It wolde lye and rest;*
> *It was propre and preste.*

So Steward's new name as a tattoo artist, like so much he did, combined a playful eroticism with a bit of poetic allusion and literary erudition.

Even as he took steps to begin work as a tattoo artist, Steward was continuing to try his hand at homoerotic illustration, contracting to sell his sexually suggestive drawings through a small company called Thor Enterprises.* He was sternly warned off that project by Kinsey, however, who reminded him that by sending such material through the mail for money he would be "subject to both Post Office and F.B.I. Investigation . . . Nearly [everyone who does so] ultimately end[s] up in trouble with the Federal government."† The best-known case of such trouble had been that of Bob Mizer, owner of *Athletic Model Guild* magazine, who had spent six months on a prison farm in California in 1947 for disseminating "obscene" bodybuilding photography. Since then, enforcement of the so-called Comstock Law against sending obscene materials through

---

*Thor's ads for Steward's drawing series appeared in the fall 1954 issue of *Physique Pictorial*.
†Steward nonetheless introduced Kinsey to Roy Hyre, the businessman who ran Thor; Hyre eventually gave the Kinsey Archive a vast collection of letters sent to "Thor" from its subscribers, many of them poignantly describing lives of intense loneliness, isolation, and sexual frustration.

the mail was increasingly vigorous, with federal agents harassing not only purveyors of erotically suggestive photography, but also publishers of literary fiction. Mail addressed to Kinsey and to the Institute for Sex Research was routinely seized as well.

As a result, Steward focused more energy on writing about his sexual activities in what he named his "Chicago Journal."* In doing so he updated his Stud File, and there made a startling discovery about his sex life: "In the past 7 years I had as many sexual contacts as I did in all my life before, up to that time. It is fantastic: 1,100 contacts to age 38, and 1,100 since then!"

As the fall term began, Steward was increasingly conscious of his advancing middle age, for his San Francisco summer had been full of sexual rejection, and on his return, Bobby Krauss rejected him as well. George Reginato, though enrolled in one of Steward's English literature classes, no longer seemed interested in exchanging sex for grades. As the semester progressed, Steward felt increasingly deprived of sexual contact with the young men he most desired. He developed a series of severe, almost incapacitating crushes on various young male pupils—but, faced with the impossibility of consummating these desires, he sank instead into despair.

Indeed, Steward's life situation at that moment was not good. His body was aging and his potency was diminishing; he was no longer the relatively carefree, attractive, and resilient young man he had once been. He had no savings and no job security, and he hated his job at DePaul. Now forty-four, he had accomplished very little as either a scholar or a writer apart from one early, promising novel. In battling depression, he had begun to rely upon Benzedrine to help him through his school day, and as soon as that day was over, he would escape down to the arcades and tattoo parlors of South State Street—for the wide-open world of skid row, however bleak, was nonetheless a welcome change from the claustrophobic faculty lounge at DePaul.

In his first attempts to establish himself as a tattoo artist, Steward had made a series of trips up to the Great Lakes Training Station on the

---

*Steward at first thought he would keep details of his private life in one journal, and details of his tattooing life in another, but by 1955 (in part because so much of his sex life was intimately connected to his work at the tattoo kiosk) he had combined the projects into a single diaristic endeavor that he later referred to as his "Tattoo Journal."

pretext of visiting with maimed and injured sailors. Once there, however, he distributed his tattooing business cards throughout the station, and loitered in the hallways and restrooms to see if anyone interesting turned up. One journal entry described these visits:

> What a warming and pleasant experience it was once more to drive in the gate at Great Lakes and see the handsome sailors—dozens and dozens of them, and watch them swagger down the halls of the recreation building, and go with them into their can, and peek from one's urinal down the line at their cocks pulled sidewise out of their incompletely unbuttoned trousers!

The visits left him in a state of such highly pitched sexual excitement that he did not hesitate when, upon a return from one of these outings, Bob Berbich telephoned to suggest a late-night meeting:

> Heated by the sight of the sailors, I said yes—put on jeans and leather jacket, and went down on the bus . . . to meet him in the parking lot by the Tribune tower. And there in full view, and with the Wrigley Tower bank of lights brilliantly illuminating the background, I went down on him . . . delighting in the thought of what my students would say if they could have seen me at that moment.

Steward's contempt for academia (and his rage at his position within it) was now such that he abandoned all academic research and largely neglected his coursework as well. Instead he focused exclusively on writing about sex and tattooing. "In the past few weeks, the tattoo mark has increased in its sexual stimulation for me," he wrote in one journal entry. "The sight of one or more on an arm becomes terrifyingly attractive; I find myself wanting to lick the tattoo, or suck it—or at the very least grab it and run my finger over it. The urge is building up in me again for the needle; if I don't get someone else to be the victim, I'll have to renew the one on my right hip." In another he confided,

> The passion overcame me today, and . . . I did [it] again, for the third time, [adding some work to] the small stylized flower on my right pelvic peak . . . then along the edge of my left palm and

forearm I put a measurement series—small red marks, barely visible to the nekkid eye after they heal [I hope] that will indicate 5,
6, 7 and 8 inches. Thus I will never be without a ruler again . . .
[and] those fantastic claims of [cocks that are] 10 and 12 inches
can now be spot-checked and disproved.

Steward would continue to add tattoos to his body for years, many of
them indelible statements of sexual rebellion. Ten days after applying the
cock-measurement marks to his forearm, he described a wildly indiscreet
new design he had created for his shoulder:

I want something added to the whip on my right [deltoid] . . . A
flying penis, a winged phallus, Pompeiian, fitted right over the
whip, wings spread, the body of it bright red. The kind of care I
would have to exercise over this obscenity might be embarrassing
and confining—and yet I do want it most powerfully. Just how
much of the sense of guilt and punishment, of the brand of the
mark of Cain, the Scarlet Letter, the mark on the minister's face
(and the black veil)* are mixed up in this? Out of what obscurities
does the feeling of the necessity for punishment arise? I am astonished to see it in myself—and of course I begin to wonder if having
the cock there is wholly the result of guilt feelings. Might it not also
be thought of as a kind of advertisement?

Dietzel applied the winged phallus to Steward's shoulder later that
week. Having placed such a radical image indelibly upon his body, Steward then reconsidered what he had done to himself, and acknowledged in
his journal that he was in the midst of a major life transition:

For some time now—say four or five years—there has been growing in me a tendency to sneer at the intellectuals . . . my disdain
for intellectual phonies, for the elegant language of art and music
criticism and literary criticism, my scorn for the *homo pedanticus*
or *academicus* have been growing for some time; and [instead I am] . . .
seeking out the opposites of the things I have long admired . . .
Oh, of course, I realize the aping and the wish-fulfillment of the

---

*"The Minister's Black Veil" is a story in Nathaniel Hawthorne's *Twice-Told Tales* (1837).

sexual—but there is also this leaving of the world I know. In an obscure way, I think that tattooing is connected with all this . . . The tattoos I have on me ally me with the herd, the toughs, the lower-class, the criminal—and I like it not only sexually but because that world [of the lower-class and the criminal] spits in the face of the one which has contained me thus far.

Kinsey, after receiving some of these writings, wrote Steward, "I have just gone over your manuscript . . . It is the most discerning analysis of the psychology of tattooing that I have seen . . . You have contributed an important document." Encouraged, Steward continued to reflect upon what he had been doing to himself:

A New Thing that I have been developing: the idea that I have become subconsciously irked with the bourgeois matrix that has contained me [because] the matrix's disapproval of homosexuality has finally become apparent to my buried self—with the result that I want to expel myself from the life which has held me thus far. Hence, tattooing . . . what better way to expel myself than to cover myself with tattoos—and to [cover] others [as well], thus drawing them down with me?

Even as he jeopardized his academic career, Steward was becoming newly aware of himself. Though strongly attracted to working-class and criminal-class males, he had previously had no easy access to such men. Tattooing, he now sensed, could change all that. In late October he wrote movingly on the subject of working-class men in his journals, in a way that makes clear that his desire to live and work as a tattoo artist was based at least in part on his persistent desire for encounters with men of this background:

Jimmy and Lonnie Knight now live on the third floor in a room about 50 x 20—used to be an old ballroom. Jimmy had said there would be lots of pretty people there; and I think I dashed him when—after meeting fifteen—I said please tell me when the pretty ones come in. I saw out of the whole crowd only one, a Dick somebody—with a low brow, big hands, a kind of bohemian

workers body, and a little expression which recalled that of Art
Craine to me. I was struck with the isolation of each one of us all,
including me; . . . There were few "movers" or mixers; most of
them stayed in the groups they came with. All of them were the
elegants, or the semi elegants,—and I felt out of place. But instead of the wretchedness borne of shyness and timidity in the
face of beauty, I was somewhat gratified to find myself caught in
violent little webs of scorn when I looked at their cufflinks and
their carefully tidied hair—oh, the glittering facades, hinting the
hollowness within . . . The fear lurking in them, the arched and
plucked eyebrows, the powdered pastiness of the skin (not hiding
the wrinkles of the neck when the head turns sidewise—so), the
elegant postures, the lines of well-cut Brooks Brothers suits, the
rings—my God, the rings! The Dick I liked most, the Neander-
thaler, ruined himself (for me) with a three-quarter inch square
black stone on one thick and hairy finger, as out of place as a dia-
per on the David.

I hate bitch parties . . . I tolerated [tonight's] better than usual,
however, for at the end of the evening I knew there lay waiting for
me the antidote to the smoke and the rings and the Cub Room and
the Knize Ten—Bob Berbich, the lanky truck-driver with his skull-
like face, his body in which each muscle stands out, with skin of
the worker who never has the time to seek out the sun and who
retains the winter whiteness all year round . . . Bob Berbich, who
has been . . . faithful all these years, with his poor grammar, his
limited view, his total and utter absence of "culture" in any form,
his proletariat pleasures (a new car every year, the old one traded
in . . .)—and [I imagine him] standing there, cock uplifted, his
hands clasped behind his head (fearful that if he should touch
me while I kneel before him, that some of my queerness will rub
off on him), and leading me here and there around the room, my
following him around the room almost on my knees—and then
his final going to the bed, where . . . his head elevated on the pillow, his hands still behind his head . . . we set to work in earnest . . .
at the moment of orgasm, there is only a slight, very slight contraction, a tiny spasm, and a little "oh!" escaping muffled from his mouth,
or a small exhalation of air. When I go to spit, I know that by the time

I get back he will be up and dressing, his shorts on—and then a final handshake, a promise to call me next week, an admonition to get some new "pitchers" to stimulate him, and off he goes.

Time and the repetitions have worn down the excitement he first brought to me to a bare nubbin—and yet as I sit here writing and thinking about it, I am certainly moved to say that I wouldn't trade him and that weekly or bi-weekly visit for any encounter with anyone of the bitches at Jimmy's party. He is . . . "pure trade"—no foolishness, very business-like and matter of fact. I sometimes wonder just what he thinks about [our meetings] . . . how he phrases it. "Well, it's Sattiday—guess I'll give him a call, and go out and let 'im have it."

Through the journal, Steward was coming to a clearer understanding of the new life he wanted to lead. He was coming, as well, to recognize some other dark desires:

[An executive I know] wanted a "party boy" for one of Young & Rubicam's clients. I said if he were to call me next week I might have some news for him . . . I called Bobby Krauss and asked him if he wanted to be a party boy for ten dollars—for someone who was about 40, tall, and "I don't know whether he's good looking or not; that's a personal matter." . . . The whole episode . . . excited me quite a little. I've arranged scores of people for people, but as far as I know, this is the first direct pimping I've done . . . maybe I'll demand fifty cents from Bobby, just for a souvenir piece. I can follow the whole thing in my mind—Bobby in slacks and jacket, knocking at the hotel room door; it opens; he's there—a bathrobe carelessly parting on a tall frame, a big cock erecting, and little Bobby earning his money, and myself demanding a cut of it. It's extremely and delightfully wicked, of course, especially since Bobby is only seventeen—something Genet himself would admire, I'm sure.

During November, while working as a curtain boy at the opera (Callas was singing *Norma* and *Traviata*, and Steward was sitting just a few feet away from her for every performance), Steward learned from Tattooed

Larry that a tattooing booth at the Sportland Arcade on South State Street was available for rent. Just south of the Loop and just a few streets in from Lake Michigan, South State Street consisted in the early 1950s of various empty lots, antiquated amusement arcades, burlesque shows, pawnshops, and flophouses. Winos lay passed out in doorways, and the gutters stank of vomit and urine. Steward recalled his first sight of the arcade years later:

> The Sportland looked dead and dingy from the outside, and darker and deader inside—long and gloomy, with dirty walls. Against the left wall, running clear back to a shooting gallery, was a tightly packed row of vintage stereopticon peepshow machines [which] dated from the 1920s . . . A glass-enclosed Egyptian fortune-telling painted plaster lady with a rotting veil peered at a row of cards . . .

•

He moved into the nine-foot-square space, which he nicknamed "the cage," on November 11, 1954,* initially planning to share it with an alcoholic tattooist whom the arcade's owner hoped to evict. That tattooist, Randy Webb, had been friends with Mickey Kellet, the wino who had sold Steward his tattooing equipment, and in fact Webb had hoped that Kellet might join him in the space. When the arcade owner chose Steward as a tenant instead, Webb took an instant dislike to him, and the feeling was mutual:

> [Webb was] a [toothless] little old man with yellow-brown hair . . . Not only did his chin nearly meet his nose . . . but he had one of the worst complexions imaginable . . . covered with rum-blossoms— big scarlet and purple pustules which he was fond of squeezing and popping out about a quarter-teaspoon full of pus and yellow matter. Beyond a doubt he was the nastiest looking person I had yet to see on the street, and [in time he would prove] the slyest and craftiest back-stabber of them all.

*Steward gives the move-in date as November 11, 1952, in *Bad Boys and Tough Tattoos* (p. 26), but he is mistaken, as both his journals and correspondence confirm that he started at the Sportland in November 1954.

At first Steward occupied the booth on Wednesdays and weekends, Webb the rest of the time. But as Steward established himself as the superior craftsman, customers in search of tattoos began abandoning Webb in favor of Steward. In retaliation, Webb put the word out that Steward was homosexual. "In those days," Steward later wrote, "you had to keep it hidden. Otherwise [you either risked a beating, or else] would be bartering blowjobs for tattoos." (Faced with a sudden influx of "barter-boys," Steward simply told them they had the wrong man, and directed them across the street to a grotesquely ugly and alcoholic tattoo artist named Shaky Jake.)

The neighboring Pacific Garden Mission also proved problematic. While it trafficked in "the usual holy-roller stuff of the far-right fundamentalist kind, derived from . . . Billy Sunday,* who had actually been 'converted' on their premises," the mission quickly revealed itself to Steward as yet another racket—one that after giving free doughnuts and coffee to sailors later milked generous donations out of their worried parents. Particularly galling to Steward was the mission's practice of sending out its temporarily reformed drunks, known as "runners," to stop sailors from getting tattooed. Steward eventually hired a lawyer to keep the mission from interfering in his business.

In opening his booth at the Sportland Arcade, Steward knew he was taking an enormous risk with his academic career. But it was, in fact, a calculated risk—for although he knew he wanted to be a tattoo artist, he did not yet know whether he would be able to make enough money at the job to survive, and he wanted to hold on to his DePaul paycheck for as long as he possibly could. While his moonlighting was surely an expression of rage against the university—for he felt extremely ill used by its administration—working as a tattoo artist was yet another form of thrill-seeking for Steward. Never before had he done anything so potentially dangerous to his livelihood and professional reputation, and never before had he worked in any place so perilous as South State Street. As a result, he wrote, "The street's miasma and excitement began to play

---

*The professional baseball player Billy Sunday (1862–1935) wandered into the Pacific Garden Mission some time in 1886 or 1887 (while playing for the Chicago White Stockings), and there began his conversion from outfielder to charismatic evangelical preacher. The most popular preacher of the first two decades of the twentieth century, he made a small fortune preaching a doctrine of conservative Christian values.

hob with my sense of reality, giving me an almost schizoid separation in my mind and emotions . . . I [had entered] . . . the seamy, sodden world of whores and pimps and pushers and winos and con-men—yes, and of tattoo artists."

While living a double life of this sort might well have been difficult for the average man, Steward was far from average. He had, after all, lived with a strongly divided consciousness since childhood, when he had appeared angelic to his aunts and teachers, yet as a renegade to neighborhood boys. As a closeted homosexual with an exceptionally dynamic sex life, he had again needed to live a life of constant concealment and trickery. For years he had courted danger and discovery as he moved between a series of highly compartmentalized personas. Now, however, he had become another person altogether: professor Sam Steward by day, tattooist Phil Sparrow by night.

There was, of course, no explaining any of it to his friends. Even among the most permissive and sympathetic of them, Steward could hardly begin to describe his erotic fixation on tattoos and tattooing, for at that moment in history, such markings were looked upon largely with horror, and were worn almost exclusively by misfits and outcasts. (Nor could he explain to his friends his overpowering attraction to delinquents, criminals, street toughs, and working-class men.) To many of his most liberal acquaintances, including Kinsey,* tattoos were a mark of degradation, and to be a tattoo artist was to traffic in corruption. In that sense, tattooing was just the opposite of Steward's vocation as a teacher, for he had by now devoted nearly twenty years to the enlightenment of young minds. Even Steward himself was quietly conflicted about this new activity, for a great deal of its allure came directly out of his gut sense that what he was doing was profoundly bad, sinful, and wrong. "[My] secret embarrassment over the whole matter," he later wrote, "led me to denigrate the skill by usually referring to it as 'tattoodling' . . . as if to show my 'intellectual' scorn of such a profession."

After Steward had set himself up as a tattoo artist down at the cage, Kinsey made a proposal, one that would add an intellectual component to the work there:

---

*"Considering Kinsey's general unshockability in almost everything," Steward wrote in his memoirs, "his forthright disapproval [of my taking up tattooing] somewhat nettled me."

After a month or two passed in my new career, [Kinsey said], "You
are probably one of a half dozen literate tattoo artists in the country—if indeed that many. And we've noticed tattoos on hundreds
of persons during our interviews. But they seem totally unable to
tell us why they got them, and we don't have the time to probe as
deeply as we would like into that aspect . . . [So] keep a journal
for us on what you can perceive as the sexual motivations for getting tattooed. You may not be a trained scientific observer, but
you have a writer's keen eye, and you should be able to unearth a
great deal.

Steward's sex-and-tattooing journal would run for six years, and ultimately amount to more than a thousand pages in single-spaced typescript;
with it he kept remarkable statistics about physical and emotional responses to tattooing, basing these statistics on interviews he conducted
informally with his clients. He later noted that along with its investigations into the psychology and sociology of tattooing, the journal evolved
into a partial record of segments of the subcultures that existed in the
1950s. "The tattoo shop was of course a magnet for the very young boot
sailors stationed at nearby Great Lakes Naval Training Station, but it also
drew into it the youth gangs of Chicago, the juvenile delinquents, the
sexually confused and rootless (sometimes illiterate) young men—the
rebels without causes. In a sense, the journal crystallize[d] a troubled
time that included McCarthyism, Korea, and the seeds of the deeper rebellion of the 1960s."

What Steward neglected to mention in this description, however, was
that the journal was also a highly detailed sexual confession—for even
as he began it, he found himself erotically transfixed by the men coming
in for tattoos, and also found himself surprisingly successful at propositioning them. Through the strange sorcery that came with applying tattoos to bodies, he discovered he was able to establish a powerfully intimate
connection with one young man after another. Sometimes he merely observed sexual responses in the men; at other times, he ended up having a
sexual interaction with them. Just as often, however, he found himself
becoming emotionally overwhelmed by these men whose bodies he was
handling so intimately, for their exceptional youth and beauty left him in
a highly responsive state. As a result their joys were his joys, their sorrows,
his sorrows:

[The other day at the tattoo kiosk] there had been standing around a young 17-year-old in a big black navy raincoat and a civvie hat . . . Came his turn—he took off the raincoat [and] he was wearing a grey corduroy jacket too small for him, and a pair of nondescript trousers . . . [I put an arrow-pierced heart on his] forearm . . . He was a little pressed for time, mentioned East Liverpool* and the train leaving shortly. It was only when he stood up to put on his Navy coat, however, that he took hold of the corduroy jacket, and said, "Navy suit." Whereat the whole story tumbled out—he had got to Great Lakes, and there been rejected for a strain or sprain, and was now going back. I was floored, and felt the emplastic unfolding within me so much that my own lip began to tremble, as his was doing, restrained only by will. I felt it all vividly, perhaps because it was so close to my own experience: the shame at rejection, the great burning to wear the uniform—and then to that I could add his feeling of loneliness in the big city, and the final desperate gesture of something to remember the Navy by—or some little sign of his all too short period of service: the tattoo, to show the folks at home, at least, a pathetic souvenir of a career cut short, and high hope extinguished.

I was more shaken by the kid than I cared to admit . . .

With entries such as these, Steward began to discover the real significance of his journal: like Lieutenant Seblon in *Querelle de Brest*, his writing would explore feelings that were otherwise denied all expression—for there was no one in his life with whom he could share them, including even the young men who evoked them. Such stories could never be published, or even told to friends. Steward was entirely alone in this new world of his own creation, but the idea of an understanding listener—the father-confessor he had so vainly sought in his conversion to Catholicism in the 1930s, and subsequently found in Alfred Kinsey—now propelled him to write about his sexual thoughts, feelings, and activities as never before. It was the only place he could tell the absolute truth. As a result, his involvment with the journal became all-consuming, and would ultimately prove the most intimate relationship of his life.

*East Liverpool, Ohio, a small town roughly ninety miles north of Steward's own hometown of Woodsfield.

•

Working at the university by day and then tattooing by night, Steward no longer had as much free time for sex. By December he was feeling the lack of it, and so he began scheduling sex meetings with his established contacts—either singly or in groups of three or four, hosting them by appointment at his home. He also began using a sign-in book down at the cage as a way of developing potential new sexual contacts via telephone and mail.

At the same time, he began taking tattooing ever more seriously. In early December he hosted Kinsey on a long visit to the tattoo cage; Kinsey was fascinated by all he observed. He also managed to obtain a rare copy of Albert Parry's *Tattoo: Secrets of a Strange Art as Practiced among the Natives of the United States*. Published in 1933, *Tattoo* was a landmark work that had taken a Freudian approach to its subject, asserting that there was a strong affinity between tattooing and sex. Like sex, tattooing featured both an active and a passive partner; insertion; strong sensation; and an experience through consensual pain of a certain kind of symbolic domination and submission. Though Steward was no Freudian, he nonetheless felt that most of Parry's conclusions were sound, for he was experiencing these sensations daily down at the tattoo parlor. He also felt that there was a great deal more to be written on the relation between sex and tattooing, and he resolved to write it. Over the next two decades, he would amass books, magazines, and articles on tattooing, as well as technical manuals, picture books, and memoirs. He did so with the ambition of someday creating the definitive work on the relation of sex to tattooing—basing it, in large part, on his own, hands-on experience.

By the end of his first two months at the Sportland Arcade, Steward was finding tattooing so satisfying on so many levels—and so much of an adventure (sexually and otherwise)—that he seemed hardly to care about his teaching duties at DePaul. Over Christmas vacation he traveled down to St. Louis to attend his sister's wedding, but rather than linger with his family he came back to Chicago on New Year's Eve, and upon his return he went directly to the cage. "I must get down to the shop," he wrote a friend who wanted to stop by the apartment for sex. "I'm sorry, but it has a greater appeal . . . I've never done anything which has made the Id purr as this thing has." As if to confirm the strange new direction his life had taken, Steward recorded a final sexual adventure for the year of 1954 in his journal, once again featuring his favorite working-class sex partner, Bob Berbich:

> And then . . . to the Sun-Times building . . . where I met Bob Berbich at 11:45. He took me in his car to the lower level, looking for a place to park so's I could give him a New Year's blow job . . . Every place we tried was too close to a bridge-tender's office looking down into the car, or there were trucks passing. Finally, we gave up and he just drove, the lights flicking past in a pattern . . . He suddenly stiffened when he came, but . . . drove straight on. It was quite an experience, and a nice way to usher in the New Year.

11

The Kothmann Affair

As 1955 began, Steward focused ever more intently on his journal writing, now recording events as they unfolded rather than trying to shape them into stories, essays, or anecdotes. "Everything [in the journal came] from direct observation," he later wrote. "[It would be wrong to] expect [it to have] the arrangement and symmetry of the scholar's monograph, [for] the order, logic, and design of the universe cannot be impressed on the chaos of life as it was observed on the skidrow of South State Street in Chicago." Even so, his daily journal entries often read as excitingly as fiction, for as Steward later explained, "tattooing furnished me with a kind of continuing drama, exciting, odd, and unusual, and quickly spoiled me for any kind of dull workaday routine occupation . . . The unusual clientele—always different, always changing—kept me fascinated and swimming in the mainstream of life—certainly in its dark rich depths . . . For anyone with even the mildest interest in people, tattooing was an ideal occupation." Then again, the journal was primarily a confessional work, and its most substantial entries concerned Steward's daily state of mind as he reflected upon the relation of his various sexual activities to his increasingly solitary life.

To his own surprise, Steward found he had a knack for running a shop, as well as a natural ability for handling the many tough guys, criminals, and drunks who frequented it. The sex researcher and psychologist Wardell Pomeroy, who visited the shop with Kinsey and, later, on his own, recalled that "[I] spent many hours in his shop watching him 'operate' [and] . . . It never ceased to amaze me how he was able to transform himself from the academic ivory-towered English professor to an entrepreneur who could handle very sticky situations and some very tough customers with an aplomb that even those raised in lower social levels would find difficult to duplicate."

Despite his primary focus on running the kiosk as a profitable business, Steward also began having a number of semipublic sexual adventures there, a form of risk-taking he found particularly exciting. One Sunday morning when Bob Berbich stopped by the arcade looking for some action, Steward did not take him back to his apartment; he simply pulled the curtain across the front of the booth:

> He came in; I drew the curtains and stood him against the back of Randy's trunk, and went down on him. He came rather quickly . . . and as I turned to get some Kleenex . . . the curtain parted a crack and it was young Ted Bott and three-four friends come for some [tattooing] work . . . I was flustered for a moment, but [then] told them that Bob had had a fly put on the head of his cock.

The danger of exposure added greatly to the thrill. Steward courted danger in other ways, too; most notably by becoming involved with Kenny Kothmann, a "boot" sailor training for the medical corps at Great Lakes who despite being quite sexually experienced was still only sixteen, and thus recognizably below the age of sexual consent. Steward, knowing this, nonethless let Kothmann stay regularly at his apartment on his weekend liberties (just as he had let Bobby Krauss do the year before), and from February through August the two had sex together twenty-three times. As with Krauss, Steward kept photographs and records of Kothmann that noted his age and background as well as their various sexual activities.

Through his relationship with Kothmann, it seems the forty-four-year-old Steward had been experiencing a second adolescence. And indeed, the new world in which he lived and worked was largely populated by adolescents:

> An astonishing day, really. After class I was visited by three [DePaul undergraduate] beauties: Bruce Smith, Dick Avery of the soft black eyes, and Ralph Johnson* of the tremendous torso— and I could not help think how generous life is to me, to surround

---

*Smith, Avery, and Johnson were not sex partners, only former students.

me with such beauty: a kind of sentimental Thornton Wilder reaction, but an honest one nonetheless. And then down to the
shop, to find a letter from Kenny [Kothmann], charming and appreciative of my "lavish apartment" and other things—and to see
him swish in a little later, accompanied by a tall southern belle in
black wool too, both of them from the medical corps school at
Great Lakes. This one, Bill Peterson, was an even wilder bitch
with a soft South Carolina accent . . . And they had not been
there long when a crowd of young Pachukes appeared at the
doorway, the central crewcut blond one fingering his cock and
saying, "can you put a fly on the head of it?" I swallowed hard and
without batting an eye said yes, whereat they all crowded inside
and we closed the curtains. I took his cock in the palm of my left
hand and carefully and methodically rubbed in the anaesthetic
cream—he got hard and enjoyed it all, I can tell—and then put
the fly on . . . it seemed to satisfy him. And then I put *chocolate*
and *vanilla* above each one of his nipples . . .

Kothmann initially treated Steward as if he were just another sailor-
trainee from Great Lakes, and Steward was in heaven, for to be a sailor
who had sex with other sailors had always been one of his great fantasies.
With Kothmann and several other boot sailors now stopping by regularly
for sex, Steward even went so far as to ask himself, "Now that the 'Navy'
is opening up for me, which is exactly what I have wanted all along, shall
I maybe give up tattooing and concentrate on sex? Else why did I take up
tattooing in the first place? But . . . I like tattooing; it's in me like a virus—
[I'd] sooner cut off my head, really."

Shortly thereafter, Kinsey came to Chicago for a visit, and the two
men met to discuss some other possible projects. Steward noted that
Kinsey "had an idea that we should all collaborate on an article on the
sexual implications of tattooing . . . I was properly modest, and we both
realized the difficulty of having anything appear under my own name,
even under that of Phil Sparrow. 'You'd be fired in a moment,' he said, and
I knew it too, perhaps not so much for tattooing as for being associated
with his name." After the meeting, however, Steward began to worry about
Kinsey's health, for he looked very ill.

Kinsey's life had become enormously difficult since the second volume of his monumental study, *Sexual Response in the Human Female*, had been published in 1953. His lifelong habit of working himself to exhaustion had taken its toll on a heart that, already weakened by childhood illness, was now further weakened by chronic work-related anxiety and tension. Since the early 1950s Kinsey had been taking both amphetamines and Nembutal daily in order to keep himself going; he was now also taking digitalis for his heart, which was enlarged and arrhythmic. After a collapse that had required hospitalization in 1953, he had suffered a number of small heart attacks in the months that followed.

Popular resentment of Kinsey, meanwhile, was growing. Unlike his *Male* volume, which had been hailed as a landmark study, *Sexual Response in the Human Female* had been roundly denounced by both Catholic and Protestant groups, and had been received throughout the country with an enormous upswell of popular anger. Part of this popular rage against Kinsey's sex research was a delayed response to the findings of the *Male* volume; but Kinsey also had to contend with the wholesale popular rejection of his statistical finding that women had strong sexual urges—a finding that many people thought deeply insulting to American womanhood.

The resentment of Kinsey was also part of a greater shift that had been going on in American culture since the late 1940s: a shift toward political and social conservatism. In the five years between *Sexual Behavior in the Human Male* and *Sexual Behavior in the Human Female*, public fears about conspiracies, spies, and enemy agents working within the United States had been wildly exaggerated at the federal level by Republicans intent on seizing and consolidating their political power. As a result of this shift, Kinsey had lost his Rockefeller Foundation funding, which was crucial to his enterprise. In his naïveté, Kinsey had expected that the knowledge gained through his statistical studies would bring about a greater understanding, tolerance, and acceptance of sexual variation within the American population. What had happened, in fact, was just the opposite: both he and his research were reviled, and sexual intolerance grew and spread. As a result, Kinsey's health collapsed, for he was worn down not only by exhaustion, but also by stress. He was also, in the the words of a close colleague, "crushed with disappointment."

•

A few days after Kinsey left Chicago, Steward made up his mind, once and for all, to place the large rose tattoo in the middle of his chest. Accordingly, he drafted up a rose image featuring a phallic meatus at its center, planning to bring it to Milwaukee to have it applied by Amund Dietzel.

The phallic rose would soon become Steward's emblem. When he left the Sportland Arcade to open his own tattoo parlor in the coming year, he would adopt it as his shop's insignia and feature it on his letterhead. One of his first significant published stories, meanwhile, would be entitled "The Sergeant with the Rose Tattoo." He was interested in the rose for its traditional symbolism: the mystic center, the heart, the garden of Eros, the flower of Venus. Originally from Persia, the rose had been considered by Arabs a masculine flower, and in ancient times was a symbol not only of joy but also of secrecy and silence. Moreover, the rose had been a staple of Western tattooing since the nineteenth century. Steward also associated the rose with Gertrude Stein, whose stationery featured a rose around which figured her famous saying, "Rose is a rose is a rose." His decision to place a large rose on his chest probably also owed something to Tennessee Williams, whose 1951 stage play *The Rose Tattoo* featured a rose tattoo (similarly placed in the middle of a man's chest) as the emblem of an overwhelming physical passion.*

Steward had an ulterior motive in going to Dietzel to have the rose put on. With his usual craftiness, he planned to extract (and absorb) as much technical information as possible from Dietzel during the process. Dietzel was, after all, a great master of the art: at the time Steward went to him, this former merchant seaman originally from Denmark was the greatest source of tattooing wisdom in the entire Midwest, and even today he is widely recognized as one of the greatest tattoo artists of the twentieth century.

While Steward would in many ways become Dietzel's successor, the two would never quite be friends, for the differences between the two men were many and great. Born in 1890, Dietzel had gone to sea as a cabin boy at age ten. Between 1912 and 1915 he had worked as a traveling tattoo artist, and in 1915 he had opened a tattoo parlor on South State Street. As his sense of style, use of shading, and ability with finer lines

---

*Steward mentions "the demand among young men for a rose tattoo on the chest, following the 1955 movie of *The Rose Tattoo* by Tennessee Williams" in *Bad Boys and Tough Tattoos* (p. 129) but makes no reference to his own rose tattoo in that paragraph.

made him sought after from coast to coast, he decided to move up to Milwaukee. There, starting in 1916, he introduced a number of designs that proved enduringly popular, including the leaping black panther. His fortunes took a turn for the better when World War II brought a tattooing boom to Milwaukee, which was just a short train ride away from the Great Lakes Naval Training Station. By the time Steward met him in 1955, Dietzel had long since become independently wealthy from real estate speculation, and had continued to work at the tattoo parlor only out of sheer love of the art. He was also a rough and somewhat vulgar man, and entirely heterosexual. "The purity and assurance of his line, the supreme and absolute confidence with which he created his tattoos, could be recognized even by a lay observer," Steward later noted. "'Dietz' was in a sense my teacher, and I learned more from him about tattooing than from any other person."

•

When not teaching at DePaul or tattooing down at the cage, Steward continued to cultivate his contacts in the world of erotic art, in part because he enjoyed introducing these men to Kinsey, and in part because he himself was still toying with the idea of publishing his visual erotica. Steward devoted the majority of his energy during this time, however, to the cultivation of his sex life, for after years of standing before handsome and aloof young male undergraduates to instruct them on grammar, composition, and the history of English literature, he was now meeting similarly handsome young men on a daily basis—handling their bodies in any way he liked, and having a great deal of sex with them. In exorcising the sexual frustrations of a seventeen-year academic career, he was incidentally discovering something Kinsey had already published in his *Male* study: namely, that the sexual lives of working-class and underclass American males were quite different from those of middle- and upper-class American males, particularly in their attitudes toward premarital intercourse, prostitution, and homosexuality. According to the Kinsey findings, young men with only a grade school education experienced four or five times as many homosexual experiences as did young men who went to college. Moreover, lower-class males tended to be quite promiscuous in the early years of marriage, had a higher tolerance for homosexuality, and were much more direct, even blunt, in their approach to sexual acts of

any sort. As a result of his move downward in the American social hierar-
chy, Steward found his sex life had been given an unexpected boost.

And yet despite Steward's sexual success on South State Street, the
stress of his double identity was beginning to wear on him. He was now
regularly popping Benzedrine to get through the teaching day at DePaul,
and people were starting to notice and comment on his erratic behavior.
In a strange way he seemed not to care: during the early summer, despite
the abundance of shocking new tattoos on his body, he began sunbathing
regularly on a DePaul University rooftop, taking only the smallest of pre-
cautions to prevent his discovery there by administrators. With this and
other actions Steward was clearly courting his own dismissal; nonetheless,
he regularly experienced anxiety attacks.

Indeed, he faced the very real possibility of being shaken down, robbed,
or possibly even murdered on South State Street. One evening, having
been informed by two tattooed minors that the cops were trying to get
them to sign a complaint against him, Steward wrote,

> A curious day, the end of it doom-filled with the same empty ter-
> ror I used to feel while drinking—that's twice within a short space
> of time. [The youngsters' story] was the beginning of the fear,
> which grew steadily all the rest of the evening. I thought of a
> dozen plans—denial, lack of proof, stopping completely . . . I left
> [a sex party with] the dread large inside me, and visions of cap-
> ture. (I can easily see that panic grows in the criminal and leads
> him to do foolish things in that tight emotional emptiness which
> he feels.)

Sensing disaster was imminent, Emmy Curtis begged Steward to
hide the great masses of erotic material and sexual records he had stock-
piled in his apartment, and even volunteered to take them into her own
home. Despite Emmy's attempt at intervention, however, Steward made
few changes to his lifestyle, for the semi-anonymous sex gatherings in his
erotica-strewn home were now a well-established way of life: "In the evening Bobby Krauss came, about eight-thirty, and we called Bert Bauer
and invited him over. He came, we spread the old chenille (freshly laun-
dered by [Emmy's cleaning lady] Mrs. Mersel, and brought back in a

hurry by Emmy when I told her it was the daisy-chain blanket: 'Oh, mercy! I'll have it there by Saturday!'—and she did.)"

The Monday after the daisy chain, Steward noted in his journal that "school is . . . awful: Every Monday, Wednesday and Friday mornings, facing my big classes, I have to take half a benny—and even then it is hard." His panic attacks continued as well: "There's a definite kind of reluctant fear in me to go down to the shop any more," he noted. "I kinda feel that each evening may be my last [as a tattooist], unless they let me tattoo in jail."

•

The situation down at the arcade became even more difficult that June, when a young man fascinated by the tattoo cage and its decor introduced himself to Steward as a magazine writer, and told him he wanted to do a feature on Steward and his work. Steward was quietly horrified, but even as he knew he ought to refuse, he worried that by declining to be interviewed he might draw even more attention to himself. So instead he gave the reporter the interview, but lied extensively about his age, training, and background. "The Ancient Art of Professor Phillip Sparrow," published in July 1955 by *Chicago* magazine, gave a fascinating glimpse of Steward's double life:

> The inside walls of the shack are covered with colored insignia: crosses encircled by thorny wreaths, lions rampant and entwined by bright green vipers, bleeding hearts capped by scrolls reading "mother" and "sweetheart," blue anchors, red roses, obsolete army tanks, daggers, mermaids, hula dancers and fierce looking eagles clutching writhing lizards in their talons.
>
> This is a tattoo parlor—the roost of professor Phillip Sparrow, one of the row's four epidermal artists.
>
> . . . Sparrow bears little resemblance in appearance or manner to any stereotyped conception of a tattooer. He is a wiry 36-year-old [sic] of medium height, with wavy blond hair and mustache and a handsome, almost patrician face. Although he carries six tattoos of his own, none are so located as to be visible to the public. His one sartorial concession to the trade is a nautical working costume of blue jeans and a dark turtle-neck sweater . . . Sparrow's

literary allusions . . . run [from the book of Leviticus in the Old Testament to] Freud and various books on the history of tattooing, and his soft polysyllabic speech helps account for his academic nickname.

. . . "He's a real perfectionist," said one of his customers. "One little flaw and he's tearing his hair."

. . . Sailors and motorcycle riders, Sparrow said, are the social groups most prominently represented among his clientele. Of approximately 400 people he has perforated here, only four have been women.

Shortly after the magazine appeared, two of Steward's students discovered it and circulated it among other members of their class. The discovery caused a sensation among the students, but even so, administrators were slow to catch on. On Friday, July 1, Steward wrote in his journal,

If DePaul should fire me, it is pleasant to think what might be done: perhaps *Life* magazine would find enough sensational shock value (pointing up the plight of the underpaid professor who had to become a tattooer to make ends meet, etc.) in my petite histoire to run something about it—which might make DePaul known in years to come as "that university where they couldn't pay one of their professors enough and he took up tattooing."

Though worried about losing his job, Steward nonetheless took pleasure in the article, and sent a copy of it to Kinsey along with the next hundred-page installment of his journal. In response to Kinsey's subsequent suggestion that he send Bill Dellenback up to Chicago to continue his documentation of Steward's apartment, Steward wrote, "As for having things to photograph—well, I just haven't been doing anything except the tattooing, and my 'art gallery' is now walking around the world."

In a subsequent journal entry, Steward described how his sex life, too, had changed: "I have now seen so many [sailors], handled so many arms, helped them on and off with jumpers, that the wonderful spell they used to cast has all but disappeared. What a shame this is! . . . If the sailor-object disappears, what in the world can be left? I am afraid my old brain can not of itself engender a new illusion to live by."

Sex with sailors had been Steward's central erotic fantasy for more than fifteen years; now the fantasy had been overtaken by quotidian reality, and Steward had temporarily lost his bearings. Part of the problem was, as he noted, overexposure. But there was another, unmentioned problem: age. Nearly all the sailors in his shop were either still adolescents or else in their early twenties. Steward, by comparison, was forty-five. The situation was particularly difficult with Kenny Kothmann, the sixteen-year-old sailor from Great Lakes who had been living at Steward's apartment on his weekend liberties—for though the two were still sexually active, Kothmann had become increasingly oblivious to Steward's thoughts and feelings. Having ceased to respond to Steward as a lover, he had begun treating him instead merely like he would any other authority figure—someone to be taken advantage of whenever possible, and otherwise simply avoided or tuned out. Over the past several months Kothmann had driven Steward half crazy with his constant stand-ups and sudden, unexplained disappearances; what had once seemed to Steward a perfect romance was now only embarrassing and humiliating. Realizing he needed to end the attachment, Steward left a note on his kitchen table asking Kothmann to return his apartment keys. Kothmann did so, with a note promising to spend the whole of the following weekend with him. When Kothmann proved a no-show the following week, Steward wrote in his journal,

> . . . the day [was] a blur of sailors . . . and more sailors, demanding anchors, hearts, skulls, daggers with snakes entwined . . . and finally, with my senses reeling, Kenny and [his friend] Peppy appearing, and Kenny saying he was going to a party, and did I mind? And all the small hopes built on the strength of last week's note . . . shattered, dusty, gone . . . with the feeling that tattooing . . . [is] spoiling my sex life almost beyond all recognition. After next Friday—I hope I never hear or see Kothmann again, ever: and I hope that when my psyche re-orients itself, gets the gyroscope of common-sense working again, I shall never again permit myself to be so entrapped . . .

Kothmann showed up at the apartment the next morning. Having started the evening at a party, he had ended it in the Clark theater,* but

---

*A Chicago movie theater known for homosexual activity, which featured all-night movie screenings.

then he had needed a place to sleep and shower before heading back to
Great Lakes—and apparently he had kept a copy of Steward's key in case
of just such an emergency. "I got out of bed [and] confess[ed that] I had
fallen in love with him three months before," Steward wrote sadly in his
journal. "[Then saying,] 'so—if my actions seem a little odd and abrupt to
you—consider why.'"

> Then I went to shave. I heard him cough a coupla times, and
> when I came back he had fallen over on the sofa, ostensibly
> asleep—but how else could we have avoided an embarrassing
> moment? I give him credit for a dramatic resolution . . . When I
> got home there was a note from Kenny, saying amongst other
> things that yes, I did a good job hiding it, he thought he was just
> someone else to go to bed with when there wasn't anyone else. "I
> can never thank you enough for all you've done. I know one sailor
> who would be awfully homesick and mixed up if it wasn't for you.
> I have a little something I'll give you next weekend."

The following Saturday, however, there was no present for Steward.
Kothmann had simply dropped him and disappeared.

That Saturday was Steward's forty-fifth birthday, and even though the
day passed in a blur of biceps and chests, he struggled hard to fight off
depression. "The $91 I took home with me this evening didn't make me
any less lonesome," he noted wearily in his journal. "I guess I'll have to
start arranging spintries again—it's just been that I'm so damned tired
after work that I don't feel like [doing] anything."

Four days later, Kothmann was caught having sex with a fellow sailor
at the Naval Training Station, and authorities there placed him in hospital
isolation for observation and intense cross-examination. In line with the
nationwide hysteria about homosexuality, naval authorities were now actively seeking to uncover any and all traces of homosexuality within the
ranks of enlisted men. In doing so, they had also decided to investigate
any person or place in the Chicago area that might be involved in promoting or encouraging homosexual activity. Steward, not yet knowing the full
extent of Kothmann's trouble, noted in his journal that a couple of days
earlier he had written "a note to Kenny, the tenor of which was that the
Navy way of life was really an abnormal one and that frequently damage
was done [by Naval authorities] in trying to create these 'young men pure'

[through forced celibacy.] As a kind of bulwark against his despair [about his life at the Training Station], I tried [using my good-luck] amulet* on him . . . [and right after that] I got his letter announcing the worst had happened."

Two days later, DePaul finished for the year, and Steward was free to immerse himself entirely in his tattooing. After putting tattoos on a pair of particularly handsome young construction workers, he noted in his journal,

> God, if teaching was a martyrdom, what is this? A very real burn-
> ing at the stake . . . I handle [these young men] so closely; I come
> so near to all these tanned young shoulders; I see the tension of
> the *serratus magnus* pattern; I feel the hair beneath the arm pit; I
> look into the eyes, I press the fainting head down between its legs
> and look at the ridge of the backbone curving like a well-fleshed
> bow; I see the hair running into a rivulet down beneath the belt
> center—my god, what is going to be left after all this? Probably
> nothing except the Catholic religion, or checking umbrellas in a
> museum.

A week later, Steward noted, "Thomas Mann died today. I re-lived the moments he and I had passed together. And wept a little . . . [Then] Kenny [Kothmann] came in, with horribly bleached hair (the underthatch quite dark), coarse and ropy; he looked like a male whore of thirty-five. He [has] got an Undesirable Discharge." Two days later, Steward had even worse news from Thurman Peppington, an effeminate black boot sailor who was a friend of Kothmann's. Peppington (or "Peppy") had heard from a mutual friend "that Kenny had spilled the whole works to the Navy—with especial reference to the Daisy Chain [with Peppington and several others at my apartment on] May 22,† and that the Navy was going to declare my shop off-limits." Steward was at that point more concerned about losing his business than with prosecution by naval authorities, since as a civilian he was technically beyond their reach. Still, he wrote, "There's

---

*Steward had purchased the amulet in Algeria in 1939, and had since used it to bring his lover Ser-
geant Bill Collins back from overseas, to help another friend obtain an automobile, and to assist
George Platt Lynes to find a new apartment and photography studio. He had used it on Kothmann in
an effort to help Kothmann adjust to naval life.
†Steward had previously described the daisy chain in his May 22 journal entry.

no describing the shock this gave me—like one swift terrible blow right to the solar plexus, leaving me kinda dark and non-functioning in the head, and unable to think or grasp what was going on externally."

While Steward instinctively knew that Kothmann had betrayed him, he could not yet bring himself to hate this damaged, troubled, and heavily promiscuous sixteen-year-old whose entire professional future had probably been irremediably compromised by his undesirable discharge. When Kothmann stopped by the shop the following day, Steward bought him a bus ticket to San Francisco and gave him a tattoo as a going-away present. Afterward he wrote, "[I] put my big rose on Kenny's shoulder, working Tab Hunter's initials into it [at Kenny's request]—half wondering if I should not have moistened the colors with curare or arsenic, or used my rustiest needles . . . I have never in my life been so glad to see anyone depart."

The next day, however, the situation worsened yet again: "The pudgy little queer negro [boot sailor], Peppington, came in—and told me [all the] details. Kenny gave way completely, told them everything about me, gave Naval Intelligence my name, picture, told of the tattoo shop, intimately described the daisy chain with Tab Buonfiglio* [right] down to the color of the [chenille] bedspread [I had] put down on the floor . . . When I got home in the early evening, I called [another sailor,] Lou Tobler . . . [who] confirmed every detail." Steward now realized that not only was his tattoo business in danger; he also faced dismissal from DePaul and public exposure as a "sexual deviant." "The one thing I wonder [most]," he wrote, "is if [Kothmann] gave them my name at school, or told the Navy I taught at DePaul."

Several days later Steward spoke with his friend Bill Bates[†] in San Francisco. "I alerted the west coast against Kenny Kothmann . . . Since we are all, as Jacques Delaunay once said, '*un grand Mafia*,' word like this can travel quickly, [since] no queer fears anything so much as one of his

---

*According to the Stud File, "nondescript sailor, brought by Kothmann."

†Bates, a strikingly handsome and very masculine six-foot-six hustler, had been introduced to Steward in December 1953 through "Bob Smith," a man Steward had picked up at the Lincoln Baths only to discover (after sex at Steward's apartment) that "Smith" was an undercover police officer. Bates, then nineteen years old, soon became a regular visitor to Steward's apartment for one-on-one encounters, *spintriae*, and photographic get-togethers. After Bates had attempted suicide, Steward helped pay for his move back to California.

own breed who's turned informer . . . I'll get Kothmann if it takes me twenty years."

The next day, while Steward was applying a tattoo, a heavily decorated chief yeoman from the Great Lakes Naval Training Station appeared at the entrance to the kiosk. When the last of Steward's customers left, he asked Steward if his name was Phil Sparrow, and if he happened to live in an apartment on Kenmore. Steward said yes, and asked how the man knew. The yeoman replied, "Let's just say it's my business to know such things":

> Here it comes, I thought. And it did. Then he asked if I knew Dion White, Kothmann . . . Peppington and Malone.* I admitted to "remembering" Peppington and Kothmann, said I didn't know the others. Then he muttered something about "living in Chicago and the police" which didn't register precisely, although I knew he was threatening . . . Then he told me, "Keep away from the sailors, you know what I mean, or the next time I won't be alone."
>
> He left, and I called after him, "Is this official?" "Yes," he said.
>
> Naturally I was in a whirl, and near-state of shock, but managed to get home, and sought solace in a sleeping pill. This looks like ruin—or was it just the "friendly" warning?

By popping a handful of Sedormid pills, Steward managed to get a few hours sleep. The next morning when he returned to work at the arcade, he was stopped at the entrance by Frank, the building's manager, who informed him that "a guy from naval intelligence was in asking just what goes [on] with Sparrow." When Steward asked Frank what he had told the intelligence man, Frank responded that he had covered for Steward: "[By] the luckiest sort of coincidence, Frank had known [the guy from naval intelligence] from way back, and gave him a song and dance in his best Lithuanian bluff manner, saying everything was on the up and up, and just let that pasty-faced little motherfucking little goddamned liar [Kothmann] come around and make his accusations face to face."

"I hope that settles it," Steward concluded, "but I am fearful still."

---

*Steward's Stud File notation: "Brought by K Kothmann. Sailor. Evanston. Involved in the Navy Scandal. Real butch-pretty type."

12

The Parting

The shock of the Kothmann incident was such that for a long time Steward took no great pleasure in recording his erotic exploits in his journal. In fact, he decided to lie low. Aside from a few entries concerning another visit from Kinsey, the journal trails off in the autumn of 1955, and in the last entry—at the end of October—he noted, "I am now so highly moral (with sailors) in the shop that I begin to look on myself as the north door to the Pacific Garden Mission." Because the journal came to a temporary halt with this entry, there was no record in it of Steward's reaction to Kinsey's news (later recounted in a memoir) that George Platt Lynes was just then nearing death from cancer. But during the fall, Steward later wrote, "George [Lynes] spoke [with me by telephone] of his aches and pains . . . 'I am taking twenty-odd kinds of pills,' he said, 'and there are terrible pains in my chest, as if an elephant is sitting on me.'"

On November 17, John Martin, the noted author and dance critic, wrote to Steward from his desk at *The New York Times* that "George . . . returned from Paris a week or so ago and went to the hospital again . . . his situation is extremely grave." Lynes died a little more than two weeks later, in early December. Steward never wrote directly about the sorrow he felt at Lynes's death, but he kept an index card with him on his desk until the end of his own life, some thirty-eight years later, on which he had typed, "George was an atheist, and so am I. But how I long now for an afterlife—a world of light or of deep dazzling darkness, where he and the others we've lost reside, unscathed, forever accessible—to have tea with, to talk nonsense with, to reinvent the world with."

•

That same autumn, a different kind of tragedy complicated Steward's life considerably when three young boys were discovered naked, bound, and strangled in a ditch near the Des Plaines River. Since police had only a vague description of a middle-aged male as a suspect, the murders triggered a citywide panic over homosexuals and homosexuality that would last for many years.

Panics over homosexual sex crimes took place all across the United States during the early 1950s, fostered by the nationwide vilification and scapegoating of homosexuals that had begun with postwar military downsizing, then intensified through the actions of various hate-mongering politicians, most notably the Wisconsin senator Joseph McCarthy. As a result, reports on predatory sexual psychopaths began to proliferate in newspapers and magazines, and in these reports homosexuals were particularly demonized, with the press routinely portraying all homosexuals as immoral, mentally ill, and a predatory threat to unsuspecting youth. The Chicago boy murders (which came to be known, after the victims, as the Peterson-Schuessler murders) were particularly incendiary because no murderer was found or taken into custody.* Chicago police deflected criticism of their failure to find the guilty party or parties by engaging in a highly visible campaign of harassment and intimidation of the city's known or suspected male homosexuals.

On January 1, 1956, Steward moved uptown to 4915 North Glenwood, an apartment building on a cul-de-sac overlooking St. Boniface Cemetery. Various diary entries note that he furnished the apartment with candles, a human skull, and a number of screens, lampshades, and sculptures of classically inspired nude males. In early January he wrote Kinsey to apologize for having fallen behind on his journal and correspondence, and explained it was partly due to his move uptown. Despite Kinsey's own very serious financial and health problems, he promptly and kindly replied, "I have thought of you repeatedly and I continue to marvel at the extent of the cooperation that you have given through these years . . . I never realized that I could learn so much more about sex as I did in the

---

*The identity of the murderer remained unknown until 1977. He turned out to be Kenneth Hansen, who at the time of the murders was a twenty-two-year-old stable hand. Hansen was finally convicted of the murders in 1995.

seven weeks in Europe . . . We will discuss this when we get together. Your help in my thinking will be very useful at this point."

Resuming his journal on Valentine's Day 1956, Steward noted that his sexual adventures had continued despite the warning he had received from the navy. Even so, he felt increasingly anxious—not only about losing his job at DePaul, but also about being threatened in the arcade. In one instance, two policemen came in for tattoos, and one of them repeatedly pointed his gun at Steward, threatening to shoot him unless he did a good job. "I laughingly pushed it away from my belly two or three times," Steward wrote, "[but] after they left . . . I sat in the corner and shook for ten minutes." In mid-February, Steward again wrote a note of apology to Kinsey for having fallen out of touch, blaming his silence on his two full-time jobs. Kinsey responded almost immediately: "Frankly I was a bit worried that something might have happened to you. I should, on the other hand, have known you well enough to know that you have managed to get through all sorts of situations that other persons wouldn't have."

Kinsey had been right to worry, for toward the end of February, DePaul administrators apparently learned about the tattoo shop. When Steward met with the dean of the school to discuss the renewal of his contract and the raise that was to go with it, the dean told him tersely that he would receive none, though everyone else in the department would. Steward then asked among his colleagues and learned, as he wrote in his diary, that "my raise had been proposed in committee and agreed upon, when word came from President O'Malley's office that I was not to be given a raise." As Steward wrote Kinsey, "I kinda feel the authorities at the school have got wind of my other job, and I think in their outraged Christian way they may be trying to force me out."

But then the situation took a wholly unexpected turn. Early Sunday morning, March 11, Steward was at home in his apartment, painting an erotic screen in the nude, when the doorbell rang. Thinking Emmy had arrived early to help him with some housework, he punched the release. As he noted in his journal afterward,

> It was two cops, the same ones that on March 8th had dropped into my shop to ask if I knew Roy Hyre,* whom they were looking for to question about the Peterson-Schuessler murder case . . .

---

*Hyre was the businessman who had marketed Steward's erotic drawings through his company, Thor Enterprises. (He was in no way implicated in the Peterson-Schuessler murder case.)

they said they'd found my [tattooing] card in [Hyre's] effects . . .
A moment I had nightmared over for years had come to sudden
shocking reality. They came in . . . looked around, commenting
on the pictures . . . one of them said he understood I had quite a
collection of obscene pictures; I did once, I said, but I gave them
all to Dr. Kinsey and got rid of them. Ah, yes, they said—well,
we'd like you to come down to the station for questioning about
these murdered boys.

During Steward's questioning at the police station, he was asked his
whereabouts for October 17–18, Monday and Tuesday. In order to give
himself an alibi for the Peterson-Schuessler murders, he had needed to
explain that he worked as a professor at DePaul. He was then released on
the condition that he return on Tuesday the thirteenth at 5:00 p.m. for a
lie detector test.

As soon as Steward returned home, he set to work transporting the
remaining photographic collections and sexual records in his apartment
to the home of Emmy Curtis, not knowing if his home was going to be
raided. He returned to the station two days later, and even though he was
told at the end of the interview that he had passed the lie detector test,
he sensed he was in trouble, writing afterward in his journal,

They'll probably pick me up from now on. So often you see the
line in the newspapers: "Police rounded up all known sex deviates
in the vicinity" of this crime or that. Can one face an existence
like that? . . .

If word of this gets to DePaul . . . it would definitely end me
there—involvement of the innocent or not.

. . . Emmy reminded me I've known I was playing with fire,
however, as I indeed have been. I seem to have some fundamen-
tal urge to destroy myself . . . Why can't I lead a dull and happy
and *carefree* life? The answer, I suppose, is that I'd rot; I have to
have excitement, even at the price of ruin.

Steward later described his questioning over the Peterson-Schuessler
murders for an oral history project: "I was cleared on . . . the murder,
largely because I had no car and [since I don't know how to drive I]
couldn't have driven out into the woods and killed the boys . . . and

take[n] them out there . . . [The police] took in six hundred people, all of them queers . . . and they never did find out who killed the three boys." Much to Steward's relief, the police did not return to his home to demand the homoerotic and pornographic materials they had stumbled across during their visit. In fact, the new apartment was much less outrageously decorated; in moving uptown he had already placed the most shocking, graphic, and incriminating of the materials into storage. Moreover, while the charge of possessing pornographic materials then carried a fine of one thousand dollars per article in the state of Illinois, the detectives had initially come to Steward without a search warrant, and they knew Steward would have cleared his apartment of everything illegal in the hours after their visit.

Nonetheless, by the end of the same week the dean of the school called an immediate meeting with Steward. In it, he simply told Steward that his contract would not be renewed:

> I tried to get him to say why, but all I could force out of him was "Shall we say for outside activities?" I said that covered a lot; yes, he said, and that I could discuss the matter with President O'Malley [the head of the university] if I wanted to. The whole business took less than 40 seconds.
>
> I staggered back to the faculty house (white-faced, I presume) . . . and then . . . retired to my office and sat for 20 minutes staring at the wall . . . all I could see was the appalling loss of face in having nothing to do except be a tattooer.
>
> . . . The thing that will be hardest to accustom myself to, of course, will be the "loss of face" and the diminishment of Gertrude's "sense of the importance of yourself inside yourself." . . . For years I have loathed teaching: the futility of it being broken all too rarely by the reward of finding an intelligent single one whom I could watch grow. I have liked being the most popular teacher in that branch; it would be silly to deny the feast such a realization furnished my ego . . . [yet] gone now will be the mornings when I had to take a halfa benny in order to face the room of witless faces in their Monday stupor.
>
> There's no denying, however, that there are still many moments of terror, when awake at night or even during the day's lulls, I wonder if I can make a go at this business of tattooing. There are so many factors . . . uncertainties at every turn—the

customers, the law, the legal age limit, mistakes possible everywhere. It requires a kind of courage and assurance very difficult
for me to summon.

　　And worst of all, of course, the remaining seven weeks of
school . . .

Steward had chosen his vocation more than twenty years earlier at
Ohio State University, and ever since then had prided himself on his extraordinary ability (and popularity) as a teacher and educator. Indeed,
quite apart from his teaching duties, he had devoted the better part of his
life to being a scholar, poet, and man of letters. And yet, over the course
of the past several years, he had been letting go of that identity, for there
was no place for him in that world. While shocked at having been fired,
he was at least strong enough not to self-destruct—unlike other, more accomplished and dedicated academics, such as Harvard's F. O. Matthies-
sen, a leftist homosexual critic who had killed himself in the midst of Senator
McCarthy's 1950 attacks on "domestic subversion," or Smith College's Newton Arvin, whose life would come to an end shortly after his home was
illegally raided by police for possession of homosexual pornography in
September 1960.*

　　Instead, Steward rallied over the weekend, taking the train up to Milwaukee and there presenting himself to Amund Dietzel with an enormous
garland-of-flowers design he had created for application to his chest. "I
plunked down a couple of $20 bills in front of him and said, 'tell me about
tattooing,'" Steward later recalled, "[and] for the 40 bucks I got five hours
of advice and teaching and a tattoo to boot—an excellent investment."
Creating the garland actually took three long, bloody sessions; the immediate physical pain may well have been both a distraction and a relief
from the much greater psychic anguish Steward was experiencing over
the abrupt termination of his academic career.

　　After describing the trip to Dietzel's in Milwaukee in his journal,
Steward noted, "James Purdy stopped into the shop today and applauded
my decision, he also having given up teaching as a shitty, futile business

---

*Seven men were convicted and given suspended sentences in the Arvin scandal. The two other
Smith College professors appealed their convictions and were later acquitted in light of a 1961 Supreme Court ruling barring illegal police searches.

(I guess he was caught in fragrant delicious.*)" He also looked forward to a visit from Kinsey, noting, "In a sense he, as a father image, will be more important to me in what he says than any other person. I am hoping he will not disapprove. He has undoubtedly known other cases . . . now, at any rate, I can collaborate on a tattoo article with him and have no fear." And indeed, Kinsey proved very supportive: "Prok[†] . . . said he would cherish me as much as a tattooer as otherwise, and suggested that I try to keep up an academic connection of some kind—reviewing, writing, teaching one course. It was he who thought I might stand a chance at Roosevelt University[‡] since they were so 'militantly broadminded'—and so indeed I might."

Steward took an upbeat tone in his next letter to Kinsey, noting on May 21, "I now have a fine and efficient new air conditioner installed in my apartment, and I look forward to Friday, the last day of school for me. With all adjustments now perfectly made, I can't for the life of me understand how I endured the restrictions of a Catholic teaching career for as long as I did."

By the end of the school term, Steward had not only reconciled himself to his departure, but also realized that he owed his adoring students at least a brief explanation of his decision to quit teaching. He delivered a farewell lecture to his last class at DePaul on Friday, May 25, 1956, and afterward described it in his journal:

> In the novel class, last of the day, I made a farewell statement in which I quoted Gide's saying to me that every man had to (ought to—"doit faire") make a complete break at least once in his life, with his home, thought, apartment or profession—and that this was it for me. A small gasp went up when I said I was retiring from teaching. And I told them that in line with my always finding a quotation of poetry to cover any situation that arose, they

---

*In flagrante delicto. Steward was of the opinion that Purdy had been caught while having sex with a student. No account of Purdy's departure from the school where he taught exists; two query letters from the author to Purdy on his friendship with Steward and life circumstances during the period of their close acquaintance went unanswered and unreturned. (Purdy died in 2009.)

†"Prok" was Kinsey's nickname, originally coined by his students as a contraction of "professor" and "Kinsey."

‡A Chicago university strongly dedicated to principles of social justice.

would find my major motivations in 1) the first four lines of Michael Drayton's sonnet, "The parting"* 2) stanzas 3, 4 and 5 of Housman's "To an Athlete Dying Young"† and 3) the last two lines of Milton's "Lycidas."‡ It was quite a little moment.

Steward then moved on in his journal entry to describe the travails of his good friend Hal McEwan, a fashion model, who had been entrapped by police on a park bench on the Near North Side: "Hal said that he felt that if he'd offered the pickup cop $25 it would all have been called off. But he didn't have it." As a result, McEwan faced legal bills of more than two hundred dollars as well as a permanent police record for homosexual solicitation.

In the first week of June, his teaching career now officially finished, Steward held fast to the notion that his work for Kinsey would sustain him intellectually as he began his full-time life as a tattoo artist:

> Prok came [down to the cage] on May 26th [and] for two hours he watched and listened . . . With his fresh and scientific eye, he saw and commented on many things which . . . have become so usual [to me] that I barely see them any more . . . he saw it, all right, he did. He . . . said he thought every clinical psychologist ought to spend five or six two-hour sessions observing [in a tattoo parlor] before going out into the field.

Having been encouraged by Kinsey to think that through his journal writing and tattoo research he would eventually find a new scholarly vocation, Steward returned to them with vigor. As he did so, he felt a new compassion for the young men who came daily into the shop, for so many of them seemed to him in desperate need of mentoring and attention. After years of simply resenting the institutions in which he had taught,

---

*"Since there's no help, come let us kiss and part / Nay, I have done, you get no more of me; / And I am glad, yea, glad with all my heart, / That thus so freely I myself can free."
†"Smart lad, to slip betimes away / From fields where glory does not stay / And early though the laurel grows / It withers quicker than the rose / Eyes the shady night has shut / Cannot see the record cut / And silence sound no worse than cheers / After earth has stopped the ears; / Now you will not swell the rout / Of lads that wore their honors out / Runners who the name outran / And the name died before the man."
‡"At last he rose, and twitch'd his mantle blew: / To morrow to fresh Woods, and Pastures new."

Steward now began to reassess his own motivations for working with and among the young. In one entry, for example, he noted the real pleasure he took in spending time among the troubled adolescents who had started to hang around the kiosk:

> I wish there were some way of getting the feel of the shop into this journal—all the double-tender* sexual talk, the gesturing, the fumbling, the hints and talk of blow-jobs, violence, purse-snatching, knifing, the thinly veiled and uncomprehended homosexual motivations of the herd-and-hero instincts. I josh with 'em, scold 'em, sympathize with them—and like a good psychiatrist, priest or scientist, never never criticize. But the life that moves into and through my shop, always changing, is the real thing, seen and touched and tasted after so many years of the counterfeit and sheltered.

Later that week, Steward took stock of his life, noting in his journal that "this first bleak look at [my] future is a hard and depressing one . . . [But] in a sense, this will weigh and judge me. I will have now to test the validity of everything I have been saying to classes for the past twenty years [about] the . . . inner strength [of] the man able to think . . . This is going to be quite a little task . . . Putting it on paper helps, as the first step." He echoed these concerns in a letter to Alice Toklas: "The end of school, the real and final end, gave me the weak willies for a day, but I recovered quickly, and hope for no recurrence. What a shallow mocking empty fraud that school was, and my life in it for eight years!"

Unfortunately, the loss of his job was not the only loss Steward was dealing with, for in letting go of his identity as a teacher, he was also letting go of his younger self. And along with letting go of that younger self, he also let go of one of the most long-standing sexual relationships that had been part of it. On June 11, he noted, "Sunday morning at two a.m. Bob Berbich rang the bell, and came up [for sex]. Afterwards, he announced he's moving to Santa Barbara next month, which will take him outa my picture, and I received the news with mild regrets. I'll miss that old baseball-bat of his, and his funny odd lower-class ways and expressions."

---

*Double-entendre.

Steward and his baby sister, Virginia, a year after they were left by their father to grow up with his aunts in Woodsfield, Ohio.

Steward's two maiden aunts, Minnie Rose and Elizabeth Rose, who sold their boardinghouse in Woodsfield to open another one at Ohio State University in Columbus.

Steward at age sixteen, his first year in Columbus, the year of his hotel encounter with Rudolph Valentino.

The Valentino reliquary, created by Steward and cherished throughout his life. (Courtesy of a private collector)

Sincerely
Rudolph Valentino

July 24, 1926

The Valentino autograph from Steward's autograph book, which features the signatures of eighteen other period celebrities, including Thornton Wilder.

Steward photographed on Sperry Glacier in Glacier Park, Montana, the summer of 1935, after Carrol College and before his yearlong appointment at Washington State University in Pullman.

A 1939 photograph by Steward of Gertrude Stein working in her tomato patch at Bilignin, taken while on vacation from his teaching position at Loyola University in Chicago.

Steward's 1939 snapshot of Thornton Wilder in the room where Oscar Wilde died, Hotel d'Alsace, Paris.

Steward, standing second from right, in a group portrait of the scholars who rewrote the *World Book Encyclopedia* in the late 1940s. His sister, Virginia, is seated at lower right.

A group photo of the four main Kinsey researchers taken shortly after Steward first met them: Wardell Pomeroy, Paul Gebhard, Alfred C. Kinsey, and Clyde Martin. (Photograph by William Dellenback, courtesy of the Kinsey Institute for Research in Sex, Gender, and Reproduction, Inc.)

A faculty portrait of Steward, circa 1950, after he had accepted an appointment at DePaul University.

A Hollywood-style portrait of Steward, probably mid-1940s.

One of the many photographss documenting Steward's apartment taken by Kinsey's photographer, Bill Dellenback. Steward's bent-wire mobile of a motorcycle tough hangs in the doorway; a number of erotic fetishes and bibelots sit atop the bookcases, which feature first-edition novels on homosexual themes as well as poetic, erotic, pornographic, and sociological titles. (Photograph by William Dellenback, courtesy of the Kinsey Institute for Research in Sex, Gender, and Reproduction, Inc.)

Steward's Polaroid of one of the rough "sex murals" that he painted on the walls of his apartment in advance of a *spintriae*.

A Polaroid of Kinsey taken by Steward at Steward's apartment.

Polaroid of a sailor looking through an album of Steward's sex Polaroids, in the same chair occupied by Kinsey in the previous photo.

A shot of Steward's Murphy bed, giving a partial glimpse of its first mural, which featured a sailor and his floozy. (Photograph by William Dellenback, courtesy of the Kinsey Institute for Research in Sex, Gender, and Reproduction, Inc.)

Polaroid of Steward in a "French gangster mask," one of the many erotic props used during *spintriae.*

A *spintriae* Polaroid.

Steward's Polaroid of a young sailor posed before the second mural he painted over his Murphy bed.

Steward frequently experimented with lighting effects and timed photography to create erotic images. Here he creates a dramatically lit self-portrait featuring a phantasmagorical other.

Steward with Sir Francis Rose and his adopted "son," Luis, summer of 1952.

Steward on the roof of 5 rue Christine with Alice B. Toklas and Basket II, summer of 1952.

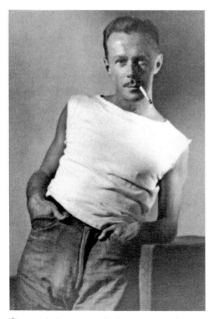

Steward, this time styled as a *jeune dur*, in a studio portrait taken in Paris, 1952.

Steward in an officer's cap. He often likened himself to Lieutenant Seblon in Jean Genet's *Querelle de Brest;* this photo may have been taken during his August 1952 trip to Brest.

A letter from Steward to George Platt Lynes on Steward's homemade erotic stationery. In this letter, Steward is describing his sexual exploits at the Embarcadero YMCA in the summer of 1953.

One of Steward's favorite photographs by George Platt Lynes, featuring his friend Johnny Leapheart, whom he introduced to Lynes in September 1952. Steward's encounters with Leapheart took place in New York, Chicago, and San Francisco. (Photograph by George Platt Lynes, courtesy of the Kinsey Institute for Research in Sex, Gender, and Reproduction, Inc., and the Estate of George Platt Lynes)

"Dr Stewart's [*sic*] Culture Club" from the De Paul yearbook. His student Douglas Martin, a close friend in later life, stands fourth from left. (Courtesy of Douglas Martin)

```
                                                    361
              11-XII-50.  Chicago.

                                           9
H B bat                                    px

12-11-50; 1-10-51; 1-31-51; 3-21; 4-11; 5-14; 5-28; 8-8;
9-18;10-23;
Figure d'ange; ame de cochon. Gangster. This is it...


[Bittersweet]  g.c. June-July 1951. Gave watch: 2-11-52
See Contract ffg ths card.
```

The "sex contract" card from the Stud File, in which Steward agrees to give George Reginato "four marks of A in four courses . . . [and] the preparation of papers of examinations" in exchange for oral sex. The reverse features a swatch of the student's pubic hair and the dates of the encounters that followed.

```
              C O N T R A C T      June   , 1951

between                 [party of the first part] and
Sam Steward [party of the second part]
   Whereas, in consideration for certain favors bestowed
upon the party of the first part by the party of the sec-
ond part [4 marks of A in 4 courses at De Paul University,
and one more to follow in August, 1951], as well as other
favors such as the preparation of papers and examinations,
party of first part agrees to let party of second part
go down on him one time during each of the months of June
thru December, 1951, with one extra time during each of
the months of June and July, 1951.

          Signed
          Signed    Sam Steward
```

Steward's Stud File, the detailed lifelong record (painstakingly alphabetized, coded, annotated, and cross-referenced) describing his thousands of sexual encounters.

Steward as shopkeeper: washing the windows of his tattoo parlor on South State Street, Chicago, circa 1957.

Steward's Polaroid of a tattooed youth, taken at the tattoo parlor.

Chuck Renslow, founder of Kris Studio and eventually owner of a small empire of sex-related businesses in Chicago. (Courtesy of the Leather Archives and Museum)

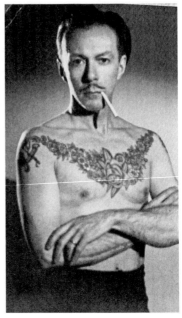

Johnny Reyes in a "beefcake" photo by Chuck Renslow. It was Renslow who introduced Reyes to Steward. (Courtesy of the Leather Archives and Museum)

Steward's chest tattoos, as photographed in Paris in 1957. Just visible on his right shoulder is his tattoo of a winged phallus overlaid by a whip.

Steward meditates at Keats's grave. Rome, Christmas, 1960.

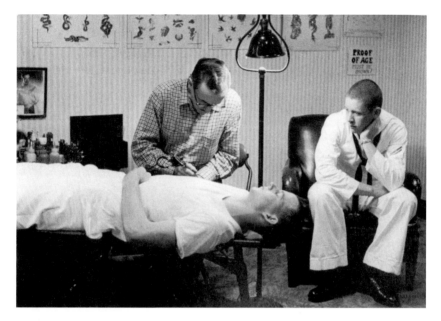

(counterclockwise from above) Steward applies a tattoo to a boot sailor (sailor trainee), 1963–64 (courtesy of the Magazine Archive, San Francisco); boot sailors waiting to be tattooed at the Phil Sparrow/Cliff Raven/Chuck Renslow Milwaukee tattoo parlor, 1963–64 (courtesy of the Magazine Archive, San Francisco); a freshly tattooed boot sailor at the Milwaukee parlor (courtesy of the Magazine Archive, San Francisco); Steward waiting on his next sailor in the Milwaukee parlor (courtesy of Don Ed Hardy)

Steward in front of his "hidden bungalow" in the Berkeley Flats, shortly after closing the Milwaukee parlor and moving to California.

Steward's Anchor Tattoo Shop on San Pablo Avenue, Oakland. The Trading Post Pawn Shop, where Herman Kartun was murdered, is directly adjacent. (Courtesy of Don Ed Hardy)

Another rare photograph of the Anchor Tattoo Shop, this time seen from across San Pablo Avenue. Just a short drive from the Hells Angels world headquarters, the Anchor was where Angels from all over California came to get their tattoos. (Courtesy of Don Ed Hardy)

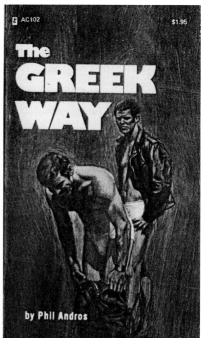

Three Phil Andros covers: *$TUD*, the 1966 Guild Press Edition with a jacket commissioned by Steward from Dom Orejudos; *The Greek Way*, typical of the gay pulp paperback editions published by Greenleaf; and *My Brother, My Self* (originally published in pulp as *My Brother, the Hustler*), in Don Allen's luxurious Perineum Press 1982 edition.

Steward in his bungalow among his collections, just a few years before his death. The squalor of Steward's home was skillfully concealed by the photographer, Robert Giard. (Courtesy of the Robert Giard Foundation.)

Steward's ever-growing awareness of his age was beginning to affect him down at the cage as well; in the same journal entry, he noted feeling "old and dirty and soiled" in front of so many "healthy and wholesome" young sailors. While his sex life remained good—he had just seen Wally Kargol, the ex-marine he had first picked up in the dunes of Indiana Harbor in 1951, and with whom he had since developed a highly satisfying "boots, whips and commands" relationship—he nonetheless found himself growing increasingly bored and impatient with his older contacts, noting, for example, that "Wally . . . has risen to be chairman of the grievance committee at Monkey Wards,* and is hard at work developing a new social consciousness, with so much talk about being the workingman's friend, that he begins . . . to wear very thin . . . I found myself wishing that he'd leave, once the encounter came to an end."

As men his own age ceased to interest him, Steward found himself more and more attracted to younger ones. In a journal entry two weeks later, he described four sensationally attractive young men who had just dropped by the cage, then added, "Sometimes I think I'll go utterly nuts having them so close and not being able to do what I'd like." However, he consoled himself with the knowledge that his business was doing better and better: "June continues good . . . total to date—$962. I was impressed by the fact that—to the dollar—I made in the week of June 17th the equivalent of a full month's pay at DePaul: $384."

It was not only closeness to so many young men in his shop that made Steward conscious of his advancing age. He was now repeatedly finding himself either ignored or passed over in sexual situations, as contact after contact instead chose someone younger and more attractive. The situation was particularly maddening for him since in most instances he was setting up the very orgies at which he was being rejected. After a daisy chain at his apartment, he recorded that among the nine young men present, only one had paid him any attention, leading him once more to wonder if he "ought to give it all up gracefully before the talking about me as an old auntie grows too painful."

But there was not much to be done about middle age. As a result, Steward began slipping into the role of the friendly mentor—a role he had long since mastered through many years of teaching. In doing so, he

*Steward's nickname for the Chicago-based department store chain Montgomery Ward.

seems to have reconciled himself to the never-ending ache of unrequited love—a sensation that had tortured him throughout his earlier, more closeted academic years in Helena and Pullman. After one particularly handsome young man named Gordon Krull stayed late with him at the tattoo shop, Steward simply abandoned himself to morose delectation, and took the rugged, unattainable youth out to dinner at a local cafeteria:

> He was a big lad, about six feet two, [with] an excellently profiled face . . . so beautiful that everything once more flowed out of me, leaving a vast emptiness behind, that terrible ache I get in front of beauty . . . I several times found myself partly erecting, an amazing phenomenon for me after all these years. He thanked me for the dinner, and finally left about seven-thirty to get his train . . . Days such as this leave me exhausted, and restless, and a little unhappy because they can have no issue in any practical fulfillment.*

On June 26, Glenway Wescott passed through Chicago. Wescott had been doing work at the Kinsey Institute on a project (never to be realized) of detailing the sexual lives of artists and writers—a project that, in the words of a Kinsey biographer, "essentially . . . seems to have been Glenway spouting intimate gossip." He visited Steward down at the tattoo cage, hoping to be invited to a *spintriae*; Steward, however, ducked out of hosting him, and declined even to invite him back to his new, uptown apartment. After receiving a note of reproach from Wescott the following week, Steward responded,

> The fantastic episodes continue to pile up here in my shabby little gold mine, and I have been so deluged with tightpantsed (!) tawny-armed beauties that I've lost nearly all sense of selectivity—handsome and ugly, they all run together. There's such a thing as having too much beauty around you, I guess; you become insensitive to everything.
>   I did not leave you for an assignation; at least, there was none intended, although after I got home one did materialize—a truck-

---

*Fifteen days later, Steward followed up by noting that "Gordon Krull, on whom I rhapsodized a bit back, is now in jail for having stolen a car. Oh, well." (Steward, *Journal*, July 10, 1956.)

driver . . . and tonight a marine sergeant, and so it goes, extremely full to the brim, and my own cup half-empty most of the time.

So let us forgive each other our own emphatic projectings, and have only a few regrets. Some time we shall make up for our delicacies.

In losing his position at DePaul—and with it, in a sense, many long-harbored pretensions about himself—Steward felt free, as well, to let go of Wescott, a pretentious literary man he had never really liked.

•

As he began tattooing full-time, Steward became more and more attuned to the life of the streets, including the lives of street gangs. "I've come closer to breaking into the closed circle of the Road Wolves than that of any other [pachuco] gang," he wrote after learning that one of its members was regularly performing oral sex on the others, even though none of them considered him homosexual. He later noted that his tattoo-artist identity gave him intimate access to the otherwise closed world of these gangs, for "a tattoo for the gang members or the delinquents was a visible sign of their rebellion, their manliness, or their affiliation with the stratum that was in revolt . . . [and since] I performed a function of which their parents disapproved . . . I was therefore one of them [and] they talked freely in front of me . . . The fact that I furnish[ed] them with their 'badges' [eventually] opened most of the [Chicago] gangs to me."

In his free time, Steward began keeping newspaper clippings relating to the tattoo cage and its "regulars." There was a nineteen-year-old named Bob Berullo, who had hung around the shop for several months, and who frequently asked Steward if he needed anyone beaten up. He subsequently disappeared. Steward discovered his name in the newspaper a short time later, in a report stating that Berullo had been given a sentence of ten years to life on one of two counts of robbery, and two to ten years on another count, with the two sentences to run concurrently.

Steward had other rough young men who interested him as well, chief among them a handsome, hulking seventeen-year-old Polish boy named Tommy Saklovitch. Saklovitch had initially tagged along with the Road Wolves gang on their visit to the cage one afternoon for gang tattoos. The gang members had shunned Saklovitch, however, thinking him "violent, stupid and crazy." Steward subsequently ascertained that when still a child, Saklovitch had been subjected to shock treatments that left him permanently confused. Rejected from the marines for lack of intelligence, he was well-nigh unemployable. Steward, however, found Saklovitch sexually attractive, and so began inviting him over to his apartment regularly for sex. The friendship between them was such that as a gift for Saklovitch's eighteenth birthday, Steward tattooed a fly on the head of his penis. An August 1 journal entry gives a sense of Steward's oddly tender relationship with this otherwise totally unloved boy-man—a sex relationship that would last, on and off, for nearly six years:*

> The night Tommy left for Milwaukee [to try to get a job] he came out to stay the night with me, and we went thru our regular ritual—first both of us climbing in the shower together, and me scrubbing that great animal body, and kneeling again to wash his feet, with my eyes centering on the little fly on his cock, dangling an inch from my mouth . . . and then going to bed, and using the vibrator on each other, and then to sleep. I suggested Tommy use my new "Heaven Hole" but he said no, he'd already tried something like that in a sponge rubber shop.

A born tinkerer and inventor, Steward was now constantly creating devices such as the "Heaven Hole" during his free time down at the cage:

> This new thing I had made up at the foam rubber shop on Broadway—a six inch cube of foam rubber with a hole down the middle the size of a silver dollar. I then got some liquid latex at the art store, and gave three-four coats to the rough inside of the center cut . . . I put the cube under one of the sofa cushions and kneel in front of it, so that by leaning on top I create pressure and squash the hole narrower. Then I insert the rubber cup of the vibrator on the far end; the latex coating picks up and transmits

_____

*Steward continued to have sex with Saklovitch until 1961, noting long afterward that "he went steadily downhill, gradually losing his good looks as he moved into his twenties . . . He ended in a state mental hospital from which he wrote to me asking me to become his sponsor so that he could get out. But had I taken care of all the lame dogs who came to me for help during the tattoo years, it would have been myself in the asylum, not they." (Steward, _BBTT_, p. 143.)

the vibration through the whole opening . . . I'll be damned if it isn't the most realistic thing I've ever felt, outside of the genuine article—and what a greater advantage, to be able to store your wife in a closet! No expense, all the pleasure. Orgasm is terrific, every time I've used it yet.

In late July, Steward encountered an old acquaintance from his Polaroid days: Bill Payson, a devastatingly handsome black weightlifter whom he later described in his Stud File as *"beau comme l'aube"*:*

I talked [him] into coming down to the shop, and he came . . . and then I suggested [a] blow-job; he was reluctant at first, and then said yes. He was no kinder than formerly . . . all my gaggings and efforts to escape from the inexorable ram availing nothing— he proceeded to thrust it in and out of my throat until I couldn't breathe and the tears ran down my face from the choking. He finally came, completely and satisfyingly uncaring about my discomfort . . . Finally he released me . . . I said goodbye to him, still blinking and breathless from my lovely ordeal, he looking at me with quiet amusement, as if saying, "Well, white boy, that's a blowjob you'll remember." And I will, too.

During that summer of 1956, Steward sensed he was being staked out again by spies from the Naval Training Station. But in the end no naval authorities harassed him. Instead, toward the end of a highly profitable summer, he had an unexpected and entirely devastating setback. In his journal for Saturday, August 25, he noted simply: "Damn, damn, and double goddamn. Prok died today, of complications of heart and pneumonia. I am too cold to think."

Throughout the upheavals of the last six years, Kinsey had remained fixed in Steward's mind as someone who understood him and sympathized with him. Through his association with Kinsey, Steward had felt he was participating in something greater than himself, something that gave his life significance and meaning. He had composed his journals, kept his sex calendars, and maintained his Stud File with Kinsey firmly in mind as

*Handsome as the dawn.

his ideal reader. As a result, Kinsey had become the most important person in his life by far—and now Kinsey was no more. "I am still frozen with shock," Steward wrote in his journal three days later. "The sense of loss is stronger than I have ever felt . . . I wanted to cry Sunday evening, but was too numb. I can't even find words to write about it."

Along with the personal loss of Kinsey himself—who had been for Steward not only a friend, but also a mentor, a confidant, and an adviser—Steward now faced another loss: of his own sense of importance. Kinsey, after all, had been Steward's one connection to the world of sex research. Set adrift from Kinsey and his monumental work, Steward now wondered what he was doing and who he was doing it for. His journals, diaries, photographs, and statistics had all been intended for Kinsey. A week after Kinsey's death, Steward confided in his journal,

> Over and over again his image returns; I re-live the moments and hours we had together. I find myself thinking: "I must get that in the journal; Prok will appreciate it"—and then find myself jerked up short, as the realization comes back. To think that this vital man, this overwhelming personality should have been struck down, and then to look at the shabby ones shuffling along outside, much older than he, leads me to distressful and adolescent cryings-out against something or other, I scarcely know what.
>
> Ward[ell] Pomeroy came to the shop to see me a few days ago; he was up here for the psychologist's convention to spread the word that the institute would still function under the double leadership of himself and Paul G[ebhard]. I reassured him of my "continuing cooperation," for whatever that may be worth. But I feel that temporarily I will have to put the journal aside, until the heart comes back into me to go on writing.
>
> It is nice to apply the *mythos* to him, and see him seated comfortably in a small anteroom, interviewing the shades. I hope he has interesting ones.

Steward reiterated this last hope many years later in his memoirs:

> If one really believed in an afterlife, it would be pleasant to consider Kinsey sitting with Socrates and Plato under the shade of an

Ilex tree discussing the *Phaedrus*,* or asking Leonardo da Vinci about his golden youths, or Michelangelo about the models he used, or Whitman to tell the real truth about himself and Peter Doyle. Questioning and questioning he would have all eternity to roam in—and if he ever came to the end, he would still be unsatisfied.

With Kinsey's death, a distinct period of Steward's own life was coming to a definitive close. In the past six years Steward had reached out to the larger artistic community of New York and Paris; he had also left the safety of the teaching life for the far riskier life of the artist, business entrepreneur, and sex enthusiast. At midlife he had dared (as few in life ever dare) to begin his life entirely anew, starting over on his own terms. But what intellectual direction his brave and adventurous new life would take, now that Kinsey was gone, was something Steward had yet to decide.

---

*One of the Platonic dialogues, a conversation between Socrates and Phaedrus on the nature and practice of love.

13

"Pleasure doesn't really make one happy"

Devastated by Kinsey's death, Steward ceased his journal. It was not until over a year later, on November 14, 1957, that he uncertainly began writing in it again, and in doing so he noted the many significant changes that had taken place in his life since he had stopped:

> I am now at the end of my first year in the new [tattoo shop I constructed in] the old bar across the street from the [Sportland] arcade . . . [and] the place has earned the deserved reputation among the young punks and juvenile delinquents and sailors of the area as being the nicest tattoo shop in town. It is really quite elegant, with more lights in the window than in a barbershop, neon signs all over the place, [and] a window display that gets a tremendous play from the passing public. The gross here is higher than [in] the old arcade . . . I won't give up this little gold mine until the civic betterment association forces me out.

Steward had had many sexual contacts during the past year, and he cataloged them all in his very long first journal entry, which concluded, "Most of all at present . . . I enjoy [the black bodybuilder] Bill Payson . . . It is his attitude of semi-cruelty, you might say, that I like; not cruelty exactly, but more a feeling of 'This is what you deserve, white boy; you scorn me because I'm a nigger, and here I am, shoving this big black tool right down in you, fucking you in the ass; that'll show you what I think of you.' . . . and man—does he."

Before Kinsey's death, Steward had felt he was doing something greater in his journal than simply gloating over his various sexual escapades, something that would serve humanity in general by serving Kinsey in particular. But now, a year after Kinsey's death, Steward was struggling with a sense of futility, for apparently he was once again back where he had started—keeping a diary of assorted sexual exploits for not much more than his own satisfaction and amusement. As a result, he struggled daily with an overwhelming sense of abandonment, hopelessness, and loss. Alice Toklas, knowing all too well what it was like to lose someone larger and more important than oneself (for she had been trying since 1946 to redefine her place in the world after the loss of Gertrude Stein), had been gently encouraging him for some time to think once again of writing for publication, asking him, "Isn't there any newspaper that pays little but more than nothing for the things you can do so very well—so naturally like the Sparrow of the dental review—less local with subjects of a wider field." Perhaps hoping to supply Steward with a little bit of "humor and diversion" of her own, she then shared with him her latest story about Sir Francis Rose, which she described, only half ironically, as "Francis and his international scandal."

Rose's "scandal" began while spending a boozy weekend in Portsmouth, England, with his old friend Lionel Kenneth Philip "Buster" Crabb.* Crabb was a retired Royal Navy commander who had been a pioneering undersea diver of the 1930s; beginning in the war years, he had been one of Rose's favorite ne'er-do-well drinking buddies, and in fact they had briefly roomed together.† Though by 1956 Crabb was forty-seven, out of shape, and deeply alcoholic, he had nonetheless managed to conduct a surreptitious underwater inspection of the Russian cruiser *Sverdlov* while the ship was docked in England. The success of this mission (Crabb had seen and described the ship's innovative steering propeller) had subsequently led MI6 to ask him to spy on the hull of the Russian cruiser *Ordzhonikidze*, which had just brought General-Secretary Nikita

---

*Crabb's nickname "Buster" was derived from the Olympic swimming star and Hollywood actor Buster Crabbe (who starred in the serials *Flash Gordon*, *Buck Rogers*, and *Tarzan*). But the two were not related.
†Crabb's life and death are chronicled in several books on what came to be known as the "Frogman" scandal. Crabb's early introduction to diving (via a friend of Picasso, who introduced him to a group of young Italian naval officers) is noted in Rose, *Saying Life* (p. 403).

Khrushchev and Premier Nikolai Bulganin to Britain on a state visit. The day of the ship's arrival in Portsmouth was the last day Crabb was seen alive; ten days later, British newspapers reported his death in a diving accident, giving no specific details.

Upon Crabb's mysterious death,* Rose had left England and attempted to hide out at his little *chambre de bonne* apartment on Ile St. Louis—but not before telling a reporter that he had received a mysteriously phrased note from Crabb the day he died. As a result, Rose suddenly found himself being stalked by British intelligence, Russian intelligence, French police, and legions of tabloid reporters. His Paris apartment was broken into soon after he arrived and the mysterious note from Crabb was reportedly stolen; subsequently Rose's "son" Luis was arrested and detained without charges in the French prison at Saint-Quentin. Hounded relentlessly by newspapermen, French plainclothes police, and the KGB, Rose had a mental breakdown. His estranged wife, Lady Frederica, arrived shortly thereafter from her home on Corsica, packed up his things and brought him back to England, and there deposited him at the former Holloway Sanatorium at Virginia Water for psychiatric observation. So began a cycle of breakdown, institutionalization, and release that would continue, on and off, for the rest of Rose's life.

Steward's existence, by comparison, had been relatively uneventful over the past year. There had been one great upset in the fall of 1956, when police had raided and shut down the Sportland Arcade for showing illegal (and highly profitable) pornographic films on its antiquated peep-show machines. As a result of the closure, Steward had lost his kiosk workspace. He had needed to find himself another space very quickly, before his business began to suffer, and so he had settled almost immediately on a shop front across the street, a former barroom and speakeasy "that Al Capone had frequented, having [once] been enamored of a barmaid [who worked] there." Steward was able to rent the place on a month-by-month lease since the building, surrounded by vacant lots, was slated for eventual demolition as part of an urban renewal scheme.

The name Steward gave his new shop—"Phil Sparrow's Tattoo Joynt"—was slyly playful. In choosing the Middle English spelling of *joint*, "joynt," Steward quietly drew attention to the word and its various meanings—for

*He had most probably been shot and killed by a Soviet sniper.

while *joint* primarily describes a place where two bodies come together or join (which is itself sexually suggestive), it also described, in slang usage, a disreputable place of entertainment, a prison, a marijuana cigarette, or (most significantly for Steward) a phallus. And indeed the Joynt contained elements of all those things. Immediately after moving in, Steward walled off the rear section of the overly large space, thereby creating a private backroom area at the Joynt devoted entirely to sex, and featuring a cot, an easy chair, a waist-high workbench for "rough fucking," and a toilet area rigged not only with a series of peepholes, but also a "glory hole" through which men could engage in anonymous oral sex.

While Steward's own sex drive was waning, he remained entirely fascinated by the rough young men he now encountered daily. As he wrote in his journal,

> my periodicity* is extending itself—from 48 hours, it has now jumped to 80 or 90—and of course my body is slowing down, for I am now 48, going on 49.
>
> One of the best of the new finds is Bill Tregoz, a boy [who] up and left a graduate fellowship in ancient languages at the University of Michigan [to come] to Chicago, [buy] a motorcycle, [play the harp] and . . . work for an engineering firm. I put three large tattoos on him . . . he wears full [motorcyclist] regalia, even down to the black leather pants . . . I have found him extremely interesting—highly intelligent . . . and a wonderful sexual thrill.†
>
> The beauties who pass through my hands [as I tattoo them], however, are the ones that torment me still a great deal . . . At any rate, I can touch them, hold their biceps, touch their knees— something I could never do with the students when I was teaching . . . So, all in all, it's been a fairly good year sexually speaking.

In January of 1957 Chuck Liston, a particularly handsome young man who had once hung around the cage en route to a military school in South Carolina, returned to Chicago in uniform and came to visit Steward at his new shop. Liston was now a soldier, and in Steward's opinion,

---

*By "periodicity," Steward means the amount of time between sexual encounters.
†Steward later described Tregoz's life in a short story entitled "The Tattooed Harpist."

"a more rugged American youth I've rarely seen." Steward developed a powerful crush on him after seeing him in uniform, one he found extremely painful, for the young man was amiable and affectionate with him, but in no way interested in sex.

In the same entry in which he described his unrequited crush on Liston, Steward nonetheless noted starting a sex relationship with a highly intelligent former student of his at DePaul named Pete Rojas. He went on to observe that "making Pete was one of the most satisfying rewards I've had for quitting teaching, for I think I could not have let myself do it (nor would he have said yes) while that other relationship [of student to teacher] existed in the background."

•

In his pursuit of sexual variety and adventure, Steward had become involved with some very troubled characters over the past year. Most notable among them was Roy Robinson, a six-foot-two, twenty-seven-year-old ex-con who had had all of his teeth removed in order to be fitted for dentures. While Steward thought Robinson an awful character, he was nonetheless fascinated by the extraordinary sensation of Robinson's toothless mouth, which Robinson made available to him (in exchange for cash) on a regular basis. Years later, after paying Robinson to perform oral sex on him a total of 230 times in the back room of the tattoo parlor, Steward observed that Robinson was without a doubt

> the most morally and ethically rotten person I had ever known, [one who] would have been easily recognized by any psychiatrist as a true sociopath . . . He had been arrested nearly eighty times and spent a good third of his life in prison . . . He was married three times . . . and was very fond of "the gurls" but that did not keep him from having a regular clientele of homosexuals whom he actively serviced for amounts ranging from two to ten dollars; he took the money thus used and spent it on his women . . . [Though he worked for me for years as a handyman] he stole from me just as easily and with no more compunction than he jack-rolled a stranger.

Writing, however, remained just as much on Steward's mind as sex. During the year following Kinsey's death, Steward's friend James Purdy had established himself as a literary novelist by privately publishing *Don't Call Me by My Right Name* and *63: Dream Palace*. The two novellas were subsequently published commercially in Britain, and then brought out in the United States (together) under the title *Color of Darkness*. With these publications, Purdy's reputation would continue to grow, and he would receive both a National Institute of Arts and Letters grant and a Guggenheim fellowship to support him in his work a short time later. While Steward did not much care for Purdy's writing and was consequently perplexed by its success, he was heartened by the thought that the dark, violent, and sexually charged urban scenes that Purdy described, so very close to the world in which Steward actually lived, described a world about which he, too, might eventually publish. Alice Toklas, who shared Steward's basic indifference to Purdy's writing, noted as well to Steward that Purdy had tried to manipulate her into writing positively on his behalf (she had met him several years earlier through both Steward and the Wilcoxes). "James Purdy bores me," she now wrote Steward. "He asked me to write something about his latest effort . . . but I ignored his request and his book. He—his subject matter and his treatment of it lack taste."

As he returned to his journal, Steward became ever more lyrical and introspective in his entries, in a way that suggested he was once again trying to find a way of turning his day-to-day experiences into some sort of publishable work. The experiences he had been chronicling in his journals were, after all, far more interesting than anything he had found in Purdy's fiction. Even as he did so, however, he seems to have been using the journal for private reflection:

> [Tattooing] has so many more compensations than anything I had ever done before in my life, that I find the utmost gratification in it. Many things are answered for me. I sit reading by the window; three sailors, heavy bowed under their enormous sea bags, pass; two wave to me and grin. They don't stop; they go on—but they are mine, and part of me is going with them . . . There is something almost terrifyingly personal and intimate about this work . . . Sailors come back just to gossip, or to ask my advice, or [ask] questions about what to do in town or where to go; I let them sew buttons on, I brush them off, I sit and watch them help each other dress and undress; I tie their ties, for the boot [sailors] often yet don't know how . . . And there is also the satisfaction of

doing a good tattoo and knowing the boy will carry it for many years, again a part of me.

Apart from his journal writing, Steward was now actively mentoring several of these young men, including the heavily tattooed former classicist Bill Tregoz. On December 6, Steward noted, "Tregoz [was told by his boss that] he'd either have to sell [his] motorcycle or stop working there . . . [He and I] fell into a discussion that turned unwarrantedly serious, about the 'suicidal urge' in us that frequently goads us to destroy ourselves right when we seem to have the world by the tail." Though Steward was wary of yet again involving himself with a charismatic young man who would ultimately abandon him, he saw enough of himself in Tregoz's sufferings—for Tregoz was decidedly homosexual in orientation—to want to help him achieve greater self-understanding. A similar desire to help and advise would later inform Steward's erotic fiction.

Business slowed as winter came on. By mid-December Steward noted being "lonesome down here at times, mainly because I have no continuing project . . . I just snooze and putter." His sex life was less dynamic as well; in September of 1957, he hosted his twenty-ninth and final daisy chain. Since on some winter days Steward earned as little as three dollars at the tattoo parlor (tattooing was, it turned out, a seasonal business), he decided to close down over the Christmas holidays to visit Alice Toklas in Paris. She seemed to him in need of company, for she was elderly and, despite being surrounded by Gertrude Stein's vast art collection, she was also very low on money. Moreover, when her new landlords bought the building at 5 Rue Christine in 1958, they had made no secret of wanting her out of her apartment. Of her late-life loneliness and recurring financial difficulties, Steward later wrote,

Some money [to cover her expenses] came from a group of her old friends who could afford it—Virgil Thomson, Carl Van Vechten, Doda Conrad, Thornton Wilder, Donald Sutherland, and Janet Flanner. Once in a while one of the pictures in the collection disappeared; the royalties from her books were certainly not enough to keep her in the grand style to which she had long been accustomed . . . To protect and preserve this deep friendship . . . I did everything I could for her, and she reciprocated by loving me in the gentle fashion that a woman in her eighties can bestow on a person three decades younger.

Not wanting to visit Paris alone, Steward invited a handsome young Chicago ballet student named Allan Mayle* along as his companion. The two were astonished upon their arrival by the extreme dark, damp, and cold of Paris in December, and in their desire to heat their garret room at the Hotel Recamier nearly poisoned themselves with a hastily purchased butane gas heater.

Steward was sorry to see how Toklas had aged in the five years since their last meeting, for her mind as well as her body seemed to have slowed down considerably, and as a result her conversations with Steward were nowhere near as interesting as they had once been. In fact, she sometimes seemed to Steward almost a caricature of her previous self:

> Alice is much feebler, walks very slowly, and with a cane. I am always a little shocked to see how much she *diminishes* between the times that I see her; she . . . is terribly humpbacked now, and *weeny*—to use a word that she herself used so much this time— and her mustache is heavier. She wears a kind of down over-the-ears cloche of fur, and with the glasses, the astrakhan coat (weighs pounds! I don't see how she supports it!) and the cane, she looks exactly like a black troll.

The sensual pleasures Steward had known in Paris during the summer of 1952 were not easily recaptured with Allan Mayle in the winter of 1957, particularly since the young dancer, however talented he may have been in bed, was largely oblivious to the beauty of the city and had a tendency to engage in endless, mindless chatter. "I must confess I had looked forward to seeing Paris somewhat through Allan's eyes," Steward wrote in his journal, "but the empty-headed little idiot might as well be living in Pumpkin Center, Ohio, for all he reacts to Paris . . . Where are the old magics that I used to feel? Gone? Or moved to Rome?"

---

*Steward's Stud File note about Allan Mayle (who also went by the name of Allan Delaney): "skinny ballet student . . . but migod, how the kid can love! Quite a sadist, with the cruelest mouth! No one has affected me so much for years!" Steward had sex with him forty-two times between March 24, 1954, and August 13, 1964, including four times during the 1957–58 trip to Paris.

Steward's next day consisted mainly of a four-and-a-half-hour visit for tea and gossip with Toklas, which included the news that "she is no longer seeing Francis [Rose] at all, having said to him that she appealed to him twice in the name of Gertrude, and wouldn't again . . . She also said that Jean Cocteau, who . . . always makes a fetish of *laisser-vivre*, went so far as to send a note to Bernard Faÿ and say 'you must NEVER see Francis Rose!' which is going pretty far, for Monsieur Cocteau." More important, however, Toklas gave Steward some advice:

> Amongst the things [Alice] told me was to write the tattoo [book], and be real about it; that reality would carry it, even without plot and love interest. She also counseled me to go to Italy with tattooing, and said, "they laugh a lot there, that's where all the gaiety has gone, not in France any more, people are too grim." And she's largely right about that. She was of the opinion that I could develop a "smart" clientele in Italy, in addition to the "bad boys" one—me, I'm not so sure.

A couple of days later, Steward ditched Mayle (who was suffering aftereffects of carbon monoxide poisoning from the butane heater, and confined to bed) to spend Christmas Day alone with his old flame Jacques Delaunay, now a well-established lawyer in Paris. The two dined together at Brasserie Lipp. There, eating Christmas dinner in a restaurant, Steward was amused to discover that the specialty of the legendary brasserie was nothing more than "sauerkraut and wieners, just like Ohio."

In the days that followed, Steward had a long visit with Julien Green, during which "we talked a lot about Prok, and tattooing—[Green] thinks maybe I could make dialogues of the [journal] material." He also visited Rudolph de Rohan again, to have photographs taken of his new rose garland tattoo. Through Pick, Steward was given an introduction to Cocteau's lover and supporter, the film star Jean Marais. Steward, who had idolized the handsome French actor for years, came away from the meeting starstruck.

On Sunday Jacques Delaunay came by again. This time, as a favor to Allan Mayle, Steward pushed the two men into each other's arms and simply retired to another room to read. Upon emerging from the bedroom, Delaunay then attempted to initiate something with Steward, but "evidently the continued excitement had been too much for Jacques and worn him down . . . we finally gave it up as a bad job [and] went and had a pizza."

At lunch with Julien Green the next day, Steward shared a realization with the author. As Steward wrote in his journal, "Julien [was] as polite and impeccable as always, and speaking so low that sometimes one could barely understand him. He . . . told me of the sad discovery he had made when he was 40, namely, that 'pleasure doesn't really make one happy,' a discovery (alas!) that I had made even before I was forty." Steward had a similarly melancholy epiphany while lunching several days later at La Mediterranée with Toklas. A simple workman, recognizing her and knowing of her long association with Gertrude Stein, briefly expressed his reverence and admiration for both women, then bent and kissed her hand. Steward was suddenly overwhelmed, for "all the past, and the perspective of a half century moved into the place, and I realized just who and what this old lady was . . . and I started to weep . . . every time I would begin to get myself in hand, the damned workman would pass through the room again, and off I'd go. Alice was quiet for a long time following his charming speech, and I imagine she too was thinking of the old days."

Steward's awareness of his advancing age was confirmed by the finished set of photographs taken by Rudolph de Rohan of Steward standing bare-chested, showing off his rose-garland tattoo. In them, Steward seemed smaller and less fit than in previous years, and his face looked older, paler, and more tired. "As I suspected, they were not so good as they were five years ago, and whose fault is that?" Steward wrote in his diary. "Ah, well, we age indeed. Still, they [are] 'documentary' as far as my tattoo [is] concerned, and fair enough."

•

Steward caught a cold during his last days in Paris that grew much worse on the flight home, "bloom[ing] into a gaudy monstrous thing, with fever and all the rest, and myself sick as a dog by the time we got to New York." The chest infection subsequently turned into a pneumonia so debilitating that only by February 6 was Steward able to get out of bed without extended coughing fits. Even during the worst of the siege, however, Steward continued to see his "regulars" for sexual encounters—for despite the real danger to his health, he worried that in turning down any of these men even once, he might lose contact with them—a loss that, considering his advancing years and ever-diminishing sex appeal, he simply could not afford.

Having received so much encouragement from Toklas and Green, Steward returned to his tattoo journal with renewed enthusiasm, describing not only his customers and daily activities, but also his various new sexual partners, including a "negro with the unbelievable name [of] Ruffian Bellows Jr." whom he had recently hired as a five-dollar hustler. But his recent illness made him ever more cautious about disease: "Soon as he left, I got to worrying about why (he said) they wouldn't take his blood [at the blood bank], and wondering if he had syphilis. [My old friend] Doc Anthony used to tell me: 'either stop fucking or stop worrying,' and I guess I should." Though Steward was strongly attracted to Bellows ("Lovely, satiny dark-brown skin. Quite a line of chatter, mostly beat"), he could not stop worrying about the possibility that he was a carrier of venereal disease, and his feelings about Bellows changed considerably when he learned several days later that Bellows had recently been treated for gonorrhea. Steward's fear was not only of another infection, but also of becoming too visible to police and city health authorities, for Roy Robinson (who had recently discovered he had tertiary syphilis) had been compelled to report Steward as a sex contact at the local venereal disease clinic just a month earlier. Since Chicago health officials were now seeking to shut down tattoo shops under any pretext, Steward wanted his name and address kept out of their records. Even so, during his last meeting with Bellows, Steward heard a story from him that made him laugh so hard he wrote it down afterward in his journal:

> He told me one fine tale about a fag who "hired" him one night. The guy made [Ruffian] take the belt out of his trousers and beat him with it, and then go into the bathroom and pee all over him, and finally, kiss his wife who'd been watching this all along and signalling to Ruffian to beat her husband harder. Ruffian was about to leave when the guy said wait, here's your money, and Ruffian said, "Whuffo you pays me for beatin' you? Why dat?" and the man said of course, and come again, and Ruffian said, "Whuffo? What kind of mens are you?" and the mens said, "I don't know."

Steward's laughter was the laughter of self-recognition, for he had been posing a similar question to himself—almost daily, and for years—on nearly every page of his journals.

•

More and more, Steward wanted to turn his endless ruminations about his sexual activities into some sort of publishable work, perhaps by incorporating these real-life events into sexually themed fiction. But while a good deal of erotic fiction was being published commercially in Paris in 1956—primarily by the Olympia Press—none of it described male homosexual sex. Steward's only means of publishing homoerotic fiction in the United States at that moment would have involved self-publishing privately (and illegally), and then distributing the work privately (which would have been even more dangerously illegal). His other alternative was to tone down the erotic content of his writing and publish it as erotically suggestive pulp fiction. But pulp fiction publishers routinely required authors to pathologize and denounce homosexuality in any fiction describing it—and Steward was opposed to doing anything of the sort.*

One of the few literary journals then interested in publishing prohomosexual short fiction was the trilingual Swiss homophile publication *Der Kreis*, to which Steward had been contributing illustrations since 1954. He had learned of the magazine through Kinsey in 1952, just as it began publishing contributions in English, and had met one of its editors, Daniel Decure, that very same year in Paris. The magazine would achieve a peak circulation, in 1959, of 2,000 copies, with only 700 of those shipped outside Switzerland, and unfortunately for Steward, its editor in chief, Karl Meier (also known as "Rolf"), was strongly disinclined toward any content (fictional or otherwise) that was openly sexual. But the editorial policy for fiction at *Der Kreis* began to change slightly after Rolf appointed a German-born English-language editor named Rudolf Burckhardt† in 1955.

---

*While some literary fiction during the late 1940s and '50s managed to suggest that homosexuality was not an illness (Gore Vidal's *The City and the Pillar* being probably the best-known example), the pulp fiction published during the same period usually carried a depressingly antihomosexual message. Then again, according to the bibliographer Ian Young, while many homosexually themed hardcover novels had faced vigorous prosecution for obscenity during the 1950s, a vast number of equally controversial pulps simply "show[ed] up [in paperback] at the local drug store or soda shop, [thus] help[ing] spread the word about a way of life that until then had largely been hidden from public view . . . [and in doing so] both reflected and influenced [an] emerging gay consciousness." Ian Young, "How Gay Paperbacks Changed America," *The Gay and Lesbian Review*, Nov.–Dec. 2001, pp. 14–17. See also Michael Bronski, *Pulp Friction: Uncovering the Golden Age of Gay Male Pulps* (New York: St. Martin's Press, 2002), and Tom Norman, *American Gay Erotic Paperbacks: A Bibliography* (Burbank, Calif.: privately printed, 1994).
†Burckhardt was a pseudonym; his real name was Rudolf Jung.

An even greater problem for Steward in writing homosexual erotic fiction was his continuing ambivalence toward his fellow homosexuals— those for whom, presumably, he would be writing. Indeed, some of his journal entries about homosexuals are so deeply loathing as to seem almost irrational. On February 17 he noted, "[Today I tattooed] the 14th queer I've tattooed in three years—out of 8900 pieces put on. I am really glad that h[omosexuals]'s don't get decorated; if they hung out in my shop, my business would be ruined. As it was, two punks eyed the fruit strangely, and laughed at him after he'd gone. I was, of course, heavily on their side as they did." (Steward's dislike of the "fruit" was not based on the man's sexual preference, however, but rather on his overt effeminacy.) A week later, Steward once again made note of his ambivalence toward homosexuals in noting the return of a homosexual couple who had been to his tattoo parlor previously: Rich, a boxer who was in the merchant marine, and Jack, his older, Ivy League lover. Steward placed a pair of bluebirds on Rich's chest and a tiger's head on one of his shoulders while Jack looked on approvingly. Steward hated the experience, for he disliked proprietary relationships between affluent homosexuals and their "bought" boys, and moreover had come to think of male homosexual "couples" of any sort as being embarrassingly unnatural. As he later wrote in an editorial piece for *Der Kreis*, "the invert, it seem[s] to me, should live alone and learn to like it, and to be self-sufficing."

Steward was now having sex regularly with a new partner, a former Nazi stormtrooper named Gerhard (soon to be "Gary") Stroh. His fascination with Stroh's Nazi past spoke to his long-standing desire to have sex with brutalizing authority figures, a desire that had increasingly colored his fantasies of the past year, as well as coming to dominate his actual sex life—for apart from Stroh, the partners he most preferred were men like Bill Payson who would physically abuse him and verbally degrade him during sex. At the same time, however, Steward continued to feel a desperate romantic longing for the relatively innocent younger men who frequented his tattoo shop, even (or particularly) those with whom no sexual relationship whatever would be possible. While the two kinds of longing may have seemed at first glance to be entirely opposite, they were, in fact, variations on the same masochistic theme of rejection and deprivation. Describing an afternoon spent with a handsome young heterosexual sailor who had a long-stemmed rose tattoo on his right hip bone,

Steward noted that after applying a new tattoo, the two had sat and talked awhile, and

> when he finally went to go he shook my hand in a grip that nigh squeezed it flat, and I said send me a postcard from a far place, and he started to say something (I'll never know what), and at the door turned and said "goodbye" with a particularly intimate inflection that left me standing weak-kneed, so that I suddenly sat down and rested my chin in my hand, and thought about youth and beauty and the ache and hunger that it can cause in one, and has caused in me such an infinite number of times . . . The warm glow that he left in my mind and heart and eyes lasted for hours . . . I remember[ed] the epitaph that Santayana wanted carved on his tomb, with two youths kneeling; I thought of Keats, of Housman, of all the golden hopes of my own youth . . .
>
> Oddly enough, I would not have had more. This contented me psychically as I have not been contented for years. It was at once an epitome and climax.

A few days after his meeting with this handsome but unattainable sailor, Steward received a letter from Rudolf Burckhardt of *Der Kreis* announcing that he would soon be coming to Chicago. "Since there was no way to get out of it gracefully, I wrote and asked him to stay the night with me if he hadn't already made his arrangements," Steward noted. And in fact, Steward was already working on some fiction. Recently while visiting his erotica collection (which was now in storage) to search for his 1954 sex calendar,* Steward had found a copy of his old motorcycle story, as well as the equally S/M-themed episode that had followed it, and he found himself thinking there was something in it that might yet be developed. "I read it over . . . it holds up well, as do the beginning pages of

---

*Although Steward donated his sex calendars to the Kinsey Institute, they are considered part of his sex history, and so are not available to any researchers, including his biographer. Copies of Steward's 1950 and 1951 sex calendars remain in his papers, showing (in calendar form) the number and type of his sexual experiences on a day-by-day basis. A letter from the sex researcher Wardell Pomeroy to Steward of January 28, 1958, noted that Steward had contributed sex calendars "from 1948 through 1953 inclusive" and also noted that his subsequent sex calendars might have been misplaced within the Kinsey archive.

episode number three," he observed. "I guess I can find it in my heart to finish them, now that the season is so slack."

As he returned to writing erotic fiction, Steward noted repeatedly in his journal how the world around him was changing, for he kept meeting younger men who seemed much more open and demonstrative in their attraction to other males than any he had known in earlier times. Two young men had, in fact, recently come into the shop for matching love tattoos featuring each other's name. "The whole episode left me rather shook up," Steward wrote after applying them. "When we were all done (I dint let my hair down—much), [one] said, 'Well, I may see you again.' And [the other] said, 'Not I!' Whereupon I said slyly, 'Not even to get it covered up?' and embarrassed them both." The experience marked the first time two outwardly masculine men had come to Steward to be thus tattooed, and Steward's response—partly jealous and partly cynical (for he thought he recognized one of them as a hustler)—was basically one of amazement: he had never imagined such expressions of loving commitment to be possible between two masculine males.

Steward had a visit a week later from his sister that proved to be unexpectedly difficult. In getting married, she had converted to her husband's religion, Catholicism, and she now pressed Steward hard to do the same. She remembered his earlier conversion, during the 1930s, and moreover she felt that, given the circumstances of his present life, he would greatly benefit from a return to the Church. "She kept after me to make a general confession; I kept telling her not to browbeat me, that I had no faith, that I couldn't, etc." Though Steward managed to give his sister the brush-off, he had an even greater surprise and shock when, a little more than a week later, Alice Toklas wrote to tell him that she, too, had been received back into the Catholic Church. The news left Steward more amazed and disturbed than he cared to admit, for, as he wrote in his journal, "She was the last person in the world except one (myself) whom I ever expected to go back to the Church—and indeed, I had always thought of her as Jewish."* He went on to note that "on top of Jinny's urg-

---

*One of Toklas's biographers has in fact noted that while Toklas "explained to friends that she had been baptized as a child . . . there is little likelihood of that early baptism . . . Alice's claim of returning to the religion of her childhood had been made, most likely, for expediency . . . Her embrace of Catholicism, in any case, was not a return to the security of her childhood beliefs, but the fulfillment of her need for an all-consuming passion, an ordered pattern of life, and, most of all, for the conception of a populated heaven where she would find Gertrude." (Simon, *The Biography of Alice B. Toklas*, p. 237.)

ing of me to return when she was here, comes now this—and I am both annoyed and pressured a great deal." Steward nonetheless responded to Toklas's news by cheerily writing that it had left him "flabber and ghasted," and then adding, "I scarcely know what to say, for my own problem gets in the way." Along with the joy he felt on her behalf, he admitted he was "wondering why I seem not able to believe any more, when once I could."

Steward was nowhere close to returning to Catholicism, however. In fact his experience of Holy Week 1958 was entirely caught up in worldly concerns. In his journal for Good Friday, he noted, "The [new light] over the john now illuminates the cocks exceedingly well, as the boys stand there to take a leak, and whenever possible, I sneak back . . . to watch them through the fruit hole." In the same entry he described how his friend Adam Norman had been entrapped by police that week at the Lincoln Park Conservatory, and how it was now going to cost Norman a thousand dollars to take care of the judge and the two cops. "More proof that you never ought to do it outside your apartment—or [your] shop, where doors can be locked." Of his own life, he concluded, "Things seem to be going fairly well at present, but I live under dread, always expecting a calamity . . . this life is full of crises."

Steward's chief concern that spring was not so much about robbery or other threats to his business, but rather with Alice Toklas, for she seemed to him so feeble as to be nearing death. With that death, Steward knew he faced yet another serious loss, for he had few significant friends left in his life, and among them Toklas was the dearest and most important. She had not only seen him gently through his drinking, but had also followed his transition from academe to tattooing without judging or condemning him. More important, she was his last living connection to that higher, better, literary life to which he had once aspired—a life once so close that now seemed entirely lost to him.

A few days after Easter, Steward wrote a friend in New York that Toklas seemed "much enfeebled . . . [and with her conversion to Catholicism] I see her getting ready [for death], for when Gertrude's last volume* appears, her work will be done." Wanting to do something truly kind and generous on her behalf, Steward forced himself to pack up all the letters that Gertrude Stein had sent to him during the 1930s and '40s, and to

---

*For several years Toklas had been overseeing publication of Stein's unpublished work by Yale University Press in conjunction with the Beinecke Library.

donate them, at long last, to the Beinecke Library at Yale. He then wrote Toklas to tell her he had done so. "The letters from Gertrude [to me] are finally now [donated to] the Yale collection," he wrote. "While they were in my house, they were a radiant center; now the hearth seems cold."

In sending the treasured letters off to Yale, Steward felt more lost than ever. Having already said goodbye to the two great mentors in his life—first Stein, then Kinsey—he was now apparently on the brink of losing Toklas, too. But the impending loss of this significant friend was just one aspect of the much greater crisis in which Steward now found himself—a crisis of self-esteem. What Stein had once termed "the question of being important inside in one" had continued to trouble Steward in the year after losing Kinsey. He was now no longer a working teacher, and could hardly even claim to be a scholar, poet, or novelist—for apart from his journals, he had written nothing of substance for nearly twenty years. Living alone without the daily support or encouragement of family or friends or even a casual lover, he was unattached to any institution or belief system that might otherwise have sustained him in his isolation. And much as Steward might have liked to think of himself as a man given over entirely to sensual debauchery, he was not entirely so. Even in dedicating his life to the exploration of his sexual nature, he was at heart too purposeful and creative a man, and moreover one with too active a mind, simply to sink into the mind-numbing repetition of sexual self-indulgence. But where was he going these days, and what was he doing with his life? Tattooing, sex, and writing were the three main activities that gave his days purpose and meaning; but how these activities might ultimately resolve Steward's "question of being important inside in one" was something he had yet to work out.

14

Kris and *Kreis*

During the spring of 1958 Steward contracted a powerful, lingering intestinal ailment, and so he recorded only a few noteworthy sexual experiences in his journal. He did, however, describe a significant emotional drama: a friend and former sex partner named Brian McKibben* came into the shop,

> looking terribly nelly in his little Ivy League clothes . . . [and] just plain terrible, as if he'd been crying for a week . . . He'd been "asked to resign" from his job—fired, in plain terms. Seems that he'd been paying [sexual] blackmail for ten years to someone in Milwaukee, as had about ten other persons, one of whom suddenly got tired of it and squealed to the cops. [When the] cops came to the store to ask him to identify the blackmailer's picture [they] went through Personnel [just as] the cops [had] verified my teaching at DePaul by going directly to the president. [So his employer learned he was homosexual and fired him.] Brian contemplated suicide for a while; I gave him a pep talk, and cheered him as best I could, which wasn't much. We are all such fools.

Steward had his own professional worries as well: the *Chicago Daily News* had recently run a column suggesting that parents file lawsuits

---

*McKibben had been a sex partner from 1953 through 1955, of whom Steward noted in the Stud File, "balding egoist exhibitionist; carrying timbre; nelly. *Does* say some funny things."

against any tattoo artist who tattooed a minor. "That's the worst possible thing that could have happened," he wrote. "[It] may be the end."

In the midst of these personal and professional dramas, the literary editor of *Der Kreis* turned up on Steward's doorstep. Steward had been dreading the visit, but to his surprise he found Rudolf Burckhardt entirely charming, for the fiftyish German had both a courtly manner and a salty sense of humor. Moreover, he professed to be deeply interested in Steward, both as an essayist and novelist. Steward was happy enough to give Burckhardt a copy of *A Hunting We Will Go!*, the novel Greenberg had declined in 1954. He also promised to write an essay for Burckhardt on the need for the older homosexual to cultivate a sense of detachment as a way of surviving the disappointments of later life. Burckhardt would publish that essay as "Detachment: A Way of Life" in August 1958, and it would be Steward's first written contribution to the magazine. Two excerpts from the novel would follow soon after. Over the next nine years, Burckhardt would establish himself as Steward's closest friend and staunchest literary ally; through his constant encouragement, Steward would publish his writings regularly in *Der Kreis*, and in the end become its strongest American voice.

•

Der Kreis was primarily a news and culture magazine for homosexual males, and the fiction in its pages tended to describe homosexual relationships largely as affairs of the heart—for, at a moment in history when homosexuality was widely feared and reviled, its editors hoped to present sexual relationships between men in the most positive (and least controversial) way possible. The extreme caution with which *Der Kreis* approached any fiction with erotic content is probably best understood in the context of European and American legal history—for while homosexuality was allowed under Swiss law during the 1950s, it remained illegal in France until 1981; and in Britain, despite the 1957 Wolfenden report (which recommended its decriminalization), it remained illegal until 1967. Homosexuality remained illegal across the United States until 1962, when Illinois became the only state in which it was legal until 1967. The editors of *Der Kreis* therefore took a cautiously "assimilationist" approach to the movement for homosexual rights—just as, in the early days of the movement for black rights, black assimilationists had taken up a similarly cautious approach to demanding racial equality. As a result, *Der Kreis** insisted that all references to sexual activity between men be kept to an absolute minimum.

Of the English and American writers who contributed to *Der Kreis* during the period 1952–67 (either with articles written specifically for the magazine or else pieces excerpted from their books), few are remembered today.† Steward was by far the most frequent American contributor, ultimately making fifty-five original contributions to the magazine, among them fifteen short stories and fifteen drawings.‡ In his unpublished memoirs he noted:

> [My] alliance with *Der Kreis* . . . last[ed] [from the early 1950s] until its demise in 1967. I had several pen-names [there]: "Donald Bishop" for sociological things such as "The Bull Market in America" (on hustling), and "Pussies in Boots" on the new leather movement. Some stories were written under "Ward Stames," a simple anagram of my real name. For poetry in the manner of Housman I became "John McAndrews." "Thomas Cave" produced more thoughtful and reflective stories.

While the editors of *Der Kreis* may have been stodgy, the magazine as a whole was not, largely because of *"das kleine blatt"* ("the little leaf"), an insert of personal ads in which (mostly Swiss) readers discreetly sought out pen pals, loving friendships, and sexual assignations. Moreover, gently provocative illustrations had begun to appear in the magazine starting in 1944. As the 1950s progressed, ever more outré physique photography

---

*For a substantial history of *Der Kreis*, see Hubert Kennedy, *The Ideal Gay Man: The Story of Der Kreis* (Binghamton, N.Y.: Harrington Park Press, 1999). Kennedy relied on Steward's bound volumes of *Der Kreis* (which Steward had donated to San Francisco State University, and which have since disappeared), as well as interviews, articles, and statements by Steward, as central, primary sources for his research.

†That list of contributors includes Alan Anthony, Richard Arlen, Victor J. Banis, James Barr, Walter Baxter, Lonnie Coleman, Clarkson Crane, Mike Dawn, Rodney Garland, James Gilmore, Marsh Harris, Ralph Harris, Arnell Larsen, Roger S. Mitchell, Jack Parrish, James H. Ramp, O. F. Simpson, Loren Wahl, William Wainwright, Chick Weston, and Frank Whitfield.

‡Five of the drawings would also be reprinted in a book published by *Der Kreis*; two of the short stories appeared not only in English, but also in German translation. In addition, in collaboration with Rudolf Jung, Steward would write two stories under the name of Philip Young, one of which appeared in German translation as well.

appeared in its pages as well. During his 1958 trip to America, Burckhardt had been actively soliciting "beefcake" contributions from various
American studios, including Chuck Renslow's Kris Studio, a physique-
photography mail order house that was just then operating out of Irv
Johnson's gym at 22 Van Buren Street, just two and a half blocks north of
Phil Sparrow's Tattoo Joynt. It was thus through Burckhardt that Steward
first met Renslow, a man who would ultimately become one of the most
successful erotic-business entrepreneurs in the history of Chicago.

On Burckhardt's first visit to Kris Studio, Renslow had given him sixty
bodybuilding photos to use in the magazine; Burckhardt had, in turn,
brought Renslow and Dom Orejudos (whom Steward initially described
in his journal as "the small sissy Italian [sic] who draws the sexy men"*)
down to the Tattoo Joynt to observe Steward at work. "They seemed a bit
out of place," Steward noted of that first visit, "but were quiet, and goggle
eyed too, at the youngsters who flocked in while they were here."

A born entrepreneur, Renslow would eventually preside over a highly
profitable business empire that catered to the many needs, interests, and
appetites of Chicago's various homosexual communities. He had been
publishing his physique-photography magazine, *Tomorrow's Man*, since
the age of twenty-two;† now, at twenty-eight, he was in the process of
buying Irv Johnson's gym, renaming it the Triumph Gym, and moving it
to a larger space on Monroe Street. He had simultaneously founded Kris
Studio (with a fellow photographer named Harry Mickelson) specifically
to shoot "beefcake" photography, an art then most visibly practiced in
Chicago by the photographer Cliff Oettinger. Renslow had sensed early
on that he might make good money through beefcake, the suggestive display of the well-muscled, scantily clad male physique. Starting in 1952,
Renslow had also helped organize AAU bodybuilding competitions
throughout the greater Chicago area, and with Cliff Oettinger he soon (in
his own words) "ran all [the Chicago] physique contests, [including] the
Mr. Chicago [and] the Mr. Illinois."

---

*Orejudos, Chuck Renslow's lover and partner, had already made a name for himself as an under-
ground homoerotic illustrator.
†The question of whether *Tomorrow's Man* was pornographic depended on local rulings. While not
considered pornographic in Illinois, copies of *Tomorrow's Man* were seized in the unwarranted raid on
Newton Arvin's home in Northampton, Massachusetts, in 1960 and (along with *Physique Pictorial*)
were described as "pornographic" by Massachusetts authorities.

By approaching bodybuilders not only as director of Physique Contest Programs for the Illinois chapter of the AAU but also as the editor and publisher of *Tomorrow's Man*, Renslow impressed bodybuilders with his credentials, and simultaneously presented them with a cost-free opportunity to be "officially" photographed by an accomplished professional. As a result, most of them gladly signed release forms giving Renslow full rights to all images. With ready access to well-muscled models willing to be photographed for free, Renslow soon built up a steady and highly profitable mail order business in soft-core homosexual pornography.* He gave the most attractive and sexually accommodating models free gym memberships, and then brought in their (bisexual and homosexual) admirers as paying gym customers. In doing so, he created a gym that was not only a home of bodybuilding champions, but also, more discreetly, a locus of male-male sexual opportunity—some of it spontaneous, some of it discreetly arranged (through Renslow) as sex-for-pay.

Sometime around 1953, Renslow had met a short, handsome twenty-year-old ballet dancer named Domingo Stephan Orejudos. Half Filipino and half Italian, Orejudos would never succeed as a dancer, in part because of his stocky build and short legs, but he would nonetheless work throughout the 1950s as a Chicago-based dance teacher and choreographer. At the same time he would channel his significant creative and erotic energies into the creation of wildly kinky murals, posters, illustrations, and comic books that he published through Renslow under the various names of "Domingo," "Stephen," and "Étienne."†

When Steward first met this unlikely younger couple, they were living in a sparsely furnished back room of their gym. As Orejudos later noted, "It was *the* gym in Chicago . . . mostly all free weights . . . Sometimes after closing hours we would entertain, and have little orgies up there, it was very adaptive. And then you had the showers right there . . . It was something like having a playroom . . . since we lived there it was [easy] entertaining that way."

Through his close daily association with the gym's many bodybuilders, Renslow knew which of them would hustle. While he would always

---

*Most of Renslow's models wore posing straps, since the possession and sale of nude photography was at that moment not only illegal, but also subject to vigorous prosecution. He did, however, sometimes photograph men in the nude.
†Étienne is French for Stephen.

maintain "I'm not a whoremaster, I'm a photographer," he never denied his role in connecting hustlers to clients, or for that matter his enjoyment of using the same hustlers for his own pleasure. Steward soon referred in his Stud File to any hustlers who came to him through Renslow (and there would be many) as "courtesy of KPS" or "Kris Pimping Service."

Steward's next meeting with Renslow began when Renslow invited him to the gym to draw tattoo designs on two bodybuilders he was going to photograph. Upon arrival, Steward was overwhelmed by the eroticism of the scene:

> I [got there] in time to see the finishing of their photographing of a breathtakingly handsome young man, a Sig Osmanos* (or some such) a big beautiful Ukrainian . . . "The next Mister America," said Chuck fondly, slapping him on his small tight buttocks. On his belly Dom had drawn his "translation" of my winged dragon . . . On a 22 inch bicep[s] there was a skull with banner, and high on the inside of his left thigh, near the crotch, an eagle's head and anchor . . . Then the next model came, a Dick Ames . . . [he] had a nice body, beautiful pectorals and *weeny* hips, and about an 18-inch bicep[s]. Privately, Chuck told me he was a hustler; and they talked quite freely in front of him. We laid him down on a long waist-high table, and went to work on him. Dom put the outline of a chest eagle on those swelling pectorals, and I filled in with the black ink I had brought . . . Dom, fiddling around, put a fly on his dong, and a small wreath of flowers in an arch above the pubic hair, just at the edge. Dick lay and took all this without comment, and if not with good nature, at least not with rancor or complaint.
>
> How to record my sensations as I worked on that fine skin (not a blemish) so intimately close to a body I knew was for hire? I was not sexually stimulated in the least, but psychically I was a tornado inside; one felt so close, and the boy seemed so attainable . . . When he posed for the back shots, he was a dream. The smooth perfection of the lines tore at this old heart . . . for I am reasonably sure that nothing on this earth could ever be so beautiful.

*The bodybuilder Sig Ulmanis.

In mid-June, Steward met another young man through Renslow, one who would eventually become his tattooing apprentice—and after that, one of the most celebrated tattoo artists in the United States. Steward initially described Cliff Ingram—later Cliff Raven—in his journals as "a nice clean-cut kid in his twenties, a friend of Bill Tregoz, about whom he inquired"—for Ingram and Tregoz, both of whom were fascinated by leather, tattoos, and motorcycles, had already had a significant sexual involvement, Tregoz having picked Ingram up on his motorcycle one night in Bughouse Square, the well-known homosexual cruising spot on the Near North Side.

Ingram, who had studied art at Indiana University in Bloomington, immediately wanted to get tattooed by Steward, for Steward was by then well-known as Chicago's most accomplished tattoo artist. "I had fantasies that I would do some dirty pictures for [Phil Sparrow] and he would give me tattoos in exchange," he later told an interviewer. "I was just a poor little working stiff, you know. I hadn't done anything about it and at that point I became more acquainted with Chuck and Dom, [and] learned that [Sparrow] was friends of theirs . . . [and] suddenly life [became] very interesting because I saw the possibility [of becoming a tattoo artist]." Ingram was at that point sexually involved with Renslow even though Renslow maintained a primary sexual relationship with Orejudos; according to Orejudos, "Cliff became part of our family; he and Chuck shared a bedroom, it was like a . . . it is hard to say like what because it was such an unusual arrangement."

Steward was glad to be making new friends, for in his isolated life at the tattoo parlor, he had begun to feel increasingly vulnerable. He noted in an early July journal entry that Charlie Costello, a former circus roustabout and hustler, had recently started stealing things out of his shop. After considering the options, Steward decided to give Costello bus fare back to his hometown of New York before Costello simply robbed the cash register outright. Several days after Costello's departure, however, the Tattoo Joynt was robbed by someone else—and Steward responded by buying his first gun. "I have come more and more to believe that the culprit was Roy Robinson," Steward wrote. "Whoever did it . . . knew the set-up well . . . [luckily he] didn't wreck my machines nor throw my colors on the floor."

Along with the constant threat of crime, Steward also had to live with various horrors relating to tattooing, for as his reputation as a tattoo artist grew, so too did visits from extremely troubled people. One day at the shop, "A man about 45 came in, tall and nervous . . . [and] showed me his chest, on which were half a dozen old pieces . . . He wanted them all covered . . . What I could hardly take my eyes off, however, was his tits: one of them was torn off completely, the other dangling by a thread of flesh. The cunt on the [tattoo of the] nude [girl on his chest] had been burned out with a cigarette. In the face of such masochism (and sadism) I turned weak, almost got sick. I could not shake this off for days." Steward had also recently been approached by a man named Ralph Mills, an Episcopalian priest with a taste for extremely heavy sadomasochistic domination: "How he settles for himself the dichotomy betwixt his activity and his religion is something I'll never know, and don't care to know," Steward wrote, "but I consider him to have something basic wrong with him if he can make the settlement, or at the least to be a bloody hypocrite. Ugh."

During this lonely and vulnerable period in his life, Steward found Renslow to be a great new friend and ally. Renslow in turn was fascinated by Steward's business, and in short order became a regular visitor down at the Tattoo Joynt. But there was more to this friendliness than Steward realized; as a businessman, Renslow saw Steward's shop as a potential gold mine, and had already started thinking about opening a chain of such storefronts. Since Steward was not only lonely, but also now dependent upon him for young bodybuilder-hustlers,* Renslow had no problem milking him for information about every aspect of his business.

Renslow's own business came under attack that October, however, when it was raided. As Steward later wrote, "The two smut-hunters from the Park District Police Force, Eli Blumenthal and Don Kelley, descended on Chuck's studio on North Clark Street and arrested him. They had in their possession some male nudes which they said Chuck had sold or given to people." After seizing what newspapers later described as "hundreds of lewd photos and negatives," the police issued a warrant for Renslow's arrest. Steward subsequently wrote Wardell Pomeroy for legal advice on

---

*Renslow was not Steward's only procurer, however; another neighborhood acquaintance, Red Jackson, frequently introduced him to rougher working-class men, mostly black, who were also willing to have sex with him for pay.

Renslow's behalf; Pomeroy responded with the name of a New York law firm that the institute had recently recommended to another individual facing similar charges. As it turned out, a municipal judge dismissed the case at its continuation on December 1, but in the process Renslow lost his commercial photography license, and with it the ability to hold any other license (including a bar license) in the city of Chicago, thus complicating his business life considerably.*

•

In December of 1958, Steward again arranged to spend Christmas with Alice Toklas in Paris, and he sent Rudolf Burckhardt some travel money so that the two men might meet there for a few days before returning to Zurich, ostensibly for a gala New Year's Eve party hosted by *Der Kreis*— but really so Steward could open a series of secret bank accounts for his undeclared tattooing income. Steward began his adventure in currency smuggling at the Marshall Field's candy department: "[I] laid a dollar bill on the foreign candy-bars until I found the right size (the saleswoman thought me crazy, I know) and then took one, which I opened carefully, and put my fifty c-notes inside, sealing it back up—and thus carried the five grand safely to Zurich."

When he saw Alice Toklas in Paris, Steward noted that she had become "much enfeebled even over last year [and] very forgetful, and frequently [she] gets quite mixed up. But . . . she spoke quite frankly about Francis [Rose] and his h[o]m[o]s[e]x[ua]l[i]ty and his affairs, so that it was a little shocking now and then to hear her." On Christmas Day, Toklas took Steward down the street to lunch at Lapérouse, one of the oldest and most famous restaurants in Paris; but she then grew so confused during the course of the meal that she caused a scene. Though he was happy to have given her the pleasure of his company, Steward found the experience excruciating; her deep confusion seemed to him yet another indication that she was not long for this world.

---

*As a result of this legal mess, Renslow decided to get involved in Chicago politics. Through carefully working the Chicago political system, he eventually assured his businesses' stability and financial success. In years to come he would own gay bars, gay gyms, gay restaurants, gay publications, and gay bathhouses, and eventually found and run IML, or International Mr. Leather, the yearly convention of leathermen and sex enthusiasts that has taken place annually in Chicago for over twenty-five years, and which is currently the largest yearly convention held in Chicago.

After visits with Jacques Delaunay, Witold Pick, and Pick's latest
boyfriend—a highly sexed young Arab bodybuilder named Bachir—
Steward and Burckhardt engaged in various Parisian adventures including a *thé dansant* hosted by the French homophile publication *Arcadie*.
Steward also made a sentimental expedition back to Rue de Lappe, where
he had had his earliest Parisian sexual adventures in 1937 and 1939. The
day before leaving for Zurich, Steward returned to Toklas's apartment
for an intimate discussion about her conversion to Catholicism—during
which, as Steward later admitted,

> I decided to tell Alice that her prayers had been answered and
> that I had returned to the church. There were many consider-
> ations: my love for her, some increase in happiness for her in the
> declining years, a strengthening of her own belief and faith. It
> was difficult to justify such a deception, but her joyful reaction
> was a partial reward, and no harm was done.

The enfeebled Toklas welcomed Steward's whopping lie with the
greatest joy and relief, afterward writing him, "What wonderfully good
news you gave me for Christmas—the best I've had since Gertrude
died . . . You are my sweet Sam, you have made your sister and me all
happy and my prayers now for you will be different ones."

From Paris, Steward and Burckhardt traveled on to Zurich for *Der
Kreis*'s New Year's Eve gala. As a recovering alcoholic who regularly
avoided the company of other homosexual males, Steward had hardly
expected to enjoy himself at the party, but even so he was surprised at just
how depressing he found the whole of Zurich, noting in his journal that
"the people [have] such dead-set earnest expressions on their faces all the
time, as if they had but two thoughts: 1) How can I make some more
money, and 2) How can I hold on to what I have? Rudolf said the suicide
rate was very high . . . Still I suppose you can't expect the bankers of the
world to be frivolous." The only bright spot to his visit was the company
of a highly intelligent and well-mannered young hustler named Antonio,
arranged for him by Burckhardt, on whom Steward would later partially
base his fictional character Phil Andros.

Immediately after opening his bank accounts Steward retreated back
to Paris, where as a joke Pick had booked him into the Hotel St. Georges,

a *maison de passe** just off the Place Pigalle. Pick and Bachir showed up shortly after his arrival, had a good laugh about the place, "and then Pick left, and Bachir undressed, needing no urging, and screwed me lovely."

After saying good-bye to Toklas and flying home to Chicago, Steward quickly fell back into his old sexual routine, noting that on January 12 he "had Berbich at noon, Adams† at 5:30, and Bob Caplowitz‡ in the evening, enough for one day." Renslow approached him for a loan to pay his legal bills, and Steward noted afterward that "with many misgivings, I lent Chuck a thousand dollars . . . He gave me a chattel mortgage of 600 shares on Perry's Gym, due in five years (without interest) . . . I do hope . . . this won't mean the breakup of things between us."

Steward also had another visit from Charlie Costello, the young hustler, circus roustabout, and criminal he had given bus fare back to New York the previous fall. Costello had made it only as far as the Chicago bus station, however, before starting a fistfight, being arrested for assault, and spending several months on a prison farm. While visiting the tattoo parlor, Costello told Steward how at the prison farm he had taken a pretty younger boy as his pogue.§ As Steward later described it in his journal,

> He said it took some time for the kid to get used to it, and then all of a sudden he liked it a lot, so Charlie fucked him every night. This story really excited me, so I took Charlie in the back room and put him in the chair, and blew him, for three bucks.
>
> So then, this morning, a letter to Phil's tattoo shop, from Charles Costello, b-1, #22 98, 2600 S. California, Cook County Jail, here in full!
>
> *Well Phil I really blew the works this time, and from the looks of it I'm really going to pay . . . I got arrested on my birthday (Feb 3), for armed robbery and then after being arrested had*

---

*House of prostitution.

†LeRoy Adams, a (married) black jazz pianist with whom Steward had sex on a regular basis from 1948 through 1960.

‡A professional wrestler and hustler whom Steward hired regularly through Renslow from 1958 through 1960.

§*Pogue* is a (now obsolete) derogatory slang term describing a young man who submits to the sexual advances of another male.

them drop two burglaries on me . . . the chances of me beating them are one in a million . . . anyway I'm hoping for about 5 years but expecting much more. Phil they took my money away . . . I realize the shape you are in but I would appreciate it very much if you sent me what you could . . . Please write soon even if you don't do anything. Respectfully yours, Charlie Costello. P.S. Your favorite customer.

I don't want to get involved, but I wrote him a little note and put four bucks in with it and sent it off. *Vale,** Charlie. By the time you get out, I may not be in Amerika any more.

During February and March, Steward recorded just a few noteworthy sexual incidents, chief among them an S/M encounter with Professor Hal Stevens, whom Steward had first met a decade earlier through the flagellist Hal Baron. Chuck Renslow and Dom Orejudos participated in the encounter, which involved heavy bondage, a mock kidnapping, various forms of whipping, and then, to cap it all off, terrorizing the blindfolded Stevens by dragging Orejudos's pet rat across Stevens's naked back. Renslow enjoyed the encounter so much that he later described it as the beginning of his life as a sexual dominant.

Shortly after the encounter with Stevens, Steward received news that one of his longtime sex partners, a high school teacher named Robert Dahm, had been "caught . . . with a seventeen-year-old [student] . . . the police got involved [and] Bob got it: about five years, with possibility of parole in 18 months . . . The thousand times I told Professor Dahm not to mix business and pleasure! And on he went." Steward then heard a similar tale of woe from Ralph Mills, the Episcopal priest, noting in his journal that Mills's vocation had come to an end after he "picked up a sixteen year old in Delaware, one of a gang of young tough tattooed Italians who were shaking down the queers. So Ralph paid blackmail for quite a while, and then went to the police, and of course his bishop, and confessed. So now he's out of a job."

Steward neglected his journal as summer came on, in part because he had increasing doubts about its usefulness to the Institute for Sex Re-

---

*Vale is Latin for "farewell."

search, but also in part because he was devoting the majority of his writing energies to a new correspondence with Burckhardt, who was strongly encouraging him to write fiction, essays, and reviews for *Der Kreis*. Steward was now writing two or three letters* a week to Burckhardt, and he later described them as "a diary if ever there was one."

Steward's business continued to be good at the tattoo parlor in 1959. In his zeal for record-keeping, he noted that he now had "a new sum for Best Day Ever ($210), a new Best Week Ever ($608); and a new Best Month Ever ($2201)." The excitement Steward felt about his correspondence with Burckhardt, his tattooing, and his moneymaking during this period was particularly important to him since his sexual adventures now consisted mainly of dullish paid encounters with Renslow's hustlers. At the same time, however, he was having intense fantasies about being sexually dominated—this time by Renslow, who in his powerful position as both pimp and erotic pornographer had come to seem to Steward a man of considerable sexual magnetism—even more so after Steward had witnessed his dominating Hal Stevens.

As early as his erotic correspondence with "Bob" in the late 1940s, Steward had fantasized about being a male prostitute "owned" by a pimp who would whore him out to others. Now, in Renslow, Steward had actually encountered just such a dominant and "pimp." In a journal entry written several months after the encounter featuring Renslow and Hal Stevens, Steward noted that Renslow's "natural aggressiveness" had, during the course of the summer, "blossomed out into as fine an example of Sadism as I've yet seen." As a result, Renslow began to loom ever larger in Steward's imagination as an exploitative sexual dominant—so much so that Steward began preferring Renslow even to sailors.

Indeed, as Steward neared his fiftieth birthday, the sailors he now met were less than half his age. While he could hardly deny their vitality or good looks, he had seen and spent time with enough of them through his tattooing as to be relatively indifferent to them as sex objects. As he wrote that summer,

The Fleet arrived for the first time in the lake waters [this July] . . . and for about ten days, Chicago was literally over-run with sailors. You

---

*Now lost; Steward kept no carbons of them, and Burckhardt's papers disappeared after his death.

saw them everywhere you turned—at night you couldn't go a
block without seeing a white uniform somewhere. Needless to
say, all the queers in Chicago were out after them, and it was a
poor pansy indeed who didn't have at least a half dozen during
that time (which makes me a poor pansy, I guess, for I had
none . . .). But what I liked was that many of the boys from the
fleet dropped in to say hello to me—kids I'd tattooed whilst they
were boots out at Great Lakes [Naval Training Station]. This was
very pleasing to me. And frequently they brought in with them a
shipmate to tattoo, or else they told someone to be sure to come
to see me while they were here.

Renslow, meanwhile, became ever more interesting to Steward. When
Renslow began to experiment with erotic films, Steward gladly participated as an extra: "Chuck decided to make a color movie of me tattoodling [a hustler named] Little Jim, putting a big peacock on his left bicep
and shoulder . . . [I had] flab under the chin, and old skin around the
jowls, [but] Little Jim [looked] absolutely beautiful and sexy as all hell . . .
Even [in] its rough state [the film] was absolutely fascinating to me: a
superb example of what Alice [Toklas] called 'letting the reality carry the
weight of it all.'"

Through Renslow, Steward was now meeting one hustler after another, and in some cases developing ongoing (paid) relationships with
them—most notably with a former Mr. Chicago and Mr. Illinois state
bodybuilding champion named Ralph Steiner.* Renslow, however, fascinated him more than any hustler ever could. "Now with the added incre-
ment of his new sadism, [he is] a tremendously stimulating figure [to
me]," Steward wrote in his journal. "I'm afraid of him, and yet strongly
drawn to him. It's all this damned new 'S'† personality of his." Renslow
unwittingly fanned the flames of Steward's desire by sharing many sexual
confidences; in one instance, "Cliff Ingram [telephoned Chuck the other
night] asking for a[n S/M] session at the gym [and] he got it; [afterward]
Chuck detailed it to me over the phone with great glee."

*Steiner, who was both Mr. Chicago and Mr. Illinois, later became a Chicago policeman. Steward
would have sex with him thirty-six times at a cost of ten dollars a time, the last encounter taking place
on a visit to Chicago in 1966.
†By "S" Steward meant "sadist" or "sexual dominant."

Steward was now finding the desire to be punished and disciplined during sex ever more central to his sexual practices. His advancing age, diminishing libido, and rapidly deteriorating self-esteem all seem to have played a part in this growing desire to be physically and verbally abused:

> Last night Frank Murphy came into the shop. [He is] a [former] roommate of Mike Miksche's in New York. I propositioned him for Chuck . . . Talk as I may, I can't get Chuck to work me over . . . Oh Lord, how I now appreciate the cruel irony of Kinsey's wry and favorite definition of a sadist [as] "a person who wouldn't even hurt a masochist." . . . Who would have thought that when I introduced [Chuck] to his first sadistic experience with Hal Stevens . . . that I would in a sense create a Frankenstein's monster that would eventually devour my peace of mind?
>
> . . . Tonight I'm supposed to have Ralph Steiner again. Chuck said he would give him some "instructions" as to how to treat me.

But the encounter with Steiner was a bust. "At least it had the saving grace of being amusing," Steward wrote the next day, "and kind of charming, for Ralph is a big sweet dumb boy, and he can't help any of it, no matter how hard he tries. I explained that I was a masochist, and [that] I'd like him to beat me a bit. 'Oh, I couldn't do that!' he said. 'I don't know you well enough.' That tied it." But Steward hadn't wanted to be "enslaved" by Steiner in any event; it was Renslow to whom he wanted to "submit." "Chuck will soon have a vast number of slaves running around town," Steward noted in his journal. "[Since] it looks as though I'll never have a chance to be [his slave] . . . I would like to put the whole g[o]dd[a]mned thing out of my head, but that's impossible I guess, with Renslow always feeding new details [of his conquests] into my overactive imagination." Renslow had in fact propelled Steward into a state of such sexual agitation that it began to cause Steward both headaches and sleeplessness. Rather than give in to Steward's importuning, however, Renslow merely offered Steward a shrug and a bottle of Miltown. When Steward continued to press him for S/M sex, Renslow finally agreed (despite misgivings) to "let him have it" once and for all.

The encounter, though ideal for neither man, nonetheless managed to convince Steward that his fantasy of being pimped out, abused, and sexually dominated by Renslow was basically impossible. "In some ways, I was a little disappointed," Steward wrote afterward; "in other ways it was a rich and gratifying experience. I think I've learned one thing from it: there is not so much masochism in me (from the point of view of physical pain) as there is the slave complex. I adore that Renslow boy, despite all the humiliations he forced upon me, or rather because of them . . . He was hardly demanding enough for me within the radius of my fantasy, but on the other hand he was working under extreme difficulties . . . [and] the fact that he pulled his punches somewhat is a witness to [our friendship]."

As fall turned to winter, Steward realized that there would be no further developments in his relationship with Renslow—for, quite apart from being a friend, Renslow was a full twenty years younger than Steward, and even if he *had* wanted to have sex with him (which he didn't), Renslow found Steward almost impossibly fussy about anything the two might have gotten up to during the course of an encounter. Since Renslow was just then surrounded by legions of handsome would-be hustlers down at the gym who were eager for any amount of no-holds-barred sexual exploitation, he really could not be bothered with Steward.

With no other outlet for his sadomasochistic obsession, Steward now began writing about Renslow on a daily basis, both in his experiments with fiction and in his journal entries. "A chorus boy from *West Side Story* [told me he wanted to be an 'm'] so I called Chuck," Steward noted one afternoon, "and to my horror [I] found myself bargaining with [Chuck], saying I'd send him this Roger Benson if he'd beat me up Monday . . . all the way home I kept saying [to myself] 'Just what the hell happened to you?'"

By the end of the month, Steward had gained some perspective on his desire to be "abused," and he had come up with a new plan for dealing with it as well:

> After the beating by Mike Miksche at Prok's, I had [the desire for S/M sex] whaled out of me for some years. Now, it is alive again. Frank Murphy the other night told me of a young husband, father of one, who was an accomplished S, and available for a fee of $15. Why not? That's only five more than Ralph Steiner charges for his mediocre performance. And [if the beating is painful

enough] it might rid me of [the desire to be an "m"] for another number of years, by which time I'll be too old to care.

The idea of hiring a violent heterosexual sadist to beat and abuse him seemed sensible enough to Steward, particularly since he knew he would get no more abuse from Renslow. While turning over the possibility in his mind, Steward attempted to understand his S/M obsession by reading Theodor Reik's *Masochism in Modern Man*.* One of Freud's first students in Vienna, Reik has suggested that patients who engaged in self-punishing or provocative behavior did so to demonstrate their emotional fortitude, as well as to induce guilt responses in others and thus to achieve a sense of "victory in defeat." Steward thought Reik's ideas on masochistic relationships chillingly accurate, and after reading Reik cover to cover, he ventured some of his own thoughts on what he termed "the 'tonic' benefit of cruelty." Specifically, he wondered if the intensity of the rejection he was experiencing at Renslow's hand might somehow be linked not merely to Renslow, but rather to Steward's own aging process:

> I don't think it's a hunger for love, because I don't know what love is: [my] heart has been dead for a long time. It's probably connected [instead] with the grand [midlife] climacteric, which I may be going through; and I may be seeing the last threads and shards of life and love being pulled away from me; this then may be a desperate attempt to stop the progression of time. At any rate, it's potent and painful. I keep feeling that there is a sentence buried in the Reik book somewhere that will make the chains fall off . . . but there [is] no magic touchstone . . .
> And so . . . despair.

On November 11, Steward celebrated the fifth anniversary of his career as a full-time tattoo artist by observing that "the prospect of retirement, or life in Europe, is not more than three years away (if all goes well)." He went on to describe a short story he had recently written about Renslow's evolution into a sexual dominant. He hoped, oddly enough, that Burckhardt might publish the story, entitled "Baby Tiger," in *Der Kreis*.

---

*New York: Farrar, Straus, 1941.

A few days later, he seemed much closer to a reconciliation with his feelings. "There's an empty saddle in the old corral, and it's mine," he wrote. "I have vacated my stall at the Renslow stables . . . [and] all morning the old battlecry of Teufelsdrockh in *Sartor Resartus* has been hammering through my brain: 'I am not thine, but free forevermore.'"* Then, to finalize the matter, Steward telephoned the heterosexual sadist hustler and set up an appointment for the beating that would hopefully clear him once and for all of his S/M obsession.

As he nervously awaited the encounter, Steward attempted to use what he had learned from Reik to make sense of his decision to pay an unknown man to beat him up. "My 'm' aggressiveness is a more intense form of the 'magic' gesture directed towards Chuck [Renslow], typified by the idea: 'You'll be sorry you wouldn't accept my love; I'll give it to someone else,'" he wrote. "Further: I seek punishment from Chuck because I am subconsciously aware that my aggressiveness [toward him] may cause me to lose him . . . So I seem to be wanting him to punish me and help me to be good so that he will love me. My violent claim to love gives me the feeling I have the right to punish him. And with this, a feeling of righteousness, possibly arising from the superego."

The next day the hustler came, beat Steward, collected his fifteen dollars, and left. Rather than achieving a much-needed release, however, Steward emerged from the experience finding it highly unsatisfactory: "Once more I am astonished to learn with what ease an 'm' can control an 'S,'" he wrote resentfully in his journal. "I was wanting to be severely marked so that I could show Chuck, and Lord, there isn't a single pink line on me anywhere today."

Since Wardell Pomeroy was just then visiting Chicago from the Institute for Sex Research, Steward sat down with him and confided the entire situation. Pomeroy, however, had no constructive suggestions for Steward on how he might take hold of his emotions. In despair, Steward ultimately turned to Gracián's *Manual*,† a book with which he had been consoling himself regularly since the early 1930s. A day later, aware of the depths of

---

*Steward is referring to *Sartor Resartus*, an enigmatic novel by Thomas Carlyle first published in 1838, whose central character, a philosopher named Diogenes Teufelsdrockh, holds that it is up to the individual to construct his or her own sense of the meaning or purpose of life.
†Better known as the *Oraculo Manual y Arte de Prudencia*, by Baltasar Gracián y Morales, first published in 1647.

despondency and self-pity into which he had sunk, he attempted once and for all to let go of the bitterness he felt toward Renslow, and in doing so to start over, "like Housman's Terence."*

By early December, Steward had regained his sense of humor about the situation, noting in his journal, "I no longer clutch at my breast or put the back of my hand to my forehead in the Lillian Gish manner when Chuck leaves—or doesn't show up at all . . . [And I had] a long talk with Dom last evening [which] was very helpful [too.]" During the course of that talk, Orejudos had apparently explained to Steward that Renslow thought of him not as a potential sex partner, but rather as a much-needed father figure. "And so," Steward wrote in his journal, "with the resignation I have generally been able to find myself at times of great stress, I decided to accept that role . . . [and] things were eased almost at once . . . This damned h complex always keeps people thinking they're younger than they are: I don't seem like 50 to myself, but I am, and to others, too."

After a lifetime of sexual adventure, Steward was now faced, through Renslow's categorical rejection, with something entirely nonnegotiable and new, and something for which, despite every precaution, he was nonetheless entirely unprepared: his transformation, at age fifty, into a sexually undesirable older man.

---

*Steward's reference is to "Terence, This Is Stupid Stuff" from *A Shropshire Lad*. His meaning about "start[ing] over" is clearer in the context of the poem:

> . . . down in lovely muck I've lain,
> Happy till I woke again.
> Then I saw the morning sky:
> Heigho, the tale was all a lie;
> The world, it was the old world yet,
> I was I, my things were wet,
> And nothing now remained to do
> But begin the game anew.

15

"Payments to hustlers"

In the months after calling it quits with Renslow, Steward nonetheless continued to seek out sadomasochistic encounters, for his desire to be "abused" remained strong. The combination of sex, pain, and terror, properly administered, was in fact so stimulating to his senses that he now craved it above all other experiences. Along with regular meetings for rough sex with Paul Jefferson (a "highly intelligent, semi-Beat Negro" who was prone to alcoholic fits of temper) and the equally abusive, stunningly handsome black bodybuilder Bill Payson (whose preferred way of having sex included heavy verbal as well as physical abuse), Steward hired a ten-dollar hustler in early December, an Italian named Pete who had recently been released from jail after serving time on a manslaughter charge.* He also noted a moment of profound self-loathing during an encounter with a hillbilly hustler named Jimmy Willers:

> [The other day] I said to [Jimmy Willers†] as I gave him his three bucks, "I'll make it five if you jack me off." So he drawled in his wretched hillbilly tones, "Waal, I don't rightly think I could, it'd make me sick to the stummick." . . . All of a sudden, everything unrolled before me . . . the nasty picture of fastidious me feasting on his dirty little cock, and then being so insulted, sent me very

---

*The Stud File entry for "Pete, a hustler" notes that the two met twice within the same week for "violent" and "enthusiastic" encounters.
†Stud File note: "Courtesy Red Jackson Pimping Service. Hillbilly. $3. White legs. Unc[ut], said: (reaching down): 'Lemme pull the hide back.'"

cold for a moment—cold in my appraisal of myself, and in the shame which I thought dead and gone.

The new series of short stories Steward wrote during this time reflected this resurgent interest in deeply humiliating, often life-threatening sex. The first, a story based on Chuck Renslow's transformation into a sexual dominant, had been fairly discreet in its handling of the subject matter, and was published; but Burckhardt sent the second one back suggesting an entirely rewritten ending—in Steward's words, "the propaganda-type of *Kreis* ending you see so much of in that silly little sentimental magazine." In attempting to describe the sexual fantasies that had taken over both his imagination and his day-to-day existence—inciting strangers and near strangers to physically abuse and degrade him—Steward was now in complete and utter conflict with *Der Kreis*, which wanted to publish life-affirming stories concerning masculine affairs of the heart, not chilling tales of semi-anonymous sadomasochistic encounters.

While Steward kept a distance from Renslow during this period, he could not break with him outright—for, apart from remaining sexually infatuated with him ("just like a 17-yr old schoolgirl"), he was largely dependent upon him for hustlers. One Latino hustler in particular caught his fancy:

> Last Monday . . . Chuck . . . sent over a $5 number named Johnny (Mendoza? Reyes?) who was one of the handsomest Puerto Rican boys I've ever seen—small, but with a perfectly developed body, and skin like silk; every muscle was in beautiful relief . . . It was a joy to look at him. I liked him so much I invited him back for Friday . . . Of course, if I "give up" Chuck, I'll miss many of these handsome young hustlers.

A teenager who played guitar and wanted to be a rock-and-roll star, Reyes seemed to Steward to have all the "sullen moods and romantic charm of a latin Heathcliff." Renslow had photographed him extensively, both in the nude and in a posing strap, for he had a very large and well-formed penis as well as a fine body. Renslow had already had sex with him repeatedly, and had sent him out to many other clients before passing him along to Steward. But Steward quickly developed a close personal bond with Reyes, one that immediately transcended the usual hustler-client relationship, and that ultimately lasted the better part of a decade.*

While Steward's use of hustlers had been minimal, even incidental, five years earlier, they were now a mainstay of his sexual life. In 1954 he had spent only $63 on hustlers, but by 1956, that amount had grown to $205, and in 1959, to $300—meaning approximately sixty paid encounters per year, or more than one per week. In 1960, the number of paid encounters would more than triple, with the lion's share of the $953 in payments, $750, going directly to Johnny Reyes.†

Unfortunately for Steward, few hustlers were interested in (or even understood) the heavy sadomasochistic role play he most craved. In his desperation he managed to negotiate one final, absurd S/M encounter with Renslow, "but it was a hasty little pudding we whipped up, with absolutely none of the ritual," Steward wrote. "In the midst of things rising to a climax, [Chuck] came spontaneously and threw himself on me panting, and it was all over. At least, he said he came; I'm not certain that I saw any evidence. The truth is more likely that he looked at his watch and saw that it was time to [pick up] Dom [down at the auditorium], and so phonied up his orgasm." In truth, both Renslow and Orejudos were by now more than indifferent to Steward; they were bored by him and irritated by his constant importunings. While Steward had once fascinated them with his vast knowledge of tattooing, they had by now largely absorbed all that they needed of that knowledge, and were putting it to use on their own. As a result, they considered him no more than a lonely, embittered, and slightly pathetic older man with little left to offer them.

Steward, however, was slow to realize the shift in their feelings toward him. Upon returning from Christmas (which he spent with his sister in Dal-

---

*Johnny Reyes, though heterosexual, had been continuously molested since the age of twelve by his uncle Mike, who also beat him and pimped him out to others. Steward wrote of Reyes's experience of childhood sexual abuse (which he only learned about several years into their relationship) in *Understanding the Male Hustler* (pp. 56–57). He also fictionalized it in the story "Jungle Cat," and enumerated its particulars in the Stud File—which has entries for both Johnny and "Uncle Mike" Reyes, because somehow in the course of knowing Johnny, Steward also negotiated a (single) sexual encounter with Johnny's abusive uncle.

†Steward's "Payments to hustlers" card in the Stud File ceases to record payments in 1969, though he did continue to hire them and record the encounters in his sex calendars. Such expenditures would peak in 1964, when Steward spent a grand total of $1,033 buying sex. The number of payments would then steadily decrease through the end of the 1960s.

las), he had been invited by Renslow and Orejudos to exchange presents with them at their home, and in a grand gesture of friendship he had bought them a hundred-dollar Zenith Super-Symphonaire Radio. They accepted the gift happily enough, but offered him no gift in return. A few days later Orejudos came down with hepatitis and Steward heard no more from the couple. "We have been drifting further and further apart," Steward noted sadly in his diary. "[Renslow] has now reached the stage of lying to me in order to stop my importuning [him for sex]—and good God, I don't bother him *that* much!"

Pondering his increasingly miserable life situation in a journal that no longer seemed to him to have any purpose, Steward observed, "Sometimes I wonder just to what extent I have profited or lost in knowing [Chuck and Dom]. I have a feeling that something in the past two years has diminished the capability with which I was guiding my life into the channel I wanted, or that my progress to my goal is being delayed, or that something has seriously undermined my faith and confidence in myself, whether in the form of my ego or simple self-respect." And, indeed, Renslow seemed more and more to Steward to have used him and cast him aside. "I try to think what my life was like before knowing them," Steward concluded. "It seemed fairly simple, peaceful, channeled and selfish. But it has become a thing of chaos and turmoil and confusion."

•

Having had no sex in Dallas over the holidays, Steward came back to Chicago hungry for something big, and so arranged for another brutal S/M "do" with the heterosexual sadist hustler Al Simpson. But news of Orejudos's very serious case of hepatitis (contracted, Steward was sure, through oral-anal contact) gave Steward second thoughts, for he knew Simpson would insist on that activity. Rather than face such a health risk himself, Steward telephoned Ralph Mills and invited the defrocked priest over to take his place on short notice. Steward then hid in another room and watched the entire encounter through a peephole:

Ralph got pissed on (and my bed too, and pillow), handed some shit and piss in a cup to drink, beat a little and hurt with a hand-shock machine, chained up, fucked in the mouth, burned with matches . . . The whole affair lasted about an hour and fifteen minutes, and built up to enough of a climax so that I . . . was suf-

ficiently stimulated [to] come all over the telephone book. But I
also concluded one thing: all further encounters with Simpson
are out. The *merde* angle's too much.

During this truly dark moment in Steward's life, he found himself
tempted into alcoholic relapse. Instead, in semidesperation, he turned to
barbiturates, which offered a similarly pleasurable sensation of alcoholic
detachment, but with fewer immediately addictive or toxic side effects.
These Seconal pills, known as "reds" (which were then being widely
abused and were relatively easy to obtain on the street) quickly became
Steward's drug of choice. Over the next decade he would develop an addiction to them that would last to the end of his life. Bob McHenry, an
amiable former sex contact from Steward's Polaroid-party days, later recalled visiting him at the tattoo parlor during this time, noting that Steward was clearly "bleary eyed and goofy" from them.

Steward had also started developing some more serious health issues,
including erectile dysfunction. His sexual problems were not so severe
that they prevented him from achieving orgasm, but they did limit the
types of sexual activity in which he could successfully engage, and they
became yet another source of personal humiliation for him, particularly since he was now frequently having sex with exceptionally virile
younger men who had no such problems.

He also developed a varicose vein in his leg that required a hospital
operation. While confined to his hospital bed, he was robbed of forty-two
dollars by a night nurse, but without friends or family to intervene on his
behalf, he could do nothing to get the money back. Steward was shocked
to find himself so vulnerable and alone in life, and this new sense of vul-
nerability prompted him, while recuperating, to write the story of an impossible love between a tattoo artist and a heterosexual serviceman. He
noted in his journal that it "was about [my experience with] Chuck Liston, and [I] called [it] 'The Sergeant with the Rose Tattoo.' To avoid
possible repercussions . . . I set the scene in Paris, and managed not to
make [the] Chuck [Liston character] until he was discharged from the
army. (What projection! Not only regarding the boutique in Paris, but the
making of that boy!) Well, midway, I got kinda disgusted: all those damned
Kreis stories are too formula-ized, too facile, ending too happily. I was
tempted to make this one bleak, but relented."

Despite his health problems and the period of introspection prompted by his hospitalization, Steward returned to rough sex within a month of his release. In the aftermath of one such encounter with Paul Jefferson, he discovered that Jefferson, while doing time in federal prison for drug pushing, had murdered another inmate by bashing in his head with a brick. Later, in his journal, Steward noted that Jefferson had said, "'I was surprised at how soft the skull was . . . like a mushmelon.' This little bit of news excited me a lot, and I thought of Genet and Weidmann.* . . . Paul worries the hell out of me when he's been drinking."

By far the greatest shock of Steward's spring came not from Paul Jefferson or Bill Payson, but from Johnny Reyes, who one afternoon let slip that he was only seventeen—and thus still a minor. Steward's old friend Robert Dahm had just spent twenty months in the Raiford penitentiary in Florida for engaging in sexual activities with a sixteen-year-old, so Steward knew all too well the danger of being sexually involved with one so young. In an attempt to swear off Reyes, Steward started up with a thuggish, chain-smoking new hustler of Renslow's named Clyde Wayne. He also resumed his sexual relationship with Pete Rojas, his former student at DePaul. Though the bookish Rojas was hardly as sexually compelling as Reyes, "[he] is still pretty charming," Steward noted in his journal that May, "and said some extraordinary and flattering things about me, that I was the only person at DePaul who had made him feel anything about the school was worthwhile, how I had 'formed' him, and so on . . . I wrote and told Rudolf, who at once said I sh[oul]d do a story [about it]."

•

That same month, while avoiding Reyes, Steward met up again with Paul Jefferson. As it happened, Jefferson had been released from a dry-out clinic that afternoon, and was on a particularly out-of-control drinking spree. During a long backroom session at the Tattoo Joynt, Jefferson caned Steward severely, forcibly sodomized him, and ultimately beat him up so violently that Steward remained black-and-blue for more than a week. Though Steward went so far as to describe the experience in the Stud File as a "rape," he became completely obsessed with Jefferson as a

---

*Eugene Weidmann (1908–1939), the killer who was the last man to be publicly executed in France, and with whom Jean Genet was obsessed.

result of the encounter—for Jefferson's heavy drinking, combined with his recently revealed real-life history as a murderer, now made encounters with him particularly thrilling.

While tending his wounds in the days that followed, Steward realized that repeated encounters like the one he had just had with Jefferson would probably one day end in his murder. Though he and Renslow were no longer particularly close, he called Renslow to discuss the situation, and Renslow, after some thought, offered to give Reyes instruction in the art of sadomasochistic "abuse." Steward wondered if doing so could possibly work, for Reyes was neither sadistic nor violent. Moreover, being so young, he lacked an authoritative or domineering presence. But when Renslow made clear to Reyes that Steward would offer him a financial bonus for being just as rough as he liked, Reyes (who had, after all, been beaten and terrorized for years by his uncle) dutifully took up the challenge—and, in the end, put in an impressive performance. Steward's intense guilt about being involved with one so young—and in so perverse a manner—intensified his pleasure at being punished and hurt by the handsome adolescent. As a result, his passion for Reyes intensified. Meetings between them became more frequent, the beatings heavier, the payments more substantial.

Instructing hustlers in sadomasochistic domination was no easy thing, however, and Steward quickly found himself exasperated with the mood-killing work of explaining to each and every young hustler sent over by Renslow just how he wanted to be abused and mistreated. Remembering similar moments of adolescent apathy from his previous life as a teacher, Steward typed up a "handout," which he began presenting to each hustler upon arrival, asking him to carefully review the material before beginning the session.

The handout read:

WHAT THIS PARTICULAR M LIKES
1. Please remember: he is your absolute slave.
2. Make him undress you.
3. Order him to take off your shoes and socks and kiss and lick your feet.
4. Make him suck your balls.
5. Piss in his mouth (a little, not too much; make him swallow it by holding your hand over his mouth and pinching his nose shut).

6. Make him swallow your come. (He may try to spit it out.)
7. Put dog collar on him. Pull him by leash.
8. It is not necessary YOU come every time. Make him jerk off in front of you.
9. Spit in his face.
10. Beat him in the face with your hard cock. Straddle his chest.
11. Talk mean and nasty to him. Call him dirty cocksucker.
12. Wear dirty socks. Cram them in his mouth.
13. Give him a few whacks on the ass with your belt. Or use whip if one present.
14. Pinch his tits, or other tender spots.
15. Make him lie on floor, and piss some on him.
16. Do NOT ask him to rim you (tongue in ass). Many M's are afraid of getting hepatitis this way or yellow jaundice.
17. Make him lick your armpits, the sweatier the better.
18. If you want to, make him give you a tongue-bath all over, or do whatever gives you pleasure.
19. In general, be as hard on him as you want to be.
20. Remember: he is your ABSOLUTE slave!

Steward was surely aware of both the irony and the pathos of this grim little document; yet rather than destroy it, he apparently decided to include it among his papers, and thus to make it a part of his sexual history.

As Steward was having these various S/M experiences, he decided to change direction in his fiction writing. Rather than write to Burckhardt's specifications, he now decided to write stories about sex that would be true to his own experience—even if it meant the stories would never be published by *Der Kreis*. His life was, after all, pornographic: Why not write pornography? He told Renslow of the decision, expecting to be congratulated; but instead, Renslow merely scoffed, telling him "you're too fuckin' old to write." These words, Steward later wrote, had an immediate and galvanizing effect:

Nothing that anyone could have said would have sent me more quickly to a typewriter. Forgotten were the years of listening to my internal critic . . . And to hell with even the question of money—I'd write just to please myself . . . and (as I have said a thousand times) lonely old men whacking off in hotel rooms at night. It is amazing how a chance remark, forgotten by the maker, can move one to violent and long-lasting activity.

•

Reyes, meanwhile, had begun pressuring Steward to pay him more money, for he wanted a car and was desperate to make a down payment. While Steward initially agreed to help him with it, he remained conflicted about his ongoing sexual patronage of one so young. In a journal entry, he noted:

He was always asking me for something to eat when he came around the shop—and I have taken to buying all sorts of cookies, and pound cake (a great favorite of his)—until one day I happened to ask him what he really liked, at which he answered "animal crackers." It is impossible to say how much that jolted me, and made me realize that though he's sexually mature, he's still just a kid. The whole vast flood of childhood memories came back—the little red boxes the crackers came in, and how we used to play suitcases with them—and suddenly I felt very ashamed of myself indeed.

Realizing his involvement with Reyes was truly wrong, Steward attempted to bring it to a conclusion by paying off all Reyes's debts—a grand total of $252—in what he described as an "existentialist, 'forever' gesture." But he then had second thoughts, fearing that in releasing Reyes from his employment he might place the young man in even greater danger.* As a result, there was no break; their paid arrangement continued. It would last well into the late 1960s, long after Steward had left Chicago.

There were a few other noteworthy events that summer and fall. Upon learning that Frederik IX, king of Denmark, would be visiting Chicago, Steward wrote and invited him to the Tattoo Joynt, for the Danish

---

*Reyes had spoken to Steward of leaving him to work in a male brothel owned by a criminal named J. P. Boyd. After Roy Robinson (who had once worked for Boyd) told Steward that Boyd routinely worked his hustlers to exhaustion and never gave them their promised cut of earnings, Steward convinced Reyes not to go there. He did so in part by continuing to employ him.

monarch was well-known for his many tattoos. When the king arrived incognito, Steward recognized him immediately, but courteously pretended not to know who he was as he applied the desired design. Steward also had the pleasure that autumn of reading about himself in James Purdy's novel *Malcolm*, noting in his journal that it "was rather hilarious . . . There was a very fine chapter laid in the Tattoo Palace of Professor Robinolte—a true portrait of [my] place in the [Sportland] arcade."

In early December, Steward took Renslow and Orejudos down to Bloomington to visit the Institute for Sex Research at the invitation of Wardell Pomeroy. While there, Pomeroy gave the three men a private screening of Genet's *Un Chant d'Amour* and the 1952 Kinsey film of Steward being dominated by Mike Miksche—the latter of which left Steward "embarrassed, with dry mouth and a fairly painful traumatic empathic reaction after all these years." Steward also had a quietly poignant encounter with a graduate student he met at the Student Union,* one who might easily have been Steward himself as a younger man:

> I took a book and sat down [in the lounge] in a big chair conveniently close to a butch-looking boy with crew-cut yaller hair, and finally got to talking with him . . . an English major, a senior . . . I just said would he like to come up to my room to talk, and he did. Goddammit, I dint have a thing to show him—no pictures, nor any licker to offer—so I just turned to him and said how would you like a blow job and he said, "What else am I here for?" It was sort of enjoyable and of course very "romantic" . . . He was h, of course, and planned to go into teaching. I'm afraid I was a bit discouraging to him about it.

Steward then traveled to Rome for Christmas—for as part of her newfound life as a Catholic, Alice Toklas had taken winter lodgings at Monteverde, the convent of the Sisters of the Most Precious Blood, close to the Vatican. Not wanting to go alone, Steward invited Pete Rojas and Rudolf Burckhardt to come with him. While paying for their companionship (like paying for sex) was not without its emotional complications,

---

*The Student Union, located at the center of the Indiana University campus, contains a hotel in which visitors to the Institute for Sex Research were usually lodged.

Steward knew that having the two along would at least make the trip less melancholy, for Rojas continued to be sexually receptive to Steward, and Burckhardt was by now his best friend.

Steward passed his first wintry afternoon in Rome by visiting the graves of Shelley and Keats at the Protestant Cemetery, during which Burckhardt snapped several photographs of him quietly meditating by Keats's grave. On the way back to the hotel, the two men had a surprise:

> We stopped to sit outside at Doney's [on Via Veneto] for an espresso. Suddenly I looked up, and there was Alice standing on the sidewalk just twenty-five feet away, all bent and shortened and looking more like a mountain troll than ever. I went over to her and bent nearly double over her, while she put out her hand to greet me, as if we had parted about thirty minutes before.

Toklas had in fact been seeing many friends since her arrival: Thornton and Isabel Wilder, Bernard Faÿ, Donald Sutherland, and Virgil Thomson had all dropped by to see how she was doing. In the days that followed, Steward escorted her on a number of extremely slow-moving visits to various Catholic monuments, as a result of which Toklas later observed that Pius XII (whom she had known as a younger man in Paris) was rather like Steward, both in his interest in Huysmans* and his generosity toward friends.

Toklas's Roman winter lasted well into spring and ended in great trauma. During Toklas's absence from Paris, Roubina Stein, the widow of Gertrude Stein's nephew Allan, entered Toklas's Paris apartment, inventoried the pictures there, and, finding several missing, secured a court order declaring the pictures endangered by Toklas's absence. She subsequently had all of them removed. The eighty-three-year-old Toklas, having received no warning of the action, returned to her Paris apartment to find it stripped of all its artwork. The shock was profound; she never recovered from it.

•

---

*Toklas's reference is specifically to Pius XII's interest in Huysmans's late novel *The Oblate of St. Benedict*, which chronicled Huysmans's acceptance of Catholicism—not Huysmans's early, "decadent" novels such as *Against the Grain*.

On Christmas Day, Steward visited Hadrian's Villa at Tivoli, and went the following day to Ostia Antica. On the twenty-seventh, he journeyed by rail to Naples and toured Pompeii in the rain. During a shared taxi ride with "about a dozen of the sleek and evil young men of Naples," he found himself "uncomfortably wondering if I had hidden my wallet well, and feeling a good deal like Sebastian surrounded by the young men who ate him in *Suddenly Last Summer*." By the thirtieth he was back in his hotel in Rome, where after a sordid encounter with a Bavarian hustler, he recalled feeling like the title character in Bunin's "The Gentleman from San Francisco." "I had a few moments of terrible revulsion after the whole experience," Steward noted. "[It] seemed so dirty, all of it."

Burckhardt, Rojas, and Steward then flew back to Zurich for the gala New Year's Eve dance organized by *Der Kreis*, after which Steward said a quick good-bye to Burckhardt and flew on to Paris, where he had arranged a meeting with Julien Green, and another with Jacques Delarue, a married, heterosexual officer of the Sûreté Nationale who had published an important book on the tattoos of the Parisian underworld. Unfortunately, Steward contracted food poisoning from a dinner of steak tartare on his first night in town. After staying up all night to be sick, he staggered over the next morning for a visit with Green, who told Steward that after some unsatisfactory correspondence with the Institute for Sex Research he had decided not to give them his diary after all.* "Well," Steward wrote afterward with disappointment, "it was a noble second try."

Steward then met Jacques Delarue for coffee at the Deux Magots. Delarue's *Les Tatouages du "Milieu,"*† a study of hand-applied amateur tattooing in French prisons and among Parisian lowlife, was one of Steward's favorite new books, not least because it featured Delarue's own photographs of the crude "hand jobs" done by men in prison, as well as a series of line drawings of gang markings and other antisocial designs favored by Parisian street criminals. Delarue himself had carefully traced these works in order to include them in his book as illustrations. The meeting between the two tattoo aficionados was so enjoyable that they immediately arranged to meet again for lunch the next day, during which

---

*As of 2008, Green's massive diary has not been published or placed in a public archive. Bowdlerized versions of certain sections have, however, appeared in both French and English.
†Robert Giraud, coauthor (Paris, 1950).

Delarue shared with Steward the most risqué photographs in his collection—a vast array of heavily tattooed penises and vaginas. "Here was an inspector of the Sûreté Nationale showing me dirty pictures!" Steward wrote delightedly in his journal. So began Steward's last significant overseas friendship, one through which he hoped he might finally establish himself in Paris as a tattoo artist—for, faced with a life in Chicago that seemed ever more empty and bleak, he was once again dreaming, as he had twenty years earlier, of relocating permanently to France.

16

Masters and Slaves

Even as he began exploring the possibility of opening a tattoo parlor in Paris, Steward continued experimenting with erotic narratives based on his sexual experiences that he vaguely intended for American publication. His decision to devote himself to erotic fiction during the early 1960s was based in part on the waning of the Chicago tattoo business, which left him plenty of free time to write; but also, paradoxically enough, on the waning of his sex drive. Steward had been charting his sexual decline since 1948, continually noting the steady increase in "periodicity" (or time elapsed) between "releases" (or orgasms) on a month-by-month basis. While still more sexually active than many, he felt the diminishment more deeply than most—for sex was by now not only a central and defining activity of his life, but also his preferred way of escaping the depression to which he was temperamentally inclined. Since his fantasizing about sex remained a constant, he seemed to have reached, like Casanova in the library at the Castle of Dux, that moment in life when creative reminiscence becomes the happiest possible way of engaging in the activity one has always most enjoyed. And indeed, in the coming years writing about sex would give his life new meaning, direction, and focus.

Steward wrote a number of essays for *Der Kreis* during this period, too, sending Burckhardt substantial reports on the changing American political and social scene. The most significant of these pieces, "What's New in Sodom?," carefully assessed the landmark legislation enacted by the Illinois state legislature in 1962 that had quietly decriminalized homosexual acts between consenting adults, and concluded,

The best "legal" opinion about the new law regarding homosexuals is that if it lasts six months without outcry for repeal, it will
be permanent . . . Meanwhile, here in Chicago . . . most of us
are . . . doing without our favorite colognes, eschewing red and
lavender neckties,* and in general trying to remain mousey, neb-
bish, and unnoticed. [Homosexual activity] may be legal now [in
Illinois], but no one can say how long it will last.

Starting in January 1962, Steward took up yet another project: mentoring Cliff Ingram in the fine art of tattooing. Under his new name of
Cliff Raven, Ingram would build on this early education with Steward to
become the most accomplished Japanese-style tattoo artist of his generation. Steward found Ingram entirely delightful, for he was a good-looking
young man brimming with enthusiasm, intelligence, good humor, and
sexual mischief. His presence in the shop would prove a bright spot for
Steward in an otherwise dismal winter, for Emmy Curtis, who had been
ailing for years, was now sinking into senility. Steward spent the better
part of his winter and spring devoting himself to her needs as a bedridden
invalid. By spring she was completely unable to care for herself, and so,
with great reluctance, he arranged to move her into a nursing home.
Steward had been close friends with Curtis since 1938—sharing meals,
seeing movies, and talking on the phone with her nearly every day. Though
their sexual relationship had lasted only until 1949, and though she had
frequently exasperated him with her peculiar and old-maidish ways, she
was in many regards his best and most constant friend, and his gloom in
watching her drift into dementia and paralysis was enormous. Some of
that sorrow is reflected in a brief piece he published over the winter in
Der Kreis:

Man's chase after happiness is a feverish and unceasing thing. As
we grow older, we search more frantically for it than formerly—
and it can be found no longer. "If I were just as happy now as I
was then," we say, and sigh. But the truth is that few men have
more to their account than a dozen hours of happiness—a frag-

---

*Wearing a red or a lavender necktie was one of the coded ways in which homosexuals identified
themselves—both to one another and to potential trade—in the years before gay liberation.

ment here and there out of the dull and sullen roll of life . . . How much happier man would be were he only to realize that a state of unhappiness or frustration or despair is the *usual* thing, the lot of nearly all men nearly all of the time! The frenetic reachings would cease, the compulsions disappear, the nervous chase smooth itself into a serene and contented acceptance.

After she died, Steward, who was coexecutor of her estate, closed up her apartment, arranged for her funeral, and oversaw the sale of her possessions. During that time Wardell Pomeroy wrote to him, "Paul [Gebhard] tells me . . . that you are now about ready to pull up stakes [for Paris] . . . Before you finally leave it would be helpful for us to secure any odds and ends, pictures, diary, calendar, observations, or you name it, before we lose you to the common market." Steward replied that, on the contrary, he was obliged to remain in Chicago until the Curtis estate had finished probate, and added, "I must say that the reality of the projected uproot [to Paris] gives me the twiddles when I think seriously about it; I don't know that at my age I still have enough git-up-&-go to dispose of my comfortable apartment and make the physical move [to Europe] . . . I keep wondering if I'd be satisfied after I got there."

One thing, however, was certain: Steward had to make a definitive change, for he had few real friends left in Chicago, and both his tattooing business and his sex life were dwindling. Renslow and Orejudos were increasingly distant, in part because their business empire—which now included two new magazines, a bathhouse, and a bar—took up most of their time and attention. The bathhouse was particularly innovative: known as Steve's Health Club, it looked on the outside like a fitness center and gym, and in that way became a model for a new generation of sex clubs.* Meanwhile, the new bar, known as the Gold Coast, had proved an even greater success, for it was the first bar in Chicago to cater specifically and openly to men interested in leather and S/M. Steward was happy enough at Renslow's commercial success, but he had no great interest in these new enterprises; if anything, he felt excluded from them, since as

---

*By 1962, all the older, syndicate-run bathhouses of Chicago had disappeared. The Congressman, in the basement of the Congress Hotel, had been torn down with the widening of the Eisenhower Expressway; the Lincoln Baths, in the basement of the Lincoln Hotel on Clark Street, had been raided and closed.

an older man he was much more comfortable paying for sex in private rather than cruising for it—and facing constant rejection—in public. Moreover, as a recovering alcoholic he was uncomfortable among drinkers and disliked spending time in bars.

He was nonetheless intrigued by Renslow's successful transferral of the "master/slave" dynamic from bedroom to workplace—for Renslow now "owned" a goodly number of "slaves," each of whom seemed entirely content to work for him full-time in exchange for regular sessions of psychic domination, a highly sexual communal living arrangement, and small amounts of spending money. Over the coming decades Renslow would continue to develop this "slave compound," with new young men joining it regularly in their desire to submit themselves to a powerful, well-connected, and sexually dominant businessman.* Describing this ever-changing assortment of young men as his "family," Renslow would eventually incorporate his various bar, restaurant, health club, and publishing businesses under the tongue-in-cheek name of Renslow Family Enterprises.

While Renslow's world had continued to expand, Steward's by comparison had shrunk almost to nothing. In response to the various sadnesses in his personal life and the growing scarcity of his friends, he might well have reached out to new acquaintances, but he seems to have chosen not to do so. Instead he continued to cultivate the state of zenlike detachment he had described for *Der Kreis* in "Detachment: A Way of Life." Even as he embraced this idea of detachment, however, Steward found himself in conflict with it, for his need for sexual variety and sexual activity continued to fascinate, compel, and distract him. Unwilling to give up the hunt for new experiences, he instead focused on what seemed to him a most reasonable course of action: protecting himself from emotional upset by having sex almost exclusively with hustlers. In doing so, Steward rationalized that despite his advancing age, he would still be able to satisfy his desire for sexual variety, and at the same time risk neither infatuation nor rejection, since the arrangement was "simply business." As he later ruefully noted in his memoirs, he had reached a new moment in his sexual history:

---

*As that desire changed or evolved the individual was free to leave, though in several instances (notably with a young man named Patrick Ryan) Renslow would attempt to keep him. (Renslow repeatedly stalked Ryan even after the young man moved to San Francisco.)

The carefree life of one's prime, and the ease with which romantic encounters had been so carelessly and happily made—those things vanished so slowly that one was scarcely aware they were diminishing. But go they did, leaving a kind of bittersweet afterglow, a flickering tapestry of golden memories, from which one now and again arose with nostalgia and a barren pleasure.

No question: one had to begin to purchase, or do without . . .

Steward had few qualms about paying for sex; he had done so whenever the mood struck him, starting in the late 1930s. Now in late midlife, he felt very strongly that there was absolutely nothing wrong with it. To his mind, no exploitation took place in the exchange of money for sex when the parties involved were consenting adult males—particularly since the roles of hustler and customer were at that time defined in a way that was entirely to the physical, psychological, and monetary advantage of the hustler. In this well-established exchange, the hustler (who was understood to be primarily heterosexual) allowed the homosexual customer to perform oral sex on him. That was all. There was no exchange of affection, no variety, and no reciprocation. As a result, the hustler retained his heterosexual identity, asserted physical and emotional dominance over the homosexual client, and at the same time profited financially from what was to him an inconsequential (and basically pleasurable) sensation. So long as the hustler was above the age of consent, not subject to coercion, and not exposed to disease, the transaction was, to Steward's way of thinking, beneficial for both parties—particularly since the male hustler, unlike his female counterpart, was basically invisible within the general population and, provided he was not exposed, suffered little or no lasting social stigmatization from his work.

Steward was adamant in his belief that hustlers and hustling were indispensable to the aging homosexual. After the well-known author Simon Raven profiled the world of the British hustler (or "rent boy") with an article in *Encounter* entitled "Boys Will Be Boys," Steward responded in *Der Kreis* with a similar survey of the American hustling scene entitled "The Bull Market in America," a surprisingly bitter polemic asserting that American society's abuse of the homosexual extended to its forbidding him to pay for sex with other men—which was after all necessary for older homosexual men such as Steward, who having consciously chosen solitary lives of sexual variety, needed to pay for sex in their later years if they were ever to have it at all. Since no harm was done to the hustler, Steward argued, the outlawing of male prostitution was just another senseless form of homosexual oppression. His impassioned argument went on to observe that hustling was, moreover, an ancient, worldwide practice:

> You have legislated against the homosexual, harried him and hounded him, permitted him by your laws and repressions to be blackmailed, sterilized him, laughed at him, kicked him, beaten him—but you cannot change his inclinations, and chances are he would not let you if you could. Is it any wonder that you have made him defiant, and made him sneer at your attempted restrictions? If he wants to buy the pleasure of a hustler's company for an evening, or ten minutes, how can you stop him?
>
> Go to the ruins of Pompeii, dear reformer. Find your way to the house of the Vetti brothers. Pay the guard a few lira and ask him to show you the small shuttered painting in the vestibule. It is of a stalwart young man, exposed, standing next to a pair of scales, and resting part of himself on one of the balances, whilst in the other—outweighed—stands a pot of gold.
>
> . . . can anyone in America, by city ordinance or state law, undo a world tradition that is centuries old?

Yet even as Steward cultivated his "detachment" by patronizing hustlers, he kept returning in his writing to those powerful fantasies of sexual domination and punishment that he had begun to describe (in his short story for Lynes, "The Motorcyclist") nearly a decade earlier. He had always hoped to make that monologue the first of a series, in the style of Schnitzler's play *Reigen*. Now, with few other projects to occupy his time, he went back to work on the series, determined to bring it to completion.

Steward's interest in confessional narratives was long-standing—his early novel *Angels on the Bough* had moved from person to person to create a group portrait of young people centered around Ohio State University. Now, however, the technique was being used not to make gentle explorations of the heart, but rather to describe explicitly a series of violent sexual acts in which each "victim" deserves his punishment: Joe is beaten up and enslaved for soliciting a homosexual encounter; Mike is blackmailed into sexual subservience for seducing an underage youth; Steve is lynched by a black man for propositioning him. Yet the collection as a whole supports the sex researcher C. A. Tripp's observation that the enjoyment of sadomasochistic techniques is usually limited to people who have had exceptionally strong social training "in either the be-kind-to-others direction, or the sex-is-sinful department, or both"—as Steward surely had. Naming the completed collection of monologues *Ring-Around-the-Rosy*, Steward toyed for a while with publishing it privately, then apparently sent his only copy to Wardell Pomeroy at the Institute for Sex Research, where the manuscript remained untouched for the better part of a year.

Steward's interest in the ultramasculine paradigms featured in the manuscript—the motorcycle tough, the cop, the gang member, the truck driver, and the sailor—links the work not only to Genet's 1947 novel *Querelle de Brest*, but also to a larger social movement that was becoming increasingly visible in the 1960s and '70s: leather. The leather movement had started during World War II, evolving out of uniform fetishism. With his early fixation on sailors and other men in uniform, and his long-standing interest in various forms of punishment and domination, Steward had been caught up in leather long before the movement had a name.

Steward was hardly a joiner, though, and as leather had evolved into a social movement during the late 1950s,* he had assiduously avoided its gatherings, remaining skeptical not only of its emerging rites and rituals, but also of the masculinity of its adherents. To the end of his life Steward would maintain that it was impossible to institutionalize a sexual practice that was, to his mind, based on the propositioning of rough, dangerous, potentially violent working-class or criminal-class men. This pursuit and seduction of an authentically masculine, primarily heterosexual, and barely civilized ideal was, to Steward's mind, essentially a solitary practice, and not one that any homosexual man could possibly engage in simply by having sex with another homosexual. To him, the new homo-

---

*By the early 1960s, the leather movement became visible in Los Angeles, New York, Chicago, and San Francisco through the establishment of various private clubs and public drinking establishments. In September 1965, Renslow, Raven, and Orejudos (along with seven other men) drew up the Constitution of the Second City Motorcycle Club, a club that was essentially an S/M sex club for gay men—whether or not they owned a motorcycle.

sexual leather crowd at Renslow's Gold Coast bar was no more than a bunch of "Pussies in Boots." As he observed about the leather scene in *Der Kreis*:

> In the first place, you call it a "movement" only by stretching the term. Granted that it is all ritualized and codified and "organized" right at the moment—but that is the fake part of it. An artificial hierarchy, a ritual, and a practice have been superimposed over a very real need of the human spirit [to locate that which is authentically masculine] . . . [but] the entire affair has become a ritual, a Fun and Games sort of thing, and in essence there is no difference today between a female impersonator or drag-queen and a leather-boy in full leather-drag. Both are dressing up to represent something they are not . . .
>
> It is difficult to say at what point in such a "movement" the degeneration sets in, and the elements of parody and caricature make their first appearance. Perhaps the decay began when the first M decided that he, too, could wear leather as well as the big butch S he so much admired. And so he bought himself a leather jacket . . .

Steward's skepticism of the leather movement (and his underlying conviction that homosexual males could never be authentically masculine) would later find confirmation in a friendship he developed with an experienced Colorado leatherman who first stopped into the tattoo parlor in April 1963. Jim Kane "came in wearing black pants and shirt, a long red necktie and a red beret, and his birdlike inflections were a marvel to hear," Steward later noted, adding that this extraordinary man would eventually "develop a reputation for being the biggest S[adist] in San Francisco—or at any rate, one of the most accomplished, with an interesting 'playroom' full of daintie devices."

Nearly twenty years younger than Steward, Jim Kane was in fact an ordained Catholic priest who had spent most of his professional years as the editor of a diocesan newspaper in Boulder, Colorado, even as he maintained a wildly active sex life. By the mid-1960s S/M was so significant a part of his sexual practice that in 1968 he would cofound the Rocky Mountaineers Motorcycle Club, an S/M sex club for men who had sex with men.* By the early 1970s, Kane would leave Colorado for San Francisco. There, without ever leaving the priesthood, he would establish himself as a central and founding member of the Society of Janus, the nation's leading BDSM group.†

Steward was both fascinated and appalled by Kane, for Steward himself had once been a Catholic, and since leaving the church he had spent nearly twenty years working for various Catholic academic institutions. He had met many a homosexual priest during that time, but never before had he met one so unabashed about his dedication to grandly theatrical homosexual BDSM sex. Steward repeatedly marveled at the outrageous and entirely unapologetic hypocrisy of this small, birdlike, leather-clad, motorcycle-riding "mad priest" who invested his domineering sexual identity with all the pomp and ceremony of a priest officiating at high mass. "How he settles his problems I'll never know," Steward observed on Kane's card in the Stud File, which also detailed Steward's thirty-five sexual encounters with Kane between 1963 and 1971, including a three-way with a bricklayer and a four-way with two black male army nurses.

Steward's skepticism about the birdlike Kane's self-proclaimed "master" status, however, spoke to his larger skepticism about the codified and ritualized forms of sexual activity that were just then emerging in the new leather subculture. These ritualized practices (which included various protocols for sexual and social encounters between leathermen both in public and private) were very different from the unscripted street pickups of thugs and ruffians that Steward and so many others of his generation had pursued in the barrooms and backstreets of the 1930s and '40s. To Steward, this new "leather" way of negotiating a sexual encounter (essentially, going out to a leather bar dressed as either "master" or "slave" in search of a fellow homosexual pickup open to sexual role play) seemed entirely scripted and inauthentic. Writing to Paul Gebhard about Kane in response to a sex-research questionnaire about the changing sexual roles enacted by homosexual men during the course of their lives, Steward later observed,

---

*Now known as the oldest gay organization in the state of Colorado, the Rocky Mountaineers later evolved into a gay social club with a mission to promote motorcycle riding in the community, and also to raise money for charitable causes.
†BDSM stands for "Bondage, Discipline, Sadism, and Masochism."

The nelly Mad Priest [has recently] discovered s/m . . . and now he plays the whole game—motorbike, full leather, whips, chains, gadgets . . . —but all you have to do is nibble his nipple to turn him all melting summer mist in bed and get his head down betwixt yr [legs] . . . To answer this question [of sexual roles] is like trying to debate the theological matter of "free will"; is your will ever free? The community, one's partners—all these have influence and effect—on many. The role I have assumed (or roles) have been pretty much matters of my own choice or perhaps— my own doing. But none of us is entirely "master of his fate, captain of his soul."*

Faced with these new developments in the American sexual underground, Steward felt more than ever that the homosexual underworld in which he had lived so adventurously over the past three decades was undergoing a radical change, and that as a result of this change, it was becoming less and less his own. His response would be to immerse himself ever more deeply in the world of his imagination, and in so doing to devote himself, as never before, to the writing of fiction.

---

*Steward is referring (not without irony) to the poem "Invictus" by William Ernest Henley, which ends: "It matters not how straight the gate, / How charged with punishments the scroll, / I am the master of my fate: / I am the captain of my soul."

17

Phil Andros, $TUD

In 1963, faced with yet another sexually suggestive story by Steward he could not possibly publish in *Der Kreis*, Rudolph Burckhardt amiably suggested that Steward try sending it to Knud Rame, a Danish bookseller who had just started a homophile publication more daring in its editorial policies. Since 1952 Rame had contributed to the Scandinavian homophile publication *Vennen* ("The Friend"); now, under the pseudonym Kim Kent, he had founded the Danish-language magazine *Eos*[*] and a related publication, *Amigo* (which featured similar content in German and English).[†] Steward's first submission to *Eos*, "The Sergeant with the Rose Tattoo," received a cash prize in the magazine's short story contest,[‡] and his subsequent story, "The Blacks and Mr. Bennett," proved even more popular. As he wrote Paul Gebhard, "[It] got lots of letters, about 200, from commentators in Yurp, + many calls for sequels, so one is comin' up." This erotic fantasy of a black man dominating a white man proved so compelling to German and Scandinavian readers that, in Steward's words, "Phil Andros [the writer[§]] was thus 'established,' and the readers clamored for a sequel, and I went on writing."[¶]

---

[*]*Eos* is Greek for "dawn" and Latin for "them."

[†]From September 1965 through June 1966, Steward would also contribute a monthly column ("Laederfront, USA") to yet another Kim Kent spinoff publication, *MANège*, which featured articles on, and images of, leather.

[‡]Steward had first published this story with *Der Kreis* in March 1960; publication in *Eos* followed a year later. *Der Kreis* would reprint the story (in German) in 1965.

[§]Though written by "Phil Andros," the story has a protagonist named Bennett.

[¶]Steward's interest in black men also led him to write "The Negro Homosexual in America," an essay for *Amigo* describing the particularly difficult lives black homosexual men faced in the United States. (*Amigo* no. 21, January 1964, pp. 31–35, 42.)

Having established himself under the pseudonym of Phil Andros, Steward began to develop a character by the same name: an "intelligent widely-read and sophisticated hustler [who would] appear as the narrator 'I' in stories which were also signed with his name as the author." In adopting this narrative technique, he was in effect conjuring an ideal self: a ruggedly handsome young man of extraordinary potency and endowment who also happened to have a heart, a brain, and a very well developed sense of the absurd. Steward had once shared his passion for hard-boiled detective fiction with Gertrude Stein; now, like Raymond Chandler's Philip Marlowe or Dashiell Hammett's Sam Spade, Sam Steward's Phil Andros would describe his erotic adventures in the American underworld with a mixture of humor and cynicism, employing his own very particular use of street vernacular for comic effect. But in his disaffected and sexually ambiguous wanderings across the American landscape (in the first Phil Andros novels, Phil describes himself as bisexual, and will only admit to having sex with men for the money; later in the series he recognizes and embraces his homosexual preference), Phil Andros would also resemble two other narrators: Sal Paradise, the young wanderer of Jack Kerouac's 1957 *On the Road*; and "youngman," the unnamed hustler-narrator of John Rechy's 1963 *City of Night*.

Steward published his first story featuring Phil Andros in *Amigo* in August 1963.* The date is telling, for he later wrote of having been both impressed and disturbed by Rechy's *City of Night*, which had explored the world of homosexual hustling through the eyes of a hustler. It had done so in a hip, darkly moody way that had appealed to heterosexual as well as homosexual readers, and so became an immediate bestseller—but its message was hardly prohomosexual, for Rechy was coy about the "true" sexuality of his hustler-protagonist, and disparaged the majority of "youngman"'s homosexual patrons, drawing them instead as pathetic, predatory grotesques.

Phil Andros took a much less angst-ridden approach to hustling, and Steward, for his part, portrayed the men on both sides of the hustling equation as basically friendly, attractive, and human characters simply

---

*The story is "The Poison Tree," a story of sexual revenge based upon an experience Steward had had while working for the summer at Glacier Park, Montana, in the summer of 1935. The title comes from Blake's poem "A Poison Tree" from *Songs of Experience* (1794).

seeking sexual release. Defending his decision to make Phil a hustler (which was not, after all, the most socially affirmative of homosexual role models), he later noted,

> I [had] had a lot of experience with hustlers, both as customers down at the tattoo shop, and as tension relievers in the shop's back room. And I had read John Rechy's *City of Night*, but . . . Rechy's waffling attitude about his nameless hustler was annoying. I had the feeling he was holding back, afraid to reveal himself, carefully cultivating the icy center of his being and saving it for—what or whom? I didn't know.
>
> I had always liked the name "Phil," and . . . as one who had once taught semantics, it was easier to return the word "philander"—its modern heterosexual matrix grossly altered from its original meaning*—to its pristine form: "philos"—to love, and "andros"—man—thus Phil Andros might be taken either as "lover-man" or "man-lover."

In time Phil Andros would express his sexual interest in other males quite openly. In the early stories, however, he simply describes himself as a stud who trades sex for pay. A drifter, he has only one great worry in life: age, and with it the eventual loss of his sexual appeal—and income.

Though bemused by the chilly ambivalence of *City of Night*, Steward had nonetheless been delighted to see John Rechy's novel published, and when its twenty-nine-year-old author wrote to him seeking a review in *Der Kreis* in July, Steward had a cordial exchange of letters with him. Rechy wrote Steward that he had actually found his way to the Phil Sparrow Tattoo Joynt in September of 1961, and had intended to introduce himself—but on finding Steward occupied with a client, he'd contented himself with simply looking through the window.

In the summer of 1963, Steward decided to shut down the Tattoo Joynt, for Illinois had recently outlawed the tattooing of all those under the age of twenty-one, and the majority of his clientele had always consisted of these younger men. As he later noted, "Every year there were

---

*Steward's reference is to the obsolete word *philander* (dating to 1731), meaning "lover."

rumors about the Illinois legislature changing the age limit for tattooing . . . New York had closed its tattoo shops in October, 1961, because of
an outbreak of hepatitis,* although the blame [for that outbreak] was
never flatly put on the tattoo artists . . . And [then] the winds of change
began to be felt in Illinois, with the result that in 1963 a law was passed
forbidding the tattooing of anyone under twenty-one." Before locking the
door to the Tattoo Joynt forever, Steward had sex there with a young black
boot sailor from Great Lakes. He was not only the last person Steward
ever had sex with in the shop, but also the first boot sailor Steward had
had sex with at his place of business since the Kenny Kothmann affair a
decade earlier.

With the shop closed, Steward found himself at loose ends. Since
Emmy Curtis's estate was still being settled and he could not yet leave
Chicago, he provisionally agreed to co-rent a small storefront shop in
Milwaukee with Chuck Renslow, doing so on a month-to-month basis. He
did so primarily to work with Renslow's "slave" Cliff Raven. Steward
and Raven would go up there only on weekends, though, for the Milwau-
kee business consisted almost exclusively of sailors coming up from the
Great Lakes training station on their weekend liberty passes.

Steward's success as Phil Andros in Denmark now led him to raid his
earlier unpublished erotic writings for material he could expand and use
in his new fiction. He wrote Wardell Pomeroy,

> I wonder if I could prevail on you to lend me, for just a little while,
> that copy of a novel I gave you some time ago: *Ring-Around-the-
> Rosy*. There is one episode in it I would like to do over a bit . . . [I
> have] won 2nd and 7th prizes in [*Eos/Amigo*'s] 1963 "Literary Con-
> test" with two s/m stories about Chuck Renslow[†] . . . I have finally
> found an editor with a less namby-pamby censorial eye than poor
> Rudolf [Burckhardt] of *Der Kreis*.

The weekly commute from Chicago to Milwaukee gave Steward the
opportunity to write his stories without interruption. By Steward's estima-
tion, most of the first twenty-five Phil Andros stories were composed, or

---

*As a result of this hepatitis scare, tattooing remained illegal in New York City until 1997.
†The stories are "Baby Tiger" and "Little Lamb, Who Made Thee?"

begun, on the electric North Shore train between Chicago and Milwaukee; for most of 1963–64 he sent Kim Kent a new Phil Andros story each month.

·

The Milwaukee tattoo parlor was a former barbershop in a hotel on Third Street, just a few blocks from Amund Dietzel's Tattooing Studio. The close proximity created "a somewhat delicate situation with the Old Master Dietzel," but after a little while Dietzel seemed not to mind: in Steward's words, "his reputation was firmly established, and all Cliff and I got was the overflow of sailors . . . there seemed to be enough to put money in everyone's pockets."

An unknown photographer, possibly Cliff Raven's artist-lover Chuck Arnett, took a series of black-and-white photographs of the Milwaukee tattoo parlor that are today the most thorough documentation of Steward's work with (and upon) the boot sailors of the Great Lakes Naval Training Station. Dom Orejudos had meanwhile revised and improved the original series of sexually suggestive placards of tattooed men Steward had made for the window of his State Street Tattoo Joynt, and Orejudos's new, hypermasculine versions established an even more outrageous butch-erotic ambiance for the Milwaukee shop. It was Cliff Raven's company that delighted Steward most about the Milwaukee gig, however, for Raven had by now developed into a formidably talented tattoo artist as well as a good friend and occasional sex partner.

Early in the fall of 1963, Steward decided to travel abroad while the weather was still warm—first to see Knud Rame in Copenhagen, then to visit Alice Toklas in Paris. "Your letter [about closing the tattoo parlor] upset me—to have to give up your work shocked me," she had written him from the bed to which she was now mostly confined. "Wouldn't Paris [be as good a place to work] as Chicago? You will understand my prejudiced point of view."

Much of Steward's gossip with Toklas during his autumn visit to her centered on Francis Rose, who had fallen on hard times since the international scandal surrounding the death of Lionel "Buster" Crabb. After being released from the mental hospital at Virginia Water, Rose had returned briefly to Paris but only to sell his tiny apartment. He subsequently found a cheap flat in a decrepit quarter of the English resort town of Brighton, and there became increasingly reliant upon a number of old friends, most notably Cecil Beaton, for handouts of used clothing and money. "He is a man who causes such extraordinary violence around him," Beaton wrote despairingly of Rose in his diary. "His life story is a long succession of suicides, killings, fatal accidents. In his wake he brings chaos."

Frederica Rose was kinder. "In England . . . his art was still appreciated by a small cluster of friends," she wrote many years after granting him the divorce and annulment that enabled him to marry another woman who had promised to support him.* "In all these changing and often unhappy circumstances, Francis was sustained, and sometimes driven, by an irrepressible zest for living . . . eccentric and capricious as he became . . . [He] was, surprisingly, a deeply serious person."

Though he still considered painting his principal vocation, Rose had worked on a sensational memoir of his early life during the late 1950s in the hope that it might bring in some sorely needed cash. The result was *Saying Life*, an autobiography so wildly improbable and so laughably self-contradictory that it was immediately dismissed by many as the work of a hopelessly eccentric fantasist.†

Though full of exaggerations, fabrications, and outright lies, *Saying Life* is a beguiling work of semifiction in the form of a celebrity memoir— one that in hindsight seems closely related to the writings of fellow Surrealists such as Dalí and Cocteau, for whom dreams and fantasies were just as "real" as everyday experience. The most bizarre aspect of the memoir—and certainly the most inflammatory—is Rose's constant denial of homosexual interest or activity, a denial that is repeatedly betrayed by the focus and interests of his narrative. Aware that he could not possibly publish a true account of his already quite notorious sex life, Rose apparently chose to play with a basic assumption of the memoir form: namely, that it be written in earnest. Instead he created a narrative that, in the best Wildean manner, delighted in its own hypocrisy, and happily chronicled things that had never happened and couldn't possibly have happened, and yet made sensationally entertaining reading. In doing so, he created what might be today considered a high-style metamemoir, one alternately

---

*In February of 1967, Rose had married Mrs. Beryl Montefiore Davis (née Norris), who thereby became Lady Rose; but in autumn of 1968, Lady Beryl had her husband forcibly removed from her home and committed to a mental hospital. She subsequently ceased supporting him.

†Cyril Connolly observed in his review that "Francis Rose can say life but not spell it."

earnest and not earnest, true and not true, entirely revealing and yet not revealing at all. It was, in its own way, a brilliant response to the sexually hypocritical culture in which he lived.

Alice Toklas, however, was not the least bit amused by it, and fumed about Rose's "endless lies" in a letter to Princess Dilkusha de Rohan. Sorry as she may have been to discover Gertrude Stein and herself included (and ridiculed) in the memoir, she nonetheless agreed to look at Rose's next project, a brief essay entitled "Gertrude Stein and Painting," doing so largely out of loyalty to the memory of Stein—who had after all adored both Rose and his painting. Around this same time, Rose also wrote several letters to Steward in which he complained of being in poor health, and confided that the memoir had proved a financial disaster. He begged Steward to write his "son" Louis (no longer Luis but Louis, he was living far from Rose in New York) to ask him for money on Rose's behalf. Steward did so. And then, for a while, the two old friends once again fell out of contact.

•

Despite receiving encouragement from Jacques Delarue, Steward returned from his November visit to Europe deeply discouraged about setting up a tattoo parlor in Paris. He laid out his problems to Paul Gebhard: "The restrictions for me as a foreigner, the terrifically high *bail** to pay to buy the 'four walls,' the difficulties of licensing—oh well, I just gave it up. Besides, I can't handle the argot well enough to be able to control my clientele completely, and that's necessary. So it's back to Milwaukee."

The highlight of Steward's lonely Wisconsin winter was sex with a Milwaukee police officer in full uniform—Jim Brashin, "a tall handsome young man, rather slender, for whom every attractive police uniform in the world seemed to have been designed." Steward later wrote that "I tattooed him . . . That uniform of his which he wore so jauntily . . . made me foolish enough to spend a considerable amount on Jim-baby." Steward had paid sex with Brashin seven times; during one of their get-togethers, Steward also painted his portrait, for he had recently taken up oil paint-

---

*Steward is employing a French word, taken from the verb *bailler*, "to hand over": in other words, key money.

ing. During this time he painted surprisingly successful oil portraits of Johnny Reyes and Dom Orejudos as well.*

Still, by early 1964 Steward had resolved to leave the Midwest, for he had come to hate the extreme cold of the long Midwestern winter, and nearly everyone he had ever cared about there was gone. The Wilcoxes, Steward's last remaining close friends, had left Chicago for North Carolina after Esther was violently attacked and repeatedly raped while her husband was asleep in the next room. During his own last lonely months in Chicago, Steward found his most sympathetic friend in Paul Gebhard, the Indiana University professor of anthropology who had become director of the Institute for Sex Research in the years after Kinsey's death. Responding immediately to Steward's news that he would probably not be moving to Paris, Gebhard reassured him,

> I'm glad you are going to be around [in the USA] for reasons of science as well as of friendship. Someday we've got to get beyond our present superficial knowledge of S/M. When we attempt this research, articulate people with insight are going to be invaluable. Which reminds me of a sad fact of which you may already be aware: Mike Miksche has been institutionalized again. I hear this time it is an unmistakable psychosis and not just an artistic revolt from reality.

A week later, perhaps prompted by news of Miksche's breakdown, Steward presented Gebhard with a new idea: he would become a psychotherapist. "As you may know," he wrote, "the law is very lax in Illinois: there are 95 of these people listed in the yellow pages in Chicago, ranging from the Hypnotism Institute to Bishop Lulu C. Trent (with an address in the heart of the negro district) who gives Spiritual Advice in All Walks of Life. For the past 25 years I have read practically everything in psychology and medicine, it being a great hobby of mine [and] when work and pleasure coincide (as they did in tattoodling), a person is very lucky indeed." Gebhard accordingly made inquiries about graduate programs on

---

*The Brashin portrait is owned by a private collector, the Reyes portrait remains with the Sam Steward papers, and the Orejudos portrait is on permanent display at the Leather Archives and Museum.

Steward's behalf at Indiana University, and encouraged him to think that psychotherapy might be a great new career: "Somehow I share the feeling that you would make an effective, if off beat therapist," he wrote Steward. "You've got a nice blend of insight, blarney, sensitivity, and con man as well as enough common sense to counteract psychological or psychiatric dogma."

•

While Steward inquired into graduate programs in psychology and pondered his next career move, he received a telephone call from a nineteen-year-old blue-collar worker named Danny Schmidt. Schmidt had heard from a benchmate in the factory where he worked that Steward often hired hustlers—and so in the interest of earning a little extra cash, he had taken down Steward's name, number, and home address. It was in this way that he initiated Steward's most significant late-life intimate relationship—one that would last, on and off, for nearly a decade.

Apart from being physically attracted to this burly young factory worker turned amateur hustler, Steward was fascinated to discover that Schmidt was a triplet with one brother who was heterosexual and another who was homosexual. Steward was moved, as well, by Schmidt's life story, for his mother had consigned Danny and his two brothers to the infamous Boys Town orphanage for delinquent youth, "from which [Danny had] escaped about twenty times in two years." Quite apart from being sympathetic to Danny's difficult upbringing, Steward was fascinated by his triplet identity: "I wondered if he and his two brothers shared one soul among three . . . They claimed to get 'flashes' of intuitive knowledge from each other, no matter how widely separated." Steward would have sex with Schmidt twenty-eight times as trade (at five dollars per encounter) between the day of their first meeting and Steward's departure from Chicago,* and would see him again (regularly) during the year of 1966, and again (after Schmidt's marriage had ended) from 1970 to 1972. Under the name of Ward Stames, Steward would write two stories about his relationship with Schmidt—the first describing the young man's introduction to the world of hustling, and the second concerning Schmidt's theft of money from

---

*In that final instance (on March 8, 1965) Steward had sex with both Danny and his triplet brother Donny, but apart from noting it in the Stud File, Steward never wrote about the experience.

him.* The tenderness he felt for Schmidt combined elements of both a father-son relationship and a teacher-student relationship despite the fact that it was primarily a sex-for-money arrangement. Steward's feelings for Schmidt were significant enough that he preserved sheet after sheet of Schmidt's awkward handwritten free verse among his papers, most of it simply describing his daily emotional ups and downs in the crudest of terms. Steward seems to have accepted these clumsy offerings without comment or criticism, and likewise to have been quietly grateful to Schmidt for his ongoing physical presence, despite the troubled young man's many shortcomings, inconsistencies, and betrayals.

Having shut down the Milwaukee tattooing operation in the spring, Steward spent the better part of his summer deciding where to move. Inspiration came to him, oddly enough, through *Life*, which published an article entitled "Homosexuality in America" in its June 26, 1964, issue.† The article expressed a number of grotesque, derogatory, and pathologizing views about both homosexuals and homosexual activity; Paul Gebhard, speaking as head of the Institute for Sex Research, was one of the few sources included in the article whose words about homosexuality were balanced and reasonable. An entirely different message, however, had been communicated to readers through the story's many photographs, which included a stunningly provocative two-page photo spread of the smoky interior of San Francisco's Tool Box leather bar. This powerful chiaroscuro image had been meant, like the article itself, to illustrate the depravity of contemporary homosexual life; but paradoxically it had instead suggested to interested men across the nation that a darkly alluring leather scene was vitally alive in the San Francisco Bay area—and it is today thought to have prompted would-be leathermen from all parts of the country to make a beeline for the historically liberal city.‡

---

*The stories are "A Trap for Tigers" and "The Pool Cue."
†Paul Welch, "Homosexuality in America," *Life*, vol. 56, no. 26 (June 26, 1964), p. 66.
‡The *Drummer* magazine editor Jack Fritscher claimed to the scholar Gayle Rubin that the classic Tool Box issue of *Life* had started the migration to San Francisco that caused both South of Market and the Castro to happen. Rubin in turn would note that while this statement was clearly hyperbole, the image certainly did have an impact. She herself felt that aside from the movie *The Wild One*, the issue of *Life* with the picture of the Tool Box was the piece of popular culture most often mentioned by the San Francisco leathermen with whom she had spoken. (Gayle Rubin, "The Valley of the Kings: Leathermen in San Francisco [1960–1990]," dissertation, University of Michigan, 1994, p. 164.) In the same essay, Rubin noted that the mural eventually became a venerated relic of the leather community (p. 159).

By 1964, a distinct and recognizable leather community had established itself both in the Tenderloin and in the South of Market Street
area. The look and feel of this popular new leather culture was probably
best described by Robert Opel in an elegaic article on the Tool Box for
Drummer magazine:

> On Saturday nights the bikes would be parked along the street
> for a whole block, lined up one against the next, a row of chrome
> and steel gleaming in the moonlight. The strains of "Stand by
> Your Man" filtered out from the jukebox . . . It was the only
> leather bar in a city named after a dude who talked to the birds,
> down there South of Market among the warehouses, the trucks
> and the loading platforms, an island apart from the social machi-
> nations of the rest of the city . . . The place smelled of sweat and
> leather and grease and beer; smoke hung in tattered patches lick-
> ing the ceiling.

While Steward had misgivings about the "institutionalization" of leather
culture, he was nonetheless intrigued by the San Francisco scene described
in the article and its photographs. Moreover, since it was a shipping port as
well as a naval center, San Francisco seemed to him a very good place to
relocate as a tattooist. The city also promised him many new sexual contacts, for San Francisco was not only a booming youth center, but also had a
well-established tradition of sex for pay that dated back at least as far as the
1849 Gold Rush. In an unpublished memoir Steward wrote of imagining
himself comfortably established there in "a little shop right next to . . . the
Embarcadero YMCA," and decided that after a brief Christmas visit to Alice
Toklas, he would travel there "to case the area with regard to opening another tattoo joynt, and also to find a place to live."

•

En route from Paris to San Francisco, Steward spent a few days in New
York, and there met a Bleecker Street bookseller named Howard Frisch.
Steward was at that moment considering self-publishing his *Eos/Amigo*
short stories in Denmark, but Frisch, who had read and enjoyed the Phil
Andros stories in *Amigo*, suggested that he meet instead with H. Lynn
Womack of Guild Press to see about publishing them in the United
States.

Ten years younger than Steward, Womack was the publisher, distributor, and editor of the Guild Press and its affiliated enterprises, which at that moment included the Guild Book Service, the Grecian Guild, the Potomac News Company, and Village Books and Press—all of which published or distributed homoerotic work of various kinds.* Womack had a terrible business reputation, but he was nonetheless a commercial dynamo: he organized and ran a large pen-pal service; published overtly sexual porn paperbacks and hardcovers; and maintained an effective distribution network for homosexual and homoerotic titles in bookstores throughout the United States. Most important, his battle against the censoring of physique magazines had resulted in the groundbreaking Supreme Court decision of *MANual Enterprises v. J. Edward Day* in 1962, which had established the legality of publishing and distributing such magazines in the United States.

Steward flew to New York in March to discuss the story collection with Womack, who turned out to be a heavyset Caucasian albino from a tenant-farming family in Hazelhurst, Mississippi. Steward was mildly horrified by his appearance and his table manners, but their lunch meeting was nonetheless productive, for Womack wanted to publish Steward, and Steward wanted to be published.

After Frisch suggested to Womack that Steward might get Wardell Pomeroy to write an introduction to the new Phil Andros story collection in order to give the book a veneer of "respectability," Womack pressed Steward (who had decided to name the book *$TUD*) to approach Pomeroy for the endorsement. But Steward thought the idea of such a foreword abominable, and wrote as much to Frisch, insisting that "the whole basic concept of the book is vicious and degenerate . . . [and] if you start drawing the line [between what is and is not obscene], where are you going to stop?"

$TUD was a story collection written in a literary style reminiscent of one of Steward's favorite short-story writers, Saki (H. H. Munro). It was

---

*Begun in 1964, Womack's Guild Book Service offered subscribers a wide array of articles as well as a list of nearly eighty books that included not only clothbound editions of homosexually themed works previously released by mainstream publishers, but also pulp paperbacks with significant homosexual themes or subtexts. Guild Press, meanwhile, was the publisher of several "physique" magazines and a series of pornographic novels entitled *Classics of the Homosexual Underground*, based on the many anonymously written pornographic stories that had circulated illegally during the 1940s and '50s.

not so much outright pornography as it was a collection of literary short stories concerning various sorts of graphically detailed sexual encounters between men—some of them brutal, some of them mercenary, some of them surprisingly tender. Its melancholy epigraph came from the Greek poet Constantin Cavafy, as translated by Phil Andros:

> *Now and again he swears*
> > *To commence a cleaner life,*
> *But when the night comes*
> > *With its dark promptings,*
> *Its uncertainties and its enterprises*
> *When the night comes*
> > *With its own dominion*
> *Over the body, he returns, lusting and searching,*
> *Lost, to that same morose delight.**

Nearly all the incidents described in the book had been taken from some sort of real-life experience: either Steward's own or that of friends. The first, "The Poison Tree," recalled Steward's 1935 seduction of a bullying heterosexual coworker in Glacier Park, Montana. "Arrangement in Black and White" described a long-standing relationship between a white bank president and his black manservant, and drew from Steward's own long-standing relationships with black men. "I (Cupid) and the Gangster" told the story of George Reginato. "Mirror, Mirror" contained Steward's recollections of George Platt Lynes and the New York scene. "H Squared" was based on his friend Robert Dahm, who had been sent to the Raiford penitentiary for having sex with an underage adolescent.† "Once in a Blue Moon" described Phil Andros's conversion of a country boy (based on Danny Schmidt) into a hustler—a project Phil undertakes because he cannot bear the purity of the love the boy offers him. "A Collar for Achil-

---

*The poem, though Steward did not give its title, is "He Swears," written in 1915. His translation is a considerable improvement over that of Rae Dalven, whose *Complete Poems of Cavafy* had been published in New York in 1961.

†This story in particular meditates on Steward's own troubled feelings about his involvement with minors. Of Dahm's character, Steward (as the hustler Phil Andros) noted, "I have never seen such total ethical and moral blindness as in that stupid, silly H squared from Milwaukee. Beside him, even I was ethical and moral."

les," meanwhile, was based on Steward's combined fascination and disgust with the bodybuilder Ralph Steiner.

Two of the strongest stories directly addressed interracial sexual domination, and were based on Steward's extensive experiences with Paul Jefferson and Bill Payson. "Ace in the Hole" set Phil Andros's love affair with a black man, Ace Hardesty, against the backdrop of Texas racism and the Kennedy assassination (the two men share a Dallas boardinghouse with Lee Harvey Oswald). The follow-up story, "Two-Bit Whore," recounted the end of the same affair in Chicago, and drew on Steward's experience of being gang-raped by a group of black thugs in 1946.

The final story in the collection was "The Blacks and Mr. Bennett," which Steward had retitled "Sea Change." Bennett, having become the sex slave of a black Muslim named Adam X, ultimately decides to "transform" himself into a black man by taking a combination of 8-methoxypsoralen tablets and sitting for long periods under a sunlamp.* Steward probably got the idea for the story from George Platt Lynes, for Lynes's friend and model Carlos Maclendon had once put himself through a similar transformation in order to perform as a dancer in all-black revues.†

Steward returned his signed contract for the $TUD collection to Womack along with an amiable letter, which noted among other things that "various of the Kris boys had a field day suggesting [titles for the book], such as 'Lavender Evenings,' 'Ding-Dong Daddy,' 'Purple Passions,' 'For Sale, Cheap,' and 'Meat Market,' all of which gave them an hilarious moment, but naturally left me cold." Assuming that Womack would produce the book within the year, Steward now turned to a much more urgent project: his relocation to San Francisco.

---

*This known treatment for psoriasis does in fact have the side effect of tinting the skin a dark yellow color.

†Maclendon described this experience—and how it ended, when white racists threatened to murder him if he continued to dance in a black revue, in David Leddick's *Naked Men: Pioneering Male Nudes* (1935–1955) (New York: Universe, 1997). Lynes knew Maclendon and had photographed him extensively in Hollywood in 1947, not long before he first met Steward.

18

A New Life in Oakland

Steward's February 1964 visit to San Francisco resulted in a chance encounter with an old Chicago acquaintance who invited him to dinner in Berkeley at a "small house built in someone's backyard, a house-behind-a-house, a 'cottage' in northern California terminology." The acquaintance, a former sex contact, was about to relocate to Europe and wanted someone to take over his lease.

The bungalow in the backyard of the house at 2016 Ninth Street was charming in an Old California way. Located in the Berkeley flatlands, the six-hundred-square-foot structure had a tiny sun porch, a tiny kitchen, a sitting room, and a bedroom. Steward liked its low rent and discreet anonymity, but his impulsive decision to assume the lease was paradoxical, for he had always dreamed of living in San Francisco, not the Berkeley flats—a neighborhood that was essentially suburban. Since Steward did not know how to drive and had no intention of ever buying a car, any visits he made to San Francisco from the bungalow would require him to take a long, slow bus ride across the Oakland Bay Bridge.* In choosing it as his future home, Steward seems to have made a conscious decision to remain perpetually at a distance from all those districts—the Tenderloin, the South of Market, and the Castro—that had attracted him to San Francisco in the first place, districts where homosexual men from across the United States were creating exciting new experimental communities for themselves. "I'd purposefully chosen to live in Berkeley, afraid that if

---

*The BART transbay tube began service only nine years after Steward had moved to Berkeley.

I actually lived in the city I would dull the excitement, or tarnish the glamour of my first visits to it a dozen years before," he would have Phil Andros later observe; "my trick had worked—each trip across the Bay still had for me the same spine-tingles of years ago." But Steward had had a lifelong ambivalence to the close company of his fellow homosexuals, and he was now fifty-five. More than a decade earlier, his advanced age had made him unattractive to most of the men he desired at the Embarcadero YMCA; living amid the rampant youth culture of mid-1960s San Francisco, he would have been even more visibly an outcast, and he knew it.

Packing up the Chicago apartment had been difficult, not only because of the huge amount of erotica, memorabilia, books, papers, photographs, and objets d'art Steward had filled it with over the years, but also because he had the vast contents of his tattoo shop to contend with as well. Overwhelmed with erotic material, he organized a large donation to the Institute for Sex Research, and burned many other things for which neither he nor the institute had further use. When after all these wrenching preparations he finally left Chicago and arrived several days later at his new home on Ninth Street in Berkeley (a place he had seen only briefly, and at night), he discovered that it stood in the middle of a crime-ridden, rubbish-strewn black ghetto. And yet, despite his misgivings, he decided simply to stay. A month later he wrote Gebhard,

> migawd, don't ever move if you can help it! . . . [But this] house-behind-a-house is very much to my liking. Of course, there was a psychological adjustment . . . I found myself acutely homesick for a while, missing the ostlers* and the tall buildings . . .
>
> I applied for a tattoodle license for Oakland, and they told me I w[oul]d h[a]v[e] to h[a]v[e] a police/vice check run on me—so I am currently sweating that out . . . It may be that I'll just sit on my ass and rot (and write!) and do nothin' else.

The question of where to open a tattoo parlor vexed Steward for some time. He initially found a location in San Francisco, across from the East Bay Bus Terminal on Mission Street, but then he apparently received some intentionally misleading advice from his fellow tattoo artist Lyle Tuttle. As Steward later explained,

---

*An ostler is a stable boy, but Steward is using the word as a homonym for "hustler," probably out of fear that an interception of the letter might result in his harassment or prosecution.

After twelve years of experience in the dog-eat-dog world of tattooing, the cut-throat unethical practices that I had seen in Chicago, I should have been prepared for anything—but I wasn't. It
was not until several years later that I discovered, or was forced
to conclude, that [Lyle Tuttle] had bribed a woman in the [San
Francisco Board of Health] to type up a phony "ordinance" for me
[stating that the minimum age for tattooing in San Francisco
was twenty-one], to keep me from being a competitor [of his] in
the city.

In September, Steward instead took a lease on a shopfront at 1727
San Pablo Avenue in Oakland. The place he had chosen to set up business was utterly desolate, but it was also cheap, close to the Oakland
naval bases, and located on a major bus route running directly to and
from Steward's bungalow—an important consideration since he had no
intentions of ever purchasing a car.

Oakland, the city about which Gertrude Stein has observed, "there is
no there there,"* certainly lived up to that epithet in Steward's new business neighborhood, a commercial strip down which few pedestrians could
venture, since it was essentially isolated by the convergence of two four-
lane commercial highways. But the new shop was serendipitously just a
five-minute ride from 4019 Foothill Boulevard, the world headquarters of
the Hells Angels motorcycle gang, a sprawling, loose-knit social club and
criminal organization that was just then in the process of cornering the
California drug trade, and whose members all regularly sought out new
tattoos to define their status and accomplishments to other members of
the gang.

The relationship of Oakland's residents to both the Hells Angels and
the Oakland police force was at that moment a complicated one, for even
as Steward opened his business, the city was under something close to
martial law, and the situation would only worsen in the coming decade.
Steward's soon-to-be-friend Ralph "Sonny" Barger, head of the Hells Angels, noted in his memoirs that "Oakland in the fifties and sixties was still
a tough town, a blue-collar area overshadowed by glittery Frisco-by-the-
Bay . . . The Oakland PD boys didn't lose a lot of fights either; they were
pretty tough . . . The OPD once came by a biker bar called Frank's Place

---

*Stein, *Everybody's Autobiography*, chapter 4, p. 289 (1937, reprinted 1971).

and jumped a bunch of our [gang] members, beat the shit out of them, and then took them to jail." Steward purchased a police shortwave radio soon after opening his shop so that he could follow the many violent crimes taking place daily in the area. He also purchased weekly transcriptions of these police conversations in an attempt to track and predict crime patterns.

Poverty, crime, and police brutality were not all Steward had to deal with at his new business location. With its large, disaffected population of African Americans, Oakland was fast becoming a national focal point of racial tension and conflict. Within months of Steward's arrival, Huey Newton and Bobby Seale formed the Black Panther Party in Oakland, calling both for armed resistance to black oppression and for the open expression of black rage. While much of that black rage would be immediately focused on the Oakland police force (which in 1966 had only 16 black officers on a force of 661), the local racial hatred was also directed at any other white "oppressor"—that is, any white businessman perceived to be exploiting black residents. White shopkeepers like Steward were therefore possible targets for race-inspired crime.

There was also student unrest. As Steward observed in his memoirs,

The [Berkeley] Free Speech movement was [just then] in full swing, and the student riots and protests over Vietnam were shortly to follow. Formerly while in Europe I had noticed that when I told anyone I was from Chicago there was a slight stiffening of the body, or even a tiny drawing away from me, as though I might have a tommy-gun concealed somewhere. And now, Berkeley achieved for a little while the same world-wide notoriety that Chicago had for so many years . . . [One day student] protesters massed at the Oakland army induction center, a building only a block away from me . . . I [constantly] feared for my plate glass windows, but [in the end] they were not broken more than once or twice.

Steward worked hard on creating a stylish new tattoo parlor in this awful new neighborhood, for he had few friends in the Bay Area and little else to do with his days. He named the place the Anchor Tattoo Shop instead of Phil Sparrow's Tattoo Joynt so that the name would come first in the phone book. The interior, however, looked much like the old shop in Chicago—black plywood panels eight feet high, topped with six feet of wall painted dark Chinese red. Outside there was a lighted sign with black "circus"-style letters spelling "Tattoo" against a yellow background. Steward placed in the window a series of placards drawn by Dom Orejudos—illustrating various tattooing styles and techniques in grand homoerotic style—that he had salvaged from the Milwaukee tattoo parlor.

•

Steward kept regular business hours five days a week, but with few customers in early daytime, he began most of his workdays by going through his tattoo journals, hoping at last to write his long-delayed general-interest book on tattooing. After years of collecting data about tattoos and tattooing from his customers, he had amassed an extraordinary amount of information, including statistics on the sorts of tattoos his customers had bought, the bodily locations on which they were placed, and the feelings and actions (many of them sexual) that customers had experienced or undertaken in the wake of their application. With these facts and statistics in hand, he felt he had more than enough material to write a unique "inside" account of contemporary American tattooing, and moreover to do so with both authority and style.

$TUD was meanwhile moving toward publication. In mid-September 1965, Steward wrote Paul Gebhard a letter detailing his hopes for the manuscript, which was then going through a final proofreading. After describing the striking dust jacket illustration he had commissioned from Dom Orejudos, he went on to describe his new life in Oakland and Berkeley as well as his various other literary projects. Gebhard, ever the anthropologist, immediately responded with a suggestion about the proposed tattoo book, namely that Steward widen its scope to include "the anthropology of tattooing," for in Gebhard's words, "to write a book on the art without tipping one's hat to the Japanese and the Maori would be impolite."

In the months that followed, Steward found the tattoo book unexpectedly difficult to write, perhaps in part because of his use of barbiturates, which had increased since his move from Chicago,* but mostly because of the overabundance of materials from which he drew. Steward's

---

*While Steward was conscientious in chronicling his sexual activities throughout his life, and was also relatively open in his descriptions of his drinking, he was not equally candid about his later-life drug use. However, a number of letters in his papers, including letters to and from his doctor, demonstrate that his barbiturate habit intensified in the period following his arrival in Berkeley, as he attempted to cope with a strong sense of dislocation, disconnection, and depression. A number of friends and acquaintances (McHenry, Kane, Barnes, Baldwin) also witnessed and described Steward's addiction.

tattoo journal had consisted of more than a thousand single-spaced typewritten pages of his own information, and on top of that he now had a vast
archive of additional information, made up of literature he had amassed
over more than a decade. His own sexuality posed yet another problem
for the project, for the tattoo journals had been primarily works of sexual
confession. Steward felt his tattoo book needed to be something entirely
different: a general-interest nonfiction book on tattooing. As a result, he
left out much of the most interesting material.

Nonetheless, within the year Steward managed to produce a lengthy
manuscript on the art, history, and practice of contemporary tattooing
he entitled *The Tattoo Jungle*. He sent it to Grove Press directly, without
the assistance of a literary agent, for at that moment he had none. At the
same time he continued to seek outlets for his erotic short fiction, repub-
lishing "Little Lamb, Who Made Thee?" with the Society of Janus magazine, *Drum*, that December. It was his first erotic story to be commercially
published in the United States.

At his sister's invitation, Steward then traveled down to Los Angeles
for the Christmas holidays. Despite his misgivings about his hard-drinking,
archconservative, deeply Catholic brother-in-law, Steward was happy
enough to pass the holidays with his sister in their beautiful Santa Monica home. On Christmas Day, however, Steward decided to fight off his
usual holiday melancholy by doing something wild and thrilling: inviting
a leather-clad parking-lot pickup named Bruce Bradbury over to the house
for sex. His arrangement with Bradbury had been made with the understanding that his sister and brother-in-law would be out making Christmas Day visits to friends. Bradbury unfortunately arrived too early, "on [a]
motorsickle, in leathers [and Jinny was] outraged. [After Jinny and Joe
left I] started to do him; [but then unexpectedly they] came back. Incom-
pleted." Walking in on the two men, his sister had been shocked and
distressed; as a result, Steward's last two days with her were distinctly
uncomfortable.*

•

In early 1966, a young man entered the Anchor who would one day become one of the most commercially successful tattoo artists in the United

---

*For a revised, fantasy version of this encounter, see the opening chapter of *The Boys in Blue*, in
which Phil Andros, while visiting his sister and brother-in-law in Santa Monica, "scores" with California Highway Patrolman Greg Wolfson, whom he has similarly picked up in a parking lot.

States. Don (later Ed) Hardy was at that moment a young printmaker working toward an MFA degree. Obsessed with William S. Burroughs, Hardy immediately recognized Steward as a similar sort of renegade intellectual—in Hardy's words, "a mysterious, inscrutable hipster cruising through dark waters with terrific élan."

Hardy had known of Phil Sparrow since taking the Milton Zeis tattooing correspondence course as a kid, since Steward, writing as Phil Sparrow, had contributed to the coursework. Upon making his way to the Oakland tattoo parlor, Hardy had been immediately dazzled by what he saw there, for the Anchor had a completely different look from Oakland's many other tattoo parlors. In Hardy's recollection, "the window display featured artists' renderings of different styles of tattooing: classic Navy work, Japanese, etc. [and] instead of walls blanketed with flash, [Sparrow] hung his sample designs like a gallery, with space in between . . . Classical music played, and the biggest change was that he did not tattoo in an enclosed area . . . but [rather] had his work desk set up in a corner of the room, open for all to observe." Hardy also thought Steward an extraordinary sight, for during that period Steward "dressed entirely in black, a black long-sleeved shirt and trousers accentuating his pencil-thin 'Errol Flynn' mustache . . . his sophistication was apparent in the first few minutes of conversation."

During that first meeting, Steward showed Hardy a recently published book on Japanese tattooing, *Irezumi*, written by the American Donald Richie and featuring Ichiro Morita's dramatic black-and-white photos of large-scale tattoos done in the classical Japanese style. "Phil said, 'the only real art tattooing in the world is done by the Japanese,'" Hardy later recalled. "I was floored [by what Phil showed me, and] my immediate thought was, if tattoos can look like this, I want to do them." Hardy got a Phil Sparrow tattoo that day—a rose—and from then on visited Steward as often as possible. He designed a few small pieces for himself that he then had Steward apply, just as Steward had once brought his pieces to Amund Dietzel.

"I was fascinated with his character," Hardy later wrote of their time together in the shop. "He told me of his background in academia, work in Chicago, and the move to California. He talked of being a writer . . . [I] knew Phil was gay but he was in the closet with most people . . . [so I] discreetly played along." After they had come to know each other as friends, Hardy asked Steward to teach him to be a tattoo artist. But "Phil firmly discouraged this, speaking of the 'deep, dark world' of this dying art, of which I had no real understanding." Steward also pointed out to Hardy that he had a wife and infant son to support, and so would probably do better by staying in graduate school and becoming an art teacher. "[His] essential message was that I was much too nice (square) to get mixed up in the strange subculture . . . At any rate, I persisted with him . . . My intention was to break tattooing into a whole new creative world [but he told me] that the mainstream tattoo clientele was not sophisticated enough to support any dramatic creativity . . . Nevertheless, he . . . advised me about purchasing a rudimentary set of equipment [and] showed me about mixing colors . . . soldering needle assemblies, cutting acetate stencils to transfer designs to skin, and a variety of other technical things. Everything about tattooing was [at that time] arcane, secretive, and jealously guarded by 'those in the know.'"

Hardy applied his first tattoo (to his own leg, a tradition among beginning tattooers) at the Anchor Tattoo Shop in early 1967, with Steward watching and giving pointers as he did so. "My apprenticeship with Phil was by no means formal or lengthy," Hardy later observed, "[but] I continued to show Phil the work I was doing [for years], both on skin and paper, [and] visit[ed] him frequently." Through him, Hardy also came to know and befriend Cliff Raven, who within a short while would relocate to California and ultimately set up a tattooing studio on Sunset Boulevard in Los Angeles. "Cliff was five years older [than me, but Phil] instilled an appreciation for Japanese work in both of us, and that is the platform that we elaborated on and made our marks with in our early careers," Hardy later explained. "Both of us . . . were book hounds, and really responded to Phil's erudition and eloquence." Steward agreed with this assessment, at one point noting that under his guidance both Hardy and Raven had developed into extremely careful workmen who had distinguished themselves through their thin and tightly controlled outlines, and also through utilizing greater varieties of pigments and colors than other American tattoo artists. "Both can insert their brilliant pigments into the skin without scarring; and both can make sure that the colors are laid in properly so that they remain," Steward observed. "Hardy excels in Oriental designs, whereas Raven succeeds in outré originality."

.

During the period that Steward was mentoring Hardy down at the tattoo shop, he received a letter from Paul Gebhard at the Institute for Sex Research inviting him to respond to a detailed questionnaire about the major life passages experienced by homosexuals. Steward did so with pleasure. He felt that documenting the texture and quality of the everyday lives of homosexual men and women was a vitally important undertaking, particularly given the historic scarcity of such information. He sent back a long response to Gebhard describing his own various life passages, a document remarkable for its clarity, comprehensiveness, and concision.

Describing his college and teaching days, Steward noted in his response to the questionnaire that as a young academic "you wore the mask and went to dull parties, and drank yourself silly because of the boredom, unless there happened to be a good-looking husband or bachelor in the crowd . . . but even so, it was a double life." To Steward's mind, the greatest change in his life had come, predictably enough, when he "took up tattoodling and said farewell to Academe," for with that change his life had become "almost entirely—if not entirely—devoted to the h element." In this he felt different from the majority of homosexuals of his generation, who had necessarily depended upon "their 'obliquity' in order to keep their jobs . . . [for] economics plays a large part [in the way our lives take shape]."

Even so, in his radical break from academe Steward did not feel entirely alone. "I have known many [homosexuals] who—reaching a certain stage in life, largely in their thirties, just say wotthehell and let [their homosexuality] be known to anyone who cares to know or is interested— and to hell with the job. It is about this time that the most curious phenomenon of 'self-destruction' arises; people begin to drift from job to job, or make a radical change as I did with tattoodling, or move to the 'death-wish' city of San Francisco, or drink themselves to death, or in some way try to destroy themselves."

Some of them, Steward thought, managed to hold on to their closeted identities. "Yet even these—like that Jenkins* in Washington—have their

---

*Walter Wilson Jenkins (1918–1985) was a longtime aide to Lyndon B. Johnson whose political career was destroyed in 1964 when he was arrested by Washington, D.C., police while engaging in a homosexual liaison in a YMCA toilet and an account of the incident was reported in the *Washington Star*. Jenkins was married with children at the time.

moments of breakthrough . . . [I think] *everyone* would break loose in his
social life, if he did not have to maintain it because of the necessities of
his job." And yet, paradoxically, Steward felt that he, too, had remained
constrained, even after opting out of conventional society: "During most
of my life . . . as far as the social side is concerned (and even in tattoodling) I've had to pretend to be something which I wasn't. I believe this
may be true of all [homosexuals] except a few 'daring' souls who flaunt
their deviation from the majority 'norm.'"

Steward continued to be remarkably candid about his own sexual
nature:

> I myself have always been usually passive [sexually] (yet here is a
> curious paradox, pointed out by Sartre in *Saint Genet*): that the
> "passive" one does all or most of the work, or even does the ask-
> ing . . . But since my particular preference has always been for
> "straight trade," naturally I must do the work and the asking. This
> "passivity" has gone through several phases: in my 20's and 30's,
> mostly masochistic with actual physical pain; now in the late 40's
> and 50s it has changed to "psychic domination."

Steward went on to explore the trauma of illness as another significant "dividing point" in every homosexual life, noting Dom Orejudos's
hepatitis as an example. He then concluded,

> I believe that the divisions in an h's life are tied up with a) experi-
> ence and the amount or lack of it, b) ageing, c) *traumae* or emo-
> tional shock (including disease), d) social position, e) availability
> of material . . . and perhaps many others which I have not even
> thought of. I am sure that aging . . . with its attendant failures of
> tumescence, has as much to do with [it.] . . . [And yet] as I grow
> older, the one thing that has impressed me in 40 years since I
> came out is the diversity of roles that people play.

In the personal letter to Gebhard that accompanied the completed
questionnaire, Steward shared his most recent bad news from the worlds
of tattooing and publishing. His business at the Anchor was a mere 15
percent of what he had once enjoyed in Chicago, he wrote; in some ways

it was hardly a business at all. Grove Press, meanwhile, had held on to Steward's tattooing manuscript for eight months, only to send it back with a letter of rejection. Worst of all, Womack had delayed releasing $TUD for more than a year, for he had been held up by "indictments for obscenity, Supreme Court decisions, and running out of money." Steward's conclusion: "Shit on this publishing business."

The situation with Womack and Guild Press was indeed about as bad as a book-publishing experience can be. Steward had expected $TUD would be published and available just a few months after his arrival in Berkeley, but Womack's legal troubles were so severe that he had retreated into a psychiatric ward at St. Elizabeth's Hospital in Washington, D.C., in order to avoid his creditors. From his improvised office in the hospital Womack could continue to run his business without restriction, but he had no money, and so $TUD was stuck in the warehouse without a binding. For the next three years Womack would evade all communication with Steward, leaving Steward unable to buy back the rights to his manuscript and incapable of publishing it elsewhere. Had the book been published in a timely manner, it might well have been recognized as a breakthrough in erotic publishing. But it had not been, and it would not be.

•

Steward spent Christmas of 1966 making his seventeenth and final visit to Alice Toklas in Paris, coming to her at her little apartment at 16 Rue de la Convention. "She was then completely bedridden," Steward noted, "eighty nine and in very poor health." The melancholy he felt at saying his final goodbye to her was intensified by a letter he received from Paul Gebhard upon his return, noting that *Querelle de Brest* was finally to be published in English by Grove Press, and suggesting that Steward volunteer them the excellent translation he had deposited at the Kinsey Archive more than a decade earlier. Steward responded by noting that he had long since volunteered Grove his translation of *Querelle* but his letter (and its offer) had been completely ignored.

Though the Oakland tattoo business remained slow, a number of noteworthy individuals stopped in to visit with Steward upon hearing he had opened the shop. Chuck Arnett, deemed by some to be "the Toulouse-Lautrec of San Francisco gay life," came by to have a large butterfly tattooed upon his chest, and later returned with his friend and lover Bill

Tellman, who recalled Steward quoting Menander in Greek to them, and translating the quotation as "a friend is a second self."* Steward also met the artist Mike McCaffee, whose "leather David," a copy of the famed Michelangelo statue clad in leather, had recently become an object of widespread kitsch fascination. (Steward himself bought one.) The British expatriate poet and tattooed leatherman Thom Gunn also popped in, having first met Steward in a San Francisco leather bar, as did the controversial French diplomat and author Roger Peyrefitte, who granted Steward the spontaneous honor of inscribing all Steward's copies of his many books.

In truth, Steward had become much more involved with the local civic and cultural scene during the past year, for his loneliness after moving to California had been extreme, and the lack of business at the tattoo parlor had forced him back out into the world. As a result, he had started volunteering for Vanguard, an outreach organization for hustlers based in and around the ultraliberal Glide Methodist Church in San Francisco—doing so mostly to meet some new hustlers, for his list of sexual contacts (paid and otherwise) had diminished greatly since leaving Chicago, and he no longer had access to dependable hustlers of quality through Chuck Renslow. To meet his immediate sexual needs, he had flown Johnny Reyes out from Chicago for a number of paid visits; hosted Bill Tregoz on a visit from New York; and even given Danny Schmidt a place to stay while he was looking for a job in the Bay Area. But by his third year in Berkeley, Steward had discovered one very talented and extraordinarily good-looking hustler he would rely upon almost exclusively for the next several years and who later took the porn name of Johnny Hardin. When the two first met, Hardin apparently had a drug problem; his Stud File card described him as a "dopedrugtheftbadboy." By 1972 he would start appearing regularly in both heterosexual and homosexual adult films and magazines[†] as well as simultaneously working as a fashion model for the Ford agency.

---

*The quotation is from Aristotle (*Ethica Magna*, II, 15, 8.), not Menander. The misattribution was most probably Tellman's, for the brief memoir in which he recounts the story contains several significant factual errors.

†Hardin (also spelled Harden) modeled for *Mandate, Blueboy, Playgirl, Jock, Playguy, All Man, Inches, Just Men, Honcho,* and *Hustler* between 1979 and 1990, and appeared in a large number of films by the Colt and Falcon studios, as well as in films by Panther, Le Salon, and HIS Video. As a model for *Playgirl,* and also in his later modeling career, he sometimes went by the name of Gene Carrier.

Between late 1966 and 1970 Steward had sex with him 155 times—approximately once a week for three years.

In January 1966, much to Steward's delight, the police raided Renslow's Kris Studio again, and this time seized a large quantity of homoerotic photography and pornographic printed materials—along with three shotguns, a hunting knife, and some whips. Renslow, his favorite "slave," Patrick Ryan, and two other young men were arrested, but Cliff Raven managed to escape through a back door. After giving Paul Gebhard a number of particularly delicious details about the raid (culled both from the newspapers and from conversations with Raven) and then describing Renslow's increasingly complicated life at the Chicago "slave compound," Steward concluded, "I am dying to write that story, but like the stuff of Mabel Dodge* and others, it c[oul]d n[e]v[e]r appear in print until 50 yrs posthumous, I reckon." When Gebhard responded by asking Steward about his current relationship to the Renslow "family," Steward wrote back, "One of the major reasons I left Chicago was that . . . they rejected me . . . But iffn you want an earful about that screwy household, believe me I can give it to you, with figures and dates."[†]

In any event, Steward had greater concerns than Renslow, for Alice Toklas had finally died in early March. She had spent several years as a bedridden and barely conscious invalid, and while Steward had been well aware that her death was imminent, the news of it had nonetheless sent him into another deep depression. "It upset me a great deal," he wrote Gebhard, "but then she'd secretly wanted it for 'all these empty years' since Gertrude died, and I hope it was a happy meeting." Indeed, Steward had been saying his good-byes to Toklas since the late 1950s, and on his last visit to her in Paris—during which he simply sat by her bedside while she slipped in and out of consciousness—he had realized that her life was essentially over.

Through an introduction by Paul Gebhard, Steward next cautiously befriended the experimental filmmaker Kenneth Anger, who like Steward had been contributing sexually themed materials to the Institute for Sex Research for many years. Anger had published *Hollywood Babylon*, a

---

*Mabel Dodge Luhan (1879–1962), a wealthy American arts patron who lived variously in New York, Florence, Provincetown, and Taos, and was notorious for her sexual indiscretions.
†Steward is referring to the Kinsey sex survey, results of which were kept in strictest confidence.

scandal-ridden picture book about mass celebrity, occultism, and kinky sex, in France in 1958.* Well before then, however, he had made a name for himself as an experimental filmmaker. Steward greatly admired his short films *Fireworks* (1947) and *Scorpio Rising* (1963), having first seen *Fireworks* in the Kinsey collection, and later having reviewed *Scorpio Rising* in both *Amigo* and *Der Kreis*. Alfred Kinsey had visited Sicily with Anger in the mid-1950s, in part to view the ruins of "Thelema Abbey," the drug-and-sex farmhouse commune of the occultist, poet-philosopher, and sexual revolutionary Aleister Crowley. Kinsey's interest in Crowley had been casual, and based only on his notorious sexual practices, but Anger was a longtime Crowley devotee.

Shortly after being introduced, Anger came to the Anchor to have Steward tattoo the word *Lucifer* across his chest in large Old English letters, and to have a similar *Lucifer* emblazoned across the chest of his young companion, a musician named Bobby. Because Ed Hardy was at that point keen to meet Anger, Steward arranged an evening with him in the Haight, during which Hardy lit up "a couple of high-powered joints" and the three men got high. Steward "got quite disoriented," Hardy later recalled. "Interestingly, the person who [had] let us in the flat was a young guy with very long hair and a top hat, who looked like Jerry Garcia did in those days. He seemed to live in a part of the house with no furniture except a set of drums. Anger introduced him as Bobby, and it turned out later that it was Bobby Beausoleil."

At nineteen, Beausoleil was just the sort of "bad boy" Steward found most attractive: a product of reform school, he had already played in a rock band, appeared in several porn films, and was now said to be the "star" of Anger's work in progress, *Lucifer Rising*. But when Beausoleil left Anger in September 1967, he stole Anger's car and allegedly stole most of the *Lucifer Rising* footage as well.† Drawing on his friendship with Mick Jagger, Anger subsequently began a new *Lucifer Rising*‡ in London, and there, through Steward, he met and befriended Sir Francis Rose. When Jagger dropped out

---

*The book would not be published in the United States until 1974, for it was laden with actionable scandal.

†The remainder would be cobbled together to create *Invocation of My Demon Brother*, a psychedelic montage of naked young men and occultist practices set largely in Anger's Haight-Ashbury apartment.

‡The introduction of Anger to Rose probably came about through Steward, but since most of Steward's contact with Anger took place either via telephone or in person, the connection is so far undocumented.

of the production, Anger recast the film to include Rose along with Jagger's girlfriend Marianne Faithfull and the filmmaker Donald Cammell, who had written the film *Performance* (1970) and was just then directing (with Nicolas Roeg) Jagger in it. The soundtrack for the twenty-eight-minute *Lucifer Rising*, which took years to complete, was composed in prison by Bobby Beausoleil—for, by 1969, the time the film was finally finished, he had been arrested and convicted for the Topanga Canyon murder of Gary Hinman in the presence of two of Charles Manson's "wives."

In *Lucifer Rising*, Steward's old friend Francis Rose, playing the character "Lord Chaos," stands in a subterranean lair, surrounded by various robed attendants and wearing an ermine cape. In a film otherwise populated by youthful beauties of both sexes, he appears aged and perhaps mentally ill: he has lank, shoulder-length gray hair, grizzled muttonchop whiskers, droopy eyelids, and spittle-coated lips. His presence is entirely disturbing; shots of him are cross-cut with shots of bubbling lava; his scene ends with a closeup of an elephant foot crushing a snake.

•

As 1967 came to a close, Steward had an encounter at his tattoo shop that he never discussed in his memoirs, and which is recorded only in his Stud File:

Dan, a Hells Angel Dec 29 1967, 1/10/68*
    Only H[ells] A[ngel] I ever had, tho tattooed scores of em.
Dint want any more.

Steward had been visited at his shop throughout 1966 and '67 by various members of the Hells Angels, including the gang's leader, Ralph "Sonny" Barger. Barger and his gang dealt widely in heroin, and two of his top gang members, Terry the Tramp and George Wetherns, sold most of the LSD and other psychedelics then available in Haight-Ashbury. Because the hippie movement had promoted the use of LSD as an aid to spiritual meditation and creative self-expression, the trade in psychedelics during the 1967 "Summer of Love" had suddenly become big business, and by cornering the LSD market the Angels had made a small fortune. When interest in LSD subsequently slacked off, the Angels

---

*The two dates indicate that Steward had sex with Dan twice.

shifted to sales of cocaine and methamphetamine, and in doing so initiated a period of great violence within and around the organization. By the time Steward opened the Anchor, Barger had already been arrested three times for assault with a deadly weapon; along with cocaine, he and most of the other Angels were now using PCP. As a result, the motorcyclists were widely feared for their sudden acts of extreme violence, which included "gang bang" rapes. Steward had dealt with many a rough character during his decade on South State Street, but he had never before witnessed such drug-crazed acts of violent rage, and he was justifiably terrified of the gang, even though they needed him for his tattooing skills and professed on a regular basis to be his friends.

Since the Angels had quickly become the financial mainstay of his business, Steward maintained a cautious friendship with the gang, and over time forged friendships with three of its top members: "Sonny" Barger, "Moldy Marvin" Tilbert, and "Saint" John Morton. Steward found the last of the three particularly engaging, for Morton was a former tattoo artist with more than a hundred tattoos on his body, and he had great appreciation for Steward's exceptionally high-quality work.

Steward befriended these three just as the motorcycle gang was beginning its ascent to quasi-mythic status. A year later, in 1967, when Hunter Thompson's *Hells Angels* became a runaway bestseller, the gang entered the popular imagination as contemporary American renegade heroes, and as a result became much more wary of would-be fans. By then Steward, for his part, had become deeply ambivalent about them, for apart from being dangerous, ignorant, violent, racist, sexist, and homophobic, they also seemed to him physically repellent: With their greasy hair, appalling hygiene, and foot-long beards, they were a far cry from the trim, muscular, leather-jacketed motorcyclists whom he had met and sometimes bedded in Chicago and San Francisco over the past two decades, and who had populated his erotic fantasies for years.

Steward became even further repulsed when he learned that many of the "secret" tattoos he was applying to the Angels were actually testaments to their participation in various beatings, rapes, maimings, and murders. In a magazine article for *Vector* in August 1970, he also noted that other tattoos made a proprietary claim: "many of their mamas [are] marked . . . on the *gluteus maximus*, or even above the celestial gate, with such phrasings as 'Property Of' followed by the member's gang-name." Tattoos also served as grim memorials: Barger's first wife, Elsie, had attempted to abort her unborn child by pumping air into her vagina, which resulted in an agonizing death; Barger subsequently had her cross-shaped headstone tattooed onto his right arm in her memory.

Many years later, Barger described how Steward had stood out from the local tattooing competition:

> Back in the late 50s and early 60s there was quite a few tattoo shops on Broadway [in Oakland]. Phil was one of the better tattooers and one of the things was, he didn't look like a normal tattooer—you knew he was something else. When I found out about his earlier life [as a university professor] I wasn't surprised at all. But he was a good tattooer!

Steward worked as the "official" tattoo artist for the Hells Angels from 1967 through 1971, regularly tattooing Angels not only from the Oakland membership, but also from Livermore, Stockton, Fresno, San Francisco, and San Bernardino.* In doing so he became intimately trusted by "Sonny" Barger, as well as several other leading club members, for all were very particular about the designs of their various emblems, all valued and respected his skill as a craftsman, and all relied on him for his discretion. "Not only did they want the skull with wings, but other designs which were arcane and esoteric—at least until the Angels started getting all their publicity," Steward wrote in his memoirs. "They got swastikas and iron crosses, the jagged 'SS' symbol, the 1% (someone had said only 1% of all motorcyclists were outlaws). They got pilot's wings—brown to mean they had screwed a man, red for cunnilingus on a menstruating old lady, or black—the same on a black woman. Or they got '13' for the letter 'M' (13th down the alphabet) meaning marijuana, 'DFFL'—Dope Forever, Forever Loaded; '666'—the number of the beast in the Apocalypse, since a preacher had called them that—and other symbols transient in meaning." There were other designs Steward tattooed onto members that he did not discuss in his memoirs, for they were secret symbols the meaning of which he was forbidden to divulge. He did, however, note being amazed

---

*The Hells Angels Ralph "Sonny" Barger and "Saint" John Morton confirmed that Steward had been their official tattoo artist during this period. (Barger, interview with author; Morton, e-mail to author.)

when Sonny Barger asked to have "a long philosophical quotation from Khalil Gibran [tattooed] on his inner right forearm."*

Steward, known among the bikers simply as "Doc," nonetheless remained uneasy in their company, and with good reason. "The Angels were terrifying," he wrote in his memoirs. "[But] gradually I acquired a kind of special status so that I could indulge in kidding and badinage with them, whereas the same words from a stranger would have resulted in a broken jaw." Despite his skill in handling them, he confessed in an unpublished draft of his memoirs that "their presence [in the shop always] put me on the thin edge between disaster and catastrophe . . . They kept my insides awash with adrenalin whenever they came a-callin.'"

On certain occasions Steward was drawn into their acts of violence. Late one evening, for instance—long after Steward had closed up the shop and taken the public bus back home to his bungalow in Berkeley—his phone rang; it was Barger, asking Steward to come back to Oakland to open up the Anchor for a special late-night tattooing job. Steward had no choice but to dress and hurry back to the storefront. There he found "four or five" Angels waiting for him, along with a banged-up young man with a blackened eye and a bloody nose. When Steward asked what was going on, one of the Angels explained that they had discovered their captive wearing a Hells Angels tattoo even though he did not belong to the organization. The Angels wanted the tattoo blacked out completely before they gave the man the rest of what he had coming.

Steward opened the shop, but insisted that for legal reasons the man needed to sign a release. After the man signed a statement saying he had been tattooed of his own free will, Steward "blacked out the design, with each of the Angels taking turns in jabbing the needle into the skin. Afterwards they threw the man into a small enclosed truck and climbed in after him. I heard later that they drove him into the country, knocked him around some more, sodomized him, stripped him naked, and dropped him on the freeway." Sonny Barger not only confirmed this story, but also noted that such incidents had taken place within his organization more than once—something Steward neglected to mention in his memoirs. Barger enthusiastically recalled in his own memoirs that after capturing a man who had stolen his motorcycle, he and the rest of his gang had taken

---

*The quotation ("I would rather that I died in yearning and longing than that I lived weary and despairing") is drawn from the Gibran poem "Tears and a Smile."

turns bullwhipping him, and then had beaten him with a spiked dog collar and broken all his fingers with a ball-peen hammer. "Despite all the news articles and studies by [popular] psychologists about the Hells Angels," Steward concluded years later, "the fact remains that they were tough and mean and had to be handled with care."

Don Ed Hardy has suggested that while Steward may have disliked the Angels, he also took a justifiable pride in his ability to handle them and move among them. "I tattooed some Hells Angels in San Francisco in the mid-seventies, but never hung out with them socially," Hardy noted; "occasionally I would meet one in Phil's shop but was not privy to a lot of contact with them. They live in their own world and it is not open to outsiders. Phil delighted in associating with 'rough trade,' and was socially very adept in getting along with a huge range of humanity."

Steward, of course, had other reasons for getting along with the Angels apart from the business they brought to his shop. After "Dan," Steward had no further sexual dealings with the Angels; but he did like to use recreational drugs such as marijuana and barbiturates. While he had no use for cocaine, PCP, methamphetamine, or LSD, he did enjoy having ready access to these other substances, and in at least one instance he traded some anti-police artwork for a jar full of "reds." Moreover, with Angels for friends, Steward felt safer on the streets of Oakland. "They were mean mothers," he later told an interviewer. "Some of them were O.K.; many of them were f[i]lthy. But I had a number of good friends amongst the group, and they were protective of you, too, if they liked you."

•

While Steward relied primarily on Johnny Hardin for sex during the later 1960s, and while he occasionally found a new sex contact down at the tattoo parlor (including a retired policeman with whom he had an ongoing liaison for several years), he met a man in 1968 who would eventually provide him with just as many new hustlers as Renslow, and who would, like Renslow, come to figure significantly in his Phil Andros fiction. J. Brian Donahue* (who went by the professional name of J. Brian) was only twenty-nine when Steward met him, but he was already running a highly successful male escort service named Golden Boys and publishing photographs

*J. Brian's first name is reported as Jeremiah ("Director J. Brian charged in second film 'conspiracy,'" *The Advocate*, March 27, 1974), but his friend Jack Fritscher remembers his first name as James. (Fritscher, e-mail to author.)

of his hustlers in a self-produced glossy magazine of the same name. Brian had hustled since the age of twenty, and had started his erotic photography business in 1963, at the age of twenty-four, after completing two and a half years at San Jose State College. Initially selling his photographs by the packet at newsstands in San Francisco's homosexual neighborhoods, he had quickly distinguished himself from his competition for his naturalistic nudes of males just above the age of consent—young "golden boy" Californians who seemed to possess the frank self-awareness of a new, less inhibited generation. He later confided to an interviewer that the secret of his success was in choosing his models with care and then treating them like friends. "I find nothing dirty or disgraceful or disgusting in pornography," he went on; "to me [the word *pornography*] means no more than the use of explicit sexual content . . . Pornography and obscenity are *not* the same thing, are not necessarily even related."

A later friend of Brian's, the *Drummer* editor Jack Fritscher, has noted that "for all his flamboyance, [J. Brian] was modest . . . a ruddy-faced, heavy-set, jolly guy with reddish-blond complexion and hair." Fritscher felt that "Sam [Steward] and J. Brian were each globally positioned with a latitude of art that intersected the longitude of sex. Both raconteurs enjoyed dropping names as much as dropping their pants . . . Sam orbited his *haute* planet of *Brideshead* literary friends . . . [while] J. Brian's map was more an archipelago of mattresses."

When Steward met him, Brian was experimenting with eight-millimeter film loops, for his secret ambition was to produce and direct fully plotted, feature-length all-male films. His call-boy service and house of prostitution were staffed by the same models who appeared in his photography and film loops—and so, as with Chuck Renslow, the various J. Brian businesses fed into one another. But Brian was hardly as street-savvy as Renslow, and he was almost immediately targeted for police investigation and prosecution—in large part because, by brazenly advertising his house of male prostitution (through his magazine, his pornographic movies, and his own direct-marketing mail campaigns*), he quickly made himself a target for police vice squads as far away as Chicago and New York.

---

*For a dollar, J. Brian Enterprises would send out a photographic portfolio of its current "models" within the larger brochure that gave details about the agency, its policies, and its pricing structure. (One of these brochures is now in the Steward Papers, a gift of Douglas Martin.)

Because Brian felt that his work as a male madam and pornographer was part of the larger sexual revolution just then sweeping America, he consciously chose not to conceal either his activities or his assets. This act of principled daring appealed mightily to Steward, as it suggested a stance on hustling that was very much in line with Steward's own. Brian was indeed so progressive in his thinking about his hustling business that he opened his brothel to an interested academic researcher who documented its comings and goings in a remarkable 1971 scholarly journal article entitled "The Male House of Prostitution." The article gave specific details of how the house worked: prospective models could not be known to the police as homosexual, nor could they have had hepatitis or veneral disease, and they were required to complete a full physical exam before starting. On the business side, Brian kept 30 percent of the take, with models allowed to keep all of their tips. Models were not allowed to give out their real names or phone numbers, and were warned not to develop attachments to their clients. However, models had to agree before starting that they would accept all the assignments they were given.

Steward was fascinated by Brian's business setup as well as with his models; never before had he been so intimately aware of the goings-on in an actual house of prostitution, or so closely connected—on a day-to-day, friendship level—to so many handsome young hustlers. He was so taken with Brian's freewheeling, sexually liberated approach to both prostitution and pornography that he allowed Brian to publish several of his stories in *Golden Boys* magazine during 1968: "The Link," a fictionalized version of his 1937 visit to Lord Alfred Douglas, and "Pig in a Poke," a Phil Andros story with a strong S/M component.

As an older man who had immersed himself in homosexual pornography for most of his life, Steward felt he had a great deal to share with Brian, including the (then unwritten and undocumented) history of underground homoerotic pornography in twentieth-century America. With Steward's encouragement, Brian decided to adapt one of the most famous of these underground stories for film. The result was Brian's first hit, *Seven in a Barn*. Though made on the tiniest of budgets (with Brian as director, chief cameraman, writer, editor, and sound dubber), the film achieved a wide circulation and had an enthusiastic following. Technologically advanced (it was the first gay porn film to feature both color and sound), it was also arguably "literary," and it ultimately impressed academics enough that Brian was invited to screen and discuss it for film classes, sociology workshops, and psychology clinics on several different California university campuses. Brian went so far as to tell one interviewer that he hoped someday to direct "a regular theater, full story-line, Hollywood-scale treatment of gay life in an open, healthy, natural way. It's a field with maybe only one title in it so far—*A Very Natural Thing** . . . I'd like to be the man who cracks that market open."

In 1969, after hearing about Steward's trouble with Womack, J. Brian offered to publish a cheap paperback edition of *$TUD*. Steward, who now considered Brian a close friend, agreed to the project with enthusiasm. Brian was able to undertake the publishing project not only because of his well-established pornographic printing contacts, but also because he already had a large distribution network in place for the sale of anything he cared to produce. His cheap, sloppy, small-magazine-format version of *$TUD* featured a number of photographs of Brian's naked young male models that had nothing at all to do with the Phil Andros text, but which served nonetheless to attract his usual buyers. While H. Lynn Womack still held the contractual rights to the book, Steward and J. Brian had undertaken their edition based on an escape clause in the Guild Press contract, one that allowed for the book's publication in paperback after a term of three years from signing. Steward later wrote that as soon as his paperback was published, the infuriated Womack had quickly printed an authorless three-volume cheap edition of the text of *$TUD*, and shortly thereafter "he evidently found the money to pay the binder [for] the hardcover edition of *$TUD* with a jacket by [Dom Orejudos]." But rather than attempt to sell the book, Womack instead remaindered it immediately, and as a result the book would never appear in bookstores, nor earn a penny in royalties for its author.

Shortly after the *$TUD* debacle, Knud Rame/Kim Kent decided to publish Steward's earlier S/M-themed, Schnitzler-inspired monologues as the porno novel *Ring-Around-the-Rosy*. He did so in Copenhagen, in a trilingual hardcover edition. Though Steward was sorry not to have the book published in the United States, he was delighted to see it in print,

---

**A Very Natural Thing* (1973), directed by Christopher Larkin, was the first mainstream commercial film to portray a loving, committed sexual relationship between two men. (For more on the film, see Russo, *Celluloid Closet*, p. 208.)

and delighted as well to publish a book with his old friend Rame. The experience seems at least temporarily to have restored his faith in book publishing.

•

Steward now wanted to write and publish more than ever, for despite his love of tattooing, he was slowly but surely coming to the conclusion that his tattoo shop's days were numbered and that his future now lay elsewhere. After being attacked and robbed in the shop, he began to acknowledge that the Anchor was in too dangerous an area. "I was strongarmed and robbed by a coupla our black soul-brothers on June 5," he wrote Paul Gebhard shortly after the incident. "I consider myself lucky not to be daid or beat-up in a hospital."

But the tattoo parlor was becoming a liability for other reasons. By the end of the 1967 Summer of Love, an estimated hundred thousand restless young people had moved to San Francisco, and during 1968, drug use among them had shifted away from "mellowing" substances such as marijuana and LSD toward agitation-producing substances such as cocaine, methamphetamine, and PCP. Violent crime was on the rise, and with it a new feeling of bitterness and disillusionment. With the stabbing murder of the rock fan Meredith Hunter by the Hells Angel Allan Passaro at the Altamont Raceway concert in December 1969,* the fortunes of the Hells Angels in particular took an abrupt turn for the worse. "After Altamont," Sonny Barger later noted, "life was one criminal cluster fuck after another." As a result, each new day at the tattoo parlor seemed to Steward to bring with it some new problem or incident relating to the Angels.

There was also the question of accidental hepatitis C transmission. Shared needle use among hippies was now a major cause of concern among local health officials, and in tattooing hippies, Steward knew that he risked spreading the disease despite his careful use of an autoclave for sterilization purposes. The explosion of hepatitis in the Bay Area led Steward to expect that both Oakland and San Francisco would soon order the closing of all area tattoo parlors—particularly since, by the end of 1968, forty-seven

---

*The murder is captured in the Rolling Stones documentary *Gimme Shelter* (1970), directed by Peter and David Maysles.

other major American cities had already enacted special ordinances against tattooing. Even if the city of Oakland did not order Steward to close his doors, however, he knew that the legal liabilities connected to hepatitis transmission had the potential to ruin him financially.

Perhaps most important for Steward, however, was the new absence of sex from the tattoo shop. Due to both his own advancing age and to the changing nature of his clientele, tattooing had simply ceased to be a locus for seduction. With fewer sexually appealing young men coming in for tattoos, Steward now found the work almost unbearably tedious. "The irritant factors in a tattoo artist's life are numerous and intense," he later wrote. "He is continually faced by an unending barrage of questions from both customers and onlookers . . . multiply the [hundred or so] questions by about a hundred and fifty thousand customers, allowing about ten questions a person, and you begin to have an idea of the kind of patience required . . . Not all of us [are] able to maintain a high degree of this virtue."

Steward was then assaulted and robbed a second time in his shop, and while still recovering both physically and psychologically from the incident, something happened that he barely ever mentioned to anyone, even the best of his friends: he witnessed a next-door robbery, then watched and held the hand of his neighbor as the shopkeeper bled to death from gunshot wounds. Steward wrote of it only briefly in his memoirs, noting in passing, "The shop next door—a pawnshop run by an elderly Jew named Herman Cartun—had been several times victimized, and between my own second and third experiences [of being robbed], poor Herman was shot and killed by a couple of blacks who disapproved of his racial remarks."

But Steward had both known and liked Cartun, whose pawnshop, the Trading Post, was adjacent to the Anchor. After hearing the loud "pop" of gunfire at close range, Steward had run to the door of the tattoo parlor to see what had happened. As he did so, Cartun, shot in the chest and bleeding heavily, appeared at his own door, and from there took five shots at his fleeing assailants with his gun. According to the newspaper account of the crime, Cartun then "fell at the door of his shop with four bullets in his body." Cartun's partner, gun in hand, chased after the robbers. Steward meanwhile bent over Cartun, who lay in a rapidly growing pool of his own blood. "Cartun asked [Steward] that the police be called," the newspaper article noted. "It was his last request [and] Steward obeyed it." Steward then attempted first aid, but nothing helped; as they waited for the ambulance, Steward simply held Cartun's hand and watched him die.

A few weeks later, Steward was robbed yet again, and seeing in this third robbery the possibility that he, too, would end up like Cartun, he made the painful decision to close down the shop. He took the place apart with his own hands. After selling off his tattooing equipment, he put all his flash and memorabilia into storage boxes and hauled them back to the bungalow.

With the closing of the Anchor, another significant period in Steward's life was coming to an end. Like Prospero breaking his staff, Steward had set down his tattoo needle, and from the fantastic life of the tattoo artist, he returned to the mundane reality of his suburban ghetto bungalow:

In March, 1970, I locked the door [to the parlor for] the last time, and retired to my house in Berkeley. Phil Sparrow, in effect, was killed, destroyed, wiped out of memory, off the books. I left no forwarding address with the post office, and became Samuel Steward once more . . . In the Tattoo shop I had been absolute boss for fifteen years . . . using the "tone of authority" which the years of teaching had developed. Now all of that was gone. No one had to do anything I ordered; in fact, there was no one to order.

19

"From the brow of Zeus"

After closing the tattoo parlor in the spring of 1970 Steward felt particularly disconnected from the world around him, for he despised the druggy, self-satisfied dropout culture of the university city in which he lived. "If you wanted to see the scruffy, barrel-bottom scrapings of the 1960s," he wrote in his memoirs, "you [needed look no further than] the Land That Time Forgot—Berkeley." To alleviate his boredom and disgust, he turned first to television (never having owned one before, he built one from an electronics kit), but then seeing in it only "the decline of Western civilization," he moved on to other hobbies, which included clock collecting, science fiction, and the inventing of various electronic gadgets—including a doorbell that he programmed to chime *gaudeamus igitur, juvenes dum sumus** "because of its melancholy view of youth."

One of his electronic inventions, an anti-telephone-bugging device, seemed commercial enough that he founded a small company called Privacy Unlimited to market it. But when legal complications ensued almost immediately, he returned once again to fiction. This time, Steward decided to try his hand at a pornographic novel. He later described the enormous pleasure he felt in "Phil Andros springing full-grown from my temple, like Athena from the brow of Zeus." James Purdy, who had been corresponding with Steward frequently since 1968, encouraged him in the project through a series of camp and teasing letters, some of them including pornographic

---

*From the drinking song and school anthem "De Brevitatae Vitae," the first stanza of which roughly translates to: "Let us rejoice therefore while we are young / After our pleasant youth and troublesome old age / The ground will have us."

"press releases" about Steward's "invisible house" and its dark erotic goings-on.

In his memoirs, Steward noted that his return to erotic writing was timely: due to a recent Supreme Court decision revisiting the 1957 case of *Roth v. United States*, "suddenly *all* the old four-letter words (and some new ones) appeared in print almost overnight [and] publishers no longer had to write prefatory notes condemning what they were printing; they could merely suggest the social significance of erotica, and lo! All was satisfied. The court's decision had more holes in it than a colander, and publishing houses sprang up like mushrooms after rain."

Steward's first challenge, of course, was to find himself one of these just-sprung-up publishing houses. After doing some networking in San Francisco, he came to an agreement with "a short, fat, greasy French Canadian" named Roland Boudreault, owner of a chain of erotic shops known as Le Salon. Boudreault would first publish a "Frenchy's Gay Line" version of *Ring-Around-the-Rosy* (which up to that point had been published only in Knud Rame's trilingual Danish edition of 1968), retitling it *The Joy Spot* and bringing it out in 1969. He would also publish the first three Phil Andros novels in 1970 and 1971 through his newly renamed publishing house, Gay Parisian Press.

While the writing of novels has never been regarded as a particularly lucrative occupation, the writing of homosexual pornography during the early 1970s was not only unprofitable but also thankless, for its disreputable publishers were entirely indifferent to the rights and expectations of their authors. These publishers wrote contracts stipulating that authors received only a small flat fee for their writing, which was sold as work for hire—meaning that the author signed away all rights to his work and all editorial control over his manuscript. The publisher then required the author to write each book to the publisher's exact specifications, including length of manuscript and percentage of text devoted to sexual description. Finally, the publisher retained complete freedom to cut, rearrange, discard, and rewrite at will, even if doing so resulted (as often happened) in a finished work that made little sense.* In later life Steward noted that in his own case "the payment for [the Phil Andros novels] from [Bou-

---

*Steward wrote cleanly and concisely, and while his publishers occasionally demanded more sexual descriptions from him, they never altered or rewrote his manuscripts. (His original, minimally altered manuscripts and page proofs remain with his archive.)

dreault] was a flat fee of $400—no royalties, no further correspondence, no nuthin'—and if any fan letters were received, they were never forwarded to the author. It was like writing into a vacuum."

In writing his Phil Andros novels, Steward was, in essence, attempting to create the sort of good-humored accounts of homosexual activity he wished had been available to him as a younger man. His writings described a wide range of sexual interests and practices with warmth, enthusiasm, and little in the way of moral judgment. By approaching the subject of homosexual activity with openness and quiet good humor, he hoped to provide not only erotic entertainment, but also a basic enlightenment about the everyday nature of the non-relationship-oriented sexual encounters that had taken up so much of his life. Doing so was relatively easy for him, since he could base his fiction on his own extensive and in-depth documentation.

The gay paperback pornography industry of 1970 was, however, a business in which lofty sociological aims were of little concern to the businessmen engaged in its highly profitable and often risky distribution and sale. Nor was good writing: atmosphere, plot, and character development were simply not important to businessmen like Boudreault, since his customers were hardly discriminating about the porn they were buying. As a result, all Boudreault needed or wanted was a series of stimulating descriptions of various sexual acts strung together with something approximating a story.

While Steward was frustrated by the basic indifference and glaring mendacity of the porn business, he was nonetheless hugely relieved to have finally found a way in which he could publish his graphic tales of sex between men, for getting writing of this sort commercially published was, in a sense, the fulfillment of his lifelong ambition. Moreover, on an immediate personal level, the novels allowed Steward a much-needed escape into fantasy at a particularly difficult and lonely period in his life—especially since, as Phil Andros, Steward was no longer a short, slight, failed English professor living alone, hooked on barbiturates, and bumping sixty. Instead he was a paragon of sexual virility, a burly professional hustler bursting with animal magnetism and attired in

a black leather jacket, black cap tipped as far back on me curly Greek locks as it will go without falling, light-colored beige chinos (which show shapes and sizes better), and black motorcycle boots about sixteen inches high . . . As for T-shirts, I like a tight black nylon one because it shows me nipples, or a tight white one, which is even better. But I very seldom wear a T-shirt at all unless I'm going "formal" for an evening. My chest hair turns 'em on.

As for my personal appearance, I'm a little over six feet with a fifty-inch chest and sixteen-inch biceps—and a good deal of hair on my body: a big triangular fan on my chest, narrowing down to a thin line as it passes through my navel, and spreading out again like a peacock's tail when it comes to my prick. My cock itself is between nine and ten inches long hard—quite a whopper—and thick enough so that you can hardly get your thumb and forefinger to touch when they circle it . . . I've got a thirty-inch waist and weigh one-eighty-five or one-ninety.

Steward's first Phil Andros novel was *My Brother, the Hustler,** a tale of the road that would ultimately distinguish itself as his most comically self-indulgent effort, and also his most surreal. In it, Phil awakens from a nap beneath the Golden Gate Bridge to find himself mistaken for a man named Denny who is apparently his doppelgänger. Various couplings with strangers ensue, with all of these men initially mistaking Phil for Denny (who is, like Phil, a hustler, and possibly Phil's long-lost twin). Phil then begins receiving a series of mysterious psychic summonses from Denny, ones that prompt him to travel across the country in search of this mysterious "brother," making stops in Chicago, Columbus, and New York.

The premise of psychic communication between separated twins was one Steward had developed out of his conversations with Danny Schmidt, who had long claimed to receive psychic messages from his two triplet brothers. Another inspiration for the story was the "lost twin" Steward had learned about in the 1947 biopsy of his amputated testicle. But Steward also had plenty of literary inspiration: the search for a second self, and more specifically for a second self through which one achieves wholeness, is at the heart of Aristophanes' speech in Plato's *Symposium*. Genet had shown a similar interest in the twin (or second self) in *Querelle de Brest*,

---

*Later republished as *My Brother, My Self*.

for in that novel not only does Querelle encounter his heterosexual twin, Robert, at the brothel, but also he feels he has met his "double" in the character of Gil Turko—a fellow criminal he both loves and betrays.

Steward's casual invocation of Whitman at the beginning of the novel* also suggests Whitman's great claim in "Song of Myself" that "all men ever born are my brothers." And, indeed, Steward returns to Whitman's idea of universal brotherhood in the last pages of the novel by paraphrasing (without attribution) Ezra Pound's poem on Whitman, "A Pact":† "O my brother! Let there be commerce between us! May we always be together." So the preoccupation with the lost brother is far more than a mere plot device.

Steward used the novel to settle an old score: Chuck Renslow and Dom Orejudos appear in its Chicago chapters as the deeply grotesque characters Mike (a low-life pimp) and Ollie (an LSD-addled foot fetishist). Phil's visit with them includes a detailed description of "The Black Castle," the bizarre series of interlinked apartments that Renslow and Orejudos inhabited on Belmont Avenue‡ that featured a dungeon play space—a home they shared not only with Renslow's many "slaves," but also, oddly enough, with Renslow's aged mother.

After two more psychic summonses—first to Columbus, to meet an evocation of Steward's adolescent self, and then to New York, to meet a tattooist—Phil returns to the San Francisco Bay area, where at last he meets with his mysterious twin. The novel concludes with their dreamlike sexual embrace.

In *My Brother, the Hustler*, Steward established Phil Andros as a peripatetic American hustler, forever on the road and forever adrift. Steward had met men of this sort in the cafés of Paris, at the Embarcadero YMCA in San Francisco, at George Lynes's New York apartment, and in his own Chicago tattoo shop. Johnny Leapheart, Mike Miksche, Bill Tregoz, Chuck Arnett, and Cliff Raven had all been sensitive, intelligent drifters and dropouts, moving from life to life and city to city in their endless, disaffected search for sexual adventure.

---

*The novel begins, "It was an afternoon that Walt Whitman himself would have loved—all sun and wind and the salt spray from the Pacific in the air." (*My Brother, My Self*, p. 1.)

†Pound's poem concludes, "We are one root and one sap / Let there be commerce between us."

‡The interlinked apartment complex with its dungeon play space had first been described as "the black castle" by a drag queen comedian working in one of Renslow's clubs who had noticed the crenellated roof of the building in which it was located.

Thematically and structurally, *My Brother, the Hustler* has much in common with the Beat novels. While Steward had never been a Beat, many of the Beats had been gay or bisexual, and their rootlessness had been predicated in part upon their sexual as well as social nonconformity. Though Jack Kerouac had once stated in an interview, "We were just a bunch of guys out trying to get laid," Ann Charters's *Kerouac* and, later, Winston Leyland's *Gay Sunshine Interviews* would clearly establish that, in the words of one scholar, "the guys didn't always have to go *out* to get laid." Steward's *My Brother, the Hustler* had been published anonymously by a fly-by-night pulp fiction publisher, with a plot so abstract and self-indulgent that it seemed half sex fantasy, half comic hallucination. But in its oddball way it posited an alternate (if later) vision of the Beat generation, one featuring a comic hero who was both an articulate social dropout and a well-adjusted sexual nonconformist.

Steward's satiric description of Renslow and Orejudos did not go unnoticed. In response, Orejudos published the erotic comic book *Locker Room* with Kris Studio in 1971 under the name Stephen, and there created a wonderfully childish revenge fantasy in which the young Sam Steward is characterized as a weakling and a snitch. As a result of informing on various sexual goings-on in the locker room, Sam gets his erotic comeuppance from a lusty, robust, and formidably endowed football team, who then go on to enjoy one another in an orgy. Renslow, meanwhile, formulated an even more substantial form of payback for Steward, for he was just then opening a transvestite cabaret in Chicago—and knowing Steward's lifelong abhorrence of effeminacy and drag queens, he both named the club after Steward and featured a wickedly accurate caricature of Steward dressed as Whistler's Mother on the club's signage and menus.*

Renslow and Orejudos were not the only people Steward caricatured in *My Brother, the Hustler*. Knud Rame appeared in the novel as Knud Gunnarson, a dentured old man with a taste for discipline who eventually reveals to Phil that he is a Catholic bishop obsessed with astrology and the occult (as Rame in fact was). Johnny Reyes made a brief appearance

---

*Located at 5220 North Sheridan Road, Sparrow's opened in 1971 and closed in 1972—but during its brief life, the restaurant sponsored the first and only float in Chicago's first gay pride parade. According to Renslow, the 1972 parade "wasn't the first gay pride [demonstration] but it was the first one that was really a parade. Before that they were really marching demonstrations."

as himself, under the name Johnny Mendoza. Even one of Steward's aunts appears in the book: she is "Aunt Ellie Andros," and Phil visits her at her boardinghouse in Columbus.

•

In the second Phil Andros novel, *San Francisco Hustler*, Phil picks up a motorcycle cop, Greg, in a parking lot while visiting his sister in Santa Monica. When the two men meet again in San Francisco, Greg has left the Highway Patrol to join the San Francisco Police Department, and he encourages Phil to join the police force, too, so that they can room together—and so have all the sex they like without attracting suspicion. A third cop then joins their ménage, and they begin a series of leather-and-uniform, BDSM erotic adventures. The speed with which Steward wrote the book suggests not only that he was enjoying his new life as Phil Andros, but also that he had quickly mastered the highly restrictive erotic-novella form—for porn novels were really short works of 50,000 to 65,000 words, of which 20 percent to 50 percent needed to be detailed descriptions of sexual acts.* In *San Francisco Hustler*, Steward's writing is deft, his plotting succinct, and his characterizations are strong; the ingenious sexual descriptions—most of them featuring some aspect of domination, uniform fetishism, and S/M—are drawn from Steward's own sexual experiences. Later republished as *The Boys in Blue*, the novel would stand as Steward's most sexually exuberant, for it featured a triangulated love relationship among three cops that allowed for every possible permutation of domination/submission sex play. The three-way relationship is also described in terms of strong and complicated feelings of both friendship and emotional attachment—even though none of these three cops requires or hopes for any kind of emotional commitment from the other two. Phil, in fact, becomes confused and upset when Greg's sexual domination of him triggers in him a response of passionate obsession, for even as he hungers for sexual domination, Phil dislikes the idea of being in a relationship:

---

*The cultural historian Michael Bronski describes the percentage as twenty, but Ellen Squires of Greenleaf, in a 1973 letter to Steward, complained that his manuscript was only 34 percent sex. In a letter shortly afterward, Steward noted to the anthologist Stephen Wright that the required amount had recently climbed to 50 percent.

If you're a hustler, you can't be tied down like that. And I had a few more years before I'd have to give it up completely. To waste even one of [those years] in an "affair" was almost beyond my ability to cope with. On the other hand—to room with a cop, and one as attractive and well-endowed as Greg (I like sex)—well, that was something else again. I didn't expect the thing to last but I might as well give it a try.

The novel also features an element of action and surprise, for Phil is kidnapped, taken by force sexually, and then rescued by his friends, who in turn take their sexual revenge on his abductors. Moreover, the story is also suspenseful, for all three cops know that if their sexual preferences are discovered, they are sure to be dismissed from the force. When rumors about Phil's past as a hustler reach the police captain, Phil realizes he must skip out of San Francisco before the rumor is confirmed. He leaves for Chicago, where he applies for a new job as a policeman, and in doing so he reconnects with his old friend the bodybuilding hustler Rudy Dax, who is now also a police officer.* Yet for all its sexual exuberance and good humor, the novel ends on a dark note as Phil learns that Greg and Pete have been sexually entrapped by a fellow officer and so have lost their jobs.

While Steward was delighted to have published *My Brother, the Hustler* and *San Francisco Hustler*, he distrusted and disliked Roland Boudreault. When he discovered that Boudreault had facilitated the pirating of *Ring-Around-the-Rosy* and probably planned to do the same with *San Francisco Hustler*, he began to network among his fellow gay erotic authors in San Francisco for a new, more trustworthy publisher, and hopefully for a better business contract.†

Shortly after publication of *My Brother, the Hustler*, Steward was asked to participate in a panel discussion entitled "The Plight of Gay Novelists" at the headquarters of SIR, or Society for Individual Rights, the leading Bay Area homophile association. He shared the panel with Richard Amory, at that moment the best-known author of gay erotic fic-

---

*Dax was based on Ralph Steiner, one of Steward's favorite bodybuilder-hustlers, who had become a Chicago police officer in the years since Steward had moved to California.

†*San Francisco Hustler* was pirated in 1974 as *Gay in San Francisco* by "Biff Thomas"; in the pirated edition, Phil Andros is renamed "Sylvon Panos."

tion in America. Amory's 1966 bestseller *Song of the Loon* and its two
sequels (*Song of Aaron* and *Listen, the Loon Sings*) were the most widely
read gay novels of the 1960s and '70s; it has been estimated that during
this period, 30 percent of all gay men in the United States had purchased
a paperback copy of *Song of the Loon*.

The panel discussion was later written up in the Los Angeles–based
newspaper *The Advocate* by Larry Townsend, an author of erotica,* who
noted that more than two hundred people had attended, and that Amory
had been the star attraction. Nonetheless, according to Townsend, "Phil
Andros [gave] quite a long, articulate statement on the writers of the past,
[noting that] back in the thirties, forties and fifties, a gay writer might occasionally find his way into print with a story about homosexual protagonists, but he was then constrained to allude only delicately to sex that
occurred between the men. Sometimes he was even forced to mask his
story by casting one of the lovers as a woman. Those who 'knew' could
read between the lines; anyone else would miss the point completely."

At the time of the SIR panel, Amory (whose real name was Richard
Love) had just separated from his wife and three children and moved to
San Jose to work as a high school Spanish teacher and participate in the
San Jose Gay Liberation Front. Steward and Amory had much in common;
like Steward, Amory had been raised in Columbus, where his father had
been a professor of psychology at Ohio State University. Like Steward,
Amory had taken up the writing of gay pulp fiction not as a way of making
a living, but rather as a way of putting his own sexual experiences with other
men into perspective, hoping that in doing so he might raise public consciousness about the true, loving nature of homosexual experience.

After serving in the military, Amory had studied anthropology in Mexico City, then married and returned to the Bay Area to take a degree in
Spanish while starting a family. His fiction was very different from Steward's as it tended to focus upon deeply felt love relationships between
men, ones originating in (but not necessarily based upon) their physical
attraction to each other. The immediate success of *Song of the Loon* in
1966 (which was partly due to its strong back-to-nature and pro–Native

---

*Townsend would write thirteen homosexually themed novels for Greenleaf (and others for Olympia
Press) before starting his own self-publishing venture, LT Publications, through which he was able
to publish his leather-oriented erotic S/M fiction without being editorially censored or financially
cheated.

American themes) had convinced Amory to continue with his writing. Nonetheless, he remained sweetly modest about the enormous popularity of his first novel in the years that followed, telling an interviewer in 1970, "I just had the good luck to hit the right market at the right time with a groovy little curiosity piece." His status as a bestselling author unfortunately brought him no financial rewards; in his work-for-hire contract with Greenleaf he had sold the novel for a flat fee and given away all rights to his own work. He would ultimately publish six novels, the last of them in 1974; none of them would ever earn him more than a modest flat fee.

Steward greatly admired the originality of *Song of the Loon* (subtitled "A Gay Pastoral in Five Books and an Interlude") even if he felt no great attraction to its plotting, characterization, or prose. A historical fantasy set on the American frontier, the novel was far from anything Steward would have cared to write; its blandly repetitive descriptions of sexual encounters and its frequent lapses into wildly self-indulgent free-verse poetry were a far cry from the lucid prose (and focused eroticism) of the Phil Andros fiction. Still, in its radical hypothesis of a world in which sexual love between men was the norm, the novel was conceptually remarkable. Steward responded positively to the book as well as to its author, who subsequently became a close friend.

Amory's emotional state was precarious. Money shortages contributed to his troubles; so did the destabilizing influence, after his separation from his wife, of psychedelic drugs. Worst of all, the knowledge that his publishers had made a small fortune off his books even as they mistreated him as an author and denigrated him as a homosexual kept him in a state of constant agitation during the time that Steward knew him. "The people at Greenleaf remind me of . . . dirty old men selling fuck-pictures in dark alleys," he observed in a 1970 *Vector* magazine* interview. "They have no real knowledge of, *or* understanding of, *or* sensitivity to a gay person's needs or circumstances. What's more, they don't *want* to understand—even if they could, which is doubtful."

As a result of their meeting for the panel discussion, Steward, Amory, and a third writer, Dirk Vanden, began working on the creation of an infor-

---

Vector magazine was published by the Society for Individual Rights (or SIR), the Bay Area homophile association.

mal organization they named the Renaissance Group. They conceived of
the Renaissance Group as a lobbying organization on behalf of gay writers
to define and advance the cause of gay literature. In addition to drafting a
list of specific demands that might be made of pulp publishers in the nego-
tiation of future contracts, Amory and Steward subsequently exchanged
copies of their published works, met frequently, and read and responded to
each other's works in progress.

Like Amory, Steward was risking the various indignities of pulp publication—including take-it-or-leave-it flat-fee contracts; bad, sloppy, and
politically insensitive editing; and unauthorized title changes and cuts to
his manuscripts—simply to get his sex-affirmative message out into public circulation. Along with Richard Amory, Larry Townsend, and others,
Steward felt he was not simply writing pornography, but rather taking part
in a vanguard action of sexual liberation—for he had now begun to consider himself as much a sexual activist as an agent provocateur. Townsend
spoke for all of these authors when he acknowledged in the April 1970
issue of *Vector* that "anything that is produced and marketed in any art
field is—and must be—a compromise between the product the artist
would like to produce and the product the publisher, studio, gallery, agent
or what-have-you is able to profitably sell." He then went on to suggest
that through fringe publishers such as Greenleaf a substantial (and au-
thentic) gay literary subculture would eventually begin to establish itself.
Others, however, doubted that the homosexual community would ever
support truly literary endeavors when the immediate interest of most of
the men reading these books was simple sexual self-gratification. One
writer for *Vector* would state as late as May 1973 that since most homosexuals turned to pulp only for sexual titillation, "a writer who tries to el-
evate the tone of the gay paperback novel is doomed to a certain and
never ending battle."

And yet, for the moment, Amory and Steward were determined to use
the "porno" houses as a means to an end. By keeping their writing just
enough inside porn-house protocols to be published, while at the same
time presenting a coherent and arguably literary vision of sex between
men and its relation to the greater world, they were playing a high-stakes
literary game. But at that moment they had no alternative; where direct
description of sex between men was concerned, the fly-by-night porn
game was the only game in town.

In writing his Phil Andros novels, moreover, Steward felt he finally had a chance to express himself. Whether or not his work as Phil Andros ever achieved any sort of recognition, he was at last creating fiction that gave his life meaning. He was also, he was sure, providing someone, somewhere, an experience not only of sexual pleasure, but also of sexual self-recognition. In the words of one such reader, the later erotic novelist and gay activist John Preston, "The Phil Andros books satisfied needs that had barely been recognized [at that time] even by ourselves. We yearned for validation of the pleasures of homosexual sex, for knowledge about other gay men and how they were dealing with this new world we were just discovering, and for wisdom from someone who had gone this way before. We needed, above all, to know we were not alone."

20

Dear Sammy

In the midst of writing his Phil Andros novels in 1970, Steward had resumed contact with his old friend Jim Kane, for the "Mad Priest" had
recently moved to San Francisco. Kane had a little vacation cabin in
Manitou Springs, Colorado, that he offered to Steward in late 1971 as a
work retreat. Steward was glad to get away from Berkeley, and spent his
December there working on a memoir of his friendship with Gertrude
Stein and Alice Toklas. As he later remembered the visit, "[Kane would]
come home to find me folded over the typewriter crying, because the
memories [of my youthful visits to Stein and Toklas] had come back [to
me] in such strength."

Steward was able to be extraordinarily detailed in his recollections
of Stein and Toklas because he had kept such extensive journal records
of their conversations and activities during his visits to them in Bilignin,
and along with the journals, he had taken their photographs and palm-
prints, too. The journals contained lengthy verbatim transcriptions of
conversations with Stein that Steward had set down using a peculiar
brand of phonetic shorthand that he had invented as a young professor, one that combined elements of Anglo-Saxon grammar, French, and
English.

Steward's visit to Manitou Springs came to an abrupt end, however,
when the cabin's wood-fired cookstove burned too hot, causing the roof
to burst into flames. The cabin burned to the ground. Steward's journals
from the Bilignin visits were lost in the blaze, but he escaped with the
draft of the memoir, which he had completed only a few days before. At

the suggestion of the Yale librarian Donald Gallup, Steward then sent the memoir to Gilbert Harrison,* who had recently purchased a small publishing house and had mentioned to Gallup his hope of publishing something by or about Stein. Harrison read the manuscript with interest but returned it to Steward with a brief, decisive note of rejection suggesting that "these are private experiences not meant for the public. So that what one has left [after these private experiences are removed] is not so much a book, as a charming, informative, affectionate memoir, something of perhaps 4,000–5,000 words." Steward then realized he would need to find an agent to represent the manuscript to other houses.

Perhaps because work on the memoir had put him in mind of his visits abroad, Steward then began a new Phil Andros novel, one that drew upon his recollections of Europe—specifically his several visits to Rome, primarily the one he had taken at the end of August 1952. In *When in Rome, Do . . .* (later published as *Roman Conquests*) Phil Andros takes a brief Roman holiday, and while seeing the sights immerses himself in the Italian world of sex for pay. For the first time in his life Phil finds he is being asked for money instead of offered it, but rather than being insulted he is delighted—for never before has he encountered such sexually uninhibited yet entirely "masculine" men.

The most romantic of the Phil Andros novels, *When in Rome, Do . . .* is also the most lighthearted. Steward dedicated it, jokingly, to his alter ego Ward Stames,† with the epigraph *"Teres Atque Rotundus‡ / Nihil Tetigit Quod Non Ornavit,"§* the first part of which came from the satires of Horace, and the second part from Samuel Johnson's epitaph for Oliver Goldsmith. In revisiting Rome through the double lens of Roman satire and English literature, Steward would salute his professorial alter ego while at the same time embellishing his own memories of sex with Roman men.

The story opens beside the Spanish Steps, as Phil tours the little house where Keats died. Phil's opening lines for the novel are perhaps some of the most outrageous ever written by a professor of English literature:

---

*Harrison had begun his career as a journalist, but then married Anne Blaine, heiress to the McCormick harvester fortune. Blaine's money had enabled Harrison first to buy *The New Republic*, and then the small publishing house of Boni and Liveright.
†"Ward Stames," an anagram of Sam Steward, was the name by which Steward signed his more serious pieces of nonfiction and occasionally some of his more serious fiction.
‡"The complete man, total, polished, and well rounded."
§"He touched nothing without embellishing it."

Keats was a tough little cookie. His pictures showed that. He had a body like a weightlifter's, a temper that made him beat up anybody that attacked him, and the greatest gift of any of the English poets. Some of his things almost gave me a hardon or made the chills crawl up my back—me, a tough American hustler with a hairy chest, a big dong, and a hand that was always out. Palm up.

Phil goes on to observe, "If I'd been alive a hundred and fifty years ago I sure as hell would have tried to make him . . . I generally don't like people with 'poetic' characteristics, but when you couple them with the talent that guy had, there's nothing I'd have liked more than to screw him." Instead, Phil does the next best thing: he seduces the soulful young English curator of the Keats house by quoting from "La Belle Dame sans Merci." The chapter ends with a passionate sexual encounter atop Keats's deathbed in the stillness of the Roman siesta.

Phil has arrived in Rome slightly in advance of his sponsor, "Bertie Messer, the duly-elected-by-women's-clubs 'Poet Laureate of New Jersey,'" who has paid Phil's way to Rome with the intention of joining him there for a trip to Greece. But Messer is delayed, with the result that, in Phil's words, "I was at present enjoying the Grandeur that was Rome. Alone."

Phil's next adventures are with a street urchin, then a carabiniere, both of whom he pays. He subsequently meets Duke, a leading American conductor traveling incognito, who pays him; a hustler (who steals his watch); a construction worker; a sailor in the Forum; a policeman, also in the Forum; a graveyard caretaker on Keats's grave in the New Protestant Cemetery; and then once again the carabiniere. The street pickups, the fantastic variety of classically handsome and impeccably tailored men in uniform, and the casual exchange of money for sex—all continually delight Phil, particularly since, as he notes with frank amazement, "sex was just a pastime here, and everyone did everything."*

After sending off this latest Phil Andros novel to Roland Boudreault, Steward began a new project: adapting the monologues of *The Joy Spot* into a film script for J. Brian. At Brian's request, the story would describe successive moments of youthful sexual initiation beginning with an episode

---

*By this, Phil means that (unlike their American counterparts) Italian men who sold themselves did not insist upon taking an exclusively active ("trade") position—rather, they happily "did everything."

based on the opening scene of *My Brother, the Hustler*.* Ultimately entitled *First Time Around*, the film achieved considerable success despite having much lower production values† than *Seven in a Barn*.

•

By August 1972, Steward had finished his next Phil Andros novel, tentatively entitled *Renegade Hustler*. He had by now realized that Boudreault was not trustworthy, and had secured a new porno publisher, Greenleaf. Its managing editor, Ginger Sisson, offered him a flat fee of eight hundred dollars for the work, but only on condition that the names of all well-known individuals be removed, "including, with all due respect, Shirley Chisholm."‡

Renegade Hustler would be the most psychologically realized of the Phil Andros novels, and also the most profoundly melancholy. It begins as Phil Andros, now twenty-eight, cruises Telegraph Avenue among the hippies and dropouts of 1972 Berkeley, and comes to the aid of a young man who has collapsed in the street while tripping on LSD. In short order Phil helps the young man, Larry Johnson, back to his bungalow and once there brings him down from his bad trip with a dose of Thorazine. Over the course of the next several months the two become involved, and Phil helps Larry turn his life around. Beginning with the promise of a highly sexual romance, the story instead becomes a dark meditation upon the impossibility of a sustained passion between two men.

As the weeks pass, Phil realizes through his newfound tenderness for Larry that his feelings about hustling have changed: he now recognizes that the sex trade has hardened him and made him feel dirty. Larry patiently teaches him by example that love requires a continuing openness, a dedicated generosity of spirit, and an ongoing willingness to trust. "I was a suspicious pragmatist," Phil then realizes, "always looking to see what was in the deal for Number One; he was an idealist, through and through."

---

*In response to this act of appropriation, Steward later did J. Brian one better: he re-created the filming scene in the opening chapter of *Blow for Blow* (later published as *Greek Ways*), with Phil Andros playing the young man being filmed.

†The film had a sound track but no dialogue; the sound track consisted of music by the Who and the Grateful Dead.

‡Shirley Chisholm (1924–2005) was the first African American woman elected to Congress and a 1972 candidate for president of the United States.

Through Phil's mentoring, Larry* lays off the heavy drugs and starts looking for a job. One day as the two are relaxing in the bungalow smoking marijuana, Phil realizes that he is becoming increasingly bored with Larry's sweetness, and fantasizes of transforming him from flower child into brutal cop. Larry is initially reluctant to consider a career as a policeman, but ultimately he follows Phil's suggestion and signs up for training at the police academy.

The early chapters of the novel are as close as Steward would ever come to describing a loving relationship between two men, and its florid descriptions of sex (which carry echoes of Steward's early, romantic writings in *Pan and the fire-bird*) are among the most detailed he ever wrote:

> Then in my loins the fire-flowers gathered, and behind my tight-clamped eyelids the patterns of green and red and gold began to fold together, and somewhere in my gut the feathered overlapping and the patterns all drew close together to form the old, the new, the bright red flower of wild unbridled passion, and gradually the petals opened wilder and wilder . . . The world exploded, the pieces dropped apart, and he collapsed against the bed, my hand wet beneath him, my body deadweight against his back . . . For a while we had been one, with one purpose, two bodies . . . breaking the isolation between ourselves. We came so close— and then the tie was broken. The final chants were sung, the soldiers and the kings departed . . . and the mopping up began. I lay listening to the heart seek its level, feeling the trickles of sweat from armpit and crotch run cooling down my ribs and thighs, and listening to the recessional hymn of Larry and the douche. Thus the high purpose and ecstasy ended in the sodden reality of bathroom mechanics.

However, even in his most intimate moments with Larry, Phil continues to take a dim view of partnered homosexual relationships, at one point observing:

---

*Steward later identified Danny Schmidt as the model for Larry Johnson (in *Understanding the Male Hustler* [p. 59]), but his description of Schmidt's sexual technique (or lack of it; "he was almost corpse-like in bed") makes clear that Schmidt was far from his erotic ideal.

A male "marriage" is a kind of lewd engraftment on the marriage of male and female, it always seemed to me, for one partner always loves less than the other and if he doesn't cheat by act, he does so by eye or intention. The basis of such affairs is quicksilver, the foundations sand, and any talk of constancy—especially, if one is a whore, a hustler—as ridiculous as it would be among rabbits in a warren.

Years ago I had removed my heart from its matrix, and carefully cemented the hollow chamber where it had pulsed. It was an empty room, a lonely room untended, with never a visitor. I inspected it regularly; there was no entrance possible.

As Larry attends the police academy, Phil begins to observe the hardening and distancing of his lover—a transformation he perversely finds compelling, for Larry's new crew cut, tight uniform, and increasingly abusive manner make him, so far as Phil is concerned, "the perfect prototype of the male": an authority figure low on compassion and high in cruelly abusive sex appeal.

As Larry then begins to physically, verbally, and sexually assault Phil on a daily basis, Phil finds himself sexually enthralled even as he realizes that both his life and his freedom are endangered. Confused and disgusted with himself, he retreats to the Berkeley hills on the morning of his twenty-ninth birthday for a full day of introspection, and in the resulting monologue, Steward conflates his own highly sexual life experience with that of his hero:

Back in the old days in Chicago, I used to spend that July anniversary entirely alone, if it could possibly be managed. I'd get on the bus and go out to Indiana Harbor . . . take off my clothes, sit on the hot sand near the tall, dry, waving grasses, look at Lake Michigan— and make what a religious person might call an examination of conscience. Well, not of conscience, really—it was more like an evaluation of the past year, what had been accomplished and what left undone . . . Such days of thinking . . . usually left me feeling ready for the final, fatal jump—lower than usual, depressed in every fiber and muscle and gray cell.

Through this afternoon of introspection, Phil realizes he hates his own abject craving for abuse, and hates as well the life he has created with Larry—for despite the intoxicating combination of physical violence with sexual pleasure, Phil recognizes that his existence with Larry has now taken on "the deadening repetitiveness you might associate with prison life."

The novel concludes with a double betrayal. When Phil accidentally discovers that Larry is planning to turn him in to the police as a hustler, he counters by informing the police about Larry's history of mental instability, drug use, and homosexuality. After one last miserable sexual encounter, Phil plants a stash of drugs in the bungalow and departs. The bungalow is then raided by the police and Larry is arrested; meanwhile, down at the Berkeley Marina heliport, Phil enjoys a final trick with an airline employee before flying off into the sunset.

By far the darkest of Steward's "pornos," the novel described the difficulty of sustaining any sort of sexual relationship based on fantasy—and in so doing detailed the complete emotional and sexual dead end Steward himself had reached in his own lengthy search for sadomasochistic fulfillment. A couple of years later, Christopher Isherwood would write to Steward, "I enjoyed all [the Phil Andros novels] greatly [but] I think what made the most impression was the drama of the relationship between Larry and Phil Andros. That would make a terrific film—it *will* make one, when gay films of that scope begin to be made." Others would agree; despite its obscure pulp paperback publication, *Renegade Hustler* received a laudatory review from Harold Fairbanks, a critic and editor at *The Advocate*, and years later the novel found an equally appreciative reader in the literary critic and social historian Michael Bronski, who singled it out for its clear-sighted awareness of "the obsessions which haunt the underside of acceptable sexuality."

After the publication of *Renegade Hustler*, Steward suspended his writing of porn. He did so partly because the policy at Greenleaf had now changed, demanding that each manuscript be "50% explicit sex," but mainly because he had now written about sexual relationships between men as thoroughly and intimately as he could, and he saw no point in repeating himself since there were no material benefits to be had for the effort. For a moment, however, he was tempted to write one more Phil Andros novel for the Olympia Press. After years of catering to specifically heterosexual tastes in erotica, Olympia had recently started a line of books for male homosexuals called the Other Traveler series, and Steward wanted very much to be published by them, for he had a great respect for Jack Kahane, its founder, who had published books so brilliantly in Paris during the 1930s.* In February 1972, Olympia offered Steward a $1,500 advance against royalties (a vast improvement on the usual work-for-hire flat fee), and Steward immediately signed. But then Olympia declared bankruptcy, for the entire future of pornographic publishing had suddenly been cast into question by a new Supreme Court ruling. As Steward later explained,

> Nine Old Men of the Supreme Court decided to take another whack at obscenity, not satisfied with the tumult and the shouting that their first decision had caused. This time they added a few nasties: they said that "community standards" could be those of any or all communities—cities, towns, villages, hamlets, states, localities, or counties. Thus San Francisco's liberal standards might allow unlimited circulation of porn, but what about Peoria or Des Moines? What's exciting and pleasurable in one place may be anathema and apoplexy-producing in another. Furthermore, "to redeeming social value" they added "literary and artistic." Confusion—devastating and complete. Alexander Pope's couplet describes it best:
>
> *Thy hand, Great Anarch! lets the curtain fall;*
> *And Universal Darkness buries All.*†

Luckily, J. Brian invited him to work on another film project just a couple of months later. For some time Brian had wanted to make $*TUD* into a movie, for he felt that these early Phil Andros stories were culturally significant works of homoerotic fiction—and he wanted, above all, that his own films be seen as something more than mere gay porn. During the filming of his $*TUD* movie, Brian spoke to *The Advocate* about wanting to create homosexual erotica that was "more than just the regular cliché-type bed scenes . . . [I want to] develop plot, characters, and real dialog for people who are interested in seeing a true male homosexual film. My idea is to take a theme or an idea and present it totally, just leaving the bedroom doors open." Since Steward liked both Brian and his hustlers,

---

*Kahane had called the house Obelisk Press, but closed it with the start of World War II. Maurice Girodias, Kahane's son, reopened the house after the war, renaming it Olympia Press.
†Steward is quoting the final couplet from Pope's *The Dunciad* (Book IV, lines 655–56).

he quickly agreed to work with them on the project, even mentioning to his former editor at Greenleaf that he was working on "a movie (still in the box) with a base of [three or four] early Phil Andros stories. The tentative title will be *Four: Money or Love.*"

Though written and shot quickly, the film—starring Joe Markum,* a swarthy, curly-haired young stud who had already worked for Brian for several years as both a hustler and a photographic model—would not appear for some time. Just as Brian began editing the footage, the J. Brian Modeling Agency was raided by the police, and Brian was arrested for running a house of prostitution. Most of his hustlers were also arrested. Brian's troubles worsened in March when police seized *Seven in a Barn* at the University of California at Irvine just before it was to be shown as part of a panel on pornography. Two months later they arrested Brian yet again, this time on felony charges of "aiding and abetting sodomy and oral copulation."

Brian responded to the arrest by speaking out in *The Advocate* against the San Francisco vice squad's persecution of the city's gay community. He also went on record as stating that the felony charge of "aiding and abetting" was unique in the history of the prosecution of erotica, and added that he was determined to "fight it into the Supreme Court if necessary." But the case against him was strong, since the police had Joe Markum as their informant and chief witness—and it was his deposition, stating that he had seen J. Brian filming oral copulation and sodomy, that had been used to present cause for the search warrant. Only after reading the deposition did Brian discover that his longtime hustler, model, and porn actor had previously worked as an informant for both the Los Angeles and the Denver police.

The second arrest was particularly catastrophic for Brian's business and finances, for during the raid of his studio the police confiscated all his available film footage, all his moviemaking equipment, and all his financial records. Over the next few months he would struggle to get the film version of *$TUD* finished and distributed (under the peculiar, punning

---

*The screen name "Markum" varies in spelling, appearing elsewhere as "Markhum" and "Markham." Markum's film work is limited to silent black-and-white and color loops and short films, including in J. Brian's *Tuesday Morning Workout* (in which he plays Phil Andros). Markum was also known as Angelo Maggio—but that, too, may have been a pseudonym, since it is the name of the character played by Frank Sinatra in *From Here to Eternity*.

title of *Four: More Than Money**) while ducking creditors, paying lawyers, and watching his entire business empire fall apart. Ultimately the case would bankrupt him.

Steward stuck with Brian through the worst of his legal troubles: in November 1972, he even filed a report on Brian with the city and county of San Francisco, vouching for Brian's character, stating that Brian had "learned from his mistakes," and suggesting Brian would certainly benefit from probation. But in January 1973, after *First Time Round* was screened at the Paris Theater in San Jose, police issued yet another warrant for Brian's arrest. Brian had not knowingly violated his probation—the screening had been arranged by a former business partner without Brian's knowledge—but even so, Brian was charged in absentia in San Jose with conspiracy to exhibit an obscene film, a felony charge that held a possible sentence of up to fifteen years imprisonment.

Jaguar, the producer-distributor for the film, meanwhile made J. Brian's editing work on *Four: More Than Money* almost impossible even as it demanded Brian hand over the completed film. The company had ceased financing Brian's editing because it had problems of its own: it, too, was being prosecuted for the production and distribution of pornography. The star witness against Jaguar was Brian's former hustler, Joe Markum. Unable to complete the film given the circumstances and facing imminent imprisonment in California, Brian simply patched the footage together as best he could, deposited it with Jaguar, and fled to Hawaii.

In April 1973, Jaguar premiered a butchered, half-finished version of *Four: More Than Money* in West Hollywood. Nearly incoherent and featuring totally botched sound, the film was a complete disaster.† Later that month it opened in San Francisco, and Steward, having seen it announced in the paper, bought himself a ticket to the screening and attended it alone. Though appalled by what he saw, he subsequently wrote a note of consolation to Brian in Hawaii suggesting that the poor San Francisco box office results might have been caused, at least in part, by Jaguar's odd decision to hold the film's premiere on Good Friday. He then went on to

---

*The premise of the title is that in each of the *four* instances portrayed in the film, the hustler does it *"for* more than money"—in other words, for personal reasons. The title was not Steward's, but Brian's (SMS to Squire, Feb. 5, 1973).

†Unlike the other works of J. Brian, all of which made the transfer to video, *Four: More Than Money* has disappeared. No copy of the film is known to have survived.

apologize for his own "momentary burst of ill-temper and downright meanness," for he had been hurt and upset when Brian had stiffed him on his (already very meager) payment for the film script. But Steward was a little insincere in this apology, for he was just then completing his (fifth and final) Phil Andros novel *Blow for Blow*, a pornographic account of Brian's calamitous downfall told from the firmly tongue-in-cheek perspective of Phil Andros.

Unlike Steward's previous novels, this final Phil Andros tale was more a black comedy than an erotic picaresque, and seems mostly to have been written out of fascination with J. Brian's disastrous recent turn of events. In it, Phil gets a job as screenwriter and "star" of a low-budget porn movie being made by a Mason Street brothel owner named Jerry.* In an effort to entrap Jerry and shut down his operation, the police place an undercover officer in the Mason Street house as a call boy, but Phil immediately recognizes the undercover cop as his former lover, Larry Johnson. Using a hidden camera, Phil and Jerry then film Larry taking real pleasure in being the passive partner in a sex act with an old friend of Phil's named Art Craine. Phil subsequently uses the footage to blackmail Larry into becoming his sex slave. Jerry, however, is undone by a second undercover agent. Police ransack his brothel, confiscate his records and equipment, and issue a warrant for his arrest. Phil is luckier; in reconnecting with the burly, charismatic Craine, he is given the opportunity to leave town. As Jerry's world falls apart, Phil spends a blissful week with Craine at his comfortable suburban home in western Pennsylvania.

Blow for Blow told the story of J. Brian's downfall with dark humor rather than anger, and J. Brian seems to have been more amused by it than anyone, for he readily resumed his friendship with Steward upon returning to San Francisco after a year of avoiding creditors (and imprisonment) by living in Hawaii. While Brian's legal problems kept him, in his own words, "out of the business for two years," he returned to erotic filmmaking in 1975 by bringing out a new film† pieced together from old footage of Joe Markum, shot before the hustler turned state's evidence.‡

---

*The name Jerry is J. Brian's real name, shortened from Jeremiah.

†The film, *Tuesday Morning Workout*, is basically plotless—an athletic fantasy shot in a San Francisco health club.

‡In *Greek Ways*, Steward notes that Jerry was able to have his film footage developed in Sunnydale before skipping town for the Hawaiian islands; J. Brian may have done something similar with the *Tuesday Morning Workout* footage.

Though J. Brian never gave up his dream of "tak[ing] that pioneer step into the regular theater market," he never managed to do so; beset by money troubles, he continued instead to make depressingly run-of-the-mill pornographic videos until his early death from unspecified causes in the early years of the AIDS epidemic.

•

Following the debacle of *Four: More Than Money*, Steward decided to take a trip to Copenhagen to visit his old friend Knud Rame. He may have been exploring the possibility of once again publishing with Rame, since the prospects for commercially published erotica in the United States were, at that moment, not good. Upon receiving the largely satiric *Blow for Blow*,* Steward's editor at Greenleaf had returned the manuscript demanding more "hots," but by the time Steward provided them, Greenleaf, like Olympia, had gone out of business.† Steward was nonetheless able to live and travel with relative financial freedom, for he had recently experienced a financial windfall. Shortly after Steward had changed all the dollars in his secret Swiss bank accounts into Swiss francs in 1972, Nixon devalued the dollar three times, and the value of his Swiss francs rose sharply. "It's sorta like the goose's golden egg," he told an old friend. "Just keeps growin'."

In early 1973,‡ however, Steward had a tremendous scare: a doctor, after taking various EKGs, diagnosed him with myocarditis, an inflammation of the heart muscle that frequently results in congestive heart failure. While the doctor was out of the examining room, Steward peeked at his medical chart and saw the words "Abnormal heart. Prognosis: very poor. Six to 12 months." Tremendously shaken, he returned home determined to disperse his vast collections of erotica and memorabilia to prevent their being thrown away en masse at the time of his death. Within a few weeks he had placed many of his most treasured possessions on consignment with rare book and manuscript dealers, and put other equally valuable items up for auction. The sales did not go unnoticed; in November 1974,

---

*The manuscript was submitted to Greenleaf as *Blow for Blow*, was later published as *The Greek Way*, and was ultimately republished by Perineum (the definitive edition, overseen by Steward) as *Greek Ways*.

†Greenleaf reorganized a year and a half later, however, ultimately publishing the manuscript in February 1975. (SMS to Wilcox, July 5, 1975.)

‡Steward describes the moment of discovery as "roughly 1972" in his memoirs but other correspondence suggests early 1973.

Donald Gallup at the Beinecke Rare Book and Manuscript Library at Yale University wrote Steward, "I am happy to report that we recently acquired your letters from Thornton Wilder [from a private dealer]. Sorry to hear that the Toklas letters* got away from us." Steward, who had since been told by his doctor that he was not going to die, responded miserably to Gallup that "disposing of all the treasures I had was a severe shock to me, but I did it, I suppose, because *timor mortis conturbat me*."† His intense regret over this hasty selling-off of his most treasured memorabilia would haunt him for the rest of his life.

•

Although Steward would be sought out frequently during the 1970s and '80s for interviews concerning his erotic fiction, he would write no more Phil Andros novels after 1972, and only a few more Phil Andros stories. From 1973 to 1975 he returned instead to his Stein-Toklas memoir, and during this time developed a friendship with the writer Christopher Isherwood, who by happy coincidence lived just around the corner from Steward's sister in Santa Monica.

In his free time Steward also helped a new friend, the independent scholar Roger Austen, to research his groundbreaking study of homosexual fiction, *Playing the Game: The Homosexual Novel in America*. Austen would quote Steward directly (as "Phil Andros") in several sections of the book, and rely heavily on information from Steward for many other sections. Steward's conversations with Austen about his Phil Andros fiction, meanwhile, informed Austen's conclusion that "the mid-seventies consensus appears to be that pornography is more 'exciting' and nonfiction more 'real' than old-fashioned homosexual novels, and thus the traditional [novel] writer is now threatened not so much by the homophobia of establishment publishers and reviewers as by the lack of interest on the part of his [sexually] preoccupied gay brothers."

Steward did some porno-book reviewing, too, after an editor at *The Advocate* who had admired his Phil Andros fiction asked him to consider

---

*Steward had by then donated the Toklas letters to the Bancroft Library at UC Berkeley, a short distance from his home, along with a number of photographs and handprints of Gertrude Stein that he had made on his two visits to Bilignin.

†Literally, "the fear of death confounds me." The line comes from the Scottish poet William Dunbar's "Lament for the Makers" (circa 1508).

reviewing various pornographic titles for the newspaper. Steward accommodated him—but grimly, for what had once seemed to him a genre full of revolutionary possibility now clearly belonged to the lowest form of hack. Discussing a novel called *Hard and Hungry* by one F. W. Love, for example, Steward noted with typical vitriol:

> If there is anyone who can successfully and single-handedly kill off homosexual pornography in the United States, that person is F.W. Love, master of the cliché, creator of the 8-year-old "hero," developer of the plotless and senseless stringing together of dull sexual encounters leading nowhere, all set down with the same lack of style you might expect to see in a fourth-grader's writing. Nothing he tries ever succeeds, but in every novel he attempts to include everything.

Indeed, pulp houses were now spewing forth such abysmally written porn that they were driving away even the least discriminate of one-handed readers. "It seems that as we got more open, with less censorship, that the literary quality has almost entirely disappeared, with only junk being produced," Steward noted about gay pornographic novels in a late-life interview. In another porno-novel review, he similarly noted that "because of the extraordinary flood of worthless pornies, fewer and fewer traditional novels are being written, and the day is probably not far off when none will be produced at all, succumbing to the unbelievable excrement that Greenleaf, Surrey House, and Blueboy produce daily."

The dumbing-down of pornography necessarily led Steward to wonder what else he might now write, for in the loneliness of retirement he found he felt happiest and most alive when seated before his typewriter. In 1975, while visiting Santa Monica, he met briefly with Jeanne Barney, a journalist whose politically minded advice column had appeared in *The Advocate* since 1970. She mentioned a new publication she hoped to start, one that would build on Steward's notion of a literature of erotic experience for the thinking male homosexual. "I told Sam, and anyone else whom I courted for the magazine . . . that my vision was for an *Evergreen Review*–type publication [called *Drummer*] for the leather/S&M crowd," she later recalled. She also specifically remembered that "there was indeed considerable contradiction between Sam Steward, the man, and Phil Andros, the writer/character. When I first met Sam, I was quite surprised to encounter the tiny, immaculately groomed gentleman that he was. But I think that it was the sweetness of his stories that made them so well received; there was a kind of nostalgia to them."

Steward returned to Berkeley interested in Barney's idea for a new magazine, sharing news of it with James Purdy. But to Barney herself he could make no promises. "I'm not sure whether Phil Andros can produce the heavy SM/leather kind of thing you prefer in *Drummer*." He did, however, do her the favor of referring her to the erotic leather artist Chuck Arnett after running into him in September 1976. In the end, he would write several stories for *Drummer* (one of them illustrated by Arnett), and at the same time become a sort of father figure for a number of writers and editors at that magazine, including Jack Fritscher, Stephen Saylor, John Preston, and Joseph Bean—all of whom would find their way to his "hidden bungalow" to pay homage to him in the coming decade.

Steward had by now withdrawn from the San Francisco gay scene, where he felt himself an entirely unwelcome older man. While he still hosted a mildly abusive hustler once a week at the bungalow (dutifully recording the event afterward in his sex calendars), he increasingly preferred reverie to reality and solitude to company. Pornographic magazines and photographs helped spur his fantasies; so too, eventually, would the VCR. To improve the physical sensation of his masturbatory experiences, he invested a substantial amount of money in a newly invented mechanical device called the Accu-Jac. Billed by its maker as "the world's first fully automatic masturbation machine," the Accu-Jac was the size and shape of a toolbox, featured "complete suction, stroke, speed and dildo depth controls," and cost a whopping $595. Steward liked the device so much that shortly after purchasing it he initiated a lengthy correspondence with its manufacturer in which he drolly identified himself as a compassionate uncle hoping to provide the best possible sexual relief to his bed-bound quadriplegic nephew. Over the course of the correspondence he suggested many possible improvements to the device, for he was by nature a tinkerer and inventor. But for the most part the device suited his needs very well. Four years into owning it, he would write Witold Pick, "There is a manufactured device called an Accu-jac; I bought one years ago, and now I don't worry about sex at all."

•

By the late 1970s Steward had become ever more like his early literary hero, Huysmans's Des Esseintes, in his desire to withdraw into a lair of decadent isolation. As he approached his seventieth year he was already quite isolated, for he had few friends in Berkeley and no friends at all in his dirty, crime-ridden, low-income neighborhood. Moreover, he could invite only the most understanding visitors into his home, for it was now so fantastically crowded with his papers, books, and erotic objets d'art that there was barely room for a guest to sit down. With age his insomnia had worsened, so his hours were highly irregular: he now read science fiction and fantasy novels late into the night, and slept into the early afternoon. In doing so he became ever more isolated, and ever more reliant upon Seconal and other barbiturates.

He did, however, continue to correspond with old friends, resuming contact in 1976 with Wendell Wilcox, who was now battling both alcoholism and liver cancer, and had recently had a colostomy. Because his wife, Esther, had always been his sole financial support, he had become nearly destitute in the years following her death. At the time Steward began corresponding with him again, he was living in a furnished room, supporting himself as best he could by taking tickets in a Chapel Hill movie theater. When he mentioned to Steward that he had long since given up writing fiction, Steward admitted that his own days of novel-writing had also come to an end: "As for Phil Andros, I think he's done for; he can no longer think of any fresh ways to describe the tongue sliding around or into or between or over or against."

•

That August, Steward surprised himself by adopting Fritz, the neglected dachshund of his recently deceased landlady. Steward had slowly befriended Fritz over the years because the little dog had frequently been let out to play in the backyard between the two homes. "I had enjoyed his company for four years [now, and when my landlady died] either I had to take him, or give him away," Steward later wrote. "For the first few weeks I kept asking all my friends if they didn't want a dog—and then gradually it all changed. I fell in love, really in love—for the first time in my life." He described in his memoirs the profundity of this relationship with Fritz, the first dog he had ever owned and the only living creature he had ever really allowed close to him: "It was as if all my life I had been waiting for an object on which to pour out all the accumulated love that I had been storing up for so many years," he admitted. "At first it was somewhat frightening, and then I succumbed and was his completely."

Apart from Fritz, Steward's only other real interest in life now was his Stein-Toklas memoir, which Houghton Mifflin bought on a proposal in 1975 on the condition that Steward publish it in tandem with the many letters Stein and Toklas had written to him. In order for those letters to make sense, Steward needed to annotate them heavily, for they referred frequently to his side of the correspondence, which unfortunately could not be included.* Steward also needed to negotiate permission from both the Stein and Toklas estates to publish the letters, a process that would end up taking over two years and would be filled with unexpected difficulties and frustrations, including persistent silence from Toklas's executor† and arguments over potential royalties. One of the Stein heirs wanted to claim 30 percent of all revenues generated by the book, and also to receive a coauthorship credit. "I am hoping (almost against hope) that Michael [Stein] will [reconsider]," Steward wrote his old friend Max White; "if not I'll give him his goddamned 30%, since 30% of zero is zero anyway."‡

•

Steward's immersion in the world of Gertrude Stein and Alice Toklas during the mid-1970s was fascinating to some of his friends but irritating to others, particularly his friends in the San Francisco leather community. Jack Fritscher, the Catholic-seminarian-turned-leatherman who edited *Drummer* magazine, bemusedly recalled Steward's "insistence on his zero degrees of separation from Gertrude and Alice [which] became his claim to fame when perhaps he thought his own notoriety and reputation was not meal ticket enough." Fritscher went on to suggest that Steward's im-

*Toklas and Stein had saved Steward's side of the correspondence and donated it to the Beinecke Library at Yale—but since Steward himself was unknown, his editor at Houghton felt that Steward's side of the correspondence did not merit publication.
†Steward's full, anguished two-year correspondence with and about Edward M. Burns, the Stein scholar who assumed the title of "Executor of the Estate of Alice B. Toklas" but who refused to answer Steward's letters, is housed in the SMS papers, BU, and includes a three-page single-spaced statement about the experience, along with copies of correspondence from James R. Mellow, Gilbert Harrison, Linda Simon, Arnold Weissberger, Virgil Thomson, Donald Gallup, Calman Levin, and the literary agent John Schaffner. Burns at last sent a note to Steward dated Dec. 1, 1975, containing "two pages of a permission of sorts," which settled the matter to Houghton's satisfaction.
‡Steward was right; the book's royalties ultimately proved minimal.

mersion in the Stein-Toklas memoir was symptomatic of his profound alienation from the new, youth-oriented, post-Stonewall gay culture:

> I thought Sam was terrif on his own terms as professor, writer, *bon vivant*. But I think that [the age of] 60-something back [in the 70s] was like 80-something now . . . the 70s left him out in the cold completely. He was a man who was old before his time . . . He could have continued on and been hot in both [the 70s and 80s]—I mean, look at his (somewhat junior) British counterpart, Thom Gunn—a gorgeous talent who [kept] on going.

To others in the new San Francisco leather community, Steward seemed merely pathetic. Guy Baldwin, a Los Angeles–based leatherman and psychotherapist, later specifically recalled Steward's addiction problems, noting,

> Sam didn't particularly stand out to me in th[e] company [of so many noteworthy San Francisco leathermen. But I do remember that] Jim [Kane] and Ike [Barnes] . . . often rushed to Sam's aid when he would overdose or threaten to do so, or had just fallen silent for too long . . . They'd drive to the East Bay to check up on him—it happened all too many times . . . I can definitely tell you that . . . Jim Kane and Ike [Barnes] came to see Sam as a sad, even tragic figure towards the end of his life . . . [for he was] dependent upon pills . . . very poor, profoundly depressed, very lonely, and intermittently suicidal* . . . I remember Jim remarking on the risks Sam took in his youth, and expressing surprise that [he] hadn't met a gruesome end long ago.

To be fair, Steward's overuse of medication—for he was now supplementing his street purchases of Seconal with a substantial prescription for it from his doctor, ostensibly to help him combat his chronic insom-

---

*Though Steward may have experienced suicidal thoughts in later life, nothing in his papers (including his medical records) suggests he actually attempted suicide, or that his indulgence in barbiturates was on a scale approximating a suicide attempt. It seems more likely that Kane and Barnes, who cared deeply for Steward, exaggerated the precariousness of his life situation in their comments to Baldwin.

nia—was not altogether different from similar dependencies that many older people develop after retirement, particularly when living alone and struggling with depression. Likewise, Steward's choice of withdrawing into his bungalow was in many ways quite reasonable, for by the mid-1970s his neighborhood had become exceptionally dangerous, particularly for an elderly man without ready access to automobile transport. The drug-dealing hippie commune two doors down from Steward had brought attack dogs and gunfire to Ninth Street; there was also a brisk sex trade taking place at Ninth and University Avenue, with "hungry males buzzing like flies around a honeypot all evening long," as Steward wrote Danny Schmidt. "In the morning we kick used condoms off the sidewalk on all four corners of the intersection." The violent crime created by so much prostitution and drug-dealing led Steward, as he wrote James Purdy, to "(anonymously) writ[e] letters about the hookers on University Avenue [to] the Brk Gazoote* [which] is using my information [for] a six-part series on 'Sex for Sale in Berkeley.' How we change. The only reason I disapprove of the hookers is probably because I'm jealous of their success with the Hot & Horny ones." To combat the disintegration of the neighborhood, Steward actually founded and led a community watchdog group named ZORRO, which undertook photographic surveillance of streetwalkers, their clients, and other potential sources of crime and vandalism.

By spring of 1977, the Stein-Toklas memoir was finally nearing publication. Since the book would be his first "legitimate" publication since his 1936 novel *Angels on the Bough*, Steward rightly worried that his Phil Sparrow and Phil Andros identities might well compromise his book's critical reception. When a series of photographs of Steward working as Phil Sparrow were featured in a museum exhibition just two months before the memoir appeared, Steward wrote to his sister, "I was interviewed and photographed [for the newspaper] yesterday (as Phil Sparrow, tattoodler) for an exhibit on [tattooing] at the Oakland Museum† . . . Impossible to compartmentalize any more, so there was talk about the [Stein-Toklas] book."

---

*Steward's nickname for *The Berkeley Gazette*, a local newspaper.
†The exhibition also featured an interview with Steward and documentation of his life. The material had been collected by Albert L. Morse for *The Tattooists*, his self-published survey of the then-intimate American tattooing community. The exhibition subsequently traveled to the Pompidou Centre in Paris.

Steward's self-consciousness about the upcoming publication was further amplified by the memoir's title. While he had originally named the book *A Love Letter to Gertrude and Alice*, his editor had thought the title "too full of girlish rapture" and in turn suggested Stein's usual salutation in the letters: "Dear Sammy." Steward was horrified, for Stein's infantilizing nickname for him had always been intended for private use only. He appealed to Christopher Isherwood for help, and together they counterproposed *They Mentioned Everything*, a title drawn from Stein's *A Long Gay Book*. But to no avail; Steward's editor at Houghton Mifflin stood firm. Feeling he had no choice in the matter, Steward bitterly wrote to a friend, "Many may take it for a biography of Sammy Davis, Jr."

Upon the book's publication in July 1977, Steward wrote a note to his World War II army lover Sergeant Bill Collins, and another to Sir Francis Rose. But the letter to Collins came back marked "deceased" and Steward received no response at all from England. "The last word I got was that [Rose] had a long white beard and was ambling around London wearing a long black raincoat," he later wrote to the publisher and activist Winston Leyland. "I . . . sent off four letters to four different addresses I had for him, including one in care of Cecil Beaton, but there was no response, nor did the letters come back."

A number of unexpected letters did arrive, however, from Steward's former students at DePaul. Some bordered on the comic, being so true to type: "I am Ralph Schuler the boxer you turned on to literature," one began. "I once posed for a drawing you were doing in your apartment." But the comedy quickly gave way to expressions of real gratitude; Schuler, now a high school teacher in Franklin Park with five teenage children, concluded his note of congratulation by writing, "Sam . . . I want to thank you very much for being a positive influence on me during those years at DePaul. To a large number of your students you were the professor Clarence Andrews you so well described in the first page of your book. In my case you taught me to think, to keep an open-mind, and above all to recognize and feel the pleasure that can be had from learning. [With] Love & Appreciation, Ralph & Donna [Schuler]." Another former student, this one female, wrote simply, "Dear Dr. Steward, I regret that you were so unhappy at DePaul, but I do not regret that you were at DePaul. You were an exceptional teacher who inspired as well as informed. I was in Mark Van Doren's final class at Columbia. The lecture hall was very large, and so was the crowd. But the emotion was no greater than that in a class-room on Kenmore Avenue, 25 May 1956."

One letter moved Steward to tears. Written by his former student Diego Martinez, it concluded,

Remember that last day of class when you wore a regular tie* for our amusement? We laughed and applauded. And when you told us that you were quite aware of our likening you (in looks) to Clifton Webb? . . . long-ago days: 1950–51 and 1951–52 at De-Paul. My freshman and sophomore years. How I hated that place! Staff and students were provincial. All, except for Dr. Steward . . . You were my first experience with a truly great and inspiring mind. So many of us felt that way. In fact, we became a cult and you our figure. This, of course, was fortified by your Arts Club. Remember that! I had just discovered ballet and was open for more. Your classes had led me to literature. Your club led me to art, opera, the symphony.

. . . Those were special days, Dr. Steward. You had the great-ness that all teachers should have . . . Still, you were not a snob. You told us this, arguing how you couldn't be both a snob and a teacher. Also, you referred to yourself as a dilettante. I thought you were the last word!

Time passed. I heard you were tattooing on South State Street. Scandalous? No. Intriguing? Yes. But how was it possible that you could have left teaching with the announcement to your students that you had nothing more to say to them (the story I heard). Impossible, I thought. Still . . .

I remembered your [teaching for] your logic in presentation, your awareness of whether or not you were holding interest, your manner that brought respect and yet imparted humor and hu-maneness. I capitalized on all these things as a [high school En-glish] teacher, adapting them, of course, to the level of juniors and seniors in a Chicago public high school. It worked. I loved it—for six years. Then came 1968 and the revolution was in full flame . . . At this point, I remembered you again. I understood

---

*Steward had favored a bow tie during his teaching years.

too well what it meant to feel you no longer had anything to say to your students. They now had all the answers, and I had nothing but questions.

If you have read these ramblings this far, Dr. Steward, you can give up trying to remember me among those thousands of "ugly pimpled face(s)." It's been too long. I was too quiet. My name in those days was different (it was Diego). But I had to write this. I remember talking with a group of students before one of your classes. We were remarking on how great we thought you were when one girl asked, "do you think he knows? Do you?"

Dear Sammy: I had to make sure that you knew.

Steward responded,

Dear Diego,

Your letter shattered me, really—left me awash in great puddles of sentimentality and appreciation, and was disturbing in a very curious way. If I had known that there were so many—as you indicate—feeling the way you did I might not ever have left teaching. And what a horror that would be! Grown old and crotchety, and telling the same jokes over and over, with everyone passing on to the next generation all the quiz questions.

Yes, long-ago days . . . I can almost come up with your face in my memory (whether you were silent or not), but the outlines are a bit fuzzy, for standing between you and me are twenty-five years, the deaths of thousands of my brain cells, and the hundred and fifty thousand customers from the tattoo shop. I wish I had a small snapshot of you . . . as for what I look like at this remove, you may see the ravaged landscape spread over the pages of the *Advocate*; a little boy is coming tomorrow to snap his lens at me . . .

I went on with the tattoo shop out here in California until 1970, when—mugged and strong-armed thrice—I decided that it was time to quit. So then I began to write, under the name of Phil Andros—and there are seven or eight cheap novels floating around, paperbacks all, pornies. This may come out in the *Advo-*

cate interview, so you'll know it anyway. That was fun, for a while.

. . . Do let me hear from you again. It was a joy, a very real pleasure.

So began the most significant and sustaining friendship of Steward's final decades. Steward's former pupil Diego Martinez, now known as Douglas Martin, conducted a warm and loving correspondence with Steward that quickly became the single greatest consolation to him in his otherwise very lonely old age.

•

Dear Sammy appeared in July 1977 to good reviews, with the exception of a slighting write-up by the *New York Times Book Review* critic James Atlas, who found Steward's "slavish devotion" to the two great literary women unseemly. The memoir did have its odd moments; to anyone unaware of Steward's fascination with Stein and Toklas, and also unaware of Steward's own lifelong obsession with record-keeping, his re-creation of their conversations may well have seemed like borderline fabrications. Steward's many explanatory footnotes, meanwhile, seemed quietly to insist upon his own significance to the Stein-Toklas story, which (as Steward was first to admit) had been minimal. The book was nonetheless a valuable contribution to Stein scholarship, for Steward had a great deal of unique and otherwise unknown biographical information to share, most particularly Stein's discussion with him about her lesbianism. Previous biographies had pussyfooted around this most obvious of topics, since open discussion of homosexuality was then relatively rare in literary biography, even in the mid-1970s. As late as 1970, Francis Steegmuller in his prizewinning biography *Cocteau* had addressed his subject's homosexuality with both hostility and contempt.

Publication of the memoir caused Steward unexpected trouble with his old friend James Purdy, who was deeply angered by Steward's inclusion of Toklas's letters featuring derogatory remarks about his fiction. "He blames me for their content!" Steward wrote Douglas Martin. In truth, Steward had attempted to shield Purdy from Toklas's slighting references to him by omitting them from his "Purdy" index entry—for Steward had, with a scholar's thoroughness, written his own index. He had also teasingly placed several phony citations into the same index entry, knowing that Purdy would almost certainly prefer to look himself up in the index rather than read the book from start to finish. Several of the pages Steward cited in the index entry bore no mention of Purdy at all; one was for page 260, even though the book had only 148 pages.

Steward played other pranks as well. He had Houghton Mifflin send a review galley to Phil Andros in care of his old friend Jim Kane. And after James Atlas's review appeared in *The New York Times*, Steward published a letter of complaint to the paper, signing it Philip M. Andros. He also telephoned James Atlas at home and, when Atlas picked up, blasted an air horn into the receiver.

While essentially reconciled to the revelation of his Phil Sparrow identity, Steward was much more concerned about what might happen to *Dear Sammy* if his pornographic work as Phil Andros came to light.* He consequently suggested to his friend Richard Hall,† the literary editor of *The Advocate*, that "this may not be exactly the time to pull all the plugs." While Hall acquiesced to Steward's request for discretion until after the memoir's publication, he nonetheless suggested that Steward then consider writing about his friendship with Thornton Wilder, for Steward had recently referred to their intimacy in an *Advocate* interview. But Steward disliked the idea of being so sexually indiscreet:

> Jonathan [Ned] Katz‡ was after me to write down the Thornton [reminiscences] . . . But alas, I am still wrestling with an old ethic (or conscience or something) . . . which made me sort of regret my remarks [about him] in the *Advocate* interview, for I think Isabel Wilder is still alive and would be wounded . . . So all this is just saying, rather tentatively, that I still don't know whether I should.

---

*The note about Steward on the *Dear Sammy* dustjacket had merely noted that he was a former English professor. No one at Houghton Mifflin was aware of his Phil Andros and Phil Sparrow identities. (Steward to Hall, March 24, 1977.)

†Richard Hall (1926–1992), novelist, short-story writer, critic, and contributing editor for books at *The Advocate* from 1976 to 1982.

‡Jonathan Ned Katz (1938–), noted historian of lesbian, gay, bisexual, transgender, and heterosexual American history and author of *Gay American History: Lesbians and Gay Men in the USA* (T. Y. Crowell, 1976).

Steward shared similar concerns with Douglas Martin, observing that "the complexities and nuances of such a subject are worrisome and vexing, and I think I'll end by not doing the article at all." By early December, Hall was pressing him instead to write a piece about his visit with Lord Alfred Douglas, who had no surviving family members who might have been hurt by such revelations. But Steward, still wary of engaging in what he described to Martin as "biograffiti," again declined.*

•

Shortly thereafter, Steward hinted in a letter to Douglas Martin that he was approaching his five thousandth documented sexual encounter. Martin immediately wrote back in amazement that he, too, had engaged in detailed sexual record-keeping for most of his adult life: "I've kept journals of my last 914 tricks," he confessed. "Beats me why I ever started . . . Methinks it has to do with the lengths my scholarly professors made me go."

"With 914 [men] you're ahead of me," Steward responded. "I've got only 801—but the total of contacts with those is near 5,000. Shall we draw straws to see who's a bigger whore? Kinsey looked at my totals, stroked his chin and said: 'Well, that's not bad . . . but I've seen better.'" When Martin complimented him by return mail on his breadth of sexual experience, Steward felt he needed to put his own statistics into clearer perspective, and wrote back,

I fear you vastly overrate my prowess. I said I was "approaching" 5000, which meant actually 4,541—but I began that count with my very first experience in high school, and if you divide that number by the years of my life you get something like once every four days . . . which, you will admit, is not as grandiose a figure as you computed, and certainly not worth a bronzing . . . [Along

---

*In his note to Hall declining to write about Lord Alfred Douglas, Steward observed, "I wrote a [fictional] story about it ([featuring] Phil Andros) under the name of "Ward Stames" (an anagram for my own name) that appeared in Der Kreis for January, 1965, and was later reprinted in H.V. Griffith's In Homage to Priapus (Greenleaf, 1970) as well as in #6 of J. Brian's Golden Boys and a German translation in Him, for October, 1971. Under the persona of Phil it tells the story of Lord Alfred and the meeting." He added, "The whole thing was more or less a debacle . . . Lord Alfred was such a thoroughly unpleasant man that it gives me heartburn just to call up those 24 hours again." (Steward to Hall, Nov. 16, 1977, Steward Papers.)

with my Stud File] I have a glass jar full of [collected] pubic hair[s] . . . and . . . a small reliquary of the pubic hair of Rodolfo Guglielmi, whom you might know by another name. It was my first "clipping."

Martin immediately responded, "Pubic Hairs? Oh, my God, you too! Only I don't use a glass jar. [I] tape them to corresponding entries." Over the course of the next few months, Steward and Martin cackled over the many other bizarre coincidences in their lives, communicating frequently by phone as well as by letter. Quite apart from being, like Steward, a schoolteacher, an art and dance aficionado, a sexual record keeper, and a bibliophile, Martin turned out to be a former patron of the J. Brian Modeling Agency, having hired hustlers from Brian at exactly the same time that Steward had been collaborating with Brian on *First Time Round* and *Four: More Than Money*. "Incidentally," Martin noted in his next letter, "did you ever meet that long-legged, hung hunk . . . who played Andros in J. Brian's film of *$TUD*? Well, I did." To which Steward replied, "Since you bedded him, and I did too, I guess we're linked together too, hey?"

⋅

A few days later, while waiting for a bus in downtown Berkeley, Steward was approached by three black youths who demanded his money. Steward refused to give it to them. The three men then attacked and beat him. After knocking him to the ground, they stole Steward's wallet and wristwatch, smashed his glasses, and kicked him until he was bloodied and unconscious. After they left, a bystander came to Steward's aid, and an ambulance came and took him to the hospital.

The experience so traumatized Steward that in the weeks and months that followed he rarely left the house except to walk his dog. His injuries from the attack, meanwhile, were so serious that they eventually required him to have hip-replacement surgery. Nonetheless, in the week that followed the beating Steward made light of his injuries to Douglas Martin, writing, "I spent the rest of the day at a hospital, getting stitched up. Me ethereal beauty is marred, and I am confined to house. They wanted money and I said 'fuck off' which was evidently a wrong trigger. Well, I'll recover— and watch my language from now on." When several months later Martin noted in passing how many of the stories in *$TUD* had featured black men,

Steward responded, "I was an old liberal when I left Chgo, but life among the blacks [of Oakland] has changed all that. So $TUD has black stories in't, but check all the rest of the sacred canon . . . blacks [are] never mentioned, all replaced by fuzz. Thus doth the world wag."

While confined for recuperation, and despite his initial reservations about doing so, Steward finally relented and wrote up the tale of his 1937 visit to Lord Alfred Douglas for his friend Richard Hall. When he published it in *The Advocate* the following February, the piece was so well received that Steward published a similar reminiscence of his visit to André Gide. Writing of this sort now became, in effect, his one source of celebrity and his one remaining lifeline to the outside world. "There are times, God knows, when I'd like to get away from all the murder and mayhem," he wrote to Knud Rame, despairing of what had happened to his neighborhood, "but I know I'd last about three weeks in the isolation of the country." Instead, Steward remained right where he was, shutting out the grim reality of his current living situation by immersing himself in various writing projects relating to his sexually active past.

Meanwhile Steward's neighborhood became ever more lawless, largely because of the ramshackle hippie commune next door, named Earth People's Park. Home to an ever-changing population of approximately sixty people, the commune created an environment on Ninth Street of constant loitering, drug dealing, drinking, littering, public urination, and gunplay. To protect their backyard marijuana crop, the drug dealers of this commune installed a pack of half-wild guard dogs in its garbage-strewn front yard; one day, while Steward was walking Fritz, one of the attack dogs escaped the yard and severely injured Steward's beloved dachshund. Steward responded by launching a letter-writing campaign to both the Berkeley police and *The Berkeley Gazette* about the many illegal activities going on at the commune. When no police action resulted, Steward began to fear that the dealers had nonetheless learned of his letter-writing activities and soon planned to retaliate with violence.* Apart from securing the bungalow with an alarm system, nailing his windows shut, and placing live-ammunition booby traps in all the bungalow's window sashes, Steward felt he could do little to protect himself, apart from carrying a loaded handgun at all times.

---

*After placing the commune under surveillance for a year, police raided and closed it (in August 1979) despite massive antipolice protests.

•

Publication of *Dear Sammy* had meanwhile brought Steward to the attention of Winston Leyland, whose *Gay Sunshine* was a leading periodical of post-Stonewall gay radicalism and activism. A former Episcopal priest, Leyland frequently interviewed established writers for *Gay Sunshine*; as a result, William Burroughs, Jean Genet, Allen Ginsberg, Christopher Isherwood, Gore Vidal, and Tennessee Williams had all discussed their homosexuality openly in its pages. Leyland, fascinated by Steward's connections to Stein, Toklas, and *Der Kreis*, recorded a lengthy interview with him that he subsequently published and anthologized.

On February 9, 1978, on one of his increasingly rare nights out, Steward had the pleasure of meeting Tom of Finland, who was just then briefly visiting California from Europe. Steward wrote Douglas Martin that "the living legend Tom of Finland . . . is actually a Finn named Tuoko Laaksonen—a nice old geezer, my age bracket, with a kind of long horsey face . . . [Since] Jim Kane and Ike Barnes wanted to meet him . . . I arranged [another] dinner [with him] + [the art dealer] Robert Opel and Robert Mapplethorpe . . . Anyway, Tom and I were toasted as the two dirtiest old men in the Westron world, and as responsible for an ocean of cum deep enough to float a battleship."

During the dinner, Steward had a long conversation with the photographer Robert Mapplethorpe, who apparently told him that his erotic studies of black males had been partly inspired by similar studies by George Platt Lynes, including the well-known studies of Steward's old friend and sex partner Johnny Leapheart. The conversation convinced Steward that the time had come for him to sell his Lynes photographs, since he knew that if he died without placing them somewhere, they might well be thrown away. After briefly corresponding about the works with Mapplethorpe's lover and patron, Sam Wagstaff, Steward placed the fifty original prints with a Los Angeles dealer. The money from their sale came in handy, as three months later, Steward's beloved dog Fritz suffered an accidental spinal cord injury, and to Steward's horror, the dog lost the use of his hind legs. In an attempt to save the dog's life, he paid a huge amount of money for an emergency veterinary operation.

Unfortunately the operation failed and, as Steward wrote Wilcox, "he had to be destroyed . . . It nearly killed me." The sudden loss of the dear little dog to which he had become so emotionally dependent left Steward devastated. Fritz had been, in a very real sense, his only family and his only living connection to the world outside his bungalow. In the coming months, Steward would compare Fritz to the "ideal companion" that the British writer J. R. Ackerley had sought in vain among other men, and ultimately found instead in his German shepherd bitch. In an attempt to come to terms with his overwhelming grief, Steward began a novel about his life with Fritz; but after composing several hundred pages he had to abandon it, for the memory of losing the dog was simply too painful.

"Porte after stormie seas"

During the 1970s, at the urging of James Purdy, Steward had worked intermittently on his memoirs, and in the year following the publication of *Dear Sammy*, a well-known New York literary agent agreed to represent the manuscript. But while Steward had lived a fascinating and highly adventurous life, he was nonetheless far from famous, and his detailed discussion of his homosexual activities proved an even greater challenge to publishers than did his near total lack of celebrity. As a result, his manuscript went unsold, and his agent returned it to him without further comment.

In drafting the memoir, Steward had grappled mightily with the question of sexual discretion, for while he had no qualms at all about exploring his own homosexuality in print, he had a long-standing respect for the right to privacy of others, particularly since so many of his sex partners had lived as heterosexuals. As a result, in writing the memoir he altered many names and left a number of significant sexual experiences unmentioned. His youthful encounter with Rudolph Valentino, which he privately considered the most extraordinary encounter of his early life, was not included at all; in fact, he would publicly share the story of it with a journalist friend only in 1989,* four years before his death. Similarly he chose not to mention his experience with Roy Fitzgerald/Rock Hudson in the elevator at Marshall Field's department store in 1946.

---

*Karl Maves, "Valentino's Pubic Hair and Me: The Many Lives of Writer Sam Steward" (*The Advocate*, June 6, 1989, pp. 72–74).

By the late 1970s many of Steward's friends felt that closeted homosexuals who were highly visible in society needed to be "outed"—since by declining to admit to their homosexuality these influential persons furthered societal perception of homosexuality as something shameful, bad, and wrong. Steward did not necessarily agree with the idea of "outing," but as various praise-filled accounts of Thornton Wilder's life began to appear, he found himself growing irritated with Wilder's biographers. As he wrote Richard Hall,

> This business of TW is a sore point with me . . . My [unpublished] autobiography has the full story in it . . . God knows I am not trying to titillate with "bedroom histories" primarily, but as we have discussed before, an understanding of TW's homosexuality makes so much clear about him. [Linda] Simon in her bio has two sentences about his hmsxlty, and one of them is mine. Well . . . [her] book is a kind of pablum [and] her veneration of the shallow old goat, the copycat, is sickening . . . His hypocrisy irritates me terribly.

In truth, Steward was puzzled by Wilder's biographers, all of whom seemed disinclined to conduct any sort of inquiry into his sexual nature. Wilder had died in 1975, just a couple of months before his former friend Richard Goldstone had published *Thornton Wilder: An Intimate Portrait** against Wilder's strenuous objections. But despite its title, the biography was anything but intimate about Wilder's sexual or emotional inner life. Malcolm Cowley, in reviewing the book, had dismissed it as "biased, shallow and misleading."

Linda Simon, the author of a lightweight biography of Alice B. Toklas, had contacted Steward after publication of *Dear Sammy* hoping to learn more of his relationship with Wilder. But even as she did so, she had suggested to Steward that Wilder's sex life would take up no great part of her work, just as (to her mind) meditations on sexual identity had taken up no great part of Wilder's literary production. Sensing yet another whitewash-

---

*New York: Dutton, 1975. Goldstone went on to write an annotated bibliography of works by and about Wilder that was published by AMS Press (New York, 1982). Richard Hall's note to Steward about Goldstone: "He is the dreariest kind of academic—small-souled and territorial . . . a deeply conventional man." (Hall to SMS, "Monday 11/12.")

in-the-making, Steward responded to Simon's awkward request for information on Wilder's sexuality by writing:

> You are perhaps not planning the definitive in-depth biography of
> him (it's a little soon for that anyway, I suppose) but rather an ap-
> preciative study. Thornton's homosexuality, his sense of guilt (and
> the New England Puritanism which kept him from ever describ-
> ing a sexual scene in his novels [consider especially *Theophilus
> North*]) were a lifelong burden to him. Just how much freedom
> he allowed himself I honestly don't know, save in matters touch-
> ing my own association with him. I don't know the names of his
> particular friends, and I doubt whether anything at all can be
> documented; his delicacy (or self-protection or whatever it was)
> made him write even his intimate letters mostly "between the
> lines." Eventually, I suppose, someone . . . will come along, and
> will pull the deepest secrets out of Thornton's stories . . . The
> only thing I could do would be to hasten the process, and since
> you put the matter to my conscience, I suppose I would have to
> say no [to you].

In a later note to Simon, Steward (who saw absolutely no advantage
in going public with the particulars of his intimate friendship with Wilder,
yet was disinclined on principle to conceal them) allowed her to mention
their seven-year affair and to paraphrase his thoughts about Wilder's puritanism. Meanwhile he obtained a copy of the Richard Goldstone biography, and wrote of it to Douglas Martin, "[G]ad, what camouflages and
exculpations!" But when Richard Hall again urged him to write his own
piece on Wilder, Steward again declined.

Years earlier Kinsey had impressed upon Steward the absolute importance of collecting and maintaining documentary evidence of the prevalence of homosexuality within American society. In contrast to Steward's
own lifelong project of saving all the names, dates, places, times, and acts
of his own sex life, the Wilder estate seemed to Steward to be engaging in
a very clear case of willful omission, one that was tantamount to the oblit-
eration of truth. Steward sensed that further acts of willful omission
would take place as Gilbert M. Harrison, who had rejected Steward's
memoir of Stein and Toklas in 1971 on the grounds that it contained

"private experiences not meant for the public," began a third biography of Wilder.

When Harrison subsequently wrote Steward asking for an interview, Steward responded,

Thank you for your letter saying you considered the friendship of Thornton and myself a valuable part of the story of his life . . .

We might as well be frank with each other. Thornton was homosexual, as you may have gathered, but was very discreet and secretive about it. Goldstone in his biography labeled him a neuter which was about all he could do since Thornton was still alive.

If you intend to do a scholarly and thorough job, then I will be most happy to be of what help I can. If, however, you are under restrictions from Isabel Wilder to maintain a cover-up of her brother's sexual nature, then I am afraid that we would both be wasting our time in discussing his life . . .

If you can assure me no posthumous purification is planned, then I will be happy to meet with you . . . It would be of great help to me in refreshing my memory if you could ask Donald Gallup to give you Xeroxes of the 24 pieces of correspondence from Thornton to me. I would also like to see my letters to him, but he was not like Gertrude in saving everything.

I do hope that you are planning to do a definitive biography of Thornton. Goldstone's essay was incomplete; [Linda] Simon's sounded like a highschool essay. It is time for a really excellent work to be done, and judging from what I know of your writing, you are capable of doing it.

In reviewing what already had been written about Wilder, Steward was particularly concerned that no one had yet mentioned the twenty-four pieces of correspondence from Wilder to Steward that Donald Gallup had purchased for the Beinecke Library at Yale. As a scholar, Steward knew such documents would by now have caught the attention of any serious biographer, and so he began to wonder if they might not have been suppressed within the library. His suspicions centered on Isabel Wilder, the spinster sister who had managed so much of Thornton Wilder's life in his later years, working through Donald Gallup, the deeply private librarian-curator at Yale whom Stein had once described as "firm as a clam"—for Gallup was both the executor of the Wilder estate and a good friend to Isabel, who lived just two miles from the Yale campus.

Steward was rightly concerned that if the correspondence were to disappear, the integrity of his own lifelong records of sexual activity might well someday be questioned. Since he had not kept copies of the Wilder letters when he sold them in 1973,* he contacted Gallup for photocopies, and upon receiving them wrote back a note of acknowledgment which, friendly enough at first glance, reminded Gallup that if scholars did not find those letters at the Beinecke, Steward would be able to produce them as required, and perhaps even to indicate their suppression by Gallup.

Anticipating that Harrison would engage in a whitewash, Steward composed a brief, bittersweet piece for Richard Hall detailing the specifics of his sexual relationship with Wilder, including dates, places, and types of sexual activity. The piece was published in *The Advocate* in May 1980, in tandem with a well-reasoned essay by Hall on the delicate question of "outing" literary figures in their biographies.

Gilbert Harrison seems to have found this account† of Wilder's homosexuality an awkward revelation, for he subsequently insinuated in a letter to Steward that if sexual acts between the two men really had occurred, they had probably occurred as the result of an aggressive homosexual seduction engineered by Steward. When Harrison then asked for particulars of their first encounter, Steward responded,

> We met in the bar of the Carleton Elite [in Zurich] the first time. After he got me to confess (early on) my homosexuality, it was himself who suggested we go to bed. I was a bit too much in awe of him to make a first move at that time. I then said, "sure" . . . This all happened on the third (or fourth) day after the first meeting in Zurich—third, I believe.
>
> Is this what you meant by "at whose initiative?"

*After Steward sold the Wilder correspondence, John Howell's bookstore sold it to the Beinecke in 1973–74. (SMS to Gilbert Harrison, January 14, 1982. BU.)

†Steward subsequently incorporated this *Advocate* piece in its entirety into his memoir, *Chapters from an Autobiography.*

In a subsequent letter to Harrison, Steward explained how he had returned Wilder's wristwatch to the Stevens Hotel after Wilder had left it on the night table in Steward's Chicago apartment, even going so far as to cite the note about it from Wilder housed in the Beinecke. In yet another note, Steward volunteered, "I am on the trail of a Norman Pittinger (not sure of the last name's spelling) who also had sexual encounters with TW. I'll let you know if I can track him down—and if he w[oul]d be willing to share the 'burden of proof' with me. Or have you already found others? Or do you want to?"

In the end, just as Steward predicted, Harrison chose not to see any significance in Wilder's homosexual activities. Harrison also suggested in the Wilder biography that Steward's lifelong project of documenting his homosexual encounters was not only bizarre but also in very poor taste. While Harrison did not go so far as to deny that Wilder had ever engaged in homosexual acts—another sexual contact, unidentified by Harrison but possibly Norman Pittinger, had by then volunteered him stories similar to Steward's—Harrison simply refused to see any importance or validity in them. "If one accepts the essentials of Steward's story," Harrison wrote, "the sexual act between them was so hurried and reticent, so barren of embrace, tenderness or passion that it might never have happened." Clearly, the desire that the sexual act "might never have happened" was Harrison's, for Wilder had instigated such sexual acts on twenty-six separate occasions over the course of seven years. Harrison had known and yet ignored this information. He had also seen (and intentionally declined to quote from) two remarkably tender letters sent by Wilder to Steward, and declined even to mention their existence in the Beinecke collections, simply because they did not fit in with the biography he wanted to publish, nor with his vision of the man about whom he wanted to write.

Though disappointed (and offended) by Harrison's whitewash, Steward could at least console himself that this lapse was far from the only one in the Harrison biography of Wilder, which appeared to largely negative reviews.

•

In July 1979, Steward celebrated a significant birthday, his seventieth. The coming year would be a relatively good one for him, for as the summer came to an end, the legendary poetry editor Donald Allen made an offer to publish a heavily revised version of Steward's memoirs. Allen was a former editor at Grove Press who had retired to San Francisco to found and run Gray Fox Press. He was motivated to publish the memoir by his long-standing friendship with Steward, for the two had first met socially during the late 1960s, after Allen had read through and declined *The Tattoo Jungle* for Grove. Upon publishing the memoir, he also offered to reprint all the Phil Andros novels. Allen had never been in the business of publishing erotica or gay pulp, so his decision to republish the Phil Andros work was in its way quite daring, for up to that point Gray Fox had primarily published the poetry and experimental fiction for which Allen himself was best known. But since he owned and ran this small press himself, he could basically publish anything he liked.

Steward's revised memoir was of very modest length, and included only a single brief chapter about his life as a pornographer. The book appeared very quietly in the fall of 1981 as the 147-page trade paperback *Chapters from an Autobiography*, and consisted primarily of adaptations of the various articles he had already published in *The Advocate* and *Gaysweek*, along with a new chapter about his friendship with Kinsey. He subsequently republished the chapter about his life as a pornographer in *The Advocate* in December 1980, perhaps as a way of promoting the book.

Steward dedicated *Chapters from an Autobiography* to Scott Andrews, a strikingly handsome twenty-five-year-old porn actor who had recently become his lover. The two had met in October of 1979 through J. Brian, for the young man was in fact one of Brian's "Golden Boys." Initially intrigued with Steward after learning of the Stein-Toklas memoir, the impressionable young Andrews had subsequently begun visiting the bungalow on a regular basis, showering Steward with small presents, and finally persuading Steward to have sex with him. Steward was of course flattered, but even so was loath to involve himself emotionally with Andrews, for experience had taught him that all handsome young men would eventually reject and abandon him. And yet, in spite of himself, Steward felt himself falling headlong into complete infatuation: "As I watched Scott," he later wrote, "I felt as I used to when I was drinking: I was a prince of the world and commanded fire and flames!" To another friend he observed, "From the very beginning I found him almost too much— too much to take in all at once, I mean. I tend to stammer or get incoherently lyrical when I try to tell someone about him. I feel like the guy in *The Duchess of Malfi* when he said: 'Cover her face. Mine eyes dazzle . . .' Just so . . . my brain sparks and crackles and becomes short circuited."

The affair gave Steward a fine, upbeat way of closing his memoirs with a chapter that ruefully admitted his philosophy of "detachment" would forever remain in conflict with his highly romantic nature. "The business between myself and Scott," he noted in his memoirs, "looms large for every aging homosexual. In what year does a good man stop it all? It seemed somehow unfair to me that so late in life I should once more be put through the—well, *agony* was not the word; *annoyance* might be more fitting—of having my emotions churned." Steward was, of course, right: just as he had predicted, the affair came to a sudden, unhappy end. Shortly after the memoir went to press, Andrews became involved with a doctor who offered to support him (and, in doing so, to enable his cocaine habit). By the time Steward's memoir was published, its dedicatee had vanished, and Steward was once again alone.

Chapters from an Autobiography was strangely produced and barely marketed. Part of its oddness lay in its packaging, for Don Allen had allowed Steward to design the book's jacket, and Steward had decided upon a semi-abstract red graphic of a phoenix (a tattoo design) on a solid black background. There was no note of explanation about Steward's identity on the jacket or in the book's interior. The little attention the book did receive was positive, however, for it was at once funny and shocking, risqué and unique.

Even as he was publishing his memoir, thereby achieving a modest literary success, Steward watched a close friend and neighbor fall apart as the result of literary rejection. The historian and literary critic Roger Austen, who had interviewed Steward extensively for *Playing the Game: The Homosexual Novel in America*, had been trying for some time to publish his second academic study of homosexuality in American literature. An independent scholar who lived in isolation and near poverty, he was so devastated by the rejection of the manuscript* that he became suicidal.

Writing a professional colleague that "dying well may be the Best Revenge," Austen had picked up a good-natured hustler in Los Angeles and flown with him to Hawaii for a final sex vacation in Waikiki. "Under the influence of Mishima, I have decided to end (?) take (?) the great adventure

---

*The problem lay not in the author's scholarship but in its subject's obscurity combined with the manuscript's excessive length. Austen's book was published posthumously through the efforts of Austen's friend and mentor John W. Crowley (who edited the manuscript to two thirds of its original word count) as *Genteel Pagan: The Double Life of Charles Warren Stoddard* (Amherst, Mass.: University of Massachusetts Press, 1991).

after a week of perfect bliss here," he wrote Steward via postcard. Upon returning to Los Angeles, Austen checked into the Hotel Carmel in Santa Monica alone, and there took a massive dose of sleeping pills. He vomited for two days but did not die, and subsequently wrote Steward again, this time asking for Steward's stash of cyanide pellets, knowing that Steward had set some by in the event that he needed to end his own life.

Saddened, angered, and repulsed by Austen's desire to self-destruct, Steward replied,

> at my age I can't fault anyone for trying suicide, [it] seems to me to be a logical extension of the pro-abortion or pro-choice point of view. And I guess there are no laws against it, against trying, that is, the way there used to be; but there ARE laws everywhere against "aiding and abetting"—so ole buddy if you think I'm gonna put anything down in writing about the whole matter, I'm sorry to say you're wrong. I will tell you this: cyanide is NOT the way to go. You can't breathe for the last five minutes, and it's worse than drowning. So I discarded mine.

Steward remained friends with Austen in the difficult months that followed, but he was unable to dissuade Austen from his objective. He attempted suicide again two years later in 1983, at a hotel in Puerto Vallarta, Mexico, only to have his plan foiled by a friend who panicked and called the police at the last minute. But in July 1984, after checking into a Seattle hotel, he apparently finally succeeded, for his drowned body was subsequently discovered in Lake Sammamish, eight miles east of the city.

•

After *Chapters from an Autobiography* was published, Steward worked with Richard Hall on several further reminiscences, including "George Platt Lynes: The Man." He also produced a general-readership article on Cardinal Newman's sexuality. By far his most exciting project, however, involved the republication of the Phil Andros novels in Don Allen's matched set of luxuriously produced trade paperbacks.

In order to publish the books, Allen decided to create a new imprint at Gray Fox, one Steward playfully suggested calling Perineum Press.* The

---

*The perineum is the area between the scrotum and the anus.

name stuck. While the creation of the imprint may have seemed at first glance a complimentary gesture toward Steward, Allen probably created it to insulate other authors at Gray Fox (as well as Gray Fox itself) from any direct association with pornography. Since the gay publishing house Alyson Publications had already contracted with Steward to reissue $*TUD* but wanted to omit six stories from the original version, Steward gave the remaining six stories from the original $*TUD* to Allen, who began the Perineum series by publishing them as *Below the Belt and Other Stories* in 1982,* specially commissioning a cover drawing for the book from Tom of Finland. Allen subsequently reissued all the other Phil Andros "pornos" (as Allen called them) with similar Tom of Finland cover drawings, renaming the books to avoid potential nuisance lawsuits from pulp publishers. In 1983 *When in Rome, Do . . .* became *Roman Conquests*, and *My Brother, the Hustler* became *My Brother, My Self*; In 1984, *Renegade Hustler* became *Shuttlecock*; *The Greek Way* became *Greek Ways*; and *San Francisco Hustler* became *The Boys in Blue*. *Different Strokes: Stories by Phil Andros & Co.*, a collection of stories previously published by Steward under various pseudonyms, came later in 1984. For each of the books, Allen advanced Steward five hundred dollars; they would remain in print for approximately five to ten years, and after earning out their advances brought in royalties for Steward in the neighborhood of three thousand dollars a year.

Absolutely delighted with the Phil Andros cover illustrations, Steward wrote to Tom of Finland,

> You have *exactly* caught the real Phil just as I had always envisioned him! That cool calculating (yet sympathetic) look in the eyes, the wonderfully sensual carving of those mobile lips, the torso—all is exact, even down to the veins in the arms! I am delighted with all . . . and the basket is superb. People will buy the book, I'm sure, as much for your illustration as for the stories inside.
>
> I am highly honored that you did it, and flattered that the two of us can appear together in or on something† . . . You are a fkn genius, man.

---

*The six stories were "The Peachiest Fuzz," "Love Me Little, Love Me Long," "I (Cupid) and the Gangster," "World Rat #III," "The Blacks and Mr. Bennett," and "The Tattooed Harpist."

†Steward's work had, in fact, been previously joined with illustrations by Tom of Finland in an article on tattooing and sex published (in Danish) by Knud Rame/Kim Kent. (Joe Raymond, as told to Donald Bishop, "Kunst pa Kroppen," *Eos* #4, April 1968.)

Though a man of few words, Tom of Finland wrote back an equally admiring note: "I feel proud to be privileged to illustrate your novels, because, as I've said before, I like them very much and feel [a] relationship to your fantasies."

With the republication of the Phil Andros novels, Steward found himself anonymous no longer—for while the Perineum books still credited only "Phil Andros" as their author, Gray Fox Press made no secret of Steward's name to anyone who asked for it. As a result, Steward began receiving letters, phone calls, and even occasional doorstep visits from new fans, many of whom were aspiring young writers hoping for guidance and advice—including the author, editor, and gay activist John Preston, who had himself once worked as a hustler. Since Preston was involved in erotic publishing, Steward soon began sharing news with him of the reissued Phil Andros novels, in one instance asking, "What do you do, or how do you handle, the increasing number of young sprouts (or twits) who want you to read their novels and 'work with' them on their *magnum opus*? Or prisoners on death row in Florida who want you to help them get a new hearing or new trial? Honestogod, the phone calls and 'appeals' are very distracting." Though he pretended irritation, Steward was in fact very moved by his fan mail, and responded to every letter he received, no matter how boring or mundane.

In December of 1982, Steward was contacted by Boyd McDonald, the founder and publisher of *Straight to Hell/The Manhattan Institute of Unnatural Acts*, a self-published newsletter that consisted of anonymously signed firsthand accounts of real-life homosexual experiences—some confessional, some diaristic, and some written as amateur erotica.* Having heard of Steward through Winston Leyland, McDonald had sent him two highly detailed questionnaires. "I hope you will feel, as I do," McDonald wrote, "that in our sex-negative culture [they] would provide inspiration and therapy to . . . thousands of men." Steward responded, "I'm not sure that the questionnaire will, as you say, 'provide inspiration & therapy' to thousands of readers, but temporary and transient giggles and hardons would be enough reward." Steward had been an interested reader of *Straight to Hell* for some time, and so was pleased to compile an account of his early sexual life for McDonald as well as a further account of his lifelong sexual habits and practices. The latter provided as close to a

---

*Gay Sunshine Press has since reprinted many of these accounts in trade paperback form.

summation of his sexual contacts as he would ever produce, noting, "I have had sex with 807 persons for a total of 4647 times. Several (4 or 5) numbered over 200 times each, though I never had a 'love affair' with anyone, nor lived with him."

Steward had another opportunity to reflect on changing social perceptions of homosexuality when he was contacted by the researcher Gregory Sprague in April 1982. Sprague was an administrator and instructor at Loyola University in Chicago, and was also coordinating the Chicago Gay and Lesbian History Project, which was documenting the development of Chicago's gay subculture. Steward responded with an immediate invitation to visit. "To say that your letter was startling would be a very mild way to put it, for back in the days when I was teaching among the Jesuits [of Loyola] the [words] *homosexual* and *gay* barely existed and were rarely heard," he wrote. "It is astonishing to learn that your activities as coordinator of the Gay/Lesbian history project are even permitted; despite the Jesuit reputation for tolerance, you might very well have found yourself on the street for such upfront work. These are new times, indeed."

Nineteen eighty-two also brought the American debut of Rainer Werner Fassbinder's *Querelle*, starring Brad Davis, Franco Nero, and Jeanne Moreau. In 1950 Genet's novel had been considered so obscene that it could only be sold illegally at a handful of Parisian bookshops, and Steward had smuggled, translated, and illustrated the book as an underground labor of love. Now it had been made into a major motion picture with an international release.

•

In spring Steward required surgery for a stomach tumor; the procedure seemed doubly dangerous to him since it required a blood transfusion. By now AIDS was rampaging through the San Francisco Bay area, and though Steward was not infected, he was justifiably worried about becoming so through the transfusion. While the surgery was successful and no AIDS infection resulted, Steward's health remained poor. Due to the chronic pulmonary emphysema he had developed over the last decade, he now needed a portable oxygen tank in order to breathe, and though he took pains to hide the device from visitors, he needed to remain connected to it for most of his day.

A number of smaller writing projects kept Steward occupied during his final years. He wrote a substantial foreword for the reissued version of James Barr's classic 1950 novel *Quatrefoil*. Paul Mariah, publisher of *Manroot Literary Journal* and Manroot Books, republished Steward's poems of the 1930s as *Love Poems: Homage to Housman* in a limited edition of three hundred signed copies featuring several of Steward's own erotic line drawings from the 1950s. Since Mariah's other poets in the same series included Jack Spicer, James Broughton, and Thom Gunn, Steward was pleased and honored to be included.

Steward published a long article in *The Advocate* in November 1983 about his experiences working with and for Alfred Kinsey. A detailed account of his visit to Thomas Mann in Zurich in 1937 appeared shortly thereafter in the same magazine, and he also contributed an essay entitled "In Defense of Erotica" for Eric Rofes's anthology *Gay Life: Leisure, Love, and Living for the Contemporary Male*.

At the suggestion of Michael Denneny, a pioneering gay editor at St. Martin's Press in New York, Steward then set to work on a series of mystery novels featuring Gertrude Stein and Alice Toklas as sleuths. The writing of these light entertainments would take up the final years of Steward's life, with *Murder Is Murder Is Murder* published in 1985 and *The Caravaggio Shawl* in 1989, but they were disappointing works of fiction, weakly plotted and of little value even to those interested in the lives of Stein and Toklas. Denneny meanwhile purchased the final revision of Steward's novel inspired by Sir Francis Rose, *A Hunting We Will Go!*, publishing it as *Parisian Lives* in 1984. The book appeared to mixed reviews, and rightly so, for the original vitality of the manuscript had been sapped by nearly thirty years of revision. Moreover, by 1984 no one in the United States knew or cared that the novel was a roman à clef about Sir Francis Rose, for the English artist had never achieved even a minor reputation in the United States, and had in fact died in poverty in 1979.* Freed of its scandalous real-life references, the novel appeared merely peculiar and anachronistic—particularly so since Oscar Wilde had used

---

*In his last years Rose had fallen into severe drug and alcohol addiction, and his mental illness had led to fits of violence that occasionally landed him in prison. "It is the last act of a tragic farce," his old friend Cecil Beaton wrote in his diary. "Anyone else who has drunk and drugged as he has would have long gone . . . It's only a tragedy that he has not left behind him a great monument of work that would justify his behaving like a Corvo." (Beaton, *The Unexpurgated Beaton* [Hugo Vickers, ed.], pp. 216–17.)

the same lover-revealed-as-son plot twist nearly a hundred years earlier in
A Woman of No Importance.

The AIDS crisis during the early 1980s was cataclysmic all over the
United States, but nowhere was it more devastating than in San Francisco. Every day Steward seemed to learn of yet another friend or acquaintance who had been diagnosed with the disease. Steward's horror at
the AIDS crisis combined with his own very severe health problems led
to a significant worsening of his depression and a marked increase in his
barbiturate use. A former DePaul student was now providing him with
large amounts of "reds" smuggled in from Mexico, even as Steward regularly pressed his doctor to prescribe him ever more Seconal for his insomnia. Among his late papers are a series of light verses addressed to that
doctor, each one begging him for more drugs. One ends,

> *You don't suppose*
> *(alas, alack!)*
> *I've got a monkey*
> *On my back?!?*
>
> *There's little chance*
> *For that to be,*
> *My bed's too small*
> *For two, you see.*
>
> *So prithee, Doc,*
> *Just once again,*
> *For this ol' senior*
> *Citizen.*

When his runaway barbiturate abuse began interfering with Steward's
other drug therapies, his doctor ordered a blood test, one that quickly revealed the magnitude of Steward's addiction. Upon being confronted with
the results, Steward professed to being thoroughly ashamed, and abjectly
wrote his doctor an apology, which concluded, "It will be easy for me, and
a relief, to let Ike Barnes have complete control of future prescriptions, if
you continue to give them to me . . . I will not go looking for more. I sometimes wonder if addiction is inherited, for my father was addicted to drugs
and also to alcohol—a helluva thing for a pharmacist to be."

•

The last significant hustler-friend Steward included in his Stud File was an easygoing former sailor turned masseur named Ervin Chance. Steward never memorialized Chance in writing, apart from mentioning him in passing in a final, unpublished revision of memoirs. On Chance's Stud File card, Steward merely noted that he had first hired the twenty-three-year-old as a ten-dollar hustler in May 1971, describing him as a "Sothron boy . . . not too smart, but . . . W[oul]dnt be ashamed to take him anywhere." In fact, by the early 1980s Steward had ceased making any new entries into the Stud File, for his sexual adventures were few, and even fewer of them seemed to him worth memorializing.

Steward wrote one last Phil Andros story, "Death and the Tattoo," for an anthology of gay mystery and suspense in early 1990. "The story in *Finale** was absolutely [Phil Andros's] last appearance. R.I.P.," Steward wrote John Preston. In the same letter he wrote of finally putting to bed his long-unpublished tattoo manuscript; now severely edited down, it would be published by a small academic press in Binghamton, New York, and it seemed to Steward destined for oblivion. "It's going to be called *Bad Boys and Tough Tattoos* and I'm on my way to the vomitorium right now," he confided to Preston. "My fairly dignified title of *The Tattoo Jungle* was consigned to the dumpster by the marketing expert boys."

While Steward's home had always been extremely cluttered, untidy, and filled with books, papers, and reading materials, it became almost horrifyingly dirty in his last years—partly because in his eccentric old age Steward became a compulsive hoarder, and partly because Cranford and Blackstone, the two dachshunds he had acquired after Fritz's death, had never been properly housebroken. As Steward lost the energy to walk the dogs, they had taken to soiling the house. Living on bottled oxygen, and without anyone to help him with housework, Steward seems to have been indifferent to the stench that so repulsed his occasional guests, for he had little remaining sense of smell. But these visitors were few, since the bungalow had become so severely congested with books, papers, ephemera, and household garbage that there was little room for anyone apart from Steward to sit. Only three narrow pathways allowed one to navigate

---

**Finale: Stories of Mystery and Suspense*, edited by Michael Nava (Boston: Alyson, 1989).

through the clutter: one from front door to armchair, one from armchair
to bed, and one from bed to bathroom.

A former schoolteacher turned librarian named Michael Williams began stopping over at the bungalow in the mid-1980s, hoping to assist
Steward in whatever way he could, for he admired Steward's writing and
he knew Steward was pretty much alone in the world. He described the
bungalow interior during Steward's last years:

> There were files and pigeon-holes and boxes and shelves every-
> where and all were overflowing with supplies, letters to answer,
> manuscripts, photographs and books. I [later] found chairs bur-
> ied under the mass of things which I had not realized were
> there . . . [Sam] had a huge TV set opposite his recliner chair and
> several bookcases filled with video copies of TV shows he had
> watched or films he had rented from adult bookstores . . . I think
> he spent most of his days in this chair—on the phone, reading,
> watching the TV, or occasionally entertaining . . . no daylight
> came in [because he kept the blinds down and curtains shut at all
> times] . . . The couch . . . had [only] one [sitting] place . . . [it
> was] covered in books and papers . . . At the other end of the
> couch was a mass of things piled up on undiscernable pieces of
> furniture. I never discovered what was here until after Sam
> died . . . The dogs would of course always be scurrying round the
> room and jumping up into Sam's lap . . .
>
> It would have been impossible to cook in the kitchen . . .
> There was [only] a very narrow path [through it] to the back door.
> At the top of the kitchen shelves were folios of pornographic
> drawings. There were tins of coins, boxes of can openers, bottle
> openers, and salt dispensers, piles of papers and lots of rinsed,
> empty dog-food cans which hadn't made it to the garbage pail . . .
> clutter everywhere . . .
>
> I suppose Sam's bedroom . . . was most representative of his
> life in his later years. There was a single bed [and] all around it
> was a heap maybe a foot high of discarded magazines, paper-
> backs, used Kleenex, support hose, and other items of clothing. It
> was like here Sam had really given up any attempt to keep a pre-
> sentable appearance. I knew that he had suffered from insom-
> nia . . . and here was proof of an endless succession of sleepless

nights and the morbid thoughts which afflicted him. There must have been hundreds of fantasy, science fiction, and mystery paperbacks, dating back to the 'sixties scattered on the floor. Most were in very poor condition as the dogs had been running around and over them for years.

The glory of the bedroom were the three nine foot high bookcases covering the wall opposite Sam's bed . . . [which] contained a wonderful [collection of books.] On another wall were some mementoes of Sam's sexual escapades, including some lingerie and gags, and a few small hand-printed labels which he had worn when serving as a masochist and [which] posed invitations to be abused. Here also was the collection of whips, brushes, and even a mace which were suggestive of punishment sessions. There were more paintings on the wall, notably the two he had painted in Chicago; one of Johnny Reyes, the other of the Milwaukee policeman [Jim Brashin].

V. K. McCarty, who wrote as "Mam'selle Victoire" for *Penthouse Forum*, also visited the bungalow during that time, and she particularly remembered how Steward had prepared for his own death:

Sammy's house was a sweet wonder and a special cautionary tale for me, since it was piled up as mine is with books and photographs and letters . . . When you went in during the last few years, there was a note pinned to the side of the first bookshelf as you opened the screen, telling you who to call if Sam had passed away in the night. It was, of course, those two wonderful friends [Jim Kane and Ike Barnes] . . . [Jim] would call [Sam] every morning and start off by saying, "Good morning, you old sport, are you still alive?"

Ike Barnes came over to Steward's place weekly to help him with his shopping, his laundry, and his medical appointments. The fragile old man and the bald, burly leather slave made a striking pair as they puttered through Berkeley in Barnes's old VW beetle.

•

Though much of his eighty-first year was taken up with severe medical problems, Steward received some unexpected attention that summer that did his spirits good. As he wrote to John Preston, "[I've met] a handsome literate cop, a fan, who's gonna invite me to a function so's I can mingle with all the gay cops in the Bay Area. I hope there'll be paramedics available, for I shall prolly faint dead away on seeing all those uniforms together in one place." Steward gave an account of the gay policemen's party in a final addendum to his never-published autobiography. He began by describing the unexpected arrival on his doorstep of "a tall good-looking man about fifty with a touch of grey at the temples" who had been hoping for some time to meet the real Phil Andros:

> And that was how I met Matthew, a real honest-to-gawd cop, who said he'd actually been launched on a peace officer's career by reading [the] Phil Andros novel about [San Francisco] cops . . . We had a dandy afternoon of talk [which] ended by his inviting me to a dinner of the organization of gay cops. And they were the Real Thing—with power to arrest, give drunk tests, handcuff bad people, and . . . order you to do all sorts of things.
>
> On that dinner night I sat benumbed and sweating among thirty-two young cops, overwhelmed by the presence of so many examples of my longtime obsession. I *think* they were all good-looking; I was really not too able to be critical that evening.
>
> "Did you enjoy yourself?" Matt asked as we were driving back across the Bay Bridge.
>
> "Sensory overload," I said, stretching my legs . . . "I was just a little disappointed, however."
>
> "How come?"
>
> "No uniforms," I said.
>
> "Ah," he said, and paused a moment. Then, "I think something can be done about that."
>
> And that's the reason that he and I were headed north on a sunny afternoon to a brunch being held—in my "honor" no less—at the country home of a gay cop, where all those invited were going to come in uniform . . .
>
> Twenty-odd young gentlemen . . . were already assembled there. The rooms were overflowing with uniforms—all kinds and colors, from the distinguished khaki of the highway patrol to the sleek dark blue of metropolitan, the gray and black of a few towns,

even the baby-shit yellow-brown of a couple of rural communities. And the haircuts and mustaches ran the whole range from neat and trim to a little shaggy and long.

The smell was everywhere—of young male bodies and soap and leather with its sharp overtone of polish—for it seemed that more than half of the crowd wore jackboots to the knee, polished until you could see your shadow moving in their lengths . . . I was continually surrounded by three or four of these paragons. I signed a lot of Phil Andros books, especially the one about cops . . .

[In the months that followed] two or three of the guys would drop in occasionally at my Berkeley home, to talk of police things, and other stuff as well—and they were very understanding about my obsession—they always came in uniform. Perhaps the most regular visitor was [the host of the brunch] Danny, who had to commute to San Francisco every evening for his night work in the City, and I got to know him better than the others. In many ways he fit my image of the ideal cop—masculine, without any sissy ways, firm enough in his take-charge manner to seem almost delightfully bossy.

Steward had been hosted that afternoon by the Golden State Peace Officers Association;* he later recalled that four of its officer-members had "let me know that one of my novels [was] responsible for their joining the force." Danny, Steward's "ideal cop," later confided to Steward that he hoped to develop a loving relationship with him, for Danny felt he had found in Steward a sort of "ideal father." Racked by both emphysema and late-life depression, Steward told Danny that he would regretfully be unable to reciprocate either sexually or emotionally. Though disappointed, Danny eventually expressed his gratitude and warm feelings toward Steward by doing chores for him down at the bungalow.

Steward's *Bad Boys and Tough Tattoos: A Social History of the Tattoo with Gangs, Sailors and Street-Corner Punks (1950–1965)* was published

---

*Founded in 1979 by a group of San Francisco police officers and deputy sheriffs meeting regularly and informally at Russian River, the club had incorporated itself in 1985 with the intention of providing peer support among gay police officers while engaging in charitable activities within the California community. By 1993 the organization would expand to include a southern division; a San Diego division followed soon after.

with little fanfare in 1990. The reviews were mixed, for no one outside the small world of American tattoo artists knew who Steward was or why he had written his book, and his academic publisher—which specialized in gay subjects rather than topics of general interest—did little to promote it in the larger world. Though Steward had told his story with a scholar's thoroughness, he had also done so in the gently comic manner of a novelist and storyteller, and in doing so created an odd, hybrid work that apparently pleased no one. Moreover, he had intended the book primarily as a social history of the tattooing world of the 1950s and '60s, and as a result, nearly all the extraordinary activities and observations relating to male sexuality that had enlivened his original journal entries for Kinsey were now absent. Of what remained, a sympathetic anthropologist noted that Steward had provided "a precious link with the gay men of the pre–gay liberation era, and their general suspicion of mainstream culture," and further noted that Steward's writings "have value as an ethnographic record of the homosocial and homosexual element in the culture of the underclass as he observed this [group] in the 'pre-Stonewall era.' Steward and other writers who describe what they saw and felt at that time will in the end allow us to see in fact just how an above-ground gay community . . . came into existence." Other reviewers were less kind, one going so far as to suggest that "the author, the topic, and the book . . . all seem to be located in a semicultural limboland between polite society and the gutter." But Steward's former pupil Don Ed Hardy later noted simply, "Phil's contribution to tattooing was in bringing a voracious intellect and multifaceted talent to a . . . field that was, in fact, largely moribund at the time. The book was a real revelation [to me and] it is still my favorite book on tattooing . . . As trenchant observation by someone with a classical education on the life on the streets and its strange markings, it is a great document."

Steward's last years were not ones of good literary work. *Understanding the Male Hustler*, published in 1991, was a distinctly feeble series of dialogues in which Phil Andros spoke with an interviewer (Steward) on the nature of hustling as a lifestyle. The book anticipated John Preston's *Hustling: A Gentleman's Guide to the Fine Art of Homosexual Prostitution*, published four years later, in which Preston discussed how a young man might set himself up as a hustler and what he might expect of a life in that business. Preston dedicated the book to Steward, noting that "[he] gave me the most helpful guides to the world of the male prostitute with his Phil Andros books, [which] helped me find and define my life as a gay man when I was younger."

AIDS had by now so devastated the world in which Steward lived that the many sorrows of his own advancing age and declining health were multiplied exponentially as he witnessed the horrific early deaths of some of his most vital and talented younger friends. Throughout the late 1980s and early 1990s, Steward kept trying to think up possible new approaches to a cure for AIDS, and among his papers are carbons of the many letters he sent to various AIDS specialists around the country offering assorted suggestions and ideas. Never one for self-pity, he only once described his own great sadness over AIDS in depth, doing so in a condolence letter to his former pupil Douglas Martin—for in October 1991, Martin's life partner of sixteen years had died of the disease.

Steward wrote Martin,

> I wish there were some magic words that I could say [to ease your pain] . . . Out here in one of the centers where the plague rages without cease, a kind of numbness has descended on all of us; we seem to be unable any longer to react . . . You have your faith, which it is good to see has not deserted you, and it will help to bring you a measure of calm. My master's thesis many years ago was written on the mutability cantos of Spenser, and it always rather comforted me to remember that the closing lines were those selected to be graven on the tombstone of Joseph Conrad: "Sleep after toyle, porte after stormie seas, / Ease after warre, death after life doth greatlie please."
>
> I sensed a small note of apology in your saying that you were not sure I wanted to read about your loss. That of course was . . . nonsense . . . Friends are *there* and *are* to be counted on—and as long as I am around, I'll expect to share in your sadness as well as your happiness. Just be yourself, old friend, and your love for Ken and your faith—and this old man—will see you through.

Apart from his early case of syphilis, a couple of later bouts of gonorrhea, and a mild case of hepatitis, Steward had enjoyed surprisingly good sexual health throughout his life. He never became infected with HIV. If any self-indulgent behavior can be said to have compromised his health, that "vice" was tobacco, for it was his chronic pulmonary emphysema that ultimately stopped his heart. Michael Williams cared for Steward during that final illness, which took place between Christmas and New Year's Eve of 1993:

> Sam called me at my dad's on Christmas Day 1993 at about noon . . . He had felt poorly [and] the doctor had recommended he call 911 and go to the hospital . . . We spent hours in Emergency while the staff assessed his condition [and we] passed the time talking. Sam was himself and not in pain . . . When a doctor asked Sam to remove the top of the gown he had been given in order to take stethoscope readings, I saw for the only time in my life the chaplet of roses tattooed round Sam's neck. It was quite faded, and of course his skin was loose, but it was clearly a beautiful tattoo. I remember feeling sorry that Sam had never volunteered to show it to me, presumably for reasons of vanity about the condition of his body.
>
> [Sam's sister] was alive and offered to come visit Sam, but she was frail and Sam asked her not to come . . . I think that she and Sam each knew that the other was likely to die at any time and had accepted the fact that they might never see each other in person again. I was aware of Don Allen visiting a number of times (daily?) and the couple from the house in front of his cottage [visited him as well]. Their little girl sent a hand-colored get-well card which touched Sam (uncharacteristically). Others may have visited, but I didn't see them and don't know of any. I do not remember if Jim [Kane] came. Sam was very afraid of dying and I know he didn't want to have to cope with small talk and encouragement. [He] died [of heart failure] on 12/31/1993.

Afterword: The Steward Papers

By the time Steward wrote his will, the world around him had changed so drastically that he doubted his lifelong sexual record-keeping remained of interest to anyone. And like many collectors, he so strongly identified with his various collections that he found the idea of parting with them impossible. As a result, nearly all of his books, papers, photos, artwork, and memorabilia remained in his bungalow at the time of his death,* and even in his will he left the decision of what to do with the various collections to his executor. Jim Kane's "slave" Ike Barnes was to have been that executor, but Barnes had developed AIDS and died just six months before Steward did. Without a sensitive executor, the contents of the bungalow might very easily have been thrown away, for the little house was a stinking, densely packed mess—and the new executor, Michael Williams, needed to sell the property relatively quickly in order to fulfill his immediate obligations to Steward's beneficiaries. At the same time, the few libraries and archives around the country that were then collecting papers relating to homosexuality were facing a glut of sudden donations as a result of deaths caused by the AIDS epidemic. In any event, no library expressed an interest in acquiring Steward's remaining papers.

Williams, however, was a trained librarian with a strong interest in gay culture, so he began sorting through Steward's things with an almost fanatical diligence. He later recalled that "the task of clearing [out the]

---

*A small collection of Steward's late-life papers had been donated by Steward to Boston University during his final decade.

six-hundred-square-foot cottage was monumental and took me over seven months [working full, eight-hour days] . . . There were books, tapes, magazines, papers, and a huge quantity of things [piled three feet high throughout the house]. All of the rooms were threaded with pathways between the furniture and the walls. I took a leave of absence from my job and dedicate[d] all my time to [it]."

Since Steward's own manuscripts, journals, photographs, letters, and papers had no financial value, Williams was eventually free to do with them as he liked. As he wrote to Don Allen six months after Steward's death:

> I [have been] going through Sam's effects and closing out his affairs. All sad work but constantly interesting as you can imagine. The "collections" are scattered throughout Sam's cottage and the basement of the front house and take considerable time to assemble . . . There are troves of photographs and photocopied articles, masses of information on tattooing, other writers, electronics, France, wordplay, etc, and of course the clocks, books, and artworks. Everything is being thought of in terms of who would cherish it most, and there will be cartons going to various archives and bibliographic centers around the country.

When Williams sold the bungalow property on Ninth Street, he removed approximately eighty boxes of material, much of it either moldy or soiled, or smelling of dog urine. Unable to face the enormous challenge of cataloging it, he simply placed the unsorted boxes in his attic along with Steward's ashes—for while Steward had prepaid his cremation costs, he had made no specific request for the ashes' dispersal, and Williams, being a man of sentiment, felt no immediate need to part with them.

In the eight years following Steward's death, few people expressed an interest in either Steward or his writings. The small group of papers that Steward had donated to Boston University's special collections library in the mid-1980s had never been requested by any researcher other than myself, nor looked at by anyone apart from the librarians who had received and cataloged them. His substantial contributions to the Institute for Sex Research, meanwhile, were closed even to sex researchers, for they were at that point considered a part of his sexual history. Only a month before my first visit to the Kinsey Institute (as the Institute for Sex Research is now known), its librarians finally generated a finding aid for the portions of the Steward papers it considered independent of his confidential sexual history, thereby opening them for reading by qualified researchers. But reading through those papers could take place only by appointment in Bloomington, Indiana. Appointments were granted only to qualified researchers (with the specific proviso that neither photocopying nor photographing would ever be permitted) for a maximum of seven hours per day, weekdays only. As a result, I was the first person outside of the institute ever to work with the Steward papers, and the first person permitted to read through the newly opened section of the papers in their entirety.

The Kinsey library was not the only one to pose significant challenges to my research. I faced a similar situation at the Beinecke Library at Yale, which had no online record of Thornton Wilder's letters to Steward. The book of Thornton Wilder–Gertrude Stein correspondence that had been published by Yale University Press in collaboration with the Beinecke Library even went so far as to state that no correspondence from Wilder to Steward was known to exist. Only when I insisted upon the existence of those letters within the library—and demonstrated that their acquisition by the Beinecke had predated the publication of the Stein-Wilder book by many years—were the letters found for me among the library's uncataloged holdings. Similarly, while the Yale library system is one of the best and most extensive in the world, it had none of Steward's Phil Andros fiction, for it was pornography. And while the library did possess a copy of Steward's *Chapters from an Autobiography*, it kept that memoir in "restricted access" off-site storage, far away from the library stacks. When I questioned a librarian about the restriction (the memoir, while risqué, is far from pornographic), I was told that books with strong sexual content were restricted because they were frequently either stolen or mutilated, and therefore were categorized as "restricted" for their own good.

I began then to realize that while some of Steward's writings had entered various public institutions, many had nonetheless remained either hidden or kept under close guard simply because of the often difficult relationship of library collections to writing that features explicit sexual content. Even the Kinsey library, despite feelings of great goodwill toward my project, withheld from me nearly all of Steward's photographic contri-

butions to the Kinsey archive, its partial copy of Steward's Stud File, all
of Steward's sexual history, his sex film with Miksche, and many of his
various other contributions to its archive, including his sex calendars. (It
had also lost the single remaining manuscript of Steward's 1939 "Chicago" novel.) Had Steward not kept so many of his papers with him until
the day of his death, and had Williams not subsequently kept them in his
attic for the near decade that followed, I very well might never have
known enough about Steward's life, work, and record-keeping to write his
life story. The vast, soiled, jumbled, and deeply disturbing collection of
papers, photographs, drawings, and objects I found in Williams's dusty
attic was, paradoxically, the best possible starting point for the researching and writing of this book.

•

Samuel Steward began his life in a time and place in which nearly any
public discussion of sexuality was discouraged, and in which the topic of
homosexuality rarely entered public discourse. As a result, the various strat-
egies by which men who had sex with men were able to function in society were essentially hidden from view. In Steward's recollection, his early
years were ones of relatively open sexual experimentation and activity
(though also painful and lonely years as well); apparently, only as society
became more conscious of the nature and statistical prevalence of homosexuality within the general population did it become more violently re-
pressive of it. Steward's lifelong documentation of his sexual activity before,
during, and after that shift into both consciousness and repression tells
the intimate story of one highly intelligent, exceptionally honest, and significantly troubled man whose life was decisively changed by his unwill-
ingness to submit to a form of social oppression he knew to be unjust.

Academic and popular accounts of homosexual life during the 1940s,
'50s, early '60s have generally been accounts of marginalization, trauma,
and victimhood. Tales of persecution and internalized self-loathing are
rarely inspiring; but prejudice, persecution, blackmail, and social ostra-
cism were, in fact, the essential conditions of an entire generation of homosexual men who lived through a period of sexual intolerance and social
opprobrium that is barely imaginable today. No wonder, then, that so few
lively accounts of everyday homosexual experience survive from that time.
But Steward was different: in quietly rejecting society's notion that both

he and his sexual nature were abhorrent, he had the presence of mind and the force of character to insist that society was wrong, not he. His various life records demonstrate, as few others have, just how difficult a set of circumstances and prejudices surrounded and shaped his everyday existence.

Steward suffered an enormous amount of artistic and professional rejection throughout his life. Though a writer and scholar of proven talent, he could find no comfortable place for himself in the literary or academic worlds. For nearly two decades the basically impossible situation in which he lived prompted him to escape into self-destructive alcoholism. But after achieving sobriety he followed Jean Genet's strategy of resolutely rejecting the world that had rejected him. In dropping out of the "respectable" world of academe to become a skid-row tattoo artist, he found a place for himself in which, though still marginalized and looked down upon, he was nonetheless basically free to live, work, and have sex as he pleased. Steward was not unscarred by the various forms of rejection he had already faced in his old life (and would continue to face in his new one), nor by the enormous loss of prestige he suffered in the descent from university professor to tattoo artist. But it was Steward's lifelong struggle with self-esteem—in other words, his lifelong search for pride, dignity, and self-respect, or what Gertrude Stein had once so plainly described to him as "the question of being important inside in one"—that was clearly his central life issue. That question of self-respect (or the lack of it) was, of course, intimately connected to his sexual identity. Only Steward's extraordinary sense of humor, his abiding love of creative play, and his equally well developed ability for "detachment" helped him to keep his lifelong psychic misery at bay. In doing so, he compiled a singular body of unique, fascinating, and highly transgressive work.

•

While Steward's later life was particularly lonely, the major sorrow he lived with during his final years was not so much that of loneliness as of literary failure. He had made a brilliant start in life, and as a young man had had grand literary ambitions; but those ambitions had been sidetracked—at first by his teaching obligations, then by his alcoholism, and finally by his obsessive immersion in sex and tattooing, both of which had taken up enormous amounts of his time, energy, and attention. They were also, of course, sidetracked by his desire to write honestly and candidly about his sexual identity and sexual practices. As a result, he never managed to repeat even the modest critical success of his first novel, and he ended his days with only a couple of substantial literary works published in his own name.

As Steward aged, the detailed records he had kept of his sex life—records that had once seemed so valuable to Kinsey—became increasingly irrelevant to anyone but Steward himself. In turning away from his diaristic endeavors of the 1950s and early '60s, Steward also unfortunately turned away from a project that might well have resulted in a groundbreaking work of literary confession, for his thousand-page sex-and-tattooing journal is perhaps the central and defining document of his life, and even in its unedited state it makes completely fascinating reading. Instead, at the age of fifty, he moved away from confession to try his hand at erotic short fiction and pornography. $TUD, the most literary of these efforts, might well have been taken seriously by critics if it had been published in a timely manner in 1966; but instead it was delayed indefinitely, and then simply remaindered. The Phil Andros novels that followed were works of significant merit, but they were part of a movement so far outside the canon of contemporary literature that they slipped by largely unnoticed at the time of their original publication. Don Allen reissued the Phil Andros novels in the early 1980s, but unwittingly did so at the height of the AIDS crisis, and as a result, critical response to the work was once again muted. Then Steward simply ran out of steam: discouraged by constant literary rejection, slowed by barbiturate use, traumatized by the AIDS epidemic, and weighed down by his own serious health concerns, he seems to have lacked the necessary stamina and ambition to persist. Accepting the fact of his literary failure during those final, isolated years, he repeatedly referred to his existence in letters to friends, only half jokingly, as "my happily wasted life."

•

Each generation of writers reinvents its perception of sexuality through novels, poetry, and autobiographical writing, and in the process rebels against the perceptions and experiences of the generation before. For male homosexuals in the twentieth-century United States, these shifts in perception have up to now been largely described merely as "pre-

Stonewall" and "post-Stonewall." But clearly there have been other equally significant generational breaks: between pre–World War II and post–World War II; pre-Kinsey and post-Kinsey; pre-McCarthy and post-McCarthy; pre-AIDS and post-AIDS; and, most recently, pre-Internet and Internet. Miraculously, Steward passed through all but the last of these periods, diligently documenting his myriad sexual and social experiences as he went.

During the course of Steward's lifetime, increasingly forthright descriptions of sex entered literary discourse, at first by being published overseas, then through the boom in pulp fiction, and then, later still, because of significant changes in American anti-obscenity laws. In retrospect Steward was, in his way, in the vanguard of all these cultural shifts, though certainly only a minor presence in any of them. During the 1930s he attempted to publish his erotic works in Paris; in the 1940s he created handmade "underground" pornography; in the 1950s he contributed to European homophile publications; in the 1960s and '70s he published homosexual pornography. He had started out in the 1930s as a published poet and a literary novelist, and by 1940 he counted a number of significant literary figures as his friends; but by 1970 he was happy enough simply to publish erotic pulp fiction under the pseudonym of Phil Andros and to live in obscurity in the slums of Berkeley. He never expected his Phil Andros novels to be read as literature, and they probably never will be. Even so, their presentation of the nature of male homosexuality is remarkably well thought out, and today these pornographic novels can easily be seen as precursors to post-Stonewall gay literary writing, in which the worlds of homoerotic experience and everyday living are one and the same. Steward's unpublished writings, meanwhile—his various journals, letters, and diaries—are even more compelling, particularly when combined with his impressively thorough visual and statistical documentation of his sex life. Through them, he has left behind an extraordinarily clear and direct record of the American homosexual experience in the middle of the twentieth century, as well as a fascinating account of how various extraordinary homosexual contemporaries—Stein, Toklas, Wilder, Rose, Wescott, Green, Lynes, and Amory, to name just a few— quietly reconciled their nonmainstream sexual orientations with their cultural and social ambitions, most of which required them to engage in various forms of hypocrisy and self-censorship in order to succeed.

Partly literary, partly diaristic, partly epistolary, partly visual, and partly statistical, Steward's lifelong documentation of his sexual activity was something he began simply as a way of creating order and sense out of his daily experience of the world. He adapted the project to suit the more rigorous demands of Alfred Kinsey, and later still he mined it for his fiction. This lifelong project was, throughout its evolution, an attempt both to demystify homosexual erotic activity and at the same time to present it in all its physical and emotional complexity.

In his intense lifelong focus on the self, Steward in some ways resembles his early literary hero, Huysmans. And indeed, he patterned his life from his earliest years on the alienated, decadent, and "wicked" ideal of Des Esseintes in *Against the Grain*. There was surely a good deal of Des Esseintes's closed-off narcissism in Steward, and in later life that closed-off quality evolved even further, into a melancholic disappointment verging on real bitterness. But unlike Des Esseintes, who abandoned himself to sensual solipsism, Steward rejected both the decadent and the mystical in his understanding of his sexual nature, and also discarded the notion of sin. The clarity, honesty, and plainspoken good humor of his sexual confessions, even at their bleakest moments, connect him instead to Kinsey's systematic, scientific study of sexuality—and through that study to an abiding belief in the healing power of truth.

NOTES

1: "WILD—HOG WILD"

3 *"stern and austere Puritanism"*: Steward, unpublished autobiography manuscript (henceforth "Early Chapters"), p. 335. Samuel M. Steward Papers.

3 *"cooking and serving, making"*: Steward, "Early Chapters," p. 35.

5 *"showy little pieces"*: Steward, *Chapters from an Autobiography* (henceforth *Chapters*), p. 3.

7 *"in my sheltered little-boy"*: Ibid., p. 7.

7 *"'Choice' had no part"*: Steward, "Early Chapters," p. 57.

8 *"Midwest American views"*: Steward, *Chapters*, p. 15.

8 *"over in less than"*: Steward, "Threefold Autobiography," unpublished manuscript, pp. 64–65. Samuel M. Steward Papers.

8 *"So began my criminal"*: Steward, "Early Chapters," p. 65.

9 *"I figured I was"*: Steward, *Straight to Hell* interview, Samuel M. Steward Papers. (N.B.: Though Steward provided this interview to McDonald for *Straight to Hell*, my citations are drawn from Steward's manuscript response to McDonald in the Samuel M. Steward Papers.)

9 *a boy who stole*: Steward, "Early Chapters," p. 46.

10 *"resolutely rejected a world"*: See Paul Robinson, *Gay Lives: Homosexual Autobiography from John Addington Symonds to Paul Monette*, p. 211, for a beautifully concise description of Genet's youthful development and worldview.

10 *"The personality which has"*: Steward, "Early Chapters," p. 48.

10 *"not only did I"*: Steward, *Chapters*, p. 12.

11 *"dabbled largely in [other]"*: "Threefold Autobiography," p. 4.

12 *"The propagandizing of my"*: Ibid., p. 72.

12 *"'I want to know'"*: Steward, "Early Chapters," p. 15.

13 *"a sad little experience"*: Ibid., p. 16.

13 *"It was not until"*: Steward to Kinsey, Feb. 8, 1950.

14 *"My aunts' house on"*: Steward, "Early Chapters," p. 22.

15 *"[Valentino] was returning"*: Carl Maves, "Valentino's Pubic Hair and Me," *Advocate*, June 6, 1989, pp. 73–74.

17 *"For my entrance essay"*: Steward, "Early Chapters," pp. 18–19.

18 *"I inhaled him"*: Ibid., pp. 110–12.

18 *"[When] I wrote a"*: Ibid., p. 111.

18 *Nonetheless Steward met a*: Ibid., p. 18.

18 *"early poetry by Pound"*: Ibid., pp. 96–97.

19 *"a single English or"*: Van Vechten quoted in Roger Austen, *Playing the Game: The Homosexual Novel in America*, p. 43.

19 *"none of us was"*: This quote comes from the Phil Andros story "Arrangement in Black and White," from *$TUD*, p. 143. The observation is made by the character Benjamin Thomas, whose background and interests are similar if not identical to those of Steward himself.

20 The Strange Confession: *The Strange Confession of Monsieur Montcairn* was published in a limited edition of 750 copies. (Austen, *Playing the Game*, pp. 46–47, footnote p. 56.) The anonymous source cited by Austen for this information was most probably Steward himself, who is quoted anonymously elsewhere in the book. Austen relied heavily on Steward for a great deal of information, only some of which he attributed to "Phil Andros."

20 *"This is yours"*: *Contemporary Verse*, vol. 25, no. 4, Oct. 1929 (Atlantic City, N.J.): n.p.

21 *The form of the poem*: Steward, "The Passion and the Soul of Petrarch," *Sewanee Review* 41 (Oct. 1933): 419–29.

21 *"Sam Steward made his"*: "Gossip on Parnassus" by Atticus Mus (Benjamin Musser), in *Bozart and C[ontemporary].V[erse].*, March–April 1930 [np; Steward Scrapbook, Samuel M. Steward Papers].

22 *"reefer, bathtub gin"*: Eric Garber, "T'Ain't Nobody's Bizness: Homosexuality in 1920s Harlem," in *Black Men—White Men: A Gay Anthology*, ed. Michael J. Smith (San Francisco: Gay Sunshine Press, 1983), p. 13.

22 *"but it drains you"*: Steward to John Preston, Nov. 21, 1980, Samuel M. Steward Papers.

22 *"That much is subtly"*: "Sophistication Is Dominant Note in Ohio Poet's Book," *Dallas News*, May 1930 (unsigned; n.p.; Steward scrapbook, Samuel M. Steward Papers).

22 *"'Pan and the fire-bird'"*: "Mostly Words" (column by Arthur J. Busch, *Brooklyn Citizen*, April 13, 1930 (np; Steward scrapbook, Samuel M. Steward Papers).

23 *"Given my loathing of"*: Steward, "Early Chapters," p. 101.

23 *"It's like backing into"*: Ibid., pp. 102–103.

24 *"I went into the church"*: Ibid., p. 115.

25 *"Having developed a passionate"*: Steward, "J.-K. Huysmans and George Moore," *Romantic Review*, vol. XXV, no. 3 (July–September 1934): 197–206.

25 *"innuendoes and crafty indictments"*: Steward, "Early Chapters," p. 115.

26 *"My allegiance to Catholicism"*: Ibid., p. 170.

2: TERES ATQUE ROTUNDUS

32 *"Trying to teach cowboys"*: Steward, *Chapters*, p. 33.

32 *"enough happened to weaken"*: Steward, "Early Chapters," p. 163.

32 *"pop[ped] out of the"*: Steward, *Chapters*, p. 33.

32 *"We had a two-week"*: Steward, "Early Chapters," p. 162.

33 *"one day in class"*: Steward to Stein, Nov. 19, 1933. Gertrude Stein and Alice B.

Toklas Papers, Yale Collection of American Literature, Beinecke Rare Book and Manuscript Library. (Unless noted, all letters from Steward to Stein are in this archive.)

33 *Steward's first letter to Stein*: Steward to Stein, Dec. 13, 1934.

33 *He quickly set up*: Toklas to Steward, March 24, 1935; *Dear Sammy*, pp. 126–27.

34 *"there are spots in"*: Stein to Steward, postmarked Sept. 2, 1935, Bilignin par Belley, Ain; *Dear Sammy*, p. 128.

34 The Commonweal: Steward, *Chapters*, p. 34.

34 *"The whole scene around"*: Steward to Stein, Oct. 26, 1935.

34 *"fine upstanding young [male]"*: Steward, *Chapters*, p. 37.

35 *"If a don of"*: Steward, "Early Chapters," p. 174.

35 *"When I wrote [Pan and the fire-bird]"*: Steward to Stein, Oct. 26, 1935.

36 *"I had two hundred"*: Steward to Stein, Feb. 2, 1936.

36 *"direct, dramatic subjectivism"*: Stanley Young, "Trouble in Academe," *New York Times*, May 31, 1936.

37 *"Four hours after the"*: "Removal Based on Rumors, Says Ousted College Professor," *Columbus Dispatch*, June 13, 1936 [np]. Steward scrapbook, Samuel M. Steward Papers.

37 *But an official investigation*: "Committee Notes and Reports: Academic Freedom and Tenure at Washington State College," *Bulletin of the American Association of University Professors*, vol. XXIII, no. 1 (Jan. 1937), pp. 19–21.

38 *"Tomorrow I am posting"*: Steward to Stein, June 11, 1936.

38 *"My Dear Sam"*: Stein to Steward, June 16, 1936, Bilignin; *Dear Sammy*, pp. 129–30.

38 *"but I sent a"*: Steward, *Chapters*, pp. 39–40.

39 *"Zabel worked us unmercifully"*: Ibid., pp. 40–41.

40 *"If I accomplished nothing"*: Steward, interview by Gregory Sprague, Chicago Historical Society. Samuel M. Steward Papers.

40 *"Whitman was no mere"*: Newton Arvin, *Whitman*, p. 277. This example of Arvin's own homophobia was first brought to my attention by Donald Webster Cory, *The Homosexual in America*, p. 164.

40 *"Zabel turned me into"*: Steward, "Early Chapters," p. 191.

40 *"If you were hypocrite"*: Ibid., pp. 189–90.

41 *"By the time I"*: Ibid., p. 88.

41 *"These were the vacant"*: Ibid., p. 83.

41 *"My classes are always"*: Steward, *Dear Sammy*, p. 53.

41 *Last to join this*: Steward, "Early Chapters," p. 192.

41 *with whom Steward had*: Steward to Jan Bouman, Aug. 15, 1988. Samuel M. Steward Papers.

42 *"sojourn the latter part"*: "All the World's a Vacationland for Professors: Loyolans Seek Diversion in Europe," Loyola newspaper [?], undated, part 3, page 2. (The citation of Wednesday, August 4, corresponds to the 1937 calendar.)

44 *"hardly . . . Wordsworth's 'pastoral farms'"*: Steward, *Chapters*, pp. 46–47.

45 *"[Lord Alfred Douglas] opened"*: Ibid., pp. 47–51.

47 *"brave and brilliant stand"*: Ibid., p. 53.

47 *As a result*: For the best and most concise reading of Gide's contribution to gay autobiography, see Paul Robinson, *Gay Lives: Homosexual Autobiography from John Addington Symonds to Paul Monette*, specifically pp. 172–73.

47 *"[While] I think that"*: *Gay Sunshine Interviews*, vol. 2, p. 228.

48 *Gide was appalled*: Steward, *Chapters*, p. 55.

49 *"I was not old enough"*: Robinson, *Gay Lives*, p. 199.

50 *For the next two years*: Steward, *Chapters*, p. 62.

50 *"We have been having"*: *Dear Sammy*, footnote, p. 177.

50 *"I am at the Carleton-Elite"*: Stein to Wilder, Sept. 7, 1937 (postcard, transcribed by Wilder). Gertrude Stein, Thornton Wilder, *The Letters of Gertrude Stein and Thornton Wilder*, ed. Edward Burns, Ulla E. Dydo, and William Rice, p. 168.

51 *"basic dishonesty [that he]"*: *Stein-Wilder*, footnote, p. 169.

51 *"My feelings about [Wilder]"*: Steward, "Early Chapters," p. 154.

51 *"Our week began"*: Steward, *Chapters*, p. 71.

52 *"During those several"*: Ibid., pp. 72–74.

53 The Magic Mountain: Ibid., p. 75.

53 *"With what nervous heart"*: Steward refers to the conversation with Wilder in "A Visit with Thomas Mann," *Advocate*, Sept. 15, 1983, pp. 28–31; Wilder notes the visit in his letter to Stein, Sept. 13, 1937 (*Stein-Wilder*, p. 175), which also remarks on Steward's visit.

53 *At Rolland's door*: "A Visit with Thomas Mann," *Advocate*, Sept. 15, 1983, pp. 28–31.

53 *"Montreux was frightfully dull"*: "Sept 12–13 Montreux. Lac Leman . . . the search for Romain Roland. 'Il est malade.' The castle of Chillon." Steward, 1937 travel diary, Samuel M. Steward Papers.

54 *"Steward [is] a fine"*: Steward to Stein, Sept. 15, 1937.

54 *"I'm glad you liked"*: Stein to Wilder, Sept. 13, 1937, *Stein-Wilder*, pp. 174–75.

54 *"the last of the"*: Wilder to Stein, Sept. 17, 1937, *Stein-Wilder*, p. 177.

3: THE CHICAGO NOVEL

56 *"I read books on the ballet"*: Steward, "Early Chapters," pp. 15–17.

57 *Erotically conceived ballets such as*: loosely paraphrased from Martin Green, *Children of the Sun: A Narrative of "Decadence" in England after 1918*, pp. 27–28, 31.

58 *"The only communal feeling"*: "Steward on Sex: Author 'Phil Andros' Looks Back" (interview by Eric Rofes), *Advocate*, Dec.11, 1984, pp. 88–90. (Henceforth, Rofes interview.)

59 *"There were two or three"*: Ibid.

59 *"I was not really 'afraid'"*: Steward, *Straight to Hell* interview. The story of being tied up is substantiated both by entries in the Stud File and in an undated letter from Wendell Wilcox to Gertrude Stein, Gertrude Stein and Alice B. Toklas Papers, Yale Collection of American Literature, Beinecke Rare Book and Manuscript Library.

60 *"feasting with panthers"*: Neil McKenna, *The Secret Life of Oscar Wilde*, pp. 203–204.

60 *"From an alley on"*: Steward, "Early Chapters," pp. 185–86.

60 *"there is a quality"*: Steward, "On Chicago," *Illinois Dental Journal* 15 (August 1946), pp. 338–39, Steward Papers.

60 *"Alice is delighted with"*: Stein to Steward, postmark illegible, Nov. ?, 1937, 27 Rue de Fleurus, Paris VI; *Dear Sammy*, p. 134.

61 *"We were all at"*: Stein to Steward, postmarked January 12, 1938, 5 Rue Christine, Paris VI; *Dear Sammy*, p. 135.

62 *"You are right"*: Steward to Stein, March 13, 1938.

62 *"Every time Thornton"*: Steward, *Chapters*, p. 76.

62 *Wilder sent a follow-up*: Wilder to Steward, March 9, 1938 (from Tucson). Thornton Wilder Papers, Yale Collection of American Literature, Beinecke Rare Book and Manuscript Library.

62 *"Now do compose yourself"*: Wilder to Steward, May 13, 1938. Thornton Wilder Papers, Yale Collection of American Literature.

63 *During early 1938, Steward*: Steward, *Dear Sammy*, footnote, p. 136.

63 *He then asked her*: Steward to Stein, June 30, 1938.

63 *"I got whapped by"*: Steward to Stein, Aug. 6, 1938.

63 *"All my sympathy on"*: Wilder to Steward, August 22, 1938. Thornton Wilder Papers, Yale Collection of American Literature.

64 *"I think I am"*: Steward to Stein, undated (probably Aug. 1938).

64 *He wrote to Stein*: Steward to Stein, Oct. 31, 1938.

64 *"What do you mean"*: Wilder to Steward, Feb. 17, 1939. Thornton Wilder Papers, Yale Collection of American Literature.

64 *"all the dirty words"*: Steward, *Dear Sammy*, p. 56. Steward attributes this comment to Gertrude Stein, to whom he showed the manuscript in July 1939.

64 *"The novel . . . is all"*: Steward to Stein, Jan. 23, 1939.

65 *"The Ides of March"*: Steward to Stein, March 18, 1939.

65 *"I have a strange"*: Steward to Stein, April 10, 1939.

65 *"Forgive a hasty [post]card"*: Wilder to Stewart [sic], April 8, 1939, postmarked New Haven, Connecticut. Thornton Wilder Papers, Yale Collection of American Literature.

65 *"I met [William] Saroyan"*: Steward to Stein, June [July?] 8, 1939.

65 *"because Paris brings it"*: Steward to Stein, postcard, June 23, 1939.

66 *"Dearest ones"*: Steward to Stein, postcard, June 30, 1939.

66 *"Yes, you know me"*: Wilder to Stein, Aug. 20, 1939; *Stein-Wilder*, p. 242.

66 *His plan was to*: Steward to Stein, June [July?] 8, 1939.

67 *"You're a motherable person"*: Steward, *Dear Sammy*, p. 54.

67 *"I suppose I might"*: Leyland, *Gay Sunshine* interview, p. 34 in manuscript, Samuel M. Steward Papers.

69 *"In 1937–38 I wrote"*: Steward, *Chapters*, p. 309.

69 *"a thoroughly hedonistic"*: Steward, *Dear Sammy*, p. 75.

69 *"[One of the Arab soldiers was]"*: Steward, "Toilet Correspondence," Kinsey Institute.

70 *"I was [always] fascinated"*: Rose, *Saying Life: The Memoirs of Sir Francis Rose* (London: Cassell, 1961) (hereafter, *Saying Life*), p. 12.

70 *As a result, Rose*: Michael De Cossart, "Sir Francis Rose (1909–1979): A Biographical Sketch," in Sir Francis Rose, *1909–1979: A Retrospective* (London: England & Co., [1988]).

71 *By his early twenties*: Rose, *Saying Life*, p. 63.

71 *Rose subsequently began*: Ibid., p. 209.

72 *"like Icarus plunging into"*: Ibid., p. 55.

72 *Though Toklas thought him*: The Rose-Stein correspondence at Yale dates from 1931.

72 *Stein had collected Rose's*: James Mellow, *Charmed Circle* (New York: Avon, 1975), p. 433.

72 *"Sam Steward, a friend"*: Rose, *Saying Life*, p. 363.

72 *"I liked Francis."*: Steward, *Dear Sammy*, p. 76.

73 *"Did [Thornton] tell you"*: Steward, *Dear Sammy*, pp. 55–57. The conversation must have taken place during this last visit with Stein, since she had only had her first opportunity to look at the "Chicago" manuscript while Steward was traveling in North Africa.

74 *"Gertrude . . . said . . . the thing"*: Steward, "Early Chapters," p. 309.

75 *"ate together, then had"*: Steward to Stein, Aug. 29, 1939 [?], Rouen.

75 *"[I have] been on"*: Steward to Stein, Sept. 15, 1939.

4: "THE NAVY HAS ALWAYS HAD AN ATTRACTION FOR ME"

76 *"Six weeks ago I"*: Steward to Stein, Dec. 14, 1939.

76 *"I remembered the village"*: Steward, *Chapters*, pp. 81–82.

76 *"My Dearest Sammy"*: Stein to Steward, postmarked March 25, 1940, Bilignin par Belley, Ain; *Dear Sammy*, pp. 147–48.

77 *"I'm writing"*: Steward to Stein, Jan. 26, 1940.

77 *"There is a lot"*: Steward to Stein, March 28, 1940.

77 *"I have been in"*: Steward to Stein, April 19, 1940.

78 *"when prowling the dark"*: Steward, "Early Chapters," p. 83.

78 *"I'm leaving tomorrow"*: Steward to Stein, July 31, 1940.

79 *"Vinalhaven, that island off"*: Steward to Preston, Jan. 14, 1981. Samuel M. Steward Papers.

79 *"Mouth of emptiness, excellent"*: Steward, Stud File, Samuel M. Steward Papers.

79 *"Forgive the hurried card"*: Wilder to Steward, Aug. 22, 1940 (postmarked Amherst, Mass.). Thornton Wilder Papers, Yale Collection of American Literature.

79 *"letters [from Stein and Toklas became]"*: Steward, *Dear Sammy*, pp. 82–83.

80 *"[The military] would probably"*: Steward to Stein, Oct. 26 [1940].

80 *"Dear Sam"*: Wilder to Steward, Oct. 13, 1940. Thornton Wilder Papers, Yale Collection of American Literature.

80 *"Sam . . . is very unhappy"*: Wilcox to Stein [nd], Gertrude Stein and Alice B. Toklas Papers, Yale Collection of American Literature.

81 *"So you do write"*: Wilder to Steward, March 31, 1941, Hotel Europa, Medellín, Colombia. Thornton Wilder Papers, Yale Collection of American Literature.

81 *"It is Quebec now"*: Steward to Stein, Aug. 14, 1941. The letter, though posted from Quebec, lists a Chicago return address—Steward's office on the downtown campus of Loyola University.

82 *By September 1942*: In 1947, the naval training center in Bainbridge, Maryland, was closed, and its recruit training program was relocated to Great Lakes. The Reserve Training Corps would grow from 2,500 recruits to 16,000. At the time, recruits were arriving at a rate of 100 per week; that number would soon rise to 400, requiring 2,935 permanent staff personnel to fill instructor and administrative billets. The Cooks and Bakers School was also moved there (195 trainee cooks, 72 stewards), and a Hospital Corpsman School was reestablished. The Naval Supply Depot was transferred there in 1947, along with the Electronic Supply Office. For these and other figures, see the naval website for Great Lakes: www.nsgreatlakes.navy.mil.

82 *"Most uniforms make"*: "(From an Unpublished Novel) by John McAndrews," *Der Kreis*, no. 1, 1963, pp. 33–34.

83 *"Everything was beginning to"*: Steward, "Early Chapters," p. 132.

83 *"Just a graceful little"*: Steward to Stein and Toklas, April 6, 1945.

84 *"gay ambiance"*: Alan Berube, *Coming Out Under Fire*, pp. 106–107.

84 *"alternating periods of crackdown"*: Ibid., pp. 106–107.

84 *"not proclaiming or parading"*: Ibid., pp. 270–71.

85 *"[These] typewritten stories [were]"*: Eric Rophes, "Steward on Sex: Author 'Phil Andros' Looks Back" *Advocate*, Dec. 11, 1984, pp. 88–90.

85 *"sailors—a coupla hundred"*: Steward, *Straight to Hell* interview [manuscript version, np, Samuel M. Steward papers].

86 *"I have been doing"*: Steward to Stein and Toklas, "13-xi-44."

86 *"At the time it"*: Roger Austen, *Playing the Game*, p. 88. The attribution Austen gives for the quote reads, "From background notes especially written for this study by 'Phil Andros,' Berkeley, California, 1975." Although Steward seems to be discussing only the 1930s, the situation remained in stasis throughout the war years; only immediately following World War II would men interested in publishing literary accounts of homosexual experience be given the opportunity to do so by commercial publishers.

86 *"My dentist in Chicago"*: Steward, "Early Chapters," p. 310.

87 *"It seems that all"*: Steward to Stein and Toklas, April 6, 1945.

87 *"It was certainly cancer"*: Steward, revised "Early Chapters" (this is a later, final version of Steward's autobiography, in manuscript form, located in the Steward Papers), pp. 216–18.

88 *"Getting readjusted to my"*: Steward to Collins, 6/19/45, from Columbus, Ohio. Steward Papers, Kinsey Institute.

89 *which Craine, to Steward's chagrin*: Steward kept no copies of his letters to Craine; all of Craine's letters, meanwhile, are missing from Steward's papers. (One empty, postmarked envelope from Craine to Steward survives, however.) Craine is mentioned with some regularity in Steward's journals. (Complete copies of these typewritten journals can be found in the Samuel M. Steward Papers at the Kinsey Institute; partial copies—some handwritten, some in typescript—also exist in the Samuel M. Steward Papers.)

90 *"I talked to Sam"*: Wilcox to Stein, undated, probably 1946. Gertrude Stein and Alice B. Toklas Papers, Yale Collection of American Literature.

90 *"there will be no"*: Steward to Stein and Toklas, April 6, 1945.

90 *"to effect my escape"*: Steward to Collins, 6-25-45, Steward Papers, Kinsey Institute.

91 *"I suppose technically you"*: Steward to Stein and Toklas, Sept. 13, 1945.

92 *"You've no idea what"*: Steward to Collins, 6-25-[19]45, Kinsey Institute.

92 *"I heard her wonderful"*: Steward, "On a Call to Paris," *Illinois Dental Journal* 15 (March 1946), pp. 124–25.

93 *"Your wire did me"*: Toklas to Steward, Aug. 22, 1946, 5, Rue Christine, Paris VI; *Dear Sammy*, pp. 155–56.

93 *"Are you being a good boy"*: Toklas to Steward, Oct. [?] 1946; *Dear Sammy*, p. 156.

93 *"incredible that I voluntarily"*: Steward, "Early Chapters," p. 233.

93 *The articles on religion*: The signed essay, entitled "With Liberty and Justice for All," was printed and distributed by World Book as part of an advertising effort. A copy of the printed document remains in the Samuel M. Steward Papers.

94 *"It seems as if"*: Wilcox to Toklas [nd], Gertrude Stein and Alice B. Toklas Papers, Yale Collection of American Literature.

95 *"the homosexual as a"*: Donald Webster Cory, *The Homosexual in America* (New York: Greenberg, 1951), pp. 94–95.

95 *And yet as he*: Steward, "Early Chapters," pp. 89–90.

95 *"Death Averted"*: Steward, "Death Averted, or Happy Days Are Here Again" (subscriber's letter to the editor, unsigned), *Der Kreis*, April 1960, p. 46.

96 *"After about four years"*: Steward, "Letter to a Young Gay Alcoholic," *Advocate* 346, July 8, 1982, pp. 35–38.

96 *"Barker put his head"*: Steward, "Early Chapters," pp. 90, 91.

96 *"Physically he does improve"*: Wilcox to Toklas, undated, but at the time of Miriam Andréas's trip to Paris. Gertrude Stein and Alice B. Toklas Papers, Yale Collection of American Literature.

97 *"Oh, Sammy, aren't you"*: Toklas to Steward, Dec. 31, 1946; *Dear Sammy*, pp. 156–58.

5: SOBRIETY AND AFTER

101 *"small tempera portrait drawings"*: Steward, "Early Chapters," p. 264.

102 *"much more interested in"*: Baron to Steward, Aug. 13, 1947. Samuel M. Steward Papers, Kinsey Institute.

102 *"Flogging was not something"*: Baron to Steward, Aug. 19, 1947. Samuel M. Steward Papers, Kinsey Institute.

103 *"While I regard my"*: Ibid.

103 *Stevens liked his beating*: Steward's Stud File card on Hal Stevens notes "2-23-59, historic s/m introduction for Renslow, Dom . . ." Renslow confirmed that this event was his first experience of S/M practices. Renslow, interview with author, June 2005.

103 *But when they met*: Steward to Lynes, Dec. 22 [nd, 1952]. Samuel M. Steward Papers.

104 *"Perhaps the first tangible"*: Steward, *Bad Boys and Tough Tattoos*, p. 9.

104 *"I got to talking"*: Steward to Baron, "Summer 1948." Samuel M. Steward Papers, Kinsey Institute.

105 *"In all those [sixteen]"*: Steward, "Early Chapters," pp. 329–30.

105 *"Oh, oh. I humbly"*: Wilder to Steward, Sept. 14, 1948.

105 *"Wendell made the mistake"*: Steward, *Chapters*, pp. 76–77.

106 *"In autumn of 1948"*: Steward, "Early Chapters," p. 244.

106 *Unemployed but unwilling*: Ibid.

106 *its students came largely*: Ibid., p. 252.

106 *"Many entering freshmen could"*: Ibid., pp. 252–53.

106 *"let the fog rise"*: Ibid., pp. 246–47.

107 *"As a minority . . . homosexuals"*: Cory, *The Homosexual in America*, p. 14.

108 *"is not quite sure"*: Ibid., p. 39.

108 *"The homosexual's chief concern"*: Ibid., p. 56.

109 *"I've kept off the subject"*: Toklas to Steward, April 8, 1949; *Dear Sammy*, p. 151.

109 *"painting as a diversion"*: Toklas to Steward, Sept. 8, 1949; *Dear Sammy*, pp. 169–72.

110 *"it's all one to"*: Toklas to Steward, quoted in *Staying on Alone*, p. 129.

6: KINSEY AND COMPANY

111 *Kinsey's study of human*: Gathorne-Hardy, *Sex, the Measure of All Things*, p. 305.

112 *Since the Kinsey data*: This summation of the Kinsey findings and its place in 1950s

cultural history comes from Bronski, *Pulp Friction*, pp. 13–14, but the statistical figures come directly from Kinsey's *Sexual Response in the Human Male*.

112 *"was only one of"*: Tripp, *Homosexual Matrix*, pp. 239–40.

113 *Moreover, since his statistical*: James H. Jones, *Alfred C. Kinsey: A Public/Private Life*, p. 519.

114 *Kinsey's belief in the*: Gathorne-Hardy, *Sex*, p. 453.

114 *In so doing, Kinsey's*: Paul Robinson, *The Modernization of Sex: Havelock Ellis, Alfred Kinsey, William Masters and Virginia Johnson*, pp. 50–51. (N.B.: Robinson's analysis of Kinsey's accomplishments is the most concise yet written.).

115 *The team obtained eighteen thousand*: Robinson, *Modernization of Sex*, p. 44.

115 *Despite being subjected to*: Gathorne-Hardy, *Sex*, pp. 272–73.

115 *Kinsey's findings about homosexual*: Robinson, *Modernization of Sex*, p. 67.

117 *"What I really wanted"*: Steward to Kinsey, Feb. 8, 1950, Kinsey Institute.

117 *"I've arranged a small"*: Steward to Kinsey, March 4, 1950, Kinsey Institute.

118 *only in 1960*: For a comprehensive account of the legal liabilities attached to possession of erotic materials during the 1950s, see Werth, *Scarlet Professor*, p. 267 *passim*.

118 *Kinsey and Pomeroy also*: Kinsey to Steward, June 6, 1950, Kinsey Institute.

119 *Toklas had reserved a room*: Toklas to Steward, Jan. 29, 1950; *Dear Sammy*, p. 174.

119 *"[It was] as if"*: Steward, *Dear Sammy*, p. 86.

121 *It was this rare*: Details of the book's publication (including details of its long-delayed publication in English) can be found in Edmund White, *Genet: A Biography*.

122 *Half French, half Russian*: White, *Genet*, p. 316. White's attribution for this statement is Roger Stephane.

124 *"8 Frenchmen in a"*: Stud File entry for "Francois, 7-VII-50," Samuel M. Steward Papers.

126 *In doing so he*: For more on this subject, see Gordon Allport, *The Use of Personal Documents in Psychological Science* (New York: Social Science Research Council, 1942).

7: LIVING IN DREAMS

128 *During that fall, Steward*: George T. Reginato (not his real name) would take time off from DePaul, eventually graduating with the class of 1954. He later became a lawyer. Reginato appears in the Stud File, in the book of drawings at the Kinsey Institute, in Steward's journals, and in Steward's erotic fiction, most notably in "I (Cupid) and the Gangster." Steward mentions that Reginato's father was Dominic Reginato in the Len Evans interview, tapes one and two, and information on him can be found in a number of publications on organized crime and the Chicago Outfit, including "US Mafia, Short History and Key Players," available on the Web at www.alternatives.com/crime/usmafia.html, and a number of documents published on the Web by the Laborers' International Union of North America, at www.laborers .org. (N.B.: Letters from the author to George T. Reginato went unanswered and unreturned.)

128 *Steward became so infatuated*: The drawing is in an album of visual fantasies addressed directly to Kinsey, and which can be found in the Kinsey archives.

129 *"the camera works wonderfully"*: Steward to Kinsey, March 1, 1951, Kinsey Institute.

130 *"so far I have"*: Steward to Kinsey, April 13, 1951, Kinsey Institute.

132 *"there is no place"*: From an American congressional report, 1950, as quoted in Patrick Higgins, *A Queer Reader*, p. 162. (Courtesy Joseph Bean.)

132 *Many homosexually active men*: Paraphrased from "Homosexual Citizens" in *Washington History*, vol. 6, no. 2, p. 47. (Courtesy Joseph Bean.)

132 *The FBI, meanwhile, began*: Jones, *Kinsey*, p. 632.

133 *"among homosexuals, learning that"*: *The Mattachine Review* quotation dates from 1956; see "Homosexual Citizens," p. 52. (Courtesy Joseph Bean.)

133 *"free"*: Steward, "Early Chapters," p. 12.

134 *And yet during the fall*: Eugene McNamara, "Meet Your Professor: Samuel M. Steward, Ph.D., Assistant Professor, English," *The DePAULIA* [Jan. 1952; np]. Samuel M. Steward Papers.

135 *"It was a pleasure"*: Toklas to Steward, Jan. 30, 1952; *Dear Sammy*, p. 196.

135 *After an introductory visit*: Kinsey to Steward, Aug. 20, 1951, features a brief acknowledgment of the donation. Kinsey Institute.

136 *"a pair of Bikinis"*: Steward to Kinsey, Aug. 2, 1951, Kinsey Institute.

136 *"I am very much"*: Kinsey to Steward, Nov. 6, 1951, Kinsey Institute.

136 *"had a great deal"*: Kinsey to Steward, Nov. 23, 1951, Kinsey Institute.

136 *"My contacts still keep apace"*: Steward to Kinsey, Dec. 20, 1951, Kinsey Institute.

136 *"Querelle seems one of"*: Steward to Wescott, Dec. 31, 1951, Glenway Wescott Papers, Yale Collection of American Literature, Beinecke Rare Book and Manuscript Library.

137 *"If Glenway Wescott could"*: Toklas to Steward, Jan. 30, 1952; *Dear Sammy*, p. 196.

137 *"horrid little penis"*: Gathorne-Hardy, *Sex*, pp. 352–53.

138 *"Irish-looking"*: Rosco, *Glenway Wescott Personally*, p. 142; Gathorne-Hardy, *Sex*, p. 323.

138 *"that horrid author"*: Wescott, *Continual Lessons*, p. 264.

138 *Certainly Wescott was jealous*: Gathorne-Hardy, *Sex*, p. 354.

139 *"a giant Paul Bunyan"*: Roscoe, *Glenway Wescott Personally*, pp. 143–44.

139 *The film of Miksche*: Paraphrased from Gathorne-Hardy, *Sex*, p. 335.

140 *"Kinsey and I"*: Steward, *Chapters*, pp. 101–103.

141 *"It was an extremely"*: Steward to Kinsey, June 10, 1952. Kinsey Institute.

146 *The next day Steward*: For a beautifully concise appreciation of Julien Green's autobiographical works, see Robinson, *Gay Lives*, pp. 233–59.

147 *"In hesitating to talk"*: Julien Green, *Julien Green Diary 1928–1957*, p. 12.

147 *"As you undoubtedly know"*: Steward to Kinsey, July 17, 1952. Kinsey Institute.

148 *She had recently become*: Steward, "Early Chapters," p. 199.

150 *Brest had long been*: White, *Genet*, pp. 146–48.

151 *"Did you ever get"*: Steward to Kinsey, dated 8-12-52 [mistakenly?], Brest.

153 *Tennessee Williams had been*: Donald Spoto, *The Kindness of Strangers: The Life of Tennessee Williams*, p. 146.

153 *"[The] stories of One Arm"*: Steward, Journals, Oct. 22, 1954. Kinsey Institute.

154 *"I had gone in"*: Steward to Williams, Jan. 5, 1976. Samuel M. Steward Papers.

157 *"George [Lynes] and I"*: Steward, "Mirror, Mirror on the Wall," $TUD, pp. 32–47.

158 *"Dear George"*: Steward to Lynes, on Taft Hotel stationery, undated. Samuel M. Steward Papers.

8: WRITING LYNES

160 *"Worry no more . . .":* Steward to Lynes, Sept. 16 [1952], Samuel M. Steward Papers.

160 *During the fall Steward:* A rough draft of Steward's letter to Morihien survives, undated; it had been tucked into an envelope addressed to Steward from Morihien. Samuel M. Steward Papers.

160 *"typewritten over what appears":* Lynes to Perlin, Oct. 27, 1952. Correspondence between George Platt Lynes and Bernard Perlin. Yale Collection of American Literature, Beinecke Rare Book and Manuscript Library.

161 *"pornographic filth":* Werth, *Scarlet Professor,* p. 166.

162 *"Right after* Finistère *was":* Steward to Edward Field, "20–I–XCIII" (Jan. 20, 1993), Samuel M. Steward Papers.

162 *At age thirty-eight, Peters:* Edward Field to Steward [nd], Samuel M. Steward Papers. Field was hoping to write a biography of Peters at the time, and so had immersed himself in the study of Peters's life, including details of his psychoanalysis and his living situation in the Gurdjieff community.

162 *Moreover, Gurdjieff:* Edward Field to Steward [nd], Samuel M. Steward Papers (see note immediately above).

162 *"burst into tears about":* Steward to Field, Feb. 1, 1993, Samuel M. Steward Papers.

162 *"[Francis] is in Portugal":* Toklas to Steward, Oct. 24, 1952; *Dear Sammy,* p. 200.

163 *"Francis had been screwing":* Steward, *Gay Sunshine* interview (Leland), original manuscript, pp. 27–28. (The passage does not appear in the printed interview.) Samuel M. Steward Papers.

163 *Apparently Rose now hoped:* See Steward, *Dear Sammy,* footnote to pp. 200–201 and elsewhere, for Steward's account, which is also supported by a letter (Rose to Steward, Toulon, Jan. 20, 1953) that remains in the Samuel M. Steward Papers.

163 *"had apparently convinced himself":* Michael DeCossart, *George Melhuish: Artist, Philosopher,* p. 123.

163 *Steward subsequently received:* The letter, along with nearly all of Rose's correspondence with Steward, was sold at auction by Steward in 1975, at a moment when he was convinced he had only a month to live. Summaries of their contents are, however, carefully documented in the sales catalog: California Book Auction Galleries, sale no. 113, Saturday, Oct. 18, 1975 (lots 331 and 332).

163 *Frederica, Lady Rose, would:* "Of Dorothy Carrington, Rose's second wife (although she herself claimed to have no knowledge of a first wife), Sir Francis left a cryptic— and perhaps not altogether reliable—account in his memoirs, *Saying Life.*" "Obituary: Frederica, Lady Rose," *Daily Telegraph,* Jan. 29, 2002, p. 27.

163 *"The tale of Francis":* Lynes to Steward, Oct. 30, 1952 (from 229 East Forty-seventh Street), Samuel M. Steward Papers.

164 *"I'm delighted you like":* Steward to Lynes, Nov. 3, 1952, Samuel M. Steward Papers.

164 *"I wish I could've been":* Steward to Lynes, Nov. 16, 1952, Samuel M. Steward Papers.

165 *"I wish I could":* Lynes to Steward, Nov. 18, 1952, Samuel M. Steward Papers.

165 *"You flatter me":* Steward to Lynes, Nov. 22, 1952, Samuel M. Steward Papers.

166 *"Something lovely happened last":* Steward to Lynes, Dec. 7, 1952, Samuel M. Steward Papers.

167 *"The combined efforts of":* Steward to Lynes, Dec. 22 [nd, 1952], Samuel M. Steward Papers.

168 *"About Francis—the story":* Toklas to Steward, Dec. 29, 1952; *Dear Sammy,* pp. 201–202.

168 *"I've developed quite a"*: Steward to Kinsey, dated Jan. 11, 1952 [but actually 1953], Kinsey Institute.

169 *By coincidence, even as*: Rose to Steward, Jan. 20, 1953. Samuel M. Steward Papers.

169 *"I wish I had"*: Lynes to Steward, Feb. 4, 1953, Samuel M. Steward Papers.

170 *"I have to catch"*: Steward to Lynes, March 1, 1953, Samuel M. Steward Papers.

171 *"Now it's your turn"*: Steward to Lynes, April 25, 1953, Samuel M. Steward Papers.

171 *"[It's] not a very"*: Steward to Kinsey, May 5, 1953, Kinsey Institute.

172 *"I'm glad you came"*: Lynes to Steward, May 12, 1953, noting in its address heading, "Also—157 East 61 Street." Samuel M. Steward Papers.

172 *"That damned novel has"*: Steward to Lynes, June 16, 1953, Samuel M. Steward Papers.

173 *"and to the equally"*: Toklas to Steward, June 28, 1953; *Dear Sammy*, pp. 203–204.

177 *"I started a rumor"*: Steward to Kinsey, July 21, 1953, Kinsey Institute.

177 *"May I save you"*: Kinsey to Steward, July 28, 1953, Kinsey Institute.

9: "A KIND OF OBSCENE DIARY, ACTUALLY"

181 *"My novel is [now]"*: Steward to Lynes, Oct. 18, 1953, Samuel M. Steward Papers.

181 *"an old-fashioned doctor got"*: Steward to August Becker, Aug. 24, 1977, Samuel M. Steward Papers, Boston University.

181 *"dear old poor old Sam"*: Lynes to Steward, Nov. 19, 1953, Samuel M. Steward Papers.

182 *"A man walking alone"*: The clipping, undated, features the headline "Judge Sees Captain, Charges Two Policemen Abused Him." Steward later donated the clipping and the letter he then sent to the judge to the Kinsey Archive. Kinsey Institute.

182 *Professor Art Lennon*: Douglas Martin, who studied with both Lennon and Steward at DePaul, recalled that Lennon was "the only cute prof[essor] at the university," but had no idea of his sexual orientation. Martin to author, August 2006.

183 *"[Art] had cruised"*: Steward, Len Evans interview, tapes one and two.

184 *"Francis has done some"*: Toklas to Steward, Jan. 28, 1954; *Dear Sammy*, p. 206.

184 *"Without any unfaithfulness to"*: Toklas to Steward, Jan. 28, 1954; *Dear Sammy*, p. 207.

184 *"[Berbich] stopped in briefly"*: Steward, Journal, Friday, Feb. 4 [1954], Kinsey Institute.

185 *"It was a lot"*: Steward to Lynes, Feb. 19 [54?], Samuel M. Steward Papers.

185 *"Ask me what I"*: Steward to Lynes, March 7, 1954, Samuel M. Steward Papers.

186 *"I simply must have"*: Steward, Journal, Thursday, March 10 [1954], Kinsey Institute.

186 *"The [motorcyclist] story you"*: Lynes to Steward, April 5, 1954, Samuel M. Steward Papers.

187 *"[Tattooed] Larry . . . said"*: Steward, Journal, April 18 [1954], Easter, Kinsey Institute.

188 *"Without too much alarm"*: Steward, Journal, May 1, 1954, Kinsey Institute.

188 *"[I have been suffering from]"*: Steward to Lynes, May 25, 1954, Samuel M. Steward Papers.

189 *"Do you do the tattooing"*: Lynes to Steward, June 30, 1954, Samuel M. Steward Papers.

190 *"Sam Steward . . . was"*: Wescott, as told to Gerry Roscoe, *Glenway Wescott Personally*, pp. 142–43.

191 *"I go out to Great Lakes"*: Steward to Kinsey, May 25, 1954, Kinsey Institute.

191 *"entre nous I have"*: Toklas to Steward, Aug. 2, 1954; *Dear Sammy*, p. 208.

10: "MR. CHIPS OF THE TATTOO WORLD"

200 *"hie me to a seaport"*: Steward to Lynes, Dec. 19, 1953. This extraordinary letter, type-written on a sheet of clear acetate, was found inserted into Steward's 1954 tattoo journal (most probably by Steward); it remains at the Kinsey Institute, its author and recipient now identified as a result of this research.

201 *"It was not until"*: Steward, *Bad Boys*, p. 12.

201 *"It took [me] a week"*: Steward, *Bad Boys*, pp. 15–16.

201 *"Could I have seen"*: Ibid., p. 17.

201 *"And why should it"*: Ibid., p. 32.

202 *"subject to both Post Office"*: Kinsey to Steward, Aug. 3, 1954, Kinsey Institute.

203 *"in the past 7"*: Steward, Journal, Sept. 12, 1954, Kinsey Institute.

204 *"Heated by the sight"*: Steward, Journal, Oct. 1, 1954, Kinsey Institute.

204 *"In the past few"*: Steward, Journal, Oct. 3, 1954 (p. 59), Kinsey Institute.

204 *"The passion overcame me"*: Steward, Journal, Sunday, Oct. 10 [1954] (p. 60), Kinsey Institute.

206 *"I have just gone"*: Kinsey to Steward, Oct. 18, 1954, Kinsey Institute.

206 *"A New Thing that"*: Steward, Journal, Sunday, Oct. 24 (p. 71, Chicago Journal), Kinsey Institute.

206 *"Jimmy and Lonnie"*: Steward, Journal, Saturday, Oct. 23, Kinsey Institute.

208 *"[An executive I know]"*: Steward, Journal, Oct. 26, Kinsey Institute.

209 *"[Webb was] a [toothless]"*: Steward, *Bad Boys*, p. 27.

210 *At first Steward occupied*: Ibid., pp. 34–35.

210 *"In those days"*: Ibid., p. 23.

210 *Steward eventually hired a lawyer*: Ibid., p. 31.

210 *"The street's miasma"*: Ibid., p. 14.

211 *"[My] secret embarrassment over"*: Ibid., p. 19.

212 *"After a month or two"*: Ibid., p. 39.

212 *Steward's sex-and-tattooing journal*: Ibid., p. 5.

214 *"I'm sorry, but it"*: Steward, Journal, Tuesday, Dec. 28 [1954], Kinsey Institute.

11: THE KOTHMANN AFFAIR

216 *"Everything [in the journal]"*: Steward, *Bad Boys*, p. 5. The latter part of this quotation deals with the manuscript of *Bad Boys* rather than the journal itself, but the statement is equally applicable to both.

216 *"tattooing furnished me with"*: Ibid., pp. 136–37.

216 *"[I] spent many hours"*: Pomeroy, Introduction, *Bad Boys*.

217 *"He came in"*: Steward, Journal, Jan. 16, 1955, Kinsey Institute.

219 *Popular resentment of Kinsey*: Gathorne-Hardy, *Sex*, p. 395.

219 *In his naïveté, Kinsey*: Jones, *Alfred C. Kinsey: A Public/Private Life*, p. 532.

219 *"crushed with disappointment"*: For more on Kinsey's death, see Gathorne-Hardy, *Sex*, pp. 430–38.

220 *He was interested in the rose*: Juan Eduardo Cirlot, *A Dictionary of Symbols* (New York: Philosophical Library, 1971).

220 *Originally from Persia*: Maria Leach and Jerome Fried, *Funk & Wagnalls Standard Dictionary of Folklore, Mythology and Legend* (New York: Funk & Wagnalls, 1949).

220 *Moreover, the rose had*: Don Ed Hardy, interview with author.

220 *With his usual craftiness*: Various publications have named Dietzel as one of the leading American tattooists of the twentieth century. In 1965 he was named one of the top ten tattoo artists in the world by the Tattoo Club of America, documentation of which can be found in the Samuel M. Steward Papers.

221 *"The purity and assurance"*: Steward, *Bad Boys*, p. 158.

221 *Moreover, lower-class males*: Robinson, *Modernization of Sex*, p. 94.

223 *"school is . . . awful"*: Steward, Journal, Friday, May 20, Kinsey Institute.

223 *"The inside walls"*: The *Chicago* magazine article (July 1955) appears without a by-line on pp. 20–21. Samuel M. Steward Papers.

224 *"As for having things"*: Steward to Kinsey, Aug. 18, 1955, Kinsey Institute.

12: THE PARTING

230 *"I am now so"*: Steward, Journal, Saturday Oct. 29, 1955, Kinsey Institute.

231 *As a result, reports*: This paragraph has been roughly paraphrased from Jones, *Alfred C. Kinsey*, p. 629.

231 *"I have thought of"*: Kinsey to Steward, Jan. 10, 1956, Kinsey Institute.

232 *"I laughingly pushed it"*: Steward, Journal, Jan. 13, 1956, Kinsey Institute.

232 *In mid-February, Steward*: Steward to Kinsey, Feb. 13, 1956, Kinsey Institute.

232 *"Frankly I was a"*: Kinsey to Steward, Feb. 17, 1956, Kinsey Institute.

232 *"my raise had been"*: This section of the journal is entitled "Crisis at DePaul" and is dated "Feb 23, *et seq.*, 1956." Kinsey Institute.

233 *"I was cleared on"*: Steward, interviewed by Len Evans on July 23, 1983, as part of Voices: The Oral History Project of the Gay, Lesbian, Bisexual and Transgendered Historical Society of Northern California. Published in *Journal of the History of Sexuality*, vol. 9, no. 4 (Oct. 2000), pp. 474–93.

235 *Steward had chosen his*: Barry Werth, *The Scarlet Professor: Newton Arvin, a Literary Life Shattered by Scandal* (New York: Nan A. Talese, 2001), p. 166.

237 *"Prok came [down to the cage]"*: Steward, Journal, June 4, 1956, Kinsey Institute.

238 *"this first bleak look"*: Steward, Journal, June 8, 1956, Friday, Kinsey Institute.

238 *"The end of school"*: Steward to Toklas, June 11, 1956, Kinsey Institute.

240 *"The fantastic episodes continue"*: Steward to Martin, May 15, 1978, Samuel M. Steward Papers, gift of Douglas Martin.

241 *"I've come closer to"*: Steward, *Bad Boys*, pp. 112–14.

242 *"violent, stupid and crazy"*: Ibid., p. 112.

242 *The friendship between them*: Ibid., p. 143.

242 *"The night Tommy left"*: Steward, Journal, Aug. 1, 1956, Kinsey Institute.

242 *"This new thing I"*: Ibid.

244 *"I am still frozen"*: Steward, Journal, Tuesday, August 28, 1956, Kinsey Institute.

244 *"Over and over again"*: Steward, Journal, Sept. 4, 1956, Kinsey Institute.

244 *"If one really believed"*: Steward, *Chapters*, p. 106.

13: "PLEASURE DOESN'T REALLY MAKE ONE HAPPY"

247 *"Francis and his international"*: Toklas to Steward, Sept. 21, 1956; *Dear Sammy*, p. 217.

248 *The day of the*: For a complete account of the Crabb scandal, see M. G. Welham

and J. A. Welham, *Frogman Spy: The Mysterious Disappearance of Commander "Buster" Crabb* (London: W. H. Allen, 1990). The précis of this book, from which this summation is adapted, appears in the June 1996 issue of *Diver* magazine. Another, earlier account of the Crabb scandal can be found in *Frogman Spy: The Incredible Case of Commander Crabb* (New York: McDowell, Obolensky, 1960). Steward gives a brief account of Rose's direct involvement in the incident in *Dear Sammy*, pp. 218–19.

248 *Upon Crabb's mysterious death*: Bryan Robertson, "Remembering Francis Rose," in *Sir Francis Rose, 1909–1979: A Retrospective* (London: England & Co., [1988]).

248 *Holloway Sanatorium at Virginia Water*: These words come directly from Michael De Cossart, *George Melhuish: Artist, Philosopher* (Wolfeboro Falls, N.H.: Alan Sutton, 1990), pp. 128–29, from which this section of the "frogman" story is adapted.

248 *"that Al Capone had"*: Steward, Revised "Early Chapters," p. 273.

250 *"the most morally and"*: Steward, *Bad Boys*, p. 147.

251 *"James Purdy bores me"*: Toklas to Steward, Sept. 14, 1957, La Brebeche–Magagnosch par Grasse; *Dear Sammy*, p. 221.

251 *"[Tattooing] has so many"*: Steward, Journal, Nov. 18, 1957, Kinsey Institute.

252 *"lonesome down here at"*: Steward, Journal, Monday, Dec. 16, 1957, Kinsey Institute.

252 *His sex life was*: Steward, Stud File, "Daisy-chain" card, Samuel M. Steward papers.

252 *Since on some winter*: Steward, Journal, Dec. 10, 1957, Kinsey Institute.

252 *"Some money [to cover her expenses]"*: Steward, *Dear Sammy*, pp. 95–96.

253 *"Alice is much feebler"*: Steward, Journal, Saturday, Dec. 21, 1957, Kinsey Institute.

253 *"I must confess I"*: Steward, Journal, Sunday, Dec. 22, 1957, Kinsey Institute.

254 *"she is no longer"*: Steward, Journal, Monday, Dec. 23, 1957, Kinsey Institute.

254 *"[sauerkraut] and wieners"*: Steward, Journal, Dec. 25, 1957, Kinsey Institute.

254 *"evidently the continued excitement"*: Steward, Journal, Dec. 29, 1957, Kinsey Institute.

255 *"Julien [was] as polite"*: Steward, Journal, Dec. 30, 1957, Kinsey Institute.

255 *"all the past, and"*: Steward, Journal, Dec. 31, 1957, Kinsey Institute.

255 *"bloom[ing] into a gaudy"*: Steward, Journal, Jan. 3, 1958, Kinsey Institute.

256 *"Soon as he left"*: Steward, Journal, Feb. 11, 1958, Kinsey Institute.

256 *"Lovely, satiny dark-brown"*: Steward, Stud File entry for Ruffian Bellows, Jr.

256 *"He told me one"*: Steward, Journal, Feb. 13, 1958, Kinsey Institute.

257 *The magazine would achieve a peak circulation*: Kennedy, *Ideal Gay Man*, p. 30.

257 *also known as "Rolf"*: Ibid., p. 10.

258 *Steward hated the experience*: Steward, Journal, Monday, Feb. 24, 1958, Kinsey Institute.

258 *"the invert, it seem[s]"*: Steward, "The Male Homosexual and Marriage," *Der Kreis*, vol. 29 (Feb. 1961), p. 29. Steward in this piece primarily surveys the potential of homosexual men to marry heterosexual women, but does take into account homosexual male partnerships as well.

259 *"when he finally went"*: Steward, Journal, Wednesday, Feb. 26, 1958, Kinsey Institute.

260 *"'Well, I may see'"*: Steward, Journal, March 17, 1958, Kinsey Institute.

260 *"She kept after me"*: Steward, Journal, Tuesday, March 25, 1958, Kinsey Institute.

261 *"wondering why I seem"*: Steward to Toklas, April 19, 1958.

261 *"much enfeebled . . ."*: Steward to Wescott, April 19, 1958, Glenway Wescott Papers, Yale Collection of American Literature.

262 *"The letters from Gertrude"*: Steward to Toklas, April 19, 1958.

14: KRIS AND *KREIS*

263 *"looking terribly nelly in"*: Steward, Journal, Wednesday, May 7, 1958, Kinsey Institute.

263 *Steward had his own*: Jack Mabley, "Teen-Agers and Tattoos," *Chicago Daily News*, May 12, 1958 [np]. A copy of the article can be found in the Samuel M. Steward Papers.

264 *He also promised to*: Steward, Journal, Monday, May 19, 1958, Kinsey Institute.

265 *Of the English and*: Kennedy, *The Ideal Gay Man*, p. 48.

265 *"[My] alliance with* Der Kreis": Steward, "Early Chapters," pp. 286–88.

266 *"ran all [the Chicago]"*: Renslow, Joseph Bean interview, Leather Archives and Museum.

267 *By approaching bodybuilders*: Ibid.

267 *"It was the gym"*: Orejudos, Bean interview, Leather Archives and Museum.

268 *"I'm not a whoremaster"*: Renslow, conversation with author, 2005.

269 *"a nice clean-cut"*: Steward, Journal, Tuesday, June 17, 1958, Kinsey Institute.

269 *Ingram, who had studied*: Cliff Ingram/Raven, Rinella interview, Leather Archives and Museum.

269 *"Cliff became part of"*: Orejudos, Bean interview, Leather Archives and Museum.

269 *Several days after Costello's*: Steward, Journal, Wednesday, Sept. 24, 1958, Kinsey Institute.

270 *"The two smut-hunters"*: Ibid.

270 *"hundreds of lewd photos"*: Steward, Journal, Dec. 12, 1958, Kinsey Institute.

271 *As it turned out*: "Photog Faces Court on Smut Charge," undated newspaper clipping, Charles Renslow Papers, Leather Archives and Museum.

272 *"I decided to tell"*: Renslow, Bean interview, Leather Archives and Museum.

272 *"What wonderfully good news"*: Steward, *Dear Sammy*, note to pp. 232–33.

273 *"and then Pick left"*: Toklas to Steward, Dec. 28, 1958; *Dear Sammy*, pp. 231–32.

273 *"with many misgivings"*: Steward, Journal. All entries describing the 1958–59 Paris/Zurich trip are dated Feb. 9, 1959. Kinsey Institute.

273 *"He said it took"*: Steward, Journal, Wednesday, Feb. 25, 1959, Kinsey Institute.

274 *Chuck Renslow and Dom Orejudos*: Steward, Journal, February 9, 1959, Kinsey Institute.

276 *"Cliff Ingram"*: Steward, Journal, Wednesday, Feb. 25, 1959, Kinsey Institute.

277 *"Last night Frank Murphy"*: Steward, Journal, Oct. 5, 1959, Kinsey Institute.

277 *despite misgivings*: Steward, Journal, Oct. 6, 1959, Kinsey Institute.

278 *"in other ways it"*: Renslow, interview with author.

278 *"A chorus boy from"*: Steward, Journal, Oct. 13, 1959, Kinsey Institute.

278 *"After the beating by"*: Steward, Journal, Oct. 26, 1959, Kinsey Institute.

279 *"victory in defeat"*: Steward, Journal, Oct. 30, 1959, Kinsey Institute.

279 *"the prospect of retirement"*: Steward, Journal, Nov. 2, 1959, Kinsey Institute.

280 *"I was wanting to"*: Steward, Journal, Nov. 16, 1959, Kinsey Institute.

281 *"like Housman's Terence"*: Steward, Journal, Nov. 20, 1959, Kinsey Institute.

15: "PAYMENTS TO HUSTLERS"

283 *"just like a 17-yr old"*: Steward, Journal, Dec. 17, 1959, Kinsey Institute.

283 *"sullen moods and romantic"*: Steward, "Early Chapters," p. 323.

284 *But Steward quickly developed*: Steward, *Understanding the Male Hustler*, pp. 56–57; the situation is also described in the Stud File, which features entry cards for both Johnny Reyes and his uncle Mike Reyes.

284 *"but it was a hasty"*: Steward, Journal, Dec. 21, 1959, Kinsey Institute.

285 *"I try to think"*: Steward, Journal, Jan. 2, 1960, Kinsey Institute.

285 *"Ralph got pissed on"*: Steward, Journal, Jan. 4, 1960, Kinsey Institute.

286 *"bleary eyed and goofy"*: Bob McHenry, interview with author.

289 *"Nothing that anyone could"*: Steward, "Early Chapters," pp. 289–90. Steward suggests elsewhere in this passage that the conversation took place in 1962, but the immersion in pornographic writing began in 1960.

290 *"He was always asking"*: Steward, Journal, Nov. 30, 1960. (The reference to December 5 is misleading, but it refers to payments made in advance for the week.) Kinsey Institute.

291 *When the king arrived*: Steward described the experience in a videotaped interview on his tattooing work. *Two Interviews on Videotape with Samuel M. Steward* (a gift of Douglas Martin), Samuel M. Steward Papers. This particular interview was conducted by Michael O. Stearns, Metamorphosis Productions, on August 23, 1983.

291 *"I took a book"*: Steward, Journal, Dec. 8, 1960, Kinsey Institute.

292 *Toklas had in fact*: Steward, *Dear Sammy*, p. 112.

292 *Toklas's Roman winter lasted*: Paraphrased from Steward's account in *Dear Sammy*, p. 112.

293 *Steward then met Jacques*: Paraphrased from Steward, *Bad Boys*, p. 195.

16: MASTERS AND SLAVES

296 *"The best 'legal' opinion"*: Donald Bishop (Sam Steward), "What's New in Sodom?" *Der Kreis*, no. 4 (1962), pp. 30–33.

296 *"Man's chase after happiness"*: John McAndrews (Sam Steward), "Man's Chase after Happiness (From an Unpublished Novel)", *Der Kreis*, no. 1 (1962), p. 36.

297 *"Paul [Gebhard] tells me"*: Pomeroy to Steward, Jan. 31, 1963, Kinsey Institute.

297 *"I must say that"*: Steward to Pomeroy, Feb. 8, 1963, Kinsey Institute.

298 *"Detachment: A Way of Life"*: Steward, "Detachment: A Way of Life," *Der Kreis*, vol. 26 (August 1958), pp. 34–35.

299 *"The carefree life"*: Steward, "Early Chapters," pp. 321–22.

299 *"The Bull Market in America"*: Steward, "The Bull Market in America," *Der Kreis*, vol. 29 (June 1961), pp. 19–24.

301 *"in either the be-kind-to-others"*: C. A. Tripp, *The Homosexual Matrix* (New York: McGraw-Hill, 1975), p. 111.

302 *"In the first place"*: Donald Bishop (Sam Steward), "Pussies in Boots," *Amigo* no. 24 (1964), pp. 183–90.

302 *"came in wearing black"*: Steward also notes that Kane and Barnes are described in two Phil Andros stories published in *Drummer*: "Baby Sitter" and "Many Happy Returns." Steward, "Early Chapters," p. 331.

304 *"the nelly Mad Priest"*: Steward to Gebhard, Oct. 10, 1966, Kinsey Institute.

17: PHIL ANDROS, $TUD

305 *"The Sergeant with the Rose Tattoo"*: Steward, Journal, May 18, 1960, Kinsey Institute.

305 *"[It] got lots of"*: Steward to Gebhard, July 23, 1964, Kinsey Institute.

305 *"Phil Andros [the writer]"*: Steward, "Early Chapters," p. 292.

306 *"intelligent widely-read and"*: Ibid., p. 313.

307 *"I [had] had a lot"*: Ibid., pp. 289–91.

307 *Rechy wrote Steward that*: Rechy to Steward ("Phil Sparrow"), July 11, 1963, Samuel M. Steward Papers.

308 *He was not only*: Steward, Stud File entry for Roy Davis. The card also notes, "Not sure this boy wasn't AWOL."

308 *"I wonder if I"*: Steward to Pomeroy, July 30, 1963, Kinsey Institute.

308 *The weekly commute from*: Steward, "Early Chapters," pp. 291, 313.

309 *The Milwaukee tattoo parlor*: Details of the location of the Dietzel Studio, 612 North Fifth Street, come from Dietzel's business card. Samuel M. Steward Papers.

309 *"his reputation was firmly"*: Steward, "Early Chapters," p. 300.

309 *It was Cliff Raven's*: Steward to John Schacht, Feb. 14, 1986, Steward Papers.

309 *"Your letter [about closing]"*: Toklas to Steward, July 20, 1963, "Chez Madame Debar—Soye-en-Septaine"; *Dear Sammy*, p. 244.

310 *"He is a man"*: Cecil Beaton, *The Unexpurgated Beaton: The Cecil Beaton Diaries as He Wrote Them (1970–1980)* ed. Hugo Vickers (New York: Random House, 2003), p. 516.

310 *"In all these changing"*: Dorothy Carrington, "Francis Rose," in *Sir Francis Rose, 1909–1979: A Retrospective* (London: England & Co., [1988]).

311 *"The restrictions for me"*: Steward to Gebhard, Dec. 2, 1963, Kinsey Institute.

311 *"I tattooed him . . . That"*: Steward, "Early Chapters," p. 334.

312 *"I'm glad you are"*: Gebhard to Steward, Dec. 10, 1963, Kinsey Institute.

312 *"As you may know"*: Steward to Gebhard, Dec. 19, 1963, Kinsey Institute.

313 *"somehow I share the"*: Gebhard to Steward, Jan. 20, 1964, Kinsey Institute.

313 *"I wondered if he"*: Steward, "Early Chapters," p. 329.

314 *By 1964, a distinct*: The history of the San Francisco leather community has been documented in Gayle Rubin, "The Valley of the Kings: Leathermen in San Francisco (1960–1990)," dissertation, University of Michigan, 1994, which is currently being revised for publication.

314 *The look and feel*: Robert Opel, "Requiem for a Tool Box," *Drummer,* no. 2 (1975), p. 28.

315 *"a little shop right"*: Steward, "Early Chapters," p. 303.

315 *"to case the area"*: Ibid., p. 342.

316 *Womack had a terrible*: Renslow, Bean interview, Leather Archives and Museum.

316 *he organized and ran*: For more on Womack, see Bronski, *Pulp Friction: Uncovering the Golden Age of Gay Male Pulps* (New York: St. Martin's Press, 2002), pp. 83–85 (from which some of this information is paraphrased), as well as the H. Lynn Womack Papers, #7441, Division of Rare and Manuscript Collections, Cornell University Library.

316 *"the whole basic concept"*: Steward to Frisch, March 20, 1965, Samuel M. Steward Papers.

318 *"'Lavender Evenings'"*: Steward to Womack, April 9, 1965, Samuel M. Steward Papers.

18: A NEW LIFE IN OAKLAND

319 *"small house built in"*: Steward, "Early Chapters," p. 342.

320 *"my trick had worked"*: Phil Andros [Samuel M. Steward], *Shuttlecock* (San Francisco: Perineum, 1984), p. 38.

320 *When after all these*: Steward, "Early Chapters," pp. 342–43.

320 *"migawd, don't ever move"*: Steward to Gebhard, May 23, 1965, Kinsey Institute.

321 *"After twelve years of"*: Steward, "Early Chapters," pp. 342–43.

321 *"Oakland in the fifties"*: Ralph "Sonny" Barger, *Hells Angel: The Life and Times of Sonny Barger and the Hells Angels Motorcycle Club*, p. 142.

322 *"The [Berkeley] Free Speech"*: Steward, "Early Chapters," pp. 344–45.

322 *Outside there was a*: Ibid., p. 345.

323 *$TUD was meanwhile moving*: Frisch to Steward, July 7, 1965, Samuel M. Steward Papers.

323 *"to write a book"*: Gebhard to Steward, Sept. 27, 1965, Kinsey Institute.

324 *Nonetheless, within the year*: *Drum*, vol. 5, no. 10 (December 1965).

324 *"on [a] motorsickle"*: Steward, Stud File, Samuel M. Steward Papers.

326 *"Cliff was five years"*: Don Ed Hardy, interview with author.

326 *"Both can insert their"*: Steward, *Bad Boys*, p. 160.

329 *"Shit on this publishing"*: Steward to Gebhard, Oct. 10, 1966, Kinsey Institute.

329 *For the next three*: John Preston, Introduction to *STUD: A Novel by Phil Andros, Introduction by John Preston* (Boston: Perineum/Alyson, 1982). (N.B.: In reprinting *$TUD*, Alyson changed the book's title to *STUD*.) Preston's information on Womack (who is not named directly in the introduction) seems to have been provided to him by Steward.

329 *"She was then completely"*: Steward, "Early Chapters," p. 313a.

329 *"the Toulouse-Lautrec of"*: Joseph Bean, e-mail to author.

329 *came by to have*: Bill Tellman ("Chuck Arnett"), *Black Sheets*, no. 15 (April 1998), pp. 39–40.

330 *By 1972 he would*: Steward, Stud File, "Payments to Hustlers" card.

331 *"It upset me a"*: Steward to Gebhard, March 11, 1967, Kinsey Institute.

334 *By the time Steward*: Barger, *Hells Angel*, pp. 257–59.

334 *"gang bang"*: Barger, *Hells Angel*, plus additional information from Barger in telephone interview with author.

335 *Barger subsequently had her*: Barger, *Hells Angel*, p. 103.

335 *"Back in the late"*: Barger, interview with author.

335 *Steward worked as the*: Steward, "Early Chapters," p. 345.

336 *"[But] gradually I acquired"*: Steward, *Chapters*, p. 90.

336 *"their presence [in the shop always]"*: Steward, "Early Chapters," p. 348.

336 *Sonny Barger not only*: Barger, interview with author.

336 *Barger enthusiastically recalled*: Barger, *Hells Angel*, p. 65.

337 *"Despite all the news"*: Steward, *Chapters*, pp. 90–92.

338 *He later confided to*: "Twelve Years Behind the Lens: The Life and Hard Times of J. Brian" by Eric Ridge (publisher and date unknown, 1975), Samuel M. Steward Papers, gift of Douglas Martin.

338 *"Sam [Steward] and J. Brian"*: Fritscher to author, Aug. 14, 2005.

339 *"'The Male House of Prostitution'"*: David J. Pittman, "The Male House of Prostitution," *TransAction*, vol. 8, nos. 5 and 6 (March/April 1971), p. 21. The article is featured

as part of "Sex and Marginality in American Men: A Special Supplement," Samuel M. Steward Papers, gift of Douglas Martin.

339 *"The Link"*: "The Link," *Golden Boys*, no. 6 (1968), pp. 2–3, 5–7, 9.

339 *a fictionalized version of*: "Pig in a Poke," *Golden Boys*, no. 9 (nd).

340 *"he evidently found the money"*: Steward, "Early Chapters," pp. 314–15.

341 *"I consider myself lucky"*: Steward to Gebhard, July 4, 1969, Kinsey Institute.

341 *"After Altamont"*: Barger, *Hells Angel*, p. 169.

341 *The explosion of hepatitis*: Steward, *Bad Boys*, p. 190.

342 *"The irritant factors in"*: Ibid., p. 175.

342 *"The shop next door"*: Steward, "Early Chapters," p. 349.

342 *"Cartun asked [Steward] that"*: "Pawnbroker Slain During Gun Battle" [unknown newspaper, nd], clipping found in the Samuel M. Steward Papers. The article mistakenly names Steward as proprietor of the "Archer" (not Anchor) tattoo parlor and gives his age (incorrectly) as forty-six (he was sixty).

343 *"In March, 1970, I"*: Steward, "Early Chapters," pp. 349–50.

19: "FROM THE BROW OF ZEUS"

344 *"If you wanted to"*: Steward, "Early Chapters," pp. 318–19.

344 *"the decline of Western"*: Steward to Martin, Aug. 1, 1977, Samuel M. Steward Papers.

344 *"because of its melancholy"*: Steward, "Early Chapters," p. 354.

344 *"Phil Andros springing full-grown"*: Ibid., pp. 318–19.

345 *"press releases"*: This quotation is published in the catalog advertising the sale of Purdy's letters to Steward, which took place on January 26, 1995. (For this and more information on the thirty-eight autographed typed letters, some signed by Purdy's pseudonym, "Babe Helps," that are now in private hands, see Lot 545, *Pacific Book Auction Galleries* catalog, Sale 66, Jan. 26, 1995.)

345 *"the payment for"*: Steward, "Early Chapters," p. 297.

346 *getting writing of this sort*: For more on the plight of gay pulp writers, see Bronski, *Pulp Friction*, p. 225 *passim*.

346 *"a black leather jacket"*: Phil Andros [Samuel M. Steward], *The Boys in Blue* (San Francisco: Perineum, 1984), p. 2.

348 *Steward used the novel*: Phil Andros [Samuel M. Steward], *My Brother, My Self*, p. 49.

349 *"the guys didn't always"*: Austen, *Playing the Game*, p. 185.

352 Song of the Loon: Bronski, *Pulp Friction*, p. 212; his citation comes from Tom Norman, author of *American Gay Erotic Paperbacks: A Bibliography*.

352 *The panel discussion was*: Larry Townsend, "Plight of Gay Novelists: Who Gauges Market Correctly, Publishers or Writers?" *Advocate*, Aug. 19, 1970, p. 19.

353 *"I just had the"*: Dirk Vanden, interview with Richard Amory, *Vector*, July 1970.

353 *"The people at Greenleaf"*: Richard Amory, *The Song of the Loon* (Vancouver: Arsenal Pulp Press, 2005), p. 244. The Vanden interview with Amory comes from *Gay* magazine, Oct. 26, 1970 [np].

354 *"a writer who tries"*: My quotation from Douglas Dean is taken from Michael Bronski, "Introduction," in *Song of the Loon* (p. 25).

355 *"The Phil Andros books"*: John Preston, "Introduction," in *STUD* (the Alyson Publications reissue of *$TUD*, published 1982).

20: DEAR SAMMY

356 *"[Kane would] come home"*: Steward to Claude Schwab, Aug. 24, 1977, Samuel M. Steward Papers, Boston University.

356 *The journals contained lengthy*: Steward to Jonathan Ned Katz, May 9, 1977, Samuel M. Steward Papers, Boston University.

356 *At the suggestion of*: Gallup to Steward, March 24, 1970, Samuel M. Steward Papers, Boston University.

357 *"these are private experiences"*: Harrison to Steward, Jan. 27, 1971 (apparently misdated; 1972), Samuel M. Steward Papers.

358 *"If I'd been alive"*: Steward, *Roman Conquests*, p. 1.

358 *"I was at present"*: Ibid., pp. 15–16.

358 *"sex was just a"*: Ibid., p. 121.

358 *At Brian's request*: Eric Ridge, "Twelve Years Behind the Lens: The Life and Hard Times of J. Brian" (publisher and date unknown, 1975). Samuel M. Steward Papers, gift of Douglas Martin.

359 *"including, with all due"*: Sisson to Steward, Aug. 1972, Samuel M. Steward Papers.

360 *"Then in my loins"*: Steward, *Shuttlecock*, pp. 55–56.

361 *"A male 'marriage'"*: Ibid., pp. 73–74.

361 *"Back in the old days"*: Ibid., pp. 99–100.

362 *"the deadening repetitiveness"*: Ibid., p. 138.

362 *"I enjoyed all"*: Isherwood to Steward, April 30, 1975, Samuel M. Steward Papers.

362 *"the obsessions which haunt"*: Michael Bronski, "S/M: The New Romance: Cruelty Without Pain," *Gay Community News*, vol. 2, no. 30.

362 *"50% explicit sex"*: Steward to Steven Wright, June 23, 1973, Samuel M. Steward Papers, Boston University.

363 *"more than just the"*: "'J. Brian' Busted Again in S.F.," *Advocate*, July 7, 1972 [np].

364 *"a movie (still in the box)"*: Steward to Ellen Squire, Greenleaf Classics, Feb. 5, 1973, Samuel M. Steward Papers.

364 *Most of his hustlers*: "S.F. Model Agencies Hit: 20 Arrested," *Advocate*, March 1, 1972 [np], Samuel M. Steward Papers, gift of Douglas Martin.

364 *"fight it into the"*: "'J. Brian' Busted Again in S.F.," *Advocate*, July 7, 1972 [np], Samuel M. Steward Papers, gift of Douglas Martin.

365 *"learned from his mistakes"*: Steward statement on J. Brian, dated Nov. 10, 1972 (copy), Samuel M. Steward Papers.

365 *The star witness against*: "Director J. Brian Charged in Second Film 'Conspiracy,'" *Advocate*, March 27, 1974 [np]. Samuel M. Steward Papers, gift of Douglas Martin.

366 *"out of the business"*: Eric Ridge, "Twelve Years Behind the Lens."

367 *demanding more "hots"*: Ellen Squire to Steward, April 25, 1973, Samuel M. Steward Papers.

367 *"It's sorta like the"*: Steward to "Donnyboy" Ireland, Sept. 27, 1979, Samuel M. Steward Papers, Boston University.

367 *Tremendously shaken, he returned*: Steward, "Early Chapters," p. 145.

368 *"I am happy to"*: Gallup to Steward, Nov. 4, 1974, Samuel M. Steward Papers.

368 *"disposing of all the"*: Steward to Gallup, Nov. 25, 1974, Samuel M. Steward Papers, Boston University.

368 *Although Steward would be*: Preston, Introduction to *STUD* (Alyson, 1982).

368 *In his free time*: Roger Austen, *Playing the Game: The Homosexual Novel in America*.

N.B.: The Roger Austen papers, which are quite limited in number, are in the Manuscripts and Archives division of the Humanities and Social Sciences Library, New York Public Library (MssCol 3608).

368 *Austen would quote Steward*: Austen, *Playing the Game*, quotes "Phil Andros" on page 88, and in his citation notes, "from background notes especially written for this study by 'Phil Andros,' Berkeley, California, 1975."

368 *"the mid-seventies consensus"*: Austen, *Playing the Game*, p. 200.

369 *"If there is anyone"*: Steward, "*Hard and Hungry* (Review)," Newswest/*Advocate*, nd, np. Samuel M. Steward Papers.

369 *"It seems that as"*: Steward, *Gay Sunshine* interview, ms. p. 25. Samuel M. Steward Papers.

369 *"because of the extraordinary"*: Steward, "*Cruising Stud* (Review)," Newswest/*Advocate*, nd, np. Samuel M. Steward Papers.

370 *Steward returned to Berkeley*: Steward to Purdy, March 1, 1976, Samuel M. Steward Papers, Boston University.

370 *"I'm not sure whether"*: Steward to Barney, Jan. 6, 1976, Samuel M. Steward Papers, Boston University.

370 *He did, however, do*: "I ran down Chuck Arnett in the City and talked with him about his drawings; la, it's been about 9 years since hearing from him!" Steward to Jeanne Barney, Sept. 17, 1976, Samuel M. Steward Papers, Boston University.

370 *In the end, he*: Barney to Steward, July 26, 1976, makes clear that "Many Happy Returns" features Jim Kane and Ike Barnes. So do the stories "Babysitter" and "Four on Ice." Samuel M. Steward Papers, Boston University.

370 *"the world's first fully"*: The ad for the machine can be found in *Drummer*, vol. 1, no. 6 (May/June 1976), p. 58.

370 *"There is a manufactured"*: Steward to Pick, May 14, 1981, Samuel M. Steward Papers.

371 *In doing so he*: Steward to Rame, Jan. 19, 1976, Samuel M. Steward Papers.

371 *"As for Phil Andros"*: Steward to Wilcox, July 5, 1975, Samuel M. Steward Papers.

371 *"I had enjoyed his"*: Steward, alternate draft of "Early Chapters," pp. 314–15.

371 *"It was as if"*: Steward, "Early Chapters," p. 355.

372 *"I am hoping"*: Steward to White, Oct. 29, 1976, Samuel M. Steward Papers.

373 *"I thought Sam was"*: Fritscher, e-mail to author.

373 *"Sam didn't particularly stand"*: Baldwin, e-mail to author.

374 *"hungry males buzzing like"*: Steward to Schmidt, Oct. 21, 1976. Samuel M. Steward Papers.

374 *"(anonymously) writ[e] letters about"*: Steward to Purdy, 1977, Samuel M. Steward Papers, Boston University.

374 *To combat the disintegration*: Documents relating to ZORRO can be found in the Samuel M. Steward Papers, Boston University.

375 *"too full of girlish"*: Steward to Martin, July 1, 1977, Samuel M. Steward Papers.

375 *But to no avail*: See the Ehrlich–Steward correspondence (1977), Samuel M. Steward Papers, Boston University.

375 *"Many may take it"*: Steward to Martin, July 1, 1977, Samuel M. Steward Papers.

375 *"Sam . . . I want to"*: Schuler to Steward, Aug. 17, 1977, Samuel M. Steward Papers.

375 *"Dear Dr. Steward"*: Student to Steward, Oct. 1977, Samuel M. Steward Papers.

376 *"Remember that last day"*: Martin to Steward, June 18, 1977, Samuel M. Steward Papers.

377 *"Dear Diego"*: Steward to Martin, July 1, 1977, Samuel M. Steward Papers.

378 *"He blames me for"*: Steward to Martin, Oct. 7, 1977, Samuel M. Steward Papers.

379 *Steward played other pranks*: Steward to *New York Times Book Review*, July 14, 1977, Samuel M. Steward Papers.

379 *"this may not be"*: Steward to Hall, March 24, 1977, Samuel M. Steward Papers.

379 *"Jonathan [Ned] Katz was"*: Steward to Hall, Sept. 21, 1977, Samuel M. Steward Papers.

380 *"the complexities and nuances"*: Steward to Martin, Oct. 7, 1977, Samuel M. Steward Papers.

380 *"I've kept journals of"*: Martin to Steward, Aug. 21, 1977, Samuel M. Steward Papers.

380 *"With 914 [men] you're"*: Steward to Martin, Sept. 12, 1977, Samuel M. Steward Papers.

380 *"I fear you vastly"*: Ibid.

381 *"Pubic Hairs? Oh, my"*: Martin to Steward, Sept. 20, 1977, Samuel M. Steward Papers.

381 *"Incidentally"*: Martin to Steward, Feb. 10, 1978, Samuel M. Steward Papers.

381 *"Since you bedded him"*: Steward to Martin, "Valentino's Day," (Feb. 14) 1978, Samuel M. Steward Papers.

381 *"I spent the rest"*: Steward to Martin, July 18, 1977, Samuel M. Steward Papers.

382 *"I was an old"*: Steward to Martin, Feb. 8, 1978, Samuel M. Steward Papers.

382 *When he published it*: Steward, "A Gift from André Gide," *Gaysweek*, no. 72 (July 10, 1978), section 2, p. 9.

382 *"There are times, God"*: Steward to Kent, Jan. 20, 1977, Samuel M. Steward Papers.

382 *Home to an ever-changing*: James Gray, "Community Rift over Lifestyles," *Berkeley Gazette*, Sept. 30, 1979 [np] (clipping), Samuel M. Steward Papers.

382 *Steward responded by launching*: Steward to *Berkeley Gazette*, March 26, 1981, Samuel M. Steward Papers, Boston University.

383 *"the living legend Tom"*: Steward to Martin, "Valentino's Day, 78," Samuel M. Steward Papers.

383 *"he had to be"*: Steward to Wilcox, June 19, 1978, Samuel M. Steward Papers.

21: "PORTE AFTER STORMIE SEAS"

386 *"This business of TW"*: Steward to Hall, Sept. 5, 1979, Samuel M. Steward Papers.

387 *"You are perhaps not"*: Steward to Simon, Nov. 22, 1976, Samuel M. Steward Papers, Boston University.

387 *"[G]ad, what camouflages and"*: Steward to Martin, May 9, 1979 [postcard], Samuel M. Steward Papers.

388 *"private experiences not meant"*: Harrison to Steward, Jan. 27, 1971, Samuel M. Steward Papers.

388 *"Thank you for your letter"*: Steward to Harrison, Nov. 23, 1979. (N.B.: Steward kept carbon and attached it to Harrison correspondence.) Samuel M. Steward Papers.

389 *"firm as a clam"*: Gertrude Stein, *Everybody's Autobiography* (New York: Random House, 1937).

389 *Steward was rightly concerned*: Steward to Gallup, Dec. 18, 1979, Samuel M. Steward Papers.

389 *Anticipating that Harrison*: "The Secret Citizen of 'Our' Town: Thornton Wilder: Samuel Steward Remembers the Man," *Advocate*, no. 293, May 29, 1980, pp. 25–29.

389 *"We met in the bar"*: Steward to Harrison, June 3, 1981, Samuel M. Steward Papers.

390 *In a subsequent letter*: Steward to Harrison, Jan. 14, 1982, Samuel M. Steward Papers.

390 *"I am on the"*: Steward to Harrison, Aug. 6, 1982. The letter also gives specific page references to the section on Wilder in *Chapters from an Autobiography*, which had been published in 1981. Samuel M. Steward Papers.

391 *Upon publishing the memoir*: Paraphrased from Don Allen finding aid, Mandeville Special Collections, UCSD/La Jolla.

391 *Steward's revised memoir was*: Eric Rofes, "The Life and Hard Times of Legendary Porn Writer Phil Andros," *Advocate*, no. 307, Dec. 11, 1980, pp. 23–27.

391 *"As I watched Scott"*: Steward, *Chapters*, p. 138.

391 *"From the very beginning"*: Steward to Darrell Inabnit, April 26–27, 1981, Samuel M. Steward Papers.

392 *"The business between myself"*: Steward, *Chapters*, p. 139.

392 *"dying well may be"*: Austen to Crowley, May 15, 1981, as published in Crowley's introduction to Roger Austen, *Genteel Pagan: The Double Life of Charles Warren Stoddard* (Amherst: University of Massachusetts Press, 1985).

392 *"Under the influence of"*: Austen to Steward, June 1, 1981, Samuel M. Steward Papers.

393 *Upon returning to Los Angeles*: Austen to Steward, undated (approximately June 16, 1981), Samuel M. Steward Papers.

393 *"at my age I"*: Steward to Austen, June 17, 1981, Samuel M. Steward Papers.

393 *"George Platt Lynes"*: Steward, "George Platt Lynes: The Man," *Advocate*, no. 332, Dec. 10, 1981, pp. 22, 24.

393 *He also produced a*: Steward, "Oxford's 'Queen Lotus Dust': Cardinal Newman & Friends," *Advocate*, no. 331, Nov. 26, 1981.

394 *"you have exactly caught"*: Steward to Laaksonen (Tom of Finland), April 20, 1982, Samuel M. Steward Papers.

395 *"I feel proud to"*: Laaksonen to Steward, Dec. 14, 1983, Samuel M. Steward Papers.

395 *"What do you do"*: Steward to Preston, Sept. 27, 1983, Samuel M. Steward Papers.

395 *"I hope you will"*: McDonald to Steward, Dec. 11, 1982. (N.B.: McDonald offered to pay Steward one hundred dollars for each of the two questionnaires.) Samuel M. Steward Papers.

395 *"I'm not sure that"*: Steward to McDonald, Dec. 20, 1982, Samuel M. Steward Papers.

395 *Steward had been an*: Steward noted his interest in *Straight to Hell* in a letter he wrote to Robert Mapplethorpe (Feb. 17, 1978; Samuel M. Steward Papers) as well as in his response to McDonald of Dec. 20, 1982. Samuel M. Steward Papers.

396 *"To say that your"*: Steward to Sprague, April 9, 1982, Samuel M. Steward Papers.

397 *Steward published a long*: "Remembering Dr. Kinsey: Sexual Scientist and Investigator," *Advocate*, no. 305, Nov. 13, 1980. See edited version in *Chapters*, pp. 95–106.

397 *A detailed account of*: Steward, "A Pilgrim's Day and Passages from a Diary: A Visit with Thomas Mann," *Advocate*, no. 376, Sept. 15, 1983, pp. 28–31, 35.

397 *At the suggestion of*: Steward to Preston, July 27, 1983, Samuel M. Steward Papers, Boston University.

398 *Steward's horror at the*: Steward to Gerald McCabe, Jan. 27, 1989, Samuel M. Steward Papers, Boston University.

398 *"It will be easy"*: Steward, letter to his doctor, Sept. 22, 1984, Samuel M. Steward Papers, Boston University.

399 *"It's going to be"*: Steward to Preston, Jan. 4, 1990, Samuel M. Steward Papers, Boston University.

399 *Living on bottled oxygen*: Robert Prager, e-mail to author; Michael Williams, e-mail to author.

400 *"There were files"*: Michael Williams, e-mail to author.

402 *"[I've met] a handsome"*: Steward to Preston, Sept. 26, 1990, Samuel M. Steward Papers, Boston University.

402 *"And that was how"*: Steward, Revised *Chapters*, pp. 328–32.

403 *Steward had been hosted*: Steward to Preston, Nov. 5, 1990, Samuel M. Steward Papers, Boston University.

403 *"let me know that"*: Steward, Revised *Chapters*, p. 297a.

403 *Though disappointed, Danny*: Steward, Revised *Chapters*, p. 332.

404 *"a precious link with"*: John Grube, "Bad Boys and Tough Tattoos" (Review), *Society of Lesbian and Gay Anthropologists Newsletter*, vol. 13, no. 1 (Feb. 1991), pp. 15–17.

404 *"the author, the topic"*: Gerald R. Gurmet, MD, "Urban Armor" (Review), *Readings: A Journal of Reviews and Commentary in Mental Health*, vol. 7, no. 1 (March 1992), pp. 8–11.

404 *Steward's last years were*: John Preston, *Hustling: A Gentleman's Guide to the Fine Art of Homosexual Prostitution* (New York: Richard Kasak/Masquerade, 1994).

405 *"I wish there were"*: Steward to Martin, Oct. 3, 1991, Samuel M. Steward Papers.

406 *"Sam called me"*: Michael Williams, e-mail to author.

AFTERWORD: THE STEWARD PAPERS

407 *Jim Kane's "slave" Ike*: Michael Williams, e-mail to author.

407 *"the task of clearing"*: Ibid.

408 *"I [have been] going"*: Michael Williams to Don Allen, July 14, 1994, Samuel M. Steward Papers.

SELECTED BIBLIOGRAPHY

The following selected bibliography focuses on published works most relevant to the researching of *Secret Historian*, for the vast majority of Steward's unpublished writings remain the property of his executor and heir, and so are currently unavailable to researchers. So, too, are the more than three hundred newspaper clippings, magazine clippings, incoming correspondence, and ephemera that Steward collected during his lifetime relating to his life and work.

Many of Steward's most interesting unpublished and out-of-print writings will be published in the coming year as *Notes from the Sexual Underground: Selected Writings of Samuel Steward, the Renegade Author Also Known as Phil Andros*, Justin Spring, ed. (New York: Hidden Bungalow Press, 2010). Similarly, a substantial selection of Steward's visual work from the Steward archive will be published in the coming year as *An Obscene Diary: The Visual World of Samuel M. Steward* by Justin Spring (North Pomfret, Vt.: Elysium Press/Antinous Press, 2010).

1. MANUSCRIPT AND ARCHIVAL COLLECTIONS OF NOTE

Donald Allen Papers, Mandeville Special Collections/Archive for New Poetry, University of California at San Diego/La Jolla, California.

Kenneth Anger Papers, Kinsey Institute Library, Kinsey Institute for Research in Sex, Gender and Reproduction, Bloomington, Indiana.

Roger Austen Papers, Manuscripts and Archives Division, New York Public Library, New York.

Edward Field Papers, Special Collections, University of Delaware Library, Newark, Delaware.

Jim Kane Papers, Leather Archives and Museum, Chicago, Illinois.

Richard G. Katzoff Collection, John Hay Library, Brown University, Providence, Rhode Island. This collection includes the Gay Pulp Fiction Collection and Database, a collection of over 30,000 titles. (This database is searchable on the Web at http://128.148.7.229:591/gaypulp/default.htm.)

The Chester H. Kirk Collection on Alcoholism and Alcoholics Anonymous, John Hay Library, Brown University.

Correspondence between George Platt Lynes and Bernard Perlin. Yale Collection of
    American Literature, Beinecke Rare Book and Manuscript Library.
Dom Orejudos Papers, Leather Archives and Museum, Chicago, Illinois.
John Preston Papers, John Hay Library, Brown University, Providence, Rhode Island.
Charles Renslow papers, Leather Archives and Museum, Chicago, Illinois.
Gertrude Stein and Alice B. Toklas Papers, Yale Collection of American Literature.
    Beinecke Rare Book and Manuscript Library, Yale University, New Haven, Connecti-
    cut. (These papers contain the majority of Steward's letters to Stein and Toklas.)
Samuel M. Steward Holdings, Leather Archives and Museum, Chicago, Illinois. A small
    collection of artworks by Steward, including a portrait of Dom Orejudos. Films in-
    cluding Steward and still photographs in which Steward appears can also be found
    in the Renslow and Orejudos holdings at the Leather Archives and Museum.
Samuel M. Steward Papers, Howard Gotlieb Archival Research Center, Boston Univer-
    sity. This is a small collection of papers donated late in life by Steward to Boston
    University. It consists primarily of printed material, manuscript material, and Stew-
    ard's late-life incoming and outgoing correspondence.
Samuel M. Steward Papers, Kinsey Institute Library, Kinsey Institute for Research in Sex,
    Gender, and Reproduction, Bloomington, Indiana. While there is no indication of a
    Steward Collection mentioned on the Kinsey Institute Library's website, the Steward
    holdings of that library are extensive, and a guide to them does exist in the form of a
    printed finding aid. However, Kinsey Institute librarians will only share that finding
    aid (and other information on their Steward holdings, which includes both visual and
    written material) pending the approval of the institute.
Alice B. Toklas Papers, Bancroft Special Collections Library, University of California,
    Berkeley. This collection contains the majority of Toklas's letters to Steward, as well
    as a substantial amount of memorabilia kept by Steward relating to his visits to Stein
    and Toklas at Paris and Bilignin.
Glenway Wescott Papers, Yale Collection of American Literature. Beinecke Rare Book
    and Manuscript Library, Yale University, New Haven, Connecticut.
Thornton Wilder Papers, Yale Collection of American Literature. Beinecke Rare Book and
    Manuscript Library, Yale University, New Haven, Connecticut.
H. Lynn Womack Papers, #7441, Division of Rare and Manuscript Collections, Cornell
    University Library, Ithaca, New York.
Morton Dauwen Zabel Papers, Newberry Library, Chicago, Illinois.

2. PUBLISHED WRITINGS AND ILLUSTRATIONS BY STEWARD

The published writings and illustrations in this section, though created by Samuel M. Steward, were often signed by Steward using various assumed names. In youth, he preferred the
shortened name of "Sam Steward," while in later life, he relied heavily on anagrams and
pseudonyms. In the interest of bibliographical clarity, I have given the names Steward himself used in signing each of the essays, articles, drawings, stories, poems, or reviews, with
the understanding that all of these names are pseudonyms or abbreviations chosen by Steward to identify himself. The writings in this section are arranged chronologically.

Steward, Sam M. "Virginia to Harlotta" (sonnet). *Contemporary Verse*. [Atlantic City, N.J.]
    25.4 (October 1929): np.

————. *Pan and the fire-bird*. Introduction by Benjamin Musser. New York: Henry Harrison, 1930. pp. 1–59.

————. "Desires" (short story). *Ohio Stater* [Columbus] 1.1 (November 1932): 1–3, 15.

————. "Mutability in Spenser." Unpublished master's thesis, Ohio State University, 1932.

————. "The Passion and the Soul of Petrarch." *The Sewanee Review* 41 (1933): 419–429.

Steward, S. M. "J.-K. Huysmans and George Moore." *The Romantic Review* 25.3 (July–September 1934): 197–206.

Steward, Samuel Morris. "Provocatives of the Oxford Movement and Its Nexus with English Literary Romanticism." Unpublished Ph.D. dissertation, Ohio State University, 1934.

Stames, Ward. "The Lay Faculty." *The Commonweal* 21.24 (April 12, 1935): 667–668. See also Jeremiah K. Durick, "The Lay Faculty: A Reply," *The Commonweal* 21.25 (April 19, 1935): 699–701.

Steward, S. M. *Angels on the Bough*. Caldwell, Idaho: Caxton, 1936.

De Mereille, Guy. *Bell Bottom Trousers* (N.D. approximately 1943, self-published.) The cover of the publication reads, "Of this story twenty five copies have been hectographed, five of which have been preserved for the author. It is particularly intended for the enjoyment of members of the Armed Services, and permission to reprint it is freely given. This is copy number ONE." (N.B.: The only known extant copy of this booklet is in the library of the Kinsey Institute for Sex, Gender, and Reproduction.)

Sparrow, Philip. "The Victim's Viewpoint: On Sublimated Sadism; or, the Dentist as Iago." *Illinois Dental Journal* 13 (February 1944): 78.

————. "The Victim's Viewpoint: On Getting an Appointment in Wartime." *Illinois Dental Journal* 13 (February 1944): 78.

————. "The Victim's Viewpoint: On the Prospect of Confinement by Porcelain Arms." *Illinois Dental Journal* 13 (March 1944): 120.

————. "The Victim's Viewpoint: On the Survival of the Medieval." *Illinois Dental Journal* 13 (April 1944): 173.

————. "The Victim's Viewpoint: On Logorrhea." *Illinois Dental Journal* 13 (May 1944): 214–15.

————. "The Victim's Viewpoint: On Psychic Somersaulting." *Illinois Dental Journal* 13 (June 1944): 248–49.

————. "The Victim's Viewpoint: On Bread and Butter." *Illinois Dental Journal* 13 (July 1944): 312–13. See also William P. Schoen, Jr., "Philip Sparrow Quits" [editorial]: 308.

————. "One Man's Viewpoint: On the Songs of War." *Illinois Dental Journal* 13 (September 1944): 419.

————. "On Cryptography." *Illinois Dental Journal* 13 (October 1944): 452–53.

————. "On Alchoholics Anonymous." *Illinois Dental Journal* 13 (November 1944): 498–99.

————. "On Christmas." *Illinois Dental Journal* 13 (December 1944): 540–41.

————. "On Fifteen Years of Lent." *Illinois Dental Journal* 14 (January 1945): 34–35.

————. "On Soldiers and Civilians." *Illinois Dental Journal* 14 (February 1945): 74–75.

————. "On How to Cook a Wolf." *Illinois Dental Journal* 14 (March 1945): 128–29.

————. "On How to Be a Spy." *Illinois Dental Journal* 14 (April 1945): 156–57.

————. "On Psychiatry." *Illinois Dental Journal* 14 (May 1945): 214–15.

———. "On Balletomania." *Illinois Dental Journal* 14 (June 1945): 248–49.

———. "On the Dilettanti." *Illinois Dental Journal* 14 (July 1945): 302–303.

———. "On Books from Prison." *Illinois Dental Journal* 14 (September 1945): 398–99.

———. Letter to Doctor Schoen ["Philip Sparrow Writes Letter"]. *Illinois Dental Journal* 14 (October–November 1945): 435.

———. "On Cemeteries." *Illinois Dental Journal* 14 (October–November 1945): 438–39.

———. "On Basic English." *Illinois Dental Journal* 14 (December 1945): 472–73.

———. "On the Laws of War." *Illinois Dental Journal* 15 (February 1946): 68–69.

———. "On a Call to Paris." *Illinois Dental Journal* 15 (March 1946): 124–25.

———. "On the Importance of Dying Young." *Illinois Dental Journal* 15 (April 1946): 152–53.

———. "On Witch-Doctoring." *Illinois Dental Journal* 15 (May 1946): 196–97.

Steward, Samuel M. "The Literature of Prophecy." *Illinois Dental Journal* 15 (June 1946): 222–224.

Sparrow, Philip. "On Reading Experiences." *Illinois Dental Journal* 15 (July 1946): 290–91.

———. "On Chicago." *Illinois Dental Journal* 15 (August 1946): 338–39.

———. "On How to Write an Encyclopedia." *Illinois Dental Journal* 15 (October 1946): 436–37.

———. "On Aviating." *Illinois Dental Journal* 15 (November 1946): 478–79.

———. "On Operas and Operating." *Illinois Dental Journal* 15 (December 1946): 520–21.

Fine arts and education editor for *World Book Encyclopedia* 1946–47. "Paris" entry [1947].

Sparrow, Philip. "On Men and Their Feathers." *Illinois Dental Journal* 16 (January 1947): 18–19.

———. "On Gertrude Stein." *Illinois Dental Journal* 16 (February 1947): 64–65.

———. "On Little White Ribbons." *Illinois Dental Journal* 16 (March 1947): 108–109.

———. "On Being Musclebound." *Illinois Dental Journal* 16 (April 1947): 152–53.

———. "On Life Insurance Agents." *Illinois Dental Journal* 16 (May 1947): 188–89.

———. "On My Poor Old Radio." *Illinois Dental Journal* 16 (August 1947): 342–43. [See "About Philip Sparrow," *Illinois Dental Journal* 16 (June 1947): 247–48. This note by the editors explains that Philip Sparrow will be on vacation "for this month only."]

———. "On the Beach and Me." *Illinois Dental Journal* 16 (September 1947): 388–89.

———. "An Open Letter to My Landlord." *Illinois Dental Journal* 16 (October 1947): 426–27.

———. "On Teaching." *Illinois Dental Journal* 16 (November 1947): 476–77.

———. "To a Chance Acquaintance." *Illinois Dental Journal* 16 (December 1947): 512–13.

———. "On Fabulous, Fabulous Field's." *Illinois Dental Journal* 17 (January 1948): 22–23.

———. "On Rooshia." *Illinois Dental Journal* 17 (February 1948): 76–77.

———. "On Fair, Fantastic Paris." *Illinois Dental Journal* 17 (April 1948): 164–65.

———. "On Ulysses, Grown Old." *Illinois Dental Journal* 17 (May 1948): 202–203.

———. "On the Comic Spirit." *Illinois Dental Journal* 17 (June 1948): 240–41.

———. "On Those Precious Two Weeks." *Illinois Dental Journal* 17 (July 1948): 294–95.

———. "On Keepsakes, Gew-Gaws, and Baubles." *Illinois Dental Journal* 17 (September 1948): 392–93.

———. "[Mohammed Zenouhin]." *Illinois Dental Journal* 17 (October 1948): 438–39.

———. "On Tipping." *Illinois Dental Journal* 17 (November 1948): 480–81.

———. "On the Dream, the Illusion." *Illinois Dental Journal* 17 (December 1948): 516–17.

———. "On Misplaced Eyebrows." *Illinois Dental Journal* 18 (January 1949): 32–33.

———. "On Time-Saving Devices." *Illinois Dental Journal* 18 (February 1949): 72–73.

———. "On Table Manners." *Illinois Dental Journal* 18 (April 1949): 126–27.

———. "On Getting to Be Forty." *Illinois Dental Journal* 18 (May 1949): 182–83.

———. "On TV." *Illinois Dental Journal* 18 (June 1949): 228–29.

———. "A Modest Proposal." *Illinois Dental Journal* 18 (July 1949): 276–77.

———. Title unavailable. *Illinois Dental Journal* 18 (September 1949): 378–79. See also William P. Schoen, Jr., "Sparrow Brings Mail" [editorial]: 374. (lost)

Phil. A drawing. *Der Kreis*, March 1958, p. 39.

Steward. "Detachment: A Way of Life." *Der Kreis*, August 1958, pp. 34–36. Reprinted as "Abstand Lernen," *Der Kreis*, February 1959, pp. 2–4.

Phillip. A drawing. *Der Kreis*, October 1958, pp. 33.

Drawing. "Friendship-twin gesture." *Der Kreis*, November 1958, pp. 36.

Phil. A drawing. *Der Kreis*, January 1959, p. 1.

Steward. "The Circle's New Year's Eve" (with drawing). *Der Kreis*, February 1959, pp. 29–30.

Young, Phillip. "Hook, Line, and Sinker" (written in collaboration with Rudolf Burkhardt-Jung). *Der Kreis*, April–May 1959, pp. 29–33.

Phil. A drawing. *Der Kreis*, June 1959, p. 36.

"Gestures" (with drawing). *Der Kreis*, July 1959, p. 36.

Phil. A drawing. *Der Kreis*, August 1959, p. 36.

Steward. "Ecco, Narcissus!" *Der Kreis*, September 1959, pp. 35–36. Reprinted as by Phil Andros in *Christopher Street* 5.7 (July 1981): 41. [Accompanied by two article reviews by John Preston, "Brothers and Fathers and Sons," pp. 36–39, and George Whitmore, "The Father of Us All," pp. 42–43.]

Young, Phillip. "Letter from Athens" (written in collaboration with Rudolf Burkhardt-Jung). *Der Kreis*, November 1959, pp. 29–32.

Steward. Translation of poem by Wang Chi'en (from French translation): "On Learning That His Friend Was Returning from the War." *Der Kreis*, November 1959, p. 36.

Phil. A drawing. *Der Kreis*, December 1959, p. 47.

———. *Der Kreis*, February 1960, p. 36.

Stames, Ward. "The Sergeant with the Rose Tattoo." *Der Kreis*, March 1960, pp. 29–36. Reprinted in *eos* (Copenhagen), 1961. Reprinted as "Der Sergeant mit der tatowierten Rose," *Der Kreis*, January 1965, pp. 1–10. (lost)

Unsigned. "Death Averted, or Happy Days Are Here Again" (subscriber's letter to editor). *Der Kreis*, April 1960, p. 46.

Stames, Ward. "The Bargain Hunters." *Der Kreis*, August 1960, pp. 29–35. Reprinted as "Die Echte Munze," *Der Kreis*, September 1964, pp. 2–9. Reprinted in *Different Strokes* as by Andros, title "The Economists."

Steward. "To the Making of a Saint" (sonnet; with drawing). *Der Kreis*, December 1960, p. 48.

McAndrews, John. "The Male Homosexual and Marriage" (published as "excerpt from novel"). *Der Kreis*, February 1961, p. 29.

———. "Dream Life" (published as "excerpt from novel"). *Der Kreis*, May 1961, p. 36.

Bishop, Donald. "The Bull Market in America." *Der Kreis*, June 1961, pp. 28–31.

Philip. Woodcut of sailor with match (Chicago). *Der Kreis*, July 1961, p.27.

McAndrews, John. "Man's Chase after Happiness" (published as "excerpt from novel"). *Der Kreis*, January 1962, p. 33.

Philip. Drawing: "The Fishing Net" (Chicago). *Der Kreis*, March 1962, p. 20.

Bishop, Donald. "What's New in Sodom?" *Der Kreis*, April 1962, pp. 30–33. Reprinted as "Was Gibt Es Neues in Sodom?" *Der Kreis*, May 1962, pp. 2–5.

Stames, Ward. "Jungle Cat." *Der Kreis*, June 1962, pp. 29–36. Reprinted as "Das Raubtier aus den Dschungel," *h i m*, February 1972, begins on p. 32.

Phil. Drawing: "Antonio." *Der Kreis*, July 1962.

Excerpt: "Consolation." Letter and drawing. *Der Kreis*, September 1962, p. 36.

Unsigned. "Is Sex a Narcotic?" (letter). *Der Kreis*, December 1962, p. 48.

McAndrews, John. "The Problem of the Uniform" ("excerpt"). *Der Kreis*, January 1963, p. 33.

Bishop, Donald. "The Lover" (vignette, with Etienne's painting *Orpheus*). *Der Kreis*, May 1963, p. 29.

Stames, Ward. "Baby Tiger." *amigo* no. 16, June 1963, pp. 207–209. Reprinted as "Handyret," *eos*, August 1963. [See "Little Lamb, Who Made Thee?" below.]

Review of John Rechy's *City of Night*. *Der Kreis*, July 1963, pp. 35–36.

Stames, Ward. "Little Lamb, Who Made Thee?" *amigo* no. 17, July 1963. Reprinted as "Sejr over Handyret," *eos*, September 1963. A bowdlerized and combined version of this story and "Baby Tiger" (listed above) were published as Phil Andros, "Little Lamb, Who Made Thee?" *Drum*, December 1965, begins on p. 8.

McAndrews, John. "My god, he's stupid . . ." ("vignette"). *Der Kreis*, August 1963, p. 35.

Andros, Phil. "The Poison Tree." *amigo* no. 18, August 1963, pp. 281–86. Reprinted as "Gifftraet," *eos*, October 1963. Included in the original edition of *$tud* (pp. 1–15).

———. "The Blacks and Mr. Bennett." *amigo* no. 21, October 1963, pp. 351–55. Reprinted as "De Sorte og Mister Bennett," *eos*, February 1964. Reprinted as "Die Schwarzen und Mr. Bennett," *amigo* no. 38, September 1965, pp. 315–19, 345. Included in the original edition of *$tud* (pp. 266–78).

Bishop, Donald. "The Negro Homosexual in America." *amigo* no. 21, January 1964, pp. 31–35, 42. Reprinted as "Den Homofile Neger i USA," *eos*, February 1964.

Andros, Phil. "Some of These Days." *amigo* no. 22, 1964, pp. 71–75. Reprinted as "Ein Skønne Dag," *eos*, January 1964.

———. "Mirror, Mirror on the Wall." *amigo* no. 23, 1964, pp. 90, 107–10, 113–14. Reprinted as "Lille Spejl pa Vaeggen Der," *eos*, April 1964. Included in the original edition of *$tud* (16–31). Reprinted in *Different: An Anthology of Homosexual Stories*, ed. Stephen Wright (New York: Bantam, 1974), pp. 35–47.

———. "Arrangement in Black and White." *amigo* no. 24, 1964, pp. 146–50. Included in the original edition of *$tud* (pp. 136–47). Reprinted in *Different: An Anthology of Homosexual Stories*, ed. Stephen Wright (New York: Bantam, 1974), pp. 62–70.

Bishop, Donald. "Pussies in Boots." *amigo* no. 25, 1964, pp. 183–90. Reprinted as "De Bestøvlede Katte," *eos*, June 1964. Reprinted as "Der Gestiefelte Kater—Susse Jungen in Stiefeln," *amigo* no. 35, 1965, pp. 168–72, 203. Truncated version reprinted as Steward, Samuel M. "The Leather Fraternity: Boys Looking for 'Real' Men," [Philadelphia] *Gay News*, April 16–29, 1982, pp. 12–13.

Stames, Ward. "The House on the Rue Erlanger." *Der Kreis*, May 1964, pp. 29–36.

Andros, Phil. "Color Him Black." *amigo* no. 26, 1964, pp. 219–25. Reprinted as "Farv Him Sort!" *eos*, August 1964. Reprinted as "Farbt Ihn Schwarz!" *amigo* no. 40, 1965, pp. 410–13, 459–63. Included in the original edition of *$tud* (pp. 279–95).

―――. "I (Cupid) and the Gangster," *amigo* no. 27, 1964, pp. 255–61. Reprinted as "Jeg, Amor―og Ham Gangsteren," *eos*, July 1964. Included in the original edition of *$tud* (pp. 234–49). Reprinted in *Different: An Anthology of Homosexual Stories*, ed. Stephen Wright (New York: Bantam, 1974), pp. 71–83. Reprinted in *Below the Belt* (pp. 48–57).

McAndrews, John. Review of Kenneth Anger's *Scorpio Rising*. *amigo* no. 28, 1964, pp. 298–300. Reprinted in *Der Kreis*, October 1964, pp. 34–36.

―――. "The Peachiest Fuzz." *Der Kreis*, August 1964, pp. 29–36. Included in the original edition of *$tud* (pp. 180–98). Reprinted in *Below the Belt* (24–35).

Andros, Phil. "Ace in the Hole." *amigo* no. 29, 1964, pp. 331–38. Reprinted as "Sa Sort Som et Kul," *eos*, October 1964 and November 1964. Included in the original edition of *$tud* (pp. 65–84).

―――. "Two-Bit Whore." *amigo* no. 30, 1964, pp. 377–82, 391. Reprinted as "De Sorte Maends Nat," *eos*, December 1964. Included in the original edition of *$tud* (pp. 85–101).

―――. "For Een Gangs Skyld" ["Once in a Blue Moon"]. *eos*, September 1964. Reprinted as "Once in a Blue Moon," *amigo* no. 32, 1965, pp. 78–83. Included in the original edition of *$tud* (pp. 148–64).

Cave, Thomas. "The Narrowing Circle." *amigo* no. 30, 1964, pp. 388–91. Reprinted as "Er Det Snart Nat Med de Homofile Glaeder," *eos*, March 1965. Reprinted as by Phil Andros, "The Narrowing Circle," *Vector*, July 1970, pp. 16–17.

Phil. End-piece. Drawing. *Der Kreis*, December 1964, p. 48.

Andros, Phil. "The Tattooed Harpist." *amigo* no. 31, 1965, pp. 33–39. Included in the original edition of *$tud* (pp. 250–65).

Stames, Ward. "The Link." *Der Kreis*, January 1965, pp. 29–36. Reprinted as "Das Bindeglied," *h i m* October 1971. Reprinted in E. V. Griffith, ed., *In Homage to Priapus* (San Diego: Greenleaf Classics, 1970), pp. 86–96. Reprinted in *Golden Boys* no. 6, no date.

Andros, Phil. "Farandring Fryder―Somme Tider." *eos*, January 1965. Reprinted as "Sea-Change," *amigo* no. 34, 1965, pp. 155–59, 162–63. Included in the original edition of *$tud* (pp. 199–215). English version reprinted in *Different: An Anthology of Homosexual Stories*, ed. Stephen Wright (New York: Bantam, 1974), pp. 48–61.

―――. "A Collar for Achilles." *amigo* nos. 33–34, 1965, pp. 118–20, 122, 160–62. Included in the original edition of *$tud* (pp. 165–79).

―――. "Paskedrengen" ["The Easter Kid"]. *eos*, April 1965. Reprinted as "The Christmas Kid," *amigo* no. 40, 1965, pp. 452–57. Included in the original edition of *$tud* (pp. 32–47) as "The Easter Kid."

―――. "The Green Monkey." *amigo* no. 35, 1965, pp. 208–14. Reprinted as "Der Grønne Abe," *eos*, December 1967. Included in the original edition of *$tud* (pp. 48–64). Reprinted, without Steward's permission, in *Gay Blades* (1975), a collection of eight short stories allegedly published in Holland, but (according to Steward) "definitely [I later learned] issuing from Los Angeles."

―――. "H²." *amigo* no. 37, 1965, pp. 299–304, 307. Included in the original edition of *$tud* (pp. 102–18).

Ole Leather-Sniffer. "Laederfront, USA" (a monthly column). *MANege* September 1965 through June 1966. This magazine was published by Kim Kent (Knut Rame) as a "leather" offshoot of *eos* and *amigo*.

Andros, Phil. "The World-Rat, Number III." *amigo* nos. 38–39, 1965: no. 38, pp. 349–52 / no. 39, pp. 395–98. Included in the original edition of *$tud* (pp. 119–35).

McAndrews, John. Poems in the Manner of Housman (ten poems). *Der Kreis*, November 1965, pp. 29–36.

———. Poems in the Manner of Housman (ten more poems). *Der Kreis*, December 1965, pp. 39–46.

Andros, Phil. *$tud*. Washington, D.C.: Guild, 1966 [hardcover]. Includes a number of earlier stories, along with "Love Me Little, Love Me Long" (pp. 216–33). Pirated, unsigned paperback reprinted by "Beaumont Classics" (Womack) in three paperback volumes, with nude photographs of a young male model. Reprinted in paperback (San Francisco: J. Brian, 1969). Reprinted in truncated paperback to meet publisher's page requirements for *$tud* (Boston: Alyson Press, 1982). This latter version includes all stories *except* "The Peachiest Fuzz," "Love Me Little, Love Me Long," "I (Cupid) and the Gangster," "World Rat #III," "The Blacks and Mr. Bennett," and "The Tattooed Harpist."

Drawing. *Der Kreis*, January 1966, p. 28.

McAndrews, John. "Cuba-Ballade" ["The Reluctant Spy"]. *MANege* March–June 1966. Reprinted in *Different Strokes* as "The Cuba Caper."

Stames, Ward. "A Trap for Tigers." *Der Kreis*, May 1966, pp. 30–36. Reprinted as "Eine Falle für Tiger," *h i m* [Hamburg, West Germany], May 1971. Reprinted in *Golden Boys* [San Francisco], no. 8, no date. Much revised version appears as by Phil Andros, "Things Are Seldom," *Gaytimes*, no. 37, December 1975, pp. 11–12. Reprinted in *Below the Belt* (pp. 16–23).

Drawing ("reprise"). *Der Kreis*, June 1966, p. 14.

Cave, Thomas. "The Better Samaritan." *Der Kreis*, September 1966, pp. 29–35. Reprinted as "Der Bessere Samariter," *h i m* November 1971. Reprinted in *Below the Belt* (pp. 81–92).

Stames, Ward. "The Family Man." *Der Kreis*, January 1967, pp. 29–36. Reprinted in *Below the Belt* (pp. 1–15).

Phil. Drawing. *Der Kreis*, January 1967, p. 16.

Stames, Ward. "The Pool Cue." *Der Kreis*, September 1967. Reprinted as "Der Billardstock," *h i m*, August 1971.

D.O.C. "Three Kinds of Love" ("excerpt"). *Der Kreis*, September 1967.

Andros, Phil. *Ring-Around-the-Rosy*. Trilingual hardback, published as *Eosbibliotek* [Copenhagen], no. 3 (1968). Reprinted as *The Joy Spot* (San Rafael, Calif.: Frenchy's Gay Line, 1969).

———. "Pig in a Poke." *Golden Boys*, no. 9, pp. 3–9. Reprinted in *Below the Belt* (pp. 58–68).

Raymond, Joe, as told to Dr. Donald Bishop. "Kunst pa Kroppen" ["Tattooing and Sex"]. *eos*, April 1968 and May 1968. Reprinted in a slightly different form as by Phil Sparrow, as told to Phil Andros, "Tattooing and Sex," *Vector*, August 1970, pp. 10–11, 36–37, 48–49, 52–53.

Andros, Phil. "A Conversation with André Gide." *Vector*, October 1970.

———. *My Brother, the Hustler*. San Francisco: Gay Parisian Press, 1970. Revised edition reprinted as *My Brother, My Self* (San Francisco: Perineum Press [Grey Fox Press], 1983).

―――. *San Francisco Hustler*. San Francisco: Gay Parisian Press, 1970. Pirated and published, with protagonists' names changed (Phil Andros becomes Sylvon Panos) and with the ten pages of material deleted from the original publication (because of Frenchy's page requirements) as Biff Thomas, *Gay in San Francisco* (Thousand Oaks, Calif.: Cameo Library, 1974). Revised edition reprinted as *The Boys in Blue* (San Francisco: Perineum Press, 1984).

―――. *When in Rome, Do . . .* San Francisco: Gay Parisian Press, 1971. Revised edition reprinted as *Roman Conquests* (San Francisco: Perineum Press, 1983).

―――. *Renegade Hustler*. San Diego: Greenleaf, 1972. Revised edition reprinted as *Shuttlecock* (San Francisco: Perineum Press, 1984).

―――. "Ring of Fire." *eos* no. 140 / *amigo* no. 90 [Copenhagen; joint issue], 1973. Revised version reprinted in *Gaytimes*, June 1975. Reprinted in *Below the Belt* (pp. 69–75).

Kramer, Ted. "Four on Ice" (Part 1). *eos* no. 145 / *amigo* no. 95 [Copenhagen; joint issue], February 1974. Accompanied by a Danish ("Fire Mand Pa Is") and a German ("Vier auf dem Eis") translation. Part 2 appeared in *eos* no. 146 / *amigo* no. 96, April–May 1974. Part 3 appeared in *eos* no. 147 / *amigo* no. 97, June–July 1974. Reprinted as by Phil Andros, in *Drummer*, vol. 10, no. 85.

Bishop, Donald. "On Growing Old." *eos* no. 145 / *amigo* no. 95 [Copenhagen; joint issue], February 1974. Accompanied by a Danish ("Om at Blive Gammel") and a German ("Das Altwerden") translation.

Steward, Dr. G. W. "Poppers." *eos* no. 145 / *amigo* no. 95 [Copenhagen; joint issue], February 1974. Accompanied by a Danish and a German translation, both under the same title.

Steward, Dr. G. W. "The Black Kiss." *eos* no. 146 / *amigo* no. 96, April–May 1974. Accompanied by a Danish ("Det Sorte Kys") and a German ("Der Schwarze Küss") translation.

Andros, Phil. "Below the Belt." *Gaytimes*, February 1975. Reprinted in *Below the Belt* (pp. 76–80).

―――. *The Greek Way*. San Diego: Greenleaf, 1975. Revised edition reprinted as *Greek Ways* (San Francisco: Perineum Press, 1984).

―――. "Babysitter." *Drummer*, April 1976. Reprinted in *Below the Belt* (pp. 103–14).

―――. "Many Happy Returns." *Drummer*, July 1976. Reprinted in *Below the Belt* (pp. 115–28).

Steward, Samuel M., ed. *Dear Sammy: Letters from Gertrude Stein and Alice B. Toklas*, with a memoir by Samuel M. Steward (Boston: Houghton Mifflin, 1977). Reprinted (paperback), New York: St. Martin's Press, 1984.

Andros, Phil. "In a Pig's Ass." *Drummer*, Fall 1977, pp. 16–21. Reprinted in *Below the Belt* (pp. 93–102).

Steward, S. M. "Tea with Lord Alfred." *Arts and Letters*, a supplement to *Gaysweek*, February 20, 1978. See edited version in *Chapters from an Autobiography* (pp. 44–51).

―――. "A Gift from André Gide." *Arts and Letters*, a supplement to *Gaysweek*, July 10, 1978. See edited version in *Chapters from an Autobiography* (pp. 52–58).

Steward, Samuel M. "The Secret Citizen of 'Our' Town: Thornton Wilder: Samuel Steward Remembers The Man" [editor's title]. *The Advocate*, May 1980. See edited version in *Chapters from an Autobiography* (pp. 70–77).

———. "Hair Today, Gone to Macho." *The Advocate*, August 7, 1980.

———. "Is Inky Kinky? The Mystique of the Tattoo." *The Advocate*, September 1980. See edited version in *Chapters from an Autobiography* (pp. 78–94).

———. "Remembering Dr. Kinsey: Sexual Scientist and Investigator." *The Advocate*, November 13, 1980. See edited version in *Chapters from an Autobiography* (pp. 95–106).

———. "The Life and Hard Times of the Legendary Porn Writer, Phil Andros." *The Advocate*, December 11, 1980. See edited version in *Chapters from an Autobiography* (pp. 107–18).

———. "France & Gertie & Sam & Alice." *The Advocate*, May 14, 1981, pp. 19–22. See edited version in *Chapters from an Autobiography* (pp. 58–70).

———. "Orpheus." *Vortex*, Spring 1981, p. 10.

———. *Chapters from an Autobiography*. San Francisco: Grey Fox Press, 1981. See review by Eric R. Rofes, "A Man for All Seasons," *Gay Community News Book Review* [Boston], October 17, 1981, p. 6.

———. "Erotica—the Purest Form of Entertainment." [Philadelphia] *Gay News*, August 7–20, 1981.

———. "Oxford's 'Queer Lotus-Dust': Cardinal Newman and Friends." *The Advocate*, November 26, 1981, pp. 25–27.

———. "George Platt Lynes: The Man" (memoir). *The Advocate*, December 10, 1981.

———. Review of Felice Picano's *An Asian Minor: The True Story of Ganymede*. *The Advocate*, June 1982.

Andros, Phil. *Below the Belt and Other Stories*. With a "Note" by Samuel M. Steward. San Francisco: Perineum Press [Grey Fox Press], 1982.

Steward, Samuel M. "To a Young Gay Alcoholic." *The Advocate*, July 8, 1982, pp. 35–38.

———. *Murder Is Murder Is Murder Is Murder*. Alyson Books, 1984.

———. *Parisian Lives*. New York: St. Martin's Press, 1984.

3. INTERVIEWS WITH SAMUEL M. STEWARD

Evans, Len. "Samuel M. Steward interviewed by Len Evans on July 23, 1983." An interview conducted as part of *Voices: The Oral History Project of the Gay, Lesbian, Bisexual and Transgendered Historical Society of Northern California*, and later published in the *Journal of the History of Sexuality*, vol. 9, no. 4 (October 2000): 474–93.

Fritscher, Jack. "Jack Fritscher Interview with Sam Steward." An unpublished typescript, dated 1974. Collection of Jack Fritscher.

Leyland, Winston. "Samuel M. Steward" (interview). *Gay Sunshine Interviews, Volume II* (San Francisco: Gay Sunshine Press, 1982).

Maves, Karl. "Samuel M. Steward" (interview). *The Advocate*, August 24, 1977, pp 25–27.

———. "Valentino's Pubic Hair and Me: The Many Lives of Writer Sam Steward." *The Advocate*, June 6, 1989, pp. 72–74

McDonald, Boyd. "Samuel M. Steward." Two interviews conducted by mail and possibly published (anonymously) in McDonald's *Straight to Hell* magazine. Steward's copy of these typed interviews remain in the Samuel M. Steward Papers. Correspondence between McDonald and Steward can be found in the Steward Papers, but no finished copy of the published *Straight to Hell* magazine has yet been located.

Rofes, Eric. "Steward on Sex: Author 'Phil Andros' Looks Back" (interview). *The Advocate*,
December 11, 1984, pp. 88–90.

Sprague, Gregory. "Samuel M. Steward" (interview). Copies of this interview, which is of
minimal interest, can be found in the Studs Terkel Center for Oral History, Chicago
History Museum.

4. INTERVIEWS WITH OTHERS

Cliff Ingram/Cliff Raven (Jack Rinella, interviewer), taped interview with transcription
available. Leather Archives and Museum.

Charles Renslow (Joseph Bean, interviewer), taped interview with transcription available,
Collection of the Leather Archives and Museum.

Dom Orejudos (Joseph Bean, interviewer), taped interview with transcription available,
Collection of the Leather Archives and Museum.

5. PUBLISHED WRITINGS BY OTHERS

Adams, Stephen. *The Homosexual as Hero in Contemporary Fiction*. New York: Barnes and
Noble Critical Studies, 1980.

Algren, Nelson. *Chicago: City on the Make*. Chicago: University of Chicago Press, 2001.

Allport, Gordon. *The Use of Personal Documents in Psychological Science*. New York: Social Science Research Council, 1942.

Amory, Richard. *The Song of the Loon*, with an introduction by Michael Bronski. Vancouver: Arsenal Pulp Press, 2005.

Anger, Kenneth. *Hollywood Babylon*. San Francisco: Straight Arrow Books, 1975.

———. *Hollywood Babylon II*. New York: Dutton, 1984.

Arvin, Newton. *Whitman*. New York: Macmillan, 1938.

Austen, Roger. *Genteel Pagan: The Double Life of Charles Warren Stoddard*. Amherst:
University of Massachusetts Press, 1985.

———. *Playing the Game: The Homosexual Novel in America*. Indianapolis, Bobbs-
Merrill, 1977.

Bachner, Evan. *At Ease: The Navy Men of World War II*. New York: Abrams, 2004.

———. *Men of World War II: Fighting Men at Ease*. New York: Abrams, 2007.

Baldwin, Guy. *Ties That Bind: The SM/Leather/Fetish Erotic Style, Issues, Commentaries
and Advice*, Joseph Bean, ed. Los Angeles: Daedalus, 1993.

Barger, Ralph "Sonny," with Keith and Kent Zimmerman. *Hells Angel: The Life and Times
of Sonny Barger and the Hells Angels Motorcycle Club*. New York: HarperCollins,
2001.

Barron, Jerome A. and C. Thomas Dienes. *MANual Enterprises v. Day*, 370 U.S. 478 in
1962; *First Amendment Law*, St. Paul, Minn.: West Publishing Co., 1993.

Bean, Joseph. *Leathersex: A Guide for the Curious Outsider and the Serious Player*. San
Francisco: Daedalus, 1994.

Beaton, Cecil. *The Unexpurgated Beaton: The Cecil Beaton Diaries as He Wrote Them
(1970–1980)*, Hugo Vickers, ed. New York: Random House, 2003.

Berube, Alan. *Coming Out Under Fire*, New York: Free Press, 1990.

Borhan, Pierre, et al. *Les Verites du Sexe: Archives du Kinsey Institute for Research in Sex, Gender and Reproduction.* Paris: Marval, 2003.

Bronski, Michael. *Pulp Friction: Uncovering the Golden Age of Gay Male Pulps.* New York: St. Martin's Press, 2002.

———. *The Pleasure Principle: Sex, Backlash and the Struggle for Gay Freedom.* New York: St. Martin's Press, 1998.

Bruno, C. *Tatoués: Qui Etes Vous?* Paris: Brodard et Topin, 1970.

Burns, John Horne. *The Gallery.* New York: Harper, 1963.

Carnes, Patrick. *Out of the Shadows: Understanding Sexual Addiction.* Center City, Minn.: Hazelden, 2001.

Carrington, Dorothy. "Francis Rose," in *Sir Francis Rose, 1909–1979: A Retrospective.* London: England & Co., 1988.

Casillo, Charles. *Outlaw: The Lives and Careers of John Rechy.* Los Angeles: Advocate Books, 2002.

Chauncey, George. *Gay New York: Gender, Urban Culture, and the Making of the Gay Male World, 1890 – 1940.* New York: Basic Books, 1994.

Christenson, Cornelia. *Kinsey: A Biography.* Bloomington: Indiana University Press, 1971.

Cocteau, Jean. *The White Book/Le Livre Blanc.* San Francisco: City Lights Books, 1989.

Cory, Donald Webster (pseudonym for Edward Sagarin.) *The Homosexual in America.* New York: Greenburg, 1951.

Crump, James. *George Platt Lynes: Photographs from the Kinsey Institute.* Boston: Little, Brown, 1993.

DeCossart, Michael. *George Melhuish: Artist, Philosopher.* Wolfeboro Falls, N.H.: Alan Sutton, 1990.

———. "Sir Francis Rose (1909 – 1979) A Biographical Sketch," in *Sir Francis Rose, 1909–1979: A Retrospective.* London: England & Co.

Delarue, Jacques, and Robert Giraud. *Les Tatouages du "Milieu."* Paris: La Roulotte, 1950.

DeMello, Margo. *Bodies of Inscription: A Cultural History of the Modern Tattoo Community.* Durham, N.C.: Duke University Press, 2000.

D'Emilio, John. *Sexual Politics, Sexual Communities: The Making of a Homosexual Minority in the United States, 1940–1970* (Chicago: University of Chicago Press, 1983).

D'Emilio, John, and Estelle Freedman. *Intimate Matters: A History of Sexuality in America* (New York: Harper and Row, 1988).

De St. Jorre, John. *Venus Bound: The Erotic Voyage of the Olympia Press and Its Writers.* New York: Random House, 1996.

Duberman, Martin. *Cures: A Gay Man's Odyssey.* New York: Dutton, 1991.

———. *The Worlds of Lincoln Kirstein.* New York: Knopf, 2008.

Duberman, Martin, Martha Vicinus, and George Chauncey, eds. *Hidden from History: Reclaiming the Gay and Lesbian Past.* New York: New American Library, 1989.

Ellenzweig, Allen, and George Stambolian. *The Homoerotic Photograph: Male Images from Durieu/Delacroix to Mapplethorpe.* New York: Columbia University Press, 1992.

Ellis, Havelock. *Psychology of Sex,* 2nd ed. New York: Harcourt, Brace, Jovanovich, 1978.

Ellman, Richard. *Oscar Wilde.* New York: Vintage, 1987.

Friedman, Mack. *Strapped for Cash: A History of American Hustler Culture*. Los Angeles: Alyson, 2003.

Fritscher, Jack. *Some Dance to Remember*. Stamford, Conn.: Knight's Press, 1990.

Gagnon, John H. *An Interpretation of Desire: Essays in the Study of Sexuality*. Chicago: University of Chicago Press, 2004.

Gallup, Donald. *Pigeons on the Granite: Memoirs of a Yale Librarian*. New Haven: Beinecke Library/Yale University, 1988.

Gathorne-Hardy, Jonathan. *Sex, the Measure of All Things: A Life of Alfred C. Kinsey*. Bloomington: Indiana University Press, 2000.

Genet, Jean. *Querelle de Brest* (Jean Cocteau, illus.). Paris: P. Morihien, 1947.

Gide, André. *Corydon* (Richard Howard, trans.). Urbana: University of Illinois Press, 2001.

———. *If It Die* (Dorothy Bussy, trans.). London: Secker & Warburg, 1950.

———. *The Immoralist* (Richard Howard, trans.) New York: Knopf, 1970.

———. *The Journals of André Gide, vol. 2. 1924–1949* (Justin O'Brien, ed. and trans.). Evanston, Ill.: Northwestern University Press, 1987.

Green, Julien. *Julien Green Diary, 1928–1957*. Selected by Kurt Wolff, translated by Anne Green. New York: Harcourt, Brace, and World, 1964.

Green, Martin. *Children of the Sun: A Narrative of "Decadence" in England after 1918*. New York: Basic Books, 1976.

Harrison, Gilbert, A. *The Enthusiast: A Life of Thornton Wilder*. New York: Fromm International, 1986.

Heap, Chad. *Slumming: Sexual and Racial Encounters in American Nightlife, 1885–1940*. Chicago: University of Chicago Press, 2009.

Higgins, Patrick. *A Queer Reader*. New York: New Press, 1993.

Hofler, Robert. *The Man Who Invented Rock Hudson: The Pretty Boys and Dirty Deals of Henry Willson*. New York: Carroll and Graf, 2005.

Hooven, F. Valentine. *Tom of Finland: His Life and Times*. New York: St. Martin's Press, 1993.

Hutton, J. Bernard. *Frogman Spy: The Incredible Case of Commander Crabb*. New York: McDowell, Obolensky, 1960.

Huysmans, J. K. *Against the Grain*. New York: Dover, 1969.

Jones, James H. *Alfred C. Kinsey: A Public Private Life*. New York: Norton, 1997.

Kaiser, Charles. *The Gay Metropolis 1940–1996*. Boston: Houghton Mifflin, 1997.

Katz, Jonathan Ned. *Gay American History: Lesbians and Gay Men in the USA*, rev. ed. New York: Meridien, 1992.

Kennedy, Hubert C. *The Ideal Gay Man: The Story of Der Kreis*. New York: Haworth, 1999.

Landis, Bill. *Anger: The Unauthorized Biography of Kenneth Anger*. New York: HarperCollins, 1995.

LaVigne, Yves. *Hells Angels: Into the Abyss*. New York: Harper Paperbacks, 1996.

Leddick, David. *George Platt Lynes, 1907–1955*. New York: Taschen, 2000.

———. *Intimate Companions: A Triography of George Platt Lynes, Paul Cadmus, Lincoln Kirstein and their Circle*. New York: St. Martin's Press, 2000.

———. *The Male Nude*. New York: Taschen, 1998.

Leyland, Winston, ed. *Gay Sunshine Interviews, Volume One*. San Francisco: Gay Sunshine Press, 1978.

———. *Gay Sunshine Interviews, Volume Two*. San Francisco: Gay Sunshine Press, 1982.

Loughery, John. *The Other Side of Silence: Men's Lives and Gay Identities: A Twentieth-Century History*. New York: Henry Holt, 1998.

Mains, Geoff. *Urban Aboriginals: A Celebration of Leather Sexuality*. Los Angeles: Daedalus, 1984.

Malcolm, Janet. *Two Lives: Gertrude and Alice*. New Haven: Yale University Press, 2007.

Manso, Peter. *Brando: The Biography*. New York: Hyperion, 1994.

McDonald, Boyd, ed. *Meat/Flesh/Sex/Cum/Juice: True Homosexual Experiences from S.T.H. Writers* (Volumes 1–5). San Francisco: Gay Sunshine Press, 1984.

McKenna, Neil. *The Secret Life of Oscar Wilde*. London: Century, 2003.

Mellow, James. *Charmed Circle*. New York: Avon, 1975.

Miller, Neil. *Out of the Past: Gay and Lesbian History from 1869 to the Present*. New York: Vintage, 1995.

Morse, Albert L. *The Tattooists*. San Francisco: Albert Morse, 1977.

Murray, Douglas. *Bosie: A Biography of Lord Alfred Douglas*. New York: Hyperion, 2000.

Norman, Tom. *American Gay Erotic Paperbacks: A Bibliography*. Burbank, Calif.: [s.n.], 1994.

Opel, Robert. "Requiem for a Tool Box," *Drummer*, no. 2, 1975, p. 28.

"Steven" (pseudonym for Don Orejudos). *Locker Room*. Chicago: Kris Studio, 1971.

Parry, Albert. *Tattoo: Secrets of a Strange Art as Practiced among the Natives of the United States*. New York: Simon & Schuster, 1933.

Peters, Fritz. *Finistère*. New York: Plume/NAL, 1986.

Pittman, David J. "The Male House of Prostitution." *TransAction* 8, nos. 5 and 6 (March/April 1971): 21–25.

Pomeroy, Wardell B. *Dr. Kinsey and the Institute for Sex Research*. New York: Harper and Row, 1972.

Preston, John. *Hustling: A Gentleman's Guide to the Fine Art of Homosexual Prostitution*. New York: Masquerade, 1994.

———. *Mr. Benson*. San Francisco: Cleis Press, 2004.

Purdy, James. *Eustace Chisholm and the Works*. New York: Bantam, 1967.

———. *Malcolm*. New York: Serpent's Tail, 1987.

Ramakers, Micha. *Dirty Pictures: Tom of Finland, Masculinity and Homosexuality*. New York: St. Martin's Press, 2000.

Rechy, John. *City of Night*. New York: Grove Press, 1963.

———. *Numbers*. New York: Grove Press, 1984.

Renslow, Chuck. *Kris: The Physique Photography of Chuck Renslow*, with an essay by Joseph W. Bean. Las Vegas, Nev.: Nazca Plains, 2008.

Robertson, Bryan. "Remembering Francis Rose," in *Sir Francis Rose, 1909–1979: A Retrospective*. London: England & Co., 1988.

Robinson, Paul. *Gay Lives: Homosexual Autobiography from John Addington Symonds to Paul Monette*. Chicago: University of Chicago Press, 1999.

———. *The Modernization of Sex: Havelock Ellis, Alfred Kinsey, William Masters, and Virginia Johnson*. New York: Harper & Row, 1976.

Roscoe, Jerry. *Glenway Wescott Personally*. Madison: University of Wisconsin Press, 2002.

Rose, Francis. *Saying Life: The Memoirs of Sir Francis Rose*. London: Cassell, 1961.

Rubin, Gayle, *The Valley of the Kings: Leathermen in San Francisco (1960–1990)*. Dissertation, University of Michigan, 1994.

Sarotte, Georges-Michel. *Like a Brother, Like a Lover: Male Homosexuality in the American Novel and Theater from Herman Melville to James Baldwin*. Garden City, N.Y.: Anchor Press/Doubleday, 1978.

Sheridan, Alan. *André Gide: A Life in the Present*. Cambridge: Harvard University Press, 1999.

Shilts, Randy. *The Mayor of Castro Street: The Life and Times of Harvey Milk*. New York: St. Martin's Press, 1982.

Simon, Linda. *The Biography of Alice B. Toklas*. Garden City, N.Y.: Doubleday, 1977.

———. *Thornton Wilder: His World*. Garden City, N.Y.: Doubleday, 1970.

Sokolowski, Thomas. *The Sailor 1930–1945* (exhibition catalog). Norfolk, Va.: The Norfolk Museum, 1983.

Souhami, Diana. *Gertrude and Alice*. London: Pandora, 1991.

Spoto, Donald. *The Kindness of Strangers: The Life of Tennessee Williams*. Boston: Little, Brown, 1985.

Steegmuller, Francis. *Cocteau: A Biography*. Boston: Little, Brown, 1970.

Stein, Gertrude. *The Autobiography of Alice B. Toklas*. New York: Harcourt, Brace, 1933.

———. *A Stein Reader* (Ulla E. Dydo, ed.). Evanston, Ill.: Northwestern University Press, 1993.

Stein, Gertrude, and Thornton Wilder. *The Letters of Gertrude Stein and Thornton Wilder*, Edward Burns, Ulla E. Dydo, and William Rice, eds. New Haven: Yale University Press, 1996.

Streitmatter, Rodger, and John C. Watson. "Herman Lynn Womack: Pornographer as First Amendment Pioneer." *Journalism History* 28:56 (Summer 2002).

Tellman, William. "Chuck Arnett." *Black Sheets*, no. 15, April 1998, pp. 39–40.

Thompson, Mark, ed. *Leatherfolk: Radical Sex, People, Politics and Practice*. Boston: Alyson, 1991.

Thompson, William R. "Sex, Lies and Photographs: Letters from George Platt Lynes." Master's thesis, Rice University, 1997.

Toklas, Alice. *The Alice B. Toklas Cook Book*. New York: Harper & Brothers, 1954.

———. *Staying On Alone: The Letters of Alice B. Toklas* (Edward Burns, ed.). New York: Liveright, 1973.

———. *What Is Remembered*. San Francisco: North Point, 1985.

Townsend, Larry. *The Leatherman's Handbook*. San Francisco: Le Salon, 1973.

———. "Plight of Gay Novelists: Who Gauges Market Correctly, Publishers or Writers?" *The Advocate*, August 19, 1970, p. 19.

Tripp, C.A. *The Homosexual Matrix*. New York: McGraw-Hill, 1975.

Vickers, Hugo. *Cecil Beaton: A Biography*. Boston: Little, Brown, 1985.

Vidal, Gore. *Palimpsest: A Memoir*. New York: Random House, 1995.

Waugh, Thomas. *Hard to Imagine: Gay Male Eroticism in Photography and Film from Their Beginnings to Stonewall*. New York: Columbia University Press, 1996.

———. *Out/Lines: Underground Gay Graphics from Before Stonewall*. Vancouver: Arsenal Pulp Press, 2002.

Webb, Spider, with Marco Vassi. *Spider Webb's Pushing Ink: The Fine Art of Tattooing*. New York: Fireside, 1979.

Weinberg, Martin S., and Colin J. Williams. *Male Homosexuals: Their Problems and Adaptations*. New York: Oxford University Press, 1974.

Welch, Paul. "Homosexuality in America," *Life*, June 26, 1964, pp. 66–78.

Welham, M. G., and J. A. Welham. *Frogman Spy: The Mysterious Disappearance of Commander "Buster" Crabb*. London: W. H. Allen, 1990.

Werth, Barry. *The Scarlet Professor Newton Arvin, a Literary Life Shattered by Scandal*. New York: Nan A. Talese, 2001.

White, Edmund. *Genet: A Biography*. New York: Alfred A. Knopf, 1993.

———. *States of Desire: Travels in Gay America*. New York: Dutton, 1980.

Wilde, Oscar. *De Profundis and Other Writings*. New York: Penguin, 1986.

Williams, Tennessee. *Memoirs*. Garden City, N.Y.: Doubleday, 1975.

Wilson, Colin. *The Occult*. New York: Vintage, 1973.

Woody, Jack. *George Platt Lynes: Photographs, 1931–1955*. Los Angeles: Twelvetrees Press, 1980.

Young, Ian. *The Male Homosexual in Literature: A Bibliography*. Metuchen, N.J.: Scarecrow Press, 1975.

6. VISUAL RECORDINGS OF STEWARD

International Tattoo Art. An interview with Samuel Steward by Michael O. Stearns, Metamorphosis Productions, 542 Chetwood Street, Oakland, California. Date of taping: August 23, 1983. A copy of this interview remains in the Steward archive.

Advocate Men Live! Fred Bissones, director. Los Angeles: Advocate Men, 1986. Color. The most significant visual interview of Samuel M. Steward. A copy of this tape remains in the Steward Archive, gift of Douglas Martin.

Olaf Odergaard interview with Samuel Steward on behalf of the International Gay and Lesbian Archives, Natalie Barney, Edward Carpenter Library, Hollywood, California. Interview taped in December 1986. A copy of this interview remains in the Steward archive.

Rick X Talks to Sam Steward, July 10, 1991, Berkeley, California. A sit-down interview by Rick X/Rick Shur, the New York–based producer of *The Closet Case Show*, a public access television show screened on New York cable television. A copy of this interview remains in the Steward archive.

Paris Was a Woman (1995). Greta Schiller, director. Los Angeles: Cicada Films/Jezebel Productions. This widely released 75-minute documentary describing women artists and writers of Paris features a substantial late-life interview of Samuel Steward about his friendship with Gertrude Stein and Alice B. Toklas.

ACKNOWLEDGMENTS

Many people helped me with the researching and publishing of this book. The most important financial assistance came from a Guggenheim Fellowship, which helped me to begin my research; and the most important personal encouragment came to me from Paul Cadmus, who at the end of his life, even as he declined to be the subject of a biography, convinced me that his generation of writers and artists needed to be better understood.

At Brown University, I'd like to thank the John Nicholas Brown American Studies Center and the Kirk Collection, both of which helped to fund my library research in Providence. I'd also like to thank the staff of the John Hay Library and the Rockefeller Library, particularly Joyce Botelho, Rosemarie Cullen, Ron Fark, Mary Jo Kline, and Sam Streit. Tovah Reis was also most helpful. At Yale University, Tim Young proved indispensable in helping me to find my way through the Beinecke Collections and in locating letters that had otherwise been invisible to all previous researchers. He was an early and enthusiastic supporter of Sam Steward's life story. Patricia Willis was also gently encouraging. A Beinecke research grant form Yale, meanwhile, helped offset my travel and lodging costs in New Haven.

Joseph Bean, the founder and organizer of the Leather Archives and Museum in Chicago, helped me immeasurably over my many years of research and in doing so became both an adviser and good friend. His successor at the Leather Archives, Rick Storer, also contributed his goodwill and expertise; so, too, did Charles "Chuck" Renslow. I would particularly like to thank Mr. Renslow for making himself available to me for interviews about his friendship with Sam Steward, and for sharing with me the extensive documentation of his life. The author Jack Rinella, a longtime associate of the Leather Archives, hosted me for a memorable evening and provided me with information about the leather community I would have found nowhere else. Douglas Martin, Steward's former pupil at DePaul, was exceptionally warm and welcoming to me during my Chicago visits. Martin was the only person to read through the manuscript in all its many drafts. He was also kind enough to offer me a place to stay during my visit to the International Mr. Leather convention in Chicago, and in so doing he shared his lifelong knowledge of Chicago with me, as well as his firsthand accounts of life at DePaul and his later-life friendship with Steward. Both Loyola and DePaul universities, meanwhile, granted me access to their special collections archives in order to research Sam Steward's career.

In San Francisco, Michael Williams was remarkably generous in sharing Sam's life story and papers with me. He was an equally generous host and guide, and over the course of nearly a decade he has become a dear and valued friend. Donald Allen shared his memories of Sam Steward with me, and gave me full access to the archives of his Gray Fox Press. In Berkeley, the manuscript dealer Burton Weiss generously shared information and gave me access to his unique collections. At UC Berkeley, Bancroft special collections librarian Peter Hanff was equally welcoming. The surviving friends and acquaintances of Sam Steward in San Francisco who were kind enough to share their memories of him included Jack Fritscher, Don Ed Hardy, Kevin Killian, Bob McHenry, Paul Padgette, and Burton Weiss. Fritscher in particular helped to expand my knowledge of gay San Francisco and the unique world of *Drummer* magazine. Various other members of the GLBTQ and kink and leather communities have explaining so many things that I would otherwise never have understood; they include Guy Baldwin, Jeanne Barney, Chad Heap, Mark Hemry, Jack Frischer, Gayle Rubin, and Bill Thompson.

In Bloomington, the Kinsey Institute gave me a warm welcome. I would particularly like to thank Catherine Johnson-Roehr, Shawn Wilson, and Liana Zhou for their patience with my project. A very special thanks goes as well to Alfred Kinsey's close associate of many years, Paul Gebhard, who candidly shared with me so many of his memories of Sam Steward and the early, pioneering years of sex research. I'd like also to thank Brenda Marston at Cornell University Library for directing me to the papers of H. Lynn Womack, and the Archives of American Art for providing information on Gertrude Abercrombie and her circle in Chicago. While I was doing my research at Boston University, George Shackelford kept me in good cheer and kindly gave me a place to sleep. George Platt Lynes II has graciously allowed me to quote extensively from the letters of George Platt Lynes to Samuel Steward; likewise, Tappan Wilder has kindly allowed me to quote from the unpublished letters of Thornton Wilder to Samuel Steward. In New York, Jennifer Milne provided indispensable copyediting and editorial help in the seemingly endless editing-down and revision of the manuscript, a process that lasted for more than a year.

Finding a publisher for *Secret Historian* took a good deal of effort, so I would particularly like to thank the writer Francine Maroukian for insisting that I continue my work on the book after other advisers suggested I abandon it in favor of something more commercial. I would like to thank Doug Stumpf for recommending the book proposal to Jeff Seroy; Jeff Seroy for recommending the proposal to Jonathan Galassi; and finally, and most important, Jonathan Galassi for daring to sign up what surely must have seemed to him a difficult and hard-to-sell book. Over the years his editorial comments have been invaluable; so, too, have been those of his assistant, Jesse Coleman. Charlotte Sheedy has been a supportive and enthusiastic agent for the book, very wise in the ways of contemporary publishing. David Deiss of Elysium Press offered not only his comments on the manuscript but also, miraculously, to publish the companion volume of Sam Steward's visual works.

And my deepest thanks, as ever, go to Anthony Korner, who lived patiently with this book for nearly a decade.

INDEX

Blaine, Anne, 357*n*
Blake, William, 306*n*
Blow for Blow, see Greek Ways
Blumenthal, Eli, 270
bodybuilding competitions, 266–67
"Boke of Phyllyp Sparrowe, The" (Skelton), 202
Boni and Liveright, 357*n*
Boston University, special collections library at, xii, 407*n*, 408
Boudreault, Roland, 345–46, 351, 358, 359
Bourges, France, 124, 125
Boyd, J. P., 290*n*
Boys in Blue, The (*San Francisco Hustler*; Andros), 165*n*, 324*n*, 350–51, 351*n*, 402–403
Boys Town, 313
"Boys Will Be Boys" (Raven), 299
Bozart: The Bi-Monthly Poetry Review, 20*n*, 21
Bradbury, Bruce, 324
Brando, Dorothy "Dode," 96, 96*n*
Brando, Marlon, Sr., 96
Braque, Georges, 48
Brash, Jeff, 174
Brashin, Jim, 311, 312*n*, 401
Brest, France, 150–51, 151*n*
Breton, André, 67
Brian, J. (J. Brian Donahue), 337–40, 337*n*; arrests of, 364–65; collaboration with Steward, 339–40, 358–59, 363–64, 381; escort and brothel business of, 337–39, 364, 384, 391; friendship with Steward, 340, 365–66; photography by, 337–38; pornographic filmmaking by, 338, 358–59, 359*n*, 363–67, 364*n*; provider of hustlers for Steward, 363, 391; publication of work by Steward, 339
Bridge of San Luis Rey, The (Wilder), 50, 63
Bronski, Michael, 350*n*, 362
Brooklyn Citizen, 22–23
brothels, male, 290, 338–39, 364
Broughton, James, 397

Brown University, John Hay Special Collections Library at, ix, x
Bulganin, Nikolai, 247–48
"Bull Market in America, The" (Bishop), 265, 299–300
Bunin, Ivan, 293
Buonfiglio, Tab, 228
Burckhardt, Rudolf (Rudolf Jung), 257, 257*n*, 259, 264, 266, 271, 272, 275, 275*n*, 279, 283, 289, 291–92, 293, 295, 305, 308
Burns, Edward M., 372*n*
Burroughs, William S., 325, 383
Butts, Mary, 70

Cabell, James Branch, 22
Cadmus, Paul, xi, 57, 82, 136, 142, 146, 146*n*, 153
"Calamus" poems (Whitman), 17, 40, 175*n*
California, University of, at Berkeley, Bancroft Library at, xii, 368*n*
Cammell, Donald, 333
Caplowitz, Bob, 273, 273*n*
Caravaggio Shawl, The (Steward), 397
Carlyle, Thomas, 280, 280*n*
Carroll College, 26, 27*n*, 32–33, 34, 34*n*
Cartun, Herman, 342–43
Cathedral, The (Huysmans), 25
Catholicism, 26*n*, 146–47, 156, 260, 260*n*, 292*n*, 302–303; SMS's conversion to, 24–26, 28–29, 213; SMS's rejection of, 32, 63–64; of Toklas, 260–61, 260*n*, 272, 291; of Virginia Harper (sister), 260–61
Cavafy, Constantin, 317, 317*n*
Cave, Thomas (pseud. of SMS), x, xii, 265
Caves du Vatican, Les (Gide), 48
Caxton Publishers, 36
120 Journées de Sodome (Sade), 120
Cerf, Bennett, 79
Chance, Ervin, 399
Chandler, Raymond, 306
Chant d'Amour, Un, 122*n*, 143–44, 291
Chapters from an Autobiography (Steward), xi, 389*n*, 391–92, 393, 409